The Complete Film Production Handbook

Third Edition

The Complete Film Production Handbook

Third Edition

Eve Light Honthaner

Focal Press

Amsterdam   Boston   Heidelberg   London   New York   Oxford
Paris   San Diego   San Francisco   Singapore   Sydney   Tokyo

Focal Press is an imprint of Elsevier.

∞ This book is printed on acid-free paper.

Library of Congress Cataloging-in-Publication Data
Honthaner, Eve Light
    The complete film production handbook / Eve Light Honthaner.—3rd. ed.
        p.   cm.
    ISBN 0-240-80419-8 (pbk. : alk. paper)
    1. Motion pictures-Production and direction-Handbooks, manuals, etc. I.
Title.

PN1995.9..P7 H66 2000
791.43'0232—dc21

                                                    00-063598

British Library Cataloguing-in-Publication Data

A catalogue record for this book is available from the British Library.

The publisher offers special discounts on bulk orders of this book.
For information, please contact:
Manager of Special Sales
Elsevier Science
200 Wheeler Road
Burlington, MA 01803
Tel: 781-313-4700
Fax: 781-313-4802

For information on all Focal Press publications available, contact our World
Wide Web homepage at http://www.focalpress.com

10 9 8 7 6 5 4 3
Printed in the United States of America

This book is lovingly dedicated to the memories of two very special women
whose strength, courage, friendship and love
have left indelible imprints on my life and in my heart.

To
Linda Ben-Ami
and
Ann Streltzer

Table of Contents

Introduction

I am thrilled to be writing the introduction to the third edition of the even *more Complete Film Production Handbook*. It has been incredibly exciting and gratifying to watch this book grow in popularity to become an industry standard.

Much has transpired since the last edition was published in 1996 to influence both the revisions and the new material contained in this version. As mentioned in previous introductions, this book is based solely on the scope of my experience, the shared experiences of friends and associates and on what I feel is important for all levels of production personnel to know (information you will not necessarily find in other publications). Every show, every project is a source of new knowledge and skills, and not only do I learn from the specific circumstances and challenges created by each new production I work on, but also from the talented, hard-working and dedicated individuals I have had the good fortune to work with. In the past few years, two additional factors have significantly impacted both my continuing education and my career. The first was the opportunity to work in Mexico (beginning with the film *Titanic*). The second is having become a teacher.

I started working on *Titanic* in April, 1996. It was the beginning of a fifteen-month odyssey that opened up many new doors for me, the most important being the experience of working in a foreign country with an international crew. This led to my writing the operations manual for Fox's new Baja Studios, followed by a subsequent job on a DreamWorks film (*In Dreams*), on which I set up and supervised a Mexico unit on yet another internationally-staffed production. *Titanic* was not only the most difficult and challenging show of my career, but it was also a source of significant

new contacts, new films, new friendships and an extensive education on filming in a foreign country.

I became a teacher in August of 1998 when asked to be the (substitute) instructor of a one-week AD-UPM-Line Producer workshop at The International Film & Television Workshops in Rockport, Maine. I had thought of teaching before, but had never gotten beyond the thinking-about-it stage. Nervous and not knowing if I even had what it took to be a good teacher, my friend Phil Wylly, who had recommended me for the position, convinced me I could to do it. So off to Maine I went.

It did not take long to discover that I love teaching. The experience was truly memorable. The school was pleased as well and asked me back for another week in October. (Have you ever been to Maine in October? It is sensationally beautiful!—an added bonus to an already terrific week.)

My teaching career continued in June of 1999 with the opportunity to create and teach a six-week course and two four-hour seminars at USC's Summer Production Workshop program. This turned out to be another special experience, for students and teacher alike.

Teaching has been the perfect balance to working on movies. I find the excitement and passion exuded by my students to be highly contagious. Their enthusiasm stays with me and acts as an effective antidote to becoming too cynical and disillusioned after one too many difficult films. It reminds me of why I got into the business to begin with, and of how satisfying and challenging the work can be. By the same token, as a working professional, I can introduce my students to the most current material, trends and attitudes. And without a doubt, being both a working professional and a teacher provides me with more and better material for this book.

For those of you who have read previous versions, you will find that each chapter has been revised, and some, substantially expanded. There are brand new chapters as well, which you will hopefully find helpful. A recurring question from my students—"Who does what?"—is how Chapter 1, "The Production Team & Who Does What," came into being. Two new chapters, Chapter 2, "The Production Office," and Chapter 3, "Basic Accounting," have incorporated the previous edition's "Establishing Company Policies" and "Setting Up Production Files." And although the book had not previously contained information on breaking down scripts, scheduling and negotiating deals, it now includes brief explanations and a general overview of these topics. (There are of course other, more detailed books on the market relating to these subjects.) In addition to a chapter pertaining to *principal* talent (Chapter 11), you will now find one on *extra talent* as well (Chapter 12). The chapter on visual effects in the last edition has now simply become "Effects" (Chapter 19), encompassing visual, physical and mechanical effects. And to complement the information pertaining to locations (Chapter 16) and working on a distant location (Chapter 17), the subject is now even more complete with a third chapter on foreign locations (Chapter 18), which incorporates the previous "Work Visas, Shipping & Customs." You will also find a new chapter pertaining to commercial production (Chapter 22).

I had wanted this edition to include information touching on the escalating profusion of digital technology, which is starting to change the way the industry makes, sells, distributes and exhibits their product. Unfortunately, much of what I would write about today would be obsolete by the time you read *this*. Since the focus of this book is physical production and not the digital revolution, and because the technology is changing so rapidly, the best I can do is to point you in the right direction. For a good overview of the digital world, I suggest another Focal Press book entitled *Digital Filmmaking: The Changing Art and Craft of Making Motion Pictures,* by Thomas A. Ohanian and Michael E. Phillips. To see the most current innovations first-hand, I strongly suggest you attend whichever conventions you can get to—ShowBiz Expo (www.showbizexpo.com), E3 (E3expo.com) and NAB (www.nab.org). Anything you want to know about digital production or post production is out there in the form of books, magazines, newspaper articles (check-out *The Wall Street Journal's Entertainment and Technology* section), a multitude of websites, classes, seminars and vendors willing to demonstrate their latest generation of digitally-based products. The information is out there for the taking, so stay apprised of these rapidly advancing technologies that affect your craft.

As noted in previous editions, a number of the forms contained in the book, such as the Day-Out-Of-Days and Shooting Schedule, are automatically prepared by computer software scheduling programs (discussed in Chapter 4, "From Script to Schedule"). They have been kept in for those who wish to break down and schedule their shows manually and for those who do not yet own the software. Several of the forms have been revised, a couple deleted and new ones have been added.

Also previously noted is the reminder to use this book as a *guideline*. The forms, releases and deal memos have been approved by an attorney, but have your own attorney look everything over before using any of them. Your attorney may want to make changes or add riders that relate to the specifics of your production.

Getting into production means you will be: networking, schmoozing and selling yourself over and over and over again; working excruciatingly long hours; having to continuously solve problems and make other people happy; giving up large chunks of your personal life and having to develop a thick skin to repel rejection, large egos and bad tempers. You will have an enormous amount of responsibility and will often be blamed for the mistakes of others. But, on the other hand, you will get to experience the thrill of putting all the people, locations, sets, equipment and details together and watching a movie come together. Each show will be the beginning of a new adventure that brings with it new challenges and skills, along with new contacts, friends and future possibilities. Your work will rarely be boring, you will have the freedom to develop your own unique style and will have opportunities to travel and work with creative, talented people from all over the world. Your job can be drudgery, or it can be a series of challenging experiences and memorable adventures. It's up to you! If you're a team player, there is no better team to be on than a film crew.

I am a firm believer in the adage that in this business, you don't have to know how to do everything—you just have to know where to *find* everything you don't know. Take this book, for example—since there are certain topics I don't know well enough to intelligently write about, I am able to find what I don't know (or discover better ways to describe what I do know) from friends and associates who generously allow me to tap into their expertise. Without their time, explanations, notes and desire to help—this and previous editions, would not have been possible.

I would especially like to acknowledge the contributions of Marc Federman, Patricia O'Brien, Nick Abdo, Stephen Marinaccio, Mark Indig, Cindy Quan, Matt Kutcher, Don Pennington, Bill Dance, Milton Reyes, Yolanda Lopez, Ned Shapiro, Christine Evey, Karen Yokomizo, Dan Schmit, Suzy Vaughan, Don Gold, Elizabeth Moseley, Mark McNair, Karon May, Cory McCrum-Abdo, Richard Wells and Mike Papadaki. I greatly value your guidance, encouragement and, most of all—your friendship.

I would like to express my love and heartfelt gratitude to my husband, Ron. I cannot imagine what my life would be like without his emotional support, help and love. To my family and other friends—thank you for being there for me and for understanding why we can't always spend as much time together as we should. And to Wayne and Nick—thanks for always being there to help out with my computer problems.

For the roles they played in my becoming a teacher, I would like to recognize Duke Underwood, who not only offered me a job teaching at USC's Summer Production Workshop program, but gave me the opportunity to design my own course and was there to cheer me on every step of the way; Phil Wylly, my mentor and dear friend, who first recommended me to teach; Alison Laslett, my first teaching assistant, who got me through my first week-long workshop and has been a friend ever since and David Lyman, who, almost a year after I taught my first workshop at his school in Maine, finally learned my name. And to all my promising, bright students—my undying appreciation for your excitement and inspiration.

With the subsequent printing of the last edition, the book was released with a companion CD instead of the two computer disks. Thank you to the folks at Focal Press for the foresight to introduce the CD, which has gone over extremely well and has been a tremendous asset to the book. A big thank you to the wonderfully professional staff at Focal who take my material and make a book out of it, and especially to Marie Lee and Terri Jadick for their faith in me and for always being so pleasant, accommodating and patient. Working with you continues to be an absolute pleasure.

Lastly, I would like to extend my gratitude to the readers, supporters and users of this book. Without you, there would have been no subsequent editions.

How To Use This Book

The Complete Film Production Handbook contains many forms, including standard production forms, contracts, deal memos and releases and an assortment of checklists and miscellaneous forms to help you stay more organized. To illustrate how each form is to be completed, they have all been fully or partially filled out. The same forms may also be found blank at the back of the book. Another source of the forms, contracts, releases, checklists, etc. can be found on the companion CD attached to the back inside cover. By utilizing the CD, you can type in all the pertinent information relating to your show and print out original documents.

In filling out the forms, I have used an assortment of fictitious names and situations. The fictitious name of our production company is *XYZ Productions*, and the name of the show is *Herby's Summer Vacation*. Note, however, that from one situation to another, *Herby's Summer Vacation* is either a feature film, a cable movie, a movie for television, or a television series, with the current episode being *Boys Night Out*.

ABBREVIATIONS

The following abbreviations are used throughout the book:

UPM	Unit Production Manager
AD	Assistant Director
DP	Director of Photography
POC	Production Office Coordinator
APOC	Assistant Production Office Coordinator
PA	Production Assistant
PR	Production Report
INT	Interior
EXT	Exterior
CGI	Computer-Generated Images
L & D	Loss and Damage
SAG	Screen Actors Guild
DGA	Directors Guild of America
WGA	Writers Guild of America
IATSE	International Alliance of Theatrical Stage Employees
AMPTP	Association of Motion Picture and Television Producers
CSATF	CONTRACT SERVICES ADMINISTRATION TRUST FUND

CHAPTER ONE

The Production Team &
Who Does What

"Who does what?" is one of the questions I am most often asked by students, interns and production assistants. Even people who have been in the business for a while are sometimes unclear as to exactly who performs which functions on any given project. While some duties can only be performed by individuals who occupy specific positions, and others can be accomplished by a number of different people, depending on the parameters of the project—there is no doubt that production requires a team effort.

From where I sit, there is a core group that comprises the production team, and they are the:

Producers
Director
Unit Production Manager
Production Accountant
Production Supervisor
Production Coordinator
First Assistant Director
Second Assistant Director

Think of casting directors, location managers, post production coordinators and the studio and network executives assigned to your show as auxiliary team members.

Unfortunately, it doesn't always happen this way, but the ideal is a team that works well together and is one in which the members understand and support each other's boundaries and goals. In other words, should you find yourself with a producer and director (or any other members of the team) who don't see eye-to-eye and can't find enough common ground to get along—you're cooked! An adversarial relationship from within this group becomes a problem for everyone.

On the other hand, efforts made to collaborate on shared common objectives, enhanced by a mutual respect for one another, will inspire the cooperation and loyalty of the cast and crew, will be helpful in promoting a pleasant working environment and will favorably influence your schedule and budget. Once you have a viable script and either a studio deal or outside financing in place, this is the group of people who will take these elements and make them into a movie. The mood and temperament of the production team is going to permeate the entire project and affect everything and everyone involved. It therefore behooves you to put together the very best team you can.

There are six phases to any film. From conception through projected finished product, they are: *development, pre-production, production, post production, distribution* and *exhibition*. Although some members are involved in more than two phases, everyone on the team is involved in both pre-production and production. These phases represent the putting together and coming together of all elements necessary to shoot a film.

The job responsibilities attributed to members of the production team will vary depending on whether the film is being made for television, cable, theatrical or Internet release; and on the project's budget, schedule, union status and location. The following is a chart that illustrates job functions (that range from acquiring the rights to a story or script through the submission of delivery elements) and indicates which position or positions generally fulfill those responsibilities. For a more in-depth interpretation as to how a production team functions, primarily from the perspective of the production manager and first assistant director, I recommend a book entitled *The Film Director's Team* by Alain Silver & Elizabeth Ward (Silman-James Press).

PRODUCTION-TEAM JOB RESPONSIBILITIES

Note: The position of PRODUCER represents a combination of producing positions. Other positions are also combined as their duties overlap and vary from show to show.

	STUDIO	PRODUCER(S)	DIRECTOR	CASTING DIRECTOR	LINE PRODUCER/ PRODUCTION MANAGER	PRODUCTION SUPERVISOR/ COORDINATOR	1ST ASSISTANT DIRECTOR	2ND ASSISTANT DIRECTOR	PRODUCTION ACCOUNTANT	LOCATION MANAGER	POST PRODUCTION COORDINATOR
Acquire rights to story/script	X	X									
Select & hire writer/have script written	X	X									
Select & hire the Director	X	X									
Select & hire the Line Producer/UPM	X	X									
Prepare preliminary budget & schedule	X	X			X						
"Pitch" the story & sell the script		X									
Make the studio deal and/or arrange financing & distribution		X									
Open bank account(s)									X		
Signatory to bank account(s)	X	X			X				X		
Arrange for completion bond and union/guild bonds as necessary		X			X						
Arrange for the legal structure of the production entity	X	X									
Prepare a more realistic board, schedule & budget					X						
Prepare a cash flow chart									X		
Sign all union agreements and contracts		X									
Select & hire a production designer	X	X			X						
Submit script to research company		X			X	X					
Secure all necessary clearances & releases		X			X	X					
Secure insurance coverage	X				X						
Set-up vendor accounts					X	X					
Approve invoices, check requests, purchase orders & time cards					X				X		
Select visual effects company & coordinator	X	X			X						
Get bids on equipment					X	X					
Check crew availabilities					X	X					
Request specific crew members	X	X	X		X						

PRODUCTION-TEAM JOB RESPONSIBILITIES

Note: The position of PRODUCER represents a combination of producing positions. Other positions are also combined as their duties overlap and vary from show to show.

	STUDIO	PRODUCER(S)	DIRECTOR	CASTING DIRECTOR	LINE PRODUCER/ PRODUCTION MANAGER	PRODUCTION SUPERVISOR/ COORDINATOR	1ST ASSISTANT DIRECTOR	2ND ASSISTANT DIRECTOR	PRODUCTION ACCOUNTANT	LOCATION MANAGER	POST PRODUCTION COORDINATOR
Select 1st Asst. Director & Script Supervisor			X								
Negotiate crew deals					X						
Prepare crew deal memos					X	X					
Issue memo re: accounting procedures to department heads									X		
Investigate potential product placement deals		X			X						
Liaison with unions & guilds		X			X	X					
Apply for permit to employ minors (if applicable)				X	X	X					
Issue pre-production schedule					X	X	X				
Cast film	X	X	X	X							
Prepare cast deal memos				X							
Station 12 cast members				X	X	X					
Select locations	X	X	X		X					X	
Secure locations					X					X	
Arrange for film permits, location parking & neighborhood approvals (if necessary)										X	
Work with the production designer in establishing the look of the film	X	X	X								
Approve wardrobe, sets & special props		X	X		X						
Make sure necessary script re-writes are made in a timely manner		X									
Set-up & run the production office						X					
Hire assistant production coordinator & production assistants						X					
Prepare & submit Taft/Hartley reports				X		X					
Sign-off on a final budget	X	X	X		X				X		
Create final board & schedule					X		X				
Create one-liner & day-out-of-days							X				
Negotiate equipment deals					X						

PRODUCTION-TEAM JOB RESPONSIBILITIES

Note: The position of PRODUCER represents a combination of producing positions. Other positions are also combined as their duties overlap and vary from show to show.

	STUDIO	PRODUCER(S)	DIRECTOR	CASTING DIRECTOR	LINE PRODUCER/ PRODUCTION MANAGER	PRODUCTION SUPERVISOR/ COORDINATOR	1ST ASSISTANT DIRECTOR	2ND ASSISTANT DIRECTOR	PRODUCTION ACCOUNTANT	LOCATION MANAGER	POST PRODUCTION COORDINATOR
Order film & equipment					X	X					
Create & distribute crew list, cast list, contact list, etc.						X					
Issue purchase orders						X			X		
Handle time cards & payroll									X		
Line-up special requirements such as animals, blue/green screens, backdrops, mock-ups, miniatures, etc.					X	X		X			
Prepare a breakdown of extras, stunts, vehicles, effects & multi-camera days							X	X			
Disseminate scripts & all essential paperwork & information					X	X		X			
Work with film commissions & local authorities		X			X	X					
Arrange for location travel & hotel accommodations					X	X					
Handle shipping & customs (when necessary)						X					
Prepare welcome packages						X					
Arrange for cast physicals & performers' special needs						X		X			
Procure cast head shots for stunt & photo doubles						X		X			
Inform Wardrobe of cast info. (including sizes)						X					
Officiate at production meetings					X	X	X				
Arrange rehearsals & still photo sessions		X				X	X	X			
Set-up editing rooms											X
Line-up lab, sound house & dubbing facilities					X						X
Submit copies of production reports to SAG on a weekly basis						X					
Set-up accounts for sound transfers, video transfers, etc.									X		X
Issue certificates of insurance						X					
Complete & submit Workers Compensation claim forms						X					
Oversee day-to-day production	X	X			X	X	X				
Responsible for keeping the production running smoothly		X			X						

PRODUCTION-TEAM JOB RESPONSIBILITIES

Note: The position of PRODUCER represents a combination of producing positions. Other positions are also combined as their duties overlap and vary from show to show.

	STUDIO	PRODUCER(S)	DIRECTOR	CASTING DIRECTOR	LINE PRODUCER/ PRODUCTION MANAGER	PRODUCTION SUPERVISOR/ COORDINATOR	1ST ASSISTANT DIRECTOR	2ND ASSISTANT DIRECTOR	PRODUCTION ACCOUNTANT	LOCATION MANAGER	POST PRODUCTION COORDINATOR
Enforce safety guidelines & hold safety meetings					X		X				
Constantly monitor budget & schedule	X	X			X				X		
Continually balance the artistic integrity of the film while maintaining the budget & schedule		X			X						
Liaison between the crew & the director							X				
Liaison between the UPM & the director							X				
Assist the director w/production details, coordinate & supervise cast & crew activities and facilitate an organized flow of activity on the set							X				
Issue work calls				X				X			
Prepare maps to location(s)										X	
Order stand-ins & extras								X			
Prepare call sheets & production reports								X			
Sign-off on call sheets & production reports					X		X				
Coordinate the delivery of film to the lab & the screening of dailies						X					X
Handle insurance claims					X	X			X		
Prepare & issue weekly cost reports									X		
Check and/or distribute weather reports					X	X		X			
Call for "QUIET ON THE SET!"							X				
Prepare daily schedules for talent & determine cast & crew calls							X				
Make sure minor cast members secure necessary work permits						X		X			
Secure extra releases & SAG contracts signed on the set								X			
Set-up on-site school room & procure teachers and baby nurses (when necessary)						X		X			
Secure police & fire officers, security & emergency medical vehicles (when necessary)					X			X		X	
Direct background action & supervise crowd control							X	X			
Liaison with actors on the set							X	X			
Liaison between the production office & the set								X			

PRODUCTION-TEAM JOB RESPONSIBILITIES

Note: The position of PRODUCER represents a combination of producing positions. Other positions are also combined as their duties overlap and vary from show to show.

	STUDIO	PRODUCER(S)	DIRECTOR	CASTING DIRECTOR	LINE PRODUCER/ PRODUCTION MANAGER	PRODUCTION SUPERVISOR/ COORDINATOR	1ST ASSISTANT DIRECTOR	2ND ASSISTANT DIRECTOR	PRODUCTION ACCOUNTANT	LOCATION MANAGER	POST PRODUCTION COORDINATOR
Distribute walkie-talkies on the set								X			
Liaison with the caterer						X		X			
Distribute paperwork sent in from the set each night						X					
Supervise daily wrap								X			
Supervise the work of DGA trainees & set production assistants								X			
Supervise wrap at the end of principal photography					X	X		X			
Contact vendors to make sure all rentals have been returned					X	X					
Compile list of remaining inventory purchased for show & decide whether to sell or store	X				X	X			X		
Collect remaining invoices for last week's rentals & any L&D (lost & damaged) items						X			X		
Inform vendors of forwarding address & phone number									X		
Arrange for wrap party and cast & crew gifts		X			X	X					
Submit final union/guild reports						X			X		
Issue post production schedule											X
Oversee post production activities											X
Compile list of screen credits	X	X			X	X					X
Turn-over files, inventory of company assets, log of insurance claims & notes re: pending issues					X	X					
Close-down production office						X					
Turn-over delivery elements		X									X

CHAPTER TWO

The Production Office

The production office is the heart of your production—its communications and operating center. It is where: decisions are made; deals are negotiated; crews are hired; valuable paperwork and vital information is generated and distributed from; logistics are handled; equipment, materials and supplies are ordered; costs are budgeted and approved; a million details are managed; problems are solved and crew needs are met. While office jobs are not perceived to be as glamorous as those of the set crew, the office staff, while functioning at a constant breakneck pace, handles massive workloads that require boundless amounts of energy, an enormous amount of patience and a good sense of humor to get through those twelve-to-fifteen-hour days. And while their talents may not be overtly creative, the ability to keep a show running smoothly and solve a multitude of spur-of-the moment problems is uniquely creative. The more organized, efficient and well-run the office, the smoother your production will run.

WHO BELONGS IN THE PRODUCTION OFFICE?

The production staff is comprised of the line producer, production manager (UPM), production supervisor, production coordinator (POC), assistant production coordinator (APOC), production secretary, production assistants and interns. Note that the production supervisor is not a traditionally standard position, but one that is continually gaining more acceptance. This person is more qualified than a production coordinator, but not being a member of the Directors Guild of America, cannot work as a production manager on DGA-signatory films. On some shows, the line producer and UPM are one and the same, and the supervisor helps handle some of the production manager duties. Other shows are busy enough and spread out enough to utilize the talents of both a UPM and supervisor.

OFFICE SPACE

You cannot always rely on the studio or production company you're working for to provide offices that are in walk-in, ready-to-go condition. Often times, you will have to locate your own production office space to occupy for a period of time ranging anywhere from two months to at least a year, depending on the project. Before the search begins, however, you must determine how much space will be needed.

Every show is set up differently. Sometimes an art department will choose to work at a different location to be closer to the set construction, the transportation department will work out of its own self-contained trailer, the wardrobe department will work out of a wardrobe house and the prop master will work out of a prop house. There are also shows where everything is set up at the same location. I have worked in production office spaces from 3,500 square feet on up. You won't know how much space is needed until you know who you need space for. Generally, production offices house:

- At least one executive producer
- At least one producer
- The director
- The production manager and/or production supervisor

- The production coordinator
- The accounting department—generally one to three offices, depending on the size of the accounting staff and the size of the offices
- The location manager and one or two assistant location managers
- Two or three assistant directors and a couple of set PAs
- The transportation department (coordinator, captain and a driver or two)
- The art department (production designer, art director, set designer, set decorator, lead person, a set dresser or two, property master, assistant property master, art department coordinator and perhaps an art department PA). This department will require one enormous space that can be sectioned off, or possibly a row of smaller interconnected offices.
- Although the stunt coordinator and director of photography are not in the office all the time (and then only during prep), desks and phones should be allocated for both
- A bullpen area for the assistant production coordinator, production secretary and at least two office production assistants
- An area for meetings
- A kitchen or area that can be set up for craft service
- A separate office or bullpen area for photocopying, faxing, assembling scripts, etc.

Now for the questions that will determine additional space requirements:

- How many more producers will need offices? And will those who won't be there on a full-time basis be willing to share an office?
- Will the casting director and casting assistants be headquartered there? If not, where will casting sessions be held for the producers and director?
- Will the wardrobe department be working out of these offices, and if so, will they need an office, fitting room, sewing room and/or space for clothing racks?
- Will Props and Set Dressing need locked storage spaces?
- Will you need a desk and phone for visiting production executives?
- Will editing rooms be set up there?
- Will Hair and Makeup department heads need space?
- If offices and stages are together, how much set construction space is needed? And will there be a need for secured rooms to lock up equipment?

Once the amount of space is determined, the search begins. If it works for you location-wise and budget-wise, many studio lots rent office and/or stage space to outside companies and come equipped with everything you could possibly need. If that isn't a viable option, you can start scouting rental space by doing any or all of the following: talk to other people who have rented office space lately, drive around the areas you're interested in and look for commercial real estate signs, check out ads for commercial space in the trade papers or other local publications, hire a location manager to scout for you and/or enlist the help of two or three commercial real estate agents. Once you have found an option or two, here are some questions to consider:

- Can you get an option for a month-to-month extension on the lease at the original rate should your schedule be pushed?
- Do you need stage space near or next to the offices? If not, how far are the offices from the stage space you might already have lined up? How far away will you be from your location sites?
- Is additional space available to rent if or as needed?
- Do the facilities provide sufficient parking, is the parking area secured and is there easy access into and out of the parking lot?
- If the parking lot will not accommodate cast, crew and production vehicles, would you have access to a sufficient amount of street parking, or could you rent additional (secured) parking facilities from someone else in the immediate vicinity?
- Does the property come with a security system or patrolling security personnel?
- Are you in an area that is safe enough so that those walking to their cars late at night won't feel apprehensive?
- Will you have access to the property twenty-four hours a day?
- Are the offices already wired for phones? Is there a phone system already in place? If not, how long will it take to have one put in?
- Do the offices come with furniture, or will you have to rent furniture from an outside source?
- Does the building have heating and air conditioning?
- Do the offices have windows, and if so, do they open?
- Are there noise factors in the surrounding area that might affect your operation?

- Are you in an area where your staff and crew cannot create any loud noise after a certain time at night or before a certain time in the morning?
- Is the wiring sufficient to accommodate a large photocopy machine and possibly editing equipment?
- Does renting office space from this individual or company obligate you to use or rent other things from them (equipment packages, services, etc.)?
- Is maintenance included in the rent, and if not, can the property management recommend an honest and reliable service that has cleaned there before?
- Will they agree to take care of such things as insect infestations, roof leaks, plumbing or electrical problems in a timely manner?
- You may not think this important at the moment, but find out if there is a policy that would prohibit your employees from bringing their (well-behaved) dogs to work with them. (I have never been on a show where at least one person didn't bring his/her dog to work, especially when on a distant location.)

Some productions look for warehouse space with offices, so their sets and offices can be at the same location. If this is the case with your show, here are some additional things to consider:

- Does the building have doors that are wide enough and tall enough to accommodate trucks driving right into the warehouse?
- Are the ceilings high enough (at least eighteen to twenty feet high)?
- Will the electrical wiring accommodate the needs of the production, or will you have to bring in generators?
- How will the set construction noise affect the production office?
- How will the production office noise affect shooting on the sets?
- If the warehouse is not soundproof, how will surrounding noises affect your shooting?
- Would you be allowed to attach a flashing red light and bell system to the outside of the warehouse and use it on shoot days?

SETTING UP

Once you have selected the office space, your attorney has approved the lease agreement, you have submitted your first rent check and have been given a key to the front door:

- If necessary, have new locks put on the doors (or possibly just the doors to certain offices or work areas), and have new keys made as needed.
- Find out how to access security codes or personnel.
- Make sure you know where to locate the electrical circuit box, the thermostats (and how they work), the phone lines coming into the building (underground or aerial/telephone pole) and the telephone equipment closet or terminal.
- Arrange for the phone system to be installed (if one is not already in place). Begin this process by determining how many rotary lines, modem lines, fax lines and extensions are needed; the type of system that will meet your needs and budget and where the phones should be placed. The local phone company will provide the phone lines, initiate service and assign you phone and fax numbers; but it is generally a separate (telecommunications) company that will install the lines and instruments, set up the system and rent you the system and phones on a monthly basis. (Note: when ordering service from the phone company, you might consider putting a block on all "900" numbers.)
- Get a floor plan of the office space from the property manager or draw one up yourself. Determine who will go into which offices or bullpen areas, where furniture will be placed, where office machines will go, etc. (The line producer, UPM, production supervisor, and/ or coordinator customarily make these decisions.)
- Order a photocopy machine that is a reliable workhorse, top-of-the-line (or close to it) model that puts out mega copies a month (you'll need it), and make sure the rental company can guarantee prompt response time to service calls. Decide where the photocopy machine is going to be placed before you schedule delivery. It's probably going to be noisy, so give it its own little area (with sufficient ventilation all around) if possible. Some companies will order one main copier and one or two smaller units for use by individual departments.
- Get bids, open accounts and order: office furniture (including a safe for Accounting and drafting tables and stools for the art department); fax machines (at least two), additional computers, monitors and printers for those who won't be bringing their own; a typewriter

(as antiquated as they may appear, every office needs one for typing forms and emergency checks); a refrigerator/freezer; bottled water and dumpsters (if needed). Schedule delivery of each.

- Have signs made (or make them up on your computer) with the name of your show/production company to hang outside the front door and at the entrance to your parking area.
- Make up name and title labels on your computer and attach them to the outside of each person's office door.
- If you are only allowed a certain number of parking spaces, have signs made and placed to indicate where everyone should park. Create reserved spaces (with their names on them) for the producer(s), director, production manager, production designer, DP and anyone else you wish to provide an exclusive spot for. The other spaces can just be labeled with the name of the production company or show.
- Make sure there are enough keys to the building for everyone who is going to need one.
- Prepare logs and sign-out sheets (see section *Inventories, Logs & Sign-Out Sheets* in Chapter 5, "Pre-production").

You have moved into the new production offices, and the setting-up continues:

- Arrange for security if necessary.
- Create a map to the office, including the address and phone number and detailed directions (coming from various areas of the city). Have a supply handy to send out or fax to those scheduled to come into work, for meetings or for casting.
- Design letterhead. The production designer is usually instrumental in creating a logo, which is then followed by approval from the studio/parent company. Have stationery printed up; or put the letterhead on computer disk, so it can be loaded into the computers of all those who will be using it. This way, it is printed out only as needed.
- Generate business cards. They can be ordered from a printing shop, or printed up right from your computer using Avery™ (Form 5371) White Business Card sheets. On tight budgets, since most printing companies require a 500-card minimum, I have ordered cards that contain the name of the show, production company, address, phone and fax numbers with an empty space in the middle of the card for

those who use them to write or print their names. When using the computer-generated cards, you can make them up individually for anyone who needs them. Those who will use them the most are the location manager and assistant location managers, but others who use business cards (especially when on distant location) tend to include the producer, production manager, production coordinator, production designer, art director and transportation coordinator.
- Print up return address and/or mailing labels. Some prefer to order rubber stamps (containing the name of the show and address) in various sizes.
- Make sure everyone knows how to operate the new phone system, and print up phone extension lists for each phone station.
- If the phone system does not come with voice mail, buy an answering machine that is compatible with your phone system.
- Make sure the office staff knows how to operate the copier and fax machines.
- Create fax cover sheets, and place a supply next to each fax machine.
- Place a subsequent furniture order if necessary (there are always items to be switched and/or added after the initial order).
- Set up the kitchen area. Assuming a refrigerator and bottled water dispenser (with hot and cold taps) have already been delivered, now consider a microwave oven, toaster oven, coffee makers and perhaps even a cappuccino maker. Depending on how long you will be there, it is often less expensive to buy these items than to rent them. Also equip the kitchen with a fire extinguisher, heavy-duty flashlight, candles, matches and first aid supplies.
- Craft service. If you don't already have one, obtain a membership to a discount warehouse store where production assistants can purchase craft service supplies and food. After the initial purchase of the basics (paper goods, coffee, tea, milk, juice, etc.), prepare and post your own *Craft Service Requests* form in the kitchen area, so favorite snack foods, fruits, cereals, etc. can be picked up on subsequent craft service runs. Many craft service areas now include a variety of headache, upset stomach and cold remedies; an assortment of vitamins and a selection of protein and power bars. And although not food-related, craft service runs should also include a liberal supply of Kleenex® and tampons.

For people who work all hours of the day and night, have little or no time to shop or cook and are more health-conscious than ever—good craft service is an essential element in creating a harmonious office.

- Contact maintenance/cleaning services to give you an estimate on cleaning the offices. Call services you have previously used or get referrals and/or references. Arrange to have the offices cleaned at least twice a week, and schedule the service to arrive after your work day has ended.
- Order at least one, half-inch VCR and TV monitor for the office (for viewing submission tapes, casting purposes, assessing location possibilities, etc.). If you are working for a studio or other production entity, check to see if they have any extra equipment they can loan you. If not, and again depending on how long it will be needed, make the decision as whether to rent or buy.

- Open accounts with a courier service and at least one overnight delivery service. Obtain waybills and packing materials from each. Also establish pick-up and delivery schedules and locate drop-off centers.
- Open accounts with the companies that will give you the best deals on reliable cell phones and pagers and place an initial order as needed.
- Establish an account with a discount office supply company that provides free, next-day delivery service and also one that is close by, where supplies can easily be picked up on an I-need-it-right-away basis. Make up and post an *Office Supply Requests* form in a designated area next to or near a supply catalog. Each request form is then attached to a purchase order and approved before the supplies are ordered. (Monitor orders carefully, as this is an area that can easily get out-of-hand and run over budget.) Here is an example of a supply request form:

OFFICE SUPPLY REQUESTS

DATE	ITEM	ITEM#	LIST PRICE	REQ. BY	DEPARTMENT

- Get bids, open an account and order at least one case each of both Polariod™ 600 and Spectra film. You will be ordering more later on, but this will get you started. The film is used by several different departments for purposes of continuity. Also make sure you have a good supply of batteries. The ones most commonly used are AA and AAA batteries.
- Have a PA pick up menus from restaurants in the area (preferably from those who deliver), and place menus in a three-ring binder, divided by the type of food (barbeque, Mexican, Chinese, Italian, vegetarian, etc.).
- Create a central information center (which is generally the reception area or a portion of a bullpen area manned by the APOC, production secretary and/or PAs) where: departmental envelopes are hung; messages are posted; out-baskets are labeled and set out for OUTGOING MAIL, OVERNIGHT DELIVERY PACKAGES, TO THE SET and TO THE STUDIO (or parent company); deadlines for outgoing mail and overnight packages are posted;

extra copies of crew lists, contact lists, the latest script changes, schedules, day-out-of-days, maps, request for pick-up and delivery slips, etc. are stacked (or placed in hanging envelopes); start paperwork, time cards, I-9s and other payroll and accounting forms that are available; the menu book and office supply catalog are available to look through; local phone books and maps are kept; extra office supplies, mailing supplies and interoffice envelopes are stored and waybills, fax cover sheets and other commonly-used forms are available.

- Strategically place designated trash cans or boxes around the office for recyclables.

THE TRAVELING PRODUCTION KIT

Whenever you start a new show, you not only bring all your past experience to the job, but you also bring your personal production boxes.

Contained in these boxes (which go with you from show to show and location to location) are items you have been accumulating since your very first show and from which comprise your "kit." In addition to your salary, most production companies will pay you a kit (also known as a "box") rental fee of generally $50 to $100 per week (although some now impose a total show cap of $1,000). I have seen production kits stored in any combination of bankers' boxes, foot lockers, suitcases on wheels and oversized fishing tackle boxes. Your need for larger receptacles will increase as you gradually collect new material. Think of your kit as a traveling office. It should contain everything you need to get started on any show at any location. Production supervisors, coordinators and assistant coordinators tend to keep more elaborate kits than do line producers and production managers, and everyone's is a little different. The following are items you might find in any one production kit:

- A computer and monitor (laptops are the most portable and most commonly used). Always keep the computer's manual close at hand.
- A printer for your computer (and an extra printer cartridge or two)
- Any other computer accessories you work with, such as a zip drive
- A surge protector
- A supply of computer disks
- A calculator (with an extra roll of tape)
- A label maker (optional, but handy)
- A flashlight
- A wall calendar
- A selection of self-inking stamps that read: Faxed, Completed, Draft, Copy, Unapproved, Confidential, File, Revised and Calls Pushed_____Hours
- A small supply of FedEx® packing materials and blank waybills
- At least one candle and matches (more for aesthetics than emergency measures)
- Basic office supplies: a three-hole punch, heavy-duty three-hole punch, two-hole punch, tape dispenser (with an extra roll of tape), scissors, in & out trays, at least one standing book/file divider, a supply of different sized laser labels, a stapler and staples, a heavy-duty stapler and staples, pens, pencils, a ruler, a roll of shipping tape, correction tape and/or fluid, a pencil sharpener, yellow writing tablets, message books, scratch pads, two or three petty cash envelopes, a pad of

Received of Petty Cash slips, various colored highlighters, permanent broad-tip markers, Sharpies®, rubber bands, paper clips and binder clips, a small supply of file folders and file folder labels, a glue stick, an assortment of Post-it™ tabs, push pins, a box of reinforcements, a small supply of batteries (C, AA, and AAA) and at least one ream of plain white paper
- A small first aid kit (with lots of Band-Aids™)
- A supply of Tylenol® and/or Advil®, antacids and throat lozenges
- A small desk clock
- A small desk lamp (some companies do not provide desk lamps, and you often have to work under those "I'm-getting-a-headache" florescent lights)
- I keep a small stash of my favorite teas, instant soup and oatmeal and small individual packets of salt and pepper
- An extra phone/modem extension line with jack plugs on each end
- An extension cord
- A headset for the phone (allowing you to talk hands-free)
- Your production binder. I carry the same large three-ring binder with me on every show. It contains the following divider tabs: Budget, Cast, Crew, Contacts, Schedule, Day-Out-of-Days, Locations, Travel, Corres/Memos, Post Production, Equipment, Script, Misc. I also have a few blank tabs/dividers that are used as needed for whatever topics are relevant to any given show. Updated lists, information and notes are continually being added to the binder throughout the production, and the binder is kept close-at-hand at all times (and goes home with me each night) for easy reference. When the production is over, I remove the contents (except for the dividers) and secure them with large brads. It now looks like a fat script and is filed or stored alongside the contents of other production binders from other shows. Once the contents are removed, the binder is ready to use on my next show.
- Resume book. Collect resumes of people you want to work with or work with again, or want to be able to recommend to others. Keep them in a large three-ring binder, divided by job categories and inserted in alphabetical order.
- Additional binders. Some production coordinators carry a few extra binders from show to show, each with alphabetical dividers. One is used to store copies of deal memos, one is for

workers compensation claims and one is for purchase orders (filed by vendor name). Some people feel that accessing this information from binders on a shelf is easier than pulling file folders out of drawers. (I've done both and have no strong preference either way.) When the show is over, the contents of the binders are transferred into the final production files, and the binders are ready to use again on your next show.

- Reference materials. This would include union and guild contract books, summaries and updates; pay scale rate charts; reference books, such as *LA 411®* (©L.A. 411 Publishing Company), *NYPG, Pacific Coast Studio Directory,* (©Pacific Coast Studio Directory), *Hollywood Creative Directory*™ (© Hollywood Creative Directory), *ifp/west Independent Filmmaker's Manual* (by Nicole Shay LaLoggia and Eden H. Wurmfeld, Published by Focal Press, ©IFP/West), Entertainment Partners' *Paymaster*, AFCI (Association of Film Commissioners International)'s listing of film commissioners, a local map book, any books you might have that would serve as quick references on budgeting and scheduling and of course—this book. And if your show will be shooting on distant location, you should have applicable airline schedules, maps, phonebooks and the production guide published by the film commission in that state and/or city.

- Production services files. Assemble a banker's box containing files that reflect an assortment of production services. From the shows you do, the trade shows you go to (such as Show-Biz Expo) and the vendors you interact with, you will amass a tremendous number of catalogs, bids, brochures and information on a wide assortment of equipment, materials, supplies and services. You may choose to reference these vendors via your collection of contact lists and/or reference books such as *LA 411®*, but if you want to save more detailed information on specific companies, production service files are for you. Keep them in alphabetical order. If you choose to save this information, update the contents of the files every year if possible. Here are some category suggestions: Animal Handlers, Bus Charters, Camera Equipment, Casting Agents, Caterers, Cell Phones & Pagers, Chartered Aircraft, Cleaning Services, Clearance & Research, Computer Rental & Repair, Counter-to-Counter Services, Courier Services, Cranes/Dollys/Camera Cars, Crew Gifts & Parties, Customs Brokers, Dumpsters, Editing Equipment, Editing Rooms, Expendables, Extra Casting Agencies, Film Commissions, Gifts, Grip and Electric Equipment, Heating & Air Conditioning, Heavy Equipment, Helicopter Work, Hotel Information, Insurance Agencies, Labs, Limo Services, Location Rentals, Location Services, Medical Services, Misc. Rentals, Office Equipment Rentals, Office Supplies, Payroll Services, Phone/Communication Systems, Picture Vehicles, Post Production Facilities/Services, Printing & Photocopying, Product Placement, Props & Set Dressing, Raw Stock & Sound Stock, Screening Facilities, Shipping Companies, Sound Equipment, Special Effects Companies, Stage Rentals, Still Photo Labs, Travel Services, Twenty-Four-Frame Video, Underwater Equipment & Services, Video Duplication, Visual Effects Houses, Walkie-Talkies, Wardrobe Houses and Weather Services.

- General reference files. You might also wish to keep files containing more general reference material, information that covers any or all of the following: Screen Actors Guild (contract information, plus a small supply of blank SAG contracts and Exhibit G forms), Directors Guild (contract information, plus a small supply of DGA deal memo forms), Misc. Forms (forms you have collected and like to use), Misc. Post Production Information, Sample Budgets, Safety Bulletins (a full set), Employment of Minors (the rules pertaining to hours, schooling, etc., a few blank applications for permits to employ minors and a few blank applications for work permits for minors), Employment of Aliens, Costs (cost information you want to save for purposes of future budgeting and negotiating). This is also where you are going to want to save your past Crew and Contact lists. It is amazing how often you will want to go back to find a specific person or vendor you had previously worked with (to use again or recommend to someone else). And if you don't have the collection of resumes you're saving in a binder, this is a good place to keep them as well—in files labeled by department.

This is quite a lot to carry from show to show, and there are times when not all of it will be relevant to your current project. After a while, you will instinctively know what to bring with you on any given show; and sometimes, you will end up bringing it in gradually as needed. Once settled into a new production office, transfer your production services and general reference files into a file cabinet (I prefer the lateral type) and your reference books, resume book and other binders onto a bookcase.

Make labels with your name on them and affix one to each item in your production kit, including the binders and file boxes. This way, there is no doubt that these things belong to you, and chances are, they will be less apt to disappear.

Also inventory the contents of your production kit, including the make, model, serial number and value of each piece of equipment; and keep the inventory in your permanent files (computer) at all times. (You only have to inventory files when traveling out of the country, and then, just by the number of file boxes.) Accounting will require a copy of your inventory when you submit your start paperwork. This inventory will provide backup for your box rental fee and for insurance purposes should anything from your kit be stolen. The inventory will also serve to meet customs requirements when traveling to foreign locations.

ANSWERING THE PHONE

You can call any production office and, chances are, someone will answer the phone by saying, "Production!" Depending on who is uttering this one-word greeting, it often comes across as "I'm-busy-what-do-you-want-make-it-fast!" Searching for an alternative to the old standard, a few years ago I started instructing my staff to answer the phone with the name of our film. Unfortunately, not all companies want to announce this information. On my last film, however, the producer convinced me that an even better way to greet callers is to say, "Production, this is (give name)." Answering the phone by identifying yourself is definitely friendlier. You may be equally as rushed as the person who just says "Production!" But this puts the person on the other end of the line at ease right off the bat; he or she knows exactly who is speaking and isn't put off. I am now convinced that this is the only (and most professional) way to answer a production office phone.

PRODUCTION ASSISTANTS

On the proverbial ladder one climbs while working one's way up to a desired position, a pro-

duction assistant (PA) is half a rung up from a ground-level intern. And, like an intern, a production assistant need not have a great deal of experience. This is where a good attitude, an eagerness to learn and help and a willingness to put in that extra effort—beyond what is expected, will propel a PA up the ladder. Good production assistants are worth their weight in gold; yet, as a group, they are the lowest paid and often the most exploited and least appreciated. While a PA's duties can be less than desirable, it is a great place to start, learn, make contacts, discover what you ultimately want to do and make yourself invaluable to everyone around—so much so that they will all want to bring you with them on their next shows.

As gratifying as it may be to give someone their very first job in the business, it takes a great deal of time to train a PA and some amount of experience to master the job. Therefore, make sure that not all the PAs you hire are rookies. Hire at least two who are seasoned and can help train those who are less experienced.

Some production assistants are assigned to work the set (under the supervision of the assistant director team), some are assigned to specific departments or to assist with cast needs and others are assigned to the office. Most production assistants want to work the set, but for that reason alone, those jobs are more difficult to come by. Those who understand that no matter where you're assigned, the trick is to get your foot in the door, will take the office jobs if there are no other (more desirable) offers at the time. The PAs referred to in this chapter are Office PAs.

Office PAs should be responsible to the production coordinator or assistant production coordinator only. They should not take directions from everyone in the office. The production coordinator (or APOC) coordinates the production assistants' duties and schedules their workday based on production priorities.

Those requesting pick-ups or deliveries generally fill out a request form (a *Request for Pick-Up/Delivery* form can be found at the end of this chapter). The form, along with any item to be delivered, is placed in a designated box—not given to a PA. The production coordinator then coordinates and schedules the runs. If an emergency should arise and a PA is not available to make a run, the production coordinator will make alternate arrangements (another PA, courier service, transportation driver, etc.). All completed pick-up/delivery forms are kept on file through the end of production. Whenever possible, production assistants should have the use of company cell phones when they are out of the office, providing you with instant access to them. If cell phones are not an option, the next best thing is pagers. If a PA does not have his or her own pager, the production should rent some (pager rentals are fairly inexpensive). Also, if a PA does not carry a cell phone, he or she should be required to call the production office after each run should there be a need for a pick-up on their way back.

INTERNS

Internships are beneficial to both the intern and the production company. Interns are students or individuals new to the industry (or new to a specific facet of the industry) who lack experience and contacts. They agree to work for a designated period of time (which is often the duration of a production) for little or no salary. An intern's compensation may include any or all of the following: experience, school credit, a small salary, free lunches, reimbursement of gas receipts, screen credit, invaluable contacts with people who have the potential of becoming future mentors. For someone who can afford to work for little or no salary for a limited amount of time, this is the best way to get your foot into the doors of the companies you want to gain access to and to meet and work with the people who have the capacity to hire and/or recommend you on other productions. And should you require even further justification for committing to hard work without a salary, merely think of this as a continuation of your education.

The overwhelming benefit to a production company is having additional employees who will not tax their budget. Many lower-budgeted films could not have been made without the contributions of their interns.

Since many colleges and universities offer internship programs to their students, contacting one or several of the schools in your area to apply for interns is a good way to start. A particular student's schedule may not always coincide with the hours you need someone to work, but more than one intern with differing schedules may do the trick. The schools will generally ask you to submit a description of the internship being offered. Here is a sample:

FILM PRODUCTION SEEKING INTERNS

On ____(date)____, _____ Productions is beginning principal
photography on a motion picture entitled _____ ,which is being produced for
_____(studio)_____.

The film stars _____ and is being directed by _____
_____.

We are currently looking for interns to work with the production, and their duties would include: answering phones, filing, running errands, photocopying and generally assisting staff members with whatever needs to be done at any given time. Part of the intern's day would also be spent on the set in a capacity yet to be determined at this time.

We are looking for team players who are self-motivated, quick learners, organized and good at follow-through. We want individuals who are good at following direction, do not mind long hours and understand the concept of paying dues. The ability to get along well with others, multitask and know when to ask questions is important. Interns should have cars that are in good working order and auto insurance; and they should know their way around the area. Previous experience is not essential, but enthusiasm and a good attitude is.

This internship would afford students the opportunity to become part of a feature film production and to interact with industry professionals. It would be a tremendous learning experience and a potential connection to vital contacts and future job opportunities.

Our production offices are headquartered at _____ , and we will be filming through
_____.

If you are interested in interning on this film, please contact _____at: ____(phone #)____.

Thank you for your interest in our film.

Interns can also be recruited by advertising in industry-related publications or just by asking everyone you know if they know of anyone who would like to intern.

When interns come through a college or university internship program, the school's workers' compensation policy covers them should they suffer a work-related injury or illness. When an intern does not come via a school internship, the production company is liable, as the interns are working under their direct supervision. Due to these liability issues, studios and production companies institute an array of differing policies with regard to interns. Some refuse to use interns unless they are part of a sanctioned school internship program. Some will pay their interns minimum wage, so they will be covered under the payroll company's workers' comp policy. Others, who carry their own workers' compensation insurance, will inform their insurance company that they wish to assume the responsibility for covering an intern and will be required to submit (in writing) general information regarding the terms of the internship. The information required is: name, address, phone number, social security number, exact work capacity and duties, department intern will be working in, work dates and hours, state(s) intern will be working in and any other applicable conditions. Details of the internship can be submitted to the insurance company via an *Intern Notification* form, a sample of which can be found at the end of this chapter.

If you are considering using the services of an intern from another country, and this person does not have a U.S. social security number or work visa (green card), discuss this with your insurance company as soon as possible. Obtaining foreign workers compensation coverage can be quite costly and may be enough to negate the worth of the intern. Under no circumstances should you allow anyone to work on your show (even someone willing to work for nothing) before workers' comp coverage is secured.

EMPLOYEES DRIVING THEIR OWN VEHICLES FOR BUSINESS PURPOSES

If an employee is driving a personal vehicle during the business day for business purposes and has an accident, insurance regulations specify that a person's own insurance is primary. The company's *non-owned auto liability policy* covers the production company, not the individual. All employees using personal vehicles for business purposes (especially PAs and interns) need to be informed of this policy and show proof of auto insurance.

STAFF SCHEDULING & ASSIGNMENT OF DUTIES

Your staff can be more effective if you do not schedule them all to work the same hours. The objective is to stagger shifts while making sure the office is always covered at first call or at the start of the business day (whichever is first), throughout lunch and through wrap or the close of the business day (whichever is last). Even when the crew call is not early in the morning, someone should be available to set up the office for the coming day, be available to deal with vendors and accessible to prepping/rigging crew members who start early. And when shooting nights, some productions require coverage in the office through wrap; while others will not require anyone in the office past midnight (usually after the first meal break) and, hopefully, after the call sheet has been finalized, copied and distributed.

When scheduling the office staff, take all factors into consideration, such as who lives the closest to the office, closest to the set, closest to the airport or closest to the lab; who can stay in the office alone late at night when necessary; who can drive to the set late at night when necessary; how are each person's strongest abilities best put to use and when are their strengths most needed; who functions best in the morning; who can run the office alone and who is better as support staff.

Once you have everyone on the right shift doing what they do best, consider alternating shifts and responsibilities. (You can always change them back.) Whenever possible, and assuming you have a big enough staff to do this— let one production assistant remain in the office manning the phones and fax machine, photocopying, handling craft service, etc., and have another out on runs all day. Then the following week, reverse their roles. This will give both a chance to earn mileage reimbursement, master different tasks and interact with different people. Along the same lines, give one production assistant the early shift one week and a later shift the following week. Or assign one PA to the office one week, and to the set, the next. Giving PAs and interns the opportunity to learn different responsibilities and work with a variety of departments will keep them motivated, anxious to keep learning and eager to do well.

A thoroughly practical and effective form designed by co-worker and production coordinator, Stephen Marinaccio, is the *Daily Office TO DO List*. Although PAs and interns are required to keep their own log of assigned tasks, details have been known to fall between the cracks amid the hecticness of a long day. This list eliminates the excuse for ever forgetting and clearly details all duties and responsibilities by the shift/time-of-day. The To Do List at the end of this chapter is a version of Stephen's form and can be used as is or as an example for creating your own.

STAFF MEETINGS

Just as you can never have enough production meetings, the same holds true with office staff meetings. A great deal of information flies around the office each day; but as many memos as you receive, questions you ask and conversations you overhear—and as much as you endeavor to stay on top of everything; different people end up with different pieces of information. The more you know, the better-informed your decisions are and the more helpful you are to others. I suggest daily meetings (either first thing in the morning or last thing at night) between the production manager, supervisor, coordinator and, possibly, assistant coordinator. If daily meetings are not possible, get together as often as your schedule permits. This time together lets you share valuable information, go over everything that has to be accomplished, decide who is going to do what and how to best handle pending issues.

I have worked with people who unfortunately believe that production assistants and interns should only be told what to do and never asked for their opinions. Nothing could be more counterproductive to promoting loyalty and team work within the production office. The production coordinator should meet regularly with his or her assistant coordinator, production secretary and all office PAs and interns; and this meeting works best at the end of the day. This is a time to let staff members know as much about what is going on with the movie you are allowed to share with them; within the realm of their world, to review what isn't working well and how to make it better; to bring up a problem someone may be having with another staff or crew member and discuss how to best resolve the issue and to share suggestions. Production assistants may be perceived to be at the bottom of the food chain and are far from decision-makers; but the good ones work hard for

little money, do the worst jobs on the show (hopefully without complaint), make your job easier and are there to back you up when needed. They have little say-so outside of this small, restricted arena, and should therefore be entitled to voice their opinions and discuss issues affecting their work environment. Their ability to participate in meetings validates their worth and further invests them in the successful running of the show.

OFFICE LUNCHES

Going on the assumption that members of any given production staff are too busy to go out to lunch and are needed in the office as much as possible, many production companies will pay for staff lunches. Again, this policy varies, depending on the company. Some will pay for lunches just during principal photography, while catered meals are being served on set. Some will also budget for a limited number of office meals (lunches and/or second meals or dinners) during prep. And some productions can both afford and are generous enough to offer their staff lunches throughout the entire prep, shoot and wrap periods, including an allowance for second meals for late nights. Once you determine if and when you are going to provide office lunches, your next step is to put a dollar limit on each person's order or a limit on each entire order. For instance, you can give everyone an $8.00 limit when each person is allowed to order off of a designated menu or give yourself a daily limit of $200 if ordering buffet style.

Ordering lunches for the staff is time-consuming, so make the process as easy as possible. Select a different restaurant each day, one that offers a variety of menu choices (accommodating both vegetarians and meat-eaters), has a majority of menu items within your price limit and that preferably delivers. Then instead of sending a PA around to take orders, just send the menu around with an attached piece of paper, so each person can write his or her name and order. You might consider making up a form with everyone's name on it and an allocated space to write in their orders. That way, you won't forget anyone. One person should be the designated orderer. And if the restaurant does not deliver, one of your PAs can pick up the food. There are also services (at least in the L.A. area) that will send you a catalog of menus from local restaurants; and if you call them, for a nominal fee, they will relay your order, pick up and deliver the food directly to your office. Choosing a restaurant, letting everyone select from the menu, ordering, picking up and passing out meals takes a lot of time. Allow yourself enough time to accomplish this in a timely manner. Otherwise, you will be eating at 3:00 every afternoon instead of the normal 12:30 or 1:00.

Staff members are almost always too busy to go to lunch, and meals are always being brought into the office, even on productions that cannot afford to provide lunches or are not providing them during a particular period of time. The only difference is that under these circumstances, everyone must pay for their own food. This can get tricky, because someone has to be responsible for collecting the money each day. While one person may have ordered a sandwich and is then called away to a meeting, someone else may realize too late that he or she doesn't have enough money that day and three other people just don't have the right amount of change. One company I worked for solved this problem by having Accounting front the money for the lunches. The Assistant Production Coordinator kept tabs on how much each person owed (including their share of the tips) and gave us all a tally at the end of the week—indicating a total amount to be paid back to Accounting.

No matter how you do it, the process of bringing food into the office is time-consuming; but that extra hour spent in the office (and not at a restaurant) is often more valuable.

TIME MANAGEMENT

The use of a Distribution Log or a To Do List, ordering supplies and/or lunches that can be delivered instead of having a PA pick them up and having staff members fill out their own request forms for craft service, office supplies and lunches are all examples of procedures that (while also fulfilling other responsibilities) will save valuable time. Any process that keeps employees on track, details more organized or replaces several steps with one will ultimately save time; and there is too much to do and accomplish each day *not* to consider any and all effective time-saving methods.

Another vital key to effective time-management is to prioritize. When you have ten things to do, ask yourself these questions about each task:

- What will happen if this is not done in an hour?
- What will happen if this is not done by the end of the day?

- Is this needed by call time tomorrow?
- Is it truly a rush?
- Who is waiting for this and how will it affect their work?
- Will it affect the schedule, a deal or someone's travel plans?
- Will not accomplishing this right away force someone to go into overtime or meal penalty?
- Will it prevent a shipment from getting out in time?

Being able to realistically answer these questions should put the importance of your tasks into the proper perspective. And prioritizing will not only save you time in the long run; but when all responsibilities do not share equal value, you are better able to accommodate new emergency situations when they arise.

RECYCLING

There is always an abundance of recyclable materials produced by a production, both in the office and on the set. The size of a staff and crew, multiplied by their work hours, equals a plethora of empty soda cans and bottles and mountains of paper created by script revisions, new schedules, outdated call sheets, maps, etc. Whether it's your craft service person or a production assistant collecting recyclables, it's important that they are collected and terribly wasteful not to.

A designated cardboard box or trash can should be allocated for the collection of empty soda cans and bottles. Place additional empty boxes or cans near the copier machine and in various locations around the office for paper. Place large, easy-to-read signs on these receptacles, so there is no mistaking the fact that you are collecting Recyclables HERE.

If your city, studio lot or building does not provide for the pick-up of recyclables, locate the nearest recycling center to your office. Have a production assistant or driver drop off recyclable items as often as it is convenient.

THE FILES

Part of running an efficient production office is establishing a complete set of files. This is a guide to organizing files and includes every category I can think of, some of which will not apply to all shows. Delete or add files as needed. Basically, any issue you deal with that necessitates or generates major paperwork deserves its own file. If there is a chance your files could get mixed-up with the files from another project, indicate the name of the show at the top of each file folder label, with the heading underneath. Secure each file with an Acco® fastener, so the contents will not fall out.

For your convenience, the file folder headings listed below can be found on the CD-ROM. They are formatted to print out Avery® (Form 5266) Laser File Folder Labels.

Files Of Blank Forms

Applications for Minors' Work Permits

Asset Inventory Logs

Box/Equipment Rental Inventory Forms

Check Requests

Courier Slips

Crew Deal Memos

Daily Office To Do Lists

DGA Deal Memos

Distribution Logs

Drive-To Sheets

Equipment Rental Logs

Extra Vouchers

Fax Cover Sheets

Filmmaker's Code of Conduct

I-9s

Insurance—Auto Accident Claim Forms

Insurance—Certificates of Insurance

Insurance—Loss & Damage Claim Forms

Insurance—Workers Compensation Claim Forms

Intern Notification Forms

Invoice Forms

Letterhead

Loanout Agreements

Location Agreements

Location—Non-Filmed Agreements

Location—Parking Release

Location Release Form

Mileage Logs

Mobile Phone/Pager Sign-Out Sheets

Petty Cash Envelopes

Production Office Information Sheets

Purchase Orders

Purchase Order Log Forms

Raw Stock Order Logs

Release Forms—Misc.

Request for Office Supplies

Request for Pick-Up/Delivery Forms

Safety—Acknowledgement of Guidelines

Safety Bulletins

Safety Checklists & Forms

SAG—Daily Contracts

SAG—Exhibit Gs

SAG—Taft/Hartley Reports

SAG—Three-Day Contracts

SAG—Weekly Contracts

SAG Contracts—Stunt Daily

SAG Contracts—Stunt Weekly

Sign-Out Sheets—Misc.

Start Paperwork

Travel Authorizations

Walkie-Talkie Sign-Out Sheets

Waybills

Wrap Reports

Files For Features, Movies For Television, Cable Or Internet

Animals

Art Department

Assets & Inventories

Budget—Preliminary

Budget—Final

Budget—Cash Flow

Budget—Chart of Accounts

Budget—Cost Reports

Call Sheets

Camera

Cast Deal Memos

Cast List

Cast Photos

Casting Information

Catering

Check Requests

Clearances

Completion Bond Company

Contact List

Continuity Breakdowns

Correspondence—Memos

Counter-to-Counter Service
Courier Log & Waybills
Crew Deal Memos
Crew Gifts—Photo—Wrap Party
Crew Lists
Crew Resumes
Customs
Day-Out-of-Days
Delivery Receipts
Director
Distribution
Distribution Agreement
Equipment (Miscellaneous)
Equipment Rental Logs
Extra Casting
Forms (Misc.)
Grip—Electric
Helicopter Work
Hotel—Motel Accommodations
Immigration
Insurance—Auto Accident Claims
Insurance—Cast Claims
Insurance—Certificates of Insurance—Equipment
Insurance—Certificates of Insurance—Locations
Insurance—Certificates of Insurance—Misc.
Insurance—Certificates of Insurance—Set Dressing, Props, Wardrobe
Insurance—Certificates of Insurance—Vehicles
Insurance—General Policy Info. & Correspondence
Insurance—Loss & Damage Claims
Insurance—Workers Compensation Claims
Interns
Legal
Locations—Local—Loc. List, Agreements & Permits
Locations—Distant—Loc. List, Agreements & Permits
Maps
Marine Department
Medical
Miscellaneous
Mobile Phones & Pagers
Music
Network (or Cable) Format

Network Standards & Practices (if applicable)
Office (Equipment, Furniture, Phones, Keys, etc.)
Office Lease Agreement
One-Line Schedule
Pager & Mobile Phone List
Personal Releases
Picture Vehicles
Post Production—Contact List, Correspondence, etc.
Post Production—Schedule & Delivery Requirements
Post Production—Screen Credits
Pre-production Schedule
Producer(s)
Product Placement
Production Reports
Projection Equipment—Projectionist
Property—Set Dressing
Prosthetics—Special Makeup Effects
Publicity
Purchase Orders—P.O. Log
Railroad Info. & Contract
Request for Pick-Up & Delivery Slips
Research Report
Resumes—General
Safety Memos & Reports
SAG—Final Reports
SAG—Fully Executed Cast Contracts
SAG—Fully Executed Stunt Contracts
SAG—Station 12
SAG—Taft-Hartleys
Script
Script—Final
Script Revisions
Script Synopsis
Script Timing
Set Construction
Shipping Info. & Logs
Shooting Schedule
Special Effects
Storyboards
Studio (or Parent Company)
Stunt Breakdown
Transportation—Vehicles

Travel—Chartered Flight Info.

Travel—Flight Schedules

Travel—Movement Lists

Underwater Info. & Equipment

Union—Guild Information

Video Playback

Visual Effects

Wardrobe

Walkie-Talkies

Wrap—Schedule & Memos

Writer(s)

Series Files

When setting up files for a television series, set up two sets—*general production files* and *episode files*. Episode files should have the name of the episode in capital letters at the top of each file folder label and the heading underneath.

General production files should contain files as listed above (as needed), except for those placed in the episode files.

Episode Files (Three For Each Episode)

1. Complete script with all changes
2. Call Sheets and Production Reports
3. Cast List, Shooting Schedule, Day-Out-of-Days, One-Liner, Research Report, etc.

Day Files

It has become a common practice for production personnel to maintain *day files*. The files are kept in chronological order and are labeled as follows, with one file for each day of shooting:

DAY #1

(Day)/(Date)

Each file contains all pertinent information for that day of shooting: call sheet, production report, camera report, sound report, film inventory, catering receipt, etc.

Individual call sheet and production report files can be kept (as indicated earlier); call sheets and production reports can be kept in day files or they can be cross-referenced and kept in both types of files. Use whichever system works best for you.

A complete set of files is particularly important when turning a show over to the studio or parent company shortly after the completion of principal photography. Before submitting files, however, go through the master set in addition to those kept by the producer(s), UPM, production supervisor, coordinator, location manager and art department coordinator. Pull out duplications (keeping originals whenever possible), so you're not sending six copies of everything. Consolidate and inventory all files—with an inventory listing the contents of each box on the outside of the box and a master inventory you can submit separately.

FORMS IN THIS CHAPTER

- Request For Pick-Up/Delivery
- Intern Notification
- Daily Office TO DO List

NOTE: File folder label headings for blank and pre-printed forms and information and for features, movies for TV, cable or Internet are formatted on the book's CD to print out on Avery™ #5266 Laser File Folder Labels.

REQUEST FOR ☑ PICK-UP ☐ DELIVERY

SHOW __HERBY'S SUMMER VACATION__ DATE __7·5·XX__

REQUESTED BY __FRED FILMER__

ITEM(S) TO BE PICKED-UP/DELIVERED __(1) COPY SAG THEATRICAL__
__CONTRACT BOOK__

PICK-UP FROM/DELIVER TO (INDIVIDUAL)_____

(COMPANY) __SCREEN ACTORS GUILD__ PHONE# __(323) 954-1600__

ADDRESS __5757 WILSHIRE BLVD.__
__LOS ANGELES__

DIRECTIONS (if needed)__
__EAST OF FAIRFAX — TURN LEFT @ MUSEUM SQUARE__

PICKUP/DELIVER BY:

☐ _____ (A.M.) (P.M.)   ☐ REFERENCE P.O.#_____
☑ AS SOON AS POSSIBLE   ☐ CHECK REQUIRED FOR PICKUP
☐ TODAY, NO SPECIFIC TIME   ☑ SEE RECEPTIONIST
☐ NO RUSH -- WHENEVER YOU CAN

COMMENTS/SPECIAL INSTRUCTIONS __BOOK IS "ON HOLD"__
__UNDER XYZ PRODUCTIONS__

DATE & TIME OF PICKUP/DELIVERY __11:30 A.M. — 7/5/XX__

ITEM(S) DELIVERED TO (PRINT NAME) __FRED FILMER__

RECEIVED BY (SIGNATURE)_____

© ELH   (ALL PICK-UP & DELIVERY SLIPS ARE TO BE KEPT ON FILE IN THE PRODUCTION OFFICE)

INTERN NOTIFICATION

PRODUCTION COMPANY ___XYZ PRODUCTIONS___

SHOW _HERBY'S SUMMER VACATION_ DATE _6.30.XX_

INTERN'S NAME ___LUCAS WANNABEE___

SOCIAL SECURITY NO. ___111-22-3333___

ADDRESS ___4327 BARRYMORE LANE___
___LOS ANGELES, CA 90003___

HOME PHONE# _555-7631_ PAGER# _555-9873_

HOME FAX# _____ MOBILE PHONE# _____

WORK CAPACITY ___OFFICE P.A.___

DEPARTMENT _PRODUCTION_ SUPERVISOR _CONNIE COORDINATES_

TO WORK AT THE FOLLOWING LOCATION(S)   IN THE FOLLOWING STATE(S)

HOME·BASE   _CALIFORNIA_

LOCATION PRODUCTION OFFICE   _WISCONSIN_

_____   _____

DATES OF SERVICE: FROM _6.30.XX_ TO _9.27.XX_

TO WORK ___5___ Days Per Week ___12___ Hrs. Per Day

☐ PAID INTERNSHIP @ $_____ ☐ per hour ☐ per day ☐ per week

☑ UNPAID INTERNSHIP

☐ SCHOOL CREDIT   College/University_____
         Phone#_____
         Contact_____

COMPANY TO PROVIDE:
   ☑ LUNCH - CATERED ON SET OR $_6_ MAX. OFF SET
   ☑ MILEAGE REIMBURSEMENT @ _.31_ ¢ PER MILE
     (DOES NOT INCLUDE DISTANCE TO & FROM REPORT-TO LOCATION)
   ☐ REIMBURSEMENT OF GAS RECEIPTS
   ☑ HOTEL ACCOMMODATIONS (IF SO, INTERNS MAY SHARE ROOMS)
   ☐ OTHER_____

AGREED TO _Lucas Wannabee_
     Intern's Signature

APPROVED BY _Fred Filmer_

© ELH

DAILY OFFICE TO DO LIST

CHECK-OFF ITEMS AS THEY ARE COMPLETED   DATE _____

IN THE MORNING

FIRST PERSON IN
- [ ] Stop on your way in to buy craft service food (donuts, bagels, fruit, juice, etc...)
- [ ] Check with front gate (or Security) to see if any packages had been dropped off during the night
- [ ] Inform Security you are in (if applicable)
- [ ] Put the coffee & hot water on, set-up craft service area, replenish bottled water supply if needed
- [ ] Turn on heat or air conditioning, open windows, unlock doors, turn on lights
- [ ] Check for messages on voice mail, write out and distribute
- [ ] Check for faxes, make copies & distribute
- [ ] Call weather service for today's weather report

LATER IN THE MORNING (DUTIES ASSIGNED BY PROD. COORDINATOR)
- [ ] Finish copying and distributing incoming faxes/messages
- [ ] Copy, file and distribute daily paperwork sent in from set
- [ ] Check office supply area to determine what needs to be replenished/ordered
- [ ] Make sure there is an ample supply of Fed-Ex® envelopes & waybills, mailing supplies & postage
- [ ] Check craft service area to determine what needs to be replenished/ordered
- [ ] Check departmental wall envelopes to determine who did not retrieve yesterday's messages or vital paperwork
      Locate those individuals, relay messages & arrange for pickup or delivery of the paperwork
- [ ] Work out schedule of daily runs with the production coordinator or assistant coordinator

DAILY
- [ ] Make sure there is an ample supply of the latest complete script (with all changes)
- [ ] Make sure there is an ample supply of current schedules, crew lists, maps, script change pages, etc.
- [ ] Monitor the supply of fax cover sheets and other forms used daily. Replenish as needed.
- [ ] Distribute incoming mail
- [ ] File contents of "To File" box
- [ ] Track down and relay important messages to those who may not be in the office
- [ ] Check updated weather report
- [ ] Keep photocopy & kitchen (craft service) areas neat
- [ ] Help with clean-up after lunch
- [ ] Check to see if additional runs need to be made during the day
- [ ] Continually check fax machines for incoming faxes
- [ ] Check area surrounding offices for loose trash and/or cigarette butts. Clean as necessary
- [ ] Take all outgoing mail to post office by 4:30 p.m.
- [ ] Make sure over-night delivery packages are dropped off before scheduled deadline
- [ ] Monitor food and water supplies
- [ ] Monitor paper supplies (white legal and letter and 3-holed white, blue, pink, etc.)
- [ ] If you run out of things to do, **ASK** what you can do to help

AT NIGHT
- [ ] Call sheet distribution
- [ ] Tomorrow's weather report
- [ ] Make sure all copiers, fax machines and printers are fully stocked with paper
- [ ] Clean kitchen area, including: counters, dirty dishes, sink, coffee pots, cutting boards, knives, etc.
- [ ] Close & seal all opened food containers, store in ziplock bags and/or in refrigerator
- [ ] Clean photocopy & fax areas, restack and reorganize paper
- [ ] On nights cleaning service is not due, collect & bag trash & close dumpsters
- [ ] Straighten bullpen areas & replenish forms
- [ ] Prepare sides for the next day

LAST PERSON OUT:
- [ ] Close & lock windows, turn off heat or air conditioning
- [ ] Turn off lights
- [ ] Activate voice mail/answering machine
- [ ] Close & lock doors
- [ ] Call Security to let them know you are last man out

FRIDAYS
- [ ] Mail approved Exhibit G's to SAG
- [ ] Mail certificates of insurance (not previously mailed) to insurance company
- [ ] Throw out old food from refrigerator
- [ ] Wash out refrigerator
- [ ] Prepare a list of who will be working over the weekend for Security

REMEMBER... KEEP A NOTEPAD & PEN WITH YOU AT ALL TIMES, TAKE NOTES AND IF YOU HAVE A QUESTION -- ASK.

© A Stephen A. Marinaccio II form

CHAPTER THREE

Basic Accounting

This chapter will not teach you how to become a qualified production accountant, nor will it teach you how to budget your film. What is intended is an understanding and appreciation of what a production accountant does, how an accounting department functions, how a budget is created, and how costs are tracked. Defining the following responsibilities and procedures will help to explain how significantly large sums of money are handled, dispersed, accounted for, and effectively managed to facilitate the needs of an entire production.

THE PRODUCTION ACCOUNTANT

This person is responsible for contributing to the preparation of the budget, monitoring all costs incurred and is essentially the guardian of the production's purse strings. He or she is instrumental in opening the production's bank account(s); is one of the signatories on the bank account; is responsible for creating cash flow charts, daily hot costs and weekly cost reports; managing and supervising the accounting department; working with department heads in overseeing and managing their individual budgets and keeping the studio, producers, bond company (if applicable) and production manager constantly apprised of where the show is financially. The accountant is frequently asked to estimate how potential changes to the schedule, cast, sets or locations will affect the budget (something that occasionally must be determined after the fact). Estimating how any given production-related decision or change will affect the budget requires a knowledge of production-related expenses, union rates and regulations, in addition to the

ability to predict costs. (This often comes intuitively after a certain amount of experience in this position.) Offsetting overages created by overtime days and meal penalties, the accountant will often pull funds not being fully utilized in one account and transfer them to an account that is over budget. If no amount of shifting money from one account to another can help the fact that the production is over budget, then the accountant will generally meet with the studio, producers and/or production manager to decide how best to remedy the situation, if it has been mandated that the show must remain on budget. Such decisions may include cutting out a location, scheduling shorter days or even shaving a day off the schedule, if necessary.

Working on foreign locations and/or with international crews, the accountant may need to open and monitor various bank accounts in multiple currencies. In many cases, an additional accountant or assistant accountant from the country you are working in will be hired to assist in paying local crew and vendors and in meeting local government and union obligations.

For those interested in becoming a production accountant, it is a position that does not necessarily require a financial background. Having been a bookkeeper or being a CPA would be helpful, but it is not mandatory. Having a good amount of common sense is. You can work your way up the accounting department ladder starting as a clerk, moving up to a second assistant, a payroll assistant, a first assistant and then an accountant. It is a position that carries with it a great deal of responsibility and innumerable challenges. And it's a job that remains the same whether you are on a $1 million-show or a $200 million-show. The only thing that changes is the volume of your work.

THE ACCOUNTING DEPARTMENT

This department, headed by the production accountant, is responsible for opening vendor accounts; processing check requests and purchase orders; paying the production's bills (accounts payable); processing payroll; dispersing petty cash; making sure studio or production company accounting procedures are being adhered to and that all State, Federal, union and contractual obligations are being met as they come due. They also play a major role in preparing insurance claims.

When it comes to the dispersing of money on a production, it seems as if everyone is in a hurry and everything is urgent. Some requests for cash or a check are indeed time-sensitive and needed immediately, but rush requests that are not crucial may stem from overzealous crew members. Part of the accounting department's job is to prioritize the needs of the production and to make sure that payments are made in a timely manner. Responsible accounting, however, dictates that prior to any funds being dispersed, certain steps (safeguards) must be taken. The first is the auditing of the check request or invoice to make sure the charges are correct and fit within the perimeters of the budget. There must be substantiating backup as well, such as an original contract, invoice, purchase order or check request (the amounts of which must match the amounts on the contract, bid, request or invoice); and approvals must be obtained from the department head and production manager, production supervisor or producer. As a last measure, the check must generally be signed by two different people (who first have to be located), making it impossible for any one person to issue funds without the other's knowledge or approval. Should you find yourself in the position of the person asking, you will now (hopefully) have an appreciation for what the accounting department must go through before you can receive your emergency check.

HANDLING PAYROLL

Most productions rely on the services of a payroll company to handle the payroll for their staff, cast and crew, and these companies are set up to pay both union and non-union employees. The payroll company becomes the *employer of record*, and being such, show employees are covered by the payroll company's workers' compensation policy. A payroll company's fees will vary depending on the payroll company, your budget and your relationship with the payroll company. Charges are generally negotiated at $7 to $10 per check for all above-the-line payments (writers, producers, director and cast), and a one-quarter to one-half percent fee based on the below-the-line (crew) payroll. The production company or studio will generally select the payroll company to be used, and the accountant will designate an individual to oversee all payroll matters. On larger shows, it would be a payroll clerk who would deal exclusively with payroll. On smaller shows, it might be a first assistant who would handle payroll along with other responsibilities. There are also times when the accountant him or herself might assume the payroll duties. Whoever this individual is, he or she is responsible for making sure start paperwork for each employee is properly and promptly submitted; comparing hours on timecards to production report hours (and making sure they match); knowing all local guild and union contracts, along with State and Federal payroll guidelines; calculating time cards (cast, crew and staff), flagging any irregular or suspicious time cards and bringing them to the attention of the accountant and/or production manager; submitting production manager-approved weekly time cards to the payroll company in a timely manner and approving the payroll company's audit on Wednesday (or the third day of your shoot-week) before checks are cut and issued on Thursday (the fourth day of your shoot-week) or Friday (the fifth day) when on distant location due to the time needed to ship the checks to location. This individual also tracks the payment of all box rentals, per diems, mileage reimbursement and car allowances; deals with actors' agents on cast payroll issues and answers all payroll-related questions from crew members. Working closely with the payroll company, this person must make sure that the payroll checks are ready on time, that they are prepared correctly, that errors are quickly remedied and that all appropriate union and guild hours and fringes are reported and submitted as required.

THE ACCOUNTING SYSTEM

Each of the major payroll companies (such as Entertainment Partners, Cast & Crew, Axium and All Payments) license accounting system software (on a show-by-show basis) to the studios and production companies they do business with. This system interfaces with your show's payroll and allows you to input accounts payable, purchase orders, petty cash expenditures, etc. It generates reports such as general ledgers, trial balances, check registers, cost reports and a "bible" (a history of all the accounting transactions on your production). It would not be practical to use one payroll company to handle your show's payroll and to license the software package from another, as you will want the ability to download your payroll records onto the software program you're using.

ACCOUNTING GUIDELINES

On their first day on a new show, crew members are given a packet of paperwork. This packet may include some or all of the following: a payroll start/close slip; a U.S. Immigration I-9 Form; a box rental inventory form; a blank deal memo form to be completed and approved by the UPM (the deal memo may also come from the production supervisor or coordinator); a set of safety procedures; a crew information sheet (this form is covered in more detail in Chapter 5, "Pre-Production"); and a memo outlining the production's accounting policies. This memo will generally cover procedures pertaining to payroll, box rental, vendor accounts, competitive bids, purchase orders, check requests, petty cash, production-owned assets, automobile allowances, mileage reimbursement, invoicing and additional taxable income. The following sections cover accepted industry guidelines pertaining to these matters.

Payroll

All individuals are subject to withholding of applicable Federal, State and local taxes, except those with *loanout* corporations. Under these circumstances, the corporation "loans out" the employee's services to the production company, the employee's compensation is paid directly to the corporation, and the corporation is responsible for all applicable payroll taxes. Most studios dictate which positions can be paid as a loanout through their corporations, and they generally include the actors, writer(s), director, producer(s), casting director, director of photography, production designer, costume designer, editor and music composer. Those who qualify are asked to complete a Loanout Agreement and provide the accounting department with a stamped copy of their articles of incorporation. The corporation

must also be qualified to do business in the state in which the production company operates, or State income taxes are assessed.

All employees (those subject to withholding as well as loanouts) must complete a U.S. Immigration I-9 Form (substantiated with a valid driver's license and social security card, birth certificate, U.S. passport, or alien registration card). Time cards are due at the end of the last working day of the week. They must include your name, project name and social security number or tax ID number, clearly printed. When indicating actual hours worked and the time taken for meals, the use of military time is preferred. On union shows, the hours worked are calculated by tenths, where each six-minute period is one-tenth of an hour. The following will help you reference military time and tenths.

MILITARY TIME	
A.M.	P.M.
1:00	+ 12 = 1300 hrs
2:00	+ 12 = 1400 hrs
3:00	+ 12 = 1500 hrs
4:00	+ 12 = 1600 hrs
5:00	+ 12 = 1700 hrs
6:00	+ 12 = 1800 hrs
7:00	+ 12 = 1900 hrs
8:00	+ 12 = 2000 hrs
9:00	+ 12 = 2100 hrs
10:00	+ 12 = 2200 hrs
11:00	+ 12 = 2300 hrs
12:00	+ 12 = 2400 hrs

TENTHS	MINUTES					
1	1	2	3	4	5	6
2	7	8	9	10	11	12
3	13	14	15	16	17	18
4	19	20	21	22	23	24
5	25	26	27	28	29	30
6	31	32	33	34	35	36
7	37	38	39	40	41	42
8	43	44	45	46	47	48
9	49	50	51	52	53	54
10	55	56	57	58	59	60

Time cards must be approved by a department head prior to being turned in. Those not turned in on time may result in late paychecks.

Paychecks are issued on the fourth work day of the following week, usually Thursday (or Friday, if Monday was a legal holiday or if you are working a six-day week on a distant location). If there is an error on your paycheck, politely discuss it with the production accountant or payroll clerk on any day except time card day (the first day of the work week), as this is the deadline to get time cards to the payroll company if Accounting is to get the paychecks back in time. If there is a valid error on your check, the payroll company will be contacted and the adjustment made. If you approach the accountant or other members of the accounting department as if they are trying to cheat you out of your hard-earned money, they will be anything but cooperative in helping you with the problem. Most payroll errors are inadvertent mistakes (often made by the payroll company) and are easily corrected. If the perceived error concerns a differing interpretation of your deal, rate, hours or union-related issues, immediately clear this up with the person you made your original deal with (producer, production manager or production supervisor).

The figure on page 29 illustrates how to correctly fill out a time card.

Box Rentals

Those who have an approved deal that includes a box rental must complete an itemized inventory of the box/kit contents. Check with Accounting to verify whether this payment can be indicated on your weekly time card or if you need to invoice for it. (See *Box/Equipment Rental Inventory* form at the end of this chapter.)

Vendor Accounts

Check to see if the production company you are working for already has established accounts with any of the vendors you wish to do business with, or if they have accounts with vendors you may not use on a regular basis but with whom the company gets discounted rates (which could be a help to your budget). Once you have done that, give Accounting a list of the remaining vendors you wish to open new accounts with and indicate who is authorized to make purchases/rentals on each account. Do not set up accounts on your own. Have the vendors fax their credit applications to Accounting. Also inform them that once the account is opened, you will be working on a purchase order system and that nothing can be ordered without a P.O.

Competitive Bids

Most studios and production companies will require you to get two or three competitive bids on all major purchases and rentals. This will especially apply to the rental of personally-owned equipment owned by department heads and other members of your crew.

Purchase Orders

The use of purchase orders is Accounting's most valuable method of tracking and forecasting costs. Many production companies so seriously and stringently enforce this policy that they refuse to pay invoices that do not have purchase orders. If your accounting department does not send out letters informing vendors of this policy, then it is your responsibility to inform the vendors you work with that all invoices must reference a P.O. number. Also, never hold a purchase order until the corresponding invoice arrives. Submit it as soon as possible, so the cost can be approved and the forthcoming invoice expected.

Purchase orders must be used whenever possible for purchases, rentals and/or services with vendors the company has, or will have, an account with. If you are not paying cash for something and Accounting has not already issued a check for it, it needs a P.O. Purchase orders are obtained from the production coordinator or accountant department and must be completely filled out and approved before an order can be made. It must also be determined that the cost of this purchase, rental or service is covered within the confines of your budget. If the purchase order is for $500 or less, it is generally approved by the production manager or production supervisor. If the purchase order is for more than $500, it may require the approval of your producer or studio executive.

When you receive a purchase order number, it will only be for the exact items and amount indicated on the P.O. If you need to add items to your order, you will need to submit a new purchase order. You cannot add on to the existing one. If you need to extend the date of a rental, some accountants will require a new purchase order, some will ask for a P.O. Extension form and still others will prefer the extended dates written on a copy of the original P.O.

Purchase orders must (legibly) indicate the name, address and phone number of the vendor; the vendor's Federal ID number (if the business entity is a corporation) or social security number

CREW TIME CARD

PICTURE ①									PROD.#			GUAR. HRS.		WEEK ENDING ⑤			
NAME ②									SOCIAL SEC..# ③			JOB CLASS ④		ACCOUNT#			
LOAN-OUT									FED. ID#			LOCATION ⑥	CITY COUNTY				
													WORK STATE	FOREIGN [ ]			

CODING	DATE	LOC	DAY	CALL	1ST MEAL OUT	1ST MEAL IN	2ND MEAL OUT	2ND MEAL IN	WRAP	RE-RATE	OCC CODE	1X	1.5X	2X	PNLTY	ACCNT#	RATE	TYPE	HRS.	TOTAL
⑦			1ST	⑧	⑨	⑩	⑪	⑫	⑬									REG		
			2ND															1.5X		
			3RD															2X		
			4TH															2.5X		
			5TH															3X		
			6TH															M.P.		
			7TH																	
										TOTAL HOURS							TOTAL AMOUNT			

ACCNT.#	MEALS-ALLOW.	MEALS-TAXABLE	PER DIEM ADV.	ACCT.#	LODGING-ALLOW.	LODGING-TAXABLE	PER DIEM ADVANCE
ACCT.#	BOX RENTAL ⑭	ACCT.#	CAR ALLOW ⑮	ACCT.#	MILEAGE-ALLOW.	MILEAGE-TAXABLE	MILEAGE ADVANCE
CHECK ONE [ ] BOX RENTAL INFORMATION ON FILE [ ] BOX RENTAL INFORMATION ATTACHED ⑯				ACCT.#	2ND CAMERA	OTHER	SALARY ADVANCE

COMMENTS

PRODUCER AND EMPLOYEE ACKNOWLEDGE BY SIGNING THIS CARD THAT IF NO HOURS ARE RECORDED, PAYROLL CO. WILL PRESUME THAT ONLY THE GUARANTEED HOURS WERE WORKED

EMPLOYEE ⑰
SIGNATURE X

APPROVED ⑱ X

PLEASE REFER TO THE ABOVE ILLUSTRATION TO MATCH THE NUMBERED NOTES. FILLING OUT YOUR TIMECARD IS A SIMPLE TASK IF YOU FOLLOW THESE GUIDELINES.

1. NAME OF YOUR SHOW
2. YOUR NAME
3. YOUR SOCIAL SECURITY NUMBER
4. YOUR JOB TITLE
5. WEEK ENDING DATE
   (Usually Saturday's date, but ask your accounting dept. if you are unsure)
6. CITY AND STATE YOU ARE WORKING IN
7. DATE(S) OF WORK (MONTH/DAY)
8. TIME OF YOUR CALL (REPORT TIME)
9. TIME YOU LEFT FOR LUNCH
10. TIME YOU RETURNED FROM LUNCH
11. TIME YOU LEFT FOR DINNER (SECOND MEAL)*
12. TIME YOU RETURNED FROM DINNER (SECOND MEAL)*
13. TIME YOU FINISHED WORK (WRAP TIME)
14. AMOUNT OF YOUR BOX RENTAL FOR WEEK*
15. AMOUNT OF YOUR CAR ALLOWANCE FOR A WEEK*
16. CHECK APPROPRIATE BOX IF YOU HAVE A BOX RENTAL*
17. YOUR SIGNATURE
18. DEPARTMENT HEAD'S APPROVAL

*THESE BOXES APPLY IF APPLICABLE

OTHER NOTES:

If you are to receive mileage, you will fill out a mileage log sheet and turn it in with your timecard. Leave the mileage box empty. Accounting will fill in the amount.

Use "COMMENTS" section only to note upgrades, etc.

Please print legibly. It will help in getting your paychecks to you on time.

Remember: The accounting department needs as much space as possible to do its calculations, so please leave the rest of the timecard blank.

(required by Federal law) and a detailed description of the work, materials ordered or items to be rented. If it is for a rental, it must indicate when the rental begins and when it will end. Purchase orders should also include a set number if applicable.

You will not get an approval on an open purchase order. If the exact dollar amount of the purchase, rental or work is not known at the time the purchase order is issued, it should reflect an estimated amount that will not be exceeded. Any charge exceeding this amount must have prior written approval, and unapproved overages could be rejected.

If the P.O. is being issued by the production department, a copy should be made for the production files before submitting it to the accounting department. Accounting will obtain approval signatures (if not already signed) and distribute fully executed copies to the department head and vendor.

Accounting keeps its own log of purchase orders, and the production coordinator generally keeps a running log of the P.O.s issued by the production department. This log should indicate the date, vendor, item(s) being purchased or rented, amount of purchase or rental, date of rental return and the department to which each P.O. is assigned. Also noted on the P.O. log are purchases that at the end of the show become part of the company's asset inventory. As these costs are entered into the system, assets generally valued at $100 (or more) are automatically scheduled on an ongoing asset list monitored by Accounting.

Check Requests

When you cannot use a purchase order and need an immediate or rush check, you will begin the process by obtaining a *Check Request* from the production coordinator or the accounting department. Fill it out completely. The UPM or production supervisor must approve it before payment can be made, and an original invoice, contract or other form of substantiation must be submitted to back up the request. If an original invoice has not yet been received, ask the vendor to fax you a copy, and attach that to the check request (noting that the original will be submitted as soon as it arrives). As with purchase orders, do not hold up the check request process by waiting for an original invoice.

Each check request should contain the following: vendor name, address, phone number, tax ID number or social security number, department/

individual requesting the check and a description that is as detailed as possible, such as:

- Is this for a purchase, rental, service, location fee, petty cash advance or deposit?
- If it is for a deposit, is it refundable or to be applied to the final bill?
- Is this a partial payment, or the first of many?
- What are the terms of the purchase, rental or service?
- Is the check to be mailed or held for pickup?
- What is the total amount to be?
- Specify date and time the check is needed.

If a check is needed immediately and the UPM is not present to approve the request, an effort should be made to locate him or her and to obtain verbal approval over the phone or via walkie-talkie. If the UPM cannot be found, approval should be obtained from the producer or studio executive. Even if this check is needed immediately, give Accounting the time they need to process the request and to obtain the necessary approvals and signatures.

Check requests (with substantiating backup) for the purchase of tools, props, wardrobe, etc. (anything that can be considered a company asset) also become part of Accounting's asset inventory log. Major assets should also be noted as such on your purchase order inventory log.

Petty Cash

Petty cash should be used for small purchases that are not covered by a purchase order or check request, generally for items such as gas or oil for company vehicles, parking fees, expendable supplies, small props and miscellaneous office supplies. Although most studios prefer petty cash to be used for items costing less than $100, most place a $250 to $300 cap on receipts that can be paid in cash. Petty cash is requested via a *Check Request* form or a specific *Petty Cash Advance Request* form that is approved by the UPM. Those receiving petty cash will receive a check in their name (or actual cash, to be determined by the production accountant) and a petty cash envelope to keep track of all petty cash expenditures.

Anyone receiving a cash advance from another person in the company will need to sign a *Received of Petty Cash* slip acknowledging receipt of the cash. The person advancing the funds will also sign the slip. When petty cash receipts are turned in, it is the responsibility of the person who had been given the cash to retrieve and discard the Received of Petty Cash slip, so he or she will no longer be responsible for the money.

Petty cash receipts should be numbered and taped to 8 1/2 x 11 sheets of paper, in sequence, each clearly labeled as to exactly what it is for. List the corresponding numbers on the front of the petty cash envelope, along with a description of each item. Petty cash should not be used for salaries (labor of any kind) or rentals, and will generally not be reimbursed for these types of expenses.

All reimbursed receipts are subject to approval, so make sure your crew is aware of the guidelines pertaining to petty cash expenditures imposed by the studio or production company you are working for, such as:

- If you advance any of your petty cash to other individuals, you are still responsible for all receipts and for the collection of any outstanding sums.
- Services of individuals or casual labor must be paid through the payroll company and not through petty cash. In case of emergencies, however, or last-minute site rental fees, have the individual you are paying write out a receipt that includes his or her name, address, telephone number, tax ID number or social security number and a signature for receipt of the cash.
- Some companies require receipts for gasoline charges to be identified by date, driver's name, vehicle license plate, quantity purchased, price per gallon and gas station.
- Meals purchased with petty cash often require preapproval by the UPM.
- It is now an IRS requirement that restaurant charges over $25 be submitted on credit card receipts.
- Each menu item ordered must be listed on restaurant receipts, and you will be required to list everyone who ate the food on (or next to) the restaurant receipt.
- Restaurant receipts in the form of check stubs are no longer acceptable (at any company). If the restaurant you eat at or order from only takes cash and only offers check stubs, ask them to write out an itemized receipt for you and to staple one of their business cards to it.
- Only original receipts are acceptable—no photocopies.
- All petty cash envelopes must be done in ink—not pencil.
- All receipts must have the vendor's name, address and telephone number imprinted or

stamped on them (if not, once again, staple one of their business cards to it).
- Note petty cash purchases that will become company assets (usually anything over $50).
- If you use cash or change for things for which there are no receipts, such as parking meters, pay phones or gratuities—make up a receipt noting what the expense was and the date it was incurred.
- If a receipt does not clearly indicate what was purchased, write a brief description on the paper next to the receipt.
- On each receipt, circle the date, vendor's name and the amount of the purchase. Do not use a highlighter for this, as the highlighter causes the printing to fade on certain paper receipts.
- Each petty cash envelope is a separate entity. You may not continue your receipts on a second envelope.
- Submit petty cash envelopes once a week or, ideally, when you've spent half your money. Date, list and total all expenditures. Do not seal the envelope. Once approved, the accounting department will either reimburse the total in cash, or issue a check for the amount of your expenditures, keeping your initial draw (or your "float") at the same balance. At the completion of principal photography or wrap, the balance of receipts and remaining cash must be accounted for before you leave the show.
- You will not be given additional petty cash prior to accounting for funds already advanced to you.
- Petty cash expenditures not accounted for by the end of one's employment on a film will generally be deducted from that person's final paycheck.

Cell Phone Reimbursement

This industry utilizes different methods of reimbursement when it comes to personal cell phone use. Establish your own policy, and make sure it is known to all those who plan to use their own phones for business purposes. Some companies reimburse only up to a certain dollar amount, such as $200. Others will ask you to determine what percentage of your bill is work-related, and they will pay that percentage. Most companies have you determine how many minutes were spent on work-related calls, and then those minutes are multiplied by your per-minute rate.

When requesting reimbursement for work-related calls, either from your personal cell phone or home (land) line, original phone bills should be submitted (not photocopies), and all work-related calls should be highlighted or circled and totaled. The bills should then be attached to a completed check request form and submitted to Accounting. You cannot use petty cash to reimburse yourself for phone calls.

Auto Allowances

Some negotiated crew deals (primarily those of department heads) include a weekly auto allowance (amounts vary depending on the show, budget of the show and anticipated use of the individual's vehicle). IRS regulations require car allowances to be paid through Payroll, and they are subject to income tax withholding.

Mileage Reimbursement

Production Assistants are the most common recipients of mileage reimbursement, because part of their job requires them to use their own vehicles to make production-related "runs." The most common form of reimbursement is made by paying a predetermined rate per mile (approximately 32¢ per mile). Some companies choose to refund gas receipts instead.

To qualify for a per-mile reimbursement, fill out a *Mileage Log*, indicating a beginning mileage, destination, purpose and ending mileage for each run. Estimated mileage is not acceptable. Mileage to and from home is not reimbursable. Employees who receive mileage reimbursement are not reimbursed for gas receipts.

In order to be reimbursed for mileage expenses, submit the Mileage Log to the UPM, production supervisor or production coordinator for approval. Once approved, the production office will pass it on to Accounting for payment. Some companies include mileage reimbursement in weekly payroll checks. Others require approved mileage logs to be submitted with a check request, and payment is made through Accounts Payable. Requests for mileage reimbursement should be submitted on a weekly basis. If your company reimburses gas receipts, this is generally done through petty cash.

Drive-To

Drive-to is another form of mileage reimbursement paid to cast, crew and extras for reporting to a local location. The mileage is determined by calculating the distance from the studio or production office to the location and back, and multiplying that distance by approximately 32¢ per mile (the exact amount is determined by individual union/guild contracts). Daily mileage to and from a location (or "report-to") site is recorded on the daily production reports. Up until recently, individuals would sign for their drive-to money and receive cash on the set on a daily basis. New IRS regulations have necessitated a change in this procedure, and now a week's accumulated drive-to is added to each person's time card and paid through Payroll. If the amount per mile is more than what the IRS allows, that amount is subject to income tax withholding.

Invoicing

Crew members should turn in their invoices for services, equipment/box rental, vehicle rental, car allowance or mileage reimbursement at the end of each week for payment the following week. Each invoice must include the employee's name, his or her corporation name, address and social security number (or Federal ID number). A complete description of what the invoice is for (i.e., services rendered or equipment rental) and a week-ending date must also be indicated on the invoice. All invoices are approved by the UPM or production supervisor before payment can be made.

Additional Taxable Income

The Federal government has set an allowable limit for mileage reimbursement, drive-to and per diems. Any amount over such limit (see your accountant for limit guidelines) is considered taxable income and will be taxed along with the weekly payroll checks. Box rental moneys are also considered taxable income but are generally not taxed on a weekly basis when the detailed inventory list is provided. Those receiving box rentals will receive a 1099 at the end of the year and will be responsible for the taxes on this additional income.

THE BUDGET

Each budget starts with a *top sheet*, which is a summary of the budget categories. The accounts are broken down into Above-the-Line or Below-the-Line categories. Above-the-line accounts include the script, writer(s), producer(s), director, cast (including casting, bits and stunts) and above-the-line expenses. Below-the-line refers to all production and post production expenses (or sometimes: shooting period, completion period and miscellaneous other expenses). The top sheet indicates each account, on what page in the budget the detail can be found and the budgeted amount for that account. Lastly, above-the-line and below-the-line costs are added together to form a grand total for the entire budget.

Each account has an account number which is listed along the left-hand column of each page. After the two-page top sheet, the budget is broken down and detailed by subaccounts. For example, if *Production Staff* is Account #20-00, then the Unit Production Manager would be #20-01, the First Assistant Director, #20-02 . . . and so on. A *Chart of Accounts* is a list of all account and sub-account numbers and is used for the purpose of *coding* all production-related expenses (on purchase orders, check requests, invoices, petty cash purchases, payroll entries, etc.). Although the budget format is generally the same, master account numbers vary depending on the studio or production company. Each uses its own budgeting format.

So much goes into the preparation, modification and monitoring of the budget, that there should be no reason why those involved should not know what the financial standing of a production is on any given week (if not day). The size of your budget does not matter. If a show is set up correctly to begin with, then you will know if, when, where and how your project is going over-budget—and, if necessary, when it's time to bring it back under control.

Preliminary Budgets are often done prior to a project ever being sold or picked up and are usually based on a first or early version of a script. They reflect how much a particular script will cost to produce and can be a major contributing factor to selling (or not selling) the project.

The first budget is prepared in conjunction with a script breakdown, production board and schedule, and the process begins as you translate this data into man hours, pay scales, cast salaries, location fees, anticipated rentals, etc. Although some individuals do budgets straight from the script, the budgeting is considerably more accurate when based on a board. Also, the more variables you are given up front, the more precise your budget will be. These variables would include knowing such things as whether this is a union or non-union film, which format it will be

shot in, which actors are being considered for specific roles, where locations are to be, etc. The more information you are provided with, the more accurate your budget.

A budget is an estimate based largely on the experience of the person preparing the budget. Anyone can look up costs, but a somewhat seasoned production manager, accountant or estimator will intuitively know where to factor-in costs not always found in books or on pay scale charts. As capable as the preparer is, however, there are always unexpected circumstances that will arise to alter the budget. That is why, whenever possible, budgets include "pads" (certain line items in the budget where you can inconspicuously forecast slightly higher costs and rates for items or crew you know will cost less) and/or "contingencies" (generally, an additional 10 percent of the total budget) to accommodate those unforeseen overages.

If a completed budget is determined not to be sufficient to make the film as envisioned, then compromises have to be made. From a budgetary standpoint, this is where pads and contingencies (or portions thereof) are removed. Changes can be made to the script to reflect smaller sets, fewer locations, fewer cast members, etc. Other compromises might include using a less-expensive cast, shooting in less-expensive locations, using a smaller crew or making this a non-union instead of a union film. Not until the budget reasonably reflects the agreed upon scope of the production is the project going to receive a "green light."

Most budgets go through several incarnations during development and pre-production as locations are changed, one actor is replaced with another and the writer adds, deletes or changes scenes. Budgets are also refined during this period as department heads research and anticipate their specific needs. If something is going to cost more than originally anticipated, and it is agreed that incurring this additional cost will benefit the film, then either permission is required from the investor(s), studio, network, company or agency to increase the budget, or other costs must be reduced to accommodate the overage.

Before the budget is finalized, department heads should feel confident that (barring any unforeseen circumstances) they can operate within the boundaries of their departmental budgets; and you should feel confident that they will endeavor to do so.

During pre-production, the accountant prepares a *Cash Flow Chart* for the investor(s), studio or production company. This schedule divides the total amount of the budget by how much cash will be needed to operate the production during any given week from the beginning of pre-production through post production and delivery. Each week, the figure varies depending on the size of the cast and crew that week; whether it's a prep, shoot or wrap week; whether the company is filming on location; etc. As in the budget, a cash flow chart is an estimate. It is the accountant's best guess as to what will keep the company operating on a week-to-week basis. Some companies will use this as a schedule for depositing funds into the production's bank account(s).

The final budget is the one everyone agrees to adhere to, and the studio executive, producer, production manager and accountant are asked to sign-off on. This means no more changes or additions are allowed that will add to the budget, unless they are studio-approved. It happens occasionally that a production manager or accountant feels it will cost more to do a picture than what the studio is allowing, and the studio is not willing to make the necessary changes to accommodate the difference. If you should find yourself in this situation, you may not wish to sign off on the budget.

Nonapproved overages from then on are deficit-financed by the studio or production company or taken from other (underutilized) areas of the budget. If neither of those options is feasible, then production- and/or post production-related cuts are made to make up for the overage. If a completion bond company is involved, and the picture has gone over budget, the bond company may have the right to take over the management of the film.

TRACKING COSTS

Daily Hot Costs represent an analysis of how much was spent versus what was budgeted and/or scheduled. Most accountants do a hot cost analysis based on each day of principal photography. It may also be called a *Daily Cost Overview*. This report indicates what was budgeted and/or scheduled for that day: the number of scenes, the number of pages, cast overtime, company shooting hours, meal penalty, catering and use of raw stock. There is a second column to indicate actual figures, and then a third to indicate the variance. These figures are fed into the accounting system by account, keeping the status of the budget as current as possible. Conscientious departments

heads often keep track of their own daily hot costs.

All expenses entered into the accounting system are used to produce *Weekly Cost Reports* (or *Estimated Final Cost Reports*). A cost report details each account listing: total cost to date, cost to complete, estimated final cost, what was budgeted and the variance. These reports continually provide you with the latest financial status of your film.

As previously mentioned, if your accounting department is set up and run properly, there should be no excuse for not knowing the financial status of your show on a weekly (if not daily) basis. You cannot operate and manage your show properly if this information is not readily available to you.

As a working (or potential) production professional, or someone who wants to become a production accountant, knowing how to accurately budget a film and how to use a good budgeting software program (such as *Movie Magic*) is an incredibly valuable asset. There are several good books on the subject and classes you can take to do just that. A few of the books you might want to look at are: *The On Production Budget Book* by Robert J. Koster (Focal Press), *ifp/west Independent Filmmaker's Manual* by Nicole Shay LaLoggia & Eden H. Wurmfeld (Focal Press), *The Hollywood Guide to Film Budgeting & Script Breakdown for Low-Budget Features* by Danford Chamness (The Stanley J. Brooks Company) and *Film & Video Budgets* by Michael Wiese and Deke Simon (Michael Wiese Productions).

FORMS IN THIS CHAPTER

- U.S. Department Of Justice I-9 Form—to be completed by all employees
- Loanout Agreement
- Box/Equipment Rental Inventory
- Vehicle Rental Sheet—not a standard form, but it should be. Keep one on file for every vehicle being rented for your show, and attach copies to respective certificates of insurance being forwarded to your insurance agency, so they have more complete information when scheduling the vehicles for coverage.
- Purchase Order—usually on NCR paper with four or five different colored pages, printed with sequential numbers in the upper right-hand corner of the page and the name of the

production, production company, address and phone number in the upper-left corner of the page.
- Purchase Order Extension
- Purchase Order Log
- Check Request
- Petty Cash Accounting—you can attach this form to the front of an envelope, or buy petty cash envelopes with this (or one of a few other standard formats) printed right on the envelope.
- Received Of Petty Cash—these usually come in pads and can be purchased at any stationery or office supply store.
- Individual Petty Cash Account—this is not a standard form but something I designed for myself to keep track of my own petty cash accounting.
- Mileage Log—mainly used by production assistants, but can be used by anyone who gets reimbursed for mileage when driving his or her own car for production-related purposes.
- Invoice—generic form that can be used for any invoicing purpose.

- Cash Or Sales Receipt—generic form that would most commonly be used at the end of a show when assets (leftover raw stock short ends, props and set dressing, office supplies, etc.) are being sold.
- Daily Cost Overview (also known as: Daily Hot Costs)—used by the production accountant and others to assist them in staying on top of costs and managing the budget.
- Crew Data Sheet—this is not a standard form, and this information can be found on Accounting's software system; but as a production coordinator/supervisor, I find it helpful in keeping track of crew members' start and wrap dates and in making sure everyone's paperwork is turned in to Accounting.
- Timecards/Invoices Weekly Check-Off List—another generic/nonstandard form that can be helpful.
- The Check's In The Mail—A good way to keep track of when checks are mailed out.

EMPLOYMENT ELIGIBILITY VERIFICATION (Form I-9)

1 **EMPLOYEE INFORMATION AND VERIFICATION:** (To be completed and signed by employee.)

Name: (Print or Type) Last	First	Middle	Birth Name
LOCKS	GOLDIE		

Address: Street Name and Number	City	State	ZIP Code
12345 MONROE LN. - MALIBU, CALIFORNIA			90265

Date of Birth (Month/Day/Year)	Social Security Number
4-12-XX	932-76-5401

I attest, under penalty of perjury, that I am (check a box):

☑ 1. A citizen or national of the United States.

☐ 2. An alien lawfully admitted for permanent residence (Alien Number A _____).

☐ 3. An alien authorized by the Immigration and Naturalization Service to work in the United States (Alien Number A _____.
or Admission Number _____ , expiration of employment authorization, if any _____).

I attest, under penalty of perjury, the documents that I have presented as evidence of identity and employment eligibility are genuine and relate to me. I am aware that federal law provides for imprisonment and/or fine for any false statements or use of false documents in connection with this certificate.

Signature *Goldie Locks*	Date (Month/Day/Year) 6.30.XX

PREPARER/TRANSLATOR CERTIFICATION (To be completed if prepared by person other than the employee). I attest, under penalty of perjury, that the above was prepared by me at the request of the named individual and is based on all information of which I have any knowledge.

Signature	Name (Print or Type)

Address (Street Name and Number)	City	State	Zip Code

2 **EMPLOYER REVIEW AND VERIFICATION:** (To be completed and signed by employer.)

Instructions:

Examine one document from List A and check the appropriate box, **OR** examine one document from List B **and** one from List C and check the appropriate boxes. Provide the **Document Identification Number** and **Expiration Date** for the document checked.

List A	List B		List C
Documents that Establish Identity and Employment Eligibility	Documents that Establish Identity	**and**	Documents that Establish Employment Eligibility

List A:

☐ 1. United States Passport

☐ 2. Certificate of United States Citizenship

☐ 3. Certificate of Naturalization

☐ 4. Unexpired foreign passport with attached Employment Authorization

☐ 5. Alien Registration Card with photograph

Document Identification

_____

Expiration Date (if any)

_____

List B:

☑ 1. A State-issued driver's license or a State-issued I.D. card with a photograph, or information, including name, sex, date of birth, height, weight, and color of eyes. (Specify State) CALIFORNIA)

☐ 2. U.S. Military Card

☐ 3. Other (Specify document and issuing authority)

_____

Document Identification

T0070733

Expiration Date (if any)

4.12.XX

List C:

☑ 1. Original Social Security Number Card (other than a card stating it is not valid for employment)

☐ 2. A birth certificate issued by State, county, or municipal authority bearing a seal or other certification

☐ 3. Unexpired INS Employment Authorization Specify form
_____

Document Identification

932.76.5401

Expiration Date (if any)

_____

CERTIFICATION: I attest, under penalty of perjury, that I have examined the documents presented by the above individual, that they appear to be genuine and to relate to the individual named, and that the individual, to the best of my knowledge, is eligible to work in the United States.

Signature *Nellie Nombers*	Name (Print or Type) NELLIE NOMBERS	Title PRODUCTION ACCOUNTANT

Employer Name	Address	Date
XYZ PRODUCTIONS · 1234 FLICK DR. - HOLLYWOOD, CA - 90038		6.30.XX

Form I-9 (05/07/87)
OMB No. 1115-0136

U.S. Department of Justice
Immigration and Naturalization Service

Employment Eligibility Verification

Section 1. Instructions to Employee/Preparer for completing this form

Instructions for the employee.

All employees, upon being hired, must complete Section I of this form. Any person hired after November 6, 1986 must complete this form. (For the purpose of completion of this form the term "hired" applies to those employed, recruited or referred for a fee.)

All employees must print or type their complete name, address, date of birth, and Social Security Number. The block which correctly indicates the employee's immigration status must be checked. If the second block is checked, the employee's Alien Registration Number must be provided. If the third block is checked, the employee's Alien Registration Number *or* Admission Number must be provided, as well as the date of expiration of that status, if it expires.

All employees whose present names differ from birth names, because of marriage or other reasons, must print or type their birth names in the appropriate space of Section I. Also, employees whose names change after employment verification should report these changes to their employer.

All employees must sign and date the form.

Instructions for the preparer of the form, if not the employee.

If a person assists the employee with completing this form, the preparer must certify the form by signing it and printing or typing his or her complete name and address.

Section 2. Instructions to Employer for completing this form

(For the purpose of completion of this form, the term "employer" applies to employers and those who recruit or refer for a fee.)

Employers must complete this section by examining evidence of identity and employment eligibility, and:
- checking the appropriate box in List A *or* boxes in both Lists B and C;
- recording the document identification number and expiration date (if any);
- recording the type of form if not specifically identified in the list;
- signing the certification section.

NOTE: Employers are responsible for reverifying employment eligibility of employees whose employment eligibility documents carry an expiration date.

Copies of documentation presented by an individual for the purpose of establishing identity and employment eligibility may be copied and retained for the purpose of complying with the requirements of this form and no other purpose. Any copies of documentation made for this purpose should be maintained with this form.

Name changes of employees which occur after preparation of this form should be recorded on the form by lining through the old name, printing the new name and the reason (such as marriage), and dating and initialing the changes. Employers should not attempt to delete or erase the old name in any fashion.

RETENTION OF RECORDS.

The completed form must be retained by the employer for:
- three years after the date of hiring; or
- one year after the date the employment is terminated, whichever is later.

Employers may photocopy or reprint this form as necessary.

U.S. Department of Justice
Immigration and Naturalization Service

OMB #1115-0136
Form I-9 (05-07 87)

LOANOUT AGREEMENT

Film: HERBY'S SUMMER VACATION

Prod. Co.: XYZ PRODUCTIONS

Address: 1234 FLICK DR.
HOLLYWOOD, CA 90038   Date: 6·25·XX

This agreement is between XYZ PRODUCTIONS ("Producer") and
GREAT RYDERS, INC. ("Company") for the services of F. SCOTT RYDER
_____ ("Employee"), in the position of WRITER   .

Company warrants that it is a bona fide Corporation, incorporated in the State of CALIFORNIA
_____ on JANUARY 5, 20XX. Federal ID# 95-33226543   , and
as a condition precedent to Company's receipt of any payment hereunder, will present a Certificate of
Incorporation to Producer evidencing corporate status.

Company and Employee warrant that Employee is under exclusive contract to Company, and that
Company has the right to loan Employee's services to Producer as herein provided. Company
understands that the lending nature of this agreement prohibits Producer from remitting any
compensation for Employee's services, rentals, living allowances, etc. due hereunder to the Employee.
By countersigning this agreement, Employee agrees to be bound hereby and agrees to render the
services provided herein, to look solely to Company for compensation for all monies due hereunder, and
to indemnify Producer against liability for withholding and payroll taxes applicable hereto.

If Company maintains a workers' compensation insurance policy under which Employee is currently
covered, Company will present a copy of documentation evidencing such coverage. Otherwise,
notwithstanding the lending nature of this agreement, the parties acknowledge that an employment
relationship exists between Producer and Employee whereby Producer or Producer's designated
Employer of Record is Employee's special employer under this agreement and Company is Employee's
general employer (as such terms are understood for purposes of workers' compensation statutes). The
parties acknowledge that their rights and the limitations on their liability pursuant to this agreement shall
be no different than those rights and limitations which would be applicable under the existing workers'
compensation statues had Employee rendered services directly for Producer as Producer's general
employee. Producer will pay, or will cause Producer's designated Employer of Record to pay, any
pension, health and welfare payments required to be made by applicable guild collective bargaining
agreements by reason of Employee's services hereunder.

If there is any inconsistency between this agreement and the terms of any applicable guild collective
bargaining agreements, then: the terms of such collective bargaining agreements shall control; this
agreement shall be deemed modified to the minimum extent necessary to resolve the conflict; and this
agreement as thus modified shall remain in full force and effect. Producer shall be entitled to the maximum
benefits permitted to Producer under any such collective bargaining agreements for the minimum
payments required, except as may be otherwise specifically provided in this agreement.

Producer's remedies and rights contained in this agreement shall be cumulative and the exercise of any
remedy or right shall not be in limitation of any other remedy or right. In the event of any failure or
omission by Producer constituting a breach of Producer's obligations under this agreement, Company's
and Employee's sole remedy (if any) shall be an action at law for damages, and neither Company nor
Employee shall have any right to rescission and/or injunctive and/or other equitable relief.

This agreement may not be altered, modified, changed, rescinded or terminated in any way except by
an instrument in writing signed by the parties hereto.

PRODUCER   COMPANY:

By _____   By GREAT RYDERS, INC.

                                  EMPLOYEE:

                                  By _____

BOX/EQUIPMENT RENTAL INVENTORY

PRODUCTION COMPANY ___XYZ PRODUCTIONS, INC.___

SHOW ___HERBY'S SUMMER VACATION___   PROD # ___0100___

EMPLOYEE ___SAM SHUTTER___   POSITION ___STILL PHOTOGRAPHER___

ADDRESS ___8436 LENS AVE.___   SOC. SEC. # ___111-12-1212___

___WONDERLAND, CA 90000___

LOAN OUT COMPANY _____   PHONE # ___(818) 555-3030___

RENTAL RATE $ ___200—___   FED. I.D. # ___95-15693276___

PER   ☐ DAY   ☑ WEEK

☐ SUBMIT WEEKLY INVOICE

☑ RECORD ON WEEKLY TIME CARD

RENTAL COMMENCES ON ___6-18-XX___

INVENTORIED ITEMS:

TWO (2) NIKON CAMERA BODIES - SER# 123456XXX
SER# 654321XXX
THREE (3) LENSES: 70-210 ZOOM (NIKON)
35-105/MACRO (VIVITAR)
28 mm (NIKON)
NIKON MOTOR DRIVE - SER# 4567890XXX
TRI-POD
BLIMP
MISC. FILTERS

Please note: 1. *Box and equipment rentals are subject to 1099 reporting.*

2. *The Production Company is not responsible for any claims of loss or damage to box/equipment rental items that are not listed on the above inventory.*

EMPLOYEE SIGNATURE _____   DATE ___6/2/XX___

APPROVED BY _____   DATE ___6/2/XX___

© ELH

VEHICLE RENTAL SHEET

PRODUCTION COMPANY __XYZ PRODUCTIONS__ DATE __9.5.XX__

ADDRESS __1234 FLICK DR.__
__HOLLYWOOD, CA 90038__

PHONE# __555-3331__

The vehicle as described below is to be rented for use on the film tentatively entitled:

__HERBY'S SUMMER VACATION__

TYPE OF VEHICLE __CAR__

YEAR, MAKE, MODEL __1992 MERCEDES BENZ SL__

VIN# __X944312967LMP3760__

LICENSE# __1PAL222__ VALUE$ __45,000—__

SPECIAL EQUIPMENT/ATTACHMENTS

RENTAL PRICE $ __250—__ PER ☑DAY ☐WEEK ☐MONTH

START DATE __2.19.XX__ COMPLETION DATE __2.20.XX__

LEGAL OWNER OF VEHICLE __ROMEO JONES__

ADDRESS __4321 BEVERLY HILLS LANE__
__BEVERLY HILLS, CA 90210__

PHONE# __555-6643__ FAX# __555-6644__

DRIVER OF VEHICLE (IF NOT OWNER)

VEHICLE TO BE USED FOR __PICTURE VEHICLE FOR Sc.25__

DEPARTMENT

INSURANCE SUPPLIED BY __XYZ PRODUCTIONS__

INSURANCE COMPANY __ABC INSURANCE CO.__

POLICY# __5362732LT__

INSURANCE AGENCY __NEAR NORTH INSURANCE BROKERAGE__

INSURANCE AGENCY REP __ERICK MEDINA__

PHONE# __556-4715__ FAX#

CERTIFICATE OF INSURANCE: ☑TO OWNER ☑IN VEHICLE ☑ON FILE

COPY OF REGISTRATION IN THE CAR: ☑YES ☐NO

AGREED TO __Romeo Jones__
(Vehicle Owner)

APPROVED BY __(signature)__ TITLE __TRANSPORTATION COORD.__

© ELH

PURCHASE ORDER

DATE __6·14·XX__

P.O.#	0125

SHOW __HERBY'S SUMMER VACATION__   PROD# __0100__

COMPANY __XYZ PRODUCTIONS__

ADDRESS __1234 FLICK DR.__   PHONE# __555-3331__

__HOLLYWOOD, CA 90038__   FAX# __555-3332__

VENDOR __EASTERN COSTUME CO.__   PHONE# __555-0900__

ADDRESS __932 HOLLYWOOD WAY__   FAX# __555-0901__

__HOLLYWOOD, CA 90028__   CONTACT __LULU__

VENDOR SOC. SEC. # OR FEDERAL ID# __95-76513215__   CORPORATION: ☑YES ☐NO

☐ PURCHASE ☑RENTAL ☐SERVICE (Indicate if amount being charged is per show-day-week- or -month)

DESCRIPTION	CODING	AMOUNT
ASSORTED T-SHIRTS & SHORTS FOR		
HERBY, MARC & JED		
$75 PER MO. X 2 MONTHS	831·56	$150—
TATTERED CLOTHES FOR JAKE		
$25 PER MO. X 2 MONTHS	831·56	50—

SET #S: _____

IF TOTAL COST CANNOT BE DETERMINED
AT THIS DATE, ESTIMATE OF COSTS
WILL NOT EXCEED $_____

INCL. TAX IF APPLICABLE _____

TOTAL COST: $ __200—__

IF P.O. IS FOR A <u>RENTAL</u>, PLEASE INDICATE RENTAL DATES: FROM __6·15·XX__ TO __8·15·XX__

ORDER PLACED BY __FRIEDA FITTER__   DEPT __WARDROBE__

APPROVED BY __Fred Filmer__   DATE __6·15·XX__

© ELH

PURCHASE ORDER EXTENSION

DATE ___8·14·XX___ ORIGINAL P.O.# _0125_

SHOW _HERBY'S SUMMER VACATION_ PROD# _0100_

VENDOR _EASTERN COSTUME CO._ PHONE# _555-0900_

CONTACT _LULU_ FAX# _555-0901_

☑ RENTAL ☐ SERVICE

DESCRIPTION	CODING	AMOUNT
ASSORTED T-SHIRTS & SHORTS FOR HERBY, MARC & JED	831·56	$75

INCL. TAX IF APPLICABLE _____

TOTAL COST: $ 75

EXTENDED RENTAL DATES: FROM _8·16·XX_ TO _9·16·XX_

P.O. EXTENDED BY _FRIEDA FITTER_ DEPT _WARDROBE_

APPROVED BY _Fred Filmer_ DATE _8·15·XX_

© ELH

PURCHASE ORDER LOG

SHOW: HERBY'S SUMMER VACATION

P.O. #	DATE	VENDOR	P.O. FOR	PRICE	CHECK ONE			DATE RENTAL RETD.	ASSET ✓	DEPARTMENT P.O. ASSIGNED TO
					PURCHASE	RENTAL	SERVICE			
1001	6/21/XX	LARRY'S LUMBER	MISC. CONSTRUCTION	$2,500	✓					CONSTRUCTION
1002	6/21/XX	ELECTRONIC CITY	TV FOR HERBY'S ROOM	$379 —	✓				✓	SET DRESSING
1003	6/21/XX	PAUL'S PROP HOUSE	MISC. HAND PROPS	$250 —		✓		8-7-XX		PROPERTY
1004	6/23/XX	JONES' SANITATION	TRASH REMOVAL	$500 —			✓			CONSTRUCTION

CHECK REQUEST

DATE _6·10·XX_   AMOUNT $180

SHOW _HERBY'S SUMMER VACATION_   PROD# _0100_

COMPANY _XYZ PRODUCTIONS_

ADDRESS _1234 FLICK DR._   PHONE# _555-3331_

HOLLYWOOD, CA 90038   FAX# _555-3332_

CHECK PAYEE _CAL'S COMPUTER CENTER_   PHONE# _555-1003_

ADDRESS _9876 FLORES ST._   FAX# _555-1004_

STUDIO VILLAGE, CA 90037   ATTN _CAL_

PAYEE SOC. SEC. # OR FEDERAL ID# _95-365421769_   CORPORATION: ☑ YES ☐ NO

☐ PURCHASE ☑ RENTAL ☐ DEPOSIT ☐ ADVANCE ☐ SERVICE ☐ 1099 ☐ ASSET

DESCRIPTION	CODING	AMOUNT
2-MONTH RENTAL OF HP LASER JET PRINTER 6·15·XX — 8·15·XX FOR USE BY ACCOUNTING DEPT.	865-55	$90/mo.

CHECK NEEDED: DAY _MON._   DATE _6/10/XX_   INCL. TAX IF APPLICABLE _____

TIME _11:00_ ☑ A.M. ☐ P.M.   TOTAL: $ _180_

☐ WITHIN NORMAL PROCESSING TIME

WHEN CHECK IS READY, PLEASE: ☐ MAIL ☑ HOLD FOR PICKUP ☐ GIVE TO: _____

CHECK REQUESTED BY _NELLIE NOMBERS_   DEPT _ACCOUNTING_

APPROVED BY _Ned Filmer_   DATE _6·10·XX_

(INVOICE SUBSTANTIATION MUST FOLLOW THIS REQUEST)

© ELH

PETTY CASH ACCOUNTING

NAME _PAULA PROPPS_   DATE _7·13·XX_   ENVELOPE# _1_

PICTURE _HERBY'S SUMMER VACATION_   AMT. RECEIVED $ _500—_

POSITION _PROPERTY MASTER_   DEPT. _PROPERTY_   [✓]CHECK [ ]CASH   CHECK# _0037_

DATE	RECEIPT NO.	PAID TO	PAID FOR	ACCOUNT	AMOUNT
7·5	1	ACE SPORTING GOODS	BASKETBALL		$ 23.50
7·6	2	JOE'S MARKET	CANNED FOOD		15.37
7·6	3	SHADES, INC.	SUNGLASSES		62.05
7·7	4	FOOD·TO·GO	COOKED DINNER		130.63
7·8	5	AL'S DRUGS	SUNTAN LOTION		6.52
7·8	6	ABC DEPARTMENT STORE	MAKE-UP		53.17
7·9	7	BED+BATH SHOP	BEACH TOWELS		33.64
7·9	8	RALPH'S OPTICAL CO.	LAURA'S GLASSES		150.06
7·9	9	AL'S DRUGS	CIGARETTES		10.36
7·11	10	ELECTRONIC CITY	WALKMAN		25.17
7·11	11	ACE SPORTING GOODS	BAT / BALL		28.39
7·12	12	HARRY'S HARDWARE	SHOVEL		43.21
7·12	13	JOE'S MARKET	SOFT DRINKS		27.09
7·12	14	PICNICS GALORE	COOLERS		43.10

UPM: _Fred Filmer_   APPROVED:

AUDITED: _Nellie Numbers_   ENTERED: _7·15·XX_

TOTAL RECEIPTS: $652.26

AMT. ADVANCED: 500.—

PETTY CASH ADVANCE/REIMBURSEMENT

RECEIVED IN CASH: $ 652.26   ON: _7·17·XX_

SIGNATURE: _Paula Propps_

CASH/CHECK RET'D:

REIMBURSEMENT DUE: $152.26

NOTE: Tape receipts to 8-1/2x11 sheets of paper and number each to correspond with numbers listed above. Receipts are to be originals, and each must be dated and clearly indicate what it is for. Circle date, vendor and total amount on each receipt.

© ELH

```
AMOUNT $ 400-                          NO. 27

              RECEIVED OF PETTY CASH

                          DATE  5.25.XX

NAME    FRIEDA FITTER
DEPARTMENT   WARDROBE
DESCRIPTION _____
_____
_____

☑ PETTY CASH TO BE ACCOUNTED FOR

APPROVED BY                RECEIVED BY
Fred Filmer, UPM           Frieda Fitter
© ELH
```

INDIVIDUAL PETTY CASH ACCOUNT

NAME PAULA PROPPS   DEPARTMENT PROPERTY

SHOW HERBY'S SUMMER VACATION   PROD # 0100

FLOAT $ 500 —

DATE	CHECK#/CASH RECV'D FROM	AMOUNT RECV'D	ACCOUNTED FOR	BALANCE
7/2/XX	CHECK #1243	$500 —		$500 —
7/10			$432 —	$ 68 —
7/11	CHECK #1536	$432 —		$500 —
7/15	CASH FROM F. FILMER	$250 —		$750 —
7/23			$830 —	$ (80)
7/28	CHECK #1732	$580 —		$500 —

© ELH

MILEAGE LOG

NAME: __GARY GOFER__   WEEK ENDING __3/25/XX__

SHOW: __HERBY'S SUMMER VACATION__   PROD # __0100__

DATE	LOCATION		PURPOSE	MILEAGE
	FROM	TO		
3/20	OFFICE	SCREEN ACTORS GUILD	PICKUP RATE BOOK	10
	SAG OFFICE	ORIN'S OFFICE SUPPLY	OFFICE SUPPLIES	5
	ORIN'S	OFFICE		15
3/21	OFFICE	SCARLET STARLET HOME	DELIVER SCRIPT	8
	SCARLET STARLET'S	KENNY SMILE'S HOME	DELIVER SCRIPT	5
	KENNY SMILE'S	NANCY NICELY'S APARTMENT	DELIVER SCRIPT	3
	NANCY NICELY'S	OFFICE		7

TOTAL MILES: __53__

__53__ MILES @ __31__ ¢ Per Mile = $ __16.43__

Approved By: _Fred Filmer_   Date: __3/30/XX__

Pd. By Check # __2976__   Date __3/31/XX__

© ELH

INVOICE

TO: XYZ PRODUCTIONS
       1234 FLICK DR.
       HOLLYWOOD, CA 90038

FROM: ASHLEY WILKES   DATE 3/17/XX
(Address)   123 TWELVE OAKS AVE.
       ATLANTA, GEORGIA
(Phone #)   555-3824

PAYEE SS# OR FED. ID#   521-76-3535   1099 ✓

FOR SERVICES RENDERED ON _____ OR WEEK/ENDING 3/15/XX

DESCRIPTION OF (SERVICE)/RENTAL/CAR ALLOWANCE

DIALOGUE COACH TO HELP CAST WITH SOUTHERN ACCENT	
22.5 HRS @ $100 PER HOUR	

TOTAL AMOUNT DUE $ 2,250

EMPLOYEE SIGNATURE *Ashley Wilkes*

APPROVED BY *Fred Gilmer*

PD. BY CHECK # 2376   DATE 3/20/XX

© ELH

CASH OR SALES RECEIPT   DATE 8/24/XX   No. 93

RECIPIENT/
SOLD TO: _IRMA'S SWAP MEET_

ADDRESS: _4226 ORANGE BOWL AVE._
PASADENA, CA

PHONE # _(818) 555-4344_

FOR PURCHASE OF: _OLD BOOKS & RECORDS_
(SET DRESSING)

WRITTEN
AMOUNT _FIFTY-TWO DOLLARS_ ———— $ 52

☑ CASH   ☐ 1099   Soc. Sec. # _123-32-1323_

☐ CHECK   Fed. I.D. # _____

ACCOUNT CODING _823-51_

APPROVED BY _Neil Filmer_   RECV'D BY _Irma Price_

© ELH

DAILY COST OVERVIEW

SHOW __HERBY'S SUMMER VACATION__ PROD # __0100__

DATE __6-7-XX__ DAY # __6__

START DATE __5-29-XX__

SCHEDULED FINISH DATE __7-8-XX__

REVISED FINISH DATE __7-9-XX__

	PER CALL SHEET	SHOT	AHEAD/BEHIND
# OF SCENES	6	4	2 BEHIND
# OF PAGES	5 3/8	4 5/8	6/8 BEHIND

	AS BUDGETED AND/OR SCHEDULED	ACTUAL	COST (OVER)/UNDER
CAST OVERTIME	$500	$650	$150
COMPANY SHOOTING HOURS	12	13	$10,000
MEAL PENALTY (5 SAG ACTORS)	$500	$300	($200)
EXTRAS & STAND-INS	$632	$577	($55)
CATERING	$840	$960	$120
RAW STOCK (5,000')	$2,250	$1,687	$563
UNANTICIPATED EXPENSES:			
ADDT'L. PROP ASST.	10 HRS. @ $22/HR.		$242
FRINGE			44

TOTAL FOR TODAY __$9,738__

PREVIOUS TOTAL __$4,000__

GRAND TOTAL __$13,738 (OVER)__

PREPARED BY _Aaron Accountant_   APPROVED BY _Ned Filmer_

© ELH

CREW DATA SHEET

NAME	POSITION	SOC. SEC. # FEDERAL ID#	ACCNTG. CODE	START DATE	DEAL MEMO	NO. OF WRAP DAYS	WRAP DATE	OVER/UNDER
CONNIE COORDINATES	PROD. COORD.	555·21·1234	20.07	5.24·XX	✓	15 DAYS	9-27	+5 DAYS
PAULA PROPPS	PROPERTY MSTR.	321·77·4476	28·01	6.14·XX	✓	10 DAYS	9·20	
F. STOPP	DIR. OF PHOTOG	132·64·3217	33·01	6·21·XX	✓	Ø	9·6	
KATIE KANDU	SCRIPT SUV'R	543·37·6732	20·04	6·21·XX	✓	10 DAYS	9·13	
MIKE BOOM	SOUND MIXER	#95-1234567	34.01	7·3·XX	✓	1 DAY	9·7	

TIME CARDS/INVOICES
WEEKLY CHECK-OFF LIST

NAME	POSITION	SOC. SEC. # / FED. I.D. #	TIME CARDS AND/OR INVOICES TURNED IN EACH WEEK							
			W/E 7·31	W/E 8·7	W/E 8·14	W/E 8·21	W/E 8·28	W/E 9·4	W/E 9·11	W/E 9·18
A. DEES	1st Asst. Dir.	555·21·1234	✓	✓	✓	✓	✓	✓	✓	
KATIE KANDU	Script Supv'r.	543·37·6732		✓	✓	✓	✓	✓	✓	
MIKE BOOM	Sound Mixer	#95-1234567		✓	✓	✓	✓	✓		
PAULA PROPPS	Property Master	321·77·4476	✓	✓	✓	✓	✓	✓	✓	✓
E. STOPP	Dir. of Photog.	132-64-3217	✓	✓	✓	✓	✓	✓	✓	✓

© ELH

THE CHECK'S IN THE MAIL

CHECK MADE OUT TO	CHECK NUMBER	CHECK DATED	ADDRESS SENT TO	DATE MAILED	PAY-ROLL	INV.
CAL'S COMPUTERS	1032	2/14/xx	9876 FLORES ST. STUDIO VILLAGE, CA	2/15		✓
XXX AUDIO SERVICES	1053	2/15	123 MAIN ST. HOLLYWOOD, CA	2/16		✓
A. PAINE, M.D.	1059	2/15	3327 INJECTION BLVD. LOS ANGELES, CA	2/16		✓
ASHLEY WILKES	1075	2/20	123 TWELVE OAKS AVE. ATLANTA, GEORGIA	2/22		✓
F. STOPP (D.P.)	1082	2/20	2486 MADONNA LN. BEVERLY HILLS, CA	2/22	✓	

© ELH

CHAPTER FOUR

From Script To Schedule

My definition of "production" is the process of taking a script and creating (or "producing") a movie (or TV show, cable movie, commercial or interactive program) from it. In simpler terms, it is the manufacturing of a product. This chapter covers (among other related issues) certain basic elements of production—the script breakdown, board and schedule, and how each step progressively leads to the next. If you are not already breaking down scripts, doing boards and schedules, or if you haven't yet prepared a one-line schedule, it's doubtful that reading this chapter would qualify you to do so. It will, however, provide you with a fundamental understanding of how it all works; why it's important to know and why these functions are the basis for the entire filmmaking process. For further information on breakdowns, boards and schedules, check out Samuel French Book Store (www.samuelfrench.com) or other book stores that sell film-related publications and check out the many books devoted to this topic. Classes and seminars on Film Scheduling are also available wherever film courses are offered.

IT ALL STARTS WITH A SCRIPT

Making a movie begins when you are handed a screenplay (script). Sometimes it's a spec script that someone is trying to sell or raise money to produce; in which case, being able to do a breakdown, board, schedule and budget based on the script will let everyone involved know the approximate length of time it should take to shoot and how much it is likely to cost—important factors in selling the project. Other times, you are hired by a studio or production company to work

on a movie after the script has been bought and the project "green lit" (given a firm "go" and start date). In this case, at least one preliminary breakdown, board, schedule and budget (probably several) have already been done, and everyone involved has their first indication of how long it should take to shoot and how much it should cost to make (although these factors continue to vary throughout the production process).

Most professional writers will submit screenplays that are formatted properly (the formatting is automatically built into all screenplay writing software). If, for whatever reason, you receive a script that is not formatted properly, it will need to be revised before anything else can be done. Standard industry writing formats create uniform-sized pages, so a film expected to be 90 to 100 minutes in length should have a screenplay that is 100 to 120-pages long—or approximately one page for each minute of screen time.

Often, you will receive a script that does not have scene numbers or where scenes are improperly identified. (A scene represents a segment of action that takes place in the same location over the same period of time.) The person who does the initial breakdown (usually a production manager) will assign properly-placed scene numbers to the script. They may change slightly when the script is turned over to the first assistant director during prep, but once finalized by the 1st AD, think of them as carved in stone. As everyone in the cast, production crew and editorial staff will organize and schedule their work according to the script's scene numbers, once finalized, they cannot change.

New material is introduced to a script by adding a letter to the previous scene number. For instance, a new scene that occurs between scenes

4 and 5 might be numbered 4A or A5—depending on which scene it is linked to. An addition to that would be scene 4B, and so on. If a scene is omitted, the scene number would remain in the script with the word "Omitted" typed next to it. The same holds true for page numbers; they should not be changed either. If you were to lengthen a scene that appeared on page 20 that now runs a page-and-a-half, do not disturb page 21, but instead type the additional half-page onto a new page that is numbered 21A. All new or omitted scene numbers and pages are issued on change pages with an asterisk (*) in the right-hand margin next to each specific change.

Script Revisions

The term final draft almost never means final. It would be ideal if all script changes could be made in the early stages of pre-production, but the reality is that changes (even small ones) are often made not only up to, but also throughout, principal photography. Script revisions need to be indicated in a precise manner in order for everyone to know if and how each change will affect them or their department.

It is not necessary to run off entire new scripts every time there are changes. The accepted standard is to distribute colored change pages. For example, the first set of change pages are copied onto blue paper, the second set onto pink, and so forth. The standard color progression runs:

white

blue

pink

yellow

green

goldenrod

buff

salmon

cherry

tan

gray

ivory

Once you have gone through each color and eleven sets of script revisions, you can begin again by using white change pages, then blue, then pink, etc. Some studios have made it a practice to come out with an entire blue-paged script once the original script has gone through all eleven sets of multicolored revision pages. Changes to a blue script would start with pink pages, and continue to progress through the same cycle of colors.

Just as important as the various colors are to differentiate between sets of changes, it is also very important to indicate the changes by typing Revised/(date) at the top left-hand corner of every change page and by indicating the individual changes with asterisks (*) in the right-hand margin next to the specific line where the change occurs.

Your script supervisor will keep track of all revised page counts and the revised number of scenes on his or her daily log, which will in turn be transferred to the Daily Production Report. With each set of new change pages, members of the cast and crew insert each of the latest pages into their scripts, replacing the original white or outdated colored change pages. By the time most shows have completed filming, the scripts are rainbow-colored.

When change pages are generated, it is imperative that they are distributed to the people who need them immediately. In addition to the producer(s), director and production manager, the first assistant director will need to know if and how these changes will affect the schedule; the casting director and/or specific cast members will need to know if there are changes in their dialogue and the location manager will need to know if any location has been deleted or new ones added. The same will hold true for each department head. Will new equipment or props have to be ordered? Will more or fewer extras be needed? Again, changes need to be distributed to those who need them as soon as possible.

Once a show has finished filming and post production is completed, a truly final script is generated. It is called a *Continuity Script* and contains the exact (word-for-word) dialogue and action as it appears in the final cut version of the picture. Continuity scripts are for purposes of distribution and are required as part of your delivery requirements.

THE BREAKDOWN

To accurately schedule a film, to know how many days each actor and stunt performer will be required to work, how many days the film will be shot at each location, and exactly what is required to accomplish each scene—a breakdown is done.

One starts the breakdown process with a few good pencils, a transparent ruler and at least one highlighter. The first step, assuming you have read the script at least once, is to create the scene numbers (or to make sure they are accurately identified), and then, in pencil, draw a horizontal line across the page at the end of each scene. Each scene is then measured by its page count, and that figure is indicated in the margin. The page count is determined by dividing each page into eighths. Given that the text of a script page does not start at the very top of the page nor does it end at the very bottom, it can be a bit confusing; but if you go with the rule-of-thumb that each eighth of a page equals approximately one inch of text, your page counts should be fairly accurate. If a scene is less than one inch, it is still counted as one-eighth of a page. And don't worry if you should end up with a page that contains more or less than eight eighths. Full pages are indicated as "1 page," not as "8 8ths"; "1 1/8 pages" would be listed as "1-1/8 pg.," not "9/8ths."

The next step is to highlight or underline the specific components in each scene. Some people use a color-coding system, assigning a color to each element and then highlighting or underlining that element by its appropriate color. Color-coded or not, these are some of the components that should be identified:

- scene headings (including: Interior or Exterior—Day or Night)
- locations
- cast members
- key props
- key wardrobe
- extras
- stunts
- visual effects
- special effects
- picture vehicles
- animals
- special equipment
- minors, babies, etc.

Also, single out scenes that can be done by a second unit. Those would be scenes shot without principal actors, such as establishing shots, certain stunts, car drive-bys, etc.

When going through the script and identifying particular elements, read more than what's on the page, and anticipate needs that aren't specifically spelled out. For instance, if you have a character or two swimming under water, you might make a note for yourself in the margin—"underwater camera operator and equipment and safety divers." If you have a scene that takes place in a bar or pool hall, you may note "atmospheric smoke" next to the scene.

Once the breakdown is done, assign a number to each speaking role in the script. These numbers, once established, never change; and the actors along with the characters they portray are forever identified by that number in schedules, Day-Out-of-Days, Call Sheets, Production Reports, SAG time sheets, etc. Generally, the character with the most scenes is listed as #1, the character with the second greatest number of scenes would be #2, and so forth. However, there are those who use different numbering criteria, such as the character's importance to the story, the value of the actor's appearance in the movie or the order in which they appear in the script.

You will now be transferring the information from the script breakdown onto breakdown pages, or entering it into the computer using a scheduling software program. Most UPMs and 1st ADs now do their scheduling on a computer. There are a few such software programs on the market, the most popular and widely used being *Movie Magic Scheduling/Breakdown* by Screenplay Systems (www.screenplay.com).

Once the particulars are entered, the programs will automatically produce production board strips, a Day-Out-of-Days, Shooting Schedule, One-Line Schedule and more.

Film schools, even those that teach the most updated scheduling software programs, are teaching students how to manually break down and schedule scripts. There are still some working professionals who prefer this method as well and some who choose to do both. Whether a script is broken down manually or on a computer, the principles are the same; and for obvious reasons, I will proceed by describing the manual method.

Okay, so now it's time to transfer the information from the script breakdown onto breakdown sheets (a sample *breakdown page* can be found at the end of this chapter). Breakdown sheets (or "pages") should be dated and numbered in sequence, with each one representing one scene, or a group of scenes that take place at the same location, with the same characters at the same time of day. Also, on each breakdown sheet, there are spaces allocated to indicate:

- the characters (listed in the order of their assigned numbers)
- the scene number(s)
- the page count

- the scripted location of where the scene is taking place
- whether it is the INT. (interior) or EXT. (exterior) of that location
- whether it is Day or Night (or possibly Dusk or Dawn, if indicated in the script)
- the story day
- a brief (one sentence) description of the scene
- a list of extras (i.e., 3-pedestrians, 2-bicyclists, 1-skateboarder)
- a list of stunt performers

Breakdown sheets also contain allocated spaces to note specific requirements in the following departments:

- wardrobe
- props
- set dressing
- vehicles
- special effects
- special equipment
- animals
- sound effects/music
- other—anything else worth noting not covered in one of the above categories

THE BOARD

It's difficult to describe a production (or "strip") board if you've never seen one. It's paneled, filled with long, thin, multicolored cardboard strips and is actually less confusing than it appears. Information from the breakdown sheets is transferred to the strips, and they are arranged, and rearranged, and rearranged again—eventually creating a shooting schedule. The board as a whole embodies your entire script.

Production boards, easy to fold up and carry around, are either 15 or 18 1/4 inches high (the 15-inch board being the most commonly used) and are generally made of vinyl-coated cardboard or wood (cardboard being the most popular). Each panel is 10 inches wide and holds twenty-five to thirty strips. Boards range from two to twelve panels, with the average feature film requiring six to eight panels.

The way information is categorized on different boards varies slightly, depending on the manufacturer of the header board and the preparer. The header board, or "header," is a wide section

of cardboard (equally as long as the strips) that fits into the far left corner of the board. Using the header as a guide, the information from each breakdown page is transferred onto the long, narrow strips. The colors of the strips generally signify the following (although variations or added colors are often used, depending on the preparer):

- Yellow strips = day exterior (EXT.)
- White strips = day interior (INT.)
- Green strips = night exterior (EXT.)
- Blue strips = night interior (INT.)
- Black and white strips = day dividers
- Solid black strips = week dividers

As with the breakdown sheets, if the characters, time of day and location are the same (generally signifying continuous action), you may combine more than one scene number on a single strip. Using the header as a guide, each strip will indicate the breakdown page it references, the scene number(s), if this scene or group of scenes takes place during Day or Night, Interior or Exterior and what the page count is. The longer box toward the top of each strip is to indicate the scripted location. Characters appearing in that (those) scene(s) are indicated by their assigned numbers, and farther down, spaces are used to list elements other than cast which need to be scheduled. Using corresponding code letters, list the elements required for your particular show, such as VFX = (for) Visual Effects, or PC = (for) Picture Cars, or A = (for) Animals.

Then, at the bottom of each strip, a very brief description of the scene(s) is inserted—with the description printed vertically from the bottom of the strip and traveling up. There is only room for a few words, just enough to get the flavor for what the scenes are about. In one of my classes, we were working on a script where a man was making breakfast for his sons, whom he was planning to take hunting right after breakfast. When the boys arrived at the kitchen table, the father flipped the last of the eggs onto their plates, then proceeded to surprise them with a gift of new rifles. It was quite a lengthy scene, but the board description merely said "guns and eggs."

The example on page 59 is not in color, and it's not to actual size, but it will give you a general idea of what the header and board strips look like.

Once the strips are completed, you're ready to start figuring out a schedule.

SAMPLE PRODUCTION (OR "STRIP") BOARD

Strips   Day Divider

Header

		5	7	9	
Breakdown Page No(s)		5	7	9	
Day or Night		D	D	D	
Scene(s)		5,7	9,10	14	
No. of Page(s)		1-1/8	48	2-4/8	
		EXT. LAURA'S HOUSE	EXT. LAURA'S BACKYARD	EXT. LAURA'S BACKYARD	1ST DAY - 4-1/8 PGS.
Title	HERBY'S SUMMER VACATION				
Director	SID CELLULOID				
Producer	SWIFTY DEALS				
Assistant Director	ALICE DEES				
Production Manager	FRED FILMER				
Character	Artist				
HERBY	CLARK GRABLE	1	1		1
JAKE	ROCKY RIZZO	2		2	
LAURA	SCARLET STARLET	3		3	3
MOM	NANCY NICELY	4			
GEORGE	HOLLYWOOD MANN	5			
BUDDY (Dog)		6	6		
EXTRAS		X	X		
		HERBY DISCOVERS HOLE IN LAURA'S FENCE	LAURA TALKS TO JAKE ABOUT HERBY	HERBY REVEALS TRUTH TO LAURA	

THE SCHEDULE

A schedule is created by way of grouping and arranging the strips. Begin by separating the strips by the following factors:

- Sets and locations (it's expensive to be jumping back and forth between locations, so one location is shot at a time whenever possible)
- Cast members (keep actors' days as consolidated as possible, the more costly their services, the faster you want them to complete their role)
- Day/night shooting
- Exteriors/interiors
- The use of child actors (remember, they can only work a limited number of hours per day)
- Changes in time periods
- Changes in a character's weight
- Time of year
- Weather conditions
- Possible cover sets
- Special effects and stunts
- Second camera days and/or second unit
- The use of special equipment

Another factor to take into consideration is the allowance of *turnaround* (the specified number of hours required between dismissal from the set at the end of one day's shooting and the next day's call time) when scheduling day-to-night or night-to-day sequences.

Once the strips are separated, take each location grouping and separate those by Interior and Exterior, Day and Night. Arrange the board by locations, then arrange them by cast numbers within each location grouping. Keep doing this with each of the factors in order of importance to your production.

When arranging strips, keep in mind that difficult stunts and effects are often planned early in the schedule, so if problems do arise, there may still be enough time to alter the schedule and facilitate changes. It's also a good idea to plan exterior location shooting as early as possible and stage (or interior) shooting at the-tail end of the schedule, so cover sets are not used up early on should there be a weather problem. On the other hand, in an effort to give the actors involved as much time as possible to get to know one another first, you would not want to plan intimate or extremely emotional scenes until later in the schedule.

Now that the strips are in order, you will want to know how many pages to schedule per day. This will depend on different factors, such as the rate of speed in which your director and director of photography work. You may be on a show (such as an episodic television series) that has a finite number of days in which to shoot, or you may have a budget that will only accommodate so many shoot days. There are also times when you may have to base your number of shoot days on an actor's availability. If you are lucky enough, you can plan for as many shoot days as you comfortably feel are necessary.

Once you determine the length of your schedule, take the number of scenes in the script and divide them by the number of days in the schedule to get the number of pages you need to shoot each day. Movies for cable or television generally shoot five to six pages per day; series, six to seven pages; and features—well, it just depends. Remember, there are certain factors you need to allow more time for: stunts, effects, animals, special equipment, working with children, making moves, working on or in the water or cold weather, working in or around aircraft, etc. Location work is also more time-consuming than stage work. If you have the luxury, schedule a lighter first day to give the cast and crew a chance to get used to working together.

Use the black and white strips to signify day breaks. The solid black ones are to separate weeks.

There is no such thing as a final board, because the schedule changes often (even if only slightly) based on changing circumstances. But once it's pretty well set, arrange your breakdown sheets in the same sequence as the strips on the board, and paper clip the grouping of sheets that comprise each week. Attach a piece of paper to the front of each week's stack and label them Week #1, (or #2, or #3, etc.); and under the week number, write in the dates for that week: for example, Monday, December 4th—through—Friday, December 8th, 200X. The breakdown sheets are now used to create the official (typewritten) *Shooting Schedule* that gets distributed to everyone associated with the picture. A shorter version of the shooting schedule is called a *One-Line Schedule*. The breakdown pages are also used to generate Day-Out-of-Days, several specific breakdowns and Call Sheets.

The following samples on pages 61 and 62 show what a Shooting Schedule and One-Line Schedule would look like.

XYZ PRODUCTIONS

HERBY'S SUMMER VACATION - PROD# 0100

SHOOTING SCHEDULE

PRODUCER:	SWIFTY DEALS	FILM SHOOTS - 36 DAYS
DIRECTOR:	SID CELLULOID	TUESDAY, JUNE 1, 20XX
PRODUCTION MANAGER:	FRED FILMER	THROUGH
1ST ASST. DIRECTOR:	ALICE DEES	FRIDAY, JULY 17, 20XX

DATE	SET/SCENES	CAST	LOCATION
1ST DAY TUESDAY 6/1/0X	EXT. LAUREL ROAD - Day Day 1 - 1-1/8 pg. Scs. 6, 7, 8	1. HERBY 2. JED 3. MARC	SWEETWATER ROAD PACIFIC PALISADES
	The boys discover a hole in the fence and look through to the other side. NOTES:	STAND-INS Herby S.I. Jed S.I. Marc S.I. ATMOS 2 elderly ladies (passers-by)	PROPS Marc's ball MAKE-UP Cut on Herby's Hand VEHICLES old truck next to fence
	EXT. LAURA'S BACKYARD - Day Day 1 - 1-4/8 pgs. Scs. 9 & 10 The boys see Laura sunbathing by her pool. NOTES:	1. HERBY 2. LAURA 3. JED 4. MARK STAND-INS Herby S.I. Laura S.I. Jed S.I. Marc S.I. SPEC. EFX. Light steam off pool	(SAME AS ABOVE) PROPS Towel Makeup bag Laura's sunglasses WARDROBE Laura's white bikini VEHICLES Laura's Mercedes (in driveway)
	EXT. LAURA'S BACKYARD - Day Day 1 - 2-4/8 pgs. Sc. 11 Steve joins Laura and chases the boys away from the fence NOTES:	1. HERBY 2. LAURA 3. JED 4. MARC 7. STEVE STAND-INS Herby S.I. Laura S.I. Jed S.I. Marc S.I Steve S.I.	(SAME AS ABOVE) WARDROBE Steve in sport shirt & jacket VEHICLES Laura's Mercedes Steve's BMW SPECIAL EQUIPMENT 1 - 60' condor
	END OF DAY #1	TOTAL PAGES:	5-1/8 pgs.

SAMPLE

XYZ PRODUCTIONS

HERBY'S SUMMER VACATION - PROD# 0100

ONE-LINE SCHEDULE

PRODUCER:	SWIFTY DEALS	FILM SHOOTS - 36 DAYS
DIRECTOR:	SID CELLULOID	TUESDAY, JUNE 1, 20XX
PRODUCTION MANAGER:	FRED FILMER	THROUGH
1ST ASST. DIRECTOR:	ALICE DEES	FRIDAY, JULY 17, 20XX

FIRST DAY - TUESDAY, JUNE 1, 20XX

Sc. 1   EXT. PIER AT SUNRISE - Day - 1/8 pg.
             Sunrise over pier at Venice Beach

Scs. 2-13   EXT. VENICE BEACH - Day - 1-6/8 Pgs.
             Steve jogs

Sc. 23   EXT. FRONT OF HOTEL - Day - 1/8 pg.
             Steve jogs up to the front of the hotel

Scs. 46-52   EXT. STRAND IN VENICE - Day - 2-3/8 pgs.
             Steve greets friends on his way out to
             job. He smiles at Laura.

Scs. 87-90   EXT. VENICE STRAND - Day - 6/8 pg.
             Nick and Cory walk together.

Sc. 95   EXT. VENICE STRAND - DAY - 4/8 pg.
             Steve and Laura talk to Herby.

Sc. 101   INT. VENICE RESTAURANT - Day - 1/8 pg.
             Couple nods hello to Seve and Laura.

Sc. 91   EXT. STRAND AREA NEAR PIER - Day - 6/8 pg.
             Marc skates for them.

END OF FIRST DAY   TOTAL PAGES: 6-4/8

Day-Out-of-Days

A Day-Out-of-Days is a chart that denotes workdays, almost always referring to the cast. It's also a handy way to chart schedules for stunt performers, extras, stand-ins, special equipment and anything that might pertain to your show. For example, if you are doing a water picture and using several different boats throughout the shoot, it would be a good idea to do a Day-Out-of-Days tracking which days each boat works.

There are code letters used on the Day-Out-of-Days that are also used on Call Sheets, Production Reports and SAG time sheets (Exhibit Gs)—all relating to cast workdays. Here is the way it works:

- S = "Start"—this denotes the first day of work, whether it's a rehearsal, travel or shoot day.
- R = "Rehearse"
- T = "Travel"
- W = "Work"—referencing a "shoot" day
- H = "Hold"—an idle day for weekly performers who remain on payroll until their roles are completed
- D = "Drop"—as in "drop/pick-up," which is when an actor has a specified period of intervening time in-between work days (for rules pertaining to consecutive employment and drop/pick-up, see Chapter 11, "Principal Talent")
- P = "Pick-up"—the second half of "drop/pick-up"
- F = "Finish"

The first entry for any actor would be an SR, ST or SW. The first day always starts with an "S" and one other letter. The exception would be if an actor works for one day only, in which case, the designation would be SWF. Just as all first days start with an "S," all last days end with an "F," as in WF or TF.

In a drop/pick-up situation, an actor's schedule may be indicated with a "SWD" or "WD" on the last day of the first part of his or her engagement, and a "PW" (following the intervening days) on the first day of the second part of his or her engagement.

Breakdowns

Breakdowns are schedules of individual elements—extras, stand-ins, stunts, effects, second-unit requirements, picture vehicles, makeup/hair, special equipment, etc. Although department heads will create their own departmental breakdowns, the 1st AD will generate specific breakdowns appropriate to the show. As discussed above, they can be detailed in the form of a Day-Out-of-Days, or may be formatted to contain more explicit information. Most will list: shoot day/date, scene number(s) and specific requirements. If you are working on a film about a road trip, you will want a breakdown of which scenes are shot in which scripted (and actual) locations. If you have potential weather issues, you might want to do a breakdown of cover sets. The more material that is broken down ahead of time, the more prepared your crew is going to be.

Continuity Breakdowns

There are different variations of the Continuity Breakdown, but basically, they all track the sequence (or progression) of events and are extremely useful tools. Here is a good basic format:

Shoot Day, Date	Story Year, Month, Day	Scene No(s)	Page Count	Story Location	Shooting Location	Brief Decription

Individual continuities should also be prepared for anything relevant to your show. If a person ages or has a weight change during the course of a script, if a car gets more damaged as the story progresses, if a building or town deteriorates or improves, or a person gradually transforms into a creature—you will want to know which stage the progression is in at all times. A continuity schedule of this type will chronologically list scene numbers and, in the next column, a description of the evolution at that point in the story. Then, no matter what order the scenes are shot, all departments will know exactly what is required of them.

FORMS IN THIS CHAPTER

- Breakdown Sheet
- Day-Out-Of-Days

BREAKDOWN SHEET

SHOW: HERBY'S SUMMER VACATION   BREAKDOWN PAGE NO: 3

LOCATION: WARNER ROAD — HOLLYWOOD LAKE   PRODUCTION NO: 0100

[ ] STAGE   [✓] LOCAL LOCATION   [ ] DISTANT LOCATION   DATE: 5·17·00

DESCRIPTION		STORY DAY:	
SCENE #S	[ ] INT. [✓] EXT. ROAD LEADING TO LAKE	[✓] DAY [ ] NIGHT [ ] DAWN [ ] DUSK	NO. OF PAGES
6	THE BOYS WALKING TOWARD THE LAKE		1/8
7	THE BOYS SPOT LAURA SUNBATHING		1/8
8&9	THE BOYS HIDE & WATCH LAURA		5/8
		TOTAL PGS:	7/8

NO.	CAST	ATMOSPHERE	PROPS-SET DRESSING
1.	HERBY	6 SUNBATHERS	BEACH CHAIRS
3.	LAURA	MAN WALKING DOG	UMBRELLAS - BALL
6.	MARC	2 KIDS PLAYING BALL	SUNTAN LOTION
7.	JED		SUNGLASSES
		CAMERA	**WARDROBE**
			LAURA IN WHITE BIKINI
		SPECIAL EFFECTS	**VISUAL EFFECTS**
STAND-INS			
HERBY S.I.			
MARC S.I.		**TRANSPORTATION-PIC. VEHICLES**	**SOUND-MUSIC**
LAURA S.I.		LAURA'S MERCEDES PARKED ON SIDE OF ROAD	
STUNTS			
		ELECTRIC-GRIP-CRANES	**SPECIAL EQUIPMENT**
			(1) 40' CONDOR
MAKEUP-HAIR			
CUT ON HERBY'S HAND		**ANIMALS-LIVESTOCK-WRANGLERS**	**OTHER**
		NO DOG + TRAINER	
SPECIAL MAKE-UP EFFECTS			[✓] TEACHER-WELFARE WORKER

© ELH

DAY-OUT-OF-DAYS

PRODUCTION COMPANY: XYZ PRODUCTIONS
PRODUCTION TITLE: HERBY'S SUMMER VACATION
EPISODE TITLE: "BOYS NIGHT OUT"
PRODUCTION #: 0100
SCRIPT DATED: FEB. 16, 19XX

DATE: JUNE 1, 19XX
PRODUCER: SWIFTY DEALS
DIRECTOR: SID CELLULOID
UNIT PRODUCTION MGR.: FRED FILMER
FIRST ASST. DIRECTOR: A. DEES

MONTH → June / July

#	NAME	CHARACTER	18 F (1)	19 S (2)	20 S	21 M (3)	22 T (4)	23 W (5)	24 TH (6)	25 F (7)	26 S (8)	27 S	28 M (9)	29 T (10)	30 W (11)	1 TH (12)	2 F (13)	3 S (14)	TRAVEL	START	FINISH	WORK	IDLE	TOTAL
1	CLARK GRABLE	HERBY	T/S	W		W	W	W	H	W	W	W	W	H	H	W	W	TR/F	2	6/18	7/3	10	2	14
2	ROCKY RIZZO	JAKE	T/S	W		W	H	H	W	H	W	W	H	H	H	W	W	TR/F	2	6/18	7/3	7	5	14
3	SCARLET STARLET	LAURA				T/S	W	W	W	H	W		W	W	TR/F				2	6/21	6/30	6	1	9
4	NANCY NICELY	MOM				T/S	W	W	H	H	W		W	W	H	W	TR/F		2	6/21	7/2	5	4	11
5	HOLLYWOOD MANN	GEORGE					T/S	W	W	W	TR/F								2	6/22	6/26	3	–	5
6	KENNY SMILES	MARC				T/S	W	W	H	W	W		W	TR/F					2	6/21	6/29	4	2	8
7	LLOYD NELSON	POLICE SGT.				T/S	W	W	H	W	W		W	TR/F					2	6/21	6/29	4	2	8
8	RAYMOND BURRMAN	ELLIOT							SW/F										1	6/24	6/24	1	–	1

CHAPTER FIVE

Pre-Production

WHAT IS PRE-PRODUCTION?

You have been successful in raising independent financing, or the studio, network or cable company has given you a "green light" on your project; and you're ready to start pre-production. Pre-production is the period of time used to plan and prepare for the filming and completion of your film. It is the time in which to:

- Produce a final script
- Breakdown, board, schedule and budget the script
- Locate and set up production offices
- Hire a staff and crew
- Cast the film
- Meet with department heads, get realistic cost estimates, refine the budget and make sure your film can be done for the amount of money it is budgeted for
- Have the script researched and all necessary clearances secured
- Evaluate locations, visual effects, special effects and stunt requirements as per your script
- Arrange for insurance and a completion bond (if necessary)
- Become signatory to the unions and guilds you wish to sign with and post any necessary bonds
- Scout and choose locations
- Contact film commissions for distant location options
- Book travel and hotel accommodations
- Secure passports, work visas, a customs broker and all necessary permits if shooting out of the country
- Build and decorate sets

- Wardrobe actors and have them fitted for wigs and prosthetics (as necessary)
- Negotiate deals with vendors, and order film, equipment, vehicles and catering
- Prepare all agreements, releases, contracts and paperwork
- Plan stunt work, aerial work and special effects
- Line up special requirements, such as picture vehicles, animals, mockups, boats, helicopters, models, etc.
- Set up accounts with labs; set up editing rooms; schedule the routing of dailies; plan a post production schedule; hire a post production crew and prebook scoring, looping and dubbing facilities
- Clear copyrighted music you wish to use in your picture

ESTABLISHING COMPANY POLICIES

Whether you are opening a temporary production office for the purpose of working on one film or you are part of an established production company that produces several shows a year, each production should operate under an established set of policy guidelines and basic operating procedures. Establishing well-defined office procedures will not only help you avoid unnecessary delays in disseminating information and paperwork, but it will enable you to maintain a more organized, more efficient production office, one that is better able to meet the needs of the entire shooting company. It is important for staff and crew members to know, coming in, what the company's policies are, what is expected of them and what they are specifically responsible for.

Most production companies distribute policy memos to all new crew members by attaching them to deal memos and/or start paperwork packages (start slip, W-4 and I-9s), integrating the acceptance of these rules as a condition of employment. In fact, this memo is commonly called *The Rules Of The Game*.

Descriptions of the types of policies can be found in Chapter 2, "The Production Office," and Chapter 3, "Basic Accounting," but here is a list of the topics that should be included in an informational-rules-procedures memo:

- Basic production office information: address, phone and fax numbers, security info, where to park, etc.
- Payroll, paychecks and timecards
- Vendor accounts
- Purchase Orders
- Check Requests
- Petty Cash and reimbursable expenses
- Competitive bids
- Assets
- Auto allowances and mileage reimbursement
- Box rentals and computer rentals
- Cell phone reimbursement

Along with *The Rules Of The Game*, deal memo and start paperwork package, it is a good idea to include a copy of the *Filmmaker's Code of Conduct* (see Chapter 16, "Locations"), copies of safety bulletins appropriate to your show and an *Acknowledgment of Safety Guidelines* form (see Chapter 15, "Safety") to be signed by each employee.

PLAN AHEAD

Plan for cover sets should the weather turn bad while filming exteriors. Know where you can exchange or get additional equipment (or raw stock) if needed at any time of the day or night. Keep names, phone numbers and resumes of additional crew members should you suddenly need an extra person or two. Line up alternative locations should your first choice not be available.

The lower the budget, the more prep time you should have. Lower budgeted films do not have the luxury of extra time or money, so on these types of projects especially, it is essential to be as prepared as possible. No matter what the budget,

unexpected and unavoidable situations (resulting in delays and/or added costs) will always arise during the course of a production, so expect and avoid as much as possible in advance. Ironically, the films needing the most prep time are the ones that can least afford it. And although it's common for independent producers to prepare as much as they can while waiting for their funding, they are somewhat limited until they can officially hire key department heads and start spending money.

Many variables, such as budget and script requirements, will determine your pre-production schedule. The following is an example of what a reasonable schedule (barring any extraordinary circumstances) might look like based on a six-week shoot with a modest budget of $4 to $6 million.

An ideal pre-production schedule would allow one and one-half weeks of prep for each week of shooting. Accordingly, a six-week shoot should have a nine-week prep period. The following eight-week schedule, however, should be more than sufficient, as well as cost-effective.

Pre-Production Schedule

Week #1 (8 weeks of prep)

Starting Crew
Producers
Director
Line Producer and/or Production Manager
Production Coordinator
Production Accountant
Location Manager
Casting Director
Secretary/Receptionist
Production Assistant #1

To Do
- Establish your company, if not done earlier
- Set up production offices
- Finalize script and budget
- Start filling out union/guild signatory papers
- Firm up insurance coverage
- Begin casting
- Start lining up your crew
- Start scouting locations
- Open accounts with vendors

Week #2 (7 weeks of prep)

Starting Crew
Production Designer

To Do

- Start music clearance procedures using either your attorney or a music clearance service to determine if the rights are available and how much the sync license fees are for each piece of music

Week #3 (6 weeks of prep)

Starting Crew

Art Director

Set Designer

Assistant Location Manager

First Assistant Director

Wardrobe Designer

Week #4 (5 weeks of prep)

Starting Crew

Assistant Production Coordinator

Assistant Accountant

Wardrobe Supervisor

Transportation Coordinator

Property Master

Set Decorator

Production Assistant #2

To Do

- Meet with person/department overseeing Product Placement and start the process
- Scouting as needed with Location Manager, Director, Producer, 1st AD and Production Designer

Week #5 (4 weeks of prep)

Starting Crew

Costumer #1

Assistant Property Master

Lead Person

To Do

- At the end of this week, you should be ready for your first production meeting

NOTE: Depending on script requirements, the production designer will determine the start dates of the construction coordinator and construction crew. The production manager will determine the start dates of the stunt coordinator and special effects crew. The producer will determine the start date of a visual effects coordinator.

Week #6 (3 weeks of prep)

Starting Crew

Director of Photography

Second Assistant Director

Transportation Captain

Swing Crew

Extra Casting, if needed

Week #7 (2 weeks of prep)

Starting Crew

Key Grip

Gaffer

Costumer #2

Production Assistant #3

To Do

- Production Executive, Producer, Director and Production Designer make final changes to sets, locations, wardrobe, cast wigs and/or hair color, prosthetics, hero props, models and anything else pertinent to the look of your show.

Week #8 (final week of prep)

Monday

Starting Crew

Script Supervisor

Set Production Assistant

Drivers (as needed)

To Do

- Post SAG bond by this date (if needed), or you will not be able to issue work calls or clear actors through Station 12
- Complete casting and send out actors' contracts
- Finalize selection of locations, make sure all applicable location agreements are signed and permits secured
- Order all equipment, vehicles, raw stock, expendables and catering
- Sometime this week, a cast read-through is usually scheduled
- Also sometime this week, a rigging crew might start (if applicable)
- Sign-off of stand-ins, photo doubles and stunt doubles
- Distribute final shooting schedule, one-line schedule, day-out-of-days, crew list and cast list

NOTE: Talk to your caterer. Many of them will graciously supply the food for a "kick-off" party, read-through and/or final production meeting at no charge.

Wednesday

Starting Crew
Best Boy, electric

Best Boy, grip

Hair Stylist

Makeup Artist

First Assistant Cameraperson

More Drivers (as necessary)

To Do
- Final location scout for camera, grip, electric

Thursday

Starting Crew
First Assistant Cameraperson

Second Assistant Cameraperson

To Do
Members of the camera, grip and electric departments begin working at the equipment houses (earlier than Thursday, if necessary), checking out equipment and loading trucks

Friday

Starting Crew
Sound Mixer

Craft Service

Still Photographer

To Do
- Hold final production meeting with all department heads
- Generate and distribute first day's call sheet
- Give out cast calls

DAILY PREP SCHEDULES

I can't overly stress the importance of publishing Daily Prep Schedules during pre-production. Unlike principal photography when all activities center around the set, during pre-production, members of the production team are scattered—scouting locations, having meetings, reading actors, working on script changes, working on the schedule or budget, etc. This is a time when good communications is essential and when everyone needs to be aware of everything else going on around them. The schedule is the best way to coordinate prep days. It keeps everyone informed as to exactly what is happening each day, who is attending each activity and when certain individuals are going to be available (so new meetings, scouts, casting sessions, etc. can be set up, and choices evaluated by and with the people who need to be involved). Keeping an accurate daily schedule tends to enhance productivity and time-efficiency while decreasing confusion and the duplication of efforts.

An updated schedule is usually distributed each morning. Sometimes, one is put out in the late afternoon as well. It can be done in a calendar format, or entries can be listed by day, date and times (either way, the individuals attending each scheduled activity would be indicated). It works best when one person, usually the First Assistant Director or Production Coordinator, is designated to collect the pertinent information from everyone involved and coordinate the schedule. The schedule can change as often as two or three times a day, so anyone wanting to set up a meeting, for instance, would contact the designated schedule-keeper ahead of time to make sure that anyone else who should be attending the meeting is available. They would then confirm when the meeting is set, so it can officially be added to the Daily Schedule.

Here are the type of items that would be listed on a Prep Schedule:

- location scouts
- casting sessions
- interviews with potential key crew positions
- department heads' first day of work
- production meetings
- script meetings
- budget meetings
- product placement meetings
- stunt and/or effects meetings
- extra casting meetings
- picture car meetings
- wardrobe fittings for lead actors
- prosthetic fittings and molds
- cast rehearsals and read-throughs
- (lead) cast appointments for wig fittings and hair coloring
- camera tests
- hair and makeup tests
- specific travel plans for cast members arriving in and out of town or for scouting parties traveling back and forth

- publicity functions
- pre-rigging
- and anything else that would be pertinent to your show.

INVENTORIES, LOGS & SIGN-OUT SHEETS

Inventories, logs and sign-out sheets are your best bets for managing the multitude of items being rented, purchased, shipped and used on your show. Keeping up the forms that track these details is time-consuming, but the effort will ultimately save you time and money. Logs and Sign-out Sheets are kept for such things as raw stock, Polariod™ film and other assets, equipment rentals, courier runs, shipments, walkie-talkies, pagers, keys and scripts. You will find examples of a selection of logs at the end of this chapter, but here are a few you can easily recreate or design versions of on your computer:

COURIER LOG

Date	Sent To	Sent From	Item(s) Sent	Waybill#

OVERNIGHT DELIVERY SERVICE LOG

Date	Sent To	Sent From	Item(s)	Anticipated Del. Date	Waybill#

POLARIOD™ SIGN-OUT LOG

600 Film				Spectra Film			
Date	# of Rolls	Dept.	Signature	Date	# of Rolls	Dept.	Signature

KEY SIGN-OUT LOG

Date	Qty.	Key(s) To	Signature

SCRIPT SIGN-OUT LOG

Date	Qty.	Script Date	Script No.	Requested by Department	Signature

Each department is responsible for inventorying its own assets. The production coordinator or assistant coordinator keeps track of all items purchased for the office on an *Asset Inventory Log* form. This would include such things as computer equipment, TVs, VCRs, coffee makers, an answering machine, etc. At the completion of principal photography, these items are turned in to the studio or parent company, stored or sold.

Equipment rented (or on loan from the studio) for the office should be logged in on an *Equipment Rental Log* form. This goes one step further than a Purchase Order Log, but when kept up, you will notice that returns are made and Loss & Damage (L & D) charges are assessed and submitted in a more timely manner.

The production coordinator or assistant coordinator is also the designated keeper of the cell phone, pager, key and (often) script sign-out sheets. (Sometimes, the producer's or director's assistant will monitor the distribution of scripts.) Walkie-talkies are traditionally handed out and collected by the Second Assistant Director (Second, Second Assistant Director or DGA Trainee). These sheets list the items, serial and/or unit numbers (if applicable), dates received and returned, department assigned to and a signature of the person being handed the phone, pager, key, script or walkie-talkie.

DISTRIBUTION

There is a staggering volume of paperwork and information that must be dispersed to cast, crew, staff, studio, network and others on any given show. It all emanates from the production office, and its distribution is crucially time-sensitive. Not being able to get vital paperwork out in time to those who need it will affect pending approvals, deals, commitments, schedules, prep times and your budget. For instance, a casting director not receiving a revised day-out-of-days in time may result in a deal being made with an actor for a part that has been shortened or no longer exists in the script. The extra casting agency that did not receive a revised call sheet may have already given a next-day call to hundreds of extras who are no longer needed. An actor who does not receive new script pages early enough may not have enough time to learn his new lines. Handing out shooting schedules, crew lists and call sheets may not seem like a big deal, but the entire production functions based on this paperwork.

Because of the sheer magnitude of the paperwork and the number of people who must receive

it, keeping a *Distribution Log* is the only way to ensure that everyone receives the information they need. A sample Distribution Log can be found at the end of the chapter.

Do not assume that because you hang departmental envelopes in the production office and place copies of essential paperwork in the envelopes or leave copies of printed material in someone's in-box that it will be promptly retrieved. That goes for faxes and phone messages as well. It is your responsibility (or that of the person you designate) to make sure all essential paperwork and information gets distributed (and acknowledged) as soon as possible. That may involve faxing, e-mailing files, tracking individuals down and asking them to come by the office, having the information delivered to them or sending it via mail or FedEx®. As things do occasionally get lost in the mail and fax machines have been known to malfunction, make sure you call to confirm that the information has been received.

COLLECTING INFORMATION & MAKING LISTS

Production offices generate massive amounts of paperwork in disseminating vital information to everyone involved with a film. Among the schedules, day-out-of-days, location lists, logs, purchase orders, sign-out sheets, script revisions, call sheets, production reports, maps, and other paperwork, the Crew, Cast and Contact lists are standard on every show. First drafts are produced during the earliest stages of pre-production, and revisions are continually being published until the final drafts are issued at the completion of principal photography.

Crew Information Sheet

This is not a standard industry form, but it should be. Stephen Marinaccio introduced me to the *Crew Information Sheet*. These forms are distributed to cast, crew and staff with their start paperwork. Once completed, they are kept in the production coordinator's office, in a binder, in alphabetical order. This form contains all the information needed to create the crew list. Additionally, it provides an emergency contact and phone number for each person (which, unfortunately, is occasionally needed), a birth date (allowing you the opportunity to celebrate co-workers birthdays if desired) and travel and hotel preferences. Being able to make as many preferred arrangements as possible, in advance, minimizes a multitude of last-minute problems. Use the form found at the end of this chapter, or design one yourself that is more specific to your show.

The Crew List

This is a listing of each member of the crew (by department) that includes their title, address, home phone number, home fax number (if they have one), cell phone and/or pager number. There are some people who prefer not to have their home address and phone number on the crew list, but there should be at least a pager number or an assis tant referenced should this person need to be reached in an emergency. In addition to crew lists, many production offices also generate quick refer ence lists that just contain titles, names and mobile phone and/or pager numbers. The following is what a crew list would look like. There is no one format that is universally used, but most are pretty similar. Some people also make a cover sheet with an index, listing each department and the page on which that department is listed. The following sample on page 73 starts by indicating how names, addresses and all pertinent numbers are listed, then just continues by department and position.

The Executive Staff List

Most shows are produced for a studio or parent production company, and you will be interacting with executives and individuals at that company on a daily basis. The studio or company will usu ally give you a staff list of in-house employees (pertinent to your project), and this list should be included at the back of your show's crew list. Some production coordinators choose to include this list with their Contact List.

The Cast List

This list references each role; the actor portray ing that role; his or her address, phone number and social security number; if incorporated, his or her corporation's name and Federal ID number and his or her agent's name and information. Cast lists should be distributed to a predetermined dis tribution list, including your wardrobe, hair, makeup and transportation people. A second cast list is often generated containing an additional column containing the actors' deals, but those are only to be given to a select few: the producer, pro duction manager, assistant directors, production

coordinator and production accountant. Actors' deals are not for general distribution.

As with crew lists, there is no one cast list for mat used by everyone, but they all end up look ing fairly similar, as in the example provided on page 76.

The Contact List

This list should include the name, address, phone/fax number and contact for all pertinent vendors, including: bank, insurance company, travel agent, equipment houses, courier service, office furniture and supplies, lab, weather ser vice, etc. If your production has various offices (home-based and location), they should be listed as well. The list is usually arranged in alphabeti cal order. Page 77 shows a sample format along with possible contact list headings.

BETTER SAFE THAN SORRY

Even with the existence of industry safety guidelines and a location code of conduct, efforts must continually be made to be aware, cautious and thorough. Although this behavior will most certainly prevent many potential problems, be assured that no production company, regardless of size or stature, is totally immune to accidents, grievances, lawsuits and insurance claims. *Be careful!* It's easy to get so busy on a shoot that, from time to time, a few small details fall between the cracks. And small details can quickly turn into big problems that come back to haunt you later on.

To best protect your own backside, and that of the company, you should:

- Keep careful inventories and note when something is lost or damaged.
- Put as much information on the back of the production report as possible, including the slightest scratch anyone might receive. When a day passes and there are no injuries, indi cate by noting, "No injuries reported today" on the back of the production report.
- When someone is injured, complete a work ers' compensation (Employer's Report of Injury) report as soon as possible, and get it to the insurance agency. Also attach a copy to the daily production report.
- Have an ambulance on the set on standby when you are doing stunts that are the least bit complicated or dangerous. Always know

SAMPLE
HERBY'S SUMMER VACATION

XYZ PRODUCTIONS
1234 Flick Drive
Hollywood, CA 90038
Tel: (323) 555-3331 - Fax: (323) 555-3332

CREW LIST
5/11/0X

PRODUCERS-DIRECTOR-WRITER

EXECUTIVE PRODUCER	MARVIN MOGUL 555 School Street Los Angeles, CA 90001	(310) 555-7250 - office (818) 555-5554 - home (310) 555-1166 - pager
PRODUCER	SWIFTY DEALS 12353 Rhodes Ave. Toluca Lake, CA 91150	(323) 555-7254 - office (818) 555-0897 - home (818) 555-0898 - home fax (310) 555-2169 - mobile phone
DIRECTOR	SID CELLULOID 2764 Carson Street Valencia, CA 90477	(818) 555-6033 - home (323) 555-6031 - mobile phone
WRITER	F. SCOTT RYDER 9336 W. Storey Street Los Angeles, CA 9000	(323) 555-7662 - home (323) 555-7663 - home fax

PRODUCTION DEPARTMENT

PRODUCTION MANAGER
PRODUCTION SUPERVISOR
PRODUCTION COORDINATOR
ASST. PRODUCTION COORDINATOR
KEY OFFICE PRODUCTION ASSISTANT
PRODUCTION ASSISTANT

ASSISTANT DIRECTORS

1ST ASSISTANT DIRECTOR
KEY 2ND ASSISTANT DIRECTOR
2ND SECOND ASSISTANT DIRECTOR
KEY SET PRODUCTION ASSISTANT
PRODUCTION ASSISTANT

ACCOUNTING DEPARTMENT

PRODUCTION ACCOUNTANT
FIRST ASST. ACCOUNTANT
PAYROLL CLERK
ASSISTANT ACCOUNTANT

ART DEPARTMENT

PRODUCTION DESIGNER
ART DIRECTOR
ASST. ART DIRECTOR
SET DESIGNER
STORYBOARD ARTIST
ART DEPT. COORDINATOR
ART DEPT. PA

CAMERA DEPARTMENT

DIRECTOR OF PHOTOGRAPHY
CAMERA OPERATOR
1ST ASST. CAMERAPERSON
2ND ASST. CAMERAPERSON
CAMERA LOADER
STILL PHOTOGRAPHER

CASTING DEPARTMENT

CASTING DIRECTOR
CASTING ASSOCIATE
CASTING ASSISTANT

CATERING DEPARTMENT

CATERING COMPANY
HEAD CHEF
ASSISTANT CHEF
CHEF ASSISTANT

CONSTRUCTION DEPARTMENT

CONSTRUCTION COORDINATOR
CONSTRUCTION FOREMAN
LABOR FOREMAN
LABORER
PROP FOREMAN
PROPMAKER
GANG BOSS
STAND-BY PAINTER
LEAD PAINTER
PAINTER
CARPENTER

CRAFT SERVICE DEPARTMENT

CRAFT SERVICE
ASST. CRAFT SERVICE

EDITORIAL DEPARTMENT

EDITOR
1ST ASSISTANT EDITOR
AVID ASST. EDITOR
APPRENTICE EDITOR
SOUND EDITOR
PROJECTIONIST
EDITORIAL PA

ELECTRIC DEPARTMENT

GAFFER (or CHIEF LIGHTING TECHNICIAN)
BEST BOY ELECTRIC
ELECTRICIAN

EXTRA CASTING

EXTRA CASTING AGENCY
EXTRA CASTING DIRECTOR
EXTRA CASTING ASSOCIATE

FIRST AID DEPARTMENT - SET MEDIC

GREENS DEPARTMENT

GREENSMAN
GREEN LABORER

GRIP DEPARTMENT

KEY GRIP
BEST BOY GRIP
DOLLY GRIP
COMPANY GRIP
RIGGING KEY GRIP
RIGGING BEST BOY GRIP
RIGGING GRIP

LOCATION DEPARTMENT

LOCATION MANAGER
ASST. LOCATION MANAGER

MAKE-UP & HAIR DEPARTMENT

DEPT. HEAD - MAKE-UP SUPERVISOR
MAKE-UP ARTIST
SPECIAL MAKE-UP EFFECTS
DEPARTMENT HEAD - HAIR SUPERVISOR
HAIR STYLIST

MUSIC DEPARTMENT - MUSIC SUPERVISOR

PROPERTY DEPARTMENT

PROPERTY MASTER
ASST. PROPERTY MASTER

PUBLICITY - UNIT PUBLICIST

SCRIPT SUPERVISOR

SET DECORATING

SET DECORATOR
LEAD PERSON
ON-SET DRESSER
SET DECORATING BUYER
SET DRESSER (OR "SWING")

SOUND DEPARTMENT

SOUND MIXER
BOOM OPERATOR
CABLE PERSON

SPECIAL EFFECTS DEPARTMENT

SPECIAL EFFECTS SUPERVISOR
SPECIAL EFFECTS COORDINATOR
SPECIAL EFFECTS FOREMAN
SPECIAL EFFECTS TECHNICIAN

STUDIO TEACHER

STUNT COORDINATOR

TRANSPORTATION DEPARTMENT

TRANSPORTATION COORDINATOR
TRANSPORTATION CAPTAIN
DRIVER

VIDEO

VIDEO ASSIST
VIDEO PLAYBACK

VISUAL EFFECTS - SUPERVISOR

WARDROBE DEPARTMENT

COSTUME DESIGNER
COSTUME SUPERVISOR
KEY SET COSTUMER
SET COSTUMER
DRAPER/STITCHER

SAMPLE

HERBY'S SUMMER VACATION

XYZ PRODUCTIONS
1234 Flick Drive
Hollywood, CA 90038
Tel: (323) 555-3331 - Fax: (323) 555-3332

CAST LIST
5/11/0X

ROLE	ACTOR	AGENT-MANAGER	START DATE	DEAL/BILLING
GEORGE	HOLLYWOOD MANN 3464 Hortense Street Wonderland, CA 90000 Tel: (818) 555-1000 Fax: (818) 555-1001 SS# 123-45-6789 Loan-out Co: Mann, Inc. Federal ID#: 95-1234567	AGENT: JOE COOL Talented Artists Agency 1515 Sunset Blvd. Hollywood, CA 90000 Tel: (310) 555-2345 Fax: (310) 555-2346 Asst: Marge MANAGER: ALEX ADMIN Total Management, Inc. 345 Dreamland Blvd. Los Angeles, CA 90000 Tel: (310) 555-9877 Fax: (310) 555-7895	JUNE, 25, 20XX	$10,000 per wk. 6-wk. guarantee 2 post prod. days Billing: main titles, single card, 4th position

SAMPLE

HERBY'S SUMMER VACATION

XYZ PRODUCTIONS
1234 Flick Drive
Hollywood, CA 90038
Tel: (323) 555-3331 - Fax: (323) 555-3332

CONTACT LIST
5/11/0X

ANIMAL HANDLERS

CUDDLY CREATURES	9870 Forest Hills Drive Sherman Oaks, CA Contact: Barry	(661) 555-7430 (661) 555- 7432 - fax (818) 555-2199 - pgr.

ART SUPPLIES

GRAPHICS PLUS	7540 Colorful Ave. Los Angeles, CA Contact: Rose	(310) 555-4332 (310) 555-4333 - fax

ATTORNEYS
BANK
CASTING
CATERING
CELLULAR PHONES
CLEANING SERVICE
CLEARANCES
COLOR COPIES
COMPUTER RENTALS
COMPUTER REPAIR
COPIER RENTAL
COURIER SERVICE
CRAFT SERVICE SUPPLIES
CREW GIFTS
DUMPSTERS
EDITING ROOMS
EDITORIAL EQUIPMENT
EQUIPMENT (Camera, Electric, Grip, Condors, etc.)
EXPENDABLES
EXTRA CASTING
FAX MACHINES
FILM COMMISSIONS
FILM STOCK
FLORIST
HOTELS
INSURANCE AGENCY
INSURANCE DOCTOR
LAB
MAKE-UP & HAIR SUPPLIES
OFFICE FURNITURE
OFFICE SUPPLIES
PAGERS
PAYROLL SERVICE
PHONE SYSTEM
PHOTO LAB (1-HR)
POST OFFICE
PRODUCT PLACEMENT
PROP HOUSES
PROPERTY MANAGER
RENTAL CARS/VANS

RESEARCH LIBRARY
SCRIPT DUPLICATION
SCRIPT RESEARCH
SECURITY
SHIPPING SERVICES
SOUND TRANSFERS
STILL FILM
STILL PHOTO LAB
TELECINE
TENTS
TRAVEL
UNIONS & GUILDS
VIDEO DUPLICATION
VIDEO RENTALS
VISUAL EFFECTS
WALKIE-TALKIES
WARDROBE HOUSE
WATER DELIVERY SERVICE
WEATHER SERVICE
WORKERS COMPENSATION

the location of the closest medical emergency facility.

- When you are experiencing difficulties with a specific employee, keep a log detailing dates and incidents.
- Confirm all major decisions and commitments in writing; and if an official agreement or contract is not drawn up, write a confirming memo detailing the arrangement.
- Do not sign an agreement and contract until your attorney has reviewed it.
- Do not sign a rental agreement for the use of equipment, motor homes, facilities, etc. until you or someone you trust can check out the quality, and you know exactly what you are getting.
- Favors involving any type of exchange are nice (i.e., the company uses a crew member's car in a chase sequence in exchange for repairs to the car) but can also backfire on you. All such agreements should be backed up with a letter in writing stating the exact terms of the exchange and releasing the company from any further obligations.

Pre-Production Checklist

You have your script and your financing (or studio deal), and you are ready to go. The following list will help you keep track of what you've done and what remains to be done:

Starting from Scratch

- ❑ Prepare a preliminary schedule and budget
- ❑ Find a good attorney who specializes in entertainment law
- ❑ Establish company structure (i.e., corporation or partnership)
- ❑ Obtain business licenses from city, county, and/or state
- ❑ Apply to the IRS for a Federal I.D. number
- ❑ If you have established a corporation, get a corporate seal and a minutes book
- ❑ Obtain workers' compensation and general liability insurance
- ❑ Secure a completion bond (if applicable)
- ❑ Find production offices and stage(s) as needed
- ❑ Start lining up staff and crew

Legal

NOTE: Your company's legal or business affairs department or an outside entertainment attorney should do this work.

- ❑ Secure the rights to the screenplay
- ❑ Make sure the script is registered with the WGA
- ❑ Negotiate (or review) and prepare the contract for the writer of the screenplay
- ❑ Review all financing and distribution agreements
- ❑ Order all copyright and title reports
- ❑ Prepare contracts for principal cast
- ❑ Prepare contracts for the producer, director, director of photography, production designer, costumer designer and editor
- ❑ Prepare minors' contracts
- ❑ Complete Errors and Omissions insurance application
- ❑ Review contracts regarding literary material to make sure all required payments are made
- ❑ Review permits and other documents having potential legal significance
- ❑ Prepare (or approve) all necessary release forms
- ❑ Start music clearance procedures
- ❑ If applicable, handle all necessary requirements related to filming in a foreign country

Set Up Production Office

- ❑ Security, if needed
- ❑ Furniture, including:
- ❑ Drafting tables and stools for the Art Department, and
- ❑ A safe for Accounting
- ❑ Contact phone company for phone numbers and phone, fax and modem lines
- ❑ Arrange for a temporary phone system
- ❑ Copier machine
- ❑ VCR/Monitor
- ❑ Computers and printers
- ❑ Typewriter
- ❑ Production and accounting software programs
- ❑ Fax machine(s)
- ❑ Office supplies
- ❑ Bottled water
- ❑ Coffee maker
- ❑ Microwave oven
- ❑ Refrigerator
- ❑ Extra keys to the office (keep a list of who has keys)

- Pagers and mobile phones for key personnel
- Prepare and post department envelopes
- Prepare a restaurant menu book
- Secure a cleaning service
- Establish account with courier service(s)
- Prepare logs for courier runs and FedEx® shipments
- Prepare sign-out sheets for keys, script, Polariod™ film, etc.
- Set up recycling receptacles and procedures

Paperwork
- Sign union and/or guild contracts (if applicable)
- Design and have letterhead and business cards printed up (the letterhead can also be put on computer disk and given to those who need it)
- Prepare fax cover sheets
- Prepare a map of how to get to the production office and/or stage
- Prepare a phone extension list to be placed next to each phone in the office
- Set up production files
- Assemble a supply of production forms
- Prepare a crew list
- Prepare a contact list
- Start a purchase order log
- Prepare and distribute asset inventory logs
- Start a raw stock inventory and order log
- If you are working on a television series, prepare a list of episodes, production dates, director, writer, and editor for each show
- Prepare DGA deal memos
- Prepare crew deal memos
- Post and distribute safety and code of conduct guidelines as required
- Distribute Acknowledgment of Safety Guidelines forms for crew to sign
- Give completed crew start slips and tax information to Payroll
- Prepare a distribution list

Visual Effects
- Hire a visual effects supervisor
- Prepare a breakdown of visual effects shots
- Have conceptual designs and storyboards prepared, clearly defining each effect

- Determine methodology and exact elements required to accomplish desired effects
- Send breakdown, designs and storyboarded scenarios out to visual effects houses for bids
- Determine time and expense necessary to accomplish each effect
- Adjust script to accommodate budgetary and scheduling limitations if necessary
- Select visual effects houses to create needed effects (i.e., creatures, animation, computer-generated characters)
- Have effects supervisor prepare a schedule integrating pre-production, production and post production activities and all work to be done at effects houses
- Determine which portion of each visual effects shot will need to be shot during production (i.e., process plates), and coordinate with the UPM and first assistant director, so requirements can be integrated into the shooting schedule
- Determine what special equipment you will need to order to be used during production (i.e., motion control camera, blue screen)
- Line up additional, specially trained crew to work on the portions of effects that are scheduled to shoot during production
- Have the effects supervisor prepare a contact list, including which effects houses are doing which effects, phone numbers and names of those who are supervising the work at each of the houses

NOTE: Complicated stunts and special effects to be shot during production should be assessed and planned during the early stages of pre-production as well. Preparation involves many of the same steps as those listed above.

Cast Related
- Secure SAG bond (if applicable)
- Finalize casting
- Prepare a cast list
- Send cast list to SAG
- Station 12 cast members
- Prepare cast deal memos
- Prepare SAG contracts
- Schedule designated cast for medical exams
- Fit wardrobe
- Hire a stunt coordinator

- ❑ Have stunt coordinator line up stunt doubles
- ❑ Hire a dialogue coach, if needed
- ❑ Make sure actors' dressing rooms and mobile homes are properly outfitted
- ❑ Check actors' deals for perks, and make sure they have everything they are contractually due
- ❑ Procure a supply of headshots from actors' agents for hair, makeup, wardrobe, stunts, extra casting, assistant directors and office copy
- ❑ Schedule wig fittings and hair coloring
- ❑ Schedule prosthetic fittings and molds, if necessary
- ❑ Schedule actors for lessons (if special skills are required for their roles)
- ❑ Schedule workouts, tanning sessions, etc. (if required)
- ❑ Schedule rehearsal(s) and read-throughs
- ❑ Schedule hair and makeup tests
- ❑ Make sure minor performers have work permits
- ❑ Hire studio teacher/welfare worker(s), as needed
- ❑ Line up an extras casting agency
- ❑ Interview stand-ins and photo doubles
- ❑ Obtain a good supply of extra vouchers (union and non-union)

Script and Schedules
- ❑ Finalize script
- ❑ Type script changes
- ❑ Duplicate script
- ❑ Distribute script and all revisions to cast, crew, staff, studio/parent production company, insurance agency, casting agencies, research company/department and product placement agencies/department
- ❑ If you are working on a television show, send scripts to network executives and Standards and Practices
- ❑ Prepare a revised Shooting Schedule
- ❑ Prepare a One-Line Schedule
- ❑ Prepare a Day-Out-Of-Days
- ❑ Prepare a script synopsis
- ❑ Have the script timed

Prepare Breakdowns
- ❑ Atmosphere
- ❑ Production vehicles

- ❑ Picture vehicles
- ❑ Stunts
- ❑ Locations ("Location List")
- ❑ Special effects
- ❑ Visual effects
- ❑ Travel ("Movement List")
- ❑ Continuity Breakdown
- ❑ Schedule of second-unit days
- ❑ Product Placement wish list
- ❑ Special equipment (condors, Technocrane, mobile lighting systems, camera remote heads, etc.)
- ❑ Schedule of train, boat or helicopter days (whatever might be applicable)
- ❑ Time-lines (as applicable)

Budgetary/Accounting
- ❑ Open bank account
- ❑ Collect departmental budgets
- ❑ Finalize budget
- ❑ Select payroll company
- ❑ Prepare cash flow chart
- ❑ Send script, budget and schedule to the completion bond company
- ❑ Prepare start paperwork packages
- ❑ Open vendor accounts
- ❑ Prepare a chart-of-accounts

Insurance
- ❑ Send script and budget to the insurance companies for bids
- ❑ Secure insurance coverage
- ❑ Make sure Errors and Omissions insurance application is submitted
- ❑ Provide information for risk management survey
- ❑ Decide on specific endorsements to meet the needs of your picture
- ❑ Secure special coverage for aircraft, boats, railroad, etc.
- ❑ If necessary, secure special coverage for working in a foreign country
- ❑ Prepare certificates of insurance for vehicles, equipment and locations
- ❑ Send travel breakdown to the insurance company

- Send stunt and effects breakdown to the insurance company, along with the resumes of the stunt coordinator and effects supervisors
- Have a supply of workers' compensation accident forms and insurance information for office, second assistant director and company nurse
- Procure a supply of loss/damage and auto accident claim forms
- Select a doctor approved by the insurance company for necessary physicals

Post Production Related

- Hire a post production supervisor
- Select lab, telecine and sound house
- Set up accounts for lab, sound transfers, telecine, supplies, etc.
- Order editing equipment
- Set up editing room(s)
- Get bids from sound effects houses
- Book dates and facility for predubbing and final mix
- Route dailies
- Schedule screening of dailies
- Prepare a tentative post production schedule
- Have script supervisor meet with editor regarding routing of daily notes and any special requests editor may have

Locations

- Hire a location manager
- Complete location agreements
- Submit signed location agreements to accounting and copies to the production office and assistant directors
- Issue certificates of insurance to property owners
- Obtain permits
- Hire fire safety and police officers as necessary
- Set up security
- Arrange for intermittent traffic control, if needed
- Post for parking
- Obtain signed releases from neighbors
- Prepare maps to locations
- Order signs with name of show and directional arrows

- Procure heaters, fans and air conditioners as needed
- Procure layout board and drop cloths
- Locate closest medical emergency facilities
- Locate closest hotels/motels, if necessary
- Set up phones, power and utilities
- Locate parking lot(s), if shuttling is necessary
- Arrange for extra tables, chairs and tents
- Allocate areas for extras, dressing rooms, eating, hair, makeup, schoolroom, rest area for minors and parents, special equipment, animals, etc.
- Allocate parking areas for equipment, vehicles and VIP cars
- Locate alternative sites to be used as cover sets
- If needed, hire service to clean locations after each one is wrapped
- Do final walk-through with property owners, have them sign Location Release form

Distant Locations

See Distant Location Checklist in Chapter 17

Foreign Locations

See Chapter 18

Order

- Raw stock (as per DP)
- Still film and Polariod™ film
- Camera equipment
- Empty cans, camera reports, black bags and cores (from lab)
- Steadicam package
- Video assist equipment
- Grip and electric equipment
- Grip, electric and camera expendables
- Dolly(s), crane(s) and condor(s)
- Generator(s)
- Sound equipment
- DAT tapes (or 1/4-inch mag stock)
- Walkie-talkies, bullhorns and headsets
- Cellular phone(s)
- Projection equipment
- Makeup/hair hydraulic lift chairs
- Portable VCR and monitor (if dailies are shown on set)
- Catering

Transportation

- ❑ Motor home(s), cast trailers and star wagon(s)
- ❑ Honeywagon(s)
- ❑ Camera car(s) and process trailer(s)
- ❑ Water truck
- ❑ Production trailer
- ❑ Hair and makeup trailer
- ❑ Wardrobe trailer
- ❑ Crew cabs and vans
- ❑ Grip and electric truck
- ❑ Camera truck
- ❑ Sound/video truck
- ❑ Prop truck
- ❑ Set dressing truck
- ❑ Effects truck and trailer
- ❑ Fuel truck
- ❑ Picture cars

Animals

- ❑ Locate the necessary animals/livestock
- ❑ Contact the American Humane Association for guidelines in the proper care, use, handling and safety of animals

Locate and hire competent:

- ❑ Animal handlers
- ❑ Trainers
- ❑ Wranglers

Specialty Items

- ❑ Technical advisor(s)
- ❑ Rear screen/process photography
- ❑ Blue or green screen for visual effects shots
- ❑ Motion control camera
- ❑ Playback
- ❑ 24-frame video playback
- ❑ Stock footage
- ❑ Cycs and backdrops
- ❑ Mockups
- ❑ Models
- ❑ Safety divers
- ❑ Nursery and baby nurse(s)

Preparing for Stage Work

- ❑ Telephones
- ❑ Security
- ❑ Power

- ❑ Remote and bell
- ❑ Heaters, fans, air conditioners
- ❑ Generator (if necessary)
- ❑ Dressing rooms
- ❑ Schoolroom
- ❑ Rest area for minors and parents
- ❑ Tables and chairs
- ❑ Area for extras
- ❑ Makeup and hair
- ❑ Darkroom
- ❑ Access to medical department or nurse/medic on set

The assistant directors will prepare a portable file box (or a legal-size accordion file) with the following paperwork to stay on the set at all times. This box should contain the following:

Copies of:

- ❑ All signed location agreements
- ❑ All permits
- ❑ Actors' deal memos
- ❑ SAG guidelines

Blanks of:

- ❑ Location agreements
- ❑ Call sheets
- ❑ Production reports
- ❑ Workers' compensation accident report forms
- ❑ Automobile accident report forms
- ❑ SAG contracts (a few of each kind)
- ❑ SAG Time Sheets (Exhibit Gs)
- ❑ SAG Taft/Hartley report forms
- ❑ Crew start paperwork packages
- ❑ Copies of safety guidelines and *Filmmaker's Code Of Conduct*
- ❑ Certificates of insurance
- ❑ Petty cash envelopes
- ❑ Release forms (an assortment)
- ❑ Extra vouchers
- ❑ Walkie-Talkie Sign-Out sheets
- ❑ Start slips, W-4s and I-9s

Extra copies of:

- ❑ Staff and crew lists
- ❑ Call sheets

- Scripts and script changes
- Cast lists
- Contact lists
- Shooting schedules
- Day-out-of-days
- Maps to the locations
- Crew pager and cell phone numbers

Keep on the set at all times:

- A complete first aid kit
- Aspirin/Tylenol®
- Several flashlights
- An assortment of office supplies
- Extra Polariod™ film
- A designated set mobile phone
- A small copier machine (if you have the room and the additional cost is within your budget), laptop computer, and printer

CREATING YOUR OWN PRODUCTION MANUAL

The best way to establish your company's policies is to have your own production manual. Having a company manual provides a substantial degree of professionalism to the smallest of production units. Assemble your manual in a large three-ring binder, and make sure all staff and freelance production personnel receive one. Keep a record of who the manuals are given to and when revisions are made.

The manual should contain the following:

- A complete listing of company operating procedures, including crew startup and payroll reporting procedures
- A contact list containing the names, addresses and phone numbers of the company's insurance representative, outside legal advisor, travel agent, vendors, storage facilities, labs and post production facilities, applicable union and guild representatives, payroll service, permit service, script research service, music clearance service, messenger service, equipment rental houses, repair contacts, etc.
- A company staff list, including department designations and phone number extensions
- Samples of the forms and releases you wish to be used on all company shows
- Pertinent union and guild rates and regulations, including rules governing the employment of minors
- Insurance guidelines, contacts, forms and claim reporting procedures
- Safety guidelines
- *Filmmaker's Code Of Conduct*
- . . . and anything else relevant to your company operations.

FORMS IN THIS CHAPTER

- Asset Inventory Log
- Equipment Rental Log
- Mobile Phone/Pager Sign-Out Sheet
- Walkie-Talkie Sign-Out Sheet
- Distribution Log
- Crew Information Sheet

ASSET INVENTORY LOG

SHOW: HERBY'S SUMMER VACATION **DEPARTMENT:** SET DRESSING

ITEM(S)	PURCHASED FROM	PURCHASE DATE	PURCHASE PRICE	P.O.# or PETTY CASH	AT COMPLETION OF PRINCIPAL PHOTOGRAPHY			
					IF PORTION USED, HOW MUCH REMAINS	IF SOLD, FOR HOW MUCH	IF RETD. TO COMPANY, IN WHAT CONDITION	LOCATION OF ITEM
(2) OIL PAINTINGS	OTTO'S GALLERY	6-12-XX	$520	1235		$260		
BOY'S BEDROOM FURNITURE SET	FURNITURE WORLD	6-18-XX	$1,575	1241			SLIGHTLY SCRATCHED	COMPANY STORAGE
(3) DOZ. BEACH TOWELS	BED & BATH SHOP	7-2-XX	$275	1256	10 TOWELS	$38		
BOOM BOX	ELECTRONIC CITY	7-5-XX	$120	P.C.		$75		

© ELH

EQUIPMENT RENTAL LOG

ITEM(S)	VENDOR ADDRESS/PHONE/FAX CONTACT	P.O.#	DEPARTMENT ASSIGNED TO	DATE PICKED-UP	LENGTH OF RENTAL	DATE RETURNED	L&D SUBMITTED
MAIN CAMERA PACKAGE	CAMERA WORLD 16730 SWEETWATER RD. HOLLYWOOD, CA 90028 CONTACT: MATT BOXX 555-2000	1321	CAMERA	7/4/XX	6 WKS.	9/8/XX	✓
GRIP PKG.	STUDIO RENTAL CO. CONTACT: BRUNO 555-9631	1325	GRIP	7/4/XX	6 WKS.	9/10/XX	✓
ELECT. PKG.	DAZZLE LIGHTING CO. CONTACT: JOE 555-4317	1328	ELECT.	7/4/XX	6 WKS.	9/10/XX	✓
FUEL TRUCK	RON'S STUDIO RENTALS CONTACT: RON 555-6201	1383	TRANSPO.	7/11/XX	2 WKS.	7/25/XX	
30' SCISSOR LIFT	ELH STUDIO EQUIP. CONTACT: SAM 555-3774	1422	SPEC. EFX.	8/7/XX	1 WK.	8/11/XX	
TECHNOCRANE	ABC REMOTE SYSTEMS CONTACT: TOM 555-4000	1471	GRIP	8/16/XX	2 DAYS	8/19/XX	
FORK LIFT	ELH STUDIO EQUIP. CONTACT: SAM 555-3774	1505	CONST.	8/21/XX	1 WK.	8/25/XX	

© ELH

[✓] MOBILE PHONE [ ] PAGER SIGN-OUT SHEET

DATE RECVD. FROM VENDOR	P.O.#	ITEM(S) & MODEL#(S) (INCLUDING ACCESSORIES)	SERIAL #	PHONE #	PRINT NAME	DATE OUT	SIGNATURE	DATE IN	DATE RETD. TO VENDOR
6/20/xx	1213	PHONE, CHARGER, CAR CHARGER	X27234	555-7637	SWIFTY DEALS	6/21	*(signature)*	9/8	9/9
6/25/xx	1227	PHONE, CHARGER, HEAD SET	X27251	555-7639	FRED FILMER	6/25	Fred Filmer	9/10	9/10

NOTES:

Vendor: HOLLYWOOD CELLULAR
Address: 321 MAIN ST. L.A. 90036
Phone#: 555 - 1372
Contact: BRIAN

© ELH

WALKIE-TALKIE SIGN-OUT SHEET

P.O.#	INDICATE ITEM & MODEL NO. (Walkie-Talkie, Charger, Headset, Bullhorn, Other Accessory, etc.)	SERIAL #	UNIT #	DEPARTMENT ASSIGNED TO	PRINT NAME	DATE OUT	SIGNATURE	DATE IN	DATE RETD. TO VENDOR
1533	W·T/NARROWBAND	AB37622	12	CAMERA	F. STOPP	4/30	*(signature)*	9/3	9/4
	"	AB37613	13	LOCATION	FRANK FEINDIT		*Frank Feindit*	9/6	9/7
	"	AB37811	15	EFX.	CAL BLOOEY		*Cal Blooey*	9/1	9/2 DAMAGED
	"	AB37865	17	STUNTS	WILL FALLE	↓	*(signature)*	8/20	8/21
↓	(1) RACK CHGR.	XR25	21					9/6	9/7
1672	W·T/HT1000	HT37600	65	UPM	FRED FUMER	7/3	*(signature)*	9/6	9/7
	W·T/HT1000	HT37503	68	A.D.	A. DEES	7/3	*(signature)*	9/6	9/7
	(1)HT1000 HEADSET	HTA37	03	↓				9/6	LOST
	(2)SINGLE CHGRS.	XR57	72					9/6	9/7
		XR93	87	↓		↓		9/6	LOST
↓	(1) BULLHORN	BH514	32	A.D.	A. DEES	7/3	*(signature)*	8/4	8/5

NOTES:

BILL'S AUDIO SERVICES
3456 GABLE BLVD.
HOLLYWOOD CA 90028
555-3456
BILL

© ELH

DISTRIBUTION LOG

Document	Marvin Mogul	Swifty Deals	Sid Celluloid	Fred Filmer	F. Stopp	A. Dees	Katie Kandu	Connie Coordinates	Nellie Numbers	Total No. of Copies Needed
SCRIPT & REVISIONS	✓	✓	✓	✓	✓	✓	✓	✓	✓	9
BUDGET	✓	✓	✓	✓				✓		4
COST REPORTS	✓	✓		✓				✓		4
PRE-PROD. SCHEDULE	✓	✓	✓	✓	✓	✓		✓	✓	8
SHOOTING SCHED. & ONE-LINER	✓	✓	✓	✓	✓	✓		✓	✓	9
DAY-OUT-OF-DAYS	✓	✓	✓	✓	✓	✓		✓	✓	9
CONTINUITY BREAKDOWN	✓	✓	✓	✓	✓	✓		✓	✓	9
STORYBOARDS	✓	✓	✓	✓	✓	✓		✓		8
CREW DEAL MEMOS	✓	✓		✓				✓	✓	5
CREW LIST	✓	✓	✓	✓	✓	✓	✓	✓	✓	9
CAST & CREW CONTRACTS	✓	✓		✓				✓	✓	5
CAST LIST W/O DEALS					✓		✓			2
CAST LIST W/DEALS	✓	✓	✓	✓	✓			✓		5
CAST PHOTOS					✓			✓		2
EXTRAS BREAKDOWN	✓	✓	✓		✓		✓	✓	✓	7
VEHICLE BREAKDOWN	✓	✓	✓		✓		✓	✓	✓	7
STUNT & EFX. BREAKDOWNS	✓	✓	✓	✓	✓		✓	✓		7
CONTACT LIST	✓	✓	✓		✓		✓	✓	✓	8
LOCATION AGREEMENTS	✓	✓	✓				✓	✓	✓	7
RELEASE FORMS	✓	✓	✓				✓	✓		5
PRODUCT PLACEMENT REPORTS	✓	✓					✓	✓	✓	5
TRAVEL INFO. & MOVEMENT LISTS	✓	✓	✓	✓		✓	✓	✓	✓	8
CALL SHEETS	✓	✓	✓	✓	✓	✓	✓	✓	✓	9
PRODUCTION REPORTS	✓	✓	✓	✓		✓	✓	✓	✓	7
WRAP REPORTS	✓	✓	✓	✓		✓		✓	✓	6
INSUR. & WORKERS COMP CLAIMS	✓	✓		✓			✓	✓	✓	5
POST PROD. SCHEDULE	✓	✓	✓	✓			✓	✓		6
MUSIC CUE SHEETS	✓	✓	✓							3
DELIVERY REQUIREMENTS	✓	✓								2

© ELH

CREW INFORMATION SHEET

Please fill in the following information **completely** and return this form to the Production Office. Thank You.

SHOW __HERBY'S SUMMER VACATION__

NAME __F. STOPP__

POSITION __DIR. OF PHOTOG.__   DEPARTMENT __CAMERA__

HOME ADDRESS __2486 MADONNA LN.__
__BEVERLY HILLS, CA 90210__

MAILING ADDRESS (If Different) _____

HOME PHONE# __555-1077__   PAGER# _____
HOME FAX# __555-1078__   MOBILE PHONE# __555-7633__
E-MAIL ADDRESS __fstopp@filmme.com__

☐ Check here if you DO NOT want any of the above information on the Crew List
☑ Check here if you just want your pager & mobile numbers on the Crew List

SOCIAL SEC# __333-63-3266__   BIRTHDAY (month & day only) __1-25__
LOAN-OUT CO. __FILMME, INC.__   FED. ID# __95-1234567__
START DATE __6/21/XX__   UNION __IA-LOCAL 600__
EMERGENCY CONTACT __STEPHANIE STOPP__
RELATIONSHIP __WIFE__   HOME PHONE# __SAME AS ABOVE__
MOBILE PHONE# __555-7634__   WORK PHONE# _____

TRAVELING PREFERENCES (We will try to accommodate your preferences to be best of our ability)

AIRLINE SEAT (check one)   ☐ Window ☐ Middle ☑ Aisle ☐ Bulkhead ☐ No Preference
AIRLINE MEAL (check one)   ☑ Vegetarian ☐ Non-Dairy ☐ Kosher ☐ No Preference

PLEASE LIST YOUR FREQUENT FLYER ACCOUNT NUMBERS

AIRLINE	ACCNT. NO.
UNITED	X23712L
AMERICAN	AM732B1Z
DELTA	432P17L3

HOTEL ROOM

LOCATION: ☐ Ground Level ☑ In the Back ☐ Near the Front ☐ No Preference
BED STYLE: ☑ King ☐ Queen ☐ 2 Beds   ROOM: ☐ Smoking ☐ Non-Smoking
IF AVAILABLE, I WOULD LIKE THE FOLLOWING IN MY ROOM:
☑ Refrigerator ☐ Microwave ☐ Extra Rollaway ☑ Desk ☑ Modem Line

The above information is solely for Production Office records and will be kept strictly confidential.

© A Stephen A. Marinaccio II form

CHAPTER SIX

Insurance Requirements

Securing insurance should be the first order of business at the start of any new production. Coverage should be obtained from an insurance agency that specializes in insurance for the entertainment industry. You may want to get bids from two or three different companies, or from one insurance broker with whom you have developed a good working relationship. There are relatively few insurance agencies that are experts in film production insurance. The major players have offices in Los Angeles, New York and London. Near North Insurance Brokerage is one such company, as is Aon/Albert G. Ruben Insurance Services, Inc.

As films continually become more complicated in terms of action, stunts, effects, technology and a reliance on highly paid actors and directors to carry entire pictures on their names alone, levels of financial exposures increase as well. Insurance companies and the agencies who represent them are taking a much closer look than ever before at each picture, vigorously investigating potential exposure and carefully assessing the risks.

In addition to budgets and schedules, insurance companies examine the track record of the production company, the producer and director; where the show is to be shot; its financing source; distribution and bond company agreements; cast; story line; all potential hazards; safety guidelines and protection methods to be utilized; proposed travel; crew specifications and anticipated payroll; rare and expensive set dressing, props or wardrobe to be used; the use of animals, motorcycles, special vehicles and equipment, watercraft, aircraft or railroad cars and all proposed action, stunts and effects.

The information necessary to complete a risk management survey is now required when applying for production insurance. Risk management personnel (i.e., in-house risk managers, brokers,

and underwriters) review all scripts, contracts and budgets, in addition to detailed breakdowns of proposed stunts and effects. The backgrounds and experience levels of stunt coordinators and effects supervisors are scrutinized, and proof of pyrotechnic licenses is required as well.

On films containing action, loss control representatives might contact stunt coordinators and effects supervisors to discuss the concerns of the underwriter, how each stunt and effect is to be accomplished, the anticipated use of personnel and the safety procedures to be implemented. These reps are extremely knowledgeable in the areas of stunts and effects and will offer advice and spend time on the set when action sequences are shot. Their sole purpose is to minimize risks and to curb the escalating losses suffered by insurance companies on action pictures. This chapter will touch on the basics of motion picture and television insurance, including both standard and supplemental coverage.

ERRORS & OMISSIONS

Errors and omissions (E&O) liability insurance provides coverage for claims made for libel, slander, invasion of privacy, infringement of copyright, defamation of character, plagiarism, piracy or unfair competition resulting from the alleged unauthorized use of titles, formats, ideas, characters, plots, performances of artists or performers or other materials. It includes coverage for any legal expenses incurred in the defense of any covered claim as well as indemnity.

Delivery requirements might dictate whether this is to be a one-year or a three-year policy. A three-year policy is cost-effective, and renewals should continue at least throughout the distribution period.

Obtain an errors and omissions liability insurance application from your insurance broker immediately upon starting pre-production. This is the only insurance application that is completed by the production company and must be signed by an authorized member of the production company. Submit the application and secure this coverage as soon as possible.

It is extremely important to make sure that your E&O application has been approved by the underwriters prior to the start of principal photography. Significant financial loss can be incurred if a part or all produced material is not approved ahead of time. It is suggested that written confirmation from the underwriters be obtained before the cameras start to roll.

COMPREHENSIVE GENERAL LIABILITY

This coverage typically provides a combined single limit of $1,000,000 per occurrence and $2,000,000 in the aggregate for bodily injury and property damage liability. The liability coverage includes: blanket contractual liability, products and completed operations, nonownership watercraft legal liability (usually restricted to vessels up to twenty-six feet in length), personal injury endorsement and fire damage legal liability (smaller limits of coverage might apply).

Evidence of this coverage is given in the form of a Certificate of Insurance. Certificates of Insurance are issued by the production office (or in some cases, the insurance agency) to a third party (e.g., a location owner) as evidence of coverage.

Frequently, you will be requested to name a certificate holder as additional insured and/or loss payee. If a certificate holder is named as an additional insured, the insurance coverage will protect the certificate holder for claims arising out of the activities of the production company. A certificate holder who is named loss payee is the owner of a vehicle or equipment being used on your film. If there is a claim resulting from the loss or damage to this vehicle or equipment, reimbursement for the loss or damage would be paid to the loss payee.

Your insurance agency may require that you call their office to request additional insured or loss payee certificates when a certificate holder requests this additional coverage. Often, however, these certificates may be issued directly from the production office.

You can order certificates of insurance that specify *Additional Insured—Managers or Lessors of Premises*, which are issued to the owner(s) of each filming location, and *Additional Insured/ Loss Payee—Equipment*, which are issued to the owners of rented equipment and vehicles. Special coverage that involves the company's use of watercraft, aircraft or a railroad is always handled through your insurance representative. Certificates involving these activities are never issued by the production office.

When filling out a Certificate of Insurance on a rental vehicle or a picture vehicle, it is a good idea to include the make, model and I.D. number of the vehicle. If the value of the vehicle exceeds the limits of the policy, additional coverage will be necessary. If you are doing a series, the episode and production number should be indicated on the certificate.

The top copy of the certificate (the original) goes to the owner of the vehicle, property or equipment. Two copies are to be sent to your insurance representative. One copy should be given to your production executive, and one is to remain in the production files. If the certificate is for a vehicle, a copy should also be kept in the vehicle's glove compartment.

HIRED, LOANED, DONATED OR NON-OWNED AUTO LIABILITY

This coverage provides liability insurance for all hired, loaned, donated and non-owned motor vehicles. Vehicles owned by or leased to the company must be scheduled separately, and a charge is incurred for each vehicle. If an employee should have an accident while driving his or her personal car for company business, his or her own insurance is primary. The company's policy only insures the production company if the employee's coverage is insufficient. Such coverage is provided under the non-owned automobile coverage.

Have your transportation coordinator keep a supply of auto accident forms (Automobile Loss Notice) on the set at all times. One should be filled out and submitted to the insurance agency immediately after an accident occurs.

HIRED, LOANED OR DONATED AUTO PHYSICAL DAMAGE

This coverage insures against physical damage to hired, loaned and donated vehicles, including the risks of loss, theft or damage and collision for certain vehicles the production company is contractually responsible for. It is not generally intended to cover physical damage to employees' vehicles being used for production activities. If coverage is required, there must be a written rental agreement between the production company and the employee. The agreement must establish that the production company is responsible for the physical damage to the subject vehicle. It is strongly suggested that the insurance agency be contacted to confirm coverage for employees' cars. Your agent must review the contract. As with the auto liability coverage, vehicles owned by or leased to the company must be scheduled separately.

If a vehicle is damaged as a result of more than one incident, notation must be made as to the specific damage caused during each incident, the date and time of each, what the vehicle was being used for (was it a picture vehicle or a production vehicle?) and how the accident occurred. The insurance company will not accept miscellaneous vehicle damage accumulated during the length of a production. It treats each occurrence as a separate accident, and a separate deductible applies to each occurrence. If you plan to use a picture vehicle for stunt work, include this information in your breakdown. Be aware that physical damage to vehicles used in stunts is generally not covered.

WORKERS' COMPENSATION & EMPLOYER'S LIABILITY

All employees are entitled to workers' compensation benefits if they are injured or acquire an illness directly resulting from or during the course of their employment. The benefits are established by state laws.

Workers' compensation coverage should be supplied by the employer of record, that is, the paying entity, which is either the payroll service or the production company. Although payroll services generally supply workers' compensation, it is a prudent practice to obtain a certificate of workers' compensation coverage from them prior to any commitment of services. Even if all employees are being paid through the payroll service, prudence further dictates that the production company still carry a minimum premium policy, insuring independent contractors, volunteers or interns who might work on your picture. A contingent workers' compensation policy would also provide employer liability coverage should the need arise.

If the employer of record is other than the production company or payroll service (for example, a stunt coordinator hiring other stunt personnel, or a special effects supervisor hiring his or her own effects crew), you should obtain a Certificate of Insurance from the employer (department head) to show evidence of workers' compensation coverage for his or her employees. If certificates are not obtained by the end of the show, this will come out at the insurance audit when payroll records and 1099s are reviewed. And in such cases, appropriate additional charges would be incurred based on the independent contractor's payroll.

If your workers' compensation coverage is coming from more than one source, generate a memo indicating which staff, crew and cast members are covered under which policy. The memo should also include information on each of the insurance companies (name, address, and phone number), the name of an insurance agency or payroll company representative to report claims to, the policy numbers of each, and a copy of the accident report form (Employer's Report of Injury) that each insurance company uses. Make sure your company medic and second assistant director have copies of this memo and a supply of accident forms on the set at all times.

When a staff, cast or crew member is injured on the set, fill out an Employer's Report of Injury form and note the incident on the back of the daily production report for that particular day. Send the report directly to the insurance agency or payroll company, keep a copy for the production files and send a copy to your production executive. Also attach an additional copy to the back of the production report. Forward all medical bills, doctor's reports and all other relevant materials to the respective insurance agency or payroll company.

When applying for workers' compensation during pre-production, declare the need for coverage for employees hired in your state of operations as well as coverage for any other state where your employees are living at the time of hire. Include an All States' Endorsement with your workers' compensation policy to protect the company if employees are hired from a state or states you had not initially declared. Injured employees will receive benefits in accordance with the compensation laws of the state in which they were living at the time of hire. Six states (Nevada, Ohio, West Virginia, Wyoming, North Dakota and Washington State) are *monopolistic*, meaning that you must purchase workers' compensation coverage directly from their state insurance program if you choose to hire employees from their state.

Inform your insurance broker if members of your shooting company are going to be working on or near the water, as USLH (United States Longshoremen's and Harborworkers) or Jones Act coverage might be required. The USLH covers workers near the water, whereas the Jones Act deals with crew (i.e., vessel crew).

Your insurance agency representative and/or the state's workers' compensation fund will supply you with appropriate injury report forms. Reporting procedures are the same in every state. Should a SAG-covered performer be injured in the course of employment with your company, the Screen Actors Guild requires that you send a copy of the accident report to them.

GUILD/UNION ACCIDENT COVERAGE

Employees traveling on company business are covered under a Travel Accident Policy, which provides coverage as specified in their governing guild or union bargaining agreements. If an employee is not a member of any union or guild, coverage is provided for a minimum amount. No employee, while on the company payroll, is allowed to fly as a pilot or as a member of a flight crew unless specifically hired for that duty and scheduled on the insurance policy. Under guild/union travel accident coverage, each production is required to keep track of (1) the number of plane and/or helicopter flights taken by any guild/union member on each show; (2) the number of hours each person may spend in a helicopter; (3) the number of days each guild/union member may be exposed to hazardous conditions; and (4) the number of days any DGA member may be exposed while filming underwater. This specific information may be requested from the insurance company at the completion of principal photography.

Coverage for guild members pursuant to guild agreements should be provided by your payroll service if one is involved. Producers might choose to obtain Guild/Union Accident coverage for non-guild members. This decision should be made by the production company.

PRODUCTION PACKAGE (PORTFOLIO POLICY)

The Production Package provides coverage for cast insurance; negative film and videotape/direct physical loss; faulty stock, camera and processing; props, sets and scenery, costumes and wardrobe; miscellaneous rented equipment and office contents; extra expense and third party property damage.

The premium for the Production Package is usually based upon what is referred to as net insurable costs—the final budget, minus the costs of post production, story, music and finance charges. Rates then range from $.75 to $1.25 (depending on negotiations, exposures, etc.) per each $100 of the net insurable costs. In some instances, however, third parties (i.e., banks or completion bond companies) have requested that story and finance charges be included as covered expenses. Under these circumstances, underwriters are usually willing to charge a lower rate for the premium. Your selection of optional coverages on any one show will be based on script and budgetary considerations, as well as requirements imposed by distributors and bond companies. Your insurance representative will discuss all variables and policy options with you and help you decide which coverage will provide the best protection for your picture.

Cast Insurance

This coverage is placed on a designated number of cast members, the director and possibly the producer or director of photography: any key person whose disability or death would cause a shutdown of the production. If an accident or illness of a covered actress, actor, director, etc. creates a postponement, interruption or cancellation of production, the production company, subject to a predetermined deductible, would be reimbursed for extra expenses if it is determined that the production must be abandoned due to an insured cast loss. The production company would then be reimbursed for all covered expenses incurred. This policy might also include coverage for kidnapping occurring during pre-production or filming, and can include coverage for the payment of ransom demands. A thorough and complete substantiation of the company's extra costs incurred due to such occurrences must be presented to the insurance company before a claim can be properly adjusted. Physical exams are required for those who are to be covered under cast insurance, and the insurance agency will furnish you with the name of a physician (or a choice of physicians) with whom you can set up appointments. The insurance company will pay closer attention to a cast member's medical history when that person is either over-aged or under-aged. When employing minors, your insurance broker needs to be aware of the childhood diseases they have had, because the diseases (e.g., chicken pox, measles, mumps) they have not yet had may be excluded from the cast insurance policy. There may also be specific exclusions imposed upon principals who have had a history of alcohol or substance abuse. If any of these circumstances do exist, they should be brought to the attention of the producer as soon as possible. At times, certain exclusions can be "bought back" or modified (i.e., by using higher deductibles, etc.).

Cast insurance usually starts three to four weeks prior to the commencement of principal photography, although additional prep coverage is often required. An example of this is a key actor who is involved with the project from the very early stages of pre-production.

If at any point during pre-production or production, the director, producer or one of the designated actors becomes ill, is injured or is incapacitated in any way, call your insurance representative immediately. If one of them feels ill yet continues working, but you are not sure how he or she will be on the following day, or how the schedule may be affected later in the week, alert the insurance agency as to the possibility of an interruption in filming. If there is ever a question as to whether you should call or not, DO IT!

If a cast claim is submitted, the director or performer who is ill or injured should be seen by a doctor as soon as possible. The doctor's report is a necessary factor in substantiating the claim.

Essential Elements

An optional endorsement, an essential element would be an actor, actress, producer or director who carries an entire show on his or her name alone, someone without whom, if this person were to die or become ill or injured, the picture could not be completed and delivered. At times, more than one key person may be designated as an essential element. If there is essential element coverage, the inability of an essential element to continue working now gives the producer the option of abandoning the project and recouping all expenses. If it is determined, however, that the essential element, after suffering an illness or injury, is likely to recover and resume his or her assigned role or position, the insurance company has the option to delay the abandonment of the insured production for up to sixty days after the occurrence of the injury or onset of the illness.

The additional insurance would begin at the start of pre-production and should be carried until at least two weeks after the completion of principal photography. In the case of an essential director, coverage might have to stay in effect through the director's cut.

Before someone is granted the status of essential element, their name must be on an "A" list of artists, or they must be approved by the underwriter. It is mandatory that he or she have an extensive medical exam and also sign a warranty agreeing to refrain from hazardous activities on and off the set during the entire span of his or her contract. The payment schedule of the artist being insured is examined, as are any previous disabling illnesses or injuries.

Family Death Endorsement (Bereavement Coverage)

This is another optional endorsement that would reimburse the production for expenses incurred when a key member of the cast or the director must interrupt his or her working schedule due to the death of an immediate family member.

Negative Film And Videotape/ Direct Physical Loss

Subject to specific exclusions, most of which are covered under Faulty Stock, Camera and Processing (described later), this coverage protects against direct physical loss, damage or destruction to all negative and videotape elements, including work prints, cutting copies, fine-grain prints, sound tracks, audiotapes, videotapes, cassettes and CDs. In addition, coverage is included for accidental magnetic erasure on videotape production and has been adapted to cover the most up-to-date technological developments of videotape production. It also includes coverage on all negative and videotape elements while in transit.

Faulty Stock, Camera, And Processing

Subject to certain exclusions, this coverage insures against the loss, damage or destruction of raw film stock or tape stock, exposed film, recorded videotape and sound tracks caused by or resulting from fogging or the use of faulty equipment, faulty developing or faulty processing. It does not cover losses due to mistakes made by the camera crew.

Props, Sets & Scenery; Costumes & Wardrobe; Miscellaneous Rented Equipment; Office Contents

Subject to specified exclusions, these provide coverage against direct physical loss, damage, or destruction to all property (contents, equipment, cameras, sets, wardrobe, lighting equipment, office furnishings, props, supplies, etc.) used in connection with the covered production. Keep running inventories of all set dressing, props, wardrobe, equipment and other items that are purchased and/or rented for each show. If anyone on your crew notices that something is missing or damaged, inform the insurance agency, make a note of it on the inventory log and on the back of the daily production report and file a police report if applicable. At the end of the show, the insurance company may not honor claims on lost or damaged equipment, props, set dressing or wardrobe without sufficient documentation. Advise all department heads to inform the production manager or production coordinator of loss and damages as they occur, and do not wait until the completion of principal photography to submit invoices for repairs and replacement costs.

In specific cases of missing equipment, props, set dressing or wardrobe, there must clearly be a theft for a claim to be honored. As soon as an item is discovered missing, file a police report to substantiate the theft. If at the end of principal photography, however, you discover you are short a few pieces of equipment, a few props or some pieces of wardrobe, and you have no idea when any of these items were taken, this is considered "mysterious disappearance." Without a police report and documentation indicating when each item was discovered missing, who discovered it missing, etc., a claim of mysterious disappearance is not covered.

No insurance reimbursements are issued for the loss of employees' personal belongings, such as purses or clothing. If an employee is using his or her own personal computer or typewriter, it is covered if substantiated in their deal memo (and scheduled on their box rental inventory), or if there is a specific contract stating that the producer will be responsible to insure these items. The problem can be with the deductible, as most policies have a deductible of at least $1,000.

Extra Expense

Claims of this type typically involve the damage or destruction of sets, props, wardrobe, locations or facilities that actually interrupt, delay or cause the cancellation of production. It also covers additional expenses resulting from the short circuiting, electrical injury or failure of any electrical generator, portable or otherwise, used in production. This added protection covers expenditures over and above the total cost normally incurred to complete principal photography when any real and/or personal property is lost due to damage or the destruction of this property.

Third Party Property Damage

This coverage pays all sums that the production company shall become legally obligated to pay as damages because of accidental injury to or destruction of property of others while such property is in the care, custody or control of the production company.

Your insurance representative will advise you as to the specific limits and deductibles of the above-mentioned coverages and any additional optional coverages you might require based on the needs of your production.

SUPPLEMENTAL (OR OPTIONAL) COVERAGE

Umbrella (Excess Liability)

There will be times, with locations, for example, when higher limits than those provided under General Liability and/or Third Party Property Damage are mandatory. This coverage carries limits of liability in excess of $1,000,000. An Umbrella Liability Policy will indemnify the insured for the ultimate net loss in excess of the underlying limit or the self-insured retention, whichever is the greater, because of bodily injury, personal injury or property damage to which the insurance applies.

Umbrella liability policies providing limits from $1 million to $25 million, and higher, are available. If, however, increased limits of liability are required for a short period of time only, excess limits can be obtained to comply with specific location or contract requirements. If your operations are to include filming at any museums, airports, major office or manufacturing locations, umbrella liability is a must.

Use Of Aircraft

Inform your insurance agency as soon as possible if you plan to use any aircraft in your show so that adequate Non-Owned Aircraft Liability and/or hull coverages can be secured. Insurance is also available to cover the use of hot air balloons, gliders, sailplanes and other types of aircraft.

To add protection for the possible negligence of the owner of the aircraft, it is also strongly advisable that the owner be asked to name your production company as additional insured under his owner's Hull and Liability Insurance policies. The production should secure a Hold Harmless and Waiver of Subrogation with respect to loss or damage to the hull of the aircraft, so that the production is not responsible for any damage to it. Request a Certificate of Insurance from the owner of the aircraft evidencing the Waiver of Subrogation and including the production company as an additional insured.

Use Of Watercraft

If you are going to be using a boat (watercraft) for the purpose of filming or carrying a film crew and/or equipment, discuss the details with your insurance representative to determine if and what type of marine coverages are necessary.

Use Of Railroads Or Railroad Facilities

For the use of railroads or railroad facilities, the production company is often required to indemnify the railroad for the production's negligence as well as the railroad's negligence. The insurance agency will need to review the contract provided by the railroad before proper coverage can be determined.

Use Of Valuables

Inform the insurance agency as to the use of fine arts, jewelry, furs and expensive antiques, and the values of each, so that limits can be increased as required. How these items are to be used with respect to the production must be discussed so that appropriate coverage can be arranged.

Use Of Livestock Or Animals

If insurance coverage is necessary for livestock or animals to be used in a production, it is arranged on a case-by-case basis and is based on contractual obligations and the value of the animal(s). Animal mortality insurance covers the death or destruction of any animal specifically insured. At no time would the limit of coverage be more than the value of the animal covered; and before coverage is issued, a veterinarian certificate on the animal is necessary. Under certain circumstances, an animal may be insured under Extra Expense, and some carriers will use the Cast Insurance section of the policy to provide this coverage. This coverage reimburses the production company for extra expenses incurred due to the accident, illness or death of a covered animal. Depending on the value of the animal, the insurance company may require that you use backup animals (i.e., doubles).

Keep in mind, should you be planning a scene that incorporates one type of animal, such as cattle, but you need another type of animal (such as horses) to wrangle the cattle, the horses would need to be covered as well as the cattle.

Signal Interruption Insurance

Insurance coverage is available to protect against exposures in the transmission of signals by satellite or closed circuit television. This coverage indemnifies the insured for loss of revenues resulting from the necessary interruption of business due to breakdown, failure or malfunction of any equipment that prevents the telecasting or presentation of the scheduled event.

Foreign Package Policy

When a production is filming outside of the United States, its territories or possessions, special coverages are necessary. Under these circumstances, it is important to procure Foreign Liability, Foreign Workers' Compensation and Foreign Auto coverage. A domestic policy will not protect you against lawsuits filed in foreign countries.

Political Risk Insurance

This coverage is recommended for production companies planning to shoot in certain (potentially dangerous) foreign countries. Under this policy, the insurance company pays for loss due to physical property damage to insured assets caused by war, civil war and insurrection. It includes forced project relocation coverage, which pays the additional costs incurred solely and directly as a result of and following relocation of the production to another country. This coverage also includes any production-related confiscation or expropriation by a foreign government.

Weather Insurance

Weather insurance is available to protect against additional costs incurred in the event your production is interrupted, postponed or canceled as a result of weather-related problems. The policy can include coverage not only for precipitation, but can be extended to include coverage for wind, fog, temperature and any other measurable weather conditions. The premium for this policy would be based on both the value of the days (or portion thereof) you wish to insure, and the degree of bad weather you wish to insure against. The rate is determined by applying an agreed rate to the daily limit of insurance, taking into consideration the time of year, location and the agreed-upon measurements of weather that would trigger an insured event.

COMPLETION BONDS

Completion guarantees, also referred to as completion bonds, insure motion picture financiers against cost overruns in excess of their approved budget. In addition, they insure that the film will be delivered in accordance with all specifications contained in the financing and distribution agreements, and in other related contracts that define the deal.

Major studios with the resources to finance pictures, including overages, do not require bonding, as the functions provided by a bond company are handled in house. Bond companies do service smaller studios and independent production companies, whose financiers and distributors will require that their picture be bonded prior to the start of principal photography.

The formal issuance of a completion guaranty involves two separate documents. The producer's agreement is signed by the producer and guarantor and is an acknowledgment and warranty by the producer to produce the film in accordance with the approved script, schedule and budget. The producer also agrees to take or cause no action that would void the approved insurance coverages or that would otherwise threaten the timely and efficient production of the film. In the event of default by the producer, this document gives the guarantor the ultimate right to take over

the film, and to complete and deliver it in the producer's stead.

The completion guaranty is signed by the financier(s) and the guarantor. In this document, the guarantor agrees to deliver the film in accordance with the approved script, schedule, budget and contractual specifications, and to pay any additional costs in excess of the approved budget required to so deliver the project. In the event that the film cannot be delivered as guaranteed, the guarantor agrees to repay all funds that have been therefore advanced by the financier(s) to cover the costs of the approved budget. If the project has to be abandoned, the financier is not put in the position of having spent money on a project that was not completed. In the event that the picture cannot be completed, the financier is repaid his or her investment. While not able to collect additional revenues from box office grosses, he or she has not lost anything either.

Completion guarantors, just as insurance underwriters, carefully assess each project before committing to a bond. They want to know that you have a script with an adequate schedule and budget, and a reputable and insurable cast and crew. They will review all major contracts relating to cast, locations, special effects, insurance, travel, etc. They will assign members of their staff to oversee projects from the beginning of pre-production through delivery; and at times, they will hire an outside person to oversee a particular picture. Bond reps will receive copies of scripts, budgets, schedules, call sheets, production reports, weekly cost reports, etc. Some will attend a production meeting or two and make occasional visits to the set during production. Other bond reps will be more hands-on and remain with the shooting company on a daily basis, involved in all major decisions pertaining to the production. Much will depend on the bond company and its particular style of involvement, the relationship and track record you have with the bond company and how each film is progressing. The ones that encounter the most difficulties are the ones more closely watched.

The traditional point where a bond company would take over a film is after the production has gone through their entire budget plus the full 10 percent contingency prior to the completion of the picture. This rarely happens, as the bond company's job is to anticipate potential problems before they occur. It works diligently with the producer, director, cast and crew to keep things on schedule and on budget. Unless you have one company that you prefer working with, shop around for a completion guarantor, as rates are competitive and often negotiable.

CLAIMS REPORTING PROCEDURES

If an accident, injury or theft occurs; if the director or a cast member becomes ill and unable to work; if you have a scratched negative or damage to equipment, props, set dressing or any of your sets, report it to the insurance agency as soon as possible. Back up each reported occurrence in writing by completing an appropriate claim form, noting such on the back of the daily production report for that particular day, and/or by writing a letter to the insurance agency containing as much detail as possible—when the incident occurred (date of loss), where it occurred, how it happened, who was there at the time, etc. Report any major theft or accident to the police, and attach a copy of the police report to your letter to the insurance agency. Even if you are not sure a loss would be covered, advise your insurance representative as to the possibility of a claim.

If a serious accident occurs, promptly record the names and phone numbers of witnesses (including staff, cast and crew members) so that an accurate description of the incident can be determined at a later date. Statements or reports should only be taken by authorized representatives of the production company, and in turn, should be submitted to your insurance representative.

Submitting Claims

When an incident occurs resulting in an insurance claim, the accounting department should begin to tag each related invoice, indicating specific costs (or portions of costs) that were directly incurred as a result of the claim. When the claim is submitted, all related costs and overages should be presented budget-style, starting with a budget top sheet indicating the exact impact to each account. Copies of invoices should be coded and placed behind the top sheet in the correct order of accounts.

In addition to applicable police and doctor reports and copies of invoices, backup should also include: call sheets; production reports; and both original and revised schedules, day-out-of-days, cast lists and anything to substantiate the changes created by the claim. Depending on the claim, copies of cast and crew deal memos, time-cards, travel movement lists, equipment rental agreements and/or location agreements may also be required. For complicated or ongoing claims, it is a good idea for the producer or production manager to either maintain a log of events pertaining to the claim on a day-to-day basis, or to write memos to the file on a regular basis.

Begin each claim with a cover letter referencing the production, date of occurrence, claim number (if available), a description of the claim and a brief summary of the backup you are providing. (I suggest binding the backup with brads or in file folders secured with Acco® fasteners.) Start processing insurance claims as soon as they occur. Submit the full claim to the insurance agency as soon as costs can be assessed and backup provided. Do not wait until the end of principal photography to start processing your claims.

Once a claim is reported to your insurance representative, it is then turned over to an insurance agency claim representative. When all the information is in order, the claim is then submitted to the insurance company, who may or may not (depending on the claim) then assign it to an independent insurance auditor. It is often advantageous for the production manager and production accountant to meet with the insurance auditor shortly after the incident occurs to better define the parameters of the claim and to know exactly what backup will be necessary.

For further information regarding any aspect of insurance, contact your insurance agent.

NOTE: Assistance for this chapter was provided by Marc J. Federman, Senior Vice President, and Erick Medina, both of Near North Insurance Brokerage in Los Angeles.

FORMS IN THIS CHAPTER

The first three forms listed below are printed by Accord™, and are standard insurance forms used in our industry. You can use these, or your insurance representative will send you a supply of blank forms.

- Certificate Of Insurance
- Property Loss Notice
- Automobile Loss Notice

The following four forms are worksheets that should be helpful when collecting information needed for the submission of claims.

- Insurance Claim Worksheet (Theft)
- Insurance Claim Worksheet (Damage)
- Insurance Claim Worksheet (Cast/Extra Expense/Faulty Stock)
- Insurance Claim Worksheet (Automobile Accident)

NOTE: Your Workers' Compensation contact will supply you with Injury/Illness forms appropriate to the states or countries in which your show will be filming/working.

ACORD™ CERTIFICATE OF LIABILITY INSURANCE

DATE (MM/DD/YY)

PRODUCER	THIS CERTIFICATE IS ISSUED AS A MATTER OF INFORMATION ONLY AND CONFERS NO RIGHTS UPON THE CERTIFICATE HOLDER. THIS CERTIFICATE DOES NOT AMEND, EXTEND OR ALTER THE COVERAGE AFFORDED BY THE POLICIES BELOW.
Near North Insurance Brokerage, Inc. 1840 Century Park East #1100 Los Angeles, California 90067 Contact: Erick Medina (310)556-4715	**COMPANIES AFFORDING COVERAGE**
INSURED	COMPANY **A** ABC Insurance Company
XYZ Productions 1234 Flick Drive Hollywood, CA 90038 RE: "Herby's Summer Vacation"	COMPANY **B**
	COMPANY **C**
	COMPANY **D**

COVERAGES

THIS IS TO CERTIFY THAT THE POLICIES OF INSURANCE LISTED BELOW HAVE BEEN ISSUED TO THE INSURED NAMED ABOVE FOR THE POLICY PERIOD INDICATED, NOTWITHSTANDING ANY REQUIREMENT, TERM OR CONDITION OF ANY CONTRACT OR OTHER DOCUMENT WITH RESPECT TO WHICH THIS CERTIFICATE MAY BE ISSUED OR MAY PERTAIN, THE INSURANCE AFFORDED BY THE POLICIES DESCRIBED HEREIN IS SUBJECT TO ALL THE TERMS, EXCLUSIONS AND CONDITIONS OF SUCH POLICIES. LIMITS SHOWN MAY HAVE BEEN REDUCED BY PAID CLAIMS.

CO LTR	TYPE OF INSURANCE	POLICY NUMBER	POLICY EFFECTIVE DATE (MM/DD/YY)	POLICY EXPIRATION DATE (MM/DD/YY)	LIMITS	
A	**GENERAL LIABILITY** [X] COMMERCIAL GENERAL LIABILITY [ ] CLAIMS MADE [X] OCCUR [ ] OWNER'S & CONTRACTOR'S PROT [ ] [ ] [ ]	GL4358609	4/13/00	4/13/01	GENERAL AGGREGATE PRODUCTS - COMP/OP AGG PERSONAL & ADV INJURY EACH OCCURRENCE FIRE DAMAGE (Any one fire) MED EXP (Any one person)	$ 2,000,000 $ 1,000,000 $ 1,000,000 $ 1,000,000 $ 50,000 $ 5,000
A	**AUTOMOBILE LIABILITY** [ ] ANY AUTO [ ] ALL OWNED AUTOS [ ] SCHEDULED AUTOS [X] HIRED AUTOS [X] NON-OWNED AUTOS [ ] [ ]	BA98374675 Hired Auto Physical Damage Limit: $250,000 per vehicle Limit: $1,000,000 Aggregate Deductible: 10% of loss subject to $2,500 min. and $7,500 max.	4/13/00	4/13/01	COMBINED SINGLE LIMIT BODILY INJURY (Per person) BODILY INJURY (Per accident) PROPERTY DAMAGE	$ 1,000,000 $ $ $
	GARAGE LIABILITY [ ] ANY AUTO [ ]				AUTO ONLY - EA ACCIDENT OTHER THAN AUTO ONLY: EACH ACCIDENT AGGREGATE	$ $ $
A	**EXCESS LIABILITY** [ ] UMBRELLA FORM [ ] OTHER THAN UMBRELLA FORM	UM984756	4/13/00	4/13/01	EACH OCCURRENCE AGGREGATE	$ 1,000,000 $ 1,000,000 $ 10,000
A	**WORKERS COMPENSATION AND EMPLOYERS' LIABILITY** THE PROPRIETOR/ PARTNERS/EXECUTIVE OFFICERS ARE: [ ] INCL [ ] EXCL	WC947630	4/13/00	4/13/01	WC STATU-TORY LIMITS [ ] OTH-ER EL EACH ACCIDENT EL DISEASE - POLICY LIMIT EL DISEASE - EA EMPLOYEE	$ 1,000,000 $ 1,000,000 $ 1,000,000
A	**OTHER** Miscellaneous Equipment Third Party Property Damage Props, Sets & Wardrobe	PKG895732 PKG895732 PKG895732	4/13/00 4/13/00 4/13/00	4/13/01 4/13/01 4/13/01	Limit: $5,000,000 Deductible: $3,500 Limit: $5,000,000 Deductible: $2,500 Limit: $5,000,000 Deductible: $2,500	

DESCRIPTION OF OPERATIONS/LOCATIONS/VEHICLES/SPECIAL ITEMS

Certificate holder is an additional insured &/or loss payee, as their interests may appear with respect to all operations ot the named insured connection with the production entitled "Herby's Summer Vacation"

CERTIFICATE HOLDER	CANCELLATION
	SHOULD ANY OF THE ABOVE DESCRIBED POLICIES BE CANCELLED BEFORE THE EXPIRATION DATE THEREOF, THE ISSUING COMPANY WILL ENDEAVOR TO MAIL _30_ DAYS WRITTEN NOTICE TO THE CERTIFICATE HOLDER NAMED TO THE LEFT, BUT FAILURE TO MAIL SUCH NOTICE SHALL IMPOSE NO OBLIGATION OR LIABILITY OF ANY KIND UPON THE COMPANY, ITS AGENTS OR REPRESENTATIVES.
	AUTHORIZED REPRESENTATIVE

ACORD 25-S (1/95)

© ACORD CORPORATION 1988

ACORD™ PROPERTY LOSS NOTICE

DATE (MM/DD/YY) 6·29·XX

PRODUCER	PHONE (A/C, No, Ext): (310) 556-4715

Near North Insurance Brokerage
1840 Century Park East
Suite 1100
Los Angeles, CA 90067

CODE: SUB CODE:

AGENCY CUSTOMER ID

MISCELLANEOUS INFO (Site & location code)

RPTD: 6·29

DATE OF LOSS AND TIME   7   ✓ AM   PM

PREVIOUSLY REPORTED YES ✓ NO

POLICY TYPE	COMPANY AND POLICY NUMBER	EFFECTIVE DATE	EXPIRATION DATE
PROP/ HOME	CO: ABC Insurance Co. POL: PKG 895732	4·13·XX	4·13·XX
FLOOD	CO: POL:		
WIND	CO: POL:		

INSURED

NAME AND ADDRESS

XYZ Productions
1234 Flick Dr.
Hollywood, CA 90038

RESIDENCE PHONE (A/C, No)   BUSINESS PHONE (A/C, No, Ext)
(XXX) 555-3331

CONTACT   CONTACT INSURED

NAME AND ADDRESS

Connie Coordinates, Prod. Coordinator
OR
Darlene Dresser, Set Decorator
@ XYZ Productions

RESIDENCE PHONE (A/C, No)   BUSINESS PHONE (A/C, No, Ext)
(XXX) 555-3331

WHERE TO CONTACT At Office

WHEN TO CONTACT 8 AM - 8 PM

LOSS

LOCATION OF LOSS Stage 5 - Hollywood Studios

POLICE OR FIRE DEPT TO WHICH REPORTED LAPD - Hollywood Div.

KIND OF LOSS FIRE   LIGHTNING   FLOOD   OTHER (explain)   ✓THEFT   HAIL   WIND

PROBABLE AMOUNT ENTIRE LOSS $3,500 —

DESCRIPTION OF LOSS & DAMAGE (Use reverse side, if necessary) XYZ Computer System, Keyboard, Monitor & Printer (used as set dressing) stolen from a dressed set during the night. It was discovered missing @ 7am the next morning.

POLICY INFORMATION

MORTGAGEE

NO MORTGAGEE

(Your insurance broker will complete or help you to complete the remainder of the form.)

HOMEOWNER POLICIES SECTION 1 ONLY (Complete for coverages A, B, C, D & additional coverages. For Homeowners Section II Liability Losses, use ACORD 3.)

A. DWELLING	B. OTHER STRUCTURES	C. PERSONAL PROPERTY	D. LOSS OF USE	DEDUCTIBLES	DESCRIBE ADDITIONAL COVERAGES PROVIDED
					ON

COVERAGE A. EXCLUDES WIND
SUBJECT TO FORMS (Insert form numbers and edition dates, special deductibles)

FIRE, ALLIED LINES & MULTI-PERIL POLICIES (Complete only those items involved in loss)

ITEM	SUBJECT OF INSURANCE	AMOUNT	% COINS	DEDUCTIBLE	COVERAGE AND/OR DESCRIPTION OF PROPERTY INSURED
	BLDG CNTS				
	BLDG CNTS				
	BLDG CNTS				

SUBJECT TO FORMS (Insert form numbers and edition dates, special deductibles)

FLOOD POLICY	BUILDING: CONTENTS:	DEDUCTIBLE: DEDUCTIBLE:	ZONE	PRE FIRM POST FIRM	DIFF IN ELEV	FORM TYPE	GENERAL DWELLING	CONDO
WIND POLICY	BUILDING	DEDUCTIBLE CONTENTS	ZONE	FORM TYPE	GENERAL DWELLING	CONDO		

REMARKS/OTHER INSURANCE (List companies, policy numbers, coverages & policy amounts)

CAT # FICO #	ADJUSTER ASSIGNED		ADJUSTER #	DATE ASSIGNED

REPORTED BY Darlene Dresser

REPORTED TO Connie Coordinates

SIGNATURE OF PRODUCER OR INSURED Connie Coordinates

ACORD 1 (2/95)   NOTE: IMPORTANT STATE INFORMATION ON REVERSE SIDE   © ACORD CORPORATION 1988

Applicable in California
Any person who knowingly presents false or fraudulent claim for the payment of a loss is guilty of a crime and may be subject to fines and confinement in state prison.

Applicable in Florida and Idaho
Any person who Knowingly and with the intent to injure, Defraud, or Deceive any Insurance Company Files a State-ment of Claim Containing any False, Incomplete or Misleading information is Guilty of a Felony.*
* In Florida - Third Degree Felony

Applicable in Indiana
A person who knowingly and with intent to defraud an insurer files a statement of claim containing any false, incomplete, or misleading information commits a felony.

Applicable in Kentucky and New Jersey
Any person who knowingly and with intent to defraud any insurance company or other persons, files a state-ment of claim containing any materially false information, or conceals for the purpose of misleading, informa-tion concerning any fact, material thereto, commits a fraudulent insurance act, which is a crime, subject to criminal prosecution and civil penalties.

Applicable in Michigan
Any person who knowingly and with intent to injure or defraud any insurer submits a claim containing any false, incomplete, or misleading information shall, upon conviction, be subject to imprisonment for up to one year for a misdemeanor conviction or up to ten years for a felony conviction and payment of a fine of up to $5,000.00.

Applicable in Minnesota
A person who files a claim with intent to defraud or helps commit a fraud against an insurer is guilty of a crime.

Applicable in Nevada
Pursuant to NRS 686A.291, any person who knowingly and willfully files a statement of claim that contains any false, incomplete or misleading information concerning a material fact is guilty of a felony.

Applicable in New Hampshire
Any person who, with purpose to injure, defraud or deceive any insurance company, files a statement of claim containing any false, incomplete or misleading information is subject to prosecution and punishment for insurance fraud, as provided in RSA 638:20.

Applicable in New York
Any person who knowingly and with intent to defraud any insurance company or other person files a statement of claim containing any materially false information, or conceals for the purpose of misleading, information con-cerning any fact material thereto, commits a fraudulent insurance act, which is a crime, and shall also be subject to a civil penalty not to exceed five thousand dollars and the stated value of the claim for each such violation.

Applicable in Ohio
Any person who, with intent to defraud or knowing that he/she is facilitating a fraud against an insurer, submits an application or files a claim containing a false or deceptive statement is guilty of insurance fraud.

Applicable in Oklahoma
WARNING: Any person who knowingly and with intent to injure, defraud or deceive any insurer, makes any claim for the proceeds of an insurance policy containing any false, incomplete or misleading information is guilty of a felony.

Applicable in Pennsylvania
Any person who knowingly and with intent to injure or defraud any insurer files a claim containing any false, incomplete or misleading information shall, upon conviction, be subject to imprisonment for up to seven years and payment of a fine of up to $15,000.

ACORD™ AUTOMOBILE LOSS NOTICE

DATE (MM/DD/YY): 6-25-XX

PRODUCER		COMPANY	MISCELLANEOUS INFO (Site & location code)
PHONE (A/C, No, Ext): (310) 556-4715		ABC INSURANCE CO.	

PRODUCER:
NEAR NORTH INSURANCE BROKERAGE
1840 CENTURY PARK EAST
SUITE 1100
LOS ANGELES, CA 90067

POLICY NUMBER	REFERENCE NUMBER	CAT #
BA 98374675		

CODE:	SUB CODE:	EFFECTIVE DATE	EXPIRATION DATE	DATE OF ACCIDENT AND TIME	✔ AM	PREVIOUSLY REPORTED
AGENCY CUSTOMER ID:		4·13·XX	4·13·XX	6·25·XX 9:23	PM	YES ✔ NO

INSURED / CONTACT

INSURED	CONTACT CONTACT INSURED

INSURED NAME AND ADDRESS
XYZ PRODUCTIONS
1234 FLICK DR.
HOLLYWOOD, CA 90038

CONTACT NAME AND ADDRESS
CONNIE COORDINATES, PROD. COORDINATOR
a TOMMY TRANSPORTS, TRANS. COORDINATOR
C/o XYZ PRODUCTIONS

WHERE TO CONTACT: AT OFFICE

WHEN TO CONTACT: 8AM - 8PM

RESIDENCE PHONE (A/C, No)	BUSINESS PHONE (A/C, No, Ext) (XXX)555-3331	RESIDENCE PHONE (A/C, No)	BUSINESS PHONE (A/C, No, Ext) (XXX)555-3331

LOSS

LOCATION OF ACCIDENT (Include city & state): CORNER OF 4th & STARLIGHT DR. STUDIO VILLAGE, CALIF.

AUTHORITY CONTACTED:
REPORT #:

VIOLATIONS/CITATIONS

DESCRIPTION OF ACCIDENT (Use reverse side, if necessary): DRIVER SHUTTLING CAST + CREW TO SET FROM PARKING AREA RAN INTO CAR IN FRONT OF HIM WHEN OTHER CAR STOPPED SHORT BEFORE TURNING LEFT @ INTERSECTION.

POLICY INFORMATION

BODILY INJURY (Per Person)	BODILY INJURY (Per Accident)	PROPERTY DAMAGE	SINGLE LIMIT	MEDICAL PAYMENT	OTC DEDUCTIBLE	OTHER COVERAGE & DEDUCTIBLES (UM, no-fault, towing, etc)
			$1,000,000			

LOSS PAYEE		COLLISION DED
TINSELTOWN MOTORS		

UMBRELLA/ EXCESS	✔ UMBRELLA	EXCESS	CARRIER: ABC INSUR. CO.	LIMITS: $1,000,000	✔ PER CLAIM	PER OCCUR

INSURED VEHICLE

VEH #	YEAR	MAKE: FORD	BODY TYPE: MINIVAN	PLATE NUMBER	STATE
X-3	'99	MODEL: AEROSTAR	V.I.N.: 1234567L7HNZ	XXX 2321	CA

OWNER'S NAME & ADDRESS: TINSELTOWN MOTORS 7305 CLUTCH RD. - TINSELTOWN, CALIF.
RESIDENCE PHONE (A/C, No):
BUSINESS PHONE (A/C, No, Ext): (XXX)555-6000

DRIVER'S NAME & ADDRESS: TERRY TEAMSTER 523 S. BIGRIG AVE. - WONDERLAND, CALIF.
(Check if same as owner)
RESIDENCE PHONE (A/C, No): (XXX)555-4427
BUSINESS PHONE (A/C, No, Ext): (XXX)555-3331

RELATION TO INSURED (Employee, family, etc.)	DATE OF BIRTH	DRIVER'S LICENSE NUMBER	STATE	PURPOSE OF USE	USED WITH PERMISSION?
EMPLOYEE	CA	T00R0378	CA	TRANSPORTING CAST + CREW	✔ YES NO

DESCRIBE DAMAGE: DENTED FRONT FENDER, BUMPER, GRILL + HOOD
ESTIMATE AMOUNT: $3750
WHERE CAN VEHICLE BE SEEN? TINSELTOWN MOTORS
WHEN CAN VEH BE SEEN? BET. 9AM + 7PM
OTHER INSURANCE ON VEHICLE

PROPERTY DAMAGED

DESCRIBE PROPERTY (If auto, year, make, model, plate #): '98 DODGE RAM PICKUP LIC PLATE: 2376573

OTHER VEH/PROP INS?	COMPANY OR AGENCY NAME:
✔ YES NO	POLICY #:

OWNER'S NAME & ADDRESS: DENNIS DRIVER 7326 N. HILLTOP DR. - STUDIO VILLAGE, CALIF.
RESIDENCE PHONE (A/C, No): (XXX) 555-4322
BUSINESS PHONE (A/C, No, Ext): (XXX) 555-8881

OTHER DRIVER'S NAME & ADDRESS: (Check if same as owner)
RESIDENCE PHONE (A/C, No):
BUSINESS PHONE (A/C, No, Ext):

DESCRIBE DAMAGE: DENTED REAR BUMPER + TAILGATE
ESTIMATE AMOUNT: $1,375
WHERE CAN DAMAGE BE SEEN? THE DRIVER HOME - 8-9 A.M. OR 6-8 P.M.

INJURED

NAME & ADDRESS	PHONE (A/C, No)	PED	INS VEH	OTH VEH	AGE	EXTENT OF INJURY

WITNESSES OR PASSENGERS

NAME & ADDRESS	PHONE (A/C, No)	INS VEH	OTH VEH	OTHER (Specify)
F. STOPP C/o XYZ PRODUCTIONS	(XXX)555-3331	✔		
PATRICK PEDESTRIAN - 123 MAIN ST. - HOLLYWOOD, CA	(XXX)555-4436			PEDESTRIAN

REMARKS (Include adjuster assigned):

REPORTED BY	REPORTED TO	SIGNATURE OF PRODUCER OR INSURED
TERRY TEAMSTER	TOMMY TRANSPORTS, TRANS. COORD.	Tommy Transports

ACORD 2 (2/95)   NOTE: IMPORTANT STATE INFORMATION ON REVERSE SIDE   © ACORD CORPORATION 1988

Applicable in California

Any person who knowingly presents false or fraudulent claim for the payment of a loss is guilty of a crime and may be subject to fines and confinement in state prison.

Applicable in Florida and Idaho

Any person who Knowingly and with the intent to injure, Defraud, or Deceive any Insurance Company Files a Statement of Claim Containing any False, Incomplete or Misleading information is Guilty of a Felony.*

    * In Florida - Third Degree Felony

Applicable in Indiana

A person who knowingly and with intent to defraud an insurer files a statement of claim containing any false, incomplete, or misleading information commits a felony.

Applicable in Kentucky and New Jersey

Any person who knowingly and with intent to defraud any insurance company or other persons, files a statement of claim containing any materially false information, or conceals for the purpose of misleading, information concerning any fact, material thereto, commits a fraudulent insurance act, which is a crime, subject to criminal prosecution and civil penalties.

Applicable in Michigan

Any person who knowingly and with intent to injure or defraud any insurer submits a claim containing any false, incomplete, or misleading information shall, upon conviction, be subject to imprisonment for up to one year for a misdemeanor conviction or up to ten years for a felony conviction and payment of a fine of up to $5,000.00.

Applicable in Minnesota

A person who files a claim with intent to defraud or helps commit a fraud against an insurer is guilty of a crime.

Applicable in Nevada

Pursuant to NRS 686A.291, any person who knowingly and willfully files a statement of claim that contains any false, incomplete or misleading information concerning a material fact is guilty of a felony.

Applicable in New Hampshire

Any person who, with purpose to injure, defraud or deceive any insurance company, files a statement of claim containing any false, incomplete or misleading information is subject to prosecution and punishment for insurance fraud, as provided in RSA 638:20.

Applicable in New York

Any person who knowingly makes or knowingly assists, abets, solicits or conspires with another to make a false report of the theft, destruction, damage or conversion of any motor vehicle to a law enforcement agency, the Department of Motor Vehicles or an insurance company, commits a fraudulent insurance act, which is a crime, and shall also be subject to a civil penalty not to exceed five thousand dollars and the value of the subject motor vehicle or stated claim for each violation.

Applicable in Ohio

Any person who, with intent to defraud or knowing that he/she is facilitating a fraud against an insurer, submits an application or files a claim containing a false or deceptive statement is guilty of insurance fraud.

Applicable in Oklahoma

WARNING: Any person who knowingly and with intent to injure, defraud or deceive any insurer, makes any claim for the proceeds of an insurance policy containing any false, incomplete or misleading information is guilty of a felony.

Applicable in Pennsylvania

Any person who knowingly and with intent to injure or defraud any insurer files a claim containing any false, incomplete or misleading information shall, upon conviction, be subject to imprisonment for up to seven years and payment of a fine of up to $15,000.

INSURANCE CLAIM WORKSHEET

(THEFT)

STOLEN ☐ EQUIPMENT
☐ WARDROBE
☐ PROPS
☑ SET DRESSING
☐ VEHICLE

PRODUCTION _HERBY'S SUMMER VACATION_

DATE ITEM(S) WERE DISCOVERED MISSING _JUNE 29, 19XX_

DESCRIPTION OF ITEM(S) STOLEN (Include I.D.#'s If Available)

MacINTOSH II si COMPUTER WITH MONITOR & KEYBOARD
SERIAL # XSF23L2762265

DEPARTMENT USED BY _SET DRESSING_
PERSON USED BY _USED AS SET DRESSING ONLY_

WHERE WERE ITEM(S) LAST SEEN _"HERBY'S BEDROOM" SET_

WHO DISCOVERED ITEM(S) MISSING _DARLENE DRESSER_

ITEM(S) ☐ PURCHASED FOR SHOW—PURCHASE PRICE $ _____
☑ RENTED FOR SHOW
RENTED FROM _CAL'S COMPUTER CENTER_
ADDRESS _8976 MAIN STREET_
STUDIO VILLAGE, CA 90000
PHONE# _(818) 555-1767_
CONTACT _CAL COLLINS_

VALUE $ _1,500_
RENTAL PRICE $ _200_ PER ☐ DAY
☐ WEEK
☑ MONTH

☑ POLICE REPORT ATTACHED
☑ OTHER ATTACHMENTS _RENTAL AGREEMENT FROM CAL'S_
COMPUTER CENTER

SUBMITTED TO INSURANCE AGENCY ON _JULY 2, 19XX_
ATTENTION _SUSIE_
CLAIM # _005327_
INSURANCE COMPANY CLAIMS REP. _CURTIS CLAIMS_

INSUR. CLAIM WORKSHEET COMPLETED BY _CONNIE COORDINATES_
DATE _JULY 2, 19XX_ TITLE _PRODUCTION COORDINATOR_

AMOUNT CREDITED TO AGGREGATE DEDUCTIBLE $ _500_ DATE _7·15·XX_
REIMBURSEMENT CHECK PAID TO _XYZ PRODUCTIONS_
AMOUNT $ _1,000_ DATE _7·20·XX_

© ELH

INSURANCE CLAIM WORKSHEET

DAMAGE TO ☑ EQUIPMENT
☐ WARDROBE
☐ PROPS
☐ SET DRESSING
☐ LOCATION/PROPERTY

PRODUCTION ___HERBY'S SUMMER VACATION___

DATE OF OCCURRENCE _6·24·XX_ TIME ___11 A.M.___

WHAT WAS DAMAGED ___MOTOROLA HT1000 WALKIE·TALKIE___

LOCATION OF OCCURRENCE ___HOLLYWOOD RIVER___

HOW DID DAMAGE OCCUR _SECOND ASSISTANT DIRECTOR ACCIDENTALLY_ _DROPPED WALKIE·TALKIE IN RIVER WHILE ARRANGING_ _ATMOSPHERE FOR SCENE 25._

WITNESS _MIKE BOOM_ POSITION _SOUND MIXER_
PHONE# _(213) 555-9993_

DAMAGED ITEM(S) ☐ PURCHASED FOR SHOW—PURCHASE PRICE $___
☑ RENTED FROM/OWNER _XXX AUDIO SERVICES_
ADDRESS _123 GRAND AVE._
HOLLYWOOD, CA 91234
PHONE # _(213) 555-5311_
CONTACT _MACK_

RENTAL PRICE $ _50_ PER ☐ DAY
☑ WEEK
☐ MONTH

VALUE OF DAMAGED ITEM(S) $ _1,000_
ESTIMATE TO REPAIR $ _600_
☑ ATTACHMENTS _COPY OF DAILY PRODUCTION REPORT (INCIDENT NOTED)_
COPY OF REPAIR INVOICE

SUBMITTED TO INSURANCE AGENCY ON _6·29·93_
ATTENTION _SUSIE_
CLAIM # _005328_
INSURANCE COMPANY CLAIMS REP. _CURTIS CLAIMS_

INSURANCE CLAIM WORKSHEET COMPLETED BY _CONNIE COORDINATES_
DATE _6·28·XX_ TITLE _PRODUCTION COORDINATOR_

AMOUNT CREDITED TO AGGREGATE DEDUCTIBLE $ _0_ DATE ___
REIMBURSEMENT CHECK PAID TO _XXX AUDIO SERVICES_
AMOUNT $ _600_ DATE _7·29·XX_

© ELH

INSURANCE CLAIM WORKSHEET

☑ CAST
☐ EXTRA EXPENSE
☐ FAULTY STOCK

PRODUCTION ___HERBY'S SUMMER VACATION___

DATE OF OCCURRENCE ___JULY 2, 19XX___ TIME ___5:00 P.M.___

DESCRIPTION OF INCIDENT ___DIRECTORS CHAIR COLLAPSED WHILE ACTRESS___
___WAS SITTING ON IT BETWEEN TAKES. SHE INJURED HER RIGHT___
___LEG AND SPRAINED HER BACK.___

IF CAST CLAIM, WHICH ARTIST ___SCARLET STARLET___

WAS A DOCTOR CALLED IN ☑ YES ☐ NO

NAME OF DOCTOR ___A. PAINE M.D.___
ADDRESS ___3327 S. INJECTION BLVD.___
___LOS ANGELES 90000___
PHONE # ___(310) 555-1177___

COULD COMPANY SHOOT AROUND INCIDENT ☐ YES ☑ NO
IF YES, FOR HOW LONG _____

HOW MUCH DOWN TIME WAS INCURRED DUE TO THIS INCIDENT ___1 DAY___

AVERAGE DAILY COST $ ___50,000___

BACKUP TO CLAIM TO INCLUDE • COPY OF DAILY PRODUCTION REPORT
• COPY OF DOCTOR'S REPORT
• BACK-UP TO COSTS INCURRED DUE TO DOWN TIME

SUBMITTED TO INSURANCE AGENCY ON ___JULY 12, 19XX___
ATTENTION ___SUSIE___
CLAIM # ___005329___
INSURANCE COMPANY CLAIMS REP. ___CURTIS CLAIMS___
INSURANCE AUDITOR ___LAWRENCE LIABILITY___

INSURANCE CLAIM WORKSHEET COMPLETED BY ___CONNIE COORDINATES___
DATE ___7·11·XX___ TITLE ___PRODUCTION COORDINATOR___

AMOUNT CREDITED TO DEDUCTIBLE $ ___0___ DATE _____
REIMBURSEMENT CHECK PAID TO ___XYZ PRODUCTIONS, INC.___
AMOUNT $ ___65,000___ DATE ___8·15·XX___

© ELH

INSURANCE CLAIM WORKSHEET

AUTOMOBILE ACCIDENT

PRODUCTION ___HERBY'S SUMMER VACATION___

DATE OF OCCURRENCE __JUNE 25, 19XX__ TIME __9:23 A.M.__

LOCATION OF OCCURRENCE __CORNER OF 4TH STREET & MAPLE DRIVE__
__STUDIO VILLAGE__

HOW DID ACCIDENT OCCUR __DRIVER SHUTTLING CAST & CREW TO SET__
__FROM PARKING AREA RAN INTO A CAR IN FRONT OF HIM__
__WHEN OTHER CAR STOPPED SHORT APPROACHING THE__
__INTERSECTION.__

INSURED VEHICLE (Year, Make, Model) __1996 FORD AEROSTAR__
VEHICLE I.D. # __1234567X2L7HNZ__ LIC. PLATE # __XXX 2321__
OWNER OF VEHICLE __TINSELTOWN FORD__
ADDRESS __7503 CLUTCH DRIVE · BURBANK, CA 91503__
PHONE # __(818) 555-3327__ CONTACT __BUDDY__

DRIVER __TERRY TEAMSTER__
POSITION __TRANSPORTATION CAPTAIN__
DRIVER'S LIC. # __S0030376__ USED W/PERMISSION ☑ YES ☐ NO
ADDRESS __523 N. BROADWAY, APT. #137__
__GLENDALE, CA 91204__
PHONE # __(818) 555-0216__

WHERE CAN CAR BE SEEN __TINSELTOWN FORD__
WHEN __BETWEEN 9:00 a.m. & 6:00 p.m.__

DAMAGE TO CAR __DENTED FRONT FENDER BUMPER, GRILL & HOOD__
__FRONT END OUT OF ALIGNMENT__
__DAMAGED RADIATOR__
ESTIMATE(S) TO REPAIR $ __2,900—__ $ __3,300—__

DAMAGE TO OTHER VEHICLE (Year, Make, Model) __1993 DODGE RAM PICK-UP__
LIC. PLATE # __2376573__
DRIVER OF OTHER VEHICLE __DENNIS DRIVER__
ADDRESS __7326 N. HILLTOP RD.__
__LOS ANGELES, CA 90000__
PHONE(S) # __(213) 555-7676__ # _____

WHERE CAN CAR BE SEEN __AT MR. DRIVER'S HOME__
WHEN __EVENINGS BETWEEN 6 p.m. & 8 p.m.__

DAMAGE TO CAR __DENTED REAR BUMPER & TAILGATE__
__BROKEN TRAILER HITCH__

ESTIMATE(S) TO REPAIR $ __1,500—__ $ __1,750—__

© ELH

INJURED __NO INJURIES__
ADDRESS
PHONE #
EXTENT OF INJURY

WITNESS(ES) __F. STOPP (DIRECTOR OF PHOTOGRAPHY)__   __PATRICK PEDESTRIAN__
    ADDRESS __3276 BEL AIR CIRCLE__   __603 N. LUMBERJACK WAY__
__BEL AIR, CA 90002__   __PASADENA, CA 91332__
    PHONE # __(310) 555-1727__   __(818) 555-1017__

☑ POLICE REPORT ATTACHED
☑ OTHER ATTACHMENTS __ESTIMATES TO REPAIR VEHICLES__

SUBMITTED TO INSURANCE AGENCY ON __6·30·XX__
                     ATTENTION __SUSIE__
                      CLAIM # __005330__
    INSURANCE COMPANY CLAIMS REP. __CURTIS CLAIMS__

INSURANCE CLAIM WORKSHEET COMPLETED BY __ALEX AUTOS__
DATE __6·28·XX__   TITLE __TRANSPORTATION COORDINATOR__

INSURANCE ADJUSTER TO SEE INSURED VEHICLE ON __7·7·XX__
           TO SEE OTHER VEHICLE ON __7·8·XX__

AMOUNT CREDITED TO DEDUCTIBLE $ __4,100__   DATE __7·12·XX__
REIMBURSEMENT CHECK PAID TO
           AMOUNT $ _____   DATE _____
                 TO
           AMOUNT $ _____   DATE _____

NOTES:

CHAPTER SEVEN

During The Shoot

THE PREP CONTINUES

Prep doesn't stop when the filming begins. As long as there is shooting to be done and changes that occur, there are preparations to be made (and remade). While pre-production activities center around the production office, during the shoot, all of the focus is on the set, and everything revolves around meeting the needs of the shooting company. Once principal photography begins, the goal of the UPM, assistant directors, production coordinator and the rest of the production staff is to keep one step ahead of everyone else by making sure sets are ready on time, special elements (i.e., equipment, prosthetics, picture cars, animals, etc.) are there when needed, filming progresses as smoothly as possible, unexpected problems are resolved quickly, the director and DP are getting the footage they envisioned, the studio is happy and kept well-informed, the set remains harmonious and the show is running on schedule and on budget. Be aware, however, that as hard as you try, there are going to be times when these things will not fall into place as they should; but never stop striving for the best results possible.

COMMUNICATION WITH THE SET

During every shoot, in addition to those working on the set and in the office, there are usually construction, set dressing and rigging crews prepping subsequent and/or wrapping previous sets. The company is spread out, and everyone not on the set wants to know what's happening on the set. The burning question of the day is, "How are they doing?" Are they on schedule, and will they finish the day on time? Was the stunt successful? Was the explosion big enough? Was the weather clear enough to make the helicopter shot? Decisions are made, schedules juggled, locations changed, scenes added or deleted—all based on the status of the filming activities occurring at any given time. Needless to say, good and constant communications between the set, the office and those prepping the next scheduled location site and/or set is vital, especially when there is a problem, delay or injury. Whether it's a dedicated land line or a mobile phone, there should always be a way for the office to reach the set, and for the set to reach the office. (The use of Nextel™ phones on film sets has become increasingly popular, as they can be used both as conventional cell phones and as walkie-talkies). The UPM, key second assistant director, the second 2nd AD should also have pagers.

Second assistant directors are required to regularly report in: the first shot of the day; when the company breaks for lunch; the first shot after lunch and wrap, including which scenes have been completed along the way. If there is an accident or injury, they should call in as soon as the situation has been contained, so the office staff can call the insurance company, help with medical arrangements, dispatch additional crew members or whatever else it takes to make sure everyone is taken care of and that filming resumes as quickly as possible.

In addition to receiving constant status reports from the set, it is also important for the line producer and/or production manager to keep a good line of communication open with department heads—checking in with each of them on a regular basis, and, when not on the set, being accessible to them when they call or come to the office to ask questions, order additional equipment or discuss impending needs and/or concerns. Being tuned in to your crew and having them know that you are there to support them to the best of your ability goes a long way to promote a well-functioning set.

THE DAILY ROUTINE

Also during the shooting period:

- An assortment of paperwork is sent in from the set each night (waiting for the office staff when they arrive each morning). It is copied, filed, acted upon and/or distributed as needed (see "Paperwork from the Set" coming up later in this chapter).
- Among the morning paperwork is an abbreviated version of the production report (also called a Daily Wrap Report), which highlights the previous day's shooting activities. This information is immediately sent to the studio or bond company, the producer(s), production manager, accountant and coordinator. When the full production report is sent in from the set, it is reviewed by the production coordinator and UPM. Corrections are made when needed, and the report is typed, signed and distributed.
- When shooting exteriors or planning to shoot exteriors, it is important to monitor weather conditions. On days when the weather is precarious at best, UPMs, ADs and/or coordinators will check the weather several times a day (possibly every hour or two, and sometimes into the night) so cover sets can be planned. If the weather has been acceptable and holding steady, checking it just once in the evening and again first thing in the morning may be sufficient. If your production has signed up with a weather service, the report should be waiting for you on the fax machine each morning. Otherwise, the information is available on the Internet (one such website is weather.com).
- Also upon arriving each morning, a call is made to a designated contact at the lab to make sure there are no problems with film sent in for processing the night before. Negative scratches or tears, out-of-focus shots, etc. could (if acceptable alternate takes are not available) necessitate reshooting and/or insurance claims. An "all clear" lab report

can also be the signal to set dressing and construction to start striking sets no longer needed.
- Runs are coordinated between the set and the office throughout the day, and cars and drivers are arranged for actors whose deals include being picked up and driven home from the set.
- New equipment is continually being ordered, and equipment no longer needed is returned. There is constant communication with vendors, new Purchase Orders to generate and pick-ups and deliveries to be scheduled.
- While the 2nd AD on the set is responsible for continually checking in with the office, it is the office staff's responsibility to regularly report in to the studio or parent company with set updates. (Some studios require status reports to be made at specifically appointed times, such as 11:00 a.m. and 4:00 p.m.).
- If you are on a distant or foreign location, on a road show that is constantly on the move or if more than one unit is operating at one time from different locations—there is a continuum of travel and hotel arrangements to be made, new crew members starting and others wrapping, new locations to set up and others to strike, a voluminous amount of shipping to coordinate and movements to keep.
- Quantities of office supplies, materials, expendables, film stock, etc. are constantly being monitored and reordered as needed.
- Raw (film) stock should be constantly monitored. This is done by keeping track of what is ordered, how much has been used (as per the production reports) and how much should be remaining at all times (see *Raw Stock Inventory* form at the end of the chapter). Approximately once a week, this amount should be compared to what the assistant cameraperson physically has on hand. This way, the film is being accounted for; and chances are, you won't be caught short. Care must be placed when ordering as well, so the DP has the stocks and quantities needed without there being too much left over at the end of the shoot (also see *Raw Stock Order Log* at the end of the chapter).
- Script and/or schedule changes are continually being generated and distributed.
- Dailies are coordinated, making them available for the producer, director and DP to view and for the studio/parent company to screen as well. The dailies schedule can change each day, and the farther away the shooting

company is from home base and/or the lab, the more complicated the coordination process.

- New cast members are starting all the time, necessitating new contracts and deal memos, wardrobe fittings, additions to the cast list, travel plans (if necessary), etc.
- "Sides" are prepared and sent to the set toward the end of each day to be used the following day. Sides are script pages that contain the scenes to be shot that day. They eliminate the need to carry around a complete script and serve as handy references for cast members and certain department heads. They are copied from an original all-white script (even the change pages are in white) at a reduced size (usually 64 percent, making them easy to tuck in a pocket or bag), and a reduced-sized call sheet is often used as a cover page. Some assistant directors will ask for the sides to include just the scenes to be shot, and others will ask the office to add the scenes preceding and following each scheduled scene. When script revisions are issued affecting sides that have already been sent to the set, new sides are issued on blue paper and sent out as soon as possible. The 2nd AD will let the office know how many sets of sides to prepare.
- Call sheets are sent (or faxed) in from the set toward the end of each shooting day, and if photocopied on or near the set, the office staff photocopies the call sheets and attaches all maps, safety bulletins and memos pertinent to the next day's shooting, sending a given amount back to the set for distribution at wrap. If the call sheets are photocopied on-set, then the original is still sent to the office to be photocopied and distributed to everyone not on the set. Copies are made and distributed to the office staff; and either call sheets are faxed or calls made to a pre-determined list of individuals (production executives, extra casting, catering, studio teacher, additional crew members needed for the next day, etc.) informing them of call times, directions and any special requirements. (Note that call times for actors are not generally made from the production office, as that is the responsibility of the 2nd AD.) If the call time changes (which may happen—sometimes, more than once), revised call sheets are distributed and new calls made to everyone on the list.
- The UPM always has a stack of P.O.s, check requests, invoices and timecards to review

and approve. Some UPMs like having the coordinator and/or accountant sit with him or her while working through the stack, so that specifics can be discussed, clarified and evaluated before approvals are granted.

- Along the same lines, the studio production executive, producer, UPM and production accountant will meet together, or any two or three at a time, at least once a week (usually after the cost report is issued) to discuss how the show and each department is doing financially (under, on or over-budget). It's important for all the key players to be able to discuss areas that are going over-budget and to agree upon realistic solutions. On a more immediate basis, it is not uncommon to come up against expenditures that could not have been predicted and are not apparent until shooting begins. Unexpected circumstances will often create a desire or need for additional (unbudgeted) scenes, days, crew members, sets, equipment, etc. Although the studio/parent company has the final word, these issues are usually discussed with the producer and production manager in an effort to reach a decision or compromise that will be in the best interest of the film. Staying on top of costs, being aware of where the budget is at all times and working out solutions to unexpected expenditures is part of the everyday challenge of efficiently managing a film shoot.

CALL SHEETS & PRODUCTION REPORTS

A Call Sheet, briefly discussed above, is a game plan for what is to be shot the following day: who is to work, what time and where they are to report and what, if any, are the special requirements needed to complete the day.

Call sheets are created by the second assistant director. A preliminary version may be prepared early in the day, and an approved version signed and photocopied by late afternoon; but in the event of changes, none are distributed until wrap. Wrapping fifteen minutes or a half-hour late may push the next day's call by fifteen minutes or a half-hour. If the call sheets are photocopied before a call is pushed, they are generally stamped: ALL CALLS PUSHED 1/4 HR., ALL CALLS PUSHED 1/2 HR., and so on. Call sheet changes affecting scenes to be shot, locations, various work times, etc. are issued on blue paper. A subsequent change would come out on pink.

The Daily Production Report (or "PR") is the official record of what was shot that day in terms of scene numbers, setups, minutes, film footage and sound rolls; who worked and the hours they worked; the locations shot at (actual and scripted); how many meals were served; vehicles and equipment that were used and the delays, accidents or notable incidents that may have occurred.

Production reports are used to help evaluate the overall progress of principal photography; help assess production costs; check invoices against equipment and vehicles used; inventory raw stock; back up workers' compensation and other insurance claims; track safety meetings and check cast, crew and extras workdays and times against submitted time cards. It is therefore imperative that they be as accurate as possible.

Also prepared by the 2nd AD, these reports include information taken from the script supervisor's daily report (indicating the exact scenes added, deleted and shot; the number of scenes, pages, setups and minutes shot; the call time, first shot, meal times [in and out], first shot after lunch and wrap time), the camera loader's camera report (indicating film footage printed, footage shot but not printed, wasted footage, short ends [leftover footage at the end of a roll] and total footage used) and the sound mixer's sound report (indicating the number of 1/4-inch rolls or DAT tapes used). Each of these items are listed in terms of what was *Previously* shot, used or taken; what was shot, used or taken *Today* and the *Total* shot, used or taken to date.

When the PR is sent in from the set, it should be stamped UNAPPROVED. The UPM and production coordinator will then go through it, making sure:

- all dates, locations, shoot days and times are properly recorded
- all figures from the previous day's PR are correctly carried over
- Start, Work, Hold and Finish days are correctly indicated, and that actors' times on the Exhibit G match those on the PR
- camera report totals are correct and accurately carried over from the previous day
- sound roll figures are correct
- partial and completed scenes are credited properly
- the caterer's daily receipt matches the recorded number of meals served
- all special equipment used for that day is indicated

- all injuries, accidents and major delays are recorded
- in and out times for the entire crew are noted
- any additional crew members working that day are indicated
- the "skins" (list of extras to work that day issued by the extras agency) match the extra talent listed on the PR
- safety meetings are noted

A separate production report should be prepared for the second unit, although one production report is often issued when the second unit is very small and shoots simultaneously at the same location, or if a splinter unit made up of first-unit crew shoots concurrently at the same location.

The UPM and/or production coordinator, after checking the PR, will discuss any discrepancies with the 2nd AD. After corrections and additions are made, both the UPM and 1st AD will review the report and may suggest additional corrections or notes. When everyone is satisfied that the PR is complete and accurate, the UPM and 1st AD will sign it. If subsequent changes are made after the report has been signed, copied and distributed, updated versions are issued and labeled "Revised."

People are handed call sheets and production reports each day, but they are easily misplaced— left at home, buried in a pile on the desk, left in a jacket pocket, in the car or in a trailer room. The production office staff is therefore often asked to assemble complete sets of each for several different people at the end of the show. To save on time, prepare two legal-sized file folders (one for call sheets and one for PRs) for the producer(s), director, UPM, 1st AD, Key 2nd AD, production supervisor and/or coordinator and studio production executive; and add a final call sheet and production report to the respective folders on a daily basis; so by the end of principal photography, full sets are already compiled and ready to distribute. (Thanks for the great suggestion, Stephen!)

PAPERWORK FROM THE SET

An assortment of paperwork is sent from the set to the production office at the end of each day's filming. One person in the office should be the designated set paperwork person (it's usually the production coordinator or assistant coordinator), and going through the daily stack (the copying, distributing and handling of) should be a first-thing-in-the-morning priority, as much of it is time-sensitive. These are the types of things that will arrive in the morning "pouch":

- Unapproved production report—to the production coordinator to check
- Completed start slips, W-4s, I-9s and time-cards—to Accounting
- Extra vouchers—to Accounting
- Completed check requests and petty cash envelopes—to Accounting
- Camera reports—a copy to Editing and a copy to the coordinator to check before being placed in the Day File
- Sound reports—same as above
- Script Supervisor's Daily Report and notes (attached to the lined script pages)—to Editing and to the coordinator to check before placing in the Day File
- Exhibit Gs—copies to Accounting, UPM, Casting, to the coordinator to check times against the PR (before placing in the Day File) and a copy in an envelope marked "SAG" (SAG is sent Exhibit Gs once a week)
- The caterer's receipt—to Accounting and the coordinator to check before filing
- Skins—to Accounting and the coordinator
- Signed SAG contracts—to the coordinator, who will then obtain the producer's signature and distribute copies accordingly
- Workers' compensation and auto accident reports—to the coordinator to complete and submit to the respective insurance companies
- Crew requests for equipment and/or expendables—to the coordinator to obtain UPM approval, prepare P.O.s, place orders and arrange for pick-up
- Completed Daily Safety Meeting reports—to be kept on file

THE SCRIPT SUPERVISOR'S ROLE

This book does not detail job descriptions, but I thought it would be worthwhile to briefly mention the responsibilities of the script supervisor. A good script supervisor is not only an essential element of a well-functioning set, but is necessary to the editing process as well. This is a position that is not always understood nor fully appreciated.

Script supervisors are part of the director's on-set team, and they are selected by directors. They use their prep time to breakdown the script and are usually asked to pre-time the script as well. Timing a script requires the visualization and act-

ing out of scenes with a stop watch in hand to come up with a reasonable estimate of the final, edited, first-cut running time of the film. Written breakdowns are submitted indicating the predicted running time of each scene. Timings are valuable in determining whether a script is too long or too short.

Positioned with the director behind the camera on-set, the script supervisor keeps track of:

- scenes, pages, setups and minutes shot
- which scenes are shot (including partially shot), which are deleted and which ones are left to be shot
- setups filmed by all cameras
- deviations from scripted dialogue
- set times: crew call, first shot, meal times (in and out), first shot after lunch, last shot and wrap
- "matching" for purposes of continuity—making sure the appearance of the set and the actors, the movements (and eyelines) of the actors and the delivery of dialogue within each take matches its original master scene, and that the progression of wardrobe, makeup, props and set dressing during any specific scene is accurate
- whether the picture is running long or short

The script supervisor keeps a set of notes each day (usually in the form of a daily log) recording each take of each scene shot, including a description detailing the action and camera movements. Also recorded is the camera roll, scene number, take number, the timing of each take, the camera lens used, and the page count credited to each take. The director will call for specific takes to be printed, and those are circled, thus the term "circled takes."

The script supervisor also:

- furnishes Camera and Sound with slate numbers
- prepares a list of pick-up shots and wild sound tracks
- assists during the blocking of scenes
- runs lines with and cues actors prior to and during rehearsals (not a required duty but very often done)
- reads offstage lines for actors not present on the set
- supplies the editor with a complete log, continuity notes and lined script pages (actual lines made through the specific scenes being

shot indicating the exact action and dialogue captured in each take)

Having the presence of mind and concentration required to stay totally aware of everything going on around them; listen to the director's instructions; be aware of camera movements; keep thorough notes and timings; account for scenes, pages, setups and minutes shot; help actors with their lines; match dialogue and movements and create a lined script for the editor (doing several of these things simultaneously) is a challenging responsibility at best. Not having a good script supervisor will have far-reaching consequences. The good ones are worth their weight in gold.

DAILY WRAP

The following steps are taken when wrapping a set for the night:

- Walkie-talkies are collected, accounted for and placed in chargers
- The location site is cleaned
- Equipment is locked in trucks or securely stored
- Remaining vehicles are locked
- Dressing rooms are cleaned
- Copies of signed agreements, contracts and permits are in-hand for the next day's filming activities
- Special arrangements for the next day (equipment, stunts, effects, etc.) are set
- Supplies of paperwork, blank forms, Polariod™ film and office supplies have been replenished
- Additional raw stock needed for the next day has been ordered and picked up
- Script notes, camera and sound reports, Exhibit Gs, time cards, etc. are collected to send to the office
- Exposed film is sent to the lab
- Pick-ups and returns for the next day are confirmed with Transportation
- Everyone has a call sheet and map for the next day
- The caterer knows how many meals to prepare for the next day
- Security is in place for the night

ON THE LIGHTER SIDE

We all work too many hours and too hard not to have some fun, and there is nothing like interjecting a bit of humor into a long, hard day to alleviate stress. When the shows we work on are over, the lasting memories we walk away with are not only linked to the work itself, but also to the camaraderie and good times we've shared with our co-workers. The following are examples of how to create some of those lighter moments.

- I collect jokes and keep a selection of the best ones in a folder marked JOKES. For the past two years, that folder has been tacked up in each of my production offices. When someone feels they need a short break, or a laugh, they walk over to the folder and pull out a joke or two.
- In addition to the folder, I will sometimes post a JOKE OF THE DAY and a QUOTE OF THE DAY. The quotes are silly, like: "If At First You Don't Succeed, Skydiving Isn't For You," "If They Don't Have Chocolate In Heaven, I Ain't Goin'!" and "What If The Hokey Pokey Is Really What It's All About?"
- Some films start the production process with just a working title of the project, and the crew is recruited to help name the film. Whether ultimately used or not, sometimes small prizes are given for the most original title, the most humorous title and/or the most fitting title. Even on shows with firm titles, someone often posts a piece of paper near the coffee machine soliciting alternative (humorous) titles. One project I worked on (called "The Thirteenth Year") was about a thirteen-year-old boy who discovers that his mother is a mermaid, while his own body is starting to change and evolve into that of a merman. Jerram Swartz, our 1st AD, posted the initial list: "When You Fish Upon A Star," "A Buoy's Life," "Oh Cod," "Sole Man," etc.
- Jerram also told me about a series he had worked on where they chose a crew *Employee of the Week*, the winner receiving an "Atta Boy!" award certificate and a prize of $50. It was a terrific morale booster and well worth the expense.
- On one show I worked on that took place largely on water, we had our own awards ceremony at the wrap party. The awards were for categories such as: The Gal the Guys Would Most Want to Be Lost at Sea With; The Guy the Gals Most Would Want to Be Lost at Sea

With; Best All-Round Sport; Best Sun Tan; etc. We bought little trophies and gag gifts to hand out, and everyone was falling off their seats with laughter. (Note: know your crew and avoid anything like this that might possibly offend anyone.)

- A UPM-friend, Mark Indig, told me that while working on picture in Miami Beach, they had a "Tackiest Souvenir" contest that was hilarious.
- A select group of crew members on one of the shows I worked on had T-shirts printed up with memorable comments that had been made by the director, producers and various crew members. They went like hot cakes. Everyone loved them!
- Amusing quips and poems on call sheets are always great.
- My friend Phil Wylly, while on a television series we worked on, wrote the funniest memos I have ever seen. He always got his point across and was able to entertain you at the same time. The titles of the memos alone were amusing. One was: "A Fate Worse than Meal Penalty!" and it dealt with the dreaded "Forced Call!" In an effort to make us all aware of exorbitant phone bills, he issued another one entitled, "The Enrichment of the Telephone Company." And when asked to order a pig for a scene we were prepping, he wrote the following, entitled "Pyramid Power." It's a bit dated, but worth repeating and sharing:

Piglet = $25
Truck to carry = $50
Driver for Truck = $200
Wrangler to Tend Pig = $200
Gov. & Union Fringes @ 40% = $160
Location Meals for Driver & Wrangler = $12
Gasoline & Oil for Truck to Carry Piglet = $10
Total Cost for 1 Poor Little Pig for 1 day = $647.00

- Most film crews don't need much encouragement when it comes to having fun, so pools and contests are always good, as are potluck dinners, kick-off parties or wear-an-unusual-hat day. On one of my shows, to honor the production coordinator (who was in his black-turtleneck phase at the time and wore one every single day), we all surprised him by wearing black turtlenecks on the last day of shooting. We had a group picture taken of all of us in our turtlenecks and will smile every time we think of it.

FORMS IN THIS CHAPTER

- Call Sheet
- Daily Production Report
- Daily Wrap Report
- Raw Stock Order Log
- Raw Stock Inventory
- Camera Department Daily Raw Stock Log
- Script Supervisor's Daily Report
- Script Supervisor's Daily Log

CALL SHEET

PRODUCTION COMPANY _XYZ PRODUCTIONS, INC._
SHOW _HERBY'S SUMMER VACATION_
SERIES EPISODE _____
PROD# _0100_ DAY # _6_ OUT OF _8_

IS TODAY A DESIGNATED DAY OFF? ☐ YES ☑ NO

CREW CALL _7A_

LEAVING CALL _—_

SHOOTING CALL _8:30 A_

DATE _FRIDAY, JULY 2, 19XX_
DIRECTOR _SID CELLULOID_
PRODUCER _SWIFTY DEALS_
LOCATION _SWEETWATER RD - HOLLYWOOD_
SUNRISE _6:20A_ SUNSET _7:40P_
ANTICIPATED WEATHER _85°_

☐ Weather Permitting   ☑ See Attached Map
☑ Report to Location   ☐ Bus to Location

Set Description	Scene Nos.	Cast	D/N	Pages	Location
EXT. ROAD TO LAKE (BOYS ON WAY TO LAKE)	6	1,6,7	D	1/8	HOLLYWOOD LAKE
EXT. BUSHES (BOYS WATCH LAURA)	7,8,9	1,3,6,7	D	6/8	
EXT. LAKE (GEORGE JOINS LAURA)	10,11	3,5	D	3 2/8	
				TOTAL: 4 1/8 PGS.	

Cast	Part Of	Leave	Makeup	Set Call	Remarks
CLARK GRABLE	HERBY (1)	7:15 A	8A	8:30 A	TO BE PICKED UP @ 7A
SCARLET STARLET	LAURA (3)	6:30 A	7A	9:30 A	TO BE PICKED UP @ 6:15A
HOLLYWOOD MANN (NEW)	GEORGE (5)	—	9A	10A	REPORT TO LOC.
KENNY SMILES	MARC (6)	—	8A	8:30A	REPORT TO LOC.
WILL PERFORMER	JED (7)	—	8A	8:30A	REPORT TO LOC.

Atmosphere & Stand-ins	
3 STANDINS	REPORT TO LOC @ 7:30A
6 SUNBATHERS	
1 MAN WALKING DOG	
2 KIDS PLAYING BALL	

NOTE: No forced calls without previous approval of unit production manager or assistant director.   All calls subject to change.

Advance Schedule Or Changes

MON. 7·5·XX
INT. HERBY'S BEDROOM (N) SCS. 5, 8, 115 THRU 123   STG. 14
INT. HERBY'S KITCHEN (N) SCS. 7, 14, 15, 22
INT. HERBY'S FRONT DOOR (N) SC. 73

Assistant Director _Alice Deer_   Production Manager _Fred Filmer_

PRODUCTION REQUIREMENT

SHOW: HERBY'S SUMMER VACATION   PROD #: 0100   DATE: 7.2.XX

NO.	STAFF & CREW	TIME	NO.	STAFF & CREW	TIME	NO.	EQUIPMENT
1	Production Mgr. FILMER	7A	1	Gaffer	7A	2	Cameras PANAFLEX ARRI
1	1st Asst. Dir. DEES	7A	1	Best Boy		1	Dolly CHAPMAN
1	2nd Asst. Dir. DURHAM	6:30A	1	Lamp Oper.			Crane
1	2nd 2nd Asst. Dir. T.C.	6:30A	1	Lamp Oper.			Condor
	DGA Trainee			Lamp Oper.			
1	Script Supervisor KANDU	8A		Local 40 Man			Sound Channel
1	Dialogue Coach WILKES	8A					
1	Prod. Coordinator	8A	1	Prod. Designer			Video
1	Prod. Sect'y	8A		Art Director			
1	Prod. Accountant	8A		Asst. Art Dir.			
1	Asst. Accountant	8A		Set Designer			Radio Mikes
1	Location Manager	6:30A		Sketch Artist		8	Walkie/talkies
1	Asst. Location Mgr.	6:30A					
1	Teacher/Welfare Worker	8A	1	Const. Coord.		5	Dressing Rooms
3	Production Assts.	6:30A	1	Const. Foreman		1	Schoolrooms
				Paint Foreman		1	Rm. for Parents
1	Dir. of Photography			Labor Foremen			
1	Camera Operator			Const. First Aid			Projector
1	Camera Operator						Moviola
	SteadyCam Operator		1	Set Decorator			
1	Asst. Cameraman		1	Lead Person			Air Conditioners
1	Asst. Cameraman		1	Swing Crew			Heaters
1	Asst. Cameraman		1	Swing Crew			Wind Machines
1	Still Photographer			Swing Crew			
	Cameraman-Process			Drapery			
	Projectionist						
1	VIDEO ASSIST	7:30A		Technical Advisor			**SUPPORT**
1	Mixer			Publicist			**PERSONNEL** — TIME
1	Boomman			**MEALS**			Policemen
1	Cableman			Caterer			Motorcycles
	Playback		25	Breakfasts ND READY @	7A		Fireman
	Video Oper.			Wlkg. Breakfasts rdy @			Guard
			10	Gals. Coffee			Night Watchman
1	Key Grip		75	Lunches rdy @ 12N Crew @	1P		
1	2nd Grip			Box Lunches			
1	Dolly Grip			Second Meal			
1	Grip						
1	Grip						
	Grip			**DRIVERS**			**VEHICLES**
			1	Trans. Coord.	6A	1	Prod. Van
	Greensman		1	Trans. Capt.	6A	1	Camera
			1	Driver	6:30A	1	Grip
	S/By Painter		1	Driver			Electric
1	Craftservice		1	Driver			Effects
1	First Aid		1	Driver		1	Props
			1	Driver		1	Wardrobe
	Spec. Efx		1	Driver		1	Makeup
	Spec. Efx		1	Driver		1	Set Dressing
			1	Driver			Crew Bus
1	Propmaster		1	Driver		1	Honeywagon
1	Asst. Props		1	Driver		2	Motorhomes
1	Asst. Props		1	Driver		1	Station Wagons
			1	Driver		2	Mini-buses
1	Costume Designer		1	Driver			Standby Cars
1	Costume Supervisor		1	Driver			Crew Cabs
1	Costumer		1	Driver			Insert Cars
1	Costumer		1	Driver		1	Generators
			1	Driver			Water Wagon
1	Makeup Artist	6:30A	1	Driver		1	Picture Cars
	Makeup Artist		1	Driver			LAURA'S CAR
	Body Makeup						
1	Hairstylist			Stunt Coord.			
1	Hairstylist			Wranglers			
			1	Animal Handlers	8A		Livestock
1	Editor	D/C				1	Animals ND DOG
1	Asst. Editor						
1	Apprentice Editor						

DEPARTMENT	SPECIAL INSTRUCTIONS
PROPS / SET DRESSING	BEACH CHAIRS, UMBRELLAS, BALL, SUNTAN LOTION, SUNGLASSES
MAKEUP	BODY MAKEUP FOR LAURA

DAILY PRODUCTION REPORT

	1st Unit	2nd Unit	Reh.	Test	Travel	Holidays	Change Over	Retakes & Add. Scs.	Total		Schedule
No. Days Sched	30	4			2				36		Ahead
No. Days Actual	6				1				7		Behind

Title **HERBY'S SUMMER VACATION**   Prod. # **0100**   Date **MON., JUNE 7, 19XX**
Producer **SWIFTY DEALS**   Director **SID CELLULOID**
Date Started **6-1-XX**   Scheduled Finish Date **7-16-XX**   Est. Finish Date **7-16-XX**

Sets (EXT.) ROAD & FENCE ALONG LAURA'S HOUSE - (EXT.) LAKE SHORE
Location SWEETWATER RD. - HOLLYWOOD LAKE
Crew Call **7A**   Shooting Call **8:30A**   First Shot **9:30A**   Lunch **1:30P**   Til **2P**
1st Shot After Lunch _____   2nd Meal _____   Til _____   Camera Wrap _____   Last Man Out _____
Company dismissed at ☐ Studio ☑ Location ☐ Headquarters   Round Trip Mileage **18 MI.**   Is Today A Designated Day Off? ☐ YES ☑ NO

SCRIPT SCENES AND PAGES			MINUTES		SETUPS		ADDED SCENES		RETAKES		
	SCENES	PAGES								PAGES	SCENES
			Prev.	31:37	Prev.	83	Prev.	4	Prev.	4 1/8	3
			Today	2:15	Today	23	Today	0	Today	4/8	1
Script	215	117 6/8	Total	33:52	Total	106	Total	4	Total	4 5/8	4
Taken Prev.	76	35 7/8	Scene No.	3, 4, 5, 26, 27, 30							
Taken Today	6	5 3/8									
Total to Date	82	40 5/8	Added Scenes								
To be Taken	133	77 1/8	Retakes	Sc. 15			Sound Tracks				

FILM STOCK	FILM USE	GROSS	PRINT	NO GOOD	WASTE	1/4" ROLLS	FILM INVENTORY 5296	
	Prev.					10	Starting Inv.	20,000
5296	Today					2	Additional Rec'd.	0
							Today	0
	To Date					12	Total	20,000

FILM STOCK	FILM USE	GROSS	PRINT	NO GOOD	WASTE		FILM INVENTORY 5293	
	Prev.	21,386	12,860	5,536	2,990		Starting Inv.	10,260
5293	Today	4,730	1,850	1,150	610		Additional Rec'd.	0
							Today	3,610
	To Date	26,116	14,710	6,686	3,600		Total	6,650

FILM STOCK	FILM USE	GROSS	PRINT	NO GOOD	WASTE		FILM INVENTORY 5247	
	Prev.						Starting Inv.	18,250
5247	Today						Additional Rec'd.	0
	To Date						Today	0
							Total	18,250

CAST - WEEKLY & DAY PLAYERS			W H S R T / TR	MAKEUP WDBE.	WORKTIME		MEALS		TRAVEL TIME				STUNT ADJ.
Worked - W Rehearsal - R Finished - F					REPORT ON SET	DISMISS ON SET	OUT	IN	LEAVE FOR LOC.	ARRIVE ON LOC.	LEAVE LOCATION	ARRIVE AT HDQ.	
Started - S Hold - H Test - T													
Travel - TR													
CAST	CHARACTER												
CLARK GRABLE	HERBY		W	8A	8:30A	6P	1:30P	2P	7A	8A	6:15P	7:15P	
SCARLET STARLET	LAURA (XX)		W	7:30A	10A	8P	1:30P	2P	6:45A	7:30A	8:15P	9P	
HOLLYWOOD MANN	GEORGE		S(W)	9A	10A	8P	1:30P	2P					
KENNY SMILES	MARC		W	8A	8:30A	6P	1:30P	2P					
WILL PERFORMER	JED		W	8A	8:30A	6P	1:30P	2P					

XX = N.D. BREAKFAST   * = DISMISS TIME INCLUDES 15 MIN. MAKEUP / WARD. REMOVAL
X = NOT PHOTOGRAPHED   S = SCHOOL ONLY

						EXTRA TALENT							
No.	Rate	1st Call	Set Dismiss	Final Dismiss	Adj.	MPV	No.	Rate	1st Call	Set Dismiss	Final Dismiss	Adj.	MPV
3	SCALE	7:30A	8P		+WARD								
2	SCALE	10A	2P										
1	SCALE	10A	2:30P		+WARD								
1	SCALE	8A	8P										

Assistant Director _____   Production Manager _____

SHOW: HERBY'S SUMMER VACATION   PROD #: 0100   DATE: 6-7-XX

NO.	STAFF & CREW	TIME	NO.	STAFF & CREW	TIME	NO.	EQUIPMENT
1	Production Mgr. F. FILMER	7A	1	Gaffer		1	Cameras PANAFLEX
1	1st Asst. Dir. A. DEES	7A	1	Best Boy		1	ARRI
1	2nd Asst. Dir. R. DURHAM	6:30A	1	Lamp Oper.		1	Dolly CHAPMAN
1	2nd 2nd Asst. Dir. T.C.	6:30A	1	Lamp Oper.			Crane
	DGA Trainee		1	Lamp Oper.			Condor
1	Script Supervisor K. KANDU	8A		Local 40 Man			
1	Dialogue Coach A. WILKES	8A					Sound Channel
1	Prod. Coordinator C. COORDINATES	8A	1	Prod. Designer			
1	Prod. Sect'y G. AIDES	7:30A	1	Art Director			Video
1	Prod. Accountant AARON A.	8A		Asst. Art Dir.			
1	Asst. Accountant	8A	1	Set Designer			Radio Mikes
1	Location Manager B. SCOUT	6:30A		Sketch Artist		8	Walkie/talkies
1	Asst. Location Mgr. BOB S.	6:30A					
1	Teacher/Welfare Worker	8A	1	Const. Coord.		5	Dressing Rooms
3	Production Assts. JONES,	6:30A	1	Const. Foreman			Schoolrooms
	SMITH, MILLER		1	Paint Foreman		1	Rm. for Parents
1	Dir. of Photography F. STOPP	7:30A	1	Labor Foremen			
1	Camera Operator S. SHUTTER	7:30A		Const. First Aid			Projector
1	Camera Operator						Moviola
	SteadyCam Operator		1	Set Decorator			
1	Asst. Cameraman		1	Lead Person			Air Conditioners
1	Asst. Cameraman		1	Swing Crew			Heaters
1	Asst. Cameraman		1	Swing Crew			Wind Machines
1	Still Photographer			Swing Crew			
	Cameraman-Process			Drapery			
	Projectionist						
				Technical Advisor			**SUPPORT**
1	Mixer			Publicist			**PERSONNEL** **TIME**
1	Boomman			**MEALS**		2	Policemen 6:30A
1	Cableman			Caterer	6:30A	2	Motorcycles 6:30A
	Playback		25	Breakfasts			Fireman
	Video Oper.		120	Wlkg. Breakfasts rdy @		1	Guard
			15	Gals. Coffee		1	Night Watchman
1	Key Grip			Lunches rdy @ Crew @			
1	2nd Grip			Box Lunches			
1	Dolly Grip			Second Meal			
1	Grip						
1	Grip						
1	Grip			**DRIVERS**			**VEHICLES**
			1	Trans. Coord.			Prod. Van
	Greensman		1	Trans. Capt.		1	Camera
			1	Driver		1 {	Grip
	S/By Painter		1	Driver		1 {	Electric
1	Craftservice		1	Driver			Effects
1	First Aid		1	Driver		1	Props
			1	Driver		1	Wardrobe
	Spec. Efx		1	Driver		1	Makeup
	Spec. Efx		1	Driver		1	Set Dressing
			1	Driver			Crew Bus
1	Propmaster			Driver		1	Honeywagon
1	Asst. Props			Driver		2	Motorhomes
	Asst. Props			Driver		1	Station Wagons
				Driver		2	Mini-buses
1	Costume Designer			Driver		2	Standby Cars
	Costume Supervisor			Driver			Crew Cabs
1	Costumer			Driver			Insert Cars
1	Costumer			Driver		2	Generators
				Driver		1	Water Wagon
1	Makeup Artist			Driver		2	Picture Cars
	Makeup Artist			Driver			LAURA'S CAR
	Body Makeup						GEORGE'S CAR
1	Hairstylist			Stunt Coord.			
1	Hairstylist			Wranglers			
				Animal Handlers			Livestock
1	Editor					1	Animals NO DOG
1	Asst. Editor						
	Apprentice Editor						

COMMENTS-DELAYS (EXPLANATIONS)-CAST, STAFF & CREW ABSENCE

- SCARLET STARLET 30 MIN. LATE TO SET
- MACINTOSH COMPUTER W/ MONITOR & KEYBOARD DISCOVERED MISSING FROM HERBY'S BEDROOM SET. POLICE REPORT FORTHCOMING.

- NO ACCIDENTS REPORTED TODAY

DAILY WRAP REPORT

SHOW __HERBY'S SUMMER VACATION__   PROD# __0100__

DAY __MONDAY__   DATE __7·12·XX__   SHOOT DAY# __6__ OUT OF __30__

LOCATION __CITY HALL - DOWNTOWN__

CREW CALL __7A__   SHOOTING CALL __8A__

FIRST SHOT __9:30A__

LUNCH __1:30__ TO __2P__   MEAL PENALTY __1__

1ST SHOT AFTER LUNCH _____

SECOND MEAL _____ TO _____   MEAL PENALTY _____

1ST SHOT AFTER 2ND MEAL _____

CAMERA WRAP __7P__   LAST OUT __8P__

OVERTIME __½ HR.__

SCHEDULED SCENE NUMBER(S) SHOT __3, 4, 5, 26, 27, 30__

UNSCHEDULED SCENE NUMBER(S) SHOT _____

SCENES SCHEDULED BUT NOT SHOT _____

PAGES SCHEDULED __5 3/8__   PAGES SHOT __5 3/8__

	SCENES	PAGES	MINUTES	SETUPS
PREVIOUS	76	35 2/8	31:37	83
TODAY	6	5 3/8	2:15	23
TOTAL	82	40 5/8	33:52	106

DAY'S WORK COMPLETED? __Yes__

OF DAYS BEHIND __1__

OF DAYS AHEAD _____

FILM FOOTAGE

GROSS TODAY __4,590__   GROSS TO DATE __28,830__

PRINT TODAY __2,720__   PRINT TO DATE __19,630__

NO GOOD __1,510__

WASTE __360__

SHORT ENDS __520__

NOTES: • SCARLET STARLET - 30 MIN. LATE REPORTING TO THE SET
• KATIE KANDU (SCRIPT SUPV'R.) TOOK ILL & REQUESTED TO BE
REPLACED. REPLACEMENT ARRIVED @ NOON.
• COMPUTER EQUIP. USED AS SET DRESSING IN HERBY'S
BEDROOM REPORTED MISSING WHEN CREW ARRIVED TO
FINISH DRESSING SET. POLICE REPORT FILED.

RAW STOCK ORDER LOG

DATE	QTY.	ROLL LENGTH	FOOTAGE PER STOCK 52 74 PRICES: 100' roll: $65.10 / 400' roll: $254.80 / 1,000' roll: $576.50	52 79 PRICES: 100' roll: $65.10 / 400' roll: $254.80 / 1,000' roll: $576.50	52 46 PRICES: 100' roll: $65.10 / 400' roll: $254.80 / 1,000' roll: $576.50	52 PRICES: 100' roll: $ / 400' roll: $ / 1,000' roll: $	P.O. #	TOTAL FOOTAGE ENTIRE ORDER	TOTAL PRICE
7/3/xx	4	1,000'	4,000'				1377	9,800'	$6,124.89
	2	400'	800'						
	5	1,000'			5,000'				
8/1/xx	5	400'		2,000'			1536	2,000'	$1,270.85
8/7/xx	2	1,000'	2,000'				1733	7,000'	$4,391.16
	5	400'			2,000'				
	3	1,000'			3,000'				

Vendor: WESTMAN FILM CO.
Address: 3376 SUNSET LN. HOLLYWOOD

Order Desk #: 555-3723
Contact: AMY JOHNSON
Contact's Dir. #: 555-5116

Account #: 3217652l
After-Hours #: 555-2227
Pick-up Hours: 9am-6pm

© ELH

RAW STOCK INVENTORY

SHOW _HERBY'S SUMMER VACATION_   PROD# _0100_

WEEK ENDING _____

	52 _46_	52 _74_	52 _79_	52 ____
WEEKLY TOTALS				
Good (Print)	7,865	6,050	7,086	
No Good	2,390	1,769	1,807	
Waste	980	823	1,230	
TOTAL EXPOSED**	11,235	8,642	10,123	

PRUCHASED

Previously Purchased	50,000	50,000	50,000	
Purchased This Week	+ 15,000	15,000	20,000	
TOTAL PURCHASED	65,000	65,000	70,000	

USED

Stock Used To Date	33,705	25,926	30,369	
Stock Used This Week**	+ 11,235	8,642	10,123	
TOTAL STOCK USED	44,940	34,568	40,492	

Total Purchased	65,000	65,000	70,000	
Total Used	- 44,940	34,568	40,492	
Estimated Remaining Stock	20,060	30,432	29,508	
Remaining Stock As per Camera Department	20,060	28,400	29,600	

RAW STOCK PURCHASES MADE THIS WEEK				
P.O.# _2076_	15,000	15,000		
P.O.# _2093_			20,000	
P.O.# _____				
P.O.# _____				
P.O.# _____				
TOTAL:	15,000	15,000	20,000	

© ELH

DAILY RAW STOCK LOG

SHOW __HERBY'S SUMMER VACATION__   PROD# __0100__

DATE __MON. – 8/21/XX__   SHOOT DAY# __40__   FILM TYPE _____

CAMERA	MAG#	ROLL	LENGTH	GOOD	NO GOOD	WASTE	TOTAL EXP.	SHORT ENDS
A	1	1	1,000'	550	350	100	1,000	
B	2	1	500'SE	210	140	60	410	90
C	3	1	400'	100	100	200	400	
A	4	1	1,000'	330	210	20	560	440
B	1	2	1,000'	190	130	140	460	540
C	3	2	400'	180	140	80	400	
A	2	2	600'SE	310	80	70	460	140
B	4	2	400'	160	140	20	320	80
A	1	3	1,000'	550	350	100	1,000	
B	2	3	550'SE	270	190	90	550	

RECEIVED			GOOD	NO GOOD	WASTE	TOTAL EXP.	SHORT ENDS
0		TODAY	2850	1830	880	5560	1290
270,000		PREVIOUS	124,210	72,760	28,500	225,470	25,915
270,000		TO DATE	127,060	74,590	29,380	231,030	27,205

– 231,030	TOTAL EXPOSED
38,970	TOTAL UNEXPOSED
+ 25,555	SHORT ENDS TO DATE UNEXPOSED
64,525	TOTAL UNEXPOSED ON HAND

S.E. EXPOSED TODAY: 1,650

S.E. TO DATE UNEXPOSED: 25,555

SCRIPT SUPERVISOR'S
DAILY REPORT

PRODUCTION CO. XYZ PRODUCTIONS   DATE 7·2·XX

SHOW HERBY'S SUMMER VACATION   SHOOT DAY# 6

LOCATION CITY HALL - DOWNTOWN

DIRECTOR SID CELLULOID   1ST AD A. DEES

UPM FRED FILMER   SCRIPT SUPV'R KATIE KANDU

CREW CALL 7A   SHOOTING CALL 730A

1ST SHOT 8:30A

LUNCH 1-1:30P

1ST SHOT AFTER LUNCH 1:50P   CAMERA ROLLS #A38 - A46

2ND MEAL

1ST SHOT AFTER 2ND MEAL   SOUND ROLLS 2: #15, 16

LAST SHOT 7P   WILD TRACKS

CAMERA WRAP 7:15P   RESHOOTS

SET DESCRIPTION   SCENES COMPLETED

EXT. CITY HALL   10, 13, 16

EXT. CITY STREET   7, 9, 12

	SCENES	PAGES	SETUPS	MINUTES
SCRIPT TOTAL	150	112 4/8		
SHOT TODAY	6	4 3/8	15	2:30
PREVIOUSLY SHOT	54	35 2/8	83	14:15
TOTAL TO DATE	60	39 5/8	106	16:45
TOTAL REMAINING	90	72 7/8		

NOTES:

SCRIPT SUPERVISOR'S
DAILY LOG

SHOW	HERBY'S SUMMER VACATION		SHOOT DAY# 6
DIRECTOR	SID CELLULOID	DAY MONDAY	DATE 7·15·XX
CAMERA 'A'	PHIL M. CANN	SCRIPT SUPERVISOR KATIE KANDU	
CAMERA 'B'	LARRY LENSCAPP	SET INT. LAURA'S HOUSE	
CREW CALL 7A	SHOOTING CALL 7³⁰A	FIRST SHOT 8¹⁵A	WEATHER OVERCAST

CAMERA ROLL	SCENE	TAKE	SOUND	PRINT	TIME	LENS	PAGE CREDIT	SHOT DESCRIPTION
A-38	19	1	ROLL 15	X	:13	44mm	4/8	MED. SHOT - LAURA & GEORGE IN BEDROOM
		2			:14			T-2 O.S. NOISE
		3			:17			T-3 LAURA STARTS LATE
		4		X	:14			
	19A	1			:05	85mm		CAMERA TRACKS IN FOR C.U. OF LAURA
		2			:07			T-2 LAURA TURNS TOO QUICKLY
		3		X	:06			
	20	1			:32	24mm	7/8	WIDE SHOT - LAURA & GEORGE ARGUE
		2		X	:30			T-2 LAURA'S GLASSES FALL OFF TABLE
		3			:25			T-3 GEORGE REACTS SLOWLY
		4			:36			T-4 DOES NOT HAVE LAURA'S LINE
		5		X	:31			

TIME CREDIT: _____   PAGE CREDIT: _____

CAMERA ROLL	SCENE	TAKE	SOUND	PRINT	TIME	LENS	PAGE CREDIT	SHOT DESCRIPTION

SHOW

PAGE#

DATE

SHOOT DAY#

TME CREDIT: PAGE CREDIT:

CHAPTER EIGHT

The Value Of Strong Industry Relationships, Making Good Deals & Saving Money

You will keep hearing over and over again that this business is built on relationships. It most definitely is! There are many different types of relationships you will enter into during your career, and many will prove to be of great mutual value. This chapter focuses on three types of relationships—those with vendors, production executives and crew. And along with negotiating tips, it will explain how these strong associations lead to the ability to make good deals, save money and elicit the cooperation and support we all need when making films.

VENDORS

Whether you are a production manager getting bids on camera equipment, a post production coordinator deciding on which lab to use, a production accountant relying on a payroll company to have everyone's check ready on Thursday or a best boy ordering gaffer's tape, chances are you are going to be dealing with a wide variety of vendors. Vendors are those people we count on for equipment, wardrobe, props, set dressing, vehicles, materials, services and supplies—from the insurance company that secures our coverage to the guy we order our office supplies from.

Why do you need to develop good relationships with your vendors? For two equally important reasons. One, the more they respect you (and like you), the better the deal or rate they are going to give you! If you are working on a low-budget show, they will bend over backwards to accommodate your budget, will throw in extras whenever possible or match a competitor's lower bid.

They will see you through the tough ones in hopes of making it up on your next show or the one after that—the one with the (hopefully) higher budget. And two, for the security of knowing that you'll be able to depend on them to cover your backside when you need them the most. Loyal vendors will be there to replace a piece of faulty equipment in the middle of the night, open up on a weekend to rush an order out, or personally deliver something to you on the set you have decided at the last moment you can't shoot without. It has also been my experience that they can be a good networking source. Always searching out new shows (just as we are), I've received several early show leads from vendors I work with often and with whom I have good relationships.

You will earn vendor loyalty, good service and good deals by:

- Dealing with them fairly and honestly (those with any amount of experience will know when you're not being honest or sincere)
- Explaining, up front (to the best of your ability at that point) exactly what your needs are going to be from start to finish
- Giving them a chance to bid on your show (even if someone else you're working with has a relationship with a competing vendor)
- Returning their calls
- Not leaving them hanging, and calling them as soon as a decision has been made, even if they are not the ones chosen for the show/order

It would also be a worthwhile gesture on your part to send your vendors show T-shirts or hats (any type of show gift), and occasionally invite them to lunch, to join you on the set or to come to your wrap party.

Most vendors will go out of their way to help you as much as they can, but no one wants to feel taken advantage of. So if you are fair, honest and up front about your needs, you will quickly earn their goodwill and support.

Negotiating With Vendors

When budgeting, don't count on the good deals you think you're going to be able to make. Budget using list prices, do better when you can and keep the amount you've saved as a pad for all the extras you hadn't anticipated. And again, your ability to successfully negotiate good deals with vendors will greatly depend on the relationships you've developed with them. Here are some general negotiating tips:

- Talk to others who do what you do. Find out which vendors they like, the service they are receiving and the deals they are getting.
- Without being obnoxious, demanding or coming across as if you expect to receive something for nothing, let your vendors know you are hoping for and would greatly appreciate a good deal. (No one likes dealing with a shyster—from either side of the table.) If you need their help and honestly ask for it, they will generally accommodate you to the best of their ability. It's all in how you ask.
- Start by getting bids, even if there is only one vendor you want to use. This way, you know his or her prices are at least comparable to other like-vendors. Many vendors will match a lower bid you receive from another. If someone you want to use does not offer to match a lower bid, ask anyway (nicely). They will usually comply.
- For years, three-day rentals on equipment (camera packages, grip, electric, etc.), props, set dressing and wardrobe were standard. The standard then became two- and one-day rentals. Now it's not uncommon to negotiate less than one-day weekly rentals. (A one-day weekly rental means that instead of a vendor charging you a per-day rate for each day you have the equipment, you will be charged the one-day rate—or for two days or a half-day, whatever the deal is—for an entire week.)
- There are vendors who cannot offer reduced weekly rentals, but they might be able to throw in "extras" that will save you some

bucks. For example, you rent an entire camera package, and the vendor throws in a couple of additional lenses at no charge. You rent an electrical package, and you get extra cable and the truck at no charge. Some vendors will supply you with additional equipment they might have extra pieces of.
- Get vendors to agree to full or partial refunds for unused expendables.
- When transporting equipment to a distant location, ask vendors to cease rental during the shipping process. If you are going to use the equipment for only part of the time on location (say, at the beginning of your schedule and then again toward the end) and it's costly to keep shipping it back and forth, many vendors will let you hold onto the equipment and just charge you rental for the days it is actually being used—if they don't need it for another customer during the intervening time.
- Make flat and package deals whenever possible.
- Based on studio guidelines, whenever possible, work out a better deal in exchange for screen credit or product placement.
- If applicable, ask for special rates for first-time filmmakers.
- If applicable, apply for student and/or low-budget rates (you may not be able to pay full rate today, but you will tomorrow; and by then, the vendor will have a loyal and steady customer).
- Try to use vendors with whom you have developed good relationships.
- On very low-budget films, ask for permission to make deferred payments.

STUDIO & NETWORK EXECUTIVES

Networks, studios, and production companies, while very involved in the development process of their projects, will, during the pre-production stage, gradually start turning over the responsibility of their films to the producers they hire. The producer and his or her crew will progressively take over the day-to-day running of a project during pre-production; and the network, studio and/or production company will oversee the operation. A studio generally has "creative" executives who are going to be concerned with the script, cast and anything to do with the look of the picture. The "physical" production department will be more interested in daily production activities, troubleshooting and making sure the film remains on budget and on schedule. Although titles may vary slightly from studio to network to independent company, physical production (also called "production management") departments are generally staffed by a vice president and director of. Some companies also have staff production coordinators who oversee the activities of the production coordinators on each of their company's shows. Studios, networks and many production companies have their own legal or business affairs departments, casting departments, post production departments, insurance departments and publicity departments—each interacting with cast and crew members as needed. Depending on the company, sometimes you will be answerable to one executive, and sometimes to several. The production executive is the liaison between the parent company and the production—not always an easy position to occupy.

It is the production executive's responsibility to stay on top of costs, schedules and all major decisions affecting the shows they are assigned to; but at times, some may appear overly involved—putting off producers, directors and production managers who prefer to keep a polite distance and are forthcoming with no more information then they are absolutely required to provide. Understand that their ultimate goal is the same as yours—to actualize a quality film that remains on budget, on schedule and as trouble-free as possible. In many instances, they are also held as accountable for the problems (or successes) of the production as you are. With few exceptions, they should be viewed as partners, not adversaries.

The network, studio and/or production company will give the producer, production manager, coordinator and accountant guidelines as to their company's forms, procedures and regulations (usually in the form of a manual). They will often give you a list of vendors you can use (who will extend the parent company's volume discount to your show) and may be able to give you access to stored equipment, supplies, wardrobe, set dressing and props left over from previous shows. Some companies will insist on your hiring certain key department heads (directors of photography, production designers, editors, etc.), others will ask that you consider individuals they have previously worked with and like and still others will just ask for final approval of department heads you wish to use. You will be required to send them copies of all budgets, cost reports, deal memos, contracts, schedules, crew lists, cast lists, call sheets and production reports. Some production executives attend production meetings, accompany you on location scouts, sit in on casting sessions, have input as to wardrobe choices and hairstyles and are just very hands-on every step of the way. Others are much less so.

As a whole, production executives are generally accessible, helpful, fair and professional. Making the time and putting forth the effort to develop good working relationships with these individuals is only going to benefit you. They are the people who are going to go to the studio and fight for you when you need an extra day to reshoot a scene, or for extra money when the director comes up with a new concept. With the influence of the studio behind them, they can often solve problems and overcome obstacles that are beyond your control, just as they may have access to resources that are beyond your reach.

Earn the support and regard of the production executive, and he or she will not only go the extra distance to help you with your show but will also fight to bring you back to work on other shows. He or she is also in an excellent position to recommend you (favorably or not-so-favorably) to prospective future employers.

YOUR CREW

I went on an interview once, and the production manager made a point of telling me that he expected the grips to be treated as well as the actors. I have always tried to treat people fairly, but I never forgot how important this was to this nice man. It didn't take me long to understand why he always attracted the best crews available.

You will be treating your crew well by:

- Paying them a fair salary within the parameters of your budget
- Being honest
- Making sure they are fed well (by providing the best catering and craft services you can afford)
- Giving them a sufficient place in which to work
- Giving them the equipment and support crew they need (again, within the parameters of your budget)
- Thanking them for a good day's work
- Not yelling
- Being accessible to them
- Listening to their ideas and suggestions

- Listening to their problems and accommodating their needs to the best of your ability
- Not saying, "No, we can't afford it," without first exploring alternatives and compromises
- Treating them with respect
- Sharing information with them
- Within reasonable limits, allowing for mistakes and room to grow
- Not changing time cards without first discussing discrepancies with the individuals who have recorded hours you don't agree with
- Addressing a problem within the privacy of your office instead of on the set in front of the entire crew
- Supplying them with comfortable accommodations while on location
- Supporting your office staff by making sure that no crew member is abusive or unfairly demanding of them
- Giving them as nice a wrap party and (Cast & Crew) gift as you can afford. Some productions throw kick-off parties prior to principal photography, so that those who haven't worked together before can start to bond.

By adopting the above policies, you will elicit a crew full of men and women who will follow you to the ends of the earth. They will work for less when you're doing lower-budgeted shows; they will waive meal penalties and overtime; they will pitch in and help with things that have nothing to do with their job titles; they will work hard to make good deals and save money; you won't have to worry as much about kickbacks, padded time cards, missing equipment or being charged for something that wasn't legitimate and you will never have to worry about your ability to assemble a good, reliable crew.

Negotiating Tips For Hiring Crew

- Department heads will generally work for less if you rent their equipment and/or vehicles.
- If you wish to pay someone more than what the studio has allotted for that position, you might be able pay him or her more by way of a (higher) box/kit rental.
- While some studios set maximum allowable salaries that are carved in stone, others may allow you to pay an individual more than what is budgeted if you can make better-than-anticipated deals elsewhere and show which account(s) the additional moneys can be taken from.

- There are always those individuals willing to work for trade-offs: experience, credit, points, advancement to a higher position, opportunity, etc.
- If you happen to be fortunate enough to be starting a show when the industry is going through a slow period, you should be able to line up a top-notch crew willing to work for less than their normal rates. People want to continue working, receiving their union benefits, renting their equipment and making new contacts. We are all the most flexible when jobs are the least plentiful.
- Appeal to your friends who are not working. They, too, may be used to higher salaries; but if they're not doing anything else at the moment, they might be willing to help you out. For those who are afraid to commit for fear that something better may come along, agree to let them replace themselves should they be offered a better-paying show before your show is completed. So many film schedules are pushed back or canceled, there is always a good chance they will be able to finish your project and not have to leave after all.
- If your budget is truly tight, and this is discussed ahead of time, crew members will often consider waiving a certain amount of meal penalty and overtime (as long as they are feeling fairly treated in all other respects). Significant amounts of meal penalty and overtime may often be exchanged for an extra day or two tacked onto a wrap schedule.

AVOID CUTTING OFF YOUR NOSE TO SPITE YOUR FACE

It takes a considerable amount of skill to make good deals and to deliver shows on or under budget; and those who are adept at this rarely have trouble finding work. Developing this expertise, however, does not come about merely by spending less money. The skill is in getting the most value for your money and knowing where to spend in order to save. Too many people in our industry are too busy trying to be heroes by slashing costs, reducing salaries and cutting corners, when in reality this is often a good way to run into trouble. Many poor decisions are made in the name of saving money; and what may appear impressive on paper, often turns out to be much costlier in the long run.

If you can afford to pay fair salaries but are paying less for the sake of saving a few bucks—your crew, if feeling unjustly treated, will find many, many ways to make up that extra money, and then some. Whether it's relating to crew salaries or renting less-expensive, less-than-adequate equipment that may break down and create expensive delays, beware of choices that will ultimately end up costing you more.

Another tough call to make is on the set at the six-hour meal break or at the end of the day when unforeseen events have created delays. Do you pull the plug? Do you avoid meal penalty and/or overtime only to have to spend another day at a particular location, incur another day (or possibly week) of rentals or have to shoot a sixth day? Taking it one step further, do you pull the plug on a schedule that is running over, taking the chance that if there is not a sufficient amount of footage, you may have to come back for reshoots at a later date? Talk to your key people (department heads and first assistant director) well in advance of making any major decision, and realize that there might be more than one clear-cut answer. Also beware that no matter how judicious your decision may be, there will always be someone second-guessing you. But don't let that stop you. Have confidence and trust yourself. In the final analysis, it's important to remember that the mere act of making a decision is often just as important as the decision you make—or you may find yourself standing around all night (on golden time) trying to decide what to do.

When you are working with a tight budget and don't think you can afford to hire someone with a significant amount of experience—think again. You can rarely afford not to. Those with the expertise in the type of project you are doing, in the operation of equipment you wish to use or with the knowledge pertaining to a distant or foreign location you wish to shoot at, are more valuable than two or three others with less experience, and they will ultimately save you both time and money. You will never be sorry hiring the very best people you can afford.

Occasionally, one of your department heads will ask you for something you know for a fact (or just instinctively know) they can do without, and approving the request would lead to unnecessary costs. But for the most part, if you are working with people who have earned your trust, and one of them tells you that he needs an extra person or an extra piece of equipment, it's probably because he does. True, it's an added expense you hadn't budgeted for, and this department may be able to do without, but there is also the chance that by denying the request, you may be compromising your schedule or the safety of your crew. This is when things tend to fall between the proverbial cracks, because all bases can't be covered at once. Do you spend more now, or risk incurring any combination of delays, overtime, second meals, loss and damages, late-payment charges, reshoots or accidents later on?

So now we're back to spending more for that experienced person who comes to the table with the most-informed, best-qualified answers as to when it's most appropriate to spend in order to save.

CHAPTER NINE

Deal Memos

Each member of a shooting company should be required to sign a contract or deal memo prior to his or her first day of work. Your attorney or legal department will generally draw up contracts for the producer(s), director, lead talent, casting director, production designer, directors of photography, costume designer, editor and music composer. Everyone else gets a deal memo, so they know up front the exact terms of their employment: what their salary will be (including overtime rates and payment for sixth and seventh days worked); how they will be traveling to location; how much their per diem will be; if they will be receiving screen credit; etc. Signed deal memos protect both the production company and the employee. It is not unusual for crew members who start shows without deal memos to have to deal with misunderstandings and disappointment later on.

With the exception of the Directors Guild of America (DGA) deal memos, the others included in this chapter are intended as basic guidelines. You and your legal advisor will want to incorporate specific provisions and/or conditions to the terms of employment as they relate to your production. Many producers also issue forms attached to deal memos, which employees are requested to sign, acknowledging that they have received, reviewed and thoroughly understand the guidelines governing general safety regulations, sexual harassment and proper location code of conduct.

Give each employee a copy of his or her signed deal memo (including all attached riders and forms of acknowledgment). Copies should also be given to the production manager, production accountant and/or payroll service. The original should be retained for the company's master files. Copies of signed DGA deal memos must be sent to the DGA's Reports Compliance Department (no later than the commencement of services), in care of the National Office of the Directors Guild of America at 7920 Sunset Blvd., Los Angeles, CA 90046. Their phone and fax numbers are as follows: (310) 289-2000 (phone), and (310) 289-2029 (fax).

NOTE: Loanouts are required to have valid corporations and Federal ID numbers. Loanouts must complete a Crew Deal Memo in addition to a Loanout Agreement (see *Loanout Agreement* form in Chapter 3, "Basic Accounting").

FORMS IN THIS CHAPTER

- Cast Deal Memo
- Crew Deal Memo
- Writer's Deal Memo
- Writing Team Deal Memo
- Director Deal Memorandum—Film (Theatrical)
- Director Deal Memorandum—Film (Television)
- Unit Production Manager & Assistant Director Deal Memorandum—Film
- Special Low Budget Project Unit Production Manager & Assistant Director Deal Memorandum—Film

CAST DEAL MEMO

PRODUCTION COMPANY _XYZ PRODUCTIONS_   DATE _5-11-XX_
ADDRESS _1234 FLICK DR._   PHONE# _555-3331_
HOLLYWOOD, CA 90038   FAX# _555-3332_
SHOW _HERBY'S SUMMER VACATION_   EPISODE _____
CASTING DIRECTOR _DEE CASTOR_   PROD# _0100_
CASTING OFFICE PHONE# _555-6636_   FAX# _555-6637_
ARTIST _SCARLET STARLET_   SOC. SEC.# _123-45-6789_
ADDRESS _555 SCHOOL ST._   PHONE# _555-3994_
STUDIO VILLAGE, CA 91604   MODILE# _555-7688_
ROLE _LAURA_   START DATE _7-5-XX_

☑ ACTOR	☑ THEATRICAL	☐ DAY PLAYER
☐ STUNT	☐ TELEVISION	☐ 3-DAY PLAYER
☐ SINGER	☐ CABLE	☑ WEEKLY
☐ PILOT	☐ MULTIMEDIA	☐ D/PU - DAILY TO WEEKLY
☐ DANCER	☐ INTERNET	☐ D/PU - DAILY TO DAILY

COMPENSATION $ _100,000_   Per ☐ DAY ☐ WEEK ☑ SHOW

	NO. OF DAYS - WEEKS	DATES
TRAVEL	2 DAYS	7·5·XX & 7·17·XX
FITTINGS	1 DAY	6·15·XX
REHEARSAL	—	
PRINCIPAL PHOTOGRAPHY	10 DAYS	7·6 THRU 7·16
ADDITIONAL SHOOT DAYS	ALLOW: 2	AS NECESSARY
POST PRODUCTION DAYS	ALLOW: 1	TBD

DRESSING ROOM _1ST CLASS DRESSING RM. WHEN WORKING ON STAGE. FULLY-EQUIPPED MOTOR HOME OR STAR TRAILER WHILE WORKING ON LOCATION (TV, VCR, MICROWAVE & CD PLAYER)_
PER DIEM - EXPENSES _$150 PER DAY ON LOCATION_
TRANSPORTATION - TRAVEL _1ST CLASS, ROUND-TRIP AIR FARE FOR MS. STARLET & A COMPANION - AND TRANSPORTATION TO & FROM AIRPORTS._
HOTEL ACCOMMODATIONS _2-BDRM. SUITE W/KITCHEN & A SINGLE ADJOINING RM. FOR MS. STARLET'S ASSISTANT_

OTHER _USE OF A CELLULAR PHONE WHILE ON THE SHOW. TRANSPORTATION TO & FROM THE SET WHILE WORKING IN TOWN._
BILLING _SINGLE CARD - MAIN TITLES - 2ND POSITION_

☑ PAID ADVERTISING

© ELH

AGENT _JOE COOL_ OFFICE# _555-5666_
AGENCY _TALENTED ARTISTS AGENCY_ FAX# _555-5667_
ADDRESS _1515 SUNSET BLVD. SUITE 100_ MOBILE# _555-3611_
HOLLYWOOD, CA 90028 PAGER# _555-7112_

MANAGER _SAMMY SLICK_ OFFICE# _555-2633_
MANAGEMENT CO._SLICK & GLICK MANAGEMENT_ FAX# _555-2634_
ADDRESS _2003 ROCKY ROAD LN._ MOBILE# _555-8321_
HOLLYWOOD, CA 90068 PAGER# _555-3533_

PUBLICIST _PATRICIA HUTCHINSON_ OFFICE# _555-1122_
P.R. FIRM _HUTCHINSON & ASSOC._ FAX# _555-1123_
ADDRESS _5600 SHELBY RD._ MOBILE# _555-4637_
HOLLYWOOD, CA 90038 PAGER# _555-8831_

☑LOANOUT
CORP. NAME _STARLET NIGHTS, INC._ FED. ID# _95-1234567_
ADDRESS (If Different From Above) _90 TAA - 1515 SUNSET BLVD., SUITE 100_
HOLLYWOOD, CA 90028

EMPLOYER OF RECORD _PREMIERE PAYROLL CO._
ADDRESS _1776 NEWMAN RD._ PHONE# _555-7000_
BEVERLY HILLS, CA 90210 FAX# _555-7001_

APPROVED BY _Swiftly Dealer_

TITLE _PRODUCER_ DATE _6.8.XX_

© ELH

CREW DEAL MEMO

PRODUCTION COMPANY _XYZ PRODUCTIONS_ DATE _5·31·XX_
SHOW _HERBY'S SUMMER VACATION_ PROD# _0100_
EMPLOYEE'S NAME _NATALIE WOODMAN_ SOC. SEC.# _123-45-6789_
ADDRESS _3133 McQUEEN AVE._ PHONE# _555-7737_
TINSELTOWN, CA 91322 MOBILE# _555-3337_
START DATE _6·1·XX_ FAX# _555-7738_
JOB TITLE _PRODUCTION SUPERVISOR_ PAGER# _555-0013_
UNION/GUILD _(NON-AFFILIATE)_ ACCOUNT# _20-06_
RATE (In Town) _$2,000—_ Per ☐ Hour ☐ Day ☑ Week for a ☑ 5 ☐ 6-day week
(Distant Location) _$2,500—_ Per ☐ Hour ☐ Day ☑ Week for a ☐ 5 ☑ 6-day week
ADDITIONAL DAY(S) @ _6ᵀᴴ DAY @ X½ — 7ᵀᴴ DAY @ XX_
OVERTIME _____ After ____ hours & _____ After ____ hours

☑ BOX/EQUIPMENT RENTAL _$100_ Per ☐ Day ☑ Week

☐ CAR ALLOWANCE _____ Per ☐ Day ☐ Week

☐ MILEAGE REIMBURSEMENT _____ Per Mile

Note: any equipment rented by the Production Company from the employee must be inventoried before rental can be paid.

TRAVEL & HOTEL ACCOMMODATIONS _BUSINESS-CLASS, ROUND TRIP AIR FARE & TRANSPORTATION TO & FROM AIRPORTS_

EXPENSES - PER DIEM _$50/DAY_
OTHER • _USE OF A CELLULAR PHONE DURING ENTIRE PRODUCTION_
• _RENTAL CAR ON LOCATION_

☐ LOANOUT

CORP. NAME _____ FED. ID# _____

ADDRESS (If Different From Above) _____

AGENT _____ AGENCY _____
ADDRESS _____ PHONE# _____
_____ FAX# _____
EMPLOYER OF RECORD _PREMIERE PAYROLL CO._
ADDRESS _1776 NEWMAN RD._ PHONE# _555-7000_
BEVERLY HILLS, FAX# _555-7001_
IF AWARDED SCREEN CREDIT, HOW WOULD YOU LIKE YOUR NAME TO READ _____
NATALIE L. WOODMAN

APPROVED BY _Swifty Deals_ TITLE _PRODUCER_

ACCEPTED BY _Natalie Woodman_ DATE _6·1·XX_

© ELH

WRITER'S DEAL MEMO

PRODUCTION COMPANY __XYZ PRODUCTIONS, INC.__ DATE __2·28·XX__

ADDRESS __1234 FLICK DRIVE__ PHONE # __(213) 555-3331__

__HOLLYWOOD, CA 90038__ FAX # __(213) 555-3332__

SHOW __HERBY'S SUMMER VACATION__ PROD # __0100__

EPISODE _____

WRITER __F. SCOTT RYDER__ PHONE # __(213) 555-7662__

SOC. SEC. # __555-00-5500__ MESSAGES _____

ADDRESS __9336 W. STOREY ST.__ FAX # __(213) 555-7660__

__LOS ANGELES, CA 90000__

DATES OF EMPLOYMENT _____
__3·1·XX THROUGH 7·31·XX__

COMPENSATION __$150,000 FOR ORIGINAL SCREENPLAY - PLUS ONE__
__ADDITIONAL REWRITE & ONE POLISH__

ADDITIONAL TERMS OF EMPLOYMENT __ONE FIRST·CLASS, ROUND·TRIP__
__AIR FARE TO LOCATION__

BILLING __SCREENPLAY BY__
__F. SCOTT RYDER__

☑ PAID ADVERTISING

WRITER'S AGENT __JOE COOL__ DIRECT # __(213) 555-5663__

AGENCY __TALENTED ARTISTS AGENCY__ PHONE # __(213) 555-2345__

ADDRESS __1515 SUNSET BLVD.__ FAX # __(213) 555-2344__

__HOLLYWOOD, CA 90000__

☑ LOAN OUT

CORPORATION NAME __GREAT RYDERS, INC.__

ADDRESS __(SAME AS ABOVE)__

FED. I.D. # __95-3367323579__

CONTRACT PREPARED BY __BARBARA BUSINESS AFFAIRS__

DATE SENT OUT __3·1·XX__

APPROVED BY __Swifty Deals__

TITLE __PRODUCER__ DATE __2·28·XX__

© ELH

WRITING TEAM DEAL MEMO

PRODUCTION COMPANY __XYZ PRODUCTIONS, INC.__ DATE __6·10·XX__
ADDRESS __1234 FLICK DR.__ PHONE # __(213) 555-3331__
__HOLLYWOOD, CA 90038__ FAX # __(213) 555-3332__
SHOW __HERBY'S SUMMER VACATION__ PROD # __0100__
EPISODE __"BOY'S NIGHT OUT"__
WRITERS __JASON PENN__   __SAMUEL INKK__
SOC.SEC. # __555-02-3657__   __555-72-7632__
ADDRESS __1723 LINCOLN BLVD.__   __313 WASHINGTON ST.__
__LOS ANGELES, CA 90000__   __CULVER CITY, CA 90230__
PHONE # __(213) 555-7321__   __(310) 555-9636__
FAX # __(213) 555-7322__   __(310) 555-9637__
DATES OF EMPLOYMENT __6·12·XX THROUGH 8·31·XX__

COMPENSATION __$80,000__

ADDITIONAL TERMS OF EMPLOYMENT _____

BILLING __SCREENPLAY BY__
__JASON PENN and SAMUEL INKK__
☑ PAID ADVERTISING
WRITER'S AGENTS __JOE COOL__   __(SAME)__
AGENCY __TALENTED ARTISTS AGENCY__
ADDRESS __1515 SUNSET BLVD.__
__HOLLYWOOD, CA 90000__
PHONE # __(213) 555-2345__
☑ LOAN OUT
CORP. NAME __PENN AND INK PRODUCTIONS, INC.__
ADDRESS __9o TAA — 1515 SUNSET BLVD.__
__HOLLYWOOD, CA 90000__
FED. I.D. # __95-7291346782__
CONTRACT PREPARED BY __BARBARA BUSINESS AFFAIRS__
DATE SENT OUT __6·15·XX__

APPROVED BY __Swifty Deals__
TITLE __PRODUCER__   DATE __6·12·XX__

© ELH

Director Deal Memorandum - FILM
(Theatrical)

DGASigPkFrm: 08AB

This confirms our agreement to employ you to direct the project described as follows:

DIRECTOR INFORMATION

Name: SID CELLULOID   SS#: 123-45-6789

Loanout (corp. name) BIG CHEEZE, INC.   Fed. ID#: 95-1234567

Address 7632 GARBO LN.   Tel#:
        MALIBU, CA 90265

Salary: $ SCALE   ☑ per film   ☐ per week   ☐ per day

Additional Time: $ SCALE ☑ per week   ☐ per day

Start Date: 6·1·XX   Guaranteed Period: 13   ☐ days   ☑ weeks

If this is your first DGA-covered employment, check here: ☐ Yes

If the Director's compensation will be $200,000 or more, is it possible that the Director's services on the project will span two (2) calendar years (i.e. commence in one calendar year and finish in a subsequent calendar year) between commencement of preparation and delivery of answer print?   ☐ Yes ☐ No

PROJECT INFORMATION

Picture Title: HERBY'S SUMMER VACATION

Project ID# (if applicable): PROD. #0100

Budget (if under $6,000,000): $

Is this Project covered by a Low Budget Sideletter?   ☐ Yes   ☑ No

Check (if applicable):   ☐ Second Unit   ☐ Replacement Director   ☐ Trailers, Talent Tests & Promos
                         ☐ Additional Photography   ☐ Freelance Shorts & Documentaries

The **INDIVIDUAL** having final cutting authority over the film is: SWIFTY DEALS (PRODUCER)

Other conditions (incl. credit above min.) $200 PER DIEM; (2) 1ST CLASS, RT AIR
FARES; 2-BDRM. HOTEL SUITE; RENTAL CAR; TRAILER ON LOC.

POST PRODUCTION INFORMATION

(Please provide all dates currently scheduled or anticipated; any revisions should be submitted as soon as practicable)

Director's Cut Start Date: 9·5·XX   Director's Cut Finish Date: 10·31·XX

Date for Special Photography & Processes (if any): _____   Date for Delivery of Answer Print: 11·30·XX

Date of Theatrical Release: 12·4·XX

This employment is subject to the provisions of the Directors Guild of America Basic Agreement of 1999

Accepted and Agreed: Signatory Co (print): XYZ PRODUCTIONS

Employee: _____   By: _____

Date: 5/31/XX   Date: 6·9·XX

Directors Guild of America
7920 Sunset Blvd.
Los Angeles, CA 90046
310-289-2000 / FAX 310-289-2029

Director Deal Memorandum - FILM
(Television)
Deal Memos must be submitted no later than
commencement of services.

DGASigPkFrm: 08BBa

This confirms our agreement to employ you to direct the project described as follows:

DIRECTOR INFORMATION

Name: FLINT WESTWOOD   SS#: 123-45-6789

Loanout (corp. name) TOUGH GUY, INC.   Fed. ID#: 95-1234567

Address 6771 RAWHIDE TRAIL RD.   Tel#: 555-7456
TINSELTOWN, CA 91344

Salary: $ SCALE   ☑ per show ☐ per week ☐ per day

Additional Time: $ SCALE   ☐ per show ☐ per week ☑ per day

Start Date (on or about): 6·1·XX   Guaranteed Period: 19 ☑ days ☐ weeks pro rata: ☐ Yes ☐ No

If this is the employee's first DGA-covered employment, check here (optional):   ☐ Yes

PROJECT INFORMATION

Project Title: HERBY'S SUMMER VACATION

Episode/Segment Title (optional): BOYS NIGHT OUT   Project ID# 0100

Length of Program: ☐ 30 min.   ☐ 90 min.
                      ☑ 60 min.   ☐ 120 min.   ☐ Other:_____

Produced Primarily for: ☑ Network Prime Time ABC   ☐ Basic Cable_____
(Please indicate which Network ☐ Network, other than Prime Time_____ ☐ Syndication
or Service, as applicable)   ☐ Pay TV_____   ☐ Disc/Cassettes

Is This a Pilot?   ☐ Yes   ☐ No

Budget (for Basic Cable "Dramatic" Projects): $_____

Pay Television:
Is the number of subscribers to the pay television service(s) to which the program is licensed at the time of
Director's employment $6,000,000 or less?   ☐ Yes ☐ No

Is the budget $5,000,000 or more?   ☐ Yes ☐ No

Check, if applicable (optional): ☐ Second Unit ☐ Segment ☐ Additional Photography ☐ Replacement Director

The **INDIVIDUAL** having final cutting authority over the Project: SWIFTY DEALS (PRODUCER)

Other conditions_____
(inc. credit above min.)_____

POST PRODUCTION INFORMATION (For Projects 90 mins. or longer)_____
(All dates must be provided upon commencement of Principal Photography. Prior to commencement of Principal Photography,
please provide all dates known or anticipated. Any revisions should be submitted as soon as practicable.)

Director's Cut Start Date:_____   Director's Cut Finish Date:_____

Date for Special Photography & Processes (if any):_____ Date for Delivery of Answer Print:_____

Date of Network Broadcast (if applicable):_____

This employment is subject to the provisions of the Directors Guild of America Basic Agreement of 1999.

Accepted and Agreed:_____   Signatory Co (print): XYZ PRODUCTIONS

Employee:_____   By:_____

Date: 6·1·XX   Date: 6·1·XX

Directors Guild of America
7920 Sunset Blvd.
Los Angeles, CA 90046
310-289-2000 / FAX 310-289-2029

**Unit Production Manager and Assistant Director
Deal Memorandum - FILM**

DGASigPkFrm: 08C

This confirms our agreement to employ you on the project described as follows:

AD/UPM INFORMATION

Name: ALICE DEES   SS#: 123-45-6789

Loanout (corp. name)_____   Fed. ID#:_____

Address 12353 AVE. OF THE LEGENDS   Tel#: 555-6541
HOLLYWOOD, CA 90068

Category:
☐ Unit Production Manager
☑ First Assistant Director
☐ Key Second Assistant Director
☐ 2nd Second Assistant Director
☐ Additional Second Assistant Director
☐ Technical Coordinator
☐ Assistant Unit Production Manager

Photography: ☑ Principal   ☐ Second Unit   ☐ Both

Salary (dollar amt): $ SCALE $ SCALE   ☑ per week
                      (Studio)   (Location)   ☐ per day

Production Fee (dollar amt): $ SCALE $ SCALE
                              (Studio)   (Location)

Start Date: 6·1·XX   Guaranteed Period: 2 WEEKS

PROJECT INFORMATION

Film or Series Title: HERBY'S SUMMER VACATION

Episode/Segment Title:_____

Length of Program:
☐ 30 min.
☐ 60 min.
☐ 90 min.
☑ 120 min.
☐ Other_____

Produced Primarily for:
☑ Theatrical
☐ Network
☐ Basic Cable
☐ Syndication
☐ Disc/Cassettes
☐ Pay-TV (service)_____

Other conditions:
(e.g., credit, suspension, per diem, etc.)
1ST CLASS ROUNDTRIP AIR FARE, $50 PER DIEM,
DGA ALLOWANCE FOR INCIDENTALS WHILE ON DIST. LOC.

☐ Studio   ☐ Distant Location   ☑ Both   ☐ Check if New York Amendment Applies

This employment is subject to the provisions of the Directors Guild of America Basic Agreement of 1999

Accepted and Agreed: Signatory Co (print): XYZ PRODUCTIONS

Employee: A. Dees   By: Swifty Deals

Date: 6·1·XX   Date: 6·1·XX

Directors Guild of America
7920 Sunset Blvd.
Los Angeles, CA 90046
310-289-2000 / FAX 310-289-2029

Special Low Budget Project
Unit Production Manager and Assistant Director
Deal Memorandum - FILM

This confirms our agreement to employ you on the project described as follows:

AD/UPM INFORMATION

Name: _FRED FILMER_   SS#: _123-45-6789_

Loanout (corp. name): _____   Fed. ID#: _____

Address _2731 N. STARLIGHT DR._   Tel#: _555-4454_
HOLLYWOOD, CA 90028

Category:
☑ Unit Production Manager   ☐ 2nd Second Assistant Director
☐ First Assistant Director   ☐ Additional Second Assistant Director
☐ Key Second Assistant Director

Photography: ☑ Principal   ☐ Second Unit   ☐ Both

Salary (dollar amt): $ _SCALE_ $ _____   ☑ per week
(Studio)   (Location)   ☐ per day

Production Fee (dollar amt): $ _____ $ _SCALE_
(Studio)   (Location)

Based on a ___6___ day/week   Based on a ___12___ hr./day
(5/6/7)

Please indcate the following if applicable: _____% is paid when services are performed
_____% is deferred

Start Date: _6·1·XX_   Guaranteed Period: _1 WK._

PROJECT INFORMATION

Film Title: _HERBY'S SUMMER VACATION_

Theatrical Film Budget:
☐ Under $1,200,000
☐ Between $1,200,000 and $2,500,000
☑ Between $2,500,000 and $3,500,000
☐ Between $3,500,000 and $6,000,000

Other conditions: _$40 PER DIEM, 1ST CLASS ROUND TRIP AIR FARE,_
(e.g., credit, per diem, etc.)   _CELL PHONE, RENTAL CAR ON LOCATION_

☐ Studio   ☐ Distant Location   ☑ Both

This employment is subject to the provisions of the Sideletter to Directors Guild of America Basic Agreement of 1999. Guild members shall understand that all conditions of employment not referenced in the Sideletter Agreement are completely negotiable, and should be specifically set forth in this deal memorandum.

Accepted and Agreed: Signatory Co (print): _XYZ PRODUCTIONS_

Employee: _Fred Filmer_   By: _Swifty Deals_

Date: _6·1·XX_   Date: _6·1·XX_

CHAPTER TEN

Unions & Guilds

INDUSTRY UNIONS & GUILDS

All major studios and many independent production companies are signatory to certain basic union and guild agreements, the most common being the Screen Actors Guild (SAG), representing actors, stunt coordinators, stunt performers, professional singers, puppeteers, airplane pilots, professional dancers (may cover swimmers and skaters as well) and extras; the Directors Guild of America (DGA), representing directors, unit production managers and assistant directors; the Writers Guild of America (WGA), representing writers; the International Alliance of Theatrical Stage Employees (IATSE or IA), covering various crew classifications (each represented by their own local) and the Teamsters, with jurisdiction over drivers and location managers. There are a few others, such as the National Association of Broadcast Employees and Technicians (NABET) and the American Federation of Television and Radio Artists (AFTRA), but when it comes to shooting a feature film or movie for television or cable, these are the primary unions and guilds you will be dealing with.

Many of the unions and guilds, in addition to having offices in both Los Angeles and New York, have additional branch offices in various other locations around the country. The IA does not have branch offices, but does maintain individual locals in different cities throughout the country. To locate the specific union or guild branch office or the IA local closest to you, contact one of their main offices or your film commission for assistance.

THE ALLIANCE OF MOTION PICTURE AND TELEVISION PRODUCERS (AMPTP)

On the West Coast, standing between the unions and guilds, the producers who employ union and guild members and those applying for union membership is the AMPTP, the Alliance of Motion Picture and Television Producers. The AMPTP provides services to studios and independent production companies covering all aspects of employment within the television and theatrical motion picture industry and other issues that affect the industry as a whole. They represent their member companies in industrywide bargaining with the unions and guilds, including grievance and arbitration decisions, and interpreting and administering agreements with the WGA, DGA, SAG, IATSE, West Coast studio local unions and basic crafts unions.

The AMPTP assists member companies in complying with the myriad of laws that impact the employment process, responds to equal employment opportunity inquiries from SAG based upon reports that are required under the existing collective bargaining agreement and oversees the Human Resources Coordinating Committee meetings for the purpose of implementing the script submission and trainee programs under the Writers Guild of America agreements. They also initiated and continue to participate in an industrywide safety committee composed of producer representatives and unions and guilds representing persons involved in the production process. The AMPTP has drafted and disseminated joint safety bulletins over the past several years in conjunction with the unions and guilds.

Under the auspices of the AMPTP, the Contract Services Administration Trust Fund (CSATF) is the entity that specifically maintains work rosters and coordinates qualifications committees; develops and administers safety, training and apprenticeship programs; administers controlled substance abuse testing; collects and maintains I-9 files; schedules expedited arbitration; handles step two conciliation grievances; handles material breach claims and provides labor relations advice.

UNION VERSUS NON-UNION SHOWS

The differences between union and non-union shows are considerably less when low-budget union and guild agreements are thrown into the equation, but generally, figure on paying approximately 15 to 18 percent for payroll fringes on non-union employees, and approximately 33 percent for union employees. (These percentages vary a bit depending on State income tax and workers' compensation rates.) And not only are salaries and fringe benefits less, but payments for overtime and other penalties are rare on non-union shows. On the other hand, free of certain regulations, a non-union DP can also operate the camera; production assistants and other crew members can drive their own trucks; you can hire a two-person sound department instead of a three-person crew and you can hire grips/electricians as needed instead of grips *and* electricians, or one extra hair/makeup person rather than one of each. Also, when filming in a right-to-work state, you are not required to hire any union employees if you choose not to.

There are advantages and disadvantages to both union and non-union shows, for the company and the employee. Determining factors as to whether a show is to be union or non-union will usually depend on your budget, where you plan to shoot and if the company releasing your film has mandatory requirements specifying union-affiliation.

Depending on what side of the fence you're sitting on, these are the things you should consider in relation to unions and guilds:

1. As an individual—should you join, what are the advantages of union membership, and are you eligible to join?

2. As a producer (and if you have a choice)—which unions and guilds, if any, should you sign with?

BECOMING A UNION MEMBER

The requirements for membership differ with each union and guild, because each has its own set of variables, depending upon the classification you are seeking. It is definitely advantageous to become a member of a union or guild with benefits such as overtime, meal penalties, health insurance, pension, vacation and holiday pay, etc. Although preferable to the longer hours and lower wages generally associated with non-union shows, union and guild membership is not open to just anyone who wants to join. It is quite difficult to join most of the unions and guilds, because a primary function of their existence is to protect the employment of their current membership by limiting the number of new members they accept.

Contact the union or guild you are interested in joining to inquire as to their membership requirements. Although you need only to sell a script to a signatory company to become a member of the Writers Guild, and you can get into SAG by way of employment on a SAG production (requiring the submission of a Taft/Hartley Report Form), many others require that you work a specified number of hours or days at a particular (non-union) job and prove a certain level of expertise in a given field. If that is the case, you will need to keep careful records documenting your work history. Even if you are far from reaching your goal, gather the substantiating data as you go along, because it is very difficult to go back and collect pieces of information long after a production has been completed. Keep copies of things such as deal memos, paycheck stubs, call sheets, production reports, and crew lists. Some unions will require letters from producers or department heads you worked under confirming work dates and job responsibilities. Occasionally, you will be asked for proof of screen credits. Find out what the requirements are, and set up a file box to start accumulating all the necessary paperwork.

BECOMING A UNION SIGNATORY

As a producer, it will be your responsibility to determine which unions and guilds to sign with. Consider the following points: Will your budget accommodate union wages and benefits? Will the film be shot in a right-to-work state or in a metropolitan area where you are likely to be visited by picketers should you not sign a particular union agreement? Are there certain people you want on your show who are union members and cannot work for you unless you become signatory to their contract? Will you be working on a studio lot that only allows for the employment of union members?

Most of the unions and guilds now offer a range of agreements to accommodate the type of show (theatrical motion picture, basic cable, prime time network television, etc.) and the budget (ranging from $500,000 or less to $1,500,000 and above). Many unions and guilds also offer affirmative action contracts as well as agreements for multimedia and Internet productions. The low-budget and affirmative action agreements offer less expensive pay scales and more flexible working conditions to those who qualify.

These special contracts are granted to companies who would not otherwise be able to sign union agreements, and allows the production entity to pay union benefits to cast and crew members who might not otherwise receive them. They also encourage keeping certain productions in town, as opposed to shooting elsewhere, where labor rates are less costly. Each agreement comes with its own qualification guidelines and requirements. Check to see if you qualify before assuming that you cannot afford to become a signatory.

DIRECTORS GUILD OF AMERICA (DGA)

The DGA offers two basic agreements, one covering theatrical motion pictures (including television, shorts and documentaries), and the other, freelance live and tape television. The Freelance Live and Tape agreement covers wages and working conditions for network, non-network, variety, primetime, non-primetime, quiz and game shows. In addition to the basic theatrical agreement, the Guild also offers a low-cost *sideletter* for films budgeted up to $6,000,000. The sideletter agreement offers varying levels of compensation based on the film's budget and is subject to the DGA members on the project being able to negotiate better terms. One of the provisions of this low-cost agreement is that films must have an initial theatrical or videocassette release in the United States. If the film is exhibited on television first, the production company is then liable for the dif-

ference in salaries between what was paid under the sideletter and applicable wages provided for in the standard basic agreement.

The Guild also offers a basic cable sideletter (for projects under the budget caps noted in the 1999 Memorandum of Agreements), national and Midwest commercial agreements, and the most recent, an agreement covering Internet projects. All DGA agreements are based upon the type of show, the show's length, budget and form of initial exhibition.

Based on a review of the financing of the project, the Guild may ask for a payroll deposit to be provided prior to principal photography to insure salary payments (and Pension, Health & Welfare contributions) to DGA-covered crew members.

For those interested, be aware that the DGA has an assistant director's training program, which is administered jointly by the DGA and the AMPTP. For more information on this program, call the Directors Guild–Producer Training Plan at: (818) 386-2545. The Guild also has a special agreement with the AMPTP, referred to as the Third Area Qualifications List, which allows production companies to hire non-union UPMs and assistant directors when shooting outside of the Southern California and New York metropolitan areas *if* the production entity has not previously signed a DGA agreement. Although non-union at the time of hire, these employees must become guild members once the company signs with the DGA (at which point, they are considered "incumbent" members). They may continue to work outside of the Southern California and New York areas under the Third Area Qualifications List while accumulating days. Once they have accumulated a required number of days, they become eligible to work on any DGA show without restrictions.

DGA members are also subject to a residency requirement, whereas they are required to declare affiliation to a specific production center (Los Angeles, New York, Chicago, Florida, etc.). Although the production center need not be the city in which they live, it is generally the area where most of their work is generated. If a DGA member were to live in Omaha, Nebraska, for example, and she were to claim Los Angeles as her production center, she could work in Los Angeles as a local (meaning the production company would be under no obligation to pay air fare, hotel or per diem for her), and she can work in Omaha as a local as well. DGA members can switch their production center once a year.

In 1964, the DGA formed the Creative Rights Committee, a special negotiating committee to obtain acknowledgment for the rights of directors. These rights are encapsulated in the *DGA Creative Rights Handbook*, used not only by directors to keep apprised of their rights but also by the companies that employ them. During the 1996 negotiations, the committee also created the *Code of Preferred Practices*. The Code is a set of guidelines that the studios and networks have agreed is the way the directing process should work. In 1999, the Creative Rights Agreement was revised, and the issues contained within continue to be addressed. While adhering to these guidelines is voluntary, they express the Committee's preferred industry practices. Contact the DGA for a copy of the *Creative Rights Handbook*.

For further information regarding the Directors Guild, their programs, and policies, call them directly or visit their website (see the list of websites at the end of the chapter). Be aware that the DGA also offers a service called *Fax on Demand*. By calling (310) 289-5355, you can request contract information, availability lists, rate cards, and other materials that will be faxed to you.

The national headquarters of the DGA is its Los Angeles office at (310) 289-2000. Additional DGA offices are located in New York at (212) 581-0370, Chicago at (312) 644-5050 and Hollywood, Florida at (954) 927-3338.

SCREEN ACTORS GUILD (SAG)

The Screen Actors Guild currently offers a low-budget agreement for productions with budgets of $2 million or under and an affirmative action agreement for productions with budgets of $2.75 million and under. These agreements provide for pay scales that are two contract terms behind the current wage structure. Films produced under this contract must be filmed entirely in the United States and have an initial theatrical release. A modified low-budget agreement is now being offered for productions with budgets under $500,000. The biggest obstacle to the modified low-budget agreement is that the film must have a theatrical release of at least two weeks. If a film made under a modified low-budget agreement is not released theatrically, the production entity is obligated to retroactively compensate all SAG performers who appeared in the film at the rate of the basic agreement at the time of principal photography.

SAG does not offer low-budget agreements for television productions, and there are separate video agreements for films made exclusively for video release. Agreements are also available for multimedia and Internet productions.

All SAG agreements require that the producer show proof of copyright ownership to the screenplay prior to the start of principal photography. This requirement impacts the guild's security interest in maintaining its rights, especially with regard to residual obligations.

SAG, DGA AND WGA—FORMS AND REPORTS

Many films are shot using non-union crews, but few production units are not signatory to the Screen Actors Guild, Directors Guild and Writers Guild. Each of these three guilds have their own very distinct forms, reports and guidelines that signatory companies are asked to adhere to. As a signatory to SAG, DGA and WGA, you will have copies of each of the guild contracts and should know the rules and rates associated with each.

At the end of this chapter, you will find a sampling of the most often used guild contracts and report forms. Note that (1) DGA deal memos are not included in this section but can be found in Chapter 9, "Deal Memos"; and (2) there are no samples of pension, health and welfare reports or gross earning reports in the following pages. The reporting of such are functions of either your production accountant or the payroll company handling your show, and are not generally prepared by production personnel.

THE WRITERS GUILD—NOTICE OF TENTATIVE WRITING CREDITS

Television

Before writing credits are finally determined, you are required to send a completed and signed copy of the WGA's Notice of Tentative Writing Credits—Television form (NTWC) to the Writers Guild and to all participating writers concurrently. At the completion of principal photography, you are required to send two copies of the revised final shooting script to each participating writer. The notice should state the company's choice of credit on a tentative basis.

A *WGA Notice of Tentative Writing Credits— Television* form can be found at the end of this chapter. Here are some guidelines in completing the form as it relates to television credits:

- List all participating writers at the top, even if not proposed for credit.
- Include network and length of show. If it is not an episodic series (sitcom or one-hour), list the type of show.
- Use an ampersand ("&") between the names of members of a writing team.
- List the "Created by" and any other continuing credits on each NTWC in the "continuing credit" space.
- The date to put after "The above tentative credits will become final . . . not later than 6:00 p.m. on . . . " is seven (7) business days from the date of dispatch of the NTWC to the Participating Writers and to the Guild. (If the writing credits need to be revised, this date must also be revised to take into consideration the new date of dispatch.) The writing credits will become final after this time period has elapsed unless the proposed credits trigger an automatic arbitration or if a protest is received from a participant and/or the Guild.
- List the Company at the bottom of the form.
- Include a contact name, phone number and address when transmitting the NTWC.
- When sending the NTWC to the Guild, it should be addressed to the attention of the Television Credits Administrator.
- For general credit waiver information, contact the TV Credits Coordinator.
- For team waivers, contact the Guild's Executive Office. Note, however, that requests for team waivers must be made prior to employing the team on the project.
- In the event a participant of the Guild protests the proposed credits or in the case of an automatic arbitration, you are required to submit three copies of all literary and source materials to the Guild.

Theatrical Motion Pictures

Before the writing credits are finally determined, you are required to file a copy of the Notice of Tentative Writing Credits—Theatrical Motion Pictures with the Writers Guild Credits Department within three days after completion of principal photography. The notice should state the company's choice of credit on a tentative

basis. Copies must be sent concurrently to all participating writers and to the Writers Guild, along with a copy of the final shooting script to each participant.

A *WGA Notice of Tentative Writing Credits— Theatrical* form can be found at the end of this chapter. Here are some guidelines in completing the form as it relates to Theatrical Motion Picture credits:

- List all participating writers at the top, even if not proposed for credit. All participating writers must receive a copy of the final shooting script.
- Include the proposed writing credit after "On Screen." For example, "Written by Writer A," or "Screenplay by Writer B and Writer C, Story by Writer A."
- Use an ampersand ("&") between the names of members of a bona fide writing team. Use an "and" to designate writers writing separately. No other punctuation is allowed.
- The date to put after "The above tentative credits will become final . . . not later than 6:00 p.m. on . . . " is twelve (12) business days from the date of dispatch of the NTWC to the Participating Writers and to the Guild. (If the writing credits need to be revised, this date must also be revised to take into consideration the new date of dispatch.) The writing credits will become final after this time period has elapsed unless proposed credits trigger an automatic arbitration, or if a protest is received from a participant and/or the Guild.
- List the Company at the bottom of the form.
- Include a contact name, phone number and address when transmitting the NTWC.
- When sending the NTWC to the Guild, it should be addressed to the attention of the Screen Credits Administrator.
- For team waivers, contact the Guild's Executive Office. Note, however, that requests for team waivers must be made prior to employing the team on the project.
- In the event a participant of the Guild protests the proposed credits or in the case of an automatic arbitration, you are required to submit three copies of all literary and source materials to the Guild.

The Notice of Tentative Writing Credits should be submitted to the Writers Guild office you signed, either:

The Writers Guild of America West

7000 W. Third Street
Los Angeles, CA 90048-4329
(323) 951-4000; Fax: (323) 782-4800

or

The Writers Guild of America East

555 W. 57th Street
New York, NY 10019
(212) 676-7800; Fax: (212) 582-1909

For further information pertaining to the NTWC and credit determinations, call the Writers Guild Credits department or refer to the WGA Minimum Basic Agreement and Credits Manuals.

UNION AND GUILDS ON THE INTERNET

For further information regarding any of the unions or guilds or the services provided by Contract Services Administration Trust Fund (CSATF), visit their websites:

The Screen Actors Guild (SAG)—www.sag.org

The Directors Guild of America (DGA)—
www.dga.org

Writers Guild of America (WGA)—www.wga.org

International Alliance of Theatrical Stage Employees (IATSE)—www.iatse.com

National Association of Broadcast Employees and Technicians (NABET)—www.nabet.org

American Federation of Television and Radio Artists (AFTRA)—www.aftra.org

Contract Services Administration Trust Fund (CSATF)—www.csatf.org

FORMS IN THIS CHAPTER

- SAG Daily Contract for Television Motion Pictures or Videotapes
- SAG Minimum Three-Day Contract for Television Motion Pictures or Videotapes
- SAG Minimum Freelance Weekly Contract for Television Motion Pictures or Videotapes
- SAG Stunt Performer's Daily Contract for Television Motion Pictures
- SAG Stunt Performer's Minimum Freelance Three-Day Contract for Television Motion Pictures
- SAG Stunt Performer's Minimum Freelance Weekly Contract for Television Motion Pictures
- SAG Daily Contract for Theatrical Motion Pictures
- SAG Minimum Freelance Contract for Theatrical Motion Pictures
- SAG Stunt Performer's Daily Contract for Theatrical Motion Pictures
- SAG Stunt Performer's Minimum Freelance Weekly Contract for Theatrical Motion Pictures
- SAG Performer Contract for Interactive Programming
- SAG Taft/Hartley Report
- SAG Taft/Hartley Report—Extra
- SAG Theatrical and Television Sign-In Sheet
- SAG Performers Production Time Report (Exhibit G)—submit copies to SAG once a week
- SAG Casting Data Report—to be submitted within ten business days of wrap
- SAG Casting Data Report for Stunt Performers Only
- SAG Casting Data Report—Low-Budget, Affirmative Action
- SAG Final Cast List Information Sheet
- SAG Member Report ADR Theatrical/Television
- DGA Weekly Work List
- DGA Employment Data Report
- WGA Notice of Tentative Writing Credits—Theatrical
- WGA Notice of Tentative Writing Credits—Television

**THE PERFORMER MAY NOT WAIVE ANY PROVISION OF THIS CONTRACT
WITHOUT THE WRITTEN CONSENT OF SCREEN ACTORS GUILD, INC.**

SCREEN ACTORS GUILD

DAILY CONTRACT
(DAY PERFORMER)
FOR TELEVISION MOTION PICTURES OR VIDEOTAPES

Company _XYZ PRODUCTIONS_   Date _JUNE 1, 19XX_

Production Title _HERBY'S SUMMER VACATION_   Performer Name _JOHN DOE_

Production Number _0100_   Address _123 ACTORS ALLEY RD. HOLLYWOOD, CA 90028_

Date Employment Starts _JUNE 2, 19XX_   Telephone No.: _(213) 555-1962_

Role _HERBY'S NEIGHBOR_   Social Security No. _124-23-9637_

* Daily Rate $ _SCALE & 10% AGENCY COMMISSION_   Date of Performer's next engagement _____

Weekly Conversion Rate $ _____

Wardrobe supplied by performer   Yes ☐   No ☑

If so, number of outfits _____ @ $ _____

       (formal) _____ @ $ _____

COMPLETE FOR "DROP-AND-PICK-UP" DEALS ONLY:

Firm recall date on _____

or on or after * _JULY 13, 19XX_

("On or after" recall only applies to pick-up as Weekly Performer)

As   ☐ Day Performer   ☑ Weekly Performer

*Means date specified or within 24 hours thereafter.

THIS AGREEMENT covers the employment of the above-named Performer by _XYZ PRODUCTIONS_ in the production and at the rate of compensation set forth above and is subject to and shall include, for the benefit of the Performer and the Producer, all of the applicable provisions and conditions contained or provided for in the applicable Screen Actors Guild Television Agreement (herein called the "Television Agreement"). Performer's employment shall include performance in non-commercial openings, bridges, etc., and no added compensation shall be payable to Performer so long as such are used in the role and episode covered hereunder in which Performer appears; for other use, Performer shall be paid the added minimum compensation, if any, required under the provisions of the Screen Actors Guild agreements with Producer.

Producer shall have all the rights in and to the results and proceeds of the Performer's services rendered hereunder, as are provided with respect to "photoplays" in Schedule A of the applicable Screen Actors Guild Codified Basic Agreement and the right to supplemental market use as defined in the Television Agreement.

Producer shall have the unlimited right throughout the world to telecast the film and exhibit the film theatrically and in supplemental markets in accordance with the terms and conditions of the Television Agreement.

If the motion picture is rerun on television in the United States or Canada and contains any of the results and proceeds of the Performer's services, the Performer will be paid for each day of employment hereunder the additional compensation prescribed therefor by the Television Agreement, unless there is an agreement to pay an amount in excess thereof as follows:

SAG MINIMUM

_____

If there is foreign telecasting of the motion picture as defined in the Television Agreement, and such motion picture contains any of the results and proceeds of the Performer's services, the Performer will be paid the amount in the blank space below for each day of employment hereunder, or if such blank space is not filled in, then the Performer will be paid the minimum additional compensation prescribed therefor by the Television Agreement. $ _____

If the motion picture is exhibited theatrically anywhere in the world and contains any of the results and proceeds of the Performer's services, the Performer will be paid $ _SAG MIN_ , or if this blank is not filled in, then the Performer will be paid the minimum additional compensation prescribed therefor by the Television Agreement.

If the motion picture is exhibited in supplemental markets anywhere in the world and contains any of the results and proceeds of the Performer's services, then Performer will be paid the supplemental market fees prescribed by the applicable provisions of the Television Agreement.

If the Performer places his or her initials in the box below, he or she thereby authorizes Producer to use portions of said television motion picture as a trailer to promote another episode or the series as a whole, upon payment to the Performer of the additional compensation prescribed by the applicable provisions of the Television Agreement.

* BILLING : END CREDITS, SHARED CARD, PLACEMENT
         AT PRODUCER'S DISCRETION.

Initial

By _~Swifty Deals~_
Producer

~John Doe~
Performer

Production time reports are available on the set at the end of each day, which reports shall be signed or initialed by the Performer.

NOTICE TO PERFORMER: IT IS IMPORTANT THAT YOU RETAIN A COPY OF THIS CONTRACT FOR YOUR PERMANENT RECORDS.

* AS AGENTS DO NOT COLLECT COMMISSION ON "SCALE", 10% IS ADDED TO THE COMPENSATION RATE FOR THOSE ACTORS WHO HAVE AGENTS & ARE RECEIVING "SCALE" FOR THEIR PERFORMANCE.

** INCLUDING THE "BILLING" (SCREEN CREDIT) IS NOT REQUIRED, BUT IT IS AN IMPORTANT PART OF THE PERFORMER'S DEAL WORTH ADDING TO THE SIGNED CONTRACT.

**THE PERFORMER MAY NOT WAIVE ANY PROVISION OF THIS CONTRACT
WITHOUT THE WRITTEN CONSENT OF SCREEN ACTORS GUILD, INC.**

SCREEN ACTORS GUILD

**MINIMUM THREE-DAY CONTRACT
FOR TELEVISION MOTION PICTURES OR VIDEOTAPES
THREE-DAY MINIMUM EMPLOYMENT**

THIS AGREEMENT is made this _____15TH_____ day of _____MAY_____, 19 XX, between _____XYZ PRODUCTIONS, INC._____, a corporation, hereinafter called "Producer," and _____RAYMOND BURRMAN_____, hereinafter called "Performer."

WITNESSETH:

1. **Photoplay: Role and Guarantee.** Producer hereby engages Performer to render service as such in the role of _____ELLIOT_____, in a photoplay produced primarily for exhibition over free television, the working title of which is now _____HERBY'S SUMMER VACATION_____. Performer accepts such engagement upon the terms herein specified. Producer guarantees that it will furnish Performer not less than _____THREE_____ days' employment. (If this blank is not filled in, the guarantee shall be three (3) days.)

2. **Salary.** The Producer will pay to the Performer, and the Performer agrees to accept for three (3) days (and pro rata for each additional day beyond three (3) days) the following salary rate: $ _____SCALE_____.

3. Producer shall have the unlimited right throughout the world to telecast the film and exhibit the film theatrically and in Supplemental Markets in accordance with the terms and conditions of the applicable Screen Actors Guild Television Agreement (herein referred to as the "Television Agreement").

4. If the motion picture is rerun on television in the United States or Canada and contains any of the results and proceeds of the Performer's services, the Performer will be paid the additional compensation prescribed therefor by the Television Agreement, unless there is an agreement to pay an amount in excess thereof as follows:

_____SAG MINIMUM_____

_____

5. If there is foreign telecasting of the motion picture as defined in the Television Agreement, and such motion picture contains any of the results and proceeds of the Performer's services, the Performer will be paid the amount in the blank space below plus an amount equal to one-third (1/3) thereof for each day of employment in excess of three (3) days, or, if such blank space is not filled in, then the Performer will be paid the minimum additional compensation prescribed therefor by the Television Agreement. $ _____SAG MIN_____.

6. If the motion picture is exhibited theatrically anywhere in the world and contains any of the results and proceeds of the Performer's services, the Performer will be paid $ _____SAG MIN_____, plus an amount equal to one-third (1/3) thereof for each day of employment in excess of three (3) days. If this blank is not filled in, the Performer will be paid the applicable minimum additional compensation prescribed therefor by the Television Agreement.

7. If the motion picture is exhibited in Supplemental Markets anywhere in the world and contains any of the results and proceeds of the Performer's services, the Performer will be paid the supplemental market fees prescribed by the applicable provisions of the Television Agreement.

8. **Term.** The term of employment hereunder shall begin on _____JUNE 20, 19XX_____, on or about* _____ and shall continue thereafter until the completion of the photography and recordation of said role.

* The "on or about clause" may only be used when the contract is delivered to the Performer at least three (3) days before the starting date.

9. **Incorporation of Television Agreement.** The applicable provisions of the Television Agreement are incorporated herein by reference. Performer's employment shall include performance in non-commercial openings, closings, bridges, etc., and no added compensation shall be payable to Performer so long as such are used in the role and episode covered hereunder and in which Performer appears; for other use, Performer shall be paid the added minimum compensation, if any, required under the provisions of the Screen Actors Guild agreements with Producer. Performer's employment shall be upon the terms, conditions and exceptions of the provisions applicable to the rate of salary and guarantee specified in Paragraphs 1. and 2. hereof.

10. **Arbitration of Disputes.** Should any dispute or controversy arise between the parties hereto with reference to this contract, or the employment herein provided for, such dispute or controversy shall be settled and determined by conciliation and arbitration in accordance with and to the extent provided in the conciliation and arbitration provisions of the Television Agreement, and such provisions are hereby referred to and by such reference incorporated herein and made a part of this agreement with the same effect as though the same were set forth herein in detail.

11. **Performer's Address.** All notices which the Producer is required or may desire to give to the Performer may be given either by mailing the same addressed to the Performer at 123 ELM ST. - HOLLYWOOD, CA 90028 or such notice may be given to the Performer personally, either orally or in writing.

12. **Performer's Telephone.** The Performer must keep the Producer's casting office or the assistant director of said photoplay advised as to where the Performer may be reached by telephone without unreasonable delay. The current telephone number of the Performer is (213) 555-3621.

13. If Performer places his initials in the box, he thereby authorizes Producer to use portions of said television motion picture as a trailer to promote another episode or the series as a whole, upon payment to the Performer of the additional compensation prescribed by the Television Agreement.

RB

14. **Furnishing of Wardrobe.** The Performer agrees to furnish all modern wardrobe and wearing apparel reasonably necessary for the portrayal of said role; it being agreed, however, that should so-called "character" or "period" costumes be required, the Producer shall supply the same. When Performer supplies any wardrobe, Performer shall receive the cleaning allowance and reimbursement specified in the Television Agreement.

15. **Next Starting Date.** The starting date of Performer's next engagement is _____.

IN WITNESS WHEREOF, the parties have executed this agreement on the day and year first above written.

BILLING: END CREDITS, SHARED CARD, POSITION AT PRODUCER'S DISCRETION.

By _Swifty Deals_
_____ Producer

Raymond Burrman
_____ Performer

173-21-6342
_____ Social Security No.

Production time reports are available on the set at the end of each day. Such reports shall be signed or initialed by the performer.

Attached hereto for your use is a Declaration Regarding Income Tax Withholding ("Part Year Employment Method of Withholding"). You may utilize such form by delivering same to Producer.

NOTICE TO PERFORMER: IT IS IMPORTANT THAT YOU RETAIN A COPY OF THIS CONTRACT FOR YOUR PERMANENT RECORDS.

SCREEN ACTORS GUILD

MINIMUM FREE LANCE WEEKLY CONTRACT
FOR TELEVISION MOTION PICTURES OR VIDEOTAPES
Continuous Employment – Weekly Basis – Weekly Salary
One Week Minimum Employment

THIS AGREEMENT is made this ___28 TH___ day of __MAY__ , 19_XX_ , between

___XYZ PRODUCTIONS, INC.___ , a corporation, hereinafter called "Producer," and

___NANCY NICELY___ , hereinafter called "Performer."

WITNESSETH:

1. **Photoplay: Role and Guarantee.** Producer hereby engages Performer to render services as such, in the role of ___Mom___ , in a photoplay produced primarily for exhibition over free television, the working title of which is now __HERBY'S SUMMER VACATION__ . Performer accepts such engagement upon the terms herein specified. Producer guarantees that it will furnish Performer not less than __TWO (2)__ weeks employment. (If this blank is not filled in, the guarantee shall be one week.)

2. **Salary.** The Producer will pay to the Performer, and the Performer agrees to accept weekly (and pro rata for each additional day beyond guarantee) the following salary rate: $ __SCALE__ per "studio week." (Schedule B Performers must receive an additional overtime payment of four (4) hours at straight time rate for each overnight location sixth day).

3. Producer shall have the unlimited right throughout the world to telecast the film and exhibit the film theatrically and in Supplemental Markets, in accordance with the terms and conditions of the applicable Screen Actors Guild Television Agreement (herein referred to as the "Television Agreement").

4. If the motion picture is rerun on television in the United States or Canada and contains any of the results and proceeds of the Performer's services, the Performer will be paid the additional compensation prescribed therefor by the Television Agreement, unless there is an agreement to pay an amount in excess thereof as follows:

___SAG MINIMUM___

5. If there is foreign telecasting of the motion picture, as defined in the Television Agreement, and such motion picture contains any of the results and proceeds of the Performer's services, the Performer will be paid $_____ plus pro rata thereof for each additional day of employment in excess of one week, or, if this blank is not filled in, the Performer will be paid the minimum additional compensation prescribed therefor by the Television Agreement.

6. If the motion picture is exhibited theatrically anywhere in the world and contains any of the results and proceeds of the Performer's services, the Performer will be paid $ _SAG MIN_ plus pro rata thereof for each additional day of employment in excess of one week, or, if this blank is not filled in, the Performer will be paid the minimum additional compensation prescribed therefor by the Television Agreement.

7. If the motion picture is exhibited in Supplemental Markets anywhere in the world and contains any of the results and proceeds of the Performer's services, the Performer will be paid the supplemental market fees prescribed by the applicable provisions of the Television Agreement.

8. **Term.** The term of employment hereunder shall begin on __JUNE 21, 19XX__ , on or about*_____ and shall continue thereafter until the completion of the photography and recordation of said role.

*The "on or about clause" may only be used when the contract is delivered to the Performer at least three (3) days before the starting date.

9. **Incorporation of Television Agreement.** The applicable provisions of the Television Agreement are incorporated herein by reference. Performer's employment shall include performance in non-commercial openings, closings, bridges, etc., and no added compensation shall be payable to Performer so long as such are used in the role and episode covered hereunder and in which Performer appears; for other use, Performer shall be paid the added minimum compensation, if any, required under the provisions of the Screen Actors Guild agreements with Producer. Performer's employment shall be upon the terms, conditions and exceptions of said provisions applicable to the rate of salary and guarantee specified in Paragraphs 1. and 2. hereof.

10. **Arbitration of Disputes.** Should any dispute or controversy arise between the parties hereto with reference to this contract, or the employment herein provided for, such dispute or controversy shall be settled and determined by conciliation and arbitration in accordance with and to the extent provided in the conciliation and arbitration provisions of the Television Agreement, and such provisions are hereby referred to and by such reference incorporated herein and made a part of this agreement with the same effect as though the same were set forth herein in detail.

11. **Performer's Address.** All notices which the Producer is required or may desire to give to the Performer may be given either by mailing the same addressed to the Performer at 4321 ORANGE RD. - LOS ANGELES, CA 90000 or such notice may be given to the Performer personally, either orally or in writing.

12. **Performer's Telephone.** The Performer must keep the Producer's casting office or the assistant director of said photoplay advised as to where the Performer may be reached by telephone without unreasonable delay. The current telephone number of the Performer is (310) 555-7997 .

13. If Performer places his initials in the box, he thereby authorizes Producer to use portions of said television motion picture as a trailer to promote another episode or the series as a whole, upon payment to the Performer of the additional compensation prescribed by the Television Agreement.

14. **Furnishing of Wardrobe.** The Performer agrees to furnish all modern wardrobe and wearing apparel reasonably necessary for the portrayal of said role; it being agreed, however, that should so-called "character" or "period" costumes be required, the Producer shall supply the same. When Performer supplies any wardrobe, Performer shall receive the cleaning allowance and reimbursement specified in the Television Agreement.

15. **Next Starting Date.** The starting date of Performer's next engagement is _____.

IN WITNESS WHEREOF, the parties have executed this agreement on the day and year first above written.

BILLING: MAIN TITLES, SINGLE CARD, 3RD POSITION

By _Swyfty Deals_____
_Nancy Nicely_____ Producer
_372·46·2232_____ Performer
Social Security No.

Production time reports are available on the set at the end of each day. Such reports shall be signed or initialed by the performer.

NOTICE TO PERFORMER: IT IS IMPORTANT THAT YOU RETAIN A COPY OF THIS CONTRACT FOR YOUR PERMANENT RECORDS.

✪ SCREEN ACTORS GUILD
STUNT PERFORMER'S
DAILY CONTRACT
FOR TELEVISION MOTION PICTURES

THE ARTIST MAY NOT WAIVE ANY PROVISION OF THIS CONTRACT
WITHOUT THE WRITTEN CONSENT OF SCREEN ACTORS GUILD, INC.

STUNT PERFORMER __JOHNNY ROCKETT__ DATE OF AGREEMENT __6·24·XX__

ADDRESS __9326 HOLLYWOOD HILLS RD.__

__HOLLYWOOD, CA 90028__

TELEPHONE _(323)_ __555-1302__ SOCIAL SECURITY NO. __123-45-6789__

COMPANY/PRODUCER __XYZ PRODUCTIONS__

PRODUCTION TITLE __HERBY'S SUMMER VACATION__ PRODUCTION NO. __0100__

AGENT/AGENCY _____

ADDRESS _____

DAILY RATE $ __SCALE__ SERIES _____

WEEKLY CONV. RATE $ _____ START DATE __6·25·XX__

1. __DESCRIPTION OF SERVICES__: Producer hereby engages Stunt Performer to render services as __STUNT DOUBLE__. Stunt Performer accepts such engagement upon the terms herein specified.

2. __TERM/GUARANTEE__: Producer guarantees to furnish Stunt Performer not less than __(1)__ days engagement. If this space is not filled in, the guarantee shall be one (1) day.

3. __STUNT ADJUSTMENTS__: It is understood that the rate of compensation specified may be adjusted depending upon the nature of the stunt activities Producer may require. If so, a stunt adjustment will be agreed upon between the parties through good faith bargaining and said adjustment shall be noted on Stunt Performer's daily time report or time card. The parties shall agree upon the compensation to be paid before the stunt is performed if they may readily do so; however, it is expressly agreed that production shall not be delayed for the purpose of first determining the compensation for a stunt. Such adjustment shall increase Stunt Performer's compensation for the day in the manner prescribed in Schedule H of the Screen Actors Guild Codified Basic Agreement.

4. __INCORPORATION OF PRODUCER-SCREEN ACTORS GUILD COLLECTIVE BARGAINING AGREEMENT__: All provisions of the Screen Actors Guild Codified Basic Agreement and Television Agreement as the same may be supplemented and/or amended to date shall be deemed incorporated herein. Stunt Performer's engagement shall include performance in non-commercial openings, closings, bridges, etc., and no added compensation shall be payable to Stunt Performer so long as such are used in the Motion Picture covered hereunder and in which Stunt Performer appears or with respect to which Stunt Performer is paid compensation hereunder. Stunt Performer's engagement shall be upon the terms, conditions and exceptions of said provisions applicable to the rate of compensation and guarantee specified.

5. __RIGHTS__: Producer shall have the unlimited right throughout the universe and in perpetuity to exhibit the Motion Picture in all media, now or hereafter known, and Producer, as employer-for-hire of Stunt Performer, shall own all rights in the results and proceeds of Stunt Performer's services hereunder.

6. __ADDITIONAL COMPENSATION__: If the Motion Picture covered hereby is exhibited, containing any of the results and proceeds of Stunt Performer's services hereunder, in any of the following media:
   (i) "Free" television reruns in the United States or Canada, or both;
   (ii) Television exhibition anywhere in the universe outside the United States and Canada;
   (iii) Theatrical exhibition anywhere in the universe;

(iv) Supplemental Market exhibition anywhere in the universe;

(v) Basic Cable exhibition anywhere in the universe,

as to each such medium in which the motion picture is so exhibited, Producer will pay, and Stunt Performer will accept as payment in full, the minimum additional compensation provided therefor in the Screen Actors Guild Codified Basic Agreement or Television Agreement, as the case may be, except as compensation in excess of such minimum, if any, has been provided in this Agreement.

7. <u>CONTINUOUS EMPLOYMENT AND RIGHT TO ROLE (when applicable)</u>: If Stunt Performer portrays a role or has dialogue, Stunt Performer shall be entitled to "continuous employment" and "Right to Role," if any, only to the extent prescribed by the Screen Actors Guild Codified Basic Agreement. Stunt Performer shall receive a separate contract for such services.

8. <u>MOTION PICTURE AND TELEVISION FUND</u>: Stunt Performer (does) (does not) hereby authorize Producer to deduct from the compensation hereinabove specified an amount equal to _____ percent of each installment of compensation due Stunt Performer hereunder, and to pay the amount so deducted to the Motion Picture and Television Fund of America, Inc.

9. <u>WAIVER</u>: Stunt Performer may not waive any provision of the Screen Actors Guild Codified Basic Agreement of Television Agreement, whichever is applicable, without the written consent of the Screen Actors Guild, Inc.

10. <u>SIGNATORY</u>: Producer makes the material representation that either it is presently a signatory to the Screen Actors Guild collective bargaining agreement covering the engagement contracted for herein, or that the Motion Picture is covered by such collective bargaining agreement under the "Independent Production" provisions (Section 24) of the General Provisions of the Screen Actors Guild Codified Basic Agreement.

Signing of this Agreement in the spaces below signified acceptance by Producer and Stunt Performer of all of the above terms and conditions hereof and attached hereto, if any, as of the date specified above.

PRODUCER _XYZ PRODUCTIONS_____ STUNT PERFORMER _Johnny Rockett_

BY _Swifty Deals_____

Production time reports and/or time cards are available on the set at the beginning and end of each day, which reports and/or time cards shall be signed or initialed by Stunt Performer and must indicate any agreed stunt adjustments.

NOTICE TO STUNT PERFORMER: IT IS IMPORTANT THAT YOU RETAIN A COPY OF THIS AGREEMENT FOR YOUR PERMANENT RECORDS.

SCREEN ACTORS GUILD
STUNT PERFORMER'S
MINIMUM FREELANCE THREE-DAY CONTRACT
FOR TELEVISION MOTION PICTURES

STUNT PERFORMER _ARNOLD WEISMULLER_ DATE OF AGREEMENT _JULY 19, 19XX_

ADDRESS _1300 TARZANA GARDENS_
TARZANA, CA 91333

TELEPHONE (213) 555-7134   SOCIAL SECURITY NO. _331-32-4476_

COMPANY/PRODUCER _XYZ PRODUCTIONS, INC._

PRODUCTION TITLE _HERBY'S SUMMER VACATION_ PRODUCTION NO. _0100_

AGENT/AGENCY _____

ADDRESS _____

---

1. **DESCRIPTION OF SERVICES:** Producer hereby engages Stunt Performer to render services as _UTILITY STUNT PERFORMER_. Stunt Performer accepts such engagement upon the terms herein specified.

2. **COMPENSATION/TERM/GUARANTEE:** Producer will pay Stunt Performer and Stunt Performer agrees to accept the following three-day compensation (excluding location premiums) of $_____ (and pro rata services). The total guaranteed compensation shall be $ _2,500_ for the total guaranteed period of _THREE (3) DAYS_. If this space is not filled in, the guarantee shall be three (3) days. Stunt Performer shall receive sixth day location premium where applicable.

3. **START DATE:** The term of engagement shall begin on _____.
   or "on or about" * _JULY 21, 19XX_ .

4. **NEXT START DATE:** The start date of Stunt Performer's next engagement is _____.

5. **STUNT ADJUSTMENTS:** It is understood that the rate of compensation specified may be adjusted depending upon the nature of the stunt activities Producer may require. If so, a stunt adjustment will be agreed upon between the parties through good faith bargaining and said adjustment shall be noted on Stunt Performer's daily time report or time card.

   The parties shall agree upon the compensation to be paid before the stunt is performed if they may readily do so; however, it is expressly agreed that production shall not be delayed for the purpose of first determining the compensation for a stunt. Such adjustment shall increase Stunt Performer's compensation for the three-days in the manner prescribed in Schedule H-II or H-III of the Screen Actors Guild Codified Basic Agreement.

6. **INCORPORATION OF PRODUCER-SCREEN ACTORS GUILD COLLECTIVE BARGAINING AGREEMENT:** All provisions of the Screen Actors Guild Codified Basic Agreement as the same may be supplemented and/or amended to date shall be deemed incorporated herein. Stunt Performer's engagement shall include performance in non-commercial openings, closings, bridges, etc., and no added compensation shall be payable to Stunt Performer so long as such are used in the Motion Picture covered hereunder and in which Stunt Performer appears or with respect to which Stunt Performer is paid compensation hereunder. Stunt Performer's engagement shall be upon the terms, conditions and exceptions of said provisions applicable to the rate of compensation specified.

The "on or about" clause may only be used when this Agreement is delivered to Stunt Performer at least three (3) days before the Start Date.

7. **RIGHTS:** Producer shall have the unlimited right throughout the universe and in perpetuity to exhibit the Motion Picture in all media, now or hereafter known, and Producer, as employer-for-hire of Stunt Performer, shall own all rights in the results and proceeds of Stunt Performer's services hereunder.

8. **ADDITIONAL COMPENSATION:** If the Motion Picture covered hereby is exhibited, containing any of the results and proceeds of Stunt Performer's services hereunder, in any of the following media:

   (i) "Free" television reruns in the United States or Canada, or both;
   (ii) Television exhibition anywhere in the universe outside the United States and Canada;
   (iii) Theatrical exhibition anywhere in the universe;
   (iv) Supplemental Market exhibition anywhere in the universe;
   (v) Basic Cable exhibition anywhere in the universe,

   as to each such medium in which the motion picture is so exhibited, Producer will pay, and Stunt Performer will accept as payment in full, the minimum additional compensation provided therefor in the Screen Actors Guild Codified Basic Agreement or Television Agreement, as the case may be, except as compensation in excess of such minimum, if any, has been provided in this Agreement.

9. **CONTINUOUS EMPLOYMENT AND RIGHT TO ROLE (when applicable):** If Stunt Performer portrays a role or has dialogue, Stunt Performer shall be entitled to "continuous employment" and "Right to Role," if any, only to the extent prescribed by the Screen Actors Guild Codified Basic Agreement. Stunt Performer shall receive a separate contract for such services.

10. **MOTION PICTURE AND TELEVISION FUND:** Stunt Performer [does] [does not] hereby authorize Producer to deduct from the compensation hereinabove specified an amount equal to _____ percent of each installment of compensation due Stunt Performer hereunder, and to pay the amount so deducted to the Motion Picture and Television Fund of America, Inc.

11. **WAIVER:** Stunt Performer may not waive any provision of the Screen Actors Guild Codified Basic Agreement or Television Agreement, whichever is applicable, without the written consent of the Screen Actors Guild, Inc.

12. **SIGNATORY:** Producer makes the material representation that either it is presently a signatory to the Screen Actors Guild collective bargaining agreement covering the engagement contracted for herein, or that the Motion Picture is covered by such collective bargaining agreement under the "Independent Production" provisions (Section 24) of the General Provisions of the Screen Actors Guild Codified Basic Agreement.

Signing of this Agreement in the spaces below signifies acceptance by Producer and Stunt Performer of all of the above terms and conditions and those on the reverse hereof and attached hereto, if any, as of the date specified above.

PRODUCER _Swifty Deals_____ STUNT PERFORMER _Arnold Ulim_____

BY ___SWIFTY DEALS_____

Production time reports and/or time cards are available on the set at the beginning and end of each day, which reports and/or time cards shall be signed or initialed by Stunt Performer and must indicate any agreed stunt adjustments.

NOTICE TO STUNT PERFORMER: IT IS IMPORTANT THAT YOU RETAIN A COPY OF THIS AGREEMENT FOR YOUR PERMANENT RECORDS.

SCREEN ACTORS GUILD
STUNT PERFORMER'S
MINIMUM FREELANCE WEEKLY CONTRACT
FOR TELEVISION MOTION PICTURES

THE ARTIST MAY NOT WAIVE ANY PROVISION OF THIS CONTRACT
WITHOUT THE WRITTEN CONSENT OF SCREEN ACTORS GUILD, INC.

STUNT PERFORMER __CLIFF HANGER__ DATE OF AGREEMENT __8·18·XX__
ADDRESS __333 ROSEBUD AVE., APT. #5__
__LOS ANGELES, CA 90035__
TELEPHONE __(310) 555-7732__ SOCIAL SECURITY NO. __123-45-6789__
COMPANY/PRODUCER __XYZ PRODUCTIONS__
PRODUCTION TITLE __HERBY'S SUMMER VACATION__ PRODUCTION NO. __0100__
AGENT/AGENCY ____
ADDRESS ____

1. **DESCRIPTION OF SERVICES**: Producer hereby engages Stunt Performer to render services as
__STUNT DOUBLE__. Stunt Performer accepts such engagement upon the terms
herein specified.

2. **COMPENSATION/TERM/GUARANTEE**: Producer will pay Stunt Performer and Stunt Performer agrees to
accept the following weekly compensation (excluding location premiums) of $ __SCALE__ (and pro rata for each
additional day beyond the guarantee until completion of services). The total guaranteed compensation shall
be $ __SCALE__ for the total guaranteed period of __ONE (1) WEEK__. If this space is not filled
in, the guarantee shall be one (1) week. Stunt Performer shall receive sixth day location premium where
applicable.

3. **START DATE**: The term of engagement shall begin on ____.
or "on or about" * __AUGUST 20, XXXX__.

4. **NEXT START DATE**: The start date of Stunt Performer's next engagement is ____.

5. **STUNT ADJUSTMENTS**: It is understood that the rate of compensation specified may be adjusted depending
upon the nature of the stunt activities Producer may require. If so, a stunt adjustment will be agreed upon
between the parties through good faith bargaining and said adjustment shall be noted on Stunt Performer's
daily time report or time card.

The parties shall agree upon the compensation to be paid before the stunt is performed if they may readily do
so; however, it is expressly agreed that production shall not be delayed for the purpose of first determining
the compensation for a stunt. Such adjustment shall increase Stunt Performer's compensation for the week
in the manner prescribed in Schedule H-II or H-III of the Screen Actors Guild Codified Basic Agreement.

6. **INCORPORATION OF PRODUCER-SCREEN ACTORS GUILD COLLECTIVE BARGAINING AGREEMENT**:
All provisions of the Screen Actors Guild Codified Basic Agreement and Television Agreement as the same
may be supplemented and/or amended to date shall be deemed incorporated herein. Stunt Performer's
engagement shall include performance in non-commercial openings, closings, bridges, etc., and no added
compensation shall be payable to Stunt Performer so long as such are used in the Motion Picture covered
hereunder and in which Stunt Performer appears or with respect to which Stunt Performer is paid
compensation hereunder. Stunt Performer's engagement shall be upon the terms, conditions and
exceptions of said provisions applicable to the rate of compensation and guarantee specified.

* The "on or about" clause may only be used when this Agreement is delivered to Stunt Performer at least three (3) days before
the Start Date.

7. <u>RIGHTS</u>: Producer shall have the unlimited right throughout the universe and in perpetuity to exhibit the Motion Picture in all media, now or hereafter known, and Producer, as employer-for-hire of Stunt Performer, shall own all rights in the results and proceeds of Stunt Performer's services hereunder.

8. <u>ADDITIONAL COMPENSATION</u>: If the Motion Picture covered hereby is exhibited, containing any of the results and proceeds of Stunt Performer's services hereunder, in any of the following media:
   (I) "Free" television reruns in the United States or Canada, or both;
   (ii) Television exhibition anywhere in the universe outside the United States and Canada;
   (iii) Theatrical exhibition anywhere in the universe;
   (iv) Supplemental Market exhibition anywhere in the universe;
   (v) Basic Cable exhibition anywhere in the universe,

   as to each such medium in which the motion picture is so exhibited, Producer will pay, and Stunt Performer will accept as payment in full, the minimum additional compensation provided therefor in the Screen Actors Guild Codified Basic Agreement or Television Agreement, as the case may be, except as compensation in excess of such minimum, if any, has been provided in this Agreement.

9. <u>CONTINUOUS EMPLOYMENT AND RIGHT TO ROLE (when applicable)</u>: If Stunt Performer portrays a role or has dialogue, Stunt Performer shall be entitled to "continuous employment" and "Right to Role," if any, only to the extent prescribed by the Screen Actors Guild Codified Basic Agreement. Stunt Performer shall receive a separate contract for such services.

10. <u>MOTION PICTURE AND TELEVISION FUND</u>: Stunt Performer (does) (does not) hereby authorize Producer to deduct from the compensation hereinabove specified an amount equal to _____ percent of each installment of compensation due Stunt Performer hereunder, and to pay the amount so deducted to the Motion Picture and Television Fund of America, Inc.

11. <u>WAIVER</u>: Stunt Performer may not waive any provision of the Screen Actors Guild Codified Basic Agreement of Television Agreement, whichever is applicable, without the written consent of the Screen Actors Guild, Inc.

12. <u>SIGNATORY</u>: Producer makes the material representation that either it is presently a signatory to the Screen Actors Guild collective bargaining agreement covering the engagement contracted for herein, or that the Motion Picture is covered by such collective bargaining agreement under the "Independent Production" provisions (Section 24) of the General Provisions of the Screen Actors Guild Codified Basic Agreement.

Signing of this Agreement in the spaces below signified acceptance by Producer and Stunt Performer of all of the above terms and conditions hereof and attached hereto, if any, as of the date specified above.

PRODUCER _XYZ PRODUCTIONS_____ STUNT PERFORMER _____

BY _____

Production time reports and/or time cards are available on the set at the beginning and end of each day, which reports and/or time cards shall be signed or initialed by Stunt Performer and must indicate any agreed stunt adjustments.

NOTICE TO STUNT PERFORMER: IT IS IMPORTANT THAT YOU RETAIN A COPY OF THIS AGREEMENT FOR YOUR PERMANENT RECORDS.

THE PERFORMER MAY NOT WAIVE ANY PROVISION OF THIS CONTRACT WITHOUT THE WRITTEN CONSENT OF SCREEN ACTORS GUILD, INC.

 SCREEN ACTORS GUILD

**DAILY CONTRACT
(DAY PERFORMER)
FOR THEATRICAL MOTION PICTURES**

Company _XYZ PRODUCTIONS, INC._   Date _JUNE 10, 19XX_

Date Employment Starts _JUNE 23, 19XX_   Performer Name _HOLLYWOOD MANN_

Production Title _HERBY'S SUMMER VACATION_   Address _3465 HORTENSE ST WONDERLAND, CA 90000_

Production Number _O100_   Telephone No.: _(818) 555-7737_

Role _GEORGE_   Social Security No. _231-56-6789_

Daily Rate $ _1,000_   Legal Resident of (State) _CALIFORNIA_

Weekly Conversion Rate $ _____   Citizen of U.S. ☑ Yes ☐ No

Wardrobe supplied by Performer   Yes ☐   No ☑

COMPLETE FOR "DROP-AND-PICK-UP" DEALS **ONLY**:

Firm recall date on _____

or on or after * _____

("On or after" recall only applies to pick-up as Weekly Performer)

As ☐ Day Performer   ☐ Weekly Performer

*Means date specified or within 24 hours thereafter.

If so, number of outfits _____ @ $_____

(formal) _____ @ $_____

Date of Stunt Performer's next engagement: _____

BILLING: END CREDITS · CO-STARRING FIRST POSITION

The employment is subject to all of the provisions and conditions applicable to the employment of DAY PERFORMER contained or provided for in the Producer-Screen Actors Guild Codified Basic Agreement as the same may be supplemented and/or amended.

The performer (does)[does not] hereby authorize the Producer to deduct from the compensation hereinabove specified an amount equal to _____.5_____ per cent of each installment of compensation due the Performer hereunder, and to pay the amount so deducted to the Motion Picture and Television Relief Fund of America, Inc.

Special Provisions: _____

PRODUCER _Swifty Deals_   PERFORMER _Hollywood Mann_

BY _SWIFTY DEALS_

Production time reports are available on the set at the end of each day. Such reports shall be signed or initialed by the Performer.

Attached hereto for your use is Declaration Regarding Income Tax Withholding.

NOTICE TO PERFORMER: IT IS IMPORTANT THAT YOU RETAIN A COPY OF THIS CONTRACT FOR YOUR PERMANENT RECORDS.

SCREEN ACTORS GUILD

**SCREEN ACTORS GUILD
MINIMUM FREE LANCE CONTRACT
FOR THEATRICAL MOTION PICTURES**

Continuous Employment—Weekly Basis—Weekly Salary
One Week Minimum Employment

THIS AGREEMENT, made this ___2ND___ day of ___MAY___, 19_____, between _____ _____XYZ PRODUCTIONS, INC._____, hereafter called "Producer," and _____CLARK GRABLE_____, hereafter called "Performer."

1. PHOTOPLAY, ROLE, SALARY AND GUARANTEE. Producer hereby engages Performer to render services as such in the role of ___HERBY___, in a photoplay, the working title of which is now HERBY'S SUMMER VACATION, at the salary of $ _2,500_ per "studio week" (Schedule B Performers must receive an additional overtime payment of four (4) hours at straight time rate for each overnight location Saturday). Performer accepts such engagement upon the terms herein specified. Producer guarantees that it will furnish Performer not less than _SIX (6)_ week's employment (if this blank is not filled in, the guarantee shall be one week). Performer shall be paid pro rata for each additional day beyond guarantee until dismissal.

2. TERM: The term of employment hereunder shall begin on

   on _JUNE 1, 19XX_

   on or about* _____

   and shall continue thereafter until the completion of the photography and recordation of said role.

3. BASIC CONTRACT. All provisions of the collective bargaining agreement between Screen Actors Guild, Inc. and Producer, relating to theatrical motion pictures, which are applicable to the employment of the Performer hereunder, shall be deemed incorporated herein.

4. PERFORMER'S ADDRESS. All notices which the Producer is required or may desire to give to the Performer may be given either by mailing the same addressed to the Performer at _1234 FIRST ST. - MALIBU, CA 90272_ or such notice may be given to the Performer personally, either orally or in writing.

5. PERFORMER'S TELEPHONE. The Performer must keep the Producer's casting office or the assistant director of said photoplay advised as to where the Performer may be reached by telephone without unreasonable delay. The current telephone number of the Performer is _(310) 555 - 7332_.

6. MOTION PICTURE AND TELEVISION RELIEF FUND. The Performer [does] [does not] hereby authorize the Producer to deduct from the compensation hereinabove specified an amount equal to _1 (ONE)_ per cent of each installment of compensation due the Performer hereunder, and to pay the amount so deducted to the Motion Picture and Television Relief Fund of America, Inc.

7. FURNISHING OF WARDROBE. The (Producer) (Performer) agrees to furnish all modern wardrobe and wearing apparel reasonably necessary for the portrayal of said role; it being agreed, however, that should so-called "character" or "period" costumes be required, the Producer shall supply the same. When Performer furnishes any wardrobe, Performer shall receive the cleaning allowance and reimbursement, if any, specified in the basic contract.

Number of outfits furnished by Performer _____ @ $_____
(formal) _____ @ $_____

*The "on or about" clause may only be used when the contract is delivered to the Performer at least seven days before the starting date. See Codified Basic Agreement, Schedule B, Schedule C, otherwise a specific starting date must be stated.

8. ARBITRATION OF DISPUTES. Should any dispute or controversy arise between the parties hereto with reference to this contract, or the employment herein provided for, such dispute or controversy shall be settled and determined by conciliation and arbitration in accordance with the conciliation and arbitration provisions of the collective bargaining agreement between the Producer and Screen Actors Guild relating to theatrical motion pictures, and such provisions are hereby referred to and by such reference incorporated herein and made a part of this Agreement with the same effect as though the same were set forth herein in detail.

9. NEXT STARTING DATE. The starting date of Performer's next engagement is _____.

10. The Performer may not waive any provision of this contract without the written consent of Screen Actors Guild, Inc.

11. Producer makes the material representation that either it is presently a signatory to the Screen Actors Guild collective bargaining agreement covering the employment contracted for herein, or that the above-referred-to photoplay is covered by such collective bargaining agreement under the Independent Production provisions of the General Provisions of the Screen Actors Guild Codified Basic Agreement as the same may be supplemented and/or amended.

IN WITNESS WHEREOF, the parties have executed this agreement on the day and year first above written.

PRODUCER _Swifty Deals_   PERFORMER _Clark Gable_ _____

BY _SWIFTY DEALS_ _____ Social Security No. _637-17-6992_ _____

BILLING: MAIN TITLES, SINGLE CARD, FIRST POSITION

Production time reports are available on the set at the end of each day, which reports shall be signed or initialed by the Performer.

Attached hereto for your use are the following: (1) Declaration Regarding Income Tax Withholding ("Part Year Employment Method of Withholding") and (2) Declaration Regarding Income Tax Withholding. You may utilize the applicable form by delivering same to Producer. Only one of such forms may be used.

NOTICE TO PERFORMER: IT IS IMPORTANT THAT YOU RETAIN A COPY OF THIS CONTRACT FOR YOUR PERMANENT RECORDS.

☃ SCREEN ACTORS GUILD
STUNT PERFORMER'S
DAILY CONTRACT
FOR THEATRICAL MOTION PICTURES

THE ARTIST MAY NOT WAIVE ANY PROVISION OF THIS CONTRACT
WITHOUT THE WRITTEN CONSENT OF SCREEN ACTORS GUILD, INC.

STUNT PERFORMER **DARREN DEVILL**   DATE OF AGREEMENT **8·5·XX**

ADDRESS **17602 VINEYARD AVE., APT. 306**

TINSELTOWN, CA 90000

TELEPHONE **(213) 555-1902**   SOCIAL SECURITY NO. **123-45-6789**

COMPANY/PRODUCER **XYZ PRODUCTIONS**

PRODUCTION TITLE **HERBY'S SUMMER VACATION**   PRODUCTION NO. **0100**

AGENT/AGENCY

ADDRESS

DAILY RATE $ **SCALE**   SERIES

WEEKLY CONV. RATE $ START DATE **8-6-XX**

1. **DESCRIPTION OF SERVICES:** Producer hereby engages Stunt Performer to render services as
ND STUNT_____. Stunt Performer accepts such engagement upon the terms
herein specified.

2. **TERM/GUARANTEE:** Producer guarantees to furnish Stunt Performer not less than **2** days
engagement. If this space is not filled in, the guarantee shall be one (1) day.

3. **STUNT ADJUSTMENTS:** It is understood that the rate of compensation specified may be adjusted depending
upon the nature of the stunt activities Producer may require. If so, a stunt adjustment will be agreed upon
between the parties through good faith bargaining and said adjustment shall be noted on Stunt Performer's
daily time report or time card. The parties shall agree upon the compensation to be paid before the stunt is
performed if they may readily do so; however, it is expressly agreed that production shall not be delayed for
the purpose of first determining the compensation for a stunt. Such adjustment shall increase Stunt
Performer's compensation for the day in the manner prescribed in Schedule H of the Screen Actors Guild
Codified Basic Agreement.

4. **INCORPORATION OF PRODUCER-SCREEN ACTORS GUILD COLLECTIVE BARGAINING AGREEMENT:**
All provisions of the Screen Actors Guild Codified Basic Agreement and Television Agreement as the same
may be supplemented and/or amended to date shall be deemed incorporated herein. Stunt Performer's
engagement shall be upon the terms, conditions and exceptions of said provisions applicable to the rate of
compensation and guarantee specified.

5. **RIGHTS:** Producer shall have the unlimited right throughout the universe and in perpetuity to exhibit the
Motion Picture in all media, now or hereafter known, and Producer, as employer-for-hire of Stunt Performer,
shall own all rights in the results and proceeds of Stunt Performer's services hereunder.

6. **ADDITIONAL COMPENSATION:** If the Motion Picture covered hereby is exhibited, containing any of the
results and proceeds of Stunt Performer's services hereunder, in any of the following media:
(i) "Free" television reruns in the United States or Canada, or both;
(ii) Television exhibition anywhere in the universe outside the United States and Canada;
(iii) Theatrical exhibition anywhere in the universe;

as to each such medium in which the motion picture is so exhibited, Producer will pay, and Stunt Performer will
accept as payment in full, the minimum additional compensation provided therefor in the Screen Actors Guild

Codified Basic Agreement, except as compensation in excess of such minimum, if any, has been provided in this Agreement.

7. <u>CONTINUOUS EMPLOYMENT AND RIGHT TO ROLE (when applicable)</u>: If Stunt Performer portrays a role or has dialogue, Stunt Performer shall be entitled to "continuous employment" and "Right to Role," if any, only to the extent prescribed by the Screen Actors Guild Codified Basic Agreement. Stunt Performer shall receive a separate contract for such services.

8. <u>MOTION PICTURE AND TELEVISION FUND</u>: Stunt Performer (does) (does not) hereby authorize Producer to deduct from the compensation hereinabove specified an amount equal to _____ percent of each installment of compensation due Stunt Performer hereunder, and to pay the amount so deducted to the Motion Picture and Television Fund of America, Inc.

9. <u>WAIVER</u>: Stunt Performer may not waive any provision of the Screen Actors Guild Codified Basic Agreement of Television Agreement, whichever is applicable, without the written consent of the Screen Actors Guild, Inc.

10. <u>SIGNATORY</u>: Producer makes the material representation that either it is presently a signatory to the Screen Actors Guild collective bargaining agreement covering the engagement contracted for herein, or that the Motion Picture is covered by such collective bargaining agreement under the "Independent Production" provisions (Section 24) of the General Provisions of the Screen Actors Guild Codified Basic Agreement.

Signing of this Agreement in the spaces below signified acceptance by Producer and Stunt Performer of all of the above terms and conditions hereof and attached hereto, if any, as of the date specified above.

PRODUCER _XYZ PRODUCTIONS_   STUNT PERFORMER _Darren Devil_

BY _Swifty Dale_

Production time reports and/or time cards are available on the set at the beginning and end of each day, which reports and/or time cards shall be signed or initialed by Stunt Performer and must indicate any agreed stunt adjustments.

NOTICE TO STUNT PERFORMER: IT IS IMPORTANT THAT YOU RETAIN A COPY OF THIS AGREEMENT FOR YOUR PERMANENT RECORDS.

THE ARTIST MAY NOT WAIVE ANY PROVISION OF THIS CONTRACT WITHOUT THE WRITTEN CONSENT OF SCREEN ACTORS GUILD, INC.

SCREEN ACTORS GUILD

STUNT PERFORMER'S
MINIMUM FREELANCE WEEKLY CONTRACT
FOR THEATRICAL MOTION PICTURES

STUNT PERFORMER _DANGEROUS DANN_   DATE OF AGREEMENT _JULY 5, 19XX_

ADDRESS _P.O. BOX 9876_

TINSELTOWN, CA 90000

TELEPHONE _(213)555-1136_   SOCIAL SECURITY NO. _961-83-2765_

COMPANY/PRODUCER _XYZ PRODUCTIONS, INC._

PRODUCTION TITLE _HERBY'S SUMMER VACATION_ PRODUCTION NO. _0100_

AGENT/AGENCY _____

ADDRESS _____

_____

1. **DESCRIPTION OF SERVICES:** Producer hereby engages Stunt Performer to render services as _UTILITY STUNT PERFORMER_ . Stunt Performer accepts such engagement upon the terms herein specified.

2. **COMPENSATION/TERM/GUARANTEE:** Producer will pay Stunt Performer and Stunt Performer agrees to accept the following weekly compensation (excluding location premiums) of $ _SCALE_ (and pro rata for each additional day beyond the guarantee until completion of services). The total guaranteed compensation shall be $ _____ for the total guaranteed period of _____ . If this space is not filled in, the guarantee shall be one (1) week. Stunt Performer shall receive sixth day location premium where applicable.

3. **START DATE:** The term of engagement shall begin on _JULY 6, 19XX_ . or "on or about" * _____ .

4. **NEXT START DATE:** The start date of Stunt Performer's next engagement is _____ .

5. **STUNT ADJUSTMENTS:** It is understood that the rate of compensation specified may be adjusted depending upon the nature of the stunt activities Producer may require. If so, a stunt adjustment will be agreed upon between the parties through good faith bargaining and said adjustment shall be noted on Stunt Performer's daily time report or time card.

   The parties shall agree upon the compensation to be paid before the stunt is performed if they may readily do so; however, it is expressly agreed that production shall not be delayed for the purpose of first determining the compensation for a stunt. Such adjustment shall increase Stunt Performer's compensation for the week in the manner prescribed in Schedule H-II or H-III of the Screen Actors Guild Codified Basic Agreement.

6. **INCORPORATION OF PRODUCER-SCREEN ACTORS GUILD COLLECTIVE BARGAINING AGREEMENT:** All provisions of the Screen Actors Guild Codified Basic Agreement as the same may be supplemented and/or amended to date shall be deemed incorporated herein. Stunt Performer's engagement shall be upon the terms, conditions and exceptions of said provisions applicable to the rate of compensation and guarantee specified.

7. **RIGHTS:** Producer shall have the unlimited right throughout the universe and in perpetuity to exhibit the Motion Picture in all media, now or hereafter known, and Producer, as employer-for-hire of Stunt Performer, shall own all rights in the results and proceeds of Stunt Performer's services hereunder.

*The "on or about" clause may only be used when this Agreement is delivered to Stunt Performer at least three (3) days before the Start Date.

8. **ADDITIONAL COMPENSATION:** If the Motion Picture covered hereby is exhibited, containing any of the results and proceeds of Stunt Performer's services hereunder, in any of the following media:

   (i)   "Free" television reruns in the United States or Canada, or both;
   (ii) Television exhibition anywhere in the universe outside the United States and Canada;
   (iii) Theatrical exhibition anywhere in the universe;
   (iv) Supplemental Market exhibition anywhere in the universe;
   (v)   Basic Cable exhibition anywhere in the universe,

   as to each such medium in which the motion picture is so exhibited, Producer will pay, and Stunt Performer will accept as payment in full, the minimum additional compensation provided therefor in the Screen Actors Guild Codified Basic Agreement or Television Agreement, as the case may be, except as compensation in excess of such minimum, if any, has been provided in this Agreement.

9. **CONTINUOUS EMPLOYMENT AND RIGHT TO ROLE (when applicable):** If Stunt Performer portrays a role or has dialogue, Stunt Performer shall be entitled to "continuous employment" and "Right to Role," if any, only to the extent prescribed by the Screen Actors Guild Codified Basic Agreement. Stunt Performer shall receive a separate contract for such services.

10. **MOTION PICTURE AND TELEVISION FUND:** Stunt Performer [does] (does not) hereby authorize Producer to deduct from the compensation hereinabove specified an amount equal to _____ percent of each installment of compensation due Stunt Performer hereunder, and to pay the amount so deducted to the Motion Picture and Television Fund of America, Inc.

11. **WAIVER:** Stunt Performer may not waive any provision of the Screen Actors Guild Codified Basic Agreement or Television Agreement, whichever is applicable, without the written consent of the Screen Actors Guild, Inc.

12. **SIGNATORY:** Producer makes the material representation that either it is presently a signatory to the Screen Actors Guild collective bargaining agreement covering the engagement contracted for herein, or that the Motion Picture is covered by such collective bargaining agreement under the "Independent Production" provisions (Section 24) of the General Provisions of the Screen Actors Guild Codified Basic Agreement.

Signing of this Agreement in the spaces below signifies acceptance by Producer and Stunt Performer of all of the above terms and conditions and those on the reverse hereof and attached hereto, if any, as of the date specified above.

PRODUCER *Swifty Deals* _____ STUNT PERFORMER *Doug von Donn* _____
BY _____ SWIFTY DEALS _____

Production time reports and/or time cards are available on the set at the beginning and end of each day, which reports and/or time cards shall be signed or initialed by Stunt Performer and must indicate any agreed stunt adjustments.

NOTICE TO STUNT PERFORMER: IT IS IMPORTANT THAT YOU RETAIN A COPY OF THIS AGREEMENT FOR YOUR PERMANENT RECORDS.

S-2 (7-92)

SCREEN ACTORS GUILD

PERFORMER CONTRACT FOR INTERACTIVE PROGRAMMING

Company __XYZ PRODUCTIONS, INC.__ Date __AUGUST 23, 19XX__

Production Title __HERBY'S SUMMER VACATION__ Performer Name __FLASH GORDON__

Production Number __0100__ Address __P.O. Box 1237 · HOLLYWOOD, CA__

Date Employment Starts __AUGUST 24, 19XX__ Telephone No.: __(213) 555-6126__

Role __POLICE SGT.__ Social Security No.: __243-76-4432__

Daily Rate $_____ Date of Performer's next engagement _____

3 Day Rate $_____

Weekly Rate $__SCALE__

Special Provisions $_____

_____

Wardrobe supplied by Performer ☐ Yes ☑ No

If so, number of outfits _____ @ $_____

(formal) _____ @ $_____

Complete for "Drop-And-Pick-Up" Deals ONLY:

Firm recall date on _____

or on or after* _____

("On or after" recall only applies to pick-up as
Weekly Performer)

As ☐ Day Performer ☐ Weekly Performer

*Means date specified or within 24 hours thereafter.

THIS AGREEMENT covers the employment of the
above-named Performer by _____XYZ PRODUCTIONS_____
in the production and at the rate of compensation set forth above and is subject to and shall include, for the benefit
of the Performer and the Producer, all of the applicable provisions and conditions contained or provided for in the
applicable Screen Actors Guild Interactive Agreement, and/or the Screen Actors Guild Television Agreement.
Performer's employment shall include performance in non-commercial openings, bridges, etc., and no added
compensation shall be payable to Performer so long as such are used in the role and project(s) covered hereunder
in which Performer appears; for other use, Performer shall be paid the added minimum compensation, if any,
required under the provisions of the Screen Actors Guild agreements with Producer.

Producer shall have all the rights in and to the results and proceeds of the Performer's services rendered
hereunder, as are provided with respect to "photoplays" in Schedule A of the applicable Screen Actors Guild
Codified Basic Agreement and the right to supplemental market use as defined in the Television Agreement.

Producer shall have the unlimited right throughout the world to telecast the film and exhibit the film theatrically and
in supplemental markets in accordance with the terms and conditions of the Television Agreement.

By _Swifty Deals_
                  Producer

Flash Gordon
                  Performer

_243·76·4432_
              Performer's Social Security No.

Production time reports are available on the set at the end of each day, which reports shall be signed or initialed by the Performer.

NOTICE TO PERFORMER: IT IS IMPORTANT THAT YOU RETAIN A COPY OF THIS CONTRACT FOR YOUR
#37A   PERMANENT RECORDS.

SCREEN ACTORS GUILD
TAFT/HARTLEY REPORT

ATTENTION: (CURRENT ADMINISTRATOR OF UNION SECURITY DEPT.)   ATTACHED?: ☑ RESUME* ☑ PHOTO

EMPLOYEE INFORMATION

NAME   GOLDIE LOCKS   SS# 111-22-1111

ADDRESS   433 BEARHOUSE LANE   AGE (IF MINOR) _____

CITY/STATE WOODLAND HILLS, CA ZIP 91364   PHONE (818) 555-6226

EMPLOYER INFORMATION

NAME   XYZ PRODUCTIONS, INC.   Check one: ☐ AD AGENCY
                                                ☐ STUDIO
ADDRESS   1234 FLICK DR.   ☑ PRODUCTION COMPANY

CITY/STATE HOLLYWOOD, CA   ZIP 90038   PHONE ( )

EMPLOYMENT INFORMATION

Check one: CONTRACT: ☑ DAILY   CATEGORY: ☑ ACTOR
                       ☐ 3-DAY   ☐ SINGER   ☐ OTHER
                       ☐ WEEKLY   ☐ STUNT

WORK DATE(S) JULY 26, 19XX   SALARY SCALE

PRODUCTION TITLE HERBY'S SUMMER VACATION PROD'N/COM'L # 0100

SHOOTING LOCATION (City & State) VENICE BEACH, CALIFORNIA

REASON FOR HIRE (be specific) WHILE SHOOTING A SCENE ON THE STRAND AT VENICE BEACH, DIRECTOR DECIDED THAT MORE "LOCAL COLOR" WAS NEEDED TO MAKE THE SCENE MORE COMPLETE. MS. LOCKS, A ROLLER-SKATING STREET PERFORMER OF EXCEPTIONAL ABILITY WHO WAS PERFORMING ON THE STRAND AT THE TIME, WAS ASKED TO PARTICIPATE IN THE SCENE AND TO INTERACT WITH THE FILM'S ACTORS.

Employer is aware of General Provision, Section 14 of the Basic Agreement that applies to Theatrical and Television production, and Schedule B of the Commercials Contract, wherein Preference of Employment shall be given to qualified professional actors (except as otherwise stated). Employer will pay to the Guild as liquidated damages, the sums indicated for each breach by the Employer of any provision of those sections.

SIGNATURE *Swifty Deals*   DATE JULY 26, 19XX
           Producer or Casting Director – Indicate which

PRINT NAME SWIFTY DEALS, PRODUCER   PHONE (213) 555-3331

*PLEASE BE CERTAIN RESUME LISTS ALL TRAINING AND/OR EXPERIENCE IN THE ENTERTAINMENT INDUSTRY.

SAG EXTRA

TAFT/HARTLEY REPORT

ATTENTION: (CURRENT ADMINISTRATOR, OF UNION SECURITY DEPT.)   ATTACHED?: ☑ RESUME   ☑ PHOTO

EMPLOYEE INFORMATION

NAME   CARY GOOPER   SS#   433-27-6327

ADDRESS   103 YORK BLVD.   AGE (IF MINOR) _____

CITY/STATE   LOS ANGELES, CA   ZIP 90000   PHONE (213) 555-6126

EMPLOYER INFORMATION

NAME   XYZ PRODUCTIONS, INC.   Check one: ☐ CASTING OFFICE
                                               ☐ STUDIO
ADDRESS   1234 FLICK DR.   ☑ PRODUCTION COMPANY

CITY/STATE   HOLLYWOOD, CA   ZIP 90038   PHONE (213) 555-3331

EMPLOYMENT INFORMATION

CHECK ONE: General Extra ☐   Special Ability Extra ☑   Dancer ☐

WORK DATE(S)   JULY 22, 19XX   SALARY   SCALE

PRODUCTION TITLE   HERBY'S SUMMER VACATION

SHOOTING LOCATION (City & State)   DOWNTOWN (5TH & BROADWAY) LOS ANGELES

REASON FOR HIRE (be specific)   MR. GOOPER WAS HIRED TO PLAY A
CARD SHARK STREET HUSTLER BECAUSE OF HIS
SPECIAL ABILITY IN "TRICK" CARD DEALING.

_____

_____

_____

Employer is aware of General Provision, Section 14.G of the Screen Actors Guild Codified Basic Agreement of 1989 for Independent Producers as amended that applies to Theatrical and Television production, wherein Preference of Employment shall be given to qualified professional extras (except as otherwise stated). Employer will pay to the Guild as liquidated damages, a sum which shall be determined by binding arbitration for each breach by the Employer of any provision of those sections.

SIGNATURE   *Swifty Deals*   DATE   7·22·XX
            Producer or Casting Director (indicate which)

PRINT NAME   SWIFTY DEALS, PRODUCER   PHONE (213) 555-3331

SCREEN ACTORS GUILD THEATRICAL & TELEVISION SIGN-IN SHEET

PRODUCER: SWIFTY DEALS
PROD'N CO: XYZ PRODUCTIONS
PROD'N OFFICE PHONE # (213) 555-3331

AUDITION DATE: 5-10-XX

CASTING REP: DEE CASTOR
CASTING REP. PHONE: (213) 555-7632
PRODUCTION TITLE: HERBYS SUMMER VACATION
EPISODE: "BOYS NIGHT OUT"

Dee Castor
Casting Director's Signature

CASTING REP:
Please fill in time seen for each actor

(1) NAME	(2) SOCIAL SECURITY	(3) ROLE	(4) AGENT	(5) PROVIDED?		(6) ARRIVAL TIME	(7) APPT. TIME	(8) TIME SEEN (Cast. rep.)	(9) TIME OUT	(10) TAPED?	(11) ACT. INI.
				PARK	SCRIPT						
CLARK GRABLE	332-62-7774	HERBY	JOE COOL	✓	✓	8:55A	9A	9A	9:25A	✓	(init.)
CARY COOPER	523-76-5351	HERBY	HOLLY WOODS	✓	✓	9:30A	9:30A	9:25A	10A		(init.)
JAMES BONDY	237-12-3678	HERBY	RON REPPS	✓	✓	10:05A	10A	10:05A	10:25A		(init.)
MARTY MELROSE	176-42-6104	HERBY	JOE COOL	✓	✓	10:25A	10:30A	10:35A	11:05A		(init.)
SCARLET STARLET	234-36-3721	LAURA	JOE COOL	✓	✓	11:10A	11A	11:15A	11:40A	✓	(init.)
MARY MARVELOUS	542-71-1134	LAURA	RON REPPS	✓	✓	11:30A	11:30A	11:45A	12:10P		(init.)
GOLDIE LOCKS	176-43-7662	LAURA	HOLLY WOODS	✓	✓	11:55A	12P	12:15A	12:35P		(init.)
BEVERLY FAIRFAX	332-27-1341	LAURA	JOE COOL	✓	✓	12:15P	12:30P	12:45A	1:15P		(init.)

SCREEN ACTORS GUILD PERFORMERS PRODUCTION TIME REPORT

Picture Title **HERBY'S SUMMER VACATION** Prod.# **0100** Date **MON, 7-15-XX** Contact **(2ND ASST. DIR.)** Phone No. (XX) **555-3331**

Shooting Location **CITY HALL - DOWNTOWN** Is Today a Designated Day Off? *Yes ___ No ✓___

Please Complete In Ink

WORK - W REHEARSAL - R FITTING - FT TRAVEL - TR
START = S HOLD - H TEST - T FINISH - F

CAST	CHARACTER	W-S-R H-F-T TR-FT	REPORT MAKEUP WDBE.	REPORT TIME Report on set	Dismiss on set	Dismiss Makeup Wardrobe	In ND MEAL	Out	MEALS 1st Meal Start	Finish	2nd Meal Start	Finish	TRAVEL TIME Leave for Location	Arrive on Location	Leave Location	Arrive at Studio	Stunt Adj.	Minors Tutoring Time	Wardrobe No. of Outfits Provided	MPVs	Forced Call	PERFORMER'S SIGNATURE
CLARK GRABLE ✓ MINORS	HERBY	W	7A	7³⁰A	4³⁰P	5P	7³⁰A 7⁴⁵A		1P	1³⁰P									2 Hrs.				Clark Grable
SCARLET STARLET	LAURA	W	6⁵⁰A	7³⁰A	6¹⁵P	6³⁰P	6⁰⁵A 6¹⁵A		1P	1³⁰P			6A	6²⁰A	6³⁰P	7P				1		Scarlett Starlett
ROCKY RIZZO	JAKE	H																				N/A
HOLLYWOOD MANN	GEORGE	WF	8A	8³⁰A	7P	7¹⁵P	8¹⁵A 8³⁰A		1P	1³⁰P										1			[signature]
CLIFF HANGER	ND STUNTS	SWF	8A- 8¹⁵A	8¹⁵A	7P	7¹⁵P	8⁰⁰A 8⁴⁵A		1P	1³⁰P							+$100⁰						Cliff Hanger

SCREEN ACTORS GUILD

CASTING DATA REPORT

#48

THIS FORM MUST BE COMPLETED FOR EACH MOTION PICTURE AND EACH EPISODE OF EACH SERIES PRODUCED FOR THE QUARTER IN WHICH PRINCIPAL PHOTOGRAPHY WAS COMPLETED.

See Reverse For Instructions

1) PRODUCTION COMPANY __XYZ PRODUCTIONS__

2) QUARTER and YEAR __3RD QUARTER - 19XX__

3) PROJECT (Title, Prod. No., etc.) __HERBY'S SUMMER VACATION - #0100__

4) DESCRIPTION (Feature, M.O.W., TV Series, etc.) __FEATURE__

5) TOTAL NO. OF DAYS OF PRODUCTION (Principal Photography Only) __58__

6) DATA SUBMITTED BY __CONNIE COORDINATES__ NAME

TELEPHONE NUMBER __(713) 555-3331__

7) CHECK IF APPROPRIATE [✓] NO STUNTS

PART I

CATEGORY		FORM OF HIRING			CAST TOTALS	NO. OF DAYS WORKED	AGE: UNDER 40	40 and OVER	UNKNOWN
		DAILY	WEEKLY	SERIES	9)	10)			11)
MALE	LEAD		3		3	170	2	1	
	SUPPORT	21			21	84	11	9	1
FEMALE	LEAD		2		2	100	2		
	SUPPORT	16			16	48	11	5	

8)

PART II

CATEGORY		FORM OF HIRING DAILY M	F	WEEKLY M	F	SERIES M	F	NO. OF DAYS WORKED M	F	AGE UNDER 40 M	F	40 and OVER M	F	UNKNOWN M	F
ASIAN/PACIFIC	LEAD	2						58	15	1	3				
	SUPPORT				3			10	50	2	1				
BLACK	LEAD	3		1	1			58	18	1	3				
	SUPPORT				3			17			1				
CAUCASIAN	LEAD	9		1	1			54	50		5		5		
	SUPPORT				10			50	15	9	5				
LATINO / HISPANIC	LEAD														
	SUPPORT	5						5		4			1		
N. AMERICAN INDIAN	LEAD														
	SUPPORT														
UNKNOWN / OTHER	LEAD														
	SUPPORT	2						2		2					

12) 13) 14)

INSTRUCTIONS

(After reading the following, if you have any further questions, please call 213/549-6644.) (For your convenience, our fax number is 213/549-6647.)

1. Indicate the name of the signatory Production Company (e.g., "THE ABC COMPANY").

2. Indicate the quarter/year when **principal photography** was completed (e.g., "1st quarter 1981"). Make one report only for full project even though it might span more than one quarter.

    The quarters consist of:

January	-	March	(1st)
April	-	June	(2nd)
July	-	September	(3rd)
October	-	December	(4th)

3. Indicate the <u>name</u> of the film for which you are reporting.

4. Indicate the <u>type</u> of project (feature, television movie, television pilot, television series, animation.

5. Use a number to respond to this question.

6. Indicate the name of person completing this form and the telephone number for same.

7. Two separate reports are required, one for <u>Performers</u> only and one for <u>Stunt Performers</u> only. If there were no Stunt Performers employed on the film, check the "No Stunt" box. If Stunt Performers were employed, complete the casting data report form for Stunt Performers.

8. **Part I.** Indicate the total number of lead and supporting Performers in each of the applicable categories. Series performers column is provided for episodic TV shows only. Daily column is for daily contract & 3-day contract performers only. Weekly column is for weekly contract and run-of-the-picture performers. A day contract performer upgraded to a weekly contract performer in a drop/pick-up situation should be listed in the weekly column (**do <u>not</u> count** the performer twice).

9. Use numbers only to indicate the total number of Performers in the category.

10. Use numbers only to indicate the total number of days worked by <u>ALL</u> Performers in the category. (Include all days paid for including hold, rehearsal days, etc.)

11. Use numbers only to indicate how many Performers were in each age group.

12. **Part II.** Indicate the total number of males and females in each category.

13. Use number only to indicate the total number of days worked by <u>ALL</u> the Performers in male and female category.

14. Use numbers only to indicate how many Performers were in each age group.

<u>NOTE</u>: PLEASE MAKE EVERY EFFORT TO INSURE THAT YOUR NUMBERS CORRESPOND ACROSS AND AMONG <u>PART I AND PART II.</u>

#48B

SCREEN ACTORS GUILD

CASTING DATA REPORT FOR STUNT PERFORMERS ONLY

THIS FORM MUST BE COMPLETED FOR EACH MOTION PICTURE AND EACH EPISODE OF EACH SERIES PRODUCED FOR THE QUARTER IN WHICH PRINCIPAL PHOTOGRAPHY WAS COMPLETED.

See Reverse For Instructions

1) PRODUCTION COMPANY   XYZ PRODUCTIONS, INC.
2) QUARTER and YEAR   3RD QUARTER, 19XX
3) PROJECT (Title, Prod. No., etc.)   HERBY'S SUMMER VACATION
4) DESCRIPTION (Feature, M.O.W., TV Series, etc.)   MOW
5) TOTAL NO. OF DAYS OF PRODUCTION (Principal Photography Only) 30

6) DATA SUBMITTED BY   CONNIE COORDINATES
   NAME
   TELEPHONE NUMBER   (213) 555-3331
7) NAME OF STUNT COORDINATOR   CLIFF HANGER

PART I

CATEGORY	8) DAILY	WEEKLY	SERIES	9) PERFORMER TOTALS	10) NUMBER DAYS WORKED	11) AGE UNDER 40	40 AND OVER	UNKNOWN	12) STUNT SUMMARY DESCRIPT	NON-DESCRIPT
MALE	6	2		8	31	3	4	1	4	4
FEMALE	2	1		3	13	2	1		2	1

PART II

CATEGORY	13) DAILY M	DAILY F	WEEKLY M	WEEKLY F	SERIES M	SERIES F	14) DAYS M	DAYS F	15) UNDER 40 M	UNDER 40 F	40 AND OVER M	40 AND OVER F	UNKNOWN M	UNKNOWN F	16) DESCRIPT M	DESCRIPT F	NON-DESCRIPT M	NON-DESCRIPT F
ASIAN/PACIFIC	1						1		1						1			
BLACK	1	1	1				17	2	1	1			1		1		1	1
CAUCASIAN	3	1	1				11	1	1	1	3				2	1	2	
LATINO / HISPANIC				1				10				1				1		
N. AMERICAN INDIAN	1						2				1						1	
OTHER / UNKNOWN																		

Unions & Guilds   177

STUNT INSTRUCTIONS

**There are two separate report forms required.
Complete one report for Performers and one report for Stunt Performers.

(After reading the following, if you have any further questions, please call 213/549-6644.) (For your convenience, our fax number is 213/549-6647.)

1. Indicate the Production Company (e.g., "THE ABC COMPANY").

2. Indicate the quarter/year (e.g., "1st quarter 1981").

    The quarters consist of:

January	-	March	(1st)
April	-	June	(2nd)
July	-	September	(3rd)
October	-	December	(4th)

3. Indicate the <u>name</u> of the film for which you are reporting.

4. Indicate the <u>type</u> of project (feature, television movie, television pilot, television series, animation.

5. Use a number to respond to this question.

6. Indicate the name of person completing this form and the telephone number for same.

7. Provide the name of the stunt coordinator for the film.

Part I

8. Indicate the total number of males and females in each category.

9. Use numbers only to indicate the total number of stunt performers in the category.

10. Use numbers only to indicate the total amount of days worked by all stunt performers in the category.

11. Use numbers only to indicate how many stunt performers are in a certain age group.

12. Use numbers only to indicate the stunts as **descript*** or **non-descript***.

    *Descript   =   A stunt performer who doubles for an actor.

    *Non-descript =   A stunt performer doing a utility or faceless stunt.

Part II

13. Indicate the total number of males and females in each category.

14. Use numbers only to indicate the total number of days worked by <u>all</u> the Performers in each category.

15. Use numbers only to indicate how many performers were in each age group.

16. Indicate the stunts as descript or non-descript.

NOTE: Please make every effort to insure that your numbers correspond across categories and among <u>Part I</u> <u>and Part II</u>.

SCREEN ACTORS GUILD

LOW-BUDGET AFFIRMATIVE ACTION CASTING DATA REPORT

See Reverse For Instructions

THIS FORM MUST BE COMPLETED FOR EACH MOTION PICTURE AND EACH EPISODE OF EACH SERIES PRODUCED FOR THE QUARTER IN WHICH PRINCIPAL PHOTOGRAPHY WAS COMPLETED.

1) PRODUCTION COMPANY XYZ PRODUCTIONS, INC.
2) QUARTER and YEAR 4TH QUARTER - 19XX
3) PROJECT (Title, Prod. No., etc.) HERBY'S SUMMER VACATION
4) DESCRIPTION (Feature, M.O.W., TV Series, etc.) FEATURE
5) TOTAL NO. OF DAYS OF PRODUCTION (Principal Photography Only) 36

6) DATA SUBMITTED BY CONNIE COORDINATES NAME
   TELEPHONE NUMBER (213) 555-3331
7) CHECK IF APPROPRIATE ☑ NO STUNTS

PART I

CATEGORY		8) DAILY	FORM OF HIRING WEEKLY	SERIES	9) CAST TOTALS	10) NO. OF DAYS WORKED	11) AGE UNDER 40	40 TO 60	60 & OVER
MALE	LEAD		1		1	36		1	
	SUPPORT	6	1		7	37	4	1	2
FEMALE	LEAD		2		2	68	2		
	SUPPORT	4	1		5	18	2	2	1

PART II

CATEGORY		12) DAILY M	DAILY F	WEEKLY M	WEEKLY F	SERIES M	SERIES F	13) DAYS M	DAYS F	14) UNDER 40 M	UNDER 40 F	40 TO 60 M	40 TO 60 F	60 & OVER M	60 & OVER F
ASIAN/PACIFIC	LEAD	1						3	2	1					
	SUPPORT		1						32	1			1		
BLACK	LEAD	2						3	2		1				
	SUPPORT	1						36	36	1	1		1		
CAUCASIAN	LEAD	3	1					6	11	2		1			
	SUPPORT	1	2					25	3	1			1	1	1
LATINO / HISPANIC	LEAD		1							1	1				
	SUPPORT														
N. AMERICAN INDIAN	LEAD														
	SUPPORT														
UNKNOWN / OTHER	LEAD														
	SUPPORT														

Unions & Guilds 179

INSTRUCTIONS

1. Indicate the Production Company (e.g., "THE ABC COMPANY").

2. Indicate the quarter/year (e.g., "1st quarter 1981").

   The quarters consist of:

January	–	March	(1st)
April	–	June	(2nd)
July	–	September	(3rd)
October	–	December	(4th)

3. Indicate the <u>name</u> of the film for which you are reporting.

4. Indicate the <u>type</u> of project (feature, television movie, television pilot, television series, animation).

5. Use a number to respond to this question.

6. Indicate the name of person completing this form and the telephone number for same.

7. Two separate reports are required, one for <u>Performers</u> only and one for <u>Stunt Performers</u> only. If there were no Stunt Performers employed on the film, check the "No Stunt" box. If Stunt Performers were employed, complete the casting data report form for Stunt Performers.

8. <u>Part I</u>. Indicate the total number of lead and supporting Performers in each of the applicable categories.

9. Use numbers only to indicate the total number of Performers in the category.

10. Use numbers only to indicate the total number of days worked by <u>ALL</u> Performers in the category.

11. Use numbers only to indicate how many Performers were in each age group.

12. <u>Part II</u>. Indicate the total number of males and females in each category.

13. Use number only to indicate the total number of days worked by <u>ALL</u> the Performers in male and female category.

14. Use numbers only to indicate how many performers were in each age group.

**<u>NOTE</u>: PLEASE MAKE EVERY EFFORT TO INSURE THAT YOUR NUMBERS CORRESPOND ACROSS AND AMONG <u>PART I AND PART II.</u>

FINAL CAST LIST INFORMATION SHEET

#10

DATE FILED: 8·2·XX

PICTURE TITLE HERBY'S SUMMER VACATION

SHOOTING LOCATION LOS ANGELES, CALIF.

PRODUCTION COMPANY XYZ PRODUCTIONS

START DATE 6·1·XX   COMPLETION DATE 7·30·XX

ADDRESS 1234 FLICK DR. - HOLLYWOOD CA 90038

FEDERAL I.D. #   STATE I.D. #

PHONE (213) 555-3331 CONTACT CONNIE COORDINATES

PICTURE # 0100

DISTRIBUTOR MIRACLE PICTURES

Check One: MP ☑   MOW ☐   OTHER TV ☐   INDUSTRIAL ☐   OTHER ☐

To establish Residual payments, see Section 5.2 of the 1980 Basic Agreement.

PLAYER NAME & SOCIAL SECURITY NUMBER	PLAYER ADDRESS INCLUDING ZIP	PERIOD WORKED (1) DYS	PERIOD WORKED (1) WKS	(1) START DATE	(1) FINISH DATE	(2) CONTRACT TYPE	(3) PLAYER TYPE	(4) TOTAL GROSS SALARY	(5) BASE SALARY	TIME UNITS	SALARY UNITS	TOTAL UNITS	FOR SAG USE ONLY
CLARK GRABLE 332·62·7749	1234 FIRST STREET MALIBU CA 90272		6	6/1	7/12	W	A	$14,325—	$2,000— PER WK.				
SCARLET STARLET 823·76·7737	555 SCHOOL STREET HOLLYWOOD CA 90038		3	6/1	6/19	W	A	$5,860—	$1,876— PER WK.				
GOLDIE LOCKS 111·22·3333	453 BEARHOUSE LANE WOODLAND HILLS CA 91364	1		7/26	7/26	D	A	$540—	$540— PER DAY				
DANGEROUS DANN 332·42·9759	P.O. BOX 456 LOS ANGELES, CA 90000		1	7/6	7/10	W	ST	$2851—	$876— PER WK.				
JOHNNY ROCKETT 552·11·7627	123 HOLLYWOOD HILLS RD. HOLLYWOOD, CA 90028	3		6/25	6/29	D	ST	$2100—	$540— PER DAY				

(1) Include days not worked, but considered worked under continuous employment provisions. Report contractually guaranteed work period or actual time worked, whichever is longer.
(2) Insert D for Daily or W for Weekly type of contract.
(3) Insert: A = Actor; ST = Stunt; P = Pilot; SG = Singer; ADR = Automated Dialogue Replacement.
(4) Include all salary, Overtime, Premium, and Stunt Adjustments. Do not include any Penalties paid (e.g., Meal Penalties, Forced Calls, etc.).
(5) List base contractual salary (e.g., $1,500.00/week or $500.00/day).

To establish Residual payments, see Section 5.2 of the 1980 Basic Agreement.

PLAYER NAME & SOCIAL SECURITY NUMBER	PLAYER ADDRESS INCLUDING ZIP	PERIOD WORKED (1) # DYS	# WKS	START DATE (1)	FINISH DATE (1)	CONTRACT TYPE (2)	PLAYER TYPE (3)	TOTAL GROSS SALARY (4)	BASE SALARY (5)	TIME UNITS	SALARY UNITS	TOTAL UNITS	FOR SAG USE ONLY

(1) Include days not worked, but considered worked under continuous employment provisions. Report contractually guaranteed work period or actual time worked, whichever is longer.
(2) Insert D for Daily or W for Weekly type of contract.
(3) Insert: A = Actor; ST = Stunt; P = Pilot; SG = Singer; ADR = Automated Dialogue Replacement.
(4) Include all salary, Overtime, Premium, and Stunt Adjustments. Do not include any Penalties paid (e.g., Meal Penalties, Forced Calls, etc.).
(5) List base contractual salary (e.g., $1,500.00/week or $500.00/day).

(THIS FORM IS USED FOR THOSE PERFORMERS NOT EMPLOYED DURING PRINCIPAL PHOTOGRAPHY OR FOR THOSE NOT "LOOPING" THEIR OWN ROLE.)

SCREEN ACTORS GUILD
MEMBER REPORT
ADR THEATRICAL/TELEVISION

It is the responsibility of the reporting member to file a copy of this report with the Screen Actors Guild within forty-eight (48) hours of each session and to deliver a copy to the employer or the employer's representative at the conclusion of each session. If there is a contractor, he shall assume these responsibilities with respect to each session.

Work Date __8/20/XX__   Title __HERBY'S SUMMER VACATION__

Episode Title __BOYS NIGHT OUT__   Prod. No. __0100__

Production Co./Employer __XYZ PRODUCTIONS__

Address __1234 FLICK DR.__

__HOLLYWOOD, CA__

__90038__

Phone # __(213) 555-3331__

Studio Facility __ABC SOUND SERVICES__

Address __9123 VINE ST.__

__HOLLYWOOD, CA__

__90028__

Phone # __(213) 555-9000__

Sound Supervisor Editor __DAN DUBBER__

Sound Engineer/Mixer __LARRY LOOPER__

ADR Supervisor __SCOTT SOUNDER__

Employer Rep. __PAULA POST__

Type of Film: Theatrical ☐   TV Series ☑   TV MOW ☐   TV Pilot ☐   Other _____

Performer's Name	Performer's Social Security #	Character of 6+ Lines (sync)	Additional sets of up to 3 characters under 5 sync lines each	Hours Employed Studio Time Report/Dismiss	Meal Period From/To	Performer's Initials
BOB HOPEFULL	332-62-7749	BALL GAME ANNOUNCER	—	7A - 11A	—	BH
ROBERT BLUFORD	432-76-7737	—	BALL GAME SPECTATOR	10A - 4P	1-1:30P	RB
LORETTA OLDER	372-44-2232	—	"	10A - 4P	1-1:30P	LO
RICKY MOONEY	173-21-6342	—	"	10A - 4P	1-1:30P	RM
BRANDON MARLOW	519-36-2173	PITCHER	—	3P - 6P	—	BM

Reel #s Recorded: __#4__

NOTES: _____

This engagement shall be governed by and be subject to the applicable terms of the Screen Actors Guild Codified Basic or Television Agreement.

Production Co./EMPLOYER __XYZ PRODUCTIONS, INC.__

Signature of Employer or Employer Representative __Paula Post__, __POST PRODUCTION SUPERVISOR__

SAG Reporter _____ (Print name) _____

SAG Reporter's Phone # (___) _____ Date _____

SCHEDULE A – EXHIBIT I

DIRECTORS GUILD OF AMERICA
WEEKLY WORK LIST

From: _XYZ PRODUCTIONS_
(signatory company)
1234 FLICK DR.
(address)
HOLLYWOOD, CA 90038

Return to:
Directors Guild of America, Inc.

Week Ending: _6·12·XX_

Name	Soc. Sec. #	Cat.	Project
SID CELLULOID	123·45·6789	DIRECTOR	HERBY'S SUMMER VACATION
FRED FILMER	234·56·7890	UPM	
ALICE DEES	456·78·9012	1ST ASST. DIR.	
WILL LIGHT	567·89·0123	2ND ASST DIR.	
LAURA LAS PALMAS	678·90·1233	2ND, 2ND A.D.	

CONNIE COORDINATES
Prepared by

_(213) 555-3331_
Phone #

RC314/031489

DGA EMPLOYMENT DATA REPORT

DATE: _8·2·XX_   PREPARED BY: _FRED FILMER_   PHONE #: _(213)555-3331_

SIGNATORY COMPANY: _XYZ PRODUCTIONS_

QUARTER COVERED: _3RD_

PROJECT: _HERBY'S SUMMER VACATION_

DIRECTOR

	C	B	H	A	AI	UNKNOWN
MALE		/				
FEMALE						

UNIT PRODUCTION MANAGER

	C	B	H	A	AI	UNKNOWN
MALE	/					
FEMALE						

FIRST ASSISTANT DIRECTOR

	C	B	H	A	AI	UNKNOWN
MALE						
FEMALE		/				

SECOND ASSISTANT DIRECTOR

	C	B	H	A	AI	UNKNOWN
MALE	/					
FEMALE			/			

FIRST TIME DIRECTOR

	C	B	H	A	AI	UNKNOWN
MALE						
FEMALE						

The minority codes utilized in this report represent the following:

C	-	CAUCASIAN
B	-	BLACK
H	-	HISPANIC
A	-	ASIAN
AI	-	AMERICAN INDIAN

When completing this report the employment statistics must be reported in order that two (2) types of statistics can be obtained; the first statistic will indicate the number of persons employed in the respective category (referenced above) during that quarter. The second statistic will indicate the number of days worked or guaranteed in the respective categories for that quarter. Therefore in each category, there will be two (2) separate sets of statistics, one on top of the other, separated by a horizontal slash (example below). The top statistic will represent the number of employees working, the bottom statistic will be the number of days worked or guaranteed during the same quarter.

Example:

DIRECTOR

	C	B	H	A	AI	UNKNOWN
MALE	1/56					
FEMALE		1/25				

In the above example there was one (1) male Caucasian Director working during the quarter for a total of fifty-six (56) days worked or guaranteed. There was one (1) female Black Director working for a total of twenty-five days worked or guaranteed.

This report is to be submitted on a per-production basis not on a per episode basis. In instances where the same DGA employee is employed for multiple episodes in a continuing series, such employee will only be counted once in the number of employee statistics but such employee's cumulative days worked shall be included in that statistic.

NOTICE OF TENTATIVE WRITING CREDITS - THEATRICAL

TO: Writers Guild of America, west, Inc. 7000 West Third Street, Los Angeles, CA 90048, or to:
Writers Guild of America, East, Inc. 555 West 57th Street, New York, NY 10019

AND

Participating Writer(s) (or current agent, if participant so elects)

NAMES OF PARTICIPATING WRITER(S)   ADDRESS(ES)

F. SCOTT RYDER   9336 W. STOREY ST.
                                          STUDIO VILLAGE, CA 91604

TITLE OF MOTION PICTURE: HERBY'S SUMMER VACATION
EXECUTIVE PRODUCER: HARRY HONCHO
PRODUCER: SWIFTY DEALS
DIRECTOR: SID CELLULOID
OTHER PRODUCTION EXECUTIVE(S), AND THEIR TITLE(S),
IF PARTICIPATING WRITER(S):

Writing Credits on this production are tentatively determined as follows:

ON SCREEN: SCREENPLAY BY F. SCOTT RYDER

ON SCREEN SOURCE MATERIAL CREDIT, IF ANY: FROM A STORY BY
AARON COUNTRYMAN
ON SCREEN AND/OR IN ADVERTISING, presentation and production credit, IF ANY:

SOURCE MATERIAL upon which the motion picture is based, IF ANY:

The final shooting script is being sent to all participating writers with the notice of tentative writing credits.

The above tentative writing credits will become final unless a protest is communicated to the undersigned not later than 6:00 p.m. on 5·31·XX .

Company: XYZ PRODUCTIONS   By: _Swifty Deals_
                                    Name: SWIFTY DEALS, PRODUCER
                                    Address: 1234 FLICK DR.
                                             HOLLYWOOD, CA 90038
Date: 5·12·XX   Phone No: 555-3331

NOTICE OF TENTATIVE WRITING CREDITS - TELEVISION

Date **5·31·XX**

TO: Writers Guild of America, west, Inc. 7000 West Third Street, Los Angeles, CA 90048, or to:
Writers Guild of America, East, Inc. 555 West 57th Street, New York, NY 10019

AND

Participating Writers

NAMES OF PARTICIPATING WRITERS	ADDRESS
JASON PENN	1723 LANCASTER RD. - LOS ANGELES, CA
SAMUEL INKK	313 FONDA CT. RD. - BEVERLY HILLS, CA

Title of Episode **BOYS NIGHT OUT**   Production# **0100**
(If Pilot or MOW or other special or unit program, indicate Network and length)

Series Title **HERBY'S SUMMER VACATION**
Producing Company **XYZ PRODUCTIONS**
Executive Producer **HARRY HONCHO**
Producer **SWIFTY DEALS**   Assoc. Producer **ADAM DARK**
Director **SID CELLULOID**   Story Editor **JACKIE MILLER**
(or Consultant)

Other Production Executives, If Participating Writers _____

Writing Credits on this episode are tentatively determined as follows:

ON SCREEN: **WRITTEN BY JASON PENN & SAMUEL INKK**

Source material credit ON THIS EPISODE (on separate card, unless otherwise indicated) if any:

Continuing source material or Created By credit APPEARING ON ALL EPISODES OF SERIES (on separate card): **CREATED BY WILLIAM LIGHT**

Revised final script was sent to participating writers on **JUNE 1, 20XX**

The above tentative credits will become final unless a protest is communicated to the undersigned not later than 6:00 p.m. on **JUNE 12, 20XX** .

XYZ PRODUCTIONS
(Company)

By **Swifty Deals**

CHAPTER ELEVEN

Principal Talent

FOLLOW-THROUGH AFTER AN ACTOR HAS BEEN SET

Once an actor has been set for a particular role, the casting office should send a booking slip to the actor's agent verifying the role, a minimum guaranteed number of days or weeks of employment and salary. A booking slip should be issued no later than the day preceding the actor's first day of employment. If engagement occurs after 6:00 P.M. of the day prior to the start of work, the booking slip may be included with the script.

Casting will notify production of the actor's name, address and phone number, and the actor's agent's name and phone number. Production then (1) notifies Wardrobe of the actor's name and phone number, (2) sends the actor a script and (3) arranges a physical examination for insurance purposes (if applicable).

The production office will request a certain number of head shots of each performer, and if the agent cannot supply enough eight-by-tens, high-quality (color) copies should be made to supplement what is needed. One copy stays on file in the production office, and others are distributed to Assistant Directors, Wardrobe, Hair, Makeup, Special Makeup Effects (if prosthetics are required), Extra Casting (as a guide in locating suitable stand-ins and photo doubles), the Stunt Coordinator (as a guide in locating appropriate stunt doubles) and to the Unit Publicist. Depending on the amount of prep time needed and the availability of a performer, Hair, Makeup and Special Makeup Effects should be notified of cast bookings as soon as possible, so wig fittings, hair coloring and/or body molds can be scheduled as needed.

A deal memo (which outlines the terms of the actor's employment on a particular film) is issued by the casting office and copies are sent to a predetermined distribution list. When the entire cast has been set, the casting office (or production office) will issue a final cast list. Partial cast lists should be done prior to all roles being set. (See Chapter 5, "Pre-Production," for a sample cast list.) A cast list should be sent to your SAG representative as soon as a majority of the roles have been set.

Cast lists should also be sent to a predetermined distribution list. Make sure cast lists are given to your wardrobe, hair, makeup and transportation people. Some cast lists may contain an additional column containing the actors' deals, but those are only to be given to a select few: the producer, production manager, assistant directors, production coordinator and production accountant. Actors' deals are not for general distribution.

A final cast list, detailed on the designated SAG Final Cast List Information Sheet, is to be submitted to the Screen Actors Guild no later than 120 days after the completion of principal photography or 90 days after the completion of post production, whichever is sooner. (If the guild is holding a security deposit, the final cast list is submitted directly after the last performer's payroll following principal photography.)

Contracts for lead talent are often prepared by the production company's legal affairs department or by the company's entertainment attorney. The casting office generally prepares standard SAG contracts (although sometimes they are prepared and sent out from the production office) with all company related riders and appropriate tax (W-4 and I-9) forms attached. Weekly and three-day player contracts are sent directly to the respective agents, with a cover letter instructing them as to where to return the contract once it has been signed by their client. Be sure all lines, spaces, boxes, etc. that need to be signed or initialed by the actor are clearly indicated with red Xs and/or paper clips to mark the spot.

The following is a sample of a cover letter that would be sent to agents with a client's contract (also enclosed would be any applicable rider[s]; all payroll forms; and a self-addressed, stamped, return envelope):

Today's Date
Agent's Name
Name of Agency
Address
City, State Zip

Dear (Agent's Name):

Enclosed please find an agreement for (actor's name)'s services on ("name of project"). Please have (him or her) sign the contract where indicated and complete the attached payroll start slip, W-4 and I-9 forms. We would appreciate it if you would send I-9 verification at the time you return the signed agreement (a copy of a driver's license and social security card or passport).

Enclosed is a self-addressed, stamped envelope for your convenience. In addition to the contract and payroll forms, please return a check authorization form if you wish (name of actor)'s checks to be sent directly to your office.

Once the contract is fully executed, a copy will be returned to you for your files. If you have any questions, please do not hesitate to call me at (production office phone number).

Sincerely yours,

If an actor does not have an agent, the contract should be sent directly to the actor and the cover letter should read:

Today's Date
Actor's Name
Address
City, State Zip

Dear (Actor's Name):

Enclosed please find an agreement for your services on ("name of project"). Please sign the contract where indicated and complete the attached

---

payroll start slip, W-4 and I-9 forms. We would appreciate it if you would send I-9 verification at the time you return the signed agreement (a copy of a drivers license and social security card or passport).

Enclosed is a self-addressed, stamped envelope for your convenience. Once the contract is fully executed, a copy will be returned to you for your files. If you have any questions, please do not hesitate to call me at (production office phone number).

Sincerely yours,

Day player contracts are often prepared with the work date left off and given to the production coordinator. The date may be filled in the evening before an actor works and the contract sent to the set the next day for signature. Standard employment contracts must be available for signature no later than the first day of employment. Be careful when communicating with a day player if there is a chance that the part may be canceled. Sending an actor a script (or sides) and/or having wardrobe contact the actor, constitutes an engagement, even if a firm work date has not yet been given and a contract has not yet been drawn up.

Stunt performer contracts are generally prepared and sent out from the production office. Specific SAG contracts exist for the employment of stunt players.

The casting office will Station 12 each actor (a SAG procedure to make sure the actors are in good standing with the guild) prior to reporting for work. The production office should Station 12 all actors (such as stunt performers) whose contracts originate from the production office and have not already been checked through the casting office. The burden is on the production company (and not the actor) to notify the Guild of all SAG performers it is employing prior to their start dates. Not only should calls be made to the Guild to Station 12 actors, but verification calls from the Guild back to the casting or production office clearing each performer should be monitored to make sure that all are okayed to work.

Reasons that performers may not be cleared through Station 12 might be (1) they are delinquent in the payment of guild dues and must pay up before being allowed to work; (2) they must be "Taft/Hartleyed" or they may fall under the category of "must join" status for membership (after being Taft/Hartleyed once before). It is therefore advantageous to clear an actor through Station 12 as soon as possible, so these additional steps (if necessary) can be taken. The fine for not clearing a performer who is not in good standing with the guild is presently $500.

Once a contract has been signed by an actor, it should be returned to the production coordinator. A copy of each contract, all accompanying W-4s and I-9s and a copy of the Exhibit G (officially called the Actors Production Time Report), which includes the actors' signatures for each day of filming, is to be turned in to the production accountant. Note that a payroll check cannot be withheld from an actor who has not yet signed a contract as long as the actor has submitted a W-4 and I-9.

Make sure the actors' work times listed on the Exhibit G are the same as the times listed on the Daily Production Report, and that the actors' signatures on the report are in ink. The top (original) copies of the SAG Time Sheets should be sent to SAG approximately once a week (to the attention of their production department). A photocopy of each time sheet should be attached to the corresponding Daily Production Report.

The production coordinator will have the producer sign the SAG contracts after they have been signed by the actors and will then distribute all fully executed copies. The white (original) copy should be sent to your production executive for the company's legal files. Subsequent copies are for the production files, the production accountant and the actor's agent (or the actor if the actor does not have an agent). A copy of each contract should also be sent to SAG.

The following is a sample of a short letter that would accompany a copy of a fully executed contract that is returned to each respective agent:

Today's Date
Agent's Name
Name of Agency
Address
City, State Zip

Dear (Agent's Name):

Enclosed you will find a fully executed copy of (actor)'s contract for (his or her) services on ("name of project"). If you have any questions, please do not hesitate to call me.

Sincerely,

Again, if the performer has no agent, the letter should read as follows:

Today's Date
Actor's Name
Address
City, State Zip

Dear (Actor's Name):

Enclosed you will find a fully executed copy of your contract for your services on ("name of project"). If you have any questions, please do not hesitate to call me.

Sincerely,

All script revisions are to be sent to actors via the production office.

WORK CALLS

The assistant director will give all "first" work calls to the casting office. They, in turn, will call all respective agents with detailed information as to time, location and scenes to be shot the following day. The assistant director will usually follow-through and call the actors that evening to confirm that they have received calls from their agents and have been given the proper information. The assistant director will also handle all work calls other than first calls.

If actors call the production or casting office to find out their calls for the next day, they should be informed as to what the call sheet reads—but it must be made clear that this is not a final call and is subject to change. Remind all actors that the assistant director will call them each evening with a definite work call for the next day.

Production should make sure casting gets a call sheet each day and is kept up to date on all schedule changes. Your SAG representative should be informed of schedule changes as well.

PERFORMER CATEGORIES

SAG members are classified by category as follows:

- Schedule A: Day performers
- Schedules B and C: Freelance weekly performers (determined by the amount of compensation paid to the performer)
- Schedule D: Multiple-picture performers
- Schedules E and F: Contract performers (determined by the amount of compensation)

- Schedule G-I: Professional singers employed by the day
- Schedule G-II: Professional singers employed by the week (a professional singer is a person who is employed primarily to sing a set piece of music on a given pitch, either as a solo or in a group requiring unison, melody and harmony)
- Schedule H-I: Stunt performers employed by the day
- Schedules H-II and H-III: Stunt performers employed by the week (depending on their salary)
- Schedule H-IV: Stunt performers under term contracts
- Schedule I: Airline pilots—a pilot who is employed to fly or taxi aircraft (including helicopters) before the camera in the photographing of motion pictures
- Schedule J: Dancers—a performer who is professionally-trained, doing choreographed routines requiring rehearsals, such as ballet, chorus dancing, modern dance, tap dancing, jazz dancing, acrobatic dancing or skating
- Schedule K-I: Stunt coordinators employed by the day at less than the "flat deal" minimum
- Schedule K-II: Stunt coordinators employed by the week at less than the "flat deal" minimum
- Schedule K-III: Stunt coordinators employed under "flat deal" contracts
- Schedule X-I: Extra performers employed in the Los Angeles, San Diego, San Francisco, Hawaii and Las Vegas Zones
- Schedule XII: Extra performers employed on motion pictures based in New York and in the New York Extra zones

Note that puppeteers do not have a separate schedule.

All categories are determined by the amount of compensation received by the performer. Compensation rates are determined at the contract year's end and are adjusted yearly.

STUNT PERFORMER CATEGORIES

- Stunt double: (Daily Performer Contract) may perform only for the character he or she agreed to double. Any other stunt work performed on any given day requires an additional contract.
- Utility stunt: (Weekly Performer Contract) may double more than one character during a single day and may perform any other stunt work that might be required without an additional contract(s) for these additional services. This type of employment is permitted only when hired under a weekly stunt contract.
- ND stunt: nondescript stunt or generic stunt work is designated on a daily contract. Such performer may not double a specific character without an additional contract for that day.

INTERVIEWS

Day performers (TV and theatrical) are not paid for interviews if they are dismissed within one hour from the time of their appointment. If detained beyond one hour, the performer is paid at straight time in one-half hour units. Three-day performers (TV) and weekly performers (TV and theatrical) do not receive compensation unless they are required to speak lines given them to learn outside the studio, or they are kept waiting for more than one hour. All interviews or auditions for television or theatrical films must have sign-in sheets available.

WORKWEEK

The performer's workweek consists of any five consecutive days out of seven consecutive days; or, on an overnight location, any six consecutive days out of seven consecutive—as designated by the producer on each production unit. Any actor or extra who works on the designated sixth or seventh day of the workweek is not entitled to premium pay unless such a day is the performer's sixth or seventh consecutive day worked.

Performers are entitled to an additional day's pay for work on the fifth day of the workweek that spills over, that is, goes past midnight, into a sixth day of work. They are not entitled to premium pay for such work on the sixth day unless they are required to report for an additional call on the sixth day.

Producers are allowed to switch the production workweek (without penalty) once, to get on a Monday through Friday workweek, or once off and then back on, to a Monday through Friday workweek. Performers shall be entitled to payment for any days off beyond four between switched workweeks. Further, performers shall be entitled to premium payment if between switched workweeks they do not receive at least one day off.

REST PERIODS

Actors working in town being given studio calls are entitled to a twelve-consecutive-hour rest period from the time of dismissal until the first call for the next day, whether for makeup, wardrobe, hairdress or any other purpose.

For a nearby location where exterior photography is required on the day preceding and the day following the rest period, the rest period may be reduced from twelve to ten hours once every fourth consecutive day. The rest period may not be reduced from twelve to ten hours on the first day of each performer's employment in a television production. There is also a provision that allows for the rest period to be reduced by fifteen minutes at the end of a workday for makeup and wardrobe removal (if no assistance is required) without the time counting toward meal penalty or rest period violations. (This provision does not apply to performers working on distant location.)

On overnight locations, the twelve-hour rest period may be reduced to eleven hours twice a week, but not on consecutive days. This is permitted on theatrical films only. If a performer reporting to an overnight location arrives at the hotel after 9:00 P.M. and does not work that night, the performer may be given a ten-hour turnaround. A performer who is required to travel by air for more than four hours to a location may not be called for work without a ten-hour rest period.

All performers are entitled to one weekly rest period of fifty-four hours provided they are not called before 6:00 A.M. on the first day of the following week. On a six-day location week, the weekly rest period is thirty-six hours. Violation of either the daily or weekly rest period is known as a forced call, and the penalty is one day's pay or $950, whichever is the lesser sum.

CONSECUTIVE EMPLOYMENT

Performers are generally paid on a consecutive day's basis from the first day they are instructed to report for work or when shooting on any overnight location, beginning with the travel day, which constitutes the first day of employment. For example, weekly freelance players scheduled to work on a Monday and Tuesday, on hold Wednesday and Thursday and scheduled again for Friday, will be paid for the entire week, even if they are not given a work call for Wednesday and Thursday. Additionally, because they are employed by the production company for the entire week, they are subject to being called in for work on Wednesday or Thursday should there be a change in schedule.

Weekly performers who are on hold for several days during the schedule and are then called back to work for another day or two cannot be taken off payroll as weekly performers and converted to a daily contract when called back for those additional days. These actors must be compensated on a weekly basis until their services on the film are completed.

A day performer can be converted to a weekly performer or may return to the show on a weekly basis as a drop/pick-up. For a drop/pick-up schedule to exist, the performer must first be on a day performer contract and must be notified of the pick-up date before wrapping the original engagement. The intervening time must be for more than ten calendar days for films produced in the United States, and fourteen calendar days for films produced outside the United States. Under these circumstances, compensation need not be given for the intervening time, and the performer is independent of any responsibility to the production. Day performers picked up on a weekly contract may be given an on-or-after pick-up date (which refers to a specific date or the following day), thus allowing the producer a twenty-four hour leeway. Day performers picked up on another day performer contract must be given a specific pick-up date. One such break in employment is allowed for each performer per production. A weekly performer may never be converted to a day performer contract. On episodic television only, day performers earning not less than two times minimum scale can be recalled once during each episode without payment for the intervening time. Consecutive employment does not apply to stunt performers, unless the stunt performer has dialogue and/or a role.

Recalls for looping, added scenes, process shots, trailers, retakes, etc. after the close of an actor's work in principal photography shall break consecutive employment. Performers may be recalled at their contractual rate provided such additional services are commenced within four months after termination of their employment. After the four-month period, performers are free to renegotiate their contracts for any additional work requested by the producer.

TRANSPORTATION AND LOCATION EXPENSES

Transportation to distant location supplied by the producer must be first class. If six or more performers travel on the same flight and in the same class on jet flights within the continental United States, then coach class shall be acceptable. For interviews and auditions only, a performer may travel other than first class on a regularly scheduled jet aircraft. Bus and train transportation (in the best class available) are acceptable.

In addition to single room accommodations, the producer is to provide per diem meal allowance at not less than the current minimum scheduled rates. If the minimum rates are not sufficient to meet prevailing reasonable costs for meals on a specific location, the producer must make appropriate adjustments. Producers must pay the per diem prior to the day or week of work. If the per diem is paid by check, then facilities must be made available to cash such checks.

LOOPING

Day performers may be recalled to loop for a four-hour session and paid one half of their contractual daily salary. A day player (not being recalled and working on a picture for the first time) must receive a full day's pay for a looping session. Weekly freelance performers recalled to loop after completion of principal photography for four hours or less are paid an additional one-half day's pay. If more than four hours are required, a full day's pay shall be required.

Producers may negotiate for a specified number of loop days to be included in a Schedule F performer's contract, and for one looping day for a day player guaranteed $5,000 or more per day.

DUBBING (FOR THEATRICAL MOTION PICTURES ONLY)

Producers are required to employ performers at rates not less than specified in SAG's current Dubbing Agreement when dubbing a SAG theatrical motion picture into a language other than English in the United States.

EMPLOYMENT OF MINORS

When finalizing a deal for the employment of minors, make sure their work permits are up to date. Most importantly, you need to be aware of both the child labor laws in the state in which minors are being hired and of SAG policies regarding the employment of minors, and to know which set of regulations apply to your production. Before you can hire minors, many states will have you apply for a Permit to Employ Minors, in addition to requiring you to supply them with a certificate of insurance to show proof of your workers' compensation coverage.

Note that California has some of the most stringent child labor laws in the country, which apply to both minors hired in California and to those hired in other states but brought to California to work. If a minor is hired in California by a California-based company and the production company chooses to shoot the film in another state, California regulations apply. If a company based in another state shoots their film in California, the minors they employ are also subject to California laws. If, however, minors are being employed by a company based in and shooting in a state other than California, where child labor laws are less stringent, then SAG regulations would take precedence.

Regulations regarding the employment of minors are very precise. Depending on the age of the children, they are allowed a required number of hours in which to work, to attend school and to rest. They cannot work earlier than a specified time in the morning nor past a specified time at night; if under sixteen years of age, minors must be accompanied by a parent or guardian. These regulations also cover the employment of teacher/welfare workers and the number of children each teacher may teach and/or supervise. Producers must hire teachers with credentials appropriate to the level of education required by the minors to be taught on the set.

For the past several years, the Screen Actors Guild and its Young Performers Committee have been actively promoting changes to the 1939 enacted Coogan Law. This law had allowed a court considering approval of a minor's contract with a studio to require a portion of the minor's net earnings to be set aside in a trust for the minor, ensuring that minors receive a portion of their earnings when they reach majority age at eighteen. Unfortunately, few contracts were reviewed by the courts, leaving over 95 percent of the children who earn money in the entertainment industry unprotected by the Coogan Law. Furthermore, little or no provision was made for the payment of the child's taxes, agents, managers and other advisors. On January 1, 2000, a SAG-sponsored California bill went into effect strengthening and updating the original Coogan Law. This new law guarantees that every time young performers work under an entertainment contract, 15 percent of their gross earnings will be set aside for them in trust until they reach legal majority (the minor or parent can petition the court to request that more than 15 percent of gross earnings be set aside). The remaining 85 percent of the minor's salary is for the payment of operating expenses such as agents, managers, attorneys, acting lessons, professional photographs, transportation costs, tutoring, publicists and accounts. The bill also makes the earnings of a minor the legal property of the minor, not the community property of the parents. And although a parent or legal guardian of the minor is appointed trustee to the child's account and is required to pay all liabilities incurred by the minor under the contract (including payments for taxes on all earnings), nothing in the new law alters any other existing responsibilities of a parent/guardian to provide for the financial support of their minor child. Producers are required to make timely deposits into the minor's trust account, allowing interest to build on the principal earnings right away.

Whether you are governed under state or SAG guidelines, make sure you and your assistant directors are fully acquainted with all the policies pertaining to the employment of minors.

TAFT/HARTLEY

The Taft/Hartley is a federal law that allows a nonmember of a union or guild to work on a union show for thirty days. At the end of that time period, he or she *must join* the union to continue working on that particular show or for another signatory company.

A producer will generally choose to hire a performer who is not a member of the Screen Actors Guild for a few different reasons. The first scenario is when a decision to hire a nonmember is made after lengthy interviews to find a specific look or type, or someone with very specific abilities that cannot be met by a SAG member. The second scenario happens on the set during filming, on the spur of the moment, when the *director* decides another performer is needed to make a scene more complete and upgrades an extra or stand-in who happens to be there at the time. This situation may also apply to well-known or famous people brought in to portray themselves.

If in doubt as to whether a non-SAG performer can be hired under the Taft/Hartley ruling, always check with the Guild first.

Whenever a nonmember is hired to perform on a SAG signatory show, a Taft/Hartley form must be completed and submitted to the Screen Actors Guild. A Taft/Hartley form submitted on a television or theatrical film must be received within fifteen calendar days of the performer's first day of work. Submissions postmarked on the fifteenth day do not count and may be subject to a fine. Submissions from commercials must be received within fifteen business days.

Taft/Hartley forms require the performer's name, address, phone number, social security number, information on your production and *reason for hire*. If the reason for hire does not satisfactorily explain why this person was hired instead of a guild member, the production may be subject to a fine.

Production companies are more apt to be fined for this type of violation when they Taft/Hartley an excessive number of performers on one show, which automatically raises doubt as to the need for so many people with special abilities or qualities that cannot be found from within the SAG membership. Damages for the employment of a performer in violation of provisions that pertain to the Taft/Hartley law are currently $500.

Also requested along with a completed Taft/Hartley Report form is a professional resume and photograph of the performer. If the performer does not have a professional photograph, a Polaroid taken on the set can be attached, but an explanation is required if a professional resume and/or photo does not exist. As soon as a performer is Taft/Hartleyed, he or she can join the guild. In all states (other than right-to-work states), a performer can work for thirty days from his or her first date of employment (or any amount of days within that thirty-day period) without having to join the Guild. Once the thirty days have lapsed, the performer must join before he or she can be employed on another SAG film.

In a right-to-work state (Alabama, Arizona, Arkansas, Florida, Georgia, Idaho, Iowa, Kansas, Louisiana, Mississippi, Nebraska, Nevada, North Carolina, North Dakota, South Carolina, South Dakota, Tennessee, Texas, Utah, Virginia and Wyoming), a performer may join but is not required to. The performer may work union or non-union films, and the production cannot be fined for hiring a non-SAG member who has worked on other SAG productions. Performers working on a union show, even if they are not guild members, must be cleared through Station 12, and Taft/Hartley letters must be submitted. In addition, pension and health benefits must be paid by the production company, and performers' employment must be reported to the guild.

NUDITY

The rules pertaining to nudity are as follows:

1. The producer's representative is to notify the performer (or their representative) of any nudity or sex acts expected in the role (if known by management at the time) prior to the first interview or audition. Producers may not require total nudity at an audition or interview, and performers must be permitted to wear pasties and a G-string or its equivalent.
2. During any production involving nudity or sex scenes, the set shall be closed to all persons having no business purpose in connection with the production.
3. No still photography of nudity or sex acts will be authorized by the producer to be made without the consent of the performer.
4. The appearance of a performer in a nude or sex scene, or the doubling of a performer in such a scene, shall be conditioned upon the performer's prior written consent. Such consent may be obtained by letter or other writing prior to a commitment or written contract being made or executed. Such consent must include a general description as to the extent of the nudity and the type of physical contact required in the scene. If a performer has agreed to appear in such scene and then withdraws consent, the producer shall also have the right to double the performer. Consent may not be withdrawn for film already photographed. The producer shall also have the right to double young children or infants in nude scenes (not in sex scenes).

Body doubles employed in scenes requiring nudity or conduct of a sexual nature shall be principal performers; however, the provisions relating to residuals, screen credit, consecutive employment and preference of employment provisions do not apply to these performers. Notwithstanding the foregoing, body doubles shall be paid for intervening days on an overnight location when required to remain at such location by the producer, and the preference of employment provisions of the applicable extra performer schedule shall apply to the employment of body doubles.

WORK IN SMOKE

Principal performers must be notified in advance when scheduled to work in smoke. If a principal performer is not notified and cannot work in smoke for health reasons, such performer shall receive a half-day's pay or payment for time actually worked, whichever is greater.

WORKING WITH ANIMALS

There is an availability of trained animals that can perform with realism and without danger of injury or death. To ensure the responsible, decent and humane treatment of animals, producers are encouraged to work with the American Humane Association pertaining to the use of animals in their films.

Producers cannot use any performer in a scene in which an animal is intentionally mistreated or killed, except when the animals being killed are subject to the provisions of a legal hunting season. Producers need to notify the American Humane Association prior to the commencement of any work involving animal(s) and to advise them as to the nature of the work to be performed. Scripted scenes involving animals should be made available to the American Humane Association, and representatives of the association may be present at any time during the filming of a motion picture in which animals are used.

SAG EXTRAS

See Chapter 12, "All About Extras," for information regarding SAG extras.

MULTIMEDIA, INTERNET AND INDUSTRIAL/EDUCATIONAL CONTRACTS

The Screen Actors Guild now offers contracts for producers hiring actors who perform in interactive/multimedia and Internet programs. SAG also offers a contract that specifically addresses the employment of principal and extra performers working on industrial and educational shows. The contract covers two categories of programs.

Category I programs are designed to train, inform, promote a product or perform a public relations function, and are exhibited in classrooms, museums, libraries or other places where no admission is charged. Included are closed-circuit television transmission and teleconferences. Also included are sales programs that are designed to promote products or services of the sponsor but will be shown on a restricted basis only.

Category II programs are intended for unrestricted exhibition to the general public. Category II programs must be designed primarily to sell specific products or services to the consuming public, (1) at locations where the products or services are sold, or (2) at public places such as coliseums, railroad stations, air/bus terminals or shopping centers. These programs may be supplied free of charge to customers as a premium or inducement to purchase specific goods or services. A five-year use limitation applies to all Category II programs.

Contact SAG for further information or to obtain contract digests outlining these agreements.

Rules pertaining to casting and the employment of actors are varied and many. Additions and revisions are enacted every three years when the Screen Actors Guild negotiates a new contract with the AMPTP. In addition to some of the basic regulations outlined in this chapter, you should have a good working knowledge of pay scales and specific rules pertaining to engagement and cancellation; makeup, hairdressing, wardrobe and fitting calls; employment contracts; billing and screen credit; overtime; location and travel time; meal penalty violations; night work; time of payment and late payments; reuse of film and affirmative action. Also be aware of the specifics on the employment of extras, minors, stunt performers, dancers, etc.

Keep a copy of the latest SAG contract (and contract digest pamphlets) close at hand. When in doubt of specific rules, contact your legal department or attorney or call your local SAG representative.

FORMS IN THIS CHAPTER

- Cast Information Sheet—a handy form used to verify that all details pertaining to the cast have been taken care of

SCREEN ACTORS GUILD OFFICES

National Headquarters
5757 Wilshire Boulevard
Los Angeles, CA 90036-3600

Main Switchboard (9 A.M. to 5 P.M.)	(323) 954-1600
Theatrical Contracts	(323) 549-6828
Television Contracts	(323) 549-6835
Production Services	(323) 549-6811
Singers' Representative	(323) 549-6864
Residuals Information and Claims	(323) 549-6505
Signatory Status	(323) 549-6869
Station 12 (9 A.M. to 6:30 P.M.)	(323) 549-6794
SAG Extras	(323) 549-6811
Affirmative Action	(323) 549-6644
Actors to Locate	(323) 549-6737
Agent Contracts	(323) 549-6745
Legal Affairs	(323) 549-6627
Industrial/Ed-Interactive-Internet	(323) 549-6850

ARIZONA
1616 E. Indian School Road, Suite 330
Phoenix, AZ 85016
Phone: (602) 265-2712   Fax: (602) 264-7571

BOSTON
11 Beacon Street, Room 512
Boston, MA 02108
Phone: (617) 742-2688   Fax: (617) 742-4904

CHICAGO
1 East Erie Street, Suite 650
Chicago, IL 60611
Phone: (312) 573-8081   Fax: (312) 573-0318

CLEVELAND
1030 Euclid Avenue, 429
Cleveland, OH 44115
Phone: (216) 579-9305   Fax: (216) 781-2257

COLORADO
950 South Cherry Street, Suite 502
Denver, CO 80246
Phone: (303) 757-6226   Fax: (303) 757-1769

DALLAS-FORT WORTH
6060 N. Central Expressway, Suite 302, LB 604
Dallas, TX 75206-5293
Phone: (214) 363-8300   Fax: (214) 363-5386

DETROIT
27770 Franklin Road
Southfield, MI 48034-2352
Phone: (248) 355-3105   Fax: (248) 355-2879

FLORIDA (CENTRAL)
646 W. Colonial Drive
Orlando, FL 32804
Phone: (407) 649-3100   Fax: (407) 649-7222

FLORIDA (MIAMI)
7300 N. Kendall Drive, Suite 620
Miami, FL 33156-7840
Phone: (305) 670-7677   Fax: (305) 670-1813

GEORGIA
455 E. Paces Ferry Road, N.E., Suite 334
Atlanta, GA 30305
Phone: (404) 239-0131, ext. 10   Fax: (404) 239-0137

HAWAII
949 Kapiolani Blvd., Suite 105
Honolulu, HI 96814
Phone: (808) 596-0388   Fax: (808) 593-2636

HOUSTON
2400 Augusta Drive, Suite 264
Houston, TX 77057
Phone: (713) 972-1806   Fax: (713) 780-0261

MINNEAPOLIS/ST. PAUL
708 N. First Street, #333
Minneapolis, MN 55401
Phone: (612) 371-9120   Fax: (612) 371-9119

NASHVILLE
P.O. Box 121087
Nashville, TN 37212
Phone: (615) 327-2944   Fax: (615) 329-2803

NEVADA
3900 Paradise Road, Suite 162
Las Vegas, NV 89109
Phone: (702) 737-8818   Fax: (702) 737-8851

NEW YORK HEADQUARTERS
1515 Broadway, 44th Floor
New York, NY 10036
Phone: (212) 944-1030   Fax: (212) 944-6774

NORTH CAROLINA
311 N. Second Street, Suite 2
Wilmington, NC 28401
Phone: (910) 762-1889   Fax: (910) 762-0881

PHILADELPHIA
230 South Broad Street, Suite 500
Philadelphia, PA 19102
Phone: (215) 732-0507   Fax: (215) 732-0086

PORTLAND
3030 SW Moody, Suite 104
Portland, OR 97201
Phone: (503) 279-9600   Fax: (503) 279-9603

PUERTO RICO
530 Ponce de Leon Avenue, Suite 312
San Juan, PR 00901
Phone: (787) 289-7832   Fax: (787) 289-8732

SAN DIEGO
7867 Convoy Court, Suite 307
San Diego, CA 92111-1214
Phone: (858) 278-7695   Fax: (858) 278-2505

SAN FRANCISCO
235 Pine Street, 11th Floor
San Francisco, CA 94104
Phone: (415) 391-7510   Fax: (415) 391-1108

SEATTLE
601 Valley Street, Suite 100
Seattle, WA 98109
Phone: (206) 270-0493   Fax: (206) 282-7073

ST. LOUIS
1310 Papin Street, Suite 103
St. Louis, MO 63101
Phone: (314) 231-8410   Fax: (314) 231-8412

WASHINGTON, D.C./BALTIMORE
4340 East West Highway, Suite 204
Bethesda, MD 20814
Phone: (301) 657-2560   Fax: (301) 656-3615

CAST INFORMATION SHEET

SHOW: Herby's Summer Vacation

ACTOR	#	ROLE	START DATE	D=DAILY, W=WEEKLY, D/P=DROP/PICKUP	# OF DAYS WORKING	DEAL MEMO	SENT SCRIPT	NOTIFIED WARDROBE	NOTIFIED MAKEUP & HAIR	STATION 12	TRAVEL/HOTEL ACCOMMODATIONS	RENTAL CAR -or- CAR & DRIVER	MEDICAL EXAM	RECEIVED HEAD-SHOTS	CONTRACT PREPARED	CONTRACT TO AGENT/ACTOR	SIGNED CONTRACT RETURNED	CONTRACT CO-SIGNED & DISTRIBUTED	WORK PERMIT, IF MINOR	SCRIPT REVISIONS (BLUE)	SCRIPT REVISIONS (PINK)	SCRIPT REVISIONS (GREEN)	DIALOGUE COACH OR LESSONS, IF NECESSARY
Clark Grable	1	Herby	6/8	W	14	5/2	5/3	5/3	5/5	5/5	✓	—	4/1	✓	5/2	5/3	4/2	4/3	✓	4/10	6/16		
Rocky Rizzo	2	Jake	6/8	W	14	5/4	5/5	5/5	5/7	5/7	✓		6/3	✓	5/5	5/6	5/21	5/23					
Scarlet Starlet	3	Laura	6/21	W	9	5/10	5/11	5/11	5/13	5/13	✓	C+D	6/15	✓	5/11	5/11	4/10	4/11					
Nancy Nicely	4	Mom	6/21	W	11	5/17	5/18	5/18	5/21	5/21	✓		6/18		5/18	5/20	4/15	4/15					
Hollywood Mann	5	George	6/22	W	5	5/17	5/17	5/18	5/21	5/21	✓	RC	6/12	✓	5/17	5/17	4/18	6/20					
Kenny Smiles	6	Marc	6/21	W	8	5/24	5/25	5/25	5/30	5/30	✓		6/14	✓	5/25	5/26	6/22	6/23	✓				
Will Performer	7	Jed	6/21	W	8	5/24	5/25	5/25	5/30	5/30	✓		6/18	✓	5/25	5/26	6/13	4/16	✓				
Lloyd Nelson	8	Police Sgt.	6/25	D	1	6/7	6/8	6/8	6/12	6/12	✓		6/17	✓	6/24	6/25	4/26	6/28		✓	✓		

© ELH

CHAPTER TWELVE

All About Extras

EXTRAS CASTING AGENCIES

You can have incredible sets, actors who are amazing, costumes that are perfect, cinematography and lighting that will take your breath away; but if your extras don't look as if they belong there, they will detract from the overall appearance of the entire film and diminish the extraordinary setting you've worked so hard to create. Extras are called *background* because they are more than just a bunch of people milling around your principal characters. They create a backdrop—one more visual element of the film the viewer is drawn into.

Once an agency secures a show, it will assign a staff casting associate to oversee the project. When selecting an agency to supply the extras and stand-ins for your show, get recommendations from friends and contacts. Go with a proven company, or make sure you have a coordinator with a good track record.

Your prime consideration is whether this agency is going to be able to effectively deliver the type of extras you need. Your decision will be a lot easier if all you require are certain numbers of people within certain age ranges. But if you need the right mix of men and women, ethnicity and physical types; people who have the just the right look, the right hair, the right complexion— people who realistically look as if they are part of an era and will completely blend into a story— then you need an agency that can fill the bill. Whether you require background players to pass for turn-of-the century blue bloods, terminally ill cancer patients, holocaust survivors or gang members, you want someone with the experience and the *"eye"* for what you're looking for—someone who can offer quality and cost-effective production value. Being able to hand-pick the right individuals is, in itself, an art form.

On a contemporary show, a good casting associate will inform extras as to what clothes to bring, eliminating the need for costumers to supply wardrobe; will know if someone's hair is the right length or color, eliminating the need for a hairstylist's time and will be able to find extras who have the exact skills that are needed (swimmers, skiers, etc.). Poor extra casting can be costly.

Agency fees are paid on a commission-basis, ranging from 8 to 10 percent. Beware of those that are the least expensive. Failing to provide you with what you need could be more costly in the long run. Compare the qualities and track records of agencies that charge less (often by providing payroll services) with other agencies (that don't offer payroll services), who may charge a little more but might offer more value for your money.

Finding Specific Types

Agencies keep extensive files and data bases full of both union and non-union extras (of every type) who have either come in to register or who have been sought out for their special abilities or looks. In addition to keeping files on individuals, agencies also establish contacts with certain organizations, special schools, medical facilities, and other groups. These connections become useful when, for example, a special education school can assist in providing extras for a film about a mentally-challenged child; or the Veterans Administration becomes a good source of extras for a film about a Vietnam vet. When very specific types cannot be found in their files, extras coordinators will often visit places that these people frequent. They become quite creative in locating the exact look you're after. They are also very good at securing intact teams with special abilities (such as bands), often for the price of a donation in lieu of a salary for each member of the group.

THE PROCESS

During pre-production, the agency/coordinator will be sent a script prior to meeting with any or all of the following: producer, director, production designer, UPM and assistant directors. The preliminary meeting will generally consist of discussions based on breakdowns (how many and which types on which days) and concepts (the "look" envisioned by the film's creative team), at which time, agency representatives will offer feedback and suggestions. This will be your first indication as to whether the extras coordinator understands the look you are searching for. Your next indication is when the agency submits pictures of possible stand-ins, photo doubles and extras for your consideration. If all continues to proceed as it should, the agency will then coordinate interview times with the assistant director, so the director (and team) can personally evaluate their choices.

The numbers of extras required for an entire show is calculated by "mandays," the number of individuals needed per day. In general terms, an average small show will require 300-400 extra mandays or less; a medium-sized show, 500-800 mandays; and a large feature (or mini-series), at least 800 mandays.

Again, in general terms and for the best possible results, you would give the extras casting agency the following number of prep weeks prior to principal photography:

	Contemporary Script	Period Script (requiring costume fittings, etc.)
Small Show	2 weeks	4 weeks
Medium Show	4 weeks	6 weeks
Large Show	6-8 weeks	8-10 weeks

Photo doubles and extras appearing in period films will have to be scheduled for costume fittings and possibly hair and makeup tests. Science fiction and/or fantasy films could require lengthy prosthetic fittings. Allow for additional fittings to accommodate changing minds or molds that have to be made more than once.

Bring the extras agency on as soon as you can; and remember, their commission is based on mandays, not on the number of days or weeks they work on your film. Bringing them in as early as possible is not going to cost more, it's just going to give them more time to do a good job for you.

If there are over 75 to 100 extras on any one shoot day, the agency may send a talent coordinator (who is included in the daily count) to check extras in, wrangle them, handle problems, etc. The assistant directors and set PAs are generally the ones who coordinate the extras, and the 2nd AD is responsible for signing off on extra vouchers (see sample vouchers at the end of this chapter).

The production company must secure appropriate areas for extras to wait when not needed on the set, to change, eat, etc. The agency will make sure minor extras have valid work permits, but it is the production company's responsibility to employ teacher/welfare workers and to provide an adequate schoolroom. For babies, nurses are required as well as a nursery.

Gathering Large Crowds And Filling Stadiums

Filling a stadium and making sure large amounts of people can be relied upon to show up at a specified location at a certain hour for an undetermined length of time is quite a chore. To make matters worse, shows are often required to fill auditoriums or stadiums with people they can't afford to pay. Since the cost of paying thousands of extras is often prohibitive, productions will pay those SAG extras they are required to have, but the remaining extras will have to be people who want to be there (and are willing to stay until no longer needed) for the mere pleasure of being a part of this movie. And not only are they not paid, sometimes they are also asked to bring their own lunch.

Although it is the agency's ultimate responsibility to fill a given space with people, the production frequently gets involved with the process as well—often with the help of the show's unit publicist. It can take the efforts of several people to fill a stadium, and those involved will do some or all of the following:

- solicit the help of marketing firms
- contact charity groups
- create website postings (if the show or an actor in the show has a fan club and/or their own website, that's a great place to start)
- place newspaper ads (I was once on a distant location, and in order to fill a small stadium, we placed ads in local newspapers that started with, "You Oughta Be In Pictures!")
- create a public interest story for publication
- offer $1 (or another specified amount) per person to be donated to charity
- procure donations of food and drink
- arrange for buses to transport large groups of people from certain locations
- line up entertainers to occupy the crowd in between shots
- set up a raffle and procure gifts and prizes for raffle winners
- make sure to have a sufficient number of portable restrooms to accommodate the crowd
- arrange for studio teachers and schoolroom space to accommodate minors in the crowd
- make sure there are enough assistant directors, production assistants and extra casting assistants (all with walkie-talkies and head mics) to coordinate the crowd

The people who commit to being part of a crowd are told what to wear and/or bring and they must often agree to stay a minimum of six to eight hours. They must also agree to return on subsequent days if needed. Signing in when they arrive, some productions will give each extra a raffle ticket, which is then forfeited should they leave early.

EXTRAS CASTING ON LOCATION

When on distant location, some companies will retain the services of a local extras casting agency, and some will bring an extras coordinator with them. Much will depend on the availability of a qualified local agency or coordinator, and also on how many and what types of extras are needed. The farther you get away from the large metropolitan areas, the fewer the resources. And the agencies you do find may not specialize, as many smaller cities have all-purpose agencies that represent models, principal talent and extras.

When on a distant/remote location, not having access to many different types of extras can be quite a challenge. Usually, the more remote the location is, the more challenging the casting. To help in the process, the extras coordinator will tap into the local community by:

- contacting the local media (public interest story)
- contacting local organizations (schools, churches, community groups, clubs, etc.)
- posting announcements throughout the town (including website postings)
- soliciting help from the local film commission and/or chamber of commerce
- soliciting help from local talent and modeling agencies
- setting up big open calls

SPECIFICALLY SAG

The different categories of SAG extras are as follows:

- General Extra: A performer of atmospheric business that includes the normal actions, gestures and facial expressions of the Extra Performer's assignment.
- Special Ability Extra: An extra specifically called and assigned to perform work requiring special skill, such as tennis, golf, choreographed social dancing (including square dancing), swimming, skating, riding animals, driving livestock, nonprofessional singing (in groups of fifteen or fewer), professional or organized athletic sports, amputees, driving that requires a special skill and a special license (such as truck driving, but not cab driving), motorcycle driving (but not bicycle riding), insert work and practical card dealing.
- Stand-In: An extra used as a substitute for another actor for the purpose of focusing shots, setting lights, etc., but not actually photographed. Stand-ins may also be used as General Extras.
- Photographic Double: An extra performer who is actually photographed as a substitute

for another actor. A General Extra who is required to do photographic doubling shall receive the Special Ability rate.

- Day Performer: A performer who delivers a speech or line of dialogue. An Extra Performer must be upgraded to Day Performer if given a line, except in the case of "omnies."
- Omnies: Any speech sounds used as general background noise rather than for its meaning. Atmospheric words such as indistinguishable background chatter in a party or restaurant scene.

Most extra casting agencies represent both union (SAG) and non-union extras. If you are a SAG signatory, you must use the following percentage of SAG extras on your project (the remainder can be non-union):

- TV Short-Form—half-hour and one-hour shows: First fifteen must be SAG extras; includes stand-ins
- TV Long-Form—one and one-half hours, two hours, and more: First fifteen must be SAG extras, plus three stand-ins
- Feature Films: First forty must be SAG extras, plus five stand-ins
- Low-Budget Features: Producer may negotiate on a show-to-show basis, and may be granted a waiver to lower the number of required SAG extras

An extra who is directed to deliver a line of dialogue or speech may be eligible for an upgrade to a principal performer. Certain circumstances allow extras to receive rate adjustments. Examples are rough or dangerous work; work requiring the performer to get wet or work in smoke; having to wear body makeup, a skull cap, hair goods, or a natural full-grown beard; and supplying wardrobe and personal props.

There are specific voucher forms supplied by SAG and extra casting agencies to be used by SAG extras (see sample at the end of this chapter). Taft/Hartley rules are the same for SAG extras as they are for other SAG performers, but there are different Taft/Hartley forms to fill out in such cases. Samples of both forms can be found in Chapter 10, "Unions & Guilds."

For more specific guidelines regarding the employment of SAG extras, contact the Screen Actors Guild and/or request a copy of their *Extra Performers Digest*.

Moving from Non-Union to Union Status

Most extras start off working non-union with the hope of eventually gaining union status. Union members are afforded higher salaries and benefits and also become eligible to accept principal speaking roles. The following are the different ways in which a non-union extra can become a member of the Screen Actors Guild:

- A non-union extra can be selected to replace a union extra who doesn't show up (earning one SAG voucher for each day this occurs).
- A non-union extra can be bumped up (to SAG status) for special business or to work as a stand-in (earning one SAG voucher for each day this occurs).
- Anytime a non-union extra gets three union vouchers (they do not have to be for consecutive days), he or she is SAG-eligible and can join after thirty days of receiving their last SAG voucher.
- If upgraded on set with a scripted line or directed scene, an extra would be Taft/Hartleyed and receive a SAG Day-Player contract.
- If thirty days have elapsed and the extra has not yet joined but continues to take SAG vouchers, the production company can be fined $453 per day. (Although he or she can choose to work non-union until joining.)

Those eligible to join SAG should save the triplicate copies of their vouchers *and* their paycheck stubs. Once in, they cannot go back to working as non-union extras. If they do and are caught, they can be fined $700 and lose their SAG membership. Anyone wishing to go back to working non-union has the option of taking a SAG withdrawal.

WITH THE EXTRA IN MIND

Becoming an extra is a good way to get into SAG or just to learn about the business. You will definitely get to see how a set is run, who does what and if you have the stamina for the work. Students and retired people find it a good way to augment their income. If you are signed up with several agencies and become a favorite, it can be a decent living in itself.

There are those who dream of progressing from extra one day to lead actor the next—many moving to Los Angeles or New York with no training, expecting to move up fast. They may have the looks but not necessarily the skill to create a character. In other words, getting three union extra vouchers does not an actor make. If you are serious about moving up, take acting classes and voice lessons, do community theatre, study dance, groom yourself, saturate yourself in your craft. Be more than just another pretty face.

When you sign up with an extras casting agency, most will collect a one-time administration fee of $20 to $25 from non-union extras only (SAG extras do not usually pay a registration fee). Avoid agencies that want to charge you $500 to take your picture and/or promise you the world. They're generally scams! SAG discourages agencies from recommending photographers or acting schools in an attempt to avoid kickbacks and/or conflicts of interest. As do the production compa-

nies who are looking for extras, make sure the agencies you sign up with are reputable and come highly recommended.

NOTE: assistance for this chapter was provided by Bill Dance of Bill Dance Casting, a Los Angeles-based extras casting agency.

FORMS IN THIS CHAPTER

- Extra Talent Voucher (can be used for union or non-union extras)—generally filled out in triplicate
- SAG Extra Voucher

EXTRA TALENT VOUCHER

VOUCHER NO: 63210P

DATE: 6·10·XX

PRODUCTION: HERBY'S SUMMER VACATION

[ ] UNION   [✓] NON-UNION

UNION NO:

PRODUCTION COMPANY: XYZ PRODUCTIONS   PROD. CO. PHONE NO: 555-3331

EXTRA CASTING AGENCY: RAZMATAZ EXTRA CASTING   PHONE NO: 555-8868

EMPLOYER OF RECORD (Payroll Co.): PAULINE'S PAYROLL CO.

CONTACT: LETSA

ADDRESS: 7322 PAYERS BLVD. BURBANK, CA 91521

NAME (Please Print): BETTE DAVISSON   AGE: 35

PHONE NO: 555-4444

ADDRESS: 1062 VOYAGER LN. HOLLYWOOD, CA 90068

[✓] NEW EMPLOYEE [ ] NEW ADDRESS

PHONE NO: 555-7614   CELL/PGR. NO: 555-1886 (PGR)

[ ] MARRIED [✓] SINGLE

SOCIAL SECURITY NO. (must be completed): 123-45-6789

OF ALLOWANCES: 1

REPORT TIME/IN: 7A	RATE: $ 46 —	INTERVIEW: $
FIRST MEAL OUT: 1P	RATE ADJUSTMENT: $	FITTING: $
FIRST MEAL IN: 1:30 P	8 HRS. OF S.T. @ $5.75 $ 46 —	SPECIAL ABILITY: $
SECOND MEAL OUT:	2 HRS. OF 1-1/2X @ $ 8.63 $ 17.26	SMOKE WORK: $
SECOND MEAL IN:	3 HRS. OF 2X @ $ 11.50 $ 34.50	BODY MAKEUP: $
DISMISSED/TIME OUT: 8:30P		HAIR: $
TOTAL MEAL TIME: ½ HR.		WET WORK: $
		BEARD: $
NET HOURS: 13 HRS.		DRESS OR UNIFORM: $ 15 —
		OTHER: $

WARDROBE: QTY: 2 $ 10 —

MEAL PENALTY: $ QTY:

USE OF AUTO: $ 15 —

MILEAGE - # OF MILES: 50

AMT. PER MILE: $ .30 $ 15 —

TOTAL: $ 40 —

TOTAL ADJUSTMENTS: $ 55 —

TOTAL: $ 15 —

GROSS TOTAL: $ 152.76

I acknowledge receipt of the compensation stated herein as payment in full for all services rendered by me on the days indicated. I hereby grant to my employer permission to photograph me and to record my voice, performances, poses, acts, plays and appearances, and use my picture, photograph, silhouette and other reproductions of my physical likeness and sound in the above-named production and in the unlimited production, advertising, promotion, exhibition and exploitation of the production by any method or device now known or hereafter devised in which the same may be used. I agree that I will not assert or maintain against you, your successors, assigns and licensees, any claim, action, suit or demand of any kind or nature whatsoever in connection with your authorized use of my physical likeness and sound in the production as herein provided.

As a condition of my employment by the Production Company on The Production, I agree that I will abide by all rules of employment as dictated by the Production Company or its agents, or by any Safety Coordinators assigned to The Production, especially those rules pertaining to safety including but not limited to: (a) remaining in areas designated as safe areas during any period that I am not asked to perform my duties as an extra, and (b) acting in a safe manner at all times so as not to injure myself or others, and (c) to refrain from taking any illegal substances that might impair my ability to do the job for which I was hired.

As a further condition of employment herein, I agree that I have the ability to perform each and every task, job assignment or special ability I have been asked to perform, and that if I knowingly make false representations that I am qualified to perform these assignments when, in fact, I know that I am not qualified, that such misrepresentation may be grounds for dismissal of any workers compensation claim should I be injured as a result of performing an assignment for which I knowingly was not qualified to perform.

I have read the entire conditions of employment and by signing this voucher, I understand and agree with the entire conditions of employment.

SIGNATURE: Bette Davisson

APPROVED BY: Elizabeth Bright

(If minor, parent or guardian must sign)

TITLE: 2ND A.D.

© ELH

SAG EXTRA VOUCHER

PRODUCER: XYZ PRODUCTIONS

DATE 6-7-XX	NAME (PRINT) THEA BERRAH	PRODUCTION NO. OR TITLE HERBY'S SUMMER VACATION #0100		DISMISSAL TIME 6P

SAG NO. 388 28 4446

TYPE OF CALL GENERAL

STARTING TIME 7A

SOCIAL SECURITY NO. MUST BE PROVIDED TO MAKE PAYMENT -0-	BASIC WAGE RATE $79—	TRAVEL TIME ARRIVE LOCATION:	PENALTIES	HOURS WORKED 10.5	MEAL PERIODS IN 1:30P OUT 2P

☒ SINGLE ☐ MARRIED ☐ MARRIED but withheld at higher single rate

Total number of allowances you are claiming: -0-

Additional amount, if any, you want deducted $ _____

	LEAVE LOCATION:		FITTING ☐	MEALS B☐ L☒ D☐	INTERVIEW ☐

If claiming exemption from withholding, write exempt and year in box [19]

ASST. DIR. APPROVED FOR PAYMENT _A. Direc_ (signature)

EMPLOYEE: PLEASE PRINT INFORMATION LISTED ABOVE AND SIGN WHERE INDICATED

	WARDROBE	PROPS	VEHICLE	MILEAGE

"I, the undersigned, certify that the number of income tax withholding exemptions claimed on this certificate does not exceed the number of which I am entitled.

"I agree to accept the sum properly computed based upon the times and the basic wage rate shown as payment in full for all services heretofore rendered by me for said employer.

"I further agree that the said sum, less all deduction required by law, may be paid to me by negotiable check issued by said company, said check to be addressed to me at my last reported address and deposited in the United States mail within the time periods provided by law.

"I hereby give and grant to the company named all rights of every kind and character whatsoever in and to all work heretofore done, and all poses, acts, plays and appearances heretofore made by me for you and in to all of the results and proceeds of my services heretofore rendered for you, as well as in and to the right to use my name, likeness and photographs, either still or moving for commercial and advertising purposes. I further give and grant to the said company the right to reproduce in any manner whatsoever any recordations heretofore made by said company of my voice and all instrumental, musical, or other sound effects produced by me. I further agree that in the event of a retake of all or any of the scenes in which I participate, or if additional scenes are required (whether originally contemplated or not) I will return to work and render my services in such scenes at the same basic rate of compensations as that paid me for the original taking.

"By signing this form, I hereby agree that said employer may take deductions from my earnings to adjust previous overpayments if and when said overpayments may occur."

Signature _Thea Borrah_ Date 6/7/XX

Address 5876 MEMORY LANE Apt # 14

City WONDERLAND State CA Zip 90000

Phone Number (818) 555-9622 PAGER: (818) 555-3226

YOUR EMPLOYER OF RECORD MUST BE COMPLETED
BACK OF WHITE COPY MUST BE COMPLETED _ABC PAYROLL CO._
IF OTHER THAN A PAYROLL COMPANY, EMPLOYER'S FEDERAL I.D. NUMBER IS _____

© ELH

DO NOT WRITE IN THIS SPACE

TYPE OF WORK	PAY CODE	HOURS		AMOUNT
		WORK	PAY	
DAY		·	·	
NIGHT		·	·	
O/T		·	·	
WET		·	·	
SMOKE		·	·	
OTHER		·	·	
OTHER		·	·	
OTHER				
OTHER				

BASIC RATE $79—

ADJUSTMENTS —

OVERTIME —

ALLOWANCES —

GROSS $79—

white—PAYROLL COPY
yellow—PRODUCTION COPY
pink—SAG COPY
golden rod—EXTRAS COPY

Screen Actors Guild
Kenmar Printing 357
Form No. 451

CHAPTER THIRTEEN

Clearances & Releases

Obtaining clearances is the process of obtaining permission to use someone's likeness, name, logo, photograph, product, premises, publication, film clip, stock footage, music or song in your film, and, in most circumstances, is in exchange for a fee. Use of stock footage and music is granted through a license. Other clearances are secured with a signed release form, each designed to grant permission for the use of that particular element (likeness, name, logo, photo, product, etc.).

Both your insurance agency and attorney will request that you have your script researched and then follow through on securing needed clearances. When you send your script to a research service, they will send back a report itemizing which elements of the script have to be cleared. You will need to follow through to make sure all such items are cleared or licensed. The distributor of your film will insist on receiving copies of all license agreements and release forms. Releasing a picture without the proper clearances may result in costly lawsuits or insurance claims.

Your attorney or legal affairs department may wish to handle any complicated clearances. Music clearances are generally handled through a music clearance service. Clearances necessary for the use of clips, stills and news footage are often cleared through a clearance service or are handled by individuals with extensive clearance experience, hired on a freelance basis to work on a particular show. You should be able to secure most routine clearances on your own. Many of the release forms found in this chapter can be used for this purpose. If you need a release form that is not here, your attorney or legal affairs department can prepare one for you. Again, even though they have all been approved by an attorney, have your own attorney look them over before you use them. The following are some general rules pertaining to clearances.

LIKENESS

Permission to use a performer's likeness is incorporated into his or her SAG contract, and extras grant permission by signing an extra voucher. Occasionally, people who are not extras are filmed as "background" or "atmosphere." This may occur when the director decides that, although there were no extras planned for the day, some atmosphere in the background would make a scene more complete. It may also occur when the director does not have enough extras, and, on the spur-of-the-moment, people walking down a street are recruited to participate in a scene. In this situation, each person filmed as background (whether being paid for their appearance or not) should sign a Personal Release, or if there are several people, a Group Release would be appropriate.

When a large group of people are recruited for an audience that will be filmed, post signs in easy-to-read locations stating that their presence as a member of this audience constitutes their permission for the production company to use their likeness. The same would apply to shooting a street scene within a confined locale, or when filming in a specific area such as a shopping center. Signs would be posted indicating that filming is taking place, people entering the area may appear in the picture and by entering the area they grant permission to the production company to use their likeness. (Exact wording for these signs is included in this chapter.) Clearance would not be required if the passersby being filmed are an incidental part of the background or if they will not be recognizable in the picture.

LOCATIONS

Permission to use a premises or property as a shooting location is obtained when the owner of the property signs a release form called a Location Agreement.

NAMES

Although a fictional character may share a common name with an actual person, the names of actual persons (printed or spoken) should not be used unless permission is granted by that person. Public figures may be referenced, providing such references are not derogatory.

NAMES OF ACTUAL BUSINESSES OR ORGANIZATIONS

The use of the actual name of a business, organization, building, etc. that is a shooting location is permissible, providing the location agreement grants the right to use such name. If the name of a business, organization or building is featured in your film but is not used as a shooting location, then permission for Use of Name or Use of Trademark or Logo is necessary.

TELEPHONE NUMBERS

Since it is difficult to clear references to identifiable phone numbers, most films use phone numbers that begin with the prefix 555, a prefix that had not appeared in any area code except for directory information. This has changed slightly, however, and currently, films use 555-4000 and up, since the phone company now uses the numbers below 4000 for their own purposes.

LICENSE PLATES

As it is also difficult to clear identifiable license plates, prop houses will manufacture fictitious plates for you.

DEPICTION OF PUBLIC AUTHORITIES

Clearance is required for the portrayal of police officers, firemen, prison guards, and other public authorities of identifiable departments or locations, whether uniforms are used or not. Wardrobe and prop departments will supply generic uniforms and related paraphernalia if clearances cannot be obtained.

STREET ADDRESSES

Referencing or identifying an actual street address must be cleared.

DEPICTION OR IDENTIFICATION OF ACTUAL PRODUCTS

A depiction or reference to an actual product does not have to be cleared if the depiction or reference is incidental and not derogatory. Featuring a product or service trademark or logo does, however, require a clearance. A *Use of Trademark or Logo* release form (included at the end of this chapter) would be appropriate in this situation.

Product Placement

Product Placement refers to the procurement of production resources, props, set dressing, vehicles and wardrobe for on-screen use—and it's big business. Most major studios have their own Product Placement departments, and there are many companies and promotional agencies that do nothing but place products in films. Some productions will hire their own product placement coordinator to supervise the entire operation while working in conjunction with the studio's product placement department and other specialized firms. This person would be required to interface with the producers, production designer and crew as well as the studio's creative executives, production executives, and the marketing, publicity and legal departments. The job requires extensive coordination and supervision of product placement deals from proposal stage through the release of the film, as well as preparation and follow-through of all legal agreements.

Productions utilize product placement to reduce the negative cost of the picture, enhance the look of their film, inject a sense of realism into a scene by using commonly-known products and maximize the production value seen on screen. And in some instances, prominent placements can generate opportunities for back-end promotions to support the release of the film.

Product placement is most effective when it creates a natural environment by featuring products in situations where they would normally appear. Depending on the film and the portrayal of the product, it is a great way for companies to receive very broad exposure and create consumer awareness for their brands.

Product placement coordinators (whether part of the crew, from the studio or from an independent company), after reading a script, will do a scene-by-scene breakdown of every opportunity to feature a product. They look for what the main characters wear, drive, eat, talk about, touch, hold and refer to by name. Special note is also taken of the locations where important scenes take place. In addition to traditional products, other items such as shopping bags, billboards, boxes, storefronts, bus signs and radio and television commercials can also provide excellent avenues for exposure.

As the process of negotiating for and acquiring goods and services can be lengthy, a product placement meeting should be scheduled as early in pre-production as possible—as soon as key department heads are on board. At this time, the product placement coordinator gets together with the production executives, producer(s), director, production designer, costume designer, transportation coordinator, prop master and set decorator to determine their vision and their specific needs for products in the film. In fact, the costume designer, transportation coordinator, prop master and set decorator should come to the meeting with "wish lists" in hand. This meeting is also the time to discuss any concerns regarding negative use or references to products in the script in the hope that some of the issues can be resolved. A subsequent meeting or two should be held as time permits to discuss prospective placement deals.

If a product is featured in a film and/or associated with a major star, it provides very valuable exposure for the manufacturer. In exchange for this placement, the product placement coordinator would negotiate a contribution of either product, an end credit in the film, a placement fee and, in some cases, a prominent exposure will lead to a company executing a tie-in promotion with the release of the film. Any funds generated from product placement may not be used to offset production costs. Once collected, these fees go against the negative cost of the picture and are not received until the film has been released theatrically.

It is very important to record the quantity, type and value of all materials provided for each film for purposes of inventory control; and a full report should be compiled summarizing all product placement deals. These details need to be managed carefully, as the production is often billed for unreturned items.

During filming, it's a good idea to have photos taken of as many products on the set as possible. These stills are presented to each company for internal purposes. They are not intended for publication or to serve as proof of exposure, and a release form should be signed prior to the company receiving any photographs. Often, after the release of a film, manufacturers will request a clip of the scene(s) in which their products appeared. The clip is also for internal use only, and unless preauthorized, a release form must be signed by the company to prevent the clip from being used for publicity purposes.

The value of product placement exposure can be evaluated on several levels: amount of screen time, box office revenue, hands-on exposure, verbal exposure and the impression of the viewer. In addition to the exposure generated by the initial release of a film, you've also got releases in foreign territories, domestic and international home video, cable, pay-per-view markets and network television. Product placement in a film now leads to worldwide exposure, so any costs associated with the placement are minimal considering the number of impressions that are generated. This exposure is particularly effective when a company is launching a new product and the release of the film coincides with the product introduction in the marketplace.

MUSIC

See Chapter 14, "A Guide To Music Clearance."

GUIDELINES FOR THE USE OF CLIPS, STILLS AND NEWS FOOTAGE IN MULTIMEDIA PROGRAMS

The following information was provided by Suzy Vaughan of Suzy Vaughan Associates, Inc., of Van Nuys, California. Suzy is an attorney with many years of clearance experience. Her firm provides clearance services for producers who are doing programs that require the use of excerpts from other projects.

Literary Works

Literary works, which include books, films, television programs, art works and still photos, among other things, must be licensed from their owners. This is because the Copyright Act gives creators of literary works the right to sell or license these works and to make money from them for the period of the copyright.

The Sonny Bono Copyright Term Extension Act of 1998, is the law that added 20 years to the duration of copyright. As a result of the Act, copyrights to pre-1978 works that would have lasted 75 years from their first publication, now last 95 years; and copyrights to 1978 and more recent works whose copyrights would have lasted for the lives of their authors plus 50 years, now last for the lives of their authors plus 70 years. This law was partially created in response to the length of copyright laws in foreign countries, which have always been anywhere from 70 years plus the life of the author, to 90 years from publication date. It is different in each country.

Once the copyright runs out, the creative works falls into the public domain and can be used freely by anyone without payment or licensing. If the work is not in the public domain, it is considered literary property, and permission must be obtained from the owner for use of the material. The Copyright Act provides substantial penalties for copyright infringement, ranging from $10,000 for accidental infringement to $250,000 for willful infringement.

News And/Or Stock Footage

News organizations can license the footage they have shot at press conferences to other entities. However, they can only license the copyright. They cannot give the licensee rights to the appearances of people who appear in the clips, including the anchor people, the news reporters, and ordinary people who are interviewed on the show. Use of these names and likenesses will require additional clearances (discussed further later).

Film Clips

Any excerpt from a feature film must be licensed from the copyright holder, and payment for use of the clips must be negotiated. Most studios charge a fee on the basis of a minute or fraction thereof. Most of them will not license footage on an aggregate basis but will base their fees on a per clip, per cut, or per minute basis.

The cost per clip depends on the rights required. It is more expensive to license all rights in perpetuity than it is to license five years of worldwide distribution, assuming that a studio would grant you perpetuity. Many studios are currently putting together their own interactive and multimedia divisions, and therefore refuse to license material for other multimedia projects. Studios rarely grant permission to use clips in advertising and promotion, even when the producer offers substantial fees for the use. Some studios have reciprocal arrangements with other studios and provide clips at a much lower fee on that basis. If your project is affiliated with a studio, it is important to determine up front if that studio has reciprocal deals in place that might apply to your project.

Contrary to popular belief, there is no rule that says you can use five seconds for free. That five seconds will cost the same as one minute. Therefore, it behooves you to use the entire scene you have licensed, rather than using two-second clips from six scenes. Studio contracts also stipulate that you may not edit scenes within a film clip. Although an interview that cuts from the interview to the clip and back again is a form of editing, the studios do not generally consider this a problem. The licensing agreements the studios send you to sign are rarely negotiable and are very stringent, demanding concessions from end credits to a guarantee that you will clear all the talent and music used in the clip, as well as an agreement that you will indemnify them against any claim that may arise as a result of the broadcast of the clip.

Television Clips

Television clips are owned by studios, independent production companies and TV networks, and are handled in the same fashion as described earlier with regard to film clips from feature films. Currently, all licensors are very concerned about usage of their material in interactive projects, fearing that the images will be manipulated and altered to the point that they are no longer recognizable. As they will not allow this to happen, the word interactive in any letter requesting permission to license clips may elicit an immediate "no," unless you can convincingly explain that the material will not be changed.

Still Photos

Still photos fall into several categories.

- Publicity photos (star headshots) have traditionally not been copyrighted. Since they are disseminated to the public, they are generally considered public domain, and therefore clearance by the studio that produced them is not necessary (even if you could determine which studio produced them).
- Production stills (photos taken on the set of a film or TV show during principal photography) must be cleared with the studio and can cost anywhere between $150 and $500.
- Lobby cards (film posters) are generally lumped into the same category as publicity photos and do not require clearance.
- Paparazzi photos must be cleared with the photographer. If not cleared, you risk a lawsuit and the possibility of the photographer showing up to demand much more money than he or she would have charged had you gone to him or her in the first place.
- Magazine and book covers involve clearances from both the magazine or book publisher and the photographer who took the photo.
- Still photo houses will generally license photos they own the rights to for $100 to $500 and up.

Samples of still photo releases are included in this chapter, both for the copyright owner of the photo and for the person(s) appearing in the photo.

Public Domain Films And Stills

Generally, a film or still is protected by copyright if it is less than 95 years old. A work of art obtains a copyright as an unpublished work as soon as it is "fixed in a tangible medium of expression." If that work of art was not registered for copyright, or does not have a notice of copyright on it and it is then published (which is accomplished by distribution to the public), it loses its unpublished copyright status and falls into the public domain. Once it is in the public domain, it can be reused by anyone without fear of copyright infringement since the copyright no longer exists. Since 1976, however, the fact that a television program may not have a visible copyright notice on it does not indicate that it is public domain, since it could have been registered with the Library of Congress. The only way to determine whether a film or television show is copyrighted is to do a copyright search at the Library of Congress. This applies to all works prior to 1988.

In 1988, the United States joined the Berne Copyright Convention, which states that no formalities are required to obtain a copyright, so therefore no copyright notice is required, nor is registration with the Library of Congress required. A program is copyrighted whether or not it has a copyright notice or is registered with the Library of Congress. However, most copyright holders still register their works with the Library of Congress and put copyright notices on them, since there are benefits to doing so with regard to lawsuits that arise out of the Copyright Act itself.

Talent Clearance

News Footage

- Public Figures in News Footage: Right of privacy: Under U.S. law, an individual has the right of privacy, and his or her image cannot be used by another until he or she either consents to that use and thereby waives this right or until he or she becomes a public figure. One becomes a public figure by placing him or herself in the limelight and making him or herself a person of public interest (such as becoming an actor or politician), or by some act that gives him or her a news significance. Consent is not required of a public figure whose likeness appears in news footage, and that includes material shot at a news conference covered by more than one news camera, or celebrities arriving at an event such as the Academy Awards for which they were not contracted but appeared in public voluntarily. They are aware that by appearing at an event such as a press conference, they give permission for use of their appearances in the footage anywhere it might appear. This situation also applies to newsreels that ran in movie theaters in the forties and fifties and are very obviously news.
- Public Figures in News Television Programs (interviewers-interviewees): Public figures who appear in news programs must be cleared because these programs were produced under a union contract. The union contracts require current consent and a negotiated payment for use of the appearance of any artist prior to the use of an excerpt from these programs in another program.

- Deceased Persons and the Right of Publicity: A deceased person has no right of privacy. The right is triggered only when a person's image is used to sell or endorse products in print ads and commercials, and does not generally apply to feature films or television programs, since they tell a story or disseminate information and do not sell a product. Music videos are a borderline situation, as they are created as tools to sell records and are occasionally considered to be musical commercials. However, the unions do require consent to be obtained from a deceased person's estate when requesting use of that person's likenesses in film clips for multimedia projects, television programs, etc.

Feature Films

- Actors: The Screen Actors Guild agreement specifies that when a producer desires to use an excerpt from a feature film, that producer must obtain current consent from all members of SAG (including actors, stunt people, helicopter and airplane pilots and estates of deceased performers) for use of the excerpt, and negotiate a fee that can be no less than the current scale payment. Stars may waive scale payment if they choose. Extras do not have to be cleared or paid. SAG also provides that if consent from an actor is not obtained prior to broadcast of the clip, the fine for violation of this regulation will be three times what the actor made the day he worked on that scene.
- Stunt Performers: Obtaining clearances from stunt performers can be a challenging objective. First of all, the identification of specific stunt players may be difficult without the help of the stunt coordinator who hired them to appear in the picture to begin with. Locating the stunt coordinator and hoping that he or she is available to help you is another matter. Clearances on stunt performers could also get quite expensive, because the clip you want may feature one action sequence in which several stunt players worked. In addition, many studios are leery of claims and refuse to license footage in which stunt performers appear. Recently, SAG changed the rules slightly to allow producers to find and pay stunt players during and after the project is completed, and stated that no negotiations are necessary with regard to fees. Stunt performers must accept SAG scale, and violations are no longer levied for late clearances.

- Pre-1960 Theatrical Feature Films: Prior to 1960, there was no provision in the SAG agreement granting actors residuals for their performances in feature films. Therefore, actors appearing in a clip from a film made prior to 1960 did not require clearance or payment. The guild recently revised this to require clearance of and payment for the use of clips, unless the name of the film is "billboarded" (either verbally as a voiceover or visually with a chyron) while the clip is on the screen. It must be readable and must appear every time the clip does, making montages impossible to do without clearing all the talent. This rule also applies to stunt players.
- SAG Waivers: Permission not to have to clear and pay actors is very difficult to obtain from SAG. Waivers may only be granted when there is a special reason, such as profits from the show going to charity. Only stars can be asked to waive. You would still be required to gain consent and pay union scale to non-stars.
- Agent's Fees: Agents are not allowed to take commission on scale payments. Therefore, when contacting an agent to obtain permission to use his or her client's performance in a clip, it is customary to offer a 10 percent agency commission over and above the scale payment you are offering to the actor.

You cannot buy out an actor for the use of clips. Each additional run requires an additional payment to the actors, with payment for the second run at 100 percent, and then 75 percent on down. If, however, you have hired the actor to appear live on your program for an over-scale fee, this fee will include the use of the actor's clips on a buyout.

Television Programs

AFTRA used to put major emphasis on obtaining current consent from talent appearing in television programs, and there was no time frame cutoff. They had to be cleared back "to the dawn of time," which in television terms is approximately 1948. Many producers assume the pre-1960 rule applies, but it does not. However, many negotiations with producers produced changes in these rules. Currently, if your program is less than 75 percent clips (meaning 74 percent clips and 26 percent new material), you do not have to obtain consent from the performers, you only have to pay them. AFTRA is good about giving you their social security numbers; and when checks are issued, you can send the payments directly to AFTRA.

AFTRA is the union governing tape programs, such as soap operas and variety shows. Many other tape programs, such as situation comedies, are governed by SAG rules, as listed earlier. AFTRA's payment schedules are more complicated than SAG's, in that there is a separate scale payment for a half-hour show, an hour show, a ninety-minute show, etc. There are also different rates for specialty acts, under five lines and special business. Dancers and singers must also be cleared and paid. You do not even have to be able to see a dancer's face, just his or her body. Once again, extras do not require clearance or payment. However, determining who is an extra can be tricky, because it does not depend on whether they speak, but how they were hired on the show. The worst-case cost for AFTRA comes in the supplemental market area, where they generally require that you approach the performers for a waiver, since supplemental markets are not addressed in the AFTRA agreement. The waiver can specify payment to each performer of double scale for television shows and single scale for videocassette. Many times, in practice, producers do not obtain waivers and simply pay single scale to all performers. These are considerations decided on a case-by-case basis.

AFTRA has an advantage over SAG, because there are no triple damage penalties. Each rerun of a show featuring AFTRA performers requires an additional payment, with the second run at 75 percent on down. A talent release for use of a performer's name and likeness in a film or TV clip is included in this chapter.

Directors And Writers Payments

- Rates: The Directors Guild and the Writers Guild have schedules of payments required each time clips are used in a multimedia program, film, or television show. There are separate schedules depending on whether the clip came from a feature film or a television show. Fees for use of feature film clips break at a thirty-second rate, while fees for television clips are much more expensive, changing rates at a ten-second cutoff. Payment schedules can be obtained from the guilds.
- Waivers: These guilds do not grant waivers, except for such things as the Oscars and the Emmys.
- One-Time Only: Payments made to the Directors and Writers Guilds for use of clips are

one-time only. There is no second payment when the show reruns or is distributed on home video.
- Schedules: A producer is required to keep track of the film or television programs in which the clips appear, the writers and directors involved with each and the amount of time used for each. This information is then submitted with a check to the appropriate guild. Episode titles are required for television shows by the Writers Guild. The guilds, in turn, issue checks to their members. DGA charges a 12.5 percent pension and welfare fee on top of the clip fee, while WGA does not charge for pension and welfare.
- Compilation Rate: If a producer is producing a program that is an anniversary show or "Best of . . . ," the DGA and WGA will levy a compilation rate, which is a penalty for using all clips and not creating new material. All of the unions would rather that a producer hire live talent rather than use clips. The compilation rate is dreaded, as it is much more than the per-clip use rate would be. There are also several versions of compilation rates, depending on the union: the daytime rate, the prime-time rate, the variety rate. The rate is arrived at by multiplying the standard writer rate times 250 percent times the number of half-hours in the program. Even if you pay a compilation rate, you must keep track of all clips used, their length and the writers and directors, so that the unions can divide up the payment you make among the various writers and directors. The only time you would benefit from the compilation rate is when you are using many short television clips. If your program is comprised of many different elements, then a clip rate is much more economical.

DISTRIBUTION OF RELEASE FORMS

Copies of fully executed release forms should be given to:

1. The person who signs the release
2. The production coordinator
3. The production accountant (when a payment is involved)
4. Assistant directors should receive copies of fully executed Location Agreements to have on the set with them at each location

5. The original release should be given to your production executive to be stored in permanent company files

NOTE: Thanks again to Suzy Vaughan for her help with this chapter. For more information on the clearance services provided by Suzy Vaughan Associates, you can contact them at (818) 988-5599, or visit their website: www.suzyvaughan.com.

FORMS IN THIS CHAPTER

Note that only the Personal Release comes in two versions, one for those who are willing to appear in a film for free, and the other for those who get paid. The remainder of the release forms grant a variety of rights "for good and valuable consideration," which means for free. If you need to alter one of these releases to fit a payment situation, change: "For good and valuable consideration" to "In consideration of the payment of the sum of $_____ and other good and valuable consideration . . ." Also make sure there is a line at the bottom of the page for the person signing the release to include their Social Security or Federal I.D. number. Other than that, they are the same.

The following release forms cover a broad range of clearances, but you will occasionally run into a situation where a clearance is needed for something not covered in this chapter. Whether you are seeking approval for the use of one of these forms or having a new one created, *always* check with your show attorney first.

- Personal Release
- Personal Release—Payment
- Group Release
- Use Of Name
- Use Of Trademark or Logo
- Use Of Literary Material
- Use Of Art Work (release from copyrighted owner)
- Use Of Still Photograph(s) (release from copyrighted owner)
- Use Of Still Photograph(s) (release from person depicted in photo)
- Use Of Poster (release from copyrighted owner)
- Use Of Vehicle
- Crowd Notice—Release (multiple copies to be placed in a studio when filming or taping before a live audience)
- Crowd Notice—Release (multiple copies to be placed in an "area" in which filming or taping is taking place)
- Supplying A Film/Tape Clip Of Your Show For Promotional Purposes
- Product Placement Release—this is a very basic release form that allows for the company providing products or services to receive screen credit in the end titles of the show. For product placement deals that entail contributions of product, a placement fee or tie-in promotion, your studio product placement executive or show attorney will prepare a comprehensive agreement more appropriate to the transaction.
- Film/Tape Footage Release
- Talent/Use Of Name & Likeness In A Film Or TV Clip
- Request For Videocassette

PERSONAL RELEASE

Film: __HERBY'S SUMMER VACATION__

Prod. Co.: __XYZ PRODUCTIONS__

Address: __1234 FLICK DR.__
__HOLLYWOOD, CA 90038__   Date: __6·23·XX__

Ladies and Gentlemen:

I, the undersigned, hereby grant permission to __XYZ PRODUCTIONS__ ("Producer") to photograph me and to record my voice, performances, poses, acts, plays and appearances, and use my picture, photograph, silhouette and other reproductions of my physical likeness and sound as part of the __MOTION PICTURE__ tentatively entitled __HERBY'S SUMMER VACATION__ (the "Picture") and the unlimited distribution, advertising, promotion, exhibition and exploitation of the Picture by any method or device now known or hereafter devised in which the same may be used, and/or incorporated and/or exhibited and/or exploited.

I agree that I will not assert or maintain against you, your successors, assigns and licensees, any claim, action, suit or demand of any kind or nature whatsoever, including but not limited to, those grounded upon invasion of privacy, rights of publicity or other civil rights, or for any other reason in connection with your authorized use of my physical likeness and sound in the Picture as herein provided. I hereby release you, your successors, assigns and licensees, and each of them, from and against any and all claims, liabilities, demands, actions, causes of action(s), costs and expenses whatsoever, at law or in equity, known or unknown, anticipated or unanticipated, which I ever had, now have, or may, shall or hereafter have by reason, matter, cause or thing arising out of your use as herein provided.

I affirm that neither I, nor anyone acting for me, gave or agreed to give anything of value to any of your employees or any representative of any television network, motion picture studio or production entity for arranging my appearance on the Picture.

I have read the foregoing and fully understand the meaning and effect thereof and, intending to be legally bound, I have signed this release.

Dated: __6/23/XX__

Signature __Haley Millstone__

If a Minor, Guardian's Signature _____

Please Print Name __HALEY MILLSTONE__

Address __123 MAIN ST.__
__HOLLYWOOD, CA 90028__

Phone No. __555-6337__

AGREED AND ACCEPTED TO:

By: __Elizabeth Bright__

PERSONAL RELEASE - PAYMENT

Film: __HERBY'S SUMMER VACATION__

Prod. Co.: __XYZ PRODUCTIONS__

Address: __1234 FLICK DR.__
__HOLLYWOOD, CA 90038__   Date: __6·25·XX__

Ladies and Gentlemen:

In consideration of payment to me of the sum of $ __50__ , receipt of which is hereby acknowledged, I, undersigned, hereby grant permission to __XYZ PRODUCTIONS__ ("Producer") to photograph me and to record my voice, performances, poses, acts, plays and appearances, and use my picture, photograph, silhouette and other reproductions of my physical likeness and sound as part of the __MOVIE FOR TELEVISION__ tentatively entitled __HERBY'S SUMMER VACATION__ (the "Picture") and the unlimited distribution, advertising, promotion, exhibition and exploitation of the Picture by any method or device now known or hereafter devised in which the same may be used, and/or incorporated and/or exhibited and/or exploited.

I agree that I will not assert or maintain against you, your successors, assigns and licensees, any claim, action, suit or demand of any kind or nature whatsoever, including but not limited to, those grounded upon invasion of privacy, rights of publicity or other civil rights, or for any other reason in connection with your authorized use of my physical likeness and sound in the Picture as herein provided. I hereby release you, your successors, assigns and licensees, and each of them, from and against any and all claims, liabilities, demands, actions, causes of action(s), costs and expenses whatsoever, at law or in equity, known or unknown, anticipated or unanticipated, which I ever had, now have, or may, shall or hereafter have by reason, matter, cause or thing arising out of your use as herein provided.

I affirm that neither I, nor anyone acting for me, gave or agreed to give anything of value to any of your employees or any representative of any television network, motion picture studio or production entity for arranging my appearance on the Picture.

I have read the foregoing and fully understand the meaning and effect thereof and, intending to be legally bound, I have signed this release.

Dated: __6·25·XX__

__Beverly Fairfax__
Signature

_____
If a Minor, Guardian's Signature

__BEVERLY FAIRFAX__
Please Print Name

__456 STATE ST.__
__HOLLYWOOD, CA__
Address

__555-4566__
Phone No.

AGREED AND ACCEPTED TO:

By: __Elizabeth Bright__

__123-45-6789__
Social Security or Federal ID No.

GROUP RELEASE

Film: HERBY'S SUMMER VACATION

Prod. Co.: XYZ PRODUCTIONS

Address: 1234 FLICK DR.

HOLLYWOOD, CA 90038   Date: 6·25·XX

Ladies and Gentlemen:

I, the undersigned, hereby grant permission to XYZ PRODUCTIONS ("Producer") to photograph me and to record my voice, performances, poses, acts, plays and appearances, and use my picture, photograph, silhouette and other reproductions of my physical likeness and sound as part of the MOVIE FOR CABLE tentatively entitled HERBY'S SUMMER VACATION (the "Picture") and the unlimited distribution, advertising, promotion, exhibition and exploitation of the Picture by any method or device now known or hereafter devised in which the same may be used, and/or incorporated and/or exhibited and/or exploited.

I agree that I will not assert or maintain against you, your successors, assigns and licensees, any claim, action, suit or demand of any kind or nature whatsoever, including but not limited to, those grounded upon invasion of privacy, rights of publicity or other civil rights, or for any other reason in connection with your authorized use of my physical likeness and sound in the Picture as herein provided. I hereby release you, your successors, assigns and licensees, and each of them, from and against any and all claims, liabilities, demands, actions, causes of action(s), costs and expenses whatsoever, at law or in equity, known or unknown, anticipated or unanticipated, which I ever had, now have, or may, shall or hereafter have by reason, matter, cause or thing arising out of your use as herein provided.

I affirm that neither I, nor anyone acting for me, gave or agreed to give anything of value to any of your employees or any representative of any television network, motion picture studio or production entity for arranging my appearance on the Picture.

I have read the foregoing and fully understand the meaning and effect thereof and, intending to be legally bound, I have signed this release.

NAME	ADDRESS	SOC. SEC.#
JACK SPRATT	4550 - 1ST AVE. - HOLLYWOOD CA	123-45-6789
MARY MUFFITT	4567 MAIN ST. #3 - LOS ANGELES	234-56-7890
H. DUMPTY	13325 WALL ST. - STUDIO VILLAGE	345-67-8901

USE OF NAME

Film: HERBY'S SUMMER VACATION

Prod. Co.: XYZ PRODUCTIONS

Address: 1234 FLICK DR.

HOLLYWOOD, CA 90038   Date: 6·28·XX

Ladies and Gentlemen:

For good and valuable consideration, receipt of which is hereby acknowledged, I grant permission to XYZ PRODUCTIONS ("Producer") and its successors, assigns, distributees and licensees forever, throughout the universe, the sole, exclusive and unconditional right and license to use, simulate and portray my name to such extent and in such manner as you in your sole discretion may elect, in or in connection with your MOTION PICTURE tentatively entitled HERBY'S SUMMER VACATION (the "Picture") including reissues, remakes of and sequels to any such production, prepared by you or any successor to your interest therein, together with the right to publish synopses thereof, and to advertise, exploit, present, release, distribute, exhibit and/or otherwise utilize said productions and publications throughout the world.

I hereby release Producer, its successors, assigns, distributees and licensees from any and all claims and demands arising out of or in connection with such use including, without limitation, any and all claims for invasion of privacy, infringement of your right of publicity, defamation (including libel and slander) and any other personal and/or property rights.

In granting of the foregoing rights and licenses, I acknowledge that I have not been induced so to do by any representative or assurance by you or on your behalf relative to the manner in which any of the rights or licenses granted hereunder may be exercised; and I agree that you are under no obligation to exercise any of the rights or licenses granted hereunder.

Sincerely yours,

Dated: 6·28·XX

Sherlock Holmes
Signature

SHERLOCK HOLMES
Please Print Name

221 BAKER STREET

AGREED AND ACCEPTED TO:

TINSELTOWN, CA 90000
Address

By: _Swifty Deals_

555-1001
Phone No.

USE OF TRADEMARK OR LOGO

Film: _HERBY'S SUMMER VACATION_
Prod. Co.: _XYZ PRODUCTIONS_
Address: _1234 FLICK DR._
HOLLYWOOD, CA 90038   Date: _6·28·XX_

Ladies and Gentlemen:

For good and valuable consideration, receipt of which is hereby acknowledged, the undersigned hereby grants to you, your agents, successors, licensees and assigns, the non-exclusive right, but not the obligation to photograph, record, reproduce or otherwise use all or part of our trademark(s), logo(s), and/or animated or identifiable characters (the "Mark(s)") listed below in the _MOVIE FOR TELEVISION_ tentatively entitled _HERBY'S SUMMER VACATION_ (the "Picture"), and to utilize and reproduce the Mark(s) in connection with the Picture, without limitation as to time or number of runs, for reproduction, exhibition and exploitation, throughout the world, in any and all manner, methods and media, whether now known or hereafter devised, and in the advertising, publicizing, promotion, trailers and exploitation thereof.

The undersign represents that the consent of no other person or entity is required to enable you to use the Mark(s) and that such use will not violate or infringe upon the rights of any third parties. I hereby release to you and your agents, successors, licensees and assigns, from any claim of any kind or nature whatsoever arising from the use of the Mark(s).

In granting of the foregoing rights and licenses, I acknowledge that I have not been induced to do so by any representative or assurance by you or on your behalf relative to the manner in which any of the rights or licenses granted hereunder may be exercised; and I agree that you are under no obligation to exercise any of the rights or licenses granted hereunder.

Mark(s): _The COUNTRY ROADS COLLECTION logo_

Very truly yours,

Barbara Hutchins
Signature

BARBARA HUTCHINS
Please Print Name

PRESIDENT
Title

COUNTRY ROADS COLLECTION
Company

11288 SUGARFOOT LN.
LOS ANGELES, CA 90027
Address

_555-7322_
Phone No.

AGREED AND ACCEPTED TO:

By: _Swifty Deals_

USE OF LITERARY MATERIAL

Film: HERBY'S SUMMER VACATION

Prod. Co.: XYZ PRODUCTIONS

Address: 1234 FLICK DR.
HOLLYWOOD, CA 90038   Date: 6-29-XX

Ladies and Gentlemen:

I am informed that you are producing a MOTION PICTURE tentatively entitled HERBY'S SUMMER VACATION (the "Picture"), and that you have requested that I grant you the right to use the title and/or portions of the following literary material owned and published by the undersigned for inclusion in the Picture:

THE COMPLETE FILM PRODUCTION HANDBOOK
(PUBLISHED BY FOCAL PRESS)

For good and valuable consideration, receipt of which is hereby acknowledged, I, the undersigned, do hereby confirm the consent hereby given you with respect to your use of the above title and/or literary material (the "Materials") in connection with the Picture, and I do hereby grant to you, your agents, successors, licensees and assigns, the perpetual right to use the Materials in connection with the Picture. I agree that you may record the Materials on film, tape or otherwise and use the Materials and recordings in and in connection with the exhibition, advertising, promotion, exploitation, and any other use of the Picture as you may desire.

I represent that the consent of no other person or entity is required to enable you to use the Materials, and that such use will not violate or infringe upon the rights of any third parties. I hereby release you, your agents, successors, licensees and assigns from and against any and all claims, liabilities, demands, actions, causes of action, costs and expenses, whatsoever, at law or in equity, known or unknown, arising out of your use of the Materials as provided herein in connection with the Picture.

In granting of the foregoing rights and licenses, I acknowledge that I have not been induced to do so by any representative or assurance by you or on your behalf relative to the manner in which any of the rights or licenses granted hereunder may be exercised; and I agree that you are under no obligation to exercise any of the rights or licenses granted hereunder.

Very truly yours,

_____
Signature

EVE LIGHT HONTHANER
Please Print Name

1233 REDFORD AVE.
STUDIO VILLAGE, CA 91604
Address

555-0723
Phone No.

AGREED AND ACCEPTED TO:

By: _____

USE OF ARTWORK
(RELEASE FROM COPYRIGHTED OWNER)

Film: __HERBY'S SUMMER VACATION__

Prod. Co.: __XYZ PRODUCTIONS__

Address: __1234 FLICK DR.__
__HOLLYWOOD, CA 90038__   Date: __6·28·XX__

Ladies and Gentlemen:

For good and valuable consideration, receipt of which is hereby acknowledged, I, the undersigned, grant to you, your agents, successors, licensees and assigns, the non-exclusive right but not the obligation to use my artwork (as described below) in the _____ tentatively entitled _____ (the "Picture"), and to utilize and reproduce the artwork in connection with the Picture, without limitation as to time or number of runs, for reproduction, exhibition and exploitation, throughout the world, in any and all manner, methods and media, whether now known or hereafter known or devised, and in the advertising, publicizing, promotion, and exploitation thereof.

I hereby release you, your agents, successors, licensees and assigns from any claim of any kind or nature whatsoever arising from the use of such artwork, including, but not limited to, those based upon defamation (including libel and slander), invasion of privacy, right of publicity, copyright, or any other personal and/or property rights and agree that I will not now or in the future assert or maintain any claims against you, your agents, successors, licensees and assigns.

I represent that I am the owner and/or authorized representative of the artwork, and that I have the authority to grant you the permission and rights herein granted, and that no one else's permission is required with respect to the rights herein granted.

In granting of the foregoing rights and licenses, I acknowledge that I have not been induced to do so by any representative or assurance by you or on your behalf relative to the manner in which any of the rights or licenses granted hereunder may be exercised; and I agree that you are under no obligation to exercise any of the rights or licenses granted hereunder.

Title of Artwork: " __CAMBRIA SHORES__ "

Very truly yours,

__Mark Key__
Signature of Owner and/or Authorized Agent

__MARK KEY__
Please Print Name

__ARTIST__
Title/Company

AGREED AND ACCEPTED TO: __4330 GALLERY ROW__

__CARMEL, CA__
Address

By: __Swifty Deals__   __555-3634__
Phone No.

USE OF STILL PHOTOGRAPH(S)
(RELEASE FROM COPYRIGHTED OWNER)

Film: _HERBY'S SUMMER VACATION_

Prod. Co.: _XYZ PRODUCTIONS_

Address: _1234 FLICK DR._
HOLLYWOOD, CA 90038　　　　Date: _6·25·XX_

Ladies and Gentlemen:

For good and valuable consideration, receipt of which is hereby acknowledged, I, the undersigned, grant to you, your agents, successors, licensees and assigns, the non-exclusive right but not the obligation to use and include the still photograph(s) (the "Still(s)") as described below, in the _TELEVISION SERIES_ tentatively entitled _HERBY'S SUMMER VACATION_ (the "Picture"), and to utilize and reproduce the Still(s) in connection with the Picture, without limitation as to time or number of runs, for reproduction, exhibition and exploitation, throughout the world, in any and all manner, methods and media, whether now known or hereafter known or devised, and in the advertising, publicizing, promotion, and exploitation thereof.

I hereby release you, your agents, successors, licensees and assigns from any claims of any kind or nature whatsoever arising from the use of the Still(s), including, but not limited to, those based upon defamation, invasion of privacy, right of publicity, copyright, or any other personal and/or property rights and agree that I will not now or in the future assert or maintain any claims against you, your agents, successors, licensees and assigns.

I represent that I am the owner and/or authorized representative of the poster, and that I have the authority to grant you the permission and rights herein granted, and that no one else's permission is required with respect to the rights herein granted.

In granting of the foregoing rights and licenses, I acknowledge that I have not been induced to do so by any representative or assurance by you or on your behalf relative to the manner in which any of the rights or licenses granted hereunder may be exercised; and I agree that you are under no obligation to exercise any of the rights or licenses granted hereunder.

Description of the Still(s): _1995 HEADSHOT OF SCARLET STARLET_

Very truly yours,

Leonardo Lenscapp
Signature of Owner and/or Authorized Agent

LEONARDO LENSCAPP
Please Print Name

DIR. OF PUBLICITY, MIRACLE PICS
Title/Company

AGREED AND ACCEPTED TO:

1003 VALENTINO BLVD.
HOLLYWOOD, CA 90028
Address

By: _Swifty Deals_

_555-1003_
Phone No.

USE OF STILL PHOTOGRAPH(S)
(RELEASE FROM PERSON DEPICTED IN PHOTO)

Film: _HERBY'S SUMMER VACATION_

Prod. Co.: _XYZ PRODUCTIONS_

Address: _1234 FLICK DR._

HOLLYWOOD, CA 90038   Date: _6·15·XX_

Ladies and Gentlemen:

For good and valuable consideration, receipt of which is hereby acknowledged, I, the undersigned, grant to you, your agents, successors, licensees and assigns, the non-exclusive right but not the obligation to use and include my physical likeness in the form of a still photograph(s) (the "Still(s)") as described below, in the _MOTION PICTURE_ tentatively entitled _HERBY'S SUMMER VACATION_ (the "Picture"), and to utilize and reproduce the Still(s) in connection with the Picture, without limitation as to time or number of runs, for reproduction, exhibition and exploitation, throughout the world, in any and all manner, methods and media, whether now known or hereafter known or devised, and in the advertising, publicizing, promotion, and exploitation thereof.

I agree that I will not assert or maintain against you, your agents, successors, licensees and assigns, a claim, action, suit or demand of any kind or nature whatsoever, including but not limited to, those grounded upon invasion of privacy, rights of publicity or other civil rights, or for any other reason in connection with your authorized use of the Still(s) in the Picture as herein provided. I hereby release you, your agents, successors, licensees and assigns from any and all such claims, actions, causes of action, suits and demands whatsoever that I may now or hereafter have against you or them.

In granting of the foregoing rights and licenses, I acknowledge that I have not been induced to do so by any representative or assurance by you or on your behalf relative to the manner in which any of the rights or licenses granted hereunder may be exercised; and I agree that you are under no obligation to exercise any of the rights or licenses granted hereunder.

Description of the Still(s): _HEADSHOT OF HOLLYWOOD MANN_

Sincerely yours,

Holly Mann
Signature

HOLLYWOOD MANN
Please Print Name

AGREED AND ACCEPTED TO:

3465 HORTENSE ST.
WONDERLAND, CA 91000
Address

By: _Swifty Deals_

_555-7654_
Phone No.

USE OF POSTER
(RELEASE FROM COPYRIGHTED OWNER)

Film: _HERBY'S SUMMER VACATION_

Prod. Co.: _XYZ PRODUCTIONS_

Address: _1234 FLICK DR._
HOLLYWOOD, CA 90038   Date: _5.15.XX_

Ladies and Gentlemen:

For good and valuable consideration, receipt of which is hereby acknowledged, I, the undersigned, grant to you, your agents, successors, licensees and assigns, the non-exclusive right but not the obligation to use and include the poster (entitled or otherwise described as _"THE BUTLER"_) (the "Poster") in the _MOVIE FOR TELEVISION_ tentatively entitled _HERBY'S SUMMER VACATION_ (the "Picture"), and to utilize and reproduce the Poster in connection with the Picture, without limitation as to time or number of runs, for reproduction, exhibition and exploitation, throughout the world, in any and all manner, methods and media, whether now known or hereafter known or devised, and in the advertising, publicizing, promotion, and exploitation thereof.

I hereby release you, your agents, successors, licensees and assigns from any claims of any kind or nature whatsoever arising from the use of the Poster, including, but not limited to, those based upon defamation (including libel and slander), invasion of privacy, right of publicity, copyright, or any other personal and/or property rights and agree that I will not now or in the future assert or maintain any claims against you, your agents, successors, licensees and assigns.

I represent that I am the owner and/or authorized representative of the poster, and that I have the authority to grant you the permission and rights herein granted, and that no one else's permission is required with respect to the rights herein granted.

In granting of the foregoing rights and licenses, I acknowledge that I have not been induced to do so by any representative or assurance by you or on your behalf relative to the manner in which any of the rights or licenses granted hereunder may be exercised; and I agree that you are under no obligation to exercise any of the rights or licenses granted hereunder.

Very truly yours,

C.F.I. Kare
Signature of Owner and/or Authorized Agent

C.F.I. KARE
Please Print Name

PRES., SPORTS POSTERS, INC.
Title/Company

AGREED AND ACCEPTED TO:

321 ARENA AVE.
LOS ANGELES, CA 90001
Address

By: _Smighty Dale_   _555-8000_
Phone No.

224 The Complete Film Production Handbook

USE OF VEHICLE

Film: _HERBY'S SUMMER VACATION_

Prod. Co.: _XYZ PRODUCTIONS_

Address: _1234 FLICK DR._

HOLLYWOOD, CA 90038   Date: _7·13·XX_

Ladies and Gentlemen:

For good and valuable consideration, receipt of which is hereby acknowledged, I, the undersigned, grant to you, your agents, successors, licensees and assigns, the right but not the obligation to use the below-mentioned vehicle, and to include all or part of the trademarks, logos, and/or identifiable characters associated therewith ("Vehicle") in the _MOTION PICTURE_ tentatively entitled _HERBY'S SUMMER VACATION_ (the "Picture"), without limitation as to time or number of runs, for reproduction, exhibition and exploitation, throughout the world, in any and all manner, methods and media, whether now known or hereafter known or devised, and in the advertising, publicizing, promotion, and exploitation thereof.

The undersigned represents that the consent of no other person or entity is required to enable Producer to use the Vehicle as described herein and that such use will not violate or infringe upon the trademarks, service marks, trade names, copyright, artistic and/or other rights of any third parties including the rights of publicity and/or privacy. The undersigned hereby releases Producer, Producer's agents, successors, licensees and assigns, from any claim of any kind or nature whatsoever arising from the use of the Vehicle, including but not limited to, those based upon defamation, invasion of privacy, right of publicity, copyright, or any other personal and/or property rights, and the undersigned agrees that the undersigned shall not now or in the future assert or maintain any such claim against Producer, Producer's agents, successors, licensees and assigns.

In granting of the foregoing rights and licenses, I acknowledge that I have not been induced to do so by any representative or assurance by you or on your behalf relative to the manner in which any of the rights or licenses granted hereunder may be exercised; and I agree that you are under no obligation to exercise any of the rights or licenses granted hereunder.

Description of Vehicle: _1963 CHEVY IMPALA CONVERTIBLE_
(BLACK BODY – WHITE TOP – WHITEWALL TIRES)
LICENSE: SCOTSJOY

Very truly yours,

[signature]

Signature of Owner and/or Authorized Agent

SCOTT DEVEROW
Please Print Name

OWNER
Title/Company

6132 COOLMAN AVE.
WONDERLAND, CA 90000
Address

_555-3322_
Phone No.

AGREED AND ACCEPTED TO:

By: _[signature]_

CROWD NOTICE - RELEASE

TO BE PLACED IN SEVERAL CLEARLY VISIBLE LOCATIONS
IN A STUDIO WHEN FILMING OR TAPING BEFORE A LIVE AUDIENCE

CROWD NOTICE - RELEASE

PLEASE BE ADVISED THAT YOUR PRESENCE AS A MEMBER OF
THIS STUDIO AUDIENCE DURING THE FILMING/TAPING OF THE
PROGRAM _____
CONSTITUTES YOUR CONSENT TO YOUR VOICE AND LIKENESS
BEING USED, WITHOUT COMPENSATION, IN THE UNLIMITED
DISTRIBUTION, ADVERTISING, PROMOTION, EXHIBITION AND
EXPLOITATION OF THE PROGRAM IN ANY AND ALL MEDIA BY ANY
METHOD OR DEVICE NOW KNOWN OR HEREAFTER DEVISED, AND
YOU RELEASE _____
FROM ANY LIABILITY IN CONNECTION WITH SUCH USAGE.

IF FOR ANY REASON YOU OBJECT TO YOUR VOICE AND LIKENESS
BEING SO USED, YOU SHOULD LEAVE THE STUDIO AT THIS TIME.
IF YOU REMAIN, YOUR PRESENCE AT THIS FILMING/TAPING WILL
CONSTITUTE YOUR APPROVAL OF THE FOREGOING.

CROWD NOTICE - RELEASE

TO BE PLACED IN SEVERAL CLEARLY VISIBLE LOCATIONS
IN THE "AREA" IN WHICH FILMING OR TAPING IS TAKING PLACE

CROWD NOTICE - RELEASE

PLEASE BE ADVISED THAT FILMING/TAPING IS TAKING PLACE IN
CONNECTION WITH THE PRODUCTION OF A _____
TENTATIVELY ENTITLED _____.
PEOPLE ENTERING THIS AREA MAY APPEAR IN THE PICTURE. BY
ENTERING THIS AREA, YOU GRANT TO _____
_____THE RIGHT TO FILM AND PHOTOGRAPH YOU AND
RECORD YOUR VOICE AND TO USE YOUR VOICE AND LIKENESS,
WITHOUT COMPENSATION, IN CONNECTION WITH THE PICTURE AND THE
DISTRIBUTION AND EXPLOITATION THEREOF, AND YOU RELEASE
_____AND ITS
LICENSEES FROM ALL LIABILITY IN CONNECTION THEREIN. YOU AGREE
AND UNDERSTAND THAT _____ WILL
PROCEED IN RELIANCE UPON SUCH GRANT AND RELEASE.

_____ DOES NOT ASSUME
RESPONSIBILITY FOR ANY INJURY TO YOUR PERSON OR DAMAGE OR
LOSS TO YOUR PROPERTY.

**THE USE OF CAMERA AND RECORDING EQUIPMENT IS
PROHIBITED DUE TO UNION AND COPYRIGHT REGULATIONS.**

SMOKING IS PROHIBITED IN THIS AREA. THANK YOU!

SUPPLYING A FILM/TAPE CLIP OF YOUR SHOW
FOR PROMOTIONAL PURPOSES

Date: __5·4·XX__

__TALK SHOW PRODUCTIONS__
__"THE EVENING SHOW"__
__1000 W. MIRACLE MILE AVE,__
__LOS ANGELES, CA 90035__

Ladies and Gentlemen:

The undersigned hereby authorizes you to use a Film/Tape Clip (the "Clip") from the __MOVIE__ __FOR TELEVISION__ entitled __HERBY'S SUMMER VACATION__ for promotional purposes only in the program entitled __THE EVENING SHOW__ currently scheduled for broadcast on __5-9-XX__ .

The undersigned hereby affirms that neither he nor anyone acting on his behalf or any company which he may represent, gave or agreed to give anything of value (except for the Clip) which was furnished for promotional purposes solely on or in connection with __THE EVENING__ __SHOW__ to any member of the production staff, anyone associated in any manner with the program or any representative of __TALK SHOW PRODUCTIONS__ for mentioning or displaying the name of any company which he may represent or any of its products, trademarks, trade-names or the like.

The undersigned understands that any broadcast identification of the Clip (or the name of any company, product, etc. which he may represent) which __XYZ PRODUCTIONS__ may furnish, shall, in no event, be beyond that which is reasonably related to the program content.

The undersigned is aware, as is the company which he may represent, that it is a Federal offense unless disclosed to __TALK SHOW PRODUCTIONS__ prior to broadcast if the undersigned gives or agrees to give anything of value to promote any product, service or venture on the air.

The undersigned represents that he is fully empowered to execute this letter on behalf of any company which he may represent.

The undersigned warrants that he or the company which he may represent has the right to grant the license herein granted, and agrees to indemnify you for all loss, damage and liability, excluding the payment of any guild-related talent fees or performing rights fees in the music included in said Clip, if any (which you agree to pay or cause to be paid), arising out of the use of the above material.

Very truly yours,

Swifty Deals
Signature

__SWIFTY DEALS__
Please Print Name

__PRODUCER__
Title

__555-3331__
Phone No.

AGREED AND ACCEPTED TO:

By: _Connie Jarson_

PRODUCT PLACEMENT RELEASE

Film: _HERBY'S SUMMER VACATION_

Prod. Co.: _XYZ PRODUCTIONS_

Address: _1234 FLICK DR._
HOLLYWOOD, CA 90038   Date: _4·21·XX_

Ladies and Gentlemen:

The undersigned ("Company") agrees to provide the following product(s) and/or service(s) to _XYZ PRODUCTIONS_ for use in the _MOTION PICTURE_ tentatively entitled _HERBY'S SUMMER VACATION_ (the "Picture"):

> _2 doz. pair - assorted sunglasses_
> _1 basketball_
> _1 bat_
> _2 softballs_

The Company grants to you, your successors, licensees and assigns, the non-exclusive right, but not the obligation to use and include all or part of the trademark(s), logo(s) and/or identifiable characters (the "Mark(s)") associated with the above listed product(s) and/or service(s) in the Picture, without limitation as to time or number of runs, for reproduction, exhibition and exploitation, throughout the world, in any and all manner, methods and media, whether now known or hereafter known or devised, and in the advertising, publicizing, promotion, trailers and exploitation thereof.

The Company warrants and represents that it is the owner of the product(s) or direct provider of the service(s) as listed above or a representative of such and has the right to enter this agreement and grant the rights granted to _XYZ PRODUCTIONS_ hereunder.

In full consideration of the Company providing the product(s) and/or service(s) to _XYZ PRODUCTIONS_, _XYZ PRODUCTIONS_ agrees to accord the Company screen credit in the end titles of the positive prints of the Picture in the following form:

> _SPORTING GOODS AND SUNGLASSES FURNISHED BY_
> _HOLLYWOOD PROMOTIONS, INC._

The Company understands that any broadcast identification of its products, trademarks, trade names or the like which may furnish, shall in no event, be beyond that which is reasonably related to the program content.

As it applies to any and all television broadcasts of the Picture, the Company is aware that it is a Federal offense to give or agree to give anything of value to promote any product, service or venture on the air. The Company affirms that it did not give or agree to give anything of value, except for the product(s) and/or service(s) to any member of the production staff, anyone associated in any manner with the Picture or any representative of _XYZ PRODUCTIONS_ for mentioning or displaying the name of the Company or any of its products, trademarks, trade names, or the like.

I represent that I am an officer of the Company and am empowered to execute this form on behalf of the Company.

Product Placement Release
Page 2

I further represent that neither I nor the Company which I represent will directly or indirectly publicize or otherwise exploit the use, exhibition or demonstration of the above product(s) and/or service(s) in the Picture for advertising, merchandising or promotional purposes without the express written consent of _XYZ PRODUCTIONS_____.

Sincerely yours,

_Anna Morphic_____
Authorized Signatory

_ANNA MORPHIC_____
Please Print Name

_V.P._____
Title

HOLLYWOOD PROMOTIONS, INC.
Name of Company

_15155 FOOTAGE AVE._____
Address

_HOLLYWOOD, CA 90028_____
Address

_555-7700_____
Phone No.

AGREED AND ACCEPTED TO:

By: _Swifty Deals_____

FILM/TAPE FOOTAGE RELEASE

Date: __6·25·XX__

LICENSOR: __STOCK SHOTS, INC.__

LICENSEE: __XYZ PRODUCTIONS__

DESCRIPTION OF THE FOOTAGE: __ESTABLISHING SHOT OF__ __DOWNTOWN SKYLINE – MILWAUKEE, WISCONSIN__

PRODUCTION: __HERBY'S SUMMER VACATION__ (the "Picture")

LENGTH OF FOOTAGE: __40'__

LICENSE FEE, if any: __$1,000__

Licensor hereby grants to Licensee, Licensor's permission to edit and include all or portion of the above-mentioned Footage in the Picture as follows:

1. Licensor grants to Licensee a non-exclusive license to edit and incorporate the Footage in the Picture. Licensee may broadcast and otherwise exploit the Footage in the Picture, and in customary advertising and publicity thereof, throughout the world in perpetuity in any media now known or hereafter devised.

2. Licensee shall not make any reproductions whatsoever of or from the Footage except as described hereunder.

3. Licensee agrees to obtain, at Licensee's expense, all required consents of any person whose appearances are contained in the Footage pursuant to this agreement, and to make any payments to such persons, guilds or unions having jurisdiction thereof and music publishers, when necessary. Licensor agrees to supply the identity of such persons, if known.

4. Licensor represents and warrants that: (1) Licensor has the right and power to grant the rights herein granted, and (2) neither Licensee's use of the Footage pursuant to this license nor anything contained therein infringes upon the rights of any third parties.

5. Licensor and Licensee each agree to indemnify and hold the other harmless from and against any and all claims, losses liabilities, damages and expenses, including reasonable attorneys' fees, which may result from any breach of their respective representations and warranties hereunder.

6. As between Licensor and Licensee, the Picture shall be Licensee's sole and exclusive property. Licensee shall not be obligated to use the Footage or the rights herein granted or to produce or broadcast the Picture.

7. Licensor acknowledges that, under the Federal Communications Act, it is a Federal offense to give or agree to give anything of value to promote any product, service or venture in the Picture, and Licensor warrants and represents that Licensor has not and will not do so.

8. This agreement constitutes the entire understanding between the parties, supersedes any prior understanding relating thereto and shall not be modified except by a writing signed by the parties. This agreement shall be irrevocable and shall be binding upon and inure to the benefit of Licensor's and Licensee's respective successors, assigns and licensees.

Kindly sign below to indicate your acceptance of the foregoing.

Licensor:

Chellon Sprockett
Signature

SHELDON SPROCKETT
Please Print Name

PRESIDENT
Title

CONFIRMED:

STOCK SHOTS, INC.
Company

51663 CULVER CIRCLE

CULVER CITY, CA 90230
Address

By: _Swifty Deals_

555-9900
Phone No.

#95-1234567
Soc. Sec. or Federal ID No:

TALENT
USE OF NAME & LIKENESS
IN A FILM OR TV CLIP

Date: 6·25·XX

MR. JOE COOL
TALENTED ARTISTS AGENCY
1515 SUNSET BLVD. SUITE 100
HOLLYWOOD, CA 90028

Dear MR. COOL:

I am writing to you with regard to a MOTION PICTURE being produced by XYZ PRODUCTIONS and tentatively entitled HERBY'S SUMMER VACATION (the "Picture"). The Picture is scheduled for release on 12·7·XX.

A brief description of the Picture is as follows:
A POIGNANT, COMING·OF·AGE STORY SET IN MILWAUKEE, WISCONSIN IN 1968. WHILE VISITING HIS GRANDMOTHER ONE SUMMER, HERBY, A 13-YR. OLD BOY, WITNESSES A MURDER, DISCOVERS HIS SEXUALITY AND LEARNS WHAT IT MEANS TO BE A FRIEND.

In conjunction with this Picture, we are requesting permission to use the appearance of SCARLET STARLET in a clip from HER 1967 APPEARANCE IN THE TELEVISION SERIES, "MARSHAL DILLON OF DODGE" - EPISODE: "THE SALOON GIRL" - SC.45.

In consideration for MS. STARLET 's permission and in conjunction with the current SAG Agreement, XYZ PRODUCTIONS hereby offers to pay MS. STARLET a fee of $ (SAG MINIMUM)+10% AGENCY COMMISSION. This sum represents the total payment for XYZ PRODUCTION 's use of SCARLET STARLET 's name and likeness in the above-described clip in and in connection with the Picture and in promotion for the picture. Compensation to MS. STARLET for any further use of the Picture in any media shall be governed by the then applicable collective bargaining agreements pertaining to such use.

I would appreciate it if you would have MS. STARLET complete the information requested below and acknowledge HER assent to the Agreement by signing below. Once executed, please return a copy of this letter to us for our records.

Please do not hesitate to call should you have any questions.

Sincerely yours,

Snifty Deals

ACCEPTED & AGREED TO:

By: *Scarlet Starlet*

STARLET NIGHTS, INC.
C/O TAA - 1515 SUNSET BLVD., #100
HOLLYWOOD, CA 90028
Loan-out Corporation Name & Address

Date: 7·5·XX
SS#: 123-45-6789
Fed. Tax ID#: #95-1234567

REQUEST FOR VIDEOCASSETTE

Date: _11·15·XX_

MR. F. STOPP
8365 SHUTTER LANE
BEVERLY HILLS, CA 90210

Dear _MR. STOPP_ :

You accept delivery of the _½" VIDEOCASSETTE_ ("Recording") of _HERBY'S SUMMER VACATION_ (the "Picture"), and in connection of our delivery of it, agree as follows:

1.   You warrant, represent and agree that the Recording shall be used solely for your private, personal library purpose or for screenings in connection with an in-house demo reel; and the Recording will never be publicly exhibited in any manner or medium whatsoever. You will not charge or authorize the charge of a fee for exhibiting the Recording. You will not duplicate or permit the duplication of the Recording. You will retain possession of the Recording at all times.

2.   All other rights in and to the Picture, under copyright or otherwise, including but not limited to title to, are retained by _XYZ PRODUCTIONS_ .

3.   The permission which we have granted to you for the use of the Recording itself will be non-assignable and non-transferable.

4.   You agree to indemnify us against and hold us harmless from claims, liabilities and actions arising out of your breach of this agreement.

5.   You agree to reimburse us for the cost of making the Recording available to you.

This will become a contract between you and us upon your acceptance of delivery of the Recording.

Sincerely yours,

Eddie Torial
Signature

EDDIE TORIAL - XYZ PRODS.
Please Print Name

1234 FLICK DR.

HOLLYWOOD, CA 90028
Address

_555-3331_
Phone No.

AGREED AND ACCEPTED TO:

By: _f. Stopp_

CHAPTER FOURTEEN

A Guide To Music Clearance

If you are planning to use anything other than originally scored music in your film, television program, music video, commercial or multimedia project, you will need the services of a music supervisor and/or a studio or production company's music clearance department or a music clearance service. You will want to know if the rights to the copyrighted musical material you wish to use are available, how much each would cost to license and if your music budget will cover the cost of the music you wish to use. Early music planning could save you a lot of time and money by knowing exactly which pieces of music you can and cannot incorporate into your project.

The following guide prepared by the *Copyright Clearinghouse, Inc.* answers the most frequently asked questions about the field of music clearance. Any additional questions you may have about music rights clearances should be directed to your attorney or music clearance service.

A TELEVISION AND FILM PRODUCER'S GUIDE TO MUSIC CLEARANCE

From *Copyright Clearinghouse, Inc.*

WHAT IS MUSIC CLEARANCE?

Simply, it is the process of securing permission to use musical compositions and recordings owned by someone else. More specifically, however, it involves: (1) determining who owns the copyright to any given musical material; (2) negotiating permission to use that material in the territories and media in which exhibition or distribution is planned; and (3) paying the negotiated license fees to the copyright owners. An agreement between a copyright owner (or its representative) and a user of the copyright is called a "license." There are many kinds of licenses that cover many different media of exploitation.

Every production presents a unique set of legal and business issues that should be addressed and resolved before production begins. The media and terms of distribution affect the rights to be obtained from music copyright owners. The clearance process should be undertaken before being committed to using specific songs and recordings in order to eliminate musical material that may be too expensive or that the copyright owners do not want used. For example, some musical compositions, while popular and in general use in areas such as radio broadcast or nightclub performance, are not available (at any price) in certain other media applications.

It is advisable that music clearance issues be addressed early in the planning stages of a project to assure the availability of the musical compositions and recordings for their intended use and subsequent exploitation. The unauthorized use of such material could result in an injunction blocking the distribution of the production, as well as other financial penalties. An early phone call to an attorney or music clearance service is highly recommended.

WHY DOES A PRODUCER HAVE TO SECURE LICENSES FOR "MUSIC RIGHTS"?

The music that is broadcast everyday on radio, television and cable, or that is performed in nightclubs and concerts, is subject to federal copyright protection. Pursuant to the U.S. Copyright Act and other related legal doctrines, the owners of copyrighted musical compositions, and the recordings thereof, have the right to control how their musical material is used and the fees that will be paid for that use. This system of law makes it possible for composers, lyricists and recording artists to earn a living from their creations and requires that music be properly cleared, it can be used to the full extent of the license terms.

HOW DOES YOUR ERRORS AND OMISSION INSURANCE POLICY RELATE TO MUSIC CLEARANCE?

Distribution and broadcast agreements require that the production be insured for such things as inadvertent copyright infringements or the unauthorized use of protected materials. Errors and Omissions insurance covers all of the parties in the production/distribution chain for reasonable errors and omissions that may occur during production.

Generally, the applicant for an E&O policy (usually the producer or distributor) will be required to follow the insurance company's written procedures for the clearance of material used in the production. The applicant must sign a written declaration stating that the detailed information required in the application for insurance (including all of the specific clearance procedures) is in all respects true, and that no information has been omitted, suppressed or misstated.

Additionally, the application for insurance must be signed by an attorney who is familiar with the clearance procedures of the insurance company. The attorney must also sign a written declaration that the attorney will use best efforts to assure that the "clearance procedures" are followed, and that he or she believes that the statements in the application are correct.

WHO ARE THE OWNERS OF MUSICAL COMPOSITIONS AND RECORDINGS?

This is a very complex question. Generally, a songwriter may sell or assign the copyright in his or her song to a music publisher who pays the writer a share of the royalties derived from its exploitation. In such cases, the publisher generally owns the copyright (or a portion of it) and is the party with authority to grant permission for its use. However, the approval of the songwriter may be required before a music publisher can grant a license. In other such cases, songwriters may own the copyright and transfer the right to grant permission and collect royalties for certain types of rights to other representatives or outside agencies, who collect royalties and generate license agreements (i.e., administration) for them.

It is now common for copyright ownership in a musical composition to be divided by percentages and territories. Several songwriters may collaborate, with each controlling his or her own interest. Several publishers could own rights in the United States, while several others could own rights for the rest of the world. All of this may result in situations where several parties must agree to the license, thereby increasing the difficulty in obtaining clearance.

Recordings are usually owned by the record company that paid for the recording session, or that had the recording artist under contract. However, the terms of recording contracts can require certain artist approvals before the record company can grant a license.

WHAT WAS THE U.S. SUPREME COURT'S "REAR WINDOW" DECISION AND HOW DOES IT AFFECT MUSIC LICENSING?

A full discussion of the so-called "rear window" decision is far beyond the scope of this book. However, you must be aware of how this decision affects music licensing.

In broad and general terms, songs copyrighted before January 1, 1978 are entitled to two terms of copyright protection: a first copyright term of 28 years, and a renewal terms of 47 years—for a total of 75 years. If the author of a song copyrighted before January 1, 1978 were to die during the first 28-year copyright term, any productions that used the song would lose the right to continue distribution of the production containing the song at the end of the first copyright term. At that point, the heirs of the songwriter would be entitled to receive additional license fees for any continued exploitation of the song in the renewal term.

For example, if a producer enters into a 10-year music license during the 25th year of the original term of a song's copyright, that license agreement may become unenforceable at the end of the 28-year term (i.e., 3 years into the 10-year license) if the songwriter dies before the end of the 28th year. In such a case, a new license agreement (for the remaining 7 years) would have to be negotiated.

Unfortunately, this is not a problem that can be easily solved. In order to do so, a producer would have to get the separate consent of all the songwriter's heirs before the songwriter dies. Even if the producer were to do so, leaving aside the additional administrative cost and license fees, there is no assurance that a songwriter would not thereafter have additional children or spouses.

No producer wants to be in a position of losing the rights to a song after he or she has recorded it into his or her production, or after he or she has paid for the rights. Your attorney or music clearance service should advise you as to which songs are affected by the decision, and the policies of distributors or broadcasters who, for legal or business reasons, may prohibit or restrict the use of such songs.

WHAT RIGHTS ARE NEEDED IN ORDER TO MAKE SURE THAT THE MUSICAL MATERIAL USED IN A PRODUCTION IS PROPERLY CLEARED?

In general, the rights commonly required in order to use musical compositions and recordings in television and film productions may be divided into the following categories:

Public Performing Rights

A public performance is a term of art that refers to the right to do such things as recite, play, sing, dance, act out or broadcast a musical composition in public. However, there is a vast difference between the rights required to merely sing a song on a bare stage and the rights required to dramatize or tell the story of a song using sets, costumes, props, etc. A detailed explanation of dramatic and nondramatic rights is beyond the scope of this chapter; however, the rights required, and the complexity of their clearance, will depend upon the way the song is to be performed.

Pursuant to the U.S. Copyright Law, a record may be "performed" in public without the permission of the record company because the U.S. Copyright Law does not provide for a performance right for sound recordings. However, legislation was enacted in 1995 that now gives owners of sound recording a limited performance right in "digital audio transmissions." The new legislation is very complicated and was written to address the seemingly narrow issue of digital audio transmissions. Traditional television and radio broadcasts are currently exempt. The Digital Millennium Copyright Act, enacted at the end of 1998, modified the 1995 legislation significantly and will have far-reaching effects when music is distributed via phone or cable lines, or as traditional broadcast media migrate to digital platforms.

Reproduction Rights

A music publisher has the right to control the reproduction (recording) of a musical composition. Reproduction Rights are referred to, in television and film production, as "synchronization rights" because the musical composition is recorded on a sound track in synchronization with visual images. "Sync rights," as they are called, should not be confused with so-called "mechanical rights," which refer to the reproduction of songs on audio CDs, records or tapes for distribution to the general public.

Record companies also have the right to control the reproduction of their recordings. A license to reproduce a record in an audio/visual work is generally referred to as a "master use" license.

Adaptation Rights

A copyright owner has the right to control the alteration or adaptation of musical compositions, including arrangements, parodies, comedic uses, lyric changes, translations, etc. If a composition is to be used in an adapted form, specific permission may be required directly from the copyright owner. Some copyright owners, while open to the use of their material as it was originally written, may not grant permission for adaptations.

The way in which a song is performed or used will determine the applicability of these various rights. The media in which distribution is planned (broadcast television, home video, feature film, etc.) will significantly affect how these rights are negotiated, with whom they are negotiated and the amount of the license fees.

FROM WHOM ARE THESE MUSIC RIGHTS OBTAINED?

The previously mentioned rights are generally not handled at one source, but instead are often licensed individually by separate parties. For certain rights, one may have to deal directly with the songwriter, the songwriter's heirs, attorneys, publishers and agents or performing artists, record companies and unions.

Musical Compositions

Public performing rights for television broadcasts have traditionally been the responsibility of the broadcasters of television programming. Networks, local stations, cable programming services and cable system operators secure these rights from the music performing rights organizations which represent composers and publishers. In the United States, those organizations are the American Society of Composers, Authors and Publishers (ASCAP), Broadcast Music, Inc. (BMI) and SESAC.

Pursuant to the U.S. Government's Consent Decrees with ASCAP and BMI, broadcasters have the choice of securing either a "blanket" or "per program" license. In either case, a broadcaster may use any or all of the songs in the ASCAP/BMI catalogs. Under the per program license, however, a broadcaster pays a performing rights society for the programs that contain music licensed by that society that has not been licensed through other means. With the advent of the per program license, an increasing number of television broadcasters are now seeking to license performance rights to the music contained in the television programs from the program producers/distributors rather than through a performing rights society. "Source Licenses," as they are called, require the producer/distributor to acquire performance rights from composers and music publishers and deliver those rights to the broadcaster without any obligation of payment to a performing rights society.

Performing rights licensing for media other than broadcast television, such as feature films, nontheatrical and nonbroadcast distribution, are generally secured directly from the copyright owner.

Synchronization rights and the right to adapt a musical composition are generally obtained by approaching the owner directly. Some music publishers, while retaining the function of quoting the fees and approving the uses, prefer to have licenses prepared and executed through an intermediary organization (e.g., The Harry Fox Agency, Inc.), which they retain to license those rights on their behalf.

Often, in the case of popular songs, the songwriter may own the copyright and designate an attorney, accountant, manager, girlfriend or boy-

friend or other representative to handle licensing for television or film use. If several parties own a composition, each may have to be contacted. If a writer is deceased and his or her rights have passed on to his or her heirs, the process can become even more difficult.

Recordings

Record companies generally control and license their recordings themselves; however, in some instances, their prior approval of the performing artist may be required. A master use license may also contain provisions requiring the user to pay any fees required, pursuant to the record company's collective bargaining agreements with the performer's unions.

A producer working in television, film or music video has no reason to personally keep track of the ownership and representation of the thousands of protected compositions and recordings that may be available. One who did would face the basic problem of where to start, with whom to talk, what paperwork to do and how to negotiate the license fees in accordance with current industry standards. All of this takes a great deal of time, even if the basic information is readily at hand.

WHAT IS A MUSIC CUE SHEET AND WHY IS IT SO IMPORTANT?

A music cue sheet is a document that lists all of the music contained in a production, including the title, composer(s), publisher(s), performing rights affiliation and the use and timing of each musical cue.

The cue sheet functions like an invoice that is used by all parties in the music licensing process to determine the amount of royalties to be paid for the public performance of the music contained in the program, and to whom those royalties are paid. For example, many broadcasters require copies of cue sheets for the television programs they broadcast in order to calculate the fees they must pay to ASCAP and BMI. Without the timely receipt of music cue sheets, they may not have access to the information necessary to correctly calculate the full amount of the license fee that would otherwise be due—resulting in a loss of income to composers and music publishers. Moreover, ASCAP and BMI use a cue sheet to identify the composers and publishers entitled to receive royalties and to calculate the share of royalties they receive. The flow of music publishing royalties should be of vital concern to the producer if musical cues composed for the production are owned by the producer.

The timely delivery of an accurate music cue sheet has always been a requirement in most production/distribution/station license agreements. Practically speaking, the music cue sheet is also a delivery requirement for music publishers and record companies whose materials have been used in the production. The practical effect of not creating an accurate cue sheet and delivering it to the proper parties may be a breach of various production/broadcast agreements and/or synchronization licenses, and may result in composers and publishers not receiving the royalties they are due.

TO WHERE SHOULD MUSIC CUE SHEETS BE SENT?

For all of the reasons listed above, producers should send cue sheets to the following organizations:

MRI (Music Reports, Inc)
405 Riverside Drive
Burbank, CA 91506
(818) 558-1400

ASCAP
One Lincoln Plaza
New York, NY 10023
(212) 595-3050

BMI
320 W. 57th Street
New York, NY 10019
(212) 586-2000

CAN A COPYRIGHT OWNER PREVENT MUSIC FROM BEING USED?

Yes. The owner of a musical composition or recording can, except in very limited situations, restrict or deny permission for its reproduction or adaptation. In certain circumstances, the performing rights organizations also allow an owner to restrict the public performance of musical compositions that are normally subject to blanket performance clearance. Some popular music, freely broadcast on radio or used in nightclub performances, may be blocked from use on commercial television or in motion pictures. The Copyright Law leaves the final decision up to the owner or owners of the work.

WHAT HAPPENS IF A SONG IS USED WITHOUT CLEARANCE?

If the copyright owner never knows—nothing. However, if the matter is discovered by the copyright owner, the producer of the project, and any broadcaster or distributor, may be held liable for copyright infringement as well as other actionable claims. Under the Copyright Act, an infringer may be liable for both the damages sustained by the copyright owner, and the producer's profits resulting from the unauthorized use of the music. Even if the copyright owner cannot show what the damages or the producer's profits are, he or she can still be awarded substantial statutory damages as provided for in the Copyright Act.

The producer may face an injunction, an out-of-court settlement with the copyright owner, or the task of going back to the finished program and making extensive changes to remove the uncleared material. A producer with a completed project from which release prints or dubs have already been made, may find him or herself incurring costs many times what the original clearance and license fees might have been.

Quite recently, several "watchdog" operations have been formed to monitor use of music in all media on behalf of composers, publishers, record companies and artists. Additionally, both ASCAP and BMI have increased their viewing of television programs and monitoring of music cue sheets in order to determine their accuracy, and to resolve questions involving performing rights payments to composers and publishers. This, of course, only increases the chance that someone may find out—particularly if the project is successful.

WHAT ABOUT OLD SONGS? AREN'T THESE SONGS IN THE PUBLIC DOMAIN AND FREE TO BE USED WITHOUT RESTRICTIONS?

There is a certain amount of music for which all copyright protection on a worldwide basis has lapsed. Some musical material that may be in the public domain in the United States may still be protected in other countries. Failure to obtain proper international copyright clearance may severely limit exploitation of the project. With the changes in the U.S. Copyright Law that became effective January 1, 1978, some older material has had its protection extended, and worldwide rights issues have become even more complicated.

If you plan to use public domain material, you must be sure that ANY arrangement created for your use is based on the original public domain version, and not on a subsequent copyrighted or protected version which would require additional clearance.

Actual clearance of the material should still be carefully undertaken to insure its public domain status and to comply with Errors and Omissions insurance procedures. It can take as much time and expense to determine whether a composition is in the public domain as to clear one that is not.

HOW LONG CAN MUSIC BE PROTECTED BY COPYRIGHT?

As previously mentioned in Chapter 13 ("Clearances & Releases"), the enactment of the Sonny Bono Copyright Term Extension Act of 1998 has added 20 years to the duration of copyright in the U.S. As a result, songs written before January 1, 1978 are protected for a total of 95 years from the end of the year the copyright was originally secured. Music created after January 1, 1978 is protected for a period of 70 years after the death of the last surviving writer.

Remember that foreign laws may provide for different copyright terms (life plus 70 years), and may have to be verified on a country-by-country basis. Moreover, as a result of the recently implemented General Agreement on Tariffs and Trade (GATT), certain works, which were previously in the public domain, have had their copyrights restored.

Also, the fact that a musical composition does not contain a copyright notice does not mean that it is in the public domain. When the United States became a member of the Berne International Copyright Convention (in order to increase foreign protection for domestic works), our copyright law had to be amended to eliminate the requirement of a copyright notice as a prerequisite for copyright protection. While a copyright notice is still required in order for a copyright owner to be entitled to certain remedies for infringement, it is not required in order for a work to be protected.

MAY I USE EIGHT BARS OF A SONG WITHOUT PAYING FOR IT?

NO! This is one of the most common misconceptions regarding music and its protection under U.S. Copyright Law. Any unauthorized use of material that is recognizable as having come from a copyrighted source is a potential infringement of copyright.

WHAT IS "FAIR USE"?

There is an exception to the exclusive rights of copyright owners called "fair use," which permits the limited use of copyrighted material in special circumstances without requiring an owner's consent. In theory, the public interest in the dissemination of ideas and information is served when the use of music for such purposes as criticism, comment, news reporting, scholarship, teaching, etc., is freely permitted. Parodies of material for humorous effect or social commentary are usually treated under the same principles. HOWEVER, caution in the area of parody is strongly recommended.

The U.S. Copyright Law lists the factors that must be considered in each case of a claimed "fair use." These factors include: (1) the purpose and character of the use; (2) the nature of the work; (3) the amount and substantiality of the portion used and (4) the effect of the use on the potential market for, or value of, the work. Although the laws of certain foreign countries contain concepts similar to the U.S. doctrine of fair use, they are not necessarily the same. Therefore, a fair use in the U.S. could be a violation of law or an author's moral right of integrity in foreign territories. Since there are no clear and definitive guidelines, it is difficult to determine in advance what may or may not be a permissible "fair use."

MAY THE TITLE OF A SONG BE USED AS THE TITLE OF A PROGRAM?

While titles are not protected by copyright law, they may be protected via other legal doctrines. Use of the title and story line of a song may involve the clearance of dramatic performing rights, or require negotiations similar to those required for the acquisition of rights in a literary property. For protection, your attorney should advise you as to whether the title may be freely used, or if specific permission should be obtained from the owner of the musical composition.

MUST A LICENSE BE SECURED IF SONG LYRICS ARE SPOKEN IN DIALOGUE?

The copyright of a song protects the lyrics as well as the music. Therefore, if an identifiable part of a song lyric is used in dialogue, a license may have to be secured in order to avoid potential liability.

MAY LYRICS TO AN EXISTING SONG BE CHANGED WITHOUT PERMISSION?

Changes made to the copyrighted lyrics of the song, including what may appear to be only minor changes, usually have to be cleared by obtaining specific permission from the copyright owner. This may even apply to the translation of the original lyrics into a foreign language.

IF A SONG IS CLEARED FOR ONE EPISODE OF A TELEVISION SERIES, MAY IT BE USED IN OTHER EPISODES WITHOUT ADDITIONAL PERMISSION?

No. Licenses are normally granted on a show-by-show basis. Specific permission is required for use in multiple episodes of a program. In addition, a new episode containing clips from previous episodes will usually require additional licenses for the music contained in the clips.

IS IT NECESSARY TO CLEAR MUSIC THAT IS TO BE USED IN COMMERCIALS?

Yes. In order for copyrighted music to be used in the advertising of products and services, the entire procedure for clearing music must be followed. Popular songs are frequently changed or adapted to fit the product or service being promoted. Accordingly, specific permission for use must be obtained from the copyright owner, based upon the markets and media to be exploited.

MAY RECORDS OR COMPACT DISCS BE USED ON A TELEVISION SHOW?

Be careful. This is a complex and gray area of both law and practice. Some use of records on television teen dance shows, for instance, has been permitted by record companies because the use is considered promotional. Other uses of records in television, home video, and motion picture productions may require permission in advance from any number of involved parties, including the music publisher, record company, artist, performer's unions, etc.

Commercial phonograph recordings made and released after February 15, 1972 are eligible for federal copyright protection. Recordings made prior to that date, though not copyrightable, may still be protected under state anti-piracy statutes and other legal theories.

IF A LICENSE IS OBTAINED TO USE A FILM CLIP FROM A TELEVISION PROGRAM OR FEATURE FILM, WILL THAT LICENSE INCLUDE THE RIGHT TO USE THE MUSIC CONTAINED ON THE CLIP?

Generally, no. Film clip licenses are usually granted with the producer acknowledging that he or she will be responsible for obtaining all third party rights and clearances. The film clip owner may not own the music, or may have acquired rights for its use in his or her production only. Therefore, if the music on the soundtrack is not specifically covered in the film clip license agreement, it will have to be cleared. The music publishing division of a motion picture company and the production or publicity division of the same company can have completely different outlooks on what you may or may not use.

IF A RECORD COMPANY ISSUES A LICENSE TO USE A MUSIC VIDEO CLIP, WILL FURTHER CLEARANCES BE REQUIRED?

The use of so-called "promotional" music videos of performing artists raises a number of music licensing issues. As with other programs, the proper licensing of the musical composition contained in a music video may require public performance rights and synchronization rights. In addition, "dramatic" performing rights may be required if the video is telling the story of the song.

A producer wishing to use a music video clip in his or her program must first determine which of the above music rights, if any, have been granted to him or her by the licensor of the music video (usually a record company). Music videos are typically licensed with the user being responsible for all third-party licensing obligations, including payment to the music publisher, and payments required to be made pursuant to the collective bargaining agreements of any performer's unions. If the performing artist has written the song and owns or controls the publishing rights, the record company, by virtue of its agreement with the artist, may be able to grant a license for promotional use of the music. However, if the performing artist has no royalty or ownership interest in the song, the record company may not be willing to assume the responsibility of securing or granting synchronization licenses for your purpose.

Since most record sales occur in the first 90 days of distribution, there is an issue as to whether use of a music video in a program intended to be distributed for a period substantially longer than 90 days would be considered promotional or commercial. The more the use is considered to be commercial, the greater the likelihood that publisher clearance will be required, along with possible payments to the record companies for continued use of the music video itself.

IS A SYNCHRONIZATION LICENSE REQUIRED FOR THE FIRST U.S. NETWORK BROADCAST OF AN ORIGINAL LIVE OR TAPED TELEVISION PROGRAM?

Generally, no! However, the law in this area is restrictive and unclear, and the answer to this question may depend on a number of factors. The Copyright Act entitles a transmitting organization (e.g., a network, local station or cable programming service) to synchronize musical compositions and recordings in a program, and to repeat that program or delay its broadcast for a period of six months, as long as the broadcaster has a license to perform the musical composition. However, U.S. network broadcasts that occur more than six months after the first network run, and syndicated broadcasts, usually require full music rights clearances.

Therefore, a program that will run for less than a six-month period on U.S. network television, and which has no value in syndication, may not need synchronization licenses for the music. If a program will be broadcast for more than six months, distributed in syndication or aired outside the U.S., a synchronization license will almost certainly be required. Even if no synchronization license is required, all other rights, such as performance and adaptation rights, must be cleared.

WHAT RIGHTS ARE REQUIRED TO RELEASE A PROGRAM FOR SALE IN THE HOME VIDEO MARKETPLACE?

Home video distribution, as that term is generally defined in the entertainment industry, requires that the producer obtain the right to reproduce the musical work on the sound track of the program (much like synchronization rights), and the right to manufacture and distribute copies of the program containing the musical work throughout the territories in which distribution is planned. Public performance rights are not required for home video distribution, as long as the program is not displayed at a place open to the public, or any place where a substantial number of people outside of a normal family and its social acquaintances is gathered.

WHAT DO MUSIC COPYRIGHT OWNERS CHARGE FOR HOME VIDEO RIGHTS?

As with all licenses, copyright owners can charge whatever they think the market will bear. Generally, they may require: (1) a flat fee or royalty per unit sold; (2) a pro-rata percentage of the wholesale or retail sales price or (3) a combination of both. These royalty arrangements usually require that the producer account to the copyright owners on a quarterly or semi-annual basis. In addition, copyright owners may seek nonrecoupable fixing fees (one-time flat fee payments similar to synchronization fees), recoupable advances or sometimes both.

It is also common (particularly with feature films, nontheatrical/educational programs, and programs using very little music), to work out arrangements similar to flat-fee licenses or "buyouts," thereby avoiding costly accounting procedures. However, some copyright owners may not agree to such license terms.

There is an additional question as to whether a music publisher can or will issue a worldwide home video license. This must be answered on a song-by-song basis, and will depend on the arrangements between the domestic publisher and its representative (subpublisher) in each foreign territory. In some cases, the right to grant licenses and collect royalties may have been contractually transferred to the subpublisher in each territory. If this is the case, the producer may have to deal with the respective subpublisher or collection society in each territory in which distribution is planned.

HOW ARE FEATURE FILMS LICENSED?

In feature films, music rights, whether for a song or a recording, are usually licensed worldwide for the duration of the copyright, on a flat-fee basis. This is partly because of the tremendous investment required to make a feature film, and the complicated contractual arrangements involved in feature film distribution. Unlike other types of productions for which rights may be licensed on a medium-by-medium basis, the producer of a feature film will usually secure a very broad grant of synchronization rights for theatrical, television, nontheatrical, home video and other rights, so that the film can be exploited in all possible media existing now or in the future.

For antitrust reasons, the performing rights organizations are not allowed to collect performing fees from motion picture theaters in the U.S. Therefore, a producer must also secure a U.S. theatrical performance license directly from the music publisher or its agent when securing a synchronization license for a musical composition.

Feature film producers must pay particular attention to the way home video and new media rights are acquired, as the major studios and distributors strongly resist paying any kind of continuing home video music royalty. There are well-known cases where studios have required producers of feature films in current theatrical release to delete, prior to home video distribution, material which carried a royalty obligation.

HOW IS MUSIC LICENSED IN RELIGIOUS PROGRAMS?

The licenses that television stations secure from the performing rights organizations include the right to broadcast religious programs that contain copyrighted musical compositions. These licenses are required even if the programs emanate from a place of worship.

However, a nonprofit organization producing the broadcast generally does not need a synchronization license to record and make copies of a program that includes songs of a religious nature (or sound recordings of such works), as long as there is no charge for the distribution of copies, and only one transmission is made by each station. However, synchronization licenses must be

secured for the use of secular songs, even if they have an underlying religious theme. Even songs of a religious nature would require clearance if the program were repeated by a station.

HOW MUCH WILL IT COST TO CLEAR A SONG FOR USE IN MY TELEVISION OR FILM PROJECT?

This depends on a number of factors, including the length of the song, whether it will be performed "on camera" or as background music, etc. A key element of the cost will be the intended distribution of the program. Many television producers can get by with a one-, three-, or five-year synchronization license for just the United States; others need more extensive worldwide rights and/or distribution terms. A license for free television only, will generally be less expensive than a license for all forms of television distribution. Feature film producers must make sure that they obtain perpetual worldwide motion picture rights, as well as television rights for eventual domestic and foreign syndication, home video and other "new" media.

The new technologies, such as CD-ROM, the Internet and digital video disks (DVDs), have complicated the matter even further, and the rights for these areas are frequently obtained on a medium-by-medium basis. There is no established pattern for these fees, as they vary from song to song, and must be computed separately for each project's specific rights and releasing requirements.

WHAT IS A NEEDLE DROP?

This refers to the use of a single portion or "cue" of an existing recording (placing the needle down on the recording and then lifting it), in synchronization with filmed or taped images.

If a needle drop or "cue" from a commercially produced popular recording has been used, one must deal with all of the normal clearance requirements previously discussed with respect to the song, the recording of the song, the recording artist and the performer's unions.

There are organizations known as "production music" libraries that provide commercially produced recordings specifically for background broadcast and film use at a variety of reasonable license rates. Most production music libraries have reporting requirements that can be satisfied by filing a music cue sheet with the performing rights societies or informing the library of the use.

The libraries will usually issue one license that includes rights for the musical composition and the master recording. Some production music companies include so-called "sound-alike" recordings of popular artists in their libraries. Remember that if such recordings are used, the producer must still secure a license from the publisher of the song. A producer that is a union signatory company must be sure to use caution, as some production music may not comply with union requirements.

WHAT HAPPENS WHEN LICENSES EXPIRE?

If the right to use music contained in a program has been granted for a limited period of time (e.g., five years) or for limited media (e.g., free television only), the licenses will have to be renewed or expanded if continued or additional exploitation of the program is contemplated. Broadcasts of the program beyond the license period or licensed media may constitute an infringement of the music copyrights. This is seldom an issue in feature films, where music is traditionally licensed in perpetuity.

Because of recent legislation, court decisions and businesses practices, it may not be a simple matter to renew all old licenses. It is also possible that the copyright owner who originally granted the license may no longer control the music. Also, there are well-known cases where composers and publishers of popular songs have refused to renew expired licenses, or have charged exorbitant fees for license renewals.

It may be possible to negotiate perpetual licenses for all media at the time of initial licensing. However, the price charged by the copyright owner may increase significantly over the normal price of a limited term or limited media license.

The Copyright Clearinghouse, Inc., located in Burbank, California, is the clearance and licensing subsidiary of Music Reports, Inc., which administers performance rights licensing for broadcasters and cable programming services. CCI maintains a staff of industry professionals who specialize in all aspects of music licensing for television and film production. Combining highly customized business affairs practices with constantly updated industry source data, CCI provides producers with complete music research, clearance, licensing and publishing administration services.

CHAPTER FIFTEEN

Safety

In an effort to promote a safer work environment, numerous states have enacted legislation implementing injury prevention programs, the training of employees in general safe and healthy work practices and the adoption of occupational safety and health standards.

In addition to state safety guidelines, the AMPTP (Association of Motion Picture and Television Producers), various unions and guilds, major television networks and studios and many independent production companies have adopted their own safety programs, many in conjunction with an Industry-Wide Labor-Management Safety Board. Sponsored by CSATF (Contract Services Administration Trust Fund), an Industry Wide Labor-Management Safety Committee meets monthly in the Los Angeles area to draft, update and disseminate a series of industry-related *Safety Bulletins*. CSATF also administers *The Safety Passport Program*, which offers health and safety training to union and guild members. Upon completion of the General Safety Passport course, each worker is issued a Safety Passport, which contains the person's photograph, name, address, emergency contacts and other pertinent information such as union affiliation. As a person receives training, that training is documented in the Passport and in the Industry Experience Roster. For those working in Southern California who would like more information on Passport Health and Safety courses, contact your local business agent or call CSATF at (818) 995-0900. If you are not from the Los Angeles area, check with the unions and/or guilds closest to you to see what type of safety training is currently being offered in your area.

Each safety bulletin (numbered in succession) details safety precautions relating to specific potentially hazardous situations and activities. Most of the unions, guilds, studios, etc. use these bulletins as the basis for their own safety program, the most recognized being The Producer's On Production Injury and Illness Prevention Program (IIPP), which is designed to comply with State and Federal OSHA guidelines (or other local, provincial, or national safety requirements). Specifically, the IIPP contains the following elements:

- Person(s) identified as being responsible for implementing the program
- Means of identifying and evaluating workplace hazards
- Methods and procedures for correcting unsafe or unhealthy conditions
- Safety training to instruct employees on general safe work practices, and specific instructions with respect to hazards for job assignments
- Means of communicating with employees on safety matters
- System of discipline to ensure compliance with safe work practices
- Systems to maintain records

Industry safety programs require that a copy of the company's safety manual be available at each work site. Safety posters and emergency procedures (including emergency numbers) must also be posted at each work site. Departmental safety guidelines and any applicable forms are given to each department head.

SAFETY MEETINGS

Safety meetings should be held with the cast and crew the first day of each new location, and on days when activities involve stunts, special effects, aircraft, wild animals or other potentially hazardous conditions. All safety meetings should be documented on the daily production report or a specific *Daily Departmental Safety Meeting Report* form (see sample form at the end of this chapter). Potentially hazardous situations must be clearly identified on the call sheet and marked at the spot, if possible. If appropriate, an AMPTP safety bulletin or other special notification addressing the particular hazard should be attached to the call sheet or posted at the location. In all cases, every attempt should be made to eliminate any hazardous situation, if possible, before it becomes a danger to cast and crew.

SAFETY TRAINING

In addition to the Safety Passport Program mentioned above, basic safety training should be introduced on each new film by emphasizing the company's intent and attitude toward safety and by familiarizing new employees with all company safety policies, rules and procedures. New employees should be provided with written job descriptions and safety procedures pertaining to their specific areas of responsibility, reinforcing actual on-the-job training. Employees should be informed of all potential exposure to any major hazards, ensuring that they fully understand the degree of hazard and all necessary precautions. After initial orientation and training has been completed, employees' work habits should be periodically evaluated, and all safety training and orientation should be documented.

DESIGNATED AREAS OF RESPONSIBILITY

The DGA has deemed that unit production managers shall have the overall responsibility for administering the On Production Injury and Illness Prevention Program (IIPP), from pre-production through completion of production, and that the first assistant director function as the On-Set Safety Coordinator. The delegation by the UPM of authority to others in order to effectuate the purposes of the IIPP does not alter such responsibil-

ity. The UPM and first and second assistant directors are asked to meet with the person responsible for the overall studio or production company IIPP. In addition to, or in lieu of, such a meeting, some studios or production companies may assign an individual to your specific production to assist in safety coordination.

The UPM, and first and second assistant directors, are each assigned different areas of responsibility in the administration of the IIPP. Together, they must (1) make sure the entire shooting company is thoroughly familiar with the safety program; (2) ensure that the safety program is working; (3) troubleshoot as necessary, addressing all hazardous conditions and concerns; (4) ensure the documentation of safety program activities; (5) deal with emergencies and serious accidents and (6) deal with OSHA inspectors and other safety investigators. The DGA provides their members with detailed guidelines relating to their individual areas of safety management.

During construction (prior to the start of principal production), the construction coordinator is responsible for set safety. He continues to administer construction safety throughout production as long as construction continues. In the production office, the production coordinator is responsible for keeping and distributing safety manuals as required, keeping a file of completed safety reports and securing the appropriate safety bulletins to be attached to call sheets when needed.

SAFETY BULLETINS

Contact the AMPTP, CSATF, DGA, SAG, your studio safety office or production company safety coordinator for a complete set of safety bulletins issued by the Industry-Wide Labor-Management Safety Committee. Copies of the bulletins should be attached to the daily call sheet when appropriate, and it should be confirmed that cast and crew members whose work and areas of responsibility involve the activities covered in the bulletins are fully aware of the detailed safety guidelines they contain. The following is a complete list of safety bulletins (with a date indicating the latest version of each):

Bulletin #1—Recommendations for Safety with Firearms (1/26/95)

Bulletin #2—Seat Belts and Harnesses (10/03/95)

Bulletin #3—Guidelines Regarding the Use of Helicopters in Motion Picture Production (11/30/94)

Bulletin #4—Stunts (3/28/97)

Bulletin #5—Safety Awareness (5/15/96)

Bulletin #6—Animal Handling Rules for the Motion Picture Industry (1/21/98)

Bulletin #7—SCUBA Equipment Recommendations for the Motion Picture Industry (10/03/95)

Bulletin #8—Guidelines for Insert Camera Cars (11/12/96)

Bulletin #9—Safety Guidelines for Multiple Dressing Room Units (10/03/95)

Bulletin #10—Guidelines Regarding the Use of Artificially Created Smokes, Fogs, and Lighting Effects (10/19/99)

Bulletin #11—Guidelines Regarding the Use of Fixed-Wing Aircraft in Motion Picture Productions (6/27/95)

Bulletin #12—Guidelines for the Use of Exotic Venomous Reptiles (9/19/95)

Bulletin #13—Gasoline Operated Equipment (10/04/95)

Bulletin #14—Code of Safe Practices: Parachuting and Skydiving (10/04/95)

Bulletin #15—Guidelines for Boating Safety for Film Crews (11/30/94)

Bulletin #16—Recommended Guidelines for Safety with Pyrotechnic Special Effects (11/30/94)

Bulletin #17—Water Hazards (1/21/98)

Bulletin #18—Guidelines for Safe Use of Air Bags (11/30/94)

Bulletin #19—Guidelines for the Use of Open Flames on Motion Picture Sets (11/30/95)

Bulletin #20—Guidelines for Use of Motorcycles (2/23/96)

Bulletin #21—Guidelines for Appropriate Clothing and Personal Protective Equipment (9/18/96)

Bulletin #22—Guidelines for the Use of Elevating Work Platforms (Scissor Lifts) and Aerial Extensible Boom Platforms (6/25/93)

Bulletin #23—Guidelines for Working with Lighting Systems and Other Electrical Equipment (6/24/93)

Bulletin #24—Recommended Safety Guidelines for Handling of Blood and Other Potentially Infectious Materials (6/24/93)

Bulletin #25—Camera Cranes (12/16/98)

Bulletin #28—Guidelines for Safety around Railroads and Railroad Equipment (11/30/94)

Bulletin #29—Guidelines for Safe Use of Hot Air Balloons (11/30/94)

Bulletin #30—Recommendations for Safety with Edged and Piercing Props (6/21/95)

Bulletin #32—Guidelines for Food Service Providers and Craft Services (11/22/96)

Addendum A to Guidelines for Food Service Providers and Craft Services (11/22/96)

Bulletin #33—Special Safety Considerations When Employing Infant Actors (15 days to six months old) (1/22/97)

GENERAL SAFETY GUIDELINES FOR PRODUCTION

Your production's safety program should include the following General Safety Guidelines in addition to the Injury and Illness Prevention Program. While most of these guidelines are common sense, others derive from federal, state or local laws and regulations. Failure to follow these guidelines and the IIPP could not only result in serious injury, but could also cost valuable production time and expense due to delays and/or shutdown enforced by either regulatory agencies or management personnel.

As you know, your working conditions may change from day to day, especially on location. To reduce the risk of accidents, you need to be aware of your work environment and the equipment that is used. Pay special attention to call sheets, as they often contain important safety information for the next day's shoot. And if you have any questions or concerns, or notice anything you believe could be hazardous to the cast and crew, do not hesitate to notify your supervisor or call the producer.

General Rules

- Obey all "No Smoking" signs. There is to be NO SMOKING on any stage. Observe designated smoking areas and always extinguish cigarettes in butt cans. Dispose of all other trash properly, not in butt cans.
- Wear appropriate clothing and any necessary protective equipment. A shirt and shoes should be worn at all times. Do not wear loose clothing, and long hair should be tied back if working around machinery. Nonessential jewelry should be left at home. Eye and/or ear protection must be worn when operating equipment or performing other work where damage to sight or hearing could occur.

- Do not work while under the influence of illegal drugs or alcoholic beverages. Medication that might interfere with your alertness or ability to work should be used only under the direction of your physician. If you feel any medication is impairing your work, discuss this with your doctor. Don't put yourself or your co-workers at risk.
- Pranks and horseplay should be kept in check. Distracting crew members operating tools or working with specialized equipment can result in accidents.
- Maintain clear walkways and exit passageways. Maintain at least a four-foot perimeter around stage areas. Keep all exit doors unlocked when working. All overhead equipment, fixtures and props should be properly secured with safety wire if needed. Cables on the floor or ground should be ramped in foot traffic areas. Fire extinguishers, hoses and hydrants must remain accessible at all times.
- Production days can be long and grueling; make sure you are getting adequate sleep. Exhaustion can cause accidents too.

Lifting And Moving

Do not attempt to lift excessive or awkward loads without getting help. Whenever possible, use dollies, carts, hand trucks, etc. If an object is too heavy to move without strain, ask for help! Proper lifting techniques can help prevent back injuries and other strains (lift with your legs, not your back).

Common Fall Risks (Catwalks, Runways, Floor Openings, Guardrails, Scaffolds And Stairwells)

Stair railings and guardrails are required by law for any elevated surface or around pits or holes. Ensure that lighting is adequate and warning signs are posted when necessary. Use safety harnesses or other fall protection equipment when needed, especially when operating above ground level or outside areas with guardrails.

Chemicals And Flammable Materials

Paints, chemicals and other hazardous materials should not accumulate on stage floors, under platforms or in other work areas. Store materials safely.

Know and observe proper handling and storage procedures for all materials. Material Safety Data Sheets should be obtained and kept on file for all materials. Set materials should be flame-retardant or made of noncombustible materials.

Hand Tools And Related Equipment

Use the right tool for the job. Ensure that all equipment is in proper working order and that protective guards are in place and in good condition. Tag and report any damaged or malfunctioning equipment. Avoid areas where others are using power tools unless your job requires you to be there. Watch for flying debris.

Do not use the top two steps of ladders. Make sure ladders are in good condition and properly supported (do not leave them free-standing against walls—secure them). Ladders should be properly stored when not in use.

Filming Equipment (Booms, Camera and Insert Cars, Cranes, Dollies, etc.)

Use the proper equipment for the job. Be aware of and observe all load capacities. Never allow more than nine people (including the driver) on an insert car. Operators and passengers of all vehicles should always use safety belts or harnesses.

Filming Vehicles (Aircraft, Helicopters, Cars, Trains, etc.)

Be especially cautious when walking, driving or traveling in congested areas. Proceed slowly and watch for sudden movement. Be cautious when working around helicopters. Remain at least fifty feet from helicopters unless you are instructed to be closer. No smoking is allowed within fifty feet of aircraft.

The use of aircraft, trains, cars or boats may require special permits and/or operator certification. All vehicles and their safety equipment must be inspected on a daily basis by qualified personnel.

Electrical Safety

Ground and properly maintain all electrical equipment and wiring. Use electrical equipment only for its intended use. Be cautions around water. DC may be required for work above, in or near water.

Water Hazards

All cast and crew members working on or above water should wear life vests or other safety equipment. Safety lines, nets, divers, observers or other precautions should be taken when working in rivers, streams or other bodies of water with currents.

Obey boat crew members instructions at all times. Observe capacity limits on all boats. Persons not essential for filming should not be on the water. Know as much as you can about the water: quality, animal life or other hazards.

Stunts And Special Effects

Stunts and special effects require an on-site dry run or walk-through with all involved parties before filming. The walk-through, safety meeting and rehearsal should be documented on the daily production report. It is the policy that all stunts and effects be reviewed by all participants prior to execution to help ensure that they are performed in the safest manner possible. The appropriate safety bulletins must be attached to the call sheet and reviewed at the safety meeting.

Effects involving pyrotechnics must be noted in advance on the call sheet. Permits must be obtained in advance as required. Performance must be by qualified, licensed persons. Regulatory agencies must be notified in advance as required by permit.

Appropriate safety equipment—eye, ear protection, shields, etc.—must be provided as needed to protect cast and crew. A planned escape route must be kept clear. Only persons necessary for the shot should be in the area.

Smoke

Be aware that the use of atmospheric smoke is regulated. Efforts should be made to reduce smoke where possible. Provide adequate ventilation and respirators where needed.

Firearms

Treat all firearms as if they are loaded. Do not handle firearms unless required and qualified to do so. Follow the direction of the property or weapon master at all times. The use of firearms may require special permits and certifications. Know all operating features and safety devices. All firearms must undergo safety inspections by qualified personnel. Live ammunition MUST NOT BE USED!

Animals

Animals are unpredictable. Animal trainers should address the cast and crew regarding safety precautions that will be in effect and answer questions about safety. Do not feed, pet or play with any animal without the permission and direct supervision of the trainer. When working with animals, the set is to be closed to outside visitors and a note made on the call sheet in advance.

Environmental Concerns

Your location should be free of hazardous materials or chemicals hazards. All hazardous waste generated by the production company (including paint) must be disposed of properly. Proper documentation of the transportation and disposal of hazardous materials must be maintained. If in doubt, ask.

Make sure all cast and crew members receive a copy of these safety guidelines and that all safety procedures, bulletins and programs (as well as local, state and federal regulations) are adhered to. All employees should be required to sign an Acknowledgment of Safety Guidelines (sample included in this chapter) attesting to having received, read and understood these procedures.

All studios and production companies should provide their production units with a supply of Safety Checklists and Worksite Safety Reports to be filled out on a daily basis. Other forms have been devised to note safety concerns while breaking down a script, and for documenting safety meetings, training sessions and various safety inspection and compliance measures. If the production company you are working for does not supply you with these forms, design your own that will specifically address the safety concerns pertaining to your production.

SCREEN ACTORS GUILD—SAFETY REGULATIONS

- A qualified first-aid person shall be present on all sets where hazardous work is planned. The producer shall properly equip this person, establish the capabilities of nearby medical facilities and provide transportation and communication with these facilities.

- Where any of the following conditions are planned as part of a driving sequence, and special expertise is necessary in order to perform such driving sequence in a safe manner, the on-camera driver shall qualify as a stunt performer under Schedule H of the SAG Agreement.

  1. When any or all wheels will leave the driving surface.

  2. When tire traction will be broken (skids, slides, etc.).

  3. When the driver's vision will be substantially impaired by dust, spray (when driving through water, mud, etc.), blinding lights, restrictive covering over the windshield, smoke or any other conditions that would substantially restrict the driver's normal vision.

  4. When the speed of the vehicle will be greater than normally safe for the conditions of the driving surface, or when other conditions, such as obstacles or difficulty of terrain, will exist, or off-road driving, other than normal low-speed driving for which the vehicle was designed, will occur.

  5. When any aircraft, fixed-wing or helicopter, is flown in close proximity to the vehicle, creating a hazardous driving condition.

  6. Whenever high speed or close proximity of two or more vehicles create conditions dangerous to the drivers, passengers, film crew or vehicles. Nothing herein shall require the performer to be doubled where the performer has the special expertise to perform the sequence in a safe manner.

  7. When for safety reasons a performer is doubled on-camera as the driver of a vehicle, the double shall qualify as a stunt performer under Schedule H of the SAG Agreement. This would also apply to passengers in a vehicle who must be doubled for their safety.

- When stunts are required, a person qualified in planning, setting up and/or performing the stunt must be present on the set. Persons involved in the planning and execution of a stunt shall be entitled to inspect any vehicle, mechanical device and/or equipment to be used in the stunt on the day prior to its use, provided it is available. In any event, such persons shall have reasonable time for such inspections. No payment shall be due for any inspection. The non-stunt performer shall have the opportunity to consult with this person before being required to perform a stunt.

- The stunt coordinator shall notify the guild whenever scripted stunts are planned involving non-stunt performers.

- The producer must always get the performer's consent before asking the performer to engage in a stunt or hazardous activity. They DO NOT have to agree; they may always request a double.

- All reasonable requests and requirements for safety equipment in connection with the performance of stunts shall be complied with by the producer or the producer's representatives on the set or location.

- Equipment provided by the producer, for example, autos, cycles, wagons, etc., shall be in suitable repair for the safe and proper performance of the stunt.

- Smoke work must be approved by the performers involved at the time of booking or prior to the work. If this does not occur, a performer may refuse the work for legitimate health reasons. Material Safety Data Sheets must also be available on the set when smoke is used.

WORKING UNDER HAZARDOUS CONDITIONS

In addition to the SAG regulations listed above, other unions and guilds impose their own regulations governing their members when they work under hazardous conditions. Many potentially dangerous situations require productions to make salary adjustments (pay bumps) for employees working under these conditions. The amount of the pay bump will vary depending on the union or guild and the dangerous activity. Pay bumps are generally paid for aerial or submarine work, working in (or under) water or under exceptionally cold conditions. Bumps are paid per occurrence with a maximum daily cap. Check your guild and union contracts to find specific regulations relating to any potentially hazardous work you are planning.

SEXUAL HARASSMENT

In promoting practices that provide for a safer and healthier work environment, the matter of sexual harassment must be addressed as well. It is imperative to inform your entire cast and crew that sexual harassment will not be tolerated on your production.

Under federal law, unwelcome sexual advances, requests for sexual favors and other verbal or physical conduct of a sexual nature constitute sexual harassment when (1) submission to such conduct is made either explicitly or implicitly a term or condition of an individual's employment; (2) submission to or rejection of such conduct by an individual is used as the basis for employment decisions affecting such individual; or (3) such conduct has the purpose or effect of unreasonably interfering with an individual's work performance or creating an intimidating, hostile or offensive working environment. This can include verbal behavior such as unwanted sexual comments, suggestions, jokes or pressure for sexual favors; nonverbal behavior, such as suggestive looks or leering and physical behavior, such as pats or squeezes, or repeatedly brushing against someone's body.

Although many assume that sexual harassment involves a male boss and a female employee, this is not always the case. Sexual harassment often involves co-workers, other employees of the company or other persons doing business with or for the company. It is against the law for females to sexually harass males or other females, as well as for males to harass other males or females.

Anyone who is being sexually harassed should, if possible, confront the harasser and ask him or her to stop. If this does not stop the behavior, the UPM should be informed of the situation as soon as possible. If, for whatever reason, the UPM cannot be told, the producer should be informed immediately. Sexual harassment or retaliation can be reported in writing or verbally, and may also be reported by someone who is not the subject of the harassment. If the UPM or producer is unable to curb the unwanted behavior, the situation must be reported to the studio or production company, and an investigation will be conducted. Where evidence of sexual harassment or retaliation is found, disciplinary action, up to and including termination, may result. If an employee is found to have engaged in sexual harassment, or if you as a manager know about the conduct and condone it, you may be personally liable for monetary damages.

"ON LOCATION"—PERSONAL SAFETY CONSIDERATIONS AND SUGGESTIONS

This information was prepared by Al Marrewa, President of Powerflex USA, Inc. of Los Angeles, California.

Visit Locations Prior To First Day Of Shooting

Familiarize yourself with locations: streets, buildings, police and fire departments, hospitals, gas stations, restaurants and pay telephones. Know the location.

Gang-Occupied Locations

- Notify the police department and/or the sheriff's department gang detail unit. Request an increase in security and visibility.
- Know which gangs can be found in the location area.
- Suggest to those in power that filming be avoided on Friday and Saturday nights.
- Remember that gang members can be as young as twelve to thirteen years old.
- While on location, avoid wearing red, blue or black clothing, such as caps, bandannas, jackets or anything similar to gang attire.
- While on location, be aware of others wearing red, blue or black clothing, such as caps, bandannas, jackets or team clothing or colors.
- Be aware of two or more individuals wearing similar clothing of any kind. Many gang members will follow a particular dress code, including having similar haircuts.
- When gang members are used as extras, notify the police or sheriff's gang detail unit in advance. Request additional security support.
- Be aware of a vehicle with three or more occupants that is parked or moving slowly down a street or alley.
- If nearby gunfire breaks out at any time, immediately drop to the ground, face first. Stay down until gunfire ceases. Then, get to a safe place.

Additional Safety Suggestions

- Whenever possible, be with other people from your group or company. There is safety in numbers.
- Whenever possible, stay in sight of other group or company members.
- Know how you appear to others at all times. Do you stand out in a particular area because of your race, sex or dress?
- Never wear expensive or showy jewelry or clothing (i.e., watch, rings, bracelets, necklace, leather jacket).
- Carry small amounts of cash at any time.
- Whenever possible, use a buddy system while on location ("I'll keep an eye on you, and you keep an eye on me").
- Consider carrying a high-powered whistle with you at all times. This can be used to notify others in an emergency.

Taking Action

- Always walk down the middle of a street, especially at night; walking on sidewalks close to buildings, alleys, bushes and hidden areas can be dangerous.
- If you notice a group of men staring at you, glancing at you one at a time or pointing toward you, run or walk away quickly. (Know where safety is.) If you must walk near them, show no fear. Show confidence in your walk and do not stop. You may choose to look directly at one of them, straight in the eye, acknowledging confidently that you see them. Remember, this should be a nonthreatening gesture.
- When dealing with street or neighborhood people, be aware of everything around you (i.e., people, physical environment).

If you get into a precarious situation, ask yourself the following questions:

Am I outnumbered?

Is he or she or are they outnumbered?

Am I concerned?

Can I get to safety if needed?

Are tempers increasing?

Is he or she or are they under the influence of alcohol or drugs?

Can I see both of his or her hands (or are they hidden)?

Can I see a weapon?

How much distance is between this person and myself?

Are my actions threatening or challenging him or her or them?

Do I feel physically threatened?

What or how am I feeling right now?

Am I prepared to fight?

Conflict Resolution

- Treat the other person with respect.
- Listen until you understand the other person's point of view.
- Express your own views, needs, feelings.
- Use body language to communicate with the other person (i.e., face him or her directly, maintain an "open" position and make eye contact).
- Avoid sarcasm.
- Negotiate.

Self-Defense Includes

- Awareness
- Assertiveness
- Communication (verbal and nonverbal)
- Instinct
- Intuition
- Planning
- Preparation
- Teamwork

FORMS IN THIS CHAPTER

- Acknowledgment Of Safety Guidelines
- Daily Departmental Safety Meeting Report
- Emergency Information Form (To be posted on the set at all times)

ACKNOWLEDGEMENT OF SAFETY GUIDELINES

This will acknowledge that in accordance with the Injury and Illness Prevention Program in place at ___XYZ PRODUCTIONS, INC.___ ,
I have received, read and understand the *Production Safety Guidelines* pertaining to the production of ___HERBY'S SUMMER VACATION___ .

I am aware that failure to adhere to these procedures could endanger me and my co-workers, and I will strive to further the company's policy of maintaining a safe work environment.

___*F. Stopp* (signature)___ ___APRIL 11, 19XX___
Employee's Signature   Date

___F. STOPP___   ___DIRECTOR OF PHOTOGRAPHY___
Employee's Name (print or type)   Job Title or Position

(Please return this form to the Production Office when signed.)

DAILY DEPARTMENTAL SAFETY MEETING REPORT

SHOW: _HERBY'S SUMMER VACATION_

DATE: _TUESDAY, 7·14·XX_   SHOOTING DAY#: _8_

TODAY'S LOCATION: _CITY HALL - DOWNTOWN_

DEPARTMENT: _SPECIAL EFFECTS_

WAS A DEPARTMENTAL SAFETY MEETING HELD BEFORE SHOOTING?   ☒ YES ☐ NO

WAS THE DAY'S WORK AND REQUIREMENTS TO COMPLETE IT BY
YOUR SPECIFIC DEPARTMENT DISCUSSED?   ☒ YES ☐ NO

WERE ANY SAFETY HAZARDS OR CONCERNS ABOUT SAFETY
RELATED TO THE DAY'S SHOOT DISCUSSED?   ☒ YES ☐ NO

SPECIFICALLY, WHAT SAFETY CONCERNS WERE DISCUSSED?

- _APPROPRIATE PROTECTIVE EQUIPMENT FOR STUNT PERSONNEL_
- _CROWD CONTROL_
- _PROPER USE OF FIREARMS_

WERE SAFETY GUIDELINES AND PROCEDURES RELATED TO THESE
CONCERNS DISCUSSED?   ☒ YES ☐ NO

WERE SAFETY BULLETINS ATTACHED TO THE CALL SHEET TODAY?   ☒ YES ☐ NO

HAS YOUR ENTIRE CREW REVIEWED THE SAFETY SHEETS?   ☒ YES ☐ NO

WERE ANY ADDITIONAL CONCERNS REGARDING THE DAY'S WORK
ADDRESSED BY THE CREW?   ☐ YES ☒ NO

IF SO, PLEASE EXPLAIN THE CONCERNS AND HOW THEY WERE
ADDRESSED:

SIGNED _____   POSITION _SPEC. EFX. COORDINATOR_

EMERGENCY INFORMATION
(To be posted on the set at all times)

SHOW: HERBY'S SUMMER VACATION   DATE: 7·23·XX

PRODUCTION CO: XYZ PRODUCTIONS

PROD. OFFICE PHONE NO: 555-3331   FAX#: 555-3332

TODAY'S LOCATION: SHAPIRO'S DINER

ADDRESS: 123 MAIN ST.
SANTA MONICA, CA 90404

LOCATION PHONE NO: 555-4117

PROPERTY OWNER(S)/MANAGER: NED SHAPIRO

OWNER/MANAGER'S PHONE NO: 555-4712 (CELL#)

ESSENTIAL PHONE NUMBERS   EMERGENCY CALLS ONLY: **911**

POLICE: 555-3000   FIRE: 555-4500

NEAREST EMERGENCY MEDICAL FACILITY: LINCOLN MEMORIAL
HOSPITAL - 576 MAIN ST. - SANTA MONICA
EMERGENCY RM. - 5TH STREET ENTRANCE

EMERGENCY ROOM PHONE NO: 555-5000

Emergency Telephone Procedures:
Indicate if you have a medical or fire emergency that requires an immediate response, then give the following information:
- Type of emergency (fire, medical, police or other) and related details (persons involved, nature of injuries, etc.)
- Location of emergency (including building, floor and room numbers)
- Your name and the telephone number you are calling from

Note: Do not hang up first as the operator may require additional information from you.

UPM: FRED FILMER
PHONE: 555-4321   PAGER: 555-1567

SET MEDIC: JOAN BURSLER
PHONE: 555-7890   PAGER: 555-6544

LOCATION MANAGER: TIFFANY WESTON
PHONE: 555-9012   PAGER: 555-8331

ON-SET SAFETY COORDINATOR: JONAS JUHLIN
PHONE: 555-8910   PAGER: 555-6776

CONSTRUCTION SAFETY COORDINATOR: GARY KRAKOFF
PHONE: 555-6788   PAGER: 555-3544

PRODUCTION SAFETY CONSULTANT: STEPHEN MARINACCIO
PHONE: 555-6543   PAGER: 555-2929

CHAPTER SIXTEEN

Locations

There are many aspects to consider before deciding to shoot at any one location besides how much the owner of the property will charge you for the right to shoot on his or her premises. How much will the permit cost? How much lead time do you need to get a permit? Will you require police and fire safety officers and how many of each? Can you use an off-duty fire officer, or must it be one on active duty? Does this location have restricted hours in which you can shoot? If you are shooting past a certain time at night, before a certain time in the morning or plan to make a great deal of noise, will you need permission from surrounding neighbors? Will you need neighborhood consent and/or special permits for the use of firearms or special effects at this location? Will you need to close a street? Will you need additional motorcycle police officers for intermittent traffic control? If so, how many? Will you need to post for parking? Will you have sufficient parking for your cast and crew at the location or will you have to find a nearby parking lot and shuttle everyone to the location site? Will you need to provide evidence of special or additional insurance coverage for use of this location?

The answers will not only depend on the particulars associated with individual locations but will also vary from city, to county, to state, to country—each having its own set of fees and regulations. The sphere of Los Angeles County film permits alone encompasses approximately thirty-five individual cities in the Los Angeles area plus Los Angeles City and Los Angeles County, each with its own filming guidelines. Each state has its own film office, and there are approximately fifty-six metropolitan U.S. cities and forty-nine international cities (outside of the U.S.) that have their own film office. These offices are set up to enforce their specific film regulations, offer information, promote filmmaking in their city and assist the filmmakers who choose to shoot in their area.

All shows require the services of a location manager, but there are independent location scouting services that will help you find all your locations as well. Commercial production companies with extremely short shooting schedules will often utilize the services of such companies. There are also companies and/or individuals who represent specific properties and others who specialize in specific types of locations (only warehouses and office buildings; only mansions; only schools and hospitals; etc.). Film permit services also exist. They will apply for and obtain permits for you; and for additional fees (and as the city or jurisdiction you're shooting in requires), they will secure police and fire officers, post for parking and collect neighborhood signatures if necessary.

The number of locations you need to find, the cost of each and consideration of your budget will determine the combination of location staff and services utilized on your show.

THE LOCATION MANAGER

A good location manager will be able to help determine not only where each location should be, but also to ascertain the specific fees, regulations and restrictions that come with each site. Most shows will employ at least one key location manager and one assistant location manager. Larger shows having many locations to find and monitor may find it necessary to staff their location department with an extra key location manager and two or three assistant location managers or location scouts utilized on an as-needed basis.

If the show is shooting in various cities, it may employ more than one location manager, each with his or her own assistants.

In Los Angeles and eleven western states, location managers and assistant location managers are members of the Teamsters union. In New York, they are members of the Directors Guild. Therefore, depending on where you are based, you cannot hire a non-union location manager if your show is signatory to one of these union agreements. Although their duties may differ somewhat based on the needs and locales of a specific production, the location manager's basic responsibilities remain the same. The following should give you an overall awareness of (and an appreciation for) their contribution to your film.

As a Location Manager, you would:

- Break down the script and identify all interior and exterior locations and the time of day they are scripted to shoot. After it has been decided which locations will be practical and which will be constructed, the next step is to discuss visual concepts of each (practical) location with the producer, director, production designer and/or art director and to share your ideas and suggestions. Also, if one hasn't already been locked-in, you would submit a departmental budget for approval (even if it's preliminary) and get a tentative schedule from the production manager or assistant director.
- Call film offices/commissioners and start gathering information. If you are in the market for government facilities, railroad facilities, hotels, private businesses, theme or ball parks, schools, etc., start setting up appointments. (Some locations can take months to line up and gather proper approvals.) Arrange for aerial scouts if necessary.
- Assemble the following items before you begin scouting: proper clothing (plan on "layered" clothing to accommodate weather changes, an extra pair of shoes and/or boots, rain gear, etc.), sun screen, sunglasses, a hat, mobile phone/pager, phone card, flashlight, business cards, compass, maps/map books, bottled water and snacks, phone numbers of vital contacts, a notebook and pen—and most importantly, a still and/or video camera and plenty of film.
- Start scouting. Presenting your business card, introduce yourself to a location contact, and make sure he or she is the owner of the property or can legally act on behalf of the owner.

(If not, get the name and number of the person you should be dealing with should this become a viable location site.) Get permission to be on a property, take still photos and/or videotapes of potential sites and initiate a discussion regarding mutually-acceptable location fees and shooting parameters with property owners and/or managers. Confirm times of access; that the site can accommodate an entire shooting company; that the perimeter of the property will accommodate production vehicles (and if not, is there alternative parking near-by?); that external sound factors in the area are within acceptable limits and if the interior of the property is needed, that ceilings are high enough (ten to twelve feet or vaulted is good) and that access into the property is sufficient. Also check out areas that might serve as potential cover sets at the same or nearby locations. If the location is a road or highway, ascertain city/county guidelines governing such.

- If a location you are scouting seems to fit all prerequisites, determine if there are other properties in the immediate vicinity that you would potentially need approvals from: neighbors, if shooting will be particularly late or early; stores whose entrances might become blocked during business hours; nearby signs/logos that could be prominent during exterior shooting and require legal clearance; neighboring properties that might be used for additional parking, etc.
- Present photos of possibilities to the producer, director and production designer. Of those they are interested in, make sure all elements involved (site fees; permit fees; fire, safety and security needs; insurance requirements; all approvals; etc.) will fit within the confines of the show's budget and schedule.
- Arrange preliminary location scouts to the sites that meet the above criteria. Early scouts are generally limited to the location manager taking the director and production designer to the sites they have shown interest in. Subsequent scouts would include the producer(s), director of photography, first assistant director, art director, set decorator, production manager and transportation coordinator. Final tech scouts (scheduled after the locations are finalized and right before the beginning of principal photography) will also include the gaffer, key grip (sometimes their best boys as well), stunt and effects coordinators and, on commercials, an agency rep or two.

- Once locations are selected, finalize negotiations for location fees with property owners (or legal representatives of the owners), have owners sign a location agreement, collect other approvals (if necessary) from neighboring property owners, request payments for location fees and permits and present property owners (or reps) with certificates of insurance.
- Make arrangements for: permits, police, fire safety officers, security, a cleaning service, lay-out board, tents, parking cones, heating/air conditioning/fans, additional phone lines, additional power, portable restrooms, ground leveling or road building if and as needed. If there is not a specific permit office in your city, start with City Hall. If they do not offer film permits, you may have to apply for a business license. Apply in a timely manner, as permits in many cities have to be applied for at least forty-eight hours (or more) in advance.
- Work closely with property owners. If shooting inside their home, make sure they are well-aware of all risks (a deposit against damages is sometimes requested). Let them know that floors will be covered with lay-out board, and that unused furniture will be covered with furniture pads or drop cloths. Suggest that they store their valuables or anything that could easily be broken. If their belongings are going to be moved around and rooms significantly altered, suggest that the set dressers take photos of the rooms before anything is done, so everything can be returned to its original state once filming has been completed. Production companies will often pay for owners to stay in a hotel while their house is being prepped, shot in, and wrapped.
- Secure parking. If there is not enough parking at your location site, you will have to negotiate for the use of space at a nearby lot (church parking lots are always a good bet during the week and may only require a small donation). Transportation will need to arrange for vans to shuttle cast and crew members back and forth. If parking is available near your location, you will need parking for the trucks and trailer that accommodate the following departments: camera, grip/electric, sound/video, props, set dressing, special effects, hair/makeup, wardrobe and catering. As needed, space should also be made available for dressing rooms and/or motor homes, a

schoolroom, honeywagon, buses and producer and director's cars. You can arrange ahead of time to have the area posted, so the space will be available when production vehicles arrive. This is called "Post for Parking" and is arranged through the permit process.
- In addition to parking, procure an area for catering to set up tables, chairs and tents from which to serve meals. Also secure an area for extras.
- If not done by Production or Transportation, line up a water truck if any scheduled production activities could result in fire (specific trucks used for this purpose hold 2,000 to 4,000 gallons of water). Arrangements need to be made with the local water department and a fee paid for hooking into fire hydrants if necessary. Also, if not done by Production, a standby ambulance should be reserved for heavy stunt days.
- Make detailed maps of how to get from the production office to each location site. Copies of maps should be available in the production office, given to prep crews and attached to the backs of call sheets whenever appropriate.
- Determine the closest major hospital with emergency facilities that would be open during filming operations (trauma centers are the best if there is one in the area). This emergency medical information should be indicated on site maps and all respective call sheets. If scheduled shooting activities include dangerous stunts and/or effects, the hospital should be contacted in advance and made aware of potential concerns. Many location managers routinely contact hospitals (regardless of stunts and effects) to inform them of upcoming filming activities in the area.
- Scout local hotels and motels in the vicinity of location sites (if necessary). There are times when even local locations might be considered far for certain cast and crew members—especially for those given exceptionally early calls, or after night shoots when, after wrap, many would prefer a hotel room to a long drive home in heavy traffic. Most hotels and motels will give film companies group rates (whether rooms are being paid for by the company or individuals) and will hold a block of rooms for you. Information about the hotels/motels should be released a week in advance of shooting at a location (usually by way of a memo attached to a call sheet). The memo should include a map, address, phone

number, contact person and cost per night for each. This information is often offered as a courtesy even when the production is not paying for the rooms, and the production office will often make reservations for those wanting rooms.

- If it is legal to post signs in the vicinity of your locations, have signs prepared with the name or initials of your show and directional arrows to be strategically placed leading up to each location. Some municipalities will charge extra for this privilege and will have their people remove the signs once filming in the area has been completed.
- Prepare a schedule which would place you or an assistant location manager at each location site (with all permits in hand) during all filming activities. Make sure all prepping and wrapping activities are also well monitored.

FILMMAKER'S CODE OF CONDUCT

If location work is set up properly, with all members of the shooting company knowing up front what is expected of them, residents who reside in the area where you are filming will not be unreasonably infringed upon. When filming in a commercial or industrial area, there should be little or no disruption of normal business activities, customer access and parking and the rights of the businesses to operate without interference are protected.

Film units that have had little regard for the location where they are shooting or the surrounding neighborhood have not only made it difficult for the next production company wanting to shoot at that location, but their behavior negatively affects the entire industry. Individual property owners and entire communities who have had poor experiences with film companies have ceased to allow any further filming activities on their premises or in their neighborhoods.

In an effort to improve the standards of the film industry and to endorse better community relations and location preservation, leaders within the industry came together to formulate the Filmmaker's Code of Professional Responsibility for location filming. These guidelines are being promoted by all the major studios and many unions, guilds and industry-related organizations. They have become an (unofficial) industry standard. The program needs to be encouraged and imple-

mented throughout the film community, worldwide and extending to the smallest of film units.

Distribute copies of the following to your entire cast and crew, and attach additional copies to daily call sheets when necessary.

Filmmaker's Code Of Conduct

1. When filming in a neighborhood or business district, proper notification is to be provided to each merchant or neighbor who is directly affected by the company (this includes parking, base camps and meal areas). Attached to the filming notification distributed to the neighborhood, the following should be included:
   a. Name of company
   b. Name of production
   c. Kind of production (e.g., feature film, movie of the week, TV pilot, etc.)
   d. Type of activity and duration (i.e., times, dates and number of days, including prep and strike)
   e. Company contacts (first assistant director, unit production manager, location manager)
2. Production vehicles arriving on location in or near a residential neighborhood shall not enter the area before the time stipulated in the permit, and they shall park one by one, turning off engines as soon as possible. Cast and crew shall observe designated parking areas.
3. Every member of the crew shall wear a production pass (badge) when issued.
4. Moving or towing of the public's vehicles is prohibited without the express permission of the municipal jurisdiction or the owner of the vehicle.
5. Do not park production vehicles in or block driveways without the express permission of the municipal jurisdiction or driveway owner.
6. Cast and crew meals shall be confined to the area designated in the location agreement or permit. Individuals shall eat within their designated meal area, during scheduled crew meals. All trash must be disposed of properly upon completion of the meal.
7. Removing, trimming and/or cutting of vegetation or trees is prohibited unless approved by the permit authority or property owner.
8. Remember to use the proper receptacles for disposal of all napkins, plates and coffee cups that you may use in the course of the working day.

9. All signs erected or removed for filming purposes will be removed or replaced upon completion of the use of that location unless otherwise stipulated by the location agreement or permit. Also remember to remove all signs posted to direct the company to the location.

10. Every member of the cast and crew shall keep noise levels as low as possible.

11. Do not wear clothing that lacks common sense and good taste. Shoes and shirts must be worn at all times, unless otherwise directed.

12. Crew members shall not display signs, posters or pictures on vehicles that do not reflect common sense or good taste (i.e., pinup posters).

13. Do not trespass onto other neighbors' or merchants' property. Remain within the boundaries of the property that has been permitted for filming.

14. The cast and crew shall not bring guests or pets to the location, unless expressly authorized in advance by the company.

15. All catering, crafts service, construction, strike and personal trash must be removed from the location.

16. Observe designated smoking areas and always extinguish cigarettes in butt cans.

17. Cast and crew will refrain from the use of lewd or improper language within earshot of the general public.

18. The company will comply with the provisions of the parking permit.

In addition to the code of conduct guidelines as listed above, remind your crew to operate with great care when shooting inside of someone's home or office. Be especially aware of potential dents, scratches and stains that can easily occur while setting up and moving equipment. Protect walls, doors, floors and carpeting to the best of your ability, and cover furniture not being used.

Once filming has been completed and a location wrapped, the location manager or assistant location manager should schedule a post-shoot walk-through with the property owner(s). At this time, if all location fees have been paid and the property has been cleaned, repaired and returned to a condition at least as good as before the company arrived, the owner is asked to sign a Location Release. This form formally releases the production from any further obligations to the owner, whether it be for location fees or restoration to the property.

FORMS IN THIS CHAPTER

- Location Agreement—Standard form securing permission to enter and film on a property.
- Non-Filmed Location Agreement—This form secures permission for use of a property for the purpose of parking, holding, serving meals, staging or other non-filming activity.
- Location Release (explained above)
- Location Information Sheet
- Location List
- Request To Film During Extended Hours

LOCATION AGREEMENT

Film __HERBY'S SUMMER VACATION__ Scripted Location __DAD'S OFFICE__
Prod. Co. __XYZ PRODUCTIONS__ Scene No(s) __7, 9, 10, 57, 99__
Address __1234 FLICK DR.__
__HOLLYWOOD, CA 90038__
Phone # __555-3331__ Date __5.11.XX__

Dear Ladies and Gentlemen:

1. I, the undersigned owner or agent, whichever is applicable, hereby irrevocably grants to __XYZ PRODUCTIONS__ ("Producer"), and its agents, employees, contractors and suppliers, the right to enter and remain upon and use the property, both real and personal, located at: __THE OFFICES OF DEWEY, CHEATEM & HOWE @ 1000 ATLANTIC BLVD, SUITE 700 - LOS ANGELES, CA 90067__
(the "Property"), including without limitation, all interior and exterior areas, buildings and other structures of the Property, and owner's name, logo, trademark, service mark and/or slogan, and any other identifying features associated therewith or which appear in, on or about the Property, for the purpose of photographing (including without limitation by means of motion picture, still or videotape photography) said premises, sets and structures and/or recording sound in connection with the production, exhibition, advertising and exploitation of the __MOTION PICTURE__
tentatively entitled __HERBY'S SUMMER VACATION__
(the "Picture").

2. Producer may take possession of said premises commencing on or about __6.1.XX__ subject to change because of weather conditions or changes in production schedule, and continuing until the completion of all scenes and work required.

3. Charges: As complete and full payment for all of the rights granted to Producer hereunder, Producer shall pay to Owner the total amount of $ __3,550__ , broken-down as follows:

	No. of Days		
Prep	1	X $ 500	= $ 500
Shoot	2	X $ 1,000	= $ 2,000
Strike	1	X $ 500	= $ 500
Hold		X $	= $
Other	PARKING ($175 X 2 SHOOT DYS)		$ 350
	PHONE ($100 X 2 SHOOT DAYS)		$ 200

All charges are payable on completion of all work completed, unless specifically agreed to the contrary. Producer is not obligated to actually use the property or produce a __MOTION PICTURE__ or include material photographed or recorded hereunder in the Picture. Producer may at any time elect not to use the Property by giving Owner or agent 24 hours written notice of such election, in which case neither party shall have any obligation hereunder.

4. Producer may place all necessary facilities and equipment, including temporary sets, on the Property, and agrees to remove same after completion of work and leave the Property in as good condition as when received, reasonable wear and tear from uses permitted herein excepted. Signs on the Property may, but need not, be removed or changed, but, if removed or changed, must be replaced. In connection with the Picture, Producer may refer to the Property or any part thereof by any fictitious name and may attribute any fictitious events as occurring on the Property. Owner irrevocably grants to Producer and Producer's successors and assigns the right, in perpetuity, throughout the universe, to duplicate and recreate all or a portion of the Property and to use such duplicates and recreations in any media and/or manner now known or hereafter devised in connection with the Picture, including without limitation sequels and remakes,

merchandising, theme parks and studio tours, and in connection with publicity, promotion and/or advertising for any or all of the foregoing.

5. Producer agrees to use reasonable care to prevent damage to the Property, and will indemnify and hold Owner harmless from and against any claims or demands arising out of or based upon personal injuries, death or property damage (ordinary wear and tear excepted), suffered by such person(s) resulting directly from any act of negligence on Producer's part in connection with the work hereunder.

6. All rights of every nature whatsoever in and to all still pictures, motion pictures, videotapes, photographs and sound recordings made hereunder, shall be owned by Producer and its successors, assigns and licensees, and neither Owner nor any tenant, or other party now or hereafter having an interest in said property, shall have any right of action against Producer or any other party arising out of any use of said still pictures, motion pictures, videotapes, photographs and or sound recordings, whether or not such use is or may claimed to be, defamatory, untrue or censurable in nature. In addition, neither Owner nor any tenant, nor any other party now or hereafter having an interest in the Property, shall have any right of action, including, but not limited to, those based upon invasion of privacy, publicity, defamation, or other civil rights, in connection with the exercise of the permission and/or rights granted by Owner to Producer. If there is a breach by Producer hereunder, Owner shall be limited to an action at law for monetary damages. In no event shall Owner have the right to enjoin the development, production, distribution or exploitation of the Picture.

7. Force Majeure: If because of illness of actors, director or other essential artists and crew, weather conditions, defective film or equipment or any other occurrence beyond Producer's control, Producer is unable to start work on the date designated above and/or work in progress is interrupted during use of the Property by Producer, then Producer shall have the right to use the Property at a later date to be mutually agreed upon and/or to extend the period set forth in Paragraph 2, and any such use shall be included in the compensation paid pursuant to Paragraph 3 above.

8. At any time within six (6) months from the date Producer completes its use of the Property hereunder, Producer may, upon not less than five (5) days prior written notice to Owner, reenter and use the Property for such period as may be reasonable necessary to photograph retakes, added scenes, etc. desired by Producer upon the same terms and conditions as contained in this agreement.

9. Owner warrants neither he or anyone acting for him, gave or agreed to give anything of value, except for use of the Property, to Producer or anyone associated with the production for using said Property as a shooting location.

10. Owner represents and warrants that he/she is the owner and/or authorized representative of the Property, and that Owner has the authority to grant Producer the permission and rights granted in this agreement, and that no one else's permission is required. If any question arises regarding Owner's authority to grant the permission and rights granted in this agreement, Owner agrees to indemnify Producer and assume responsibility for any loss and liability incurred as a result of its breach of the representation of authority contained in this paragraph, including reasonable attorneys' fees.

AGREED AND ACCEPTED TO:

XYZ PRODUCTIONS
Production Company ("Producer")

By: _Tiffany Weston_
Its Authorized Signatory

Charles Cheatem, partner
("Owner")

1000 ATLANTIC BLVD. SUITE 700
LOS ANGELES, CA 90067
Address
555-4400
Phone No.

By: LOCATION MANAGER
Its:
#95-1234567
Social Security or Federal ID No.

555-3332
Fax No.

NON-FILMED LOCATION AGREEMENT

Property Owner ___Tom Jones___   Location ___Marc's House___

Property Address ___807 S. 3rd Street___   Set# ___08___
___Studio Village, CA 91604___

Production Co. ___XYZ Productions___ ("Producer")

Address ___1234 Flick Dr.___
___Hollywood, CA 90038___

Re: ___Herby's Summer Vacation___ (the "Picture")

To the Producer:

I, the undersigned owner or agent, whichever is applicable, hereby irrevocably grants to Producer, its employees, agents, contractors and suppliers, and such other parties as it may authorize or designate, to enter and use, for the purpose of: ___Production's Base Camp___
___(Crew Parking, Honeywagon, Trailers, Catering Truck & Meals)___
(indicate whether parking, holding, meals, staging, etc.) the Property located at the address set forth above hereinafter referred to as the "Property" which Property consists of: ___½ Acre___
___Parking Lot___
(description), which permission includes access to and from the Property and the rights to bring and utilize thereon personnel, personal property, material and equipment. Producer shall leave the Property in substantially as good condition as when received by Producer, excepting reasonable wear and tear and use of the Property for the purposes herein permitted.

Access to the Property is granted for ___2 Days___, commencing approximately
___6·2·XX___ ("the Term").

In full consideration of the above, Producer will pay the undersigned the sum of $ _____ .

In the event that any loss and liability is incurred as a direct result of any property damage to the Property occurring on the Property caused by Producer in connection with the aforementioned use of the Property, Producer agrees to pay for all reasonable costs of actual and verifiable damage. In this connection, the undersigned agrees to participate in a walk-through of the Property with Producer's representative (Location Manager) to inspect the property so damaged.

Producer further agrees to hold the undersigned harmless from any and all third-party suits, claims, or loss or liabilities caused by Producer in connection with the aforementioned use of the Property.

It is further agreed that the undersigned's rights and remedies in the event of a failure or an omission constituting a breach of the provisions of this Agreement shall be limited to the undersigned's right, if any, to recover damages in an action at law, but in no event shall the undersigned be entitled by reason of any such breach to terminate this Agreement, or to enjoin or restrain the distribution, exhibition or other exploitation of the Picture or the advertising or publicizing thereof.

This Agreement may not be altered except by a written instrument signed by both parties. This Agreement shall be binding upon and inure to the benefit of the undersigned and Producer and their respective successors and assigns.

The undersigned warrants that the undersigned has the full right to enter into this Agreement and that the consent of no other party is necessary to effectuate the full and complete permission granted herein.

AGREED & ACCEPTED:

By. ___Tom Jones___
(Property owner or designated signatory)

AGREED & ACCEPTED for Producer:

Phone#: ___555-7556___ Fax#: ___555-7555___

By: ___Tiffany Weston___

Social Security# or Federal ID#: ___123·45·6789___

LOCATION RELEASE

Property Owner _DEWEY, CHEATEM & HOWE_   Location _DAD'S OFFICE_

Property Address _1000 ATLANTIC BLVD., SUITE 700_   Set# _#10_
LOS ANGELES, CA 90067

Production Co. _XYZ PRODUCTIONS_   ("Producer")

Address _1234 FLICK DR._
HOLLYWOOD, CA 90038

Re: _HERBY'S SUMMER VACATION_   (the "Picture")

To the Producer:

Owner hereby acknowledges that the Property as referred to in the LOCATION AGREEMENT between Producer and Owner dated _5.11.XX_ , (the "Agreement") has been returned to Owner in substantially the same condition as it was in prior to Producer's use thereof:

Owner hereby acknowledges that:

(a)   all payments required under the Agreement have been paid;

(b)   no additional restoration work is required in connection with the Property;

(c)   Owner and any individual who entered the Property at the invitation or on behalf of Owner, suffered no personal loss or damage in connection with the use of the Property by Producer; and

(d)   Producer has no other responsibilities in connection with the Property other than to continue to hold Owner harmless from any and all third-party suits, claims, or loss or liabilities directly resulting from Producer's use of the Property.

Owner hereby releases and forever discharges Producer, its parent, subsidiary, affiliated and associated companies and its and their officers, employees and agents, and their successors and assigns of and from any and all claims, debts, demands, liabilities, obligations, costs, expenses, damages, actions and causes of action of whatsoever kind or nature, whether known or unknown, which Owner has ever had, now has or which Owner or any of its successors or assigns hereafter can, shall or may have against Producer based on or arising out of, relating to or in connection with the Agreement.

Producer may assign, transfer, license, delegate and/or grant all or any part of its rights, privileges and property hereunder to any person or entity. This Agreement shall be binding upon and shall inure to the benefit of the parties hereto and their respective heirs, executors, administrators, successors and assigns. This Agreement and Owner's rights and obligations hereunder may not be assigned by Owner.

ACCEPTED AND AGREED TO:

Charles Cheatem, partner   _6.4.XX_
Owner   Date

LOCATION INFORMATION SHEET

SHOW **HERBY'S SUMMER VACATION**
LOCATION MANAGER **B. SCOUT**
PERMIT SERVICE **PAT'S PERMIT SERVICE**
    CONTACT **PAT**
    PHONE # **(213) 555-7662**

PRODUCTION # **0100**
(SCRIPTED) LOCATION **HERBY'S DAD'S**
LAW OFFICE
DATE(S) **6-15-XX**
☑ INT.   ☐ EXT.   ☑ DAY   ☐ NIGHT

ACTUAL LOCATION
(Address & Phone #)
1000 ATLANTIC BLVD., SUITE 1200
LOS ANGELES, CA 90000
(213) 555-6000

CONTACTS

OFFICES OF:
DEWEY, CHEATEM & HOWE
Owner(s) Name(s) **CHARLES CHEATEM**
    Address **1000 ATLANTIC BLVD., # 1200**
    LOS ANGELES, CA 90000
Phone/FAX # **(310) 555-6000**
Beeper # **(310) 555-1626**

DATE & DAYS

	# of days	dates
Prep:	1	6-14-XX
Shoot:	1	6-15-XX
Strike:	1	6-16-XX

Representative(s)

Company: **LOCATION FINDERS, INC.**
Contact: **DORIS**
Address: **5153 RAILROAD DR.**
LOS ANGELES CA 90000
Phone/FAX # **(213) 555-2222**
Beeper # **(213) 555-1246**

LOCATION OF NEAREST EMERGENCY
MEDICAL FACILITY
BEVERLY HILLS HOSPITAL
1000 TINSELTOWN RD.
BEVERLY HILLS

LOCATION SITE RENTAL FEE

Full Amount	$ **2,000**	
Amount for PREP days	$ **500**	
Amount for SHOOT days	$ **1,000**	
Amount for STRIKE days	$ **500**	

Deposit $ **500**   Due on **6/1/XX**
☐ Refundable ☑ Apply to total fee
Balance $ **1,500**   Due on **6/13/XX**

O.T. after **12** hrs. per day @ $ **100** per hr.
ANY Additional days @ $ **1,000** per day
Additional charges: Phone $ **50/DAY**
    Utilities $ **INCL.**
    Parking $ **150**
(Other) _____ $ _____

CHECKLIST

☑ Location Agreement
☑ Certificate of Insurance
☑ Permit
☑ Fire Safety Officer(s)
☐ Police
☑ Location Fee
☑ Security
☐ Intermittent Traffic Control
☑ Post for Parking
☑ Signed Release from Neighbors
☑ Prepared Map to Location

☐ Heaters/Fans/Air Conditioners
☑ Lay-out Board/Drop Cloths
☐ Utilities/Power Supply
Allocated Areas For
☑ Extras
☑ Dressing Rms.
☑ Eating
☑ Hair/Makeup
☐ School
☑ Equipment
☑ Special Equipment
☐ Animals

Allocated Parking For
☑ Equipment
☑ Honeywagons
☑ Motor Homes
☑ Catering Truck
☑ Cast Vehicles
☑ Crew Vehicles
☐ Buses
☐ Picture Vehicles
☑ Extra Tables & Chairs/Tent
☐ Locate Parking Lot if
    Shuttle is Necessary

© ELH

LOCATION LIST

SHOW **HERBY'S SUMMER VACATION** PRODUCTION # **0100**

SET LOCATION	ACTUAL LOCATION (ADDRESS & PHONE)	DATE & DAYS (PREP/SHOOT/STRIKE)	CONTACTS (OWNER & REPRESENTATIVE)
HERBY'S DAD'S OFFICE	OFFICES OF: DEWEY, CHEATEM & HOWE 1000 ATLANTIC BLVD., SUITE 1200 L.A. 90000 (213) 555-6000	PREP: 6-14-XX SHOOT: 6-15-XX STRIKE: 6-16-XX	CHARLES CHEATEM (213) 555-6000 LOCATION FINDERS, INC. (213) 555-1222 ATTN: BORIS
HERBY'S HOUSE	WESTER HOME 12436 SOUNDMAN RD. STUDIO VILLAGE, CA 91111	PREP: 6-16-XX SHOOT: 6-17&18 STRIKE: 6-19-XX	K. WESTER H: (818) 555-3221 O: (818) 555-1223

REQUEST TO FILM DURING EXTENDED HOURS

Dear Resident:

This is to inform you that **XYZ PRODUCTIONS** will be shooting a film entitled **"HERBY'S SUMMER VACATION"** in your neighborhood at the following address: **12353 Rose Street.** Filming activities in residential areas is normally allowed only between the hours of **8:00 a.m.** and **8:00 p.m.** In order to extend the hours before and/or after these times, the City requires that we obtain a signature of approval from the neighbors. The following information pertains to the dates and times of our scheduled shoot and any specific information you may need to know regarding our filming activities.

We have obtained or applied for all necessary City permits and maintain all legally required liability insurance. A copy of our film permit will be on file at the City Film Office and will also be available at our shooting location.

<u>FILMING DAYS/HOURS REQUESTED:</u> on **August 3rd and 4th, 19XX**
> from **10:00 a.m.** to **10:00 p.m.**
> and **August 5th and 6th, 19XX**
> from **12:00 noon** to **12:00 midnight**

<u>THE FOLLOWING ACTIVITIES ARE PLANNED FOR THE EXTENDED HOURS:</u>
A backyard party to include approximately 80 extras, a minimal amount of loud music and a stunt where ten guests fall into the swimming pool.

We appreciate your hospitality and cooperation. We wish to make filming on your street a pleasant experience for both you and us. If you have any questions or concerns before or during the filming, please feel free to call our Production Office and ask for me or the Production Manager.

Sincerely yours,

_____   _____
Location Manager   Production Company

                                          _____
                                          Phone No.

We would very much appreciate it if you would complete and sign where indicated below.
A representative from our company will be by within the next day or two to pick up this form.

— —— —— — —— —— — —— —— —— —— — —— —— —— —— — —— —— —— —— —— —

☐ I DO NOT OBJECT TO THE EXTENDED FILMING HOURS
☐ I DO OBJECT TO THE EXTENDED FILMING HOURS

COMMENTS:

NAME: _____

ADDRESS: _____

_____

PHONE #: (Optional) _____

© ELH

CHAPTER SEVENTEEN

Distant Location

Some films are shot at a combination of local and distant locations, some are entirely shot at one distant location and still others are shot at multiple locations—each scenario requiring a different type of prep. The production staff of a show scheduled to be based in one location will generally start prepping locally from their home base, then move to and set up offices on location, continuing to prep while finalizing all necessary arrangements. The crew would start gradually as needed. Once filming has started, however, and additional major moves are slated, it becomes difficult to finish prepping subsequent locations. In this situation, many productions will hire smaller, separate teams to set up subunits at the other locations, so that everything is ready when the main unit arrives (hotel rooms, temporary offices, phone lines, location sites, sets, local crew and extras, rigging, etc.). After the first unit has left, this same team would remain to tie up all the loose ends, making sure location sites and sets are wrapped properly, bills are paid, equipment is returned, etc.

THE TRAVELING PRODUCTION OFFICE

If you have a show that incorporates various locations that are not great distances apart, but far enough apart to necessitate new hotels and new bases of operation every few days or week or two, you might want to consider a mobile office trailer. These custom-built units are being used more and more, especially for road pictures (a story that unfolds while its characters are traveling). They can save you a great deal of time by eliminating the need to constantly set up temporary offices at every stop. Once everything is set up, that's it. A traveling office will run more efficiently while conveniently remaining in one place (which is close to the set with the other production vehicles and not back at the hotel). The trailers are outfitted with office furniture; phones are cellular, digital and/or satellite; faxes are sent and received via satellite and the power to run the lights and office machines is generator-driven or from outside electrical lines. The downside to all of this is that once in a while, a location is so remote (or surrounded by so many mountains), that not even the satellite phones will give you adequate reception. And when that happens, you're back at the hotel making your calls.

The following checklist, while not reflecting a multiple-unit scenario, does cover the basics and should prove to be extremely helpful.

DISTANT LOCATION CHECKLIST

❑ Contact film commissions representing areas you are considering as location sites. (Some productions will have their home-based location manager make all initial contacts with film commission representatives and will send the location manager ahead to pre-scout.)

❑ Review location photos while weighing the advantages (and disadvantages) of shooting at each site.

❑ Select a travel agent who is accustomed to working with production companies (see more on this under "Travel Considerations" below).

❑ Scout location sites under consideration.

- Check out hotels, motels and rental units in the areas you are considering.
- Make final location site selections.
- Develop a good working relationship with local film commission representatives in the area(s) where you will be shooting.
- Contact the SAG branch office closest to where you will be shooting for jurisdictional guidelines.
- Based on the recommendations of others who have shot at that location, find and hire a local location manager (if necessary).
- Based on the recommendations of others who have shot at that location, find and hire a local production manager, coordinator or assistant coordinator.
- Hire a local extras casting agency (or extras coordinator), if necessary.
- Obtain a local phone book to locate needed services.
- Secure living accommodations (i.e., hotel, motel, rental units) for arriving cast and crew.
- Establish and set up a temporary location-based production office.
- Have outside phone lines installed in the production office (including lines for fax and Internet access).
- Have business cards made up with the production's local address, phone and fax numbers.
- Set up accounts for gasoline, rental cars, motor homes, office supplies, etc.
- Arrange to rent a refrigerator, coffee machine, and other items for the production office.
- Determine the availability of local crew, drivers, office help, etc. and set up interviews.
- Determine the availability of local equipment, supplies and services (items that will not have to be transported to location).
- Determine whether suitable catering is available locally, or if you will have to bring a caterer (with truck and crew) to location.
- Prepare a list of airline schedules to and from the location(s), along with the airlines' phone numbers and the names of their contact reps.
- Make travel arrangements for cast and crew.
- Prepare a movement list and individual travel itineraries.
- Arrange with the airline or travel agency to have someone at the airport to meet cast and crew members and help with arriving equipment.
- Open an account with the airline for the shipment of dailies.
- Obtain a supply of packing slips, waybills, labels, heavy tape and other supplies for the shipping of film each night.
- Order pagers and cellular phones (for key cast and crew) while on location (sometimes you can get better monthly plans on the pagers and phones you bring with you as opposed to getting them on location).
- Order long distance phone cards for those who will need them while on location.
- Open a local bank account.
- As necessary, rent computers and printers, a copier machine, typewriter and other office equipment.
- Order a portable screen and projector and/or a VCR and monitor to screen dailies, and/or make arrangements to screen dailies in one of the hotel's banquet rooms or at a local theatre.
- Prepare a room list.
- Get recommendations (from the film commission or hotel management) for a good doctor, dentist and chiropractor. Call to introduce yourself to the doctors' assistants, letting them know about your pending shooting activities; and ask if you can call upon them if necessary. Confirm that you can give cast and crew members their names and numbers to contact in emergency situations during non-working hours. Ask for their recommendations for the best hospital/trauma center in the area.
- Prepare welcome packages (see description of welcome packages under "Welcome to Location" later in the chapter).
- Distribute safety and code of conduct guidelines to cast and crew.
- Check extended weather reports for the area (daily).
- Prepare a list of local shooting locations.
- Locate a source for flowers, fruit baskets and gift shops for cast and VIP arrival gifts.
- Locate clothing racks for the wardrobe department (if needed).
- Find out if refrigerators and microwave ovens are available for cast and crew to rent (if not already in hotel rooms).

❏ Keep maps of how to get to each location in the production office at all times. Tack a call sheet and map to the next day's location on the production office door when you close up for the night.

TRAVEL CONSIDERATIONS

It is the production company's responsibility to transport members of their shooting company to and from a distant location; and assuming that obligation, they are required to carry a *Travel Accident Policy* as part of their insurance package. Union and guild regulations go a step further by dictating which class of travel certain individuals must be afforded. It is therefore frowned upon when cast and crew members wish to make their own (alternative) travel arrangements, and the studios (along with many other production companies) make it perfectly clear that they are not responsible for individuals who wish to travel on their own. Smaller independent companies tend to be more flexible with this, and those who decide to drive instead of taking a company-arranged flight or the company-provided bus may be reimbursed for their mileage or paid the equivalent price of the plane ticket. And some who choose not to fly when the rest of the company is doing so may be given a plane ticket anyway (fulfilling the production company's obligation), but it would be an exchangeable ticket that can be traded in and used at another time. Understand that you are responsible for yourself should you choose to make your own travel arrangements. Just make sure to inform the production office of your decision and give them a copy of your itinerary. Also, if possible, let them know where and how they can reach you if necessary.

Along the same lines, some cast and crew members wish to make their own housing arrangements, especially when staying in one location for an extended period of time. Some companies will offer you a housing allowance in lieu of a hotel room. Find out what your company's policy is, how much of an allowance (if any) they are offering and how often it will be paid. Then if you choose to make your own arrangements, make sure to inform the production office as to where you are staying and how they can reach you.

The production coordinator is the one who has traditionally handled all travel and housing arrangements when a film unit shoots on a distant location. Some shows, however, are so large or their many locations so spread out, that their production coordinators would end up with little time for anything other than travel. It is therefore no longer uncommon for larger shows to employ a dedicated travel coordinator. (On *Titanic*, in addition to three production coordinators, we had a full-time travel coordinator and a two-person housing department to accommodate all the cast, crew, stunt performers and extras working in Mexico.)

An issue that comes up often that I would like to clarify is that it is not the production or travel coordinators' responsibility to make personal travel arrangements for the friends and family of cast and crew members who wish to visit on location. If asked nicely, and if they can find the time in their already hectic day, they might be willing to do so; but this would be their choice and not something that should be expected.

Major studios and several independent production companies have their own in-house travel departments; when you are doing a show for them, one of their travel reps will be assigned to your project. The production or travel coordinator will then interact with this person for all the production's travel, limo, rental car and chartered flight needs. You will also be given an after-hours contact and number to call for travel needs that may arise after your rep has gone home for the evening. The way the process generally works is that the production or travel coordinator will fill out a travel request form called a TA (travel authorization). Information is verbally given to the travel rep, so he or she can start checking reservations and tentatively lining up itineraries. At the same time, the TA is sent to the show's designated production executive for approval. Once approved, a copy of the signed TA is faxed or handed over to the travel office, so arrangements can be finalized and tickets purchased. The travel rep will then fax a confirmed itinerary back to the production office. Tickets are either picked up from the travel department, or electronic tickets are arranged for and picked up at the airport.

If you are not associated with a studio or production company that has it's own travel department, you will be enlisting the services of an independent agency and agent to help you with your show. The number one rule is, use an agency that is familiar with how film companies operate (and can take ever-changing travel arrangements in their stride), and ask for (and check out) references from other people who have used them on other shows. Also, make sure they:

- can offer an after-hours contact and phone number
- have good relationships with airline reps who can offer group discounts and help with product placement deals
- have good rental car and limo service contacts
- if desired, can offer *Meet & Greet* services at the airport (this service entails having someone at the airport to meet arriving cast and crew, help them with their luggage and check-in, escort them to a VIP waiting room, etc.)
- can help with chartered and helicopter flights if necessary

The production or travel coordinator would be responsible for the following:

- If applicable, filling out TAs.
- Scheduling direct, nonstop flights whenever possible.
- If desired, arranging for *Meet & Greet* and/or the use of the VIP waiting room at the airport.
- If everyone is not traveling in one group, making sure cast and crew members know where they are going to be met when they arrive—at the arrival gate in the terminal, in baggage or outside of baggage. (Awaiting drivers generally hold up signs with the name of the show or the names of arriving passengers.)
- Maintaining an updated list of airlines that fly to and from your location, phone numbers of the airlines, contact names of the airline reps and a schedule of all flights to and from location.
- Preparing Movement Lists and Individual Travel Itineraries.

Movement Lists And Individual Travel Itineraries

It is essential to keep certain people informed as to who is traveling and when—most of all, the people who are doing the traveling. Movement lists provide a basic schedule of who is traveling, when and how. They are generally distributed to the producer(s); director; production manager, supervisor and coordinator; production accountant; transportation coordinator; location manager

(if applicable); studio or production company executives and the insurance company. This information is used to determine per diem payments, schedule vans and drivers for airport runs, establish how many hotel rooms will be needed on a given night, etc. Department heads from Hair, Makeup, Wardrobe and Props and the stunt coordinator will also often request copies of movement lists, so they know when cast members are arriving on locations and can schedule fittings and meetings and Props can fit performers with jewelry, eyeglasses, etc. At the end of this chapter, you will find a general *Travel Movement* form which would primarily be used if many (or all) members of a shooting company are scheduled to travel at the same time. Also included is a *Quick Reference Travel Movement* form, which can be used to track any number of individuals traveling to any location.

An *Individual Travel Itinerary* (also located at the end of the chapter) would be used to inform each person traveling of all the specifics associated with their trip, details relating to: ground transportation to and from the airport; their flight; their plane ticket and per diem; where they will be staying; the address, phone and fax numbers of the temporary location-based production office and when they are currently scheduled to return.

WELCOME TO LOCATION

Most productions will arrange to have some sort of gift basket or flower arrangement left in the rooms of arriving principal cast members. On one show I worked on, the producer had flowers awaiting every female crew member as well (there were only three of us, and what a nice way to walk into an empty hotel room). Some productions will host a kick-off party or small welcoming reception at the hotel once everyone has arrived, a day or two before filming begins. The goal is to make arriving cast and crew feel welcome and comfortable and to acquaint them with both their new co-workers and their new surroundings as soon as possible. They will be working long, hard hours, so try to find enjoyable ways they can spend their scant amount of time off. Much of what you can do to accomplish this will of course depend on the flexibility of your budget, but it's amazing what you can achieve with a little imagination and just a little time to make some arrangements.

While on location, the film crew is everyone's surrogate family, and we all want to feel as if we belong. Not everyone will partake of extracurricular activities—and on some shoots, any spare time will be spent catching up on sleep—but do as much as you can. Informal parties are always good, such as barbeques or group dinners at local restaurants, especially on the nights preceding a day off. Ask the film commission office to help set up sightseeing packages (if there is anything of interest to see); tours of local attractions (while I was working on a picture in Northern California, our crew was treated to tours of the local wineries on Sundays); or to get tickets to plays or amusement parks. Bowling nights are popular, as are shopping excursions (find out if there are any outlet malls nearby). Find out where the local movie theatres are, the golf courses and where one can get a massage or a workout.

Having good food on location is a vital part of keeping your crew happy and comfortable. Make sure the caterer you hire is the best you can afford and comes with rave recommendations. The same holds true for your craft service department. If you are working nights and it's cold, make sure to have hot soups, chili and plenty of warm drinks available. If you are working under exceptionally hot conditions, plenty of cool water, fresh fruit, salads and anything refreshing is much appreciated (as are small towels or neckerchiefs soaked in Sea Breeze™ and cold water and extra bottles of sunblock). Not only is good food important; sometimes, just having access to food is crucial. After wrap, some people are too tired to go out to eat, or it may be so late (or early) that most restaurants are closed. Find out the hours of several local restaurants (especially the ones closest to the hotel), and scout out the ones that deliver. Also make arrangements with the hotel for their restaurant, coffee shop and/or room service to accommodate crew hours. Never strand anyone without access to food.

Most production offices provide *Welcome Packages* to arriving cast and crew. These packages of valuable information will not only prove useful to those who receive them, but the more complete they are, the fewer questions the production office will have to answer over and over again. This will let everyone know who they can call should they need medical attention during nonwork hours, where they can get their checks cashed, where they can get their laundry done, what they can do on their day off—everything they could possibly need or want to know about this new location you've transported them to. The information for the package can be collected from the film commission, hotel management, local chamber of commerce and the contact lists of others who have shot there before. The most important part of any welcome package is the local contact list. It should contain:

- The name and phone number of the nearest hospital emergency room and/or trauma center
- The names and numbers of a local doctor, dentist and chiropractor (see "Distant Location Checklist")
- The location of the closest laundry facilities and cleaners
- The location and business hours of nearby grocery stores and pharmacies
- The location and business hours of the bank the production has opened an account with and any other nearby ATMs
- The location and business hours of the closest post office
- Locations and numbers of the closest gym, exercise and/or yoga classes and where one can get a massage
- Phone numbers of a taxicab service and rental car agencies (for those not provided with a rental car or for friends and relatives coming to visit)
- A restaurant list, noting restaurants by price range and cuisines—also noting restaurants that deliver
- A list of nightclubs, karaoke bars, any type of night life
- Information on local golf courses, bowling alleys, movie theatres and shopping centers
- And anything else you can think of . . .

In addition to the contact list, the welcome package should include:

- Hotel guidelines (including how to make long distance calls, information on Internet access, coffee shop hours, etc.; some hotels will supply you with maps of the facilities)
- A map of the area
- A map indicating shooting locations in relation to the hotel
- In applicable, bus and subway schedules and routes
- Brochures describing local points of interest, attractions and entertainment
- A listing of local events

Please understand that as hard as you try to keep your cast and crew comfortable and content, and as wonderful as most of them are, when on location, there are always one or two individuals who can make you wish you had become an insurance broker. There are these perfectly normal functioning adults, who, when taken out of their familiar surroundings and worked twelve to sixteen hours a day, tend to become totally inept at taking care of themselves. Some just whine and complain a lot. They are tired and impatient; and no matter what you do to try to help, it's never enough. All you can do is your best (which includes trying to keep *your* patience in check). If it gets too bad, ask the producer to intercede on your behalf; but don't worry about it too much. Taking care of an entire shooting company on distant location is a difficult job at best; so give yourself the credit you deserve, and don't let a couple of boobs get to you. They probably whine when they're at home and drive their husbands and wives crazy, too.

INTERACTING WITH LOCAL COMMUNITIES

Meeting, working with and interacting with local people on a shooting location can be a rewarding experience and produce friendships that long outlast your shooting schedule. Most people living outside of big film centers are thrilled to have a film shooting in their town and will extend a great deal of hospitality and support to the visiting production. Keep in mind, however, that the perception any local community has of your shooting company will reflect on the entire film industry. The reaction by the community, good or bad, will directly affect your company's (and future companies') access to location sites, cooperation from local merchants, rates on hotel rooms, site rentals, local services and everything connected to that location. A negative experience with one film company can motivate an entire city to ban all future film production in that area.

Inform local cast and crew members, in addition to reminding those traveling from home base, of Code of Conduct guidelines. This should be done verbally as well as in memo form. In dealing with local merchants, pay your bills in a timely manner and make sure to get what you need without being overly demanding. Be courteous and treat people with respect. Jackets and T-shirts that display vulgarities should not be worn, and noise levels should not get out of hand. Do not interfere with the normal activities of the neighborhood unless these activities are authorized as part of your scheduled shoot. Leave location sites cleaned and as you originally found them (if not better). As time permits, involve the community in your activities as much as possible. A positive rapport with the community will not only help to promote a positive image of the film industry, but it will guarantee that you will be welcomed back with open arms and increasing cooperation on your next shoot at that location.

FILM COMMISSIONS

The purpose of a film commission is to promote and aid film production in a particular city, region, state or country. Film commissions are government-sanctioned and are found throughout the United States and in many other countries as well. Some film offices are independent entities, some operate as part of various governors' offices and others are divisions of tourism boards. Most are members of the Association of Film Commissioners International (AFCI), an international, nonprofit, educational organization of government employees serving as film commissioners. The Association's purpose is to act as a liaison between the visual communications industry and local public and private sectors to facilitate on-location production, and to stimulate economic benefit for member governments.

General information on shooting in various locations can be obtained through *Locations Magazine*, the official publication of the AFCI, and also by attending Location Expo, a yearly, three-day convention (held in February in Los Angeles) where national and international film commissions exhibit a vast array of locations and location services. You will find a full list of AFCI-member film commissions on their website at www.afci.org. Many individual film commissions have their own websites, which can also be accessed through www.afci.org.

In an effort to persuade you to shoot your picture and spend your production dollars in their state or country, film commission representatives are most helpful in the process of selecting locations and also during production when shooting on a distant location. When you are considering different locations in which to shoot, contact the film office representing each of those locations. They will not only answer questions over the phone, but will also be happy to send you photographs of location sites that might meet your needs and a complimentary copy of their resource guide. This book provides information on local crew, living accommodations, equipment, services, restaurants, local talent agencies, pertinent tax and/or permit requirements, etc.

If you plan to scout a number of locations before making a final selection, call the film commission representing each area ahead of time. Film commissioners or members of their staff will generally meet with you, show you around and help in any way they can—from cutting through government red tape, to obtaining permits, to helping you get a good rate on hotel rooms. They will make your decision to shoot in their area as desirable as possible, using whatever state or city resources available to them in doing so.

Once you select a location, working with the local film commission will save you valuable time, energy and money. You need a person, or persons, who know that area well and are at the same time familiar with the demands of filming and production coordination.

The relationship between production company and film commission is almost always a mutually beneficial one. While it is the film commissioner's job to lure you to a particular location, it is the rapport you develop with this person that will ultimately promote even more help, cooperation, good deals and open doors. Whether it's helping you cut red tape to get a film permit, getting you great hotel room rates, introducing you to reliable vendors, helping you fill a stadium full of extras, recommending great local crew members and supplying you with brochures and maps to local attractions, they become your best and most valuable friends while at that location. That is why film commission representatives often become unofficial crew members, are invited to lunch on the set and to cast and crew parties and are sent letters (or gifts) of thanks and appreciation before visiting productions wrap and head back home.

SAG BRANCH OFFICES

Even if you have signed an agreement and posted a bond (in one of SAG's main offices) prior to leaving for a distant location, contact the local SAG branch office upon arriving at your location. Local SAG representatives are your best source of information for matters such as what constitutes a local hire within that state, current guidelines on right-to-work state laws (if applicable), casting procedures in that area, the hiring of local extras, drive-to reimbursements, etc. A current list of

SAG branch offices can be found at the end of Chapter 11, "Principal Talent."

THE HOTEL

Choosing hotels, motels and rental units on location will depend on where your location is, the availability of lodging in that town, how long you are going to be staying and your budget. Not all hotels can accommodate an entire shooting company, so while one is generally selected to serve as the production's headquarters, often two or three are used to house cast and crew members.

Factors to consider when scouting hotels:

* The most obvious—the cleanliness of their rooms. (No matter how inexpensive they are, if they are not clean—keep looking.)
* Will they give you a fair group rate (based on the going room rates in the area)?
* Will they give you the same per room rate whether a room's furnished with a king bed, two queens or is occupied by one person or two?
* Have they housed other film companies before? If the answer is yes and they still want your business, great.
* Do they have suites available for the producer, director and cast?
* Do they have a restaurant and/or coffee shop, and would they be willing to open early or stay open late to accommodate shooting hours?
* Do they offer room service? If so, during which hours?
* Do they have ample parking for all company vehicles (trucks and trailers included)?
* Would your catering and/or camera trucks be able to pull up to an electrical outlet, so they could plug in for the night?
* If necessary, do they have a banquet or meeting room that could be used for meetings or for screening dailies?
* If you are going to be shooting nights, would they be willing to reschedule housekeeping— cleaning rooms in the evening and not vacuuming or doing anything noisy near crew-occupied rooms during the day?
* Do they accept pets? (There are always a few people who travel to location with their dogs.) If so, is there an additional charge or any special requirements?
* If needed, would you have access to their copier and fax machines? If so, how much per

page would they charge? And if so, would you have access to these machines at any hour of the day or night?

- Would they be willing to throw in a meeting or banquet room, or two-to-three adjoining guest rooms that could be converted into temporary offices at no extra cost? If so, would you be allowed to have outside phone lines installed in those rooms (enough to accommodate phone, fax and modem lines)?
- Would they be able to supply refrigerators and/or microwaves in the rooms (if not already there)?
- For those people who might need to work from their rooms, would their rooms have a phone that's located on a table or desk and would it have a sufficiently long cord? (It's not easy to work from a phone with a short cord that's right next to the bed.)
- Would they be willing to waive the cost of local phone calls?
- Would they mind posting a call sheet and map in their lobby each evening?

Not many hotels or motels will be able to accommodate everything on your wish list, but the more they can say yes to, the more desirable they become.

Once you have selected a hotel, they will ask you to sign a contract and request a deposit (to be applied to the final bill). Most deposit requests are for one night's stay for the entire shooting company. The agreement you sign should include provisions for schedule changes or cancellation. As the hotel has agreed to block a significant number of rooms for a specified period of time, much will depend on how much notice you can give them in the event of a change and whether they have sufficient time to rebook the rooms. Many of the larger hotels will give you the flexibility of canceling up to seven days prior to your scheduled arrival. After that, the minimum they may require is a cancellation fee equal to your first night's reservations. With sufficient notice, you should be able to postpone your hotel dates without penalty.

Make sure the hotel understands that the production is paying for rooms and tax only. Everyone staying there will be responsible for their own incidental charges, and the hotel is responsible for obtaining a credit card from each individual against their incidentals. As this is standard procedure, most crew members are good about doing this.

As part of their deals, principal cast members, producers, directors and DPs are often given a weekly living allowance while on location that incorporates their housing. If there are individuals on your show who have this type of deal, the hotel should be given a list of their names and informed that they will be responsible for their own hotel bills. Also under these circumstances, inform those involved of their room choices before reserving suites for them. Since they are paying for it, they may want less-expensive rooms (or maybe not)—but ask.

Your main hotel contact is generally the sales manager and possibly one other individual from the sales department or front desk. Production-related requests should be directed toward these people only. Likewise, inform your crew that any complaints they might have about their rooms or the facilities are to go through the production office. The greater the number of people who get involved, the greater the chance for miscommunications and mistakes.

Without even being asked, cast and crew members will generally inform you (prior to traveling to location) as to their preferences in hotel rooms. And if you use the *Crew Information Sheet* (found in Chapter 5, "Pre-Production"), it asks for hotel preferences. Supply the hotel with a listing of arrivals (names, dates and approximate times of arrival); the type of room each person has requested (if available)—a suite, king-size bed, two beds, a room on the ground floor, etc. and indicate when each person is scheduled to check out. Keep the sales manager or reservations clerk alerted as to any last-minute additions or changes in arrivals and departures.

Make sure the hotel rooms are ready for cast and crew members when they arrive, even if they arrive early in the day (before check-in time). If you let the hotel know in advance of your need for early check-ins, they may waive the extra night's fee if the hotel has vacancies anyway; or they may just charge you a half-day fee for an early check-in.

Your hotel office space should be able to accommodate a UPM, production coordinator, assistant coordinator and a couple of PAs, as well as a two or three-person accounting office and possibly a transportation office. The camera, sound and wardrobe departments generally work off of their trucks or trailers, but occasionally you will need rooms to store equipment. Editing rooms are also sometimes set up in the hotel. Rooms for equipment, editing and wardrobe should be on the ground floor and should have deadbolt locks on the doors.

Keep your own list (see the *Hotel Room Log* at the end of the chapter) of when each person checks in and out, and compare it against the hotel bills. It may be helpful to keep a second list (in alphabetical order) for quick reference in addition to the Hotel Room Log that categorizes everyone by department and the date they arrive.

If the hotel is busy, think about reserving a couple of extra rooms, just in case the schedule changes and additional cast or crew have to be brought to location earlier than anticipated. Most hotels will not charge you for holding the extra rooms, as long as you release the ones you won't be needing early each afternoon, so they can be rented that night. Find out the status of available rooms should your show run over schedule and the company have to stay longer than anticipated. Check out the availability of rooms at other hotels and motels in the area should they be needed.

SHIPPING DAILIES

While on location, you will be shipping the film shot each day to the lab each night (except Friday and Saturday's film, which is sent on Sunday). The film negative is developed during the night, the sound is synced up to picture the next morning and *dailies* (made from the director's selected takes) are shipped back to location the next day in the form of a work print and/or VHS or Beta SP cassettes. The method of shipping film and dailies back and forth will greatly depend on how far away your location is from the lab. Unless close enough to have the film driven in each night, most productions will ship their film via counter-to-counter air service.

You would start this process by opening an account with the air cargo division of the airline you choose for the shipment of dailies. Select an airline that flies nonstop to your destination, with the most evening flights. If it is impossible to get a direct flight, choose a route that has as few stops as possible. This will lessen the chances of the film being unloaded at the wrong stop.

If you call the airline, a representative may come to your office to open an account, or will fax you a credit application to fill out and fax back. The airline rep will then send you preprinted waybills (with your company name and account number on them) and flight schedules. Keep the flight schedules of more than the one airline in case flights are canceled or an unscheduled rush situation on your end necessitates the use of another carrier. Depending on how many different airlines you might use, it may be worthwhile to open accounts with at least two of them. On the rare occasion in which you would be using a carrier you don't have an account with, your driver can pay cash and fill out a new waybill at the counter.

Be sure to keep a copy of each waybill in case your shipment is delayed, mislaid or lost. (They also provide backup to the shipping bills.) Also keep a log of every shipment that leaves the production office, indicating the date, waybill number, flight number, arrival and departure times and the contents of your shipment—the number of reels you are shipping, number of sound rolls, still film, any equipment you may be returning, etc. (See the *Dailies Shipment Log* form at the end of this chapter.)

A production assistant from your home base office or a courier service (there are those that specialize in the handling of dailies) will pick up your daily shipment each night. If it's a PA, he or she should go to the airport before you start shipping dailies and introduce him or herself to the airline personnel who will be handling the film shipment when it comes in each night. (Consider having the PA take a few show T-shirts along as introduction gifts.) Should there be a problem with the flight or the routing of the dailies, it helps to know the airport routine and to be on good terms with the staff.

Once the film starts arriving, your PA or courier will open the box(es) and separate the film for the lab, the sound tapes, the still film, the envelope(s) for the office (you should pouch copies of all your daily paperwork back to the home office via the daily shipment each night) and whatever else you have sent. The PA will drop the film and sound off that night, and deliver the remainder to the office first thing the next morning for distribution.

Labels on the box(es) should be addressed to the production office (always include the office phone number), with the notation: HOLD FOR PICK-UP. Boxes should also indicate or have labels that read: UNDEVELOPED FILM—DO NOT X-RAY.

It is best to ship film on the same flight each evening. Taking the lab's cutoff time into consideration as well as the time needed to transport the film to the lab, pick the latest flight available in order to get the film there on time. If it works for you, the last flight is the one usually selected to allow a full day's worth of shooting (or most of one) to be sent out. If shooting for the day is not completed by the time the driver has to leave for the airport, the camera crew will have to "break film" at a designated time, sending what they have.

The driver making the airport run should have the packed boxes, a completed waybill and a memo indicating the flight information and a description of what is in each of the boxes you are sending. The driver should call the production coordinator from the airport to confirm that the boxes got onboard and that the flight was on schedule. If there is a problem, he or she should call to inform Production that the boxes had to be sent on another airline or that the flight is going to be delayed. The production coordinator will in turn call the PA or courier service at the other end to confirm an estimated arrival time and to give them the waybill number. When the driver returns, he or she should give the production coordinator a completed copy of the waybill. Because most labs are closed from Friday night to Sunday night, Friday and Saturday's footage is shipped on Sunday afternoon so that it arrives before midnight on Sunday.

FORMS IN THIS CHAPTER

- Travel Movement—primarily used when many (or all) members of a shooting company are scheduled to travel at the same time
- Quick Reference Travel Movement—used to track any number of individuals traveling to any location
- Individual Travel Itinerary
- Hotel Room Log
- Hotel Room List
- Meal Allowance—form used for individuals signing for their per diem
- Dailies Shipment Log

TRAVEL MOVEMENT

SHOW __HERBY'S SUMMER VACATION__ PROD # __0100__
TRAVEL FROM __LOS ANGELES, CA__ TO __MILWAUKEE WISCONSIN__
DAY/DATE __MON. SEPT. 20, 19XX__ AIRLINE __WISCONSIN AIR__
TYPE OF AIRCRAFT __747__
FLIGHT # __230__ MEAL(S) __LUNCH__ MOVIE __YES__
CHANGE TO FLIGHT # _____ DEPARTURE TIME __11:00 A.M.__ ARRIVAL __5:15 P.M.__ FLIGHT STOPS IN _____
                                      DEPARTURE _____ ARRIVAL _____

NAME	POSITION	GROUND TRANSPORTATION TO AIRPORT	TO BE PICKED UP @	GROUND TRANSPORTATION FROM AIRPORT
SWIFTY DEALS	PRODUCER	LOU'S LIMO SER.	10:00 A.M.	MILWAUKEE DRIVER TO PICK UP CREW
SID CELLULOID	DIRECTOR	LOU'S LIMO SER.	9:45 A.M.	OUTSIDE OF BAGGAGE AREA
FRED FILMER	UPM	DRIVER TO PICKUP	9:30 A.M.	
F. STOPP	DIR. OF PHOTOG.	DRIVER TO PICKUP	9:45 A.M.	

HOTEL __MILWAUKEE GRAND__ DIRECT # TO PRODUCTION OFFICE __(414) 555-2376__
Address __12345 WISCONSIN BLVD.__ FAX # __(414) 555-2352__
__MILWAUKEE, WISCONSIN__ ADDITIONAL INFO. _____
Phone # __(414) 555-2000__

© ELH

TRAVEL MOVEMENT

SHOW: HERBY'S SUMMER VACATION

DATE: 8·6·XX

NOTE -- the following information is subject to change

NAME	POSITION	DATE LEAVING	GROUND TRANSPORTATION TO AIRPORT	FLIGHT INFO.	GROUND TRANSPORTATION FROM AIRPORT	HOTEL ACCOMMODATIONS
SWIFTY DEALS	PRODUCER	8/7	LOU'S LIMO SERVICE	WISCONSIN AIR #2003 - LV. L.A. 9A ARR. MILWAUKEE 3:15P	LOCAL LOC. MGR.	THE MILWAUKEE GRAND (555-2000)
SID CELLULOID	DIRECTOR	8/7	LOU'S LIMO SERVICE			
FRED FILMER	UPM	8/7	LOU'S LIMO SERVICE	→	→	→
KATIE KANDU	SCRIPT SUP'R.	8/12	TRANSPO. DRIVER	WISCONSIN AIR #2009 - LV. L.A. 7A ARR. MILWAUKEE 1:15P	HOTEL VAN	GOOD NIGHT INN (555-7220)
PHIL M. CANN	CAMERA OPERATOR	8/12	SELF	SAME AS ABOVE	HOTEL VAN	SAME AS ABOVE
CAL BLOOEY	SPEC. EFX. COORDINATOR	8/15	TRANSPO. DRIVER	WISCONSIN AIR #2006 LV. LA 11:15A - ARR. 5:30P	CAB	WINDSOR APARTMENTS (555-7632)

© ELH

INDIVIDUAL TRAVEL ITINERARY

SHOW __HERBY'S SUMMER VACATION__   DATE __5·22·XX__
COMPANY __XYZ PRODUCTIONS__
ADDRESS __1234 FLICK DR.__   PHONE# __555-3331__
__HOLLYWOOD, CA 90038__   FAX# __555-3332__

NAME __PHIL M. CANN__   POSITION __CAMERA OPERATOR__
DATE SCHEDULED TO TRAVEL __WEDNESDAY, 6-2-XX__
LOCATION(S) __MILWAUKEE, WISCONSIN__

Current weather conditions are: __70's & 80's__
We will be shooting __5__ nights, and the weather at night during this time of year is anticipated to be:
__WARM-BALMY (BRING INSECT REPELLENT)__ . Please pack accordingly.

GROUND TRANSPORTATION TO: [ ] THE AIRPORT [ ] LOCATION
[✓] Company will send a car for you @ __7:15__ [✓]a.m. [ ]p.m.
[ ] Report to_____to take shuttle bus at_____ [ ]a.m. [ ]p.m.
[ ] Please provide your own ground transportation to the airport, and the production will reimburse you
for the airport shuttle van or cab fare
Be at the airport no later than_____ [ ]a.m. [ ]p.m. for check-in

---

FLIGHT INFORMATION
Airport __LAX__
Airline __WISCONSIN AIR__   Flight # __2003__   Departs at __9:00__ [✓]a.m. [ ]p.m.
Change of plane in_____
Airline_____ Flight#_____ Departs at_____ [ ]a.m. [ ]p.m.
Arrives in __MILWAUKEE__   at __2:15__ [ ]a.m. [✓]p.m.

YOUR AIRLINE TICKET
[ ] Pick-up @ the production office
[ ] It will be delivered to your home
[✓] You have an electronic ticket waiting for you at the airport
Record Locator No: __X2345LMNP376__
(Note: be sure to bring a picture ID with you to the airport)

YOUR PER DIEM
Your per diem will be $__50__ per day
[ ] Pick-up @ the prod. office before you leave
[✓] You will receive it when you get to location

GROUND TRANSPORTATION FROM THE AIRPORT
[✓] You will be picked-up by a company driver: [✓] at the arrival gate [ ] in the baggage area [ ] outside of baggage
[ ] The driver will have a sign with: [ ] your name on it [ ] the name of the show on it
[ ] A rental car will be waiting for you at the airport - Rental Car Company_____
Type of car_____ Confirmation No._____
[ ] Take a cab from the airport to the hotel [ ] Take the hotel shuttle van from the airport to the hotel

---

HOTEL/MOTEL ACCOMMODATIONS
Hotel/Motel __THE MILWAUKEE GRAND__
Address __12345 WISCONSIN BLVD.__
__MILWAUKEE, WI 53210__
Phone No. __555-3000__
Fax No. __555-3001__

LOCATION PRODUCTION OFFICE
Address __THE MILWAUKEE GRAND__
← SAME
(THE BREWERS SUITE)
Phone No. DIR#: __555-3022__
Fax No. __555-3025__

IF YOU ARE HAVING YOUR MAIL FORWARDED TO YOU WHILE YOU ARE ON LOCATION, HAVE IT SENT:
[ ] to the home office (it will be forwarded to location) [ ] to the production office on location [✓] to the hotel

RETURN: You are tentatively scheduled to return on __6·25·XX__

© ELH

HOTEL ROOM LOG

SHOW: HERBY'S SUMMER VACATION

HOTEL: THE MILWAUKEE GRAND

ADDRESS: 12345 WISCONSIN BLVD.

MILWAUKEE, WI 53210

PHONE#: (414) 555-3000   FAX#: (414) 555-3001

DATE(S): From 5·15·XX To 6·30·XX

WEEK/ENDING: _____

CONTACT: CINDY

NAME	POSITION	CONF.#	PO/TA#	ROOM TYPE	ROOM #	ROOM RATE	DATE IN	DATE OUT	LATE CHECK-IN NOTES	TOTAL DAYS
SWIFTY DEALS	PRODUCER	30072	1055	SUITE	402	$120	5·15	6·23		39
SID CELLULOID	DIRECTOR	30073	1055	SUITE	412	$120	5·15	6·20		36
FRED FILMER	PROD. MGR.	30077	1059	KING	370	$70	5·15	6·25		41

© ELH

HOTEL ROOM LIST

SHOW __HERBY'S SUMMER VACATION__ PROD # __0100__

HOTEL __MILWAUKEE, GRAND__ LOCATION __MILWAUKEE, WIS.__

ADDRESS __12345 WISCONSIN BLVD.__

__MILWAUKEE, WISCONSIN__ LOCATION DATES __9-20-XX__

Through
__10-30-XX__

PHONE # __(414) 555-6000__ FAX # __(414) 555-6001__

NAME	POSITION	ROOM #	DIRECT #
Production Office	----------	103	555-6376
Accounting Office	----------	101	555-6374
Transportation Office	----------	105	555-6372
Editing Room	----------	107	555-6370
SWIFTY DEALS	PRODUCER	215	
SID CELLULOID	DIRECTOR	220	
A. DEES	1ST ASST. DIR.	330	
KATIE KANDU	SCRIPT SUPV'R.	307	
PAULA PROPS	PROPERTY MASTER	217	
MIKE BOOM	SOUND MIXER	302	

© ELH

MEAL ALLOWANCE

SHOW __HERBY'S SUMMER VACATION__   PROD # __0100__

LOCATION __MILWAUKEE, WISCONSIN__   WEEK OF __SEPT. 20 - 26, 19XX__

MEAL RATES
BREAKFAST $ 8
LUNCH $ 12
DINNER $ 20

NAME	MON B	L	D	TUE B	L	D	WED B	L	D	THUR B	L	D	FRI B	L	D	SAT B	L	D	SUN B	L	D	TOTAL	SIGNATURE
DATE	9-20			9-21			9-22			9-23			9-24			9-25			9-26				
A. DEES	-	-	20	8	-	20	8	-	20	8	-	20	8	-	20	8	-	20	8	12	20	200	_A. Dees_
K. KANDY	-	-	20	8	-	20	8	-	20	8	-	20	8	-	20	8	-	20	8	12	20	200	_K. Kandy_
M. BOOM	-	-	20	8	-	20	8	-	20	8	-	20	8	-	20	8	-	20	8	12	20	200	_M. Boom_
P. PROPS	-	-	20	8	-	20	8	-	20	8	-	20	8	-	20	8	-	20	8	12	20	200	_P. Props_
C. COORDINATES	8	12	20	8	12	20	8	12	20	8	12	20	8	12	20	8	12	20	8	12	20	280	_C. Coordinates_
A. ACCOUNTANT	8	12	20	8	12	20	8	12	20	8	12	20	8	12	20	8	12	20	8	12	20	280	_A. Accountant_

TOTAL: $ 1360

APPROVED _(signature)_

© ELH

DAILIES SHIPMENT LOG

SHOW: HERBY'S SUMMER VACATION

DATE: 5·25-XX

DATE	CHECK ONE — TO OFFICE	CHECK ONE — TO LOC.	ITEM(S) BEING SHIPPED	AIRLINE	FLIGHT NO.	LEAVES	ARRIVES	# OF PIECES	WAYBILL #	DRIVER-SERVICE DELIVERING TO AIRPORT	DRIVER-SERVICE PICKING UP FROM AIRPORT	✓
5/20	✓		Day #1 Film + Paperwork	Wisconsin Air	2006	7:20P	9:35P	3	WA 123-45678	Driver: Josh	Dailies Express	✓
5/21		✓	Day #1 Dailies	United	723	2:15P	8:30P	2	UA 732-71-6331	P.A. - Erik	Driver: Josh	✓
5/21	✓		Day #2 Film, Paperwork & Equip. Return	Wisconsin Air	2008	8:30P	10:45P	4	WA 123-45993	Driver: Skip	Dailies Express	✓
5/22		✓	Day #2 Dailies	United	723	2:15P	8:30P	2	UA 721-71-6355	Erik	Skip	✓
5/22	✓		Day #3 Film	United	774	8P	10:15P	3	UA 363-75-7321	Josh	Dailies Express	

© ELH

CHAPTER EIGHTEEN

Foreign Locations

Our business continues to become increasingly international as more U.S.-based films are being shot in other countries and filmmakers from other countries are coming to the U.S. to work here. The controversy also continues to grow over the issue of "runaway" production (a significantly growing number of U.S. films being shot in other countries). But no matter where you stand on the subject, many films (or portions of films) are being shot in more than one country, and you should have a basic working knowledge of the following guidelines.

U.S. COMPANIES SHOOTING IN FOREIGN COUNTRIES

If you think preparing and shooting a picture in your own city is a formidable task, and that taking a film on distant location provides you with an even bigger challenge—just wait until you take your picture out of the country! While you will likely experience the wonder and excitement of being on foreign soil, chances are, your patience may be put to new tests, you may at times feel totally overwhelmed and the word *challenge* may take on a whole new meaning to you. Passports; immunizations; immigration and work visas; crossing borders; customs, carnets, bonds, registrations, shipping and mountains of documents; possible language and culture barriers; exchange rates and alternative currencies; unfamiliar regulations and laws—and that's just for starters. There is so much to know about working on foreign locations—getting there, setting up and filming—the topic could fill an entire book in itself. Being limited to a single chapter, however, I'll stick to the highlights and urge you

not to stop here. Talk to the people you need to, become thoroughly familiar with the process and start preparing as early as possible.

Before You Cross the Border

Consider the following before you take your production across the border:

- Start by contacting the film commission, tourism board and/or embassy associated with the location you are considering and learn as much as you can about filming in that country. Collect photos, brochures, resource guides, anything you can.
- Talk to other people who have shot there, and get recommendations on production managers or coordinators with prior experience at that location, or at least someone who speaks the language (if relevant).
- Scout the foreign location(s) you are considering.
- Contact Immigration for their policies, requirements and restrictions pertaining to the number of work visas your production is eligible for (which will determine how many cast and crew members you would be allowed to bring with you). Remember, in an effort to protect their nation's film industry and workforce, some countries are quite restrictive.
- Explore other guidelines such as tax incentives, labor rebates, etc.
- Get recommendations on and hire a local production or unit manager, one who speaks English and has worked with other U.S. companies shooting in his or her country.

- If you are going to be working at or through a local studio facility or production company, ask if they have an operations manual or resource guide they can send you.
- You and your attorney should decide whether it would be in your best interest to retain the services of a local attorney (who has previously represented U.S. film companies, if possible). If the answer is yes, make sure to get recommendations, and have your attorney interview those under consideration (over the phone) before making a final decision.
- Determine if you will be required to form a new corporation in that country or must be sponsored or represented by a local entity.
- Contact the CDC (Center for Disease Control) or check out their website (www.cdc.bov/travel) to ascertain whether any vaccines or immunizations are required for those traveling to that country. Arrange for your cast and crew to receive their shots prior to traveling.
- Through your travel agent, contact the airlines that fly to your destination. If you have enough people traveling at one time, many will negotiate reasonable group rates or chartered flights and will allow you to transport equipment, props, set dressing, wardrobe and materials (freight) on the same flight taken by cast and crew.
- Make sure anyone you are traveling abroad with has a current passport that will not expire before the completion of the project.
- With the help of your local production manager, work and negotiate with the local film unions. Establish the availability of a qualified local work force (technicians, craftspeople, office staff, actors, stunt performers and extras) and determine whether you will be responsible for any displacement fees. (Displacement fees are payments made for each employee you bring with you, who, in essence, displaces one of their workers. A displacement fee is sometimes based on a percentage of an individual's wage up to a maximum amount, or it can be a flat negotiated rate.) In certain instances, you may not have to pay displacement fees, but you may be required to hire one local person for everyone you bring. In many countries, without the approval of their local film unions, Immigration will not process your requests for work visas.
- Begin the process of procuring work visas as soon as possible.
- Get recommendations on and retain a good freight forwarder and/or customs broker that specializes in the entertainment industry. This is important, so talk to several brokers and get more than one recommendation before making a decision. You will need one on both sides of the border; and hopefully, the two of them will already have a good working relationship with each other.
- As much confidence as you may have in your customs brokers, do your own homework. Determine your port of entry, find out who the administrators are, what their specific policies are and how they operate (within the same country, different ports are often subject to different regulations). Find out what materials are restricted and will require special permits, and how long it will take to get the permits. Find out if the country accepts carnets, and if there are any materials or items the country will not import. (Carnet is pronounced "car-nay," and it is a customs document that lists specific pieces of equipment to be taken into and back out of other countries.) Find out everything you can regarding the process. Meet with the Customs border officials (of both countries) if at all possible, introduce yourself and inform them of your upcoming project. If you can't do this in person, sometimes a formal letter will have to do. (Also see "Customs & Shipping" later in this chapter.)
- Make sure your insurance representative is informed of all your planned activities out of the country, so the proper coverage can be secured. Adding *Foreign Coverage* to your U.S. policy will provide liability coverage, protecting you in the U.S. against lawsuits that may arise out of your activities in a foreign country. It will also provide workers' compensation coverage for any third-country nationals on your payroll. (An example of a third-country national would be a Brit going to Mexico to work on an American film.) Employees from the U.S. are covered for workers' compensation by your producing entity or respective payroll company, but a policy from your host-country will cover local employees working for you while you are there.
- Foreign countries do not honor U.S. insurance policies, so have your local production manager secure all necessary coverage required for that country through a local insurance carrier, or make the arrangements through your insurance broker who may have a reciprocal relationship with a broker in that country.

- Investigate local emergency medical facilities and procedures (including those pertaining to the landing of medivac helicopters), and secure the services of an ambulance service, local paramedic and/or a doctor to remain with your shooting unit. Also, locate a highly-recommended doctor and dentist in the area who speak English.
- Determine the currency exchange rate and open local bank accounts. On some shows, (if local businesses accept U.S. currency) two accounts are opened, one in dollars and the other in the national currency. To open an account, you will probably be asked to provide documentation that may include a copy of your incorporation papers, copies of passports belonging to those who will be signing on the account and a letter of introduction from a film union, tourism ministry or local production company.
- Determine union, employment and payroll guidelines governing local labor. (Can you hire non-union employees?)
- Secure the services of local casting and extras casting agencies if needed.
- Investigate the availability of services, supplies and materials that can be purchased locally.
- Meet with local authorities, find out what type of permits are required. If needed, procure a special seal (stamp) sanctioning your presence by the authorities that can be placed in each company-driven vehicle. Also have windshield placards made up identifying your company and show.
- Prepare individual photo I.D. cards for cast and crew. On the back of the I.D. card, indicate emergency medical information (who to call and what to do should a medical emergency occur during nonwork hours). Also include that person's nationality and passport number (should they lose consciousness and have to be transported to the nearest medical facility). Ask cast and crew members traveling to location to bring (at least) two extra I.D. photos with them for this or similar purposes.
- Determine if you will need converters. Does this country use PAL or NTSC? Is their power 120 or 210?
- Determine the most effective way for you to receive mail while on location. Pouch it with the dailies? FedEx®? Air freight? For items other than mail, be aware that at this time, DHL® and Emery® accept carnet shipments. UPS and FedEx® generally do not. (Note: counter-to-counter airline service is only available on domestic flights.)

Supplying Information to Cast and Crew

In addition to the standard welcome package described in Chapter 17, "Distant Location," you will need to provide cast and crew traveling to a foreign location with the following additional information. (Remember, the more thorough the information, the easier your life will be.)

- The basics: the time difference, how to direct-dial to the production office and/or hotel, predicted weather conditions, whether they need to bring converters, etc.
- Guidelines on shipping personal belongings
- How per diem will be paid, what the exchange rate is and where to go to exchange currencies
- Common phrases in the local language
- Relevant cultural guidelines
- A description of municipal, state and federal police authorities; basic local laws; instructions as to what to do if stopped by a police officer and regulations relating to driving, D.U.I. and drug and weapons violations (Did you know that Manila executes drug smugglers?)
- Procedures for packing, labeling and documenting their equipment, materials and supplies being transported to location
- Guidelines for crossing the border and going through Customs
- Housing information (condo and apartment complexes, rental agents, etc.)
- A list of good, reliable and recommended restaurants
- Contacts for local cell phones or pagers, rental car agencies, an auto insurance agency that can provide coverage for those who drive their personal vehicles across the border (if applicable), etc.
- A detailed map (or maps) that illustrate the border, airport, hotel, location site(s) and studio and the closest emergency medical facilities
- Detailed information on emergency medical procedures, including contact names and numbers for a doctor, dentist, hospital or ambulance
- Local holidays (if applicable)
- Weight and measure conversions (if applicable)

Instructions for Crossing into a Foreign Country

General Rule

If you are not asked, do not volunteer any information. If asked, be honest. As you enter a foreign country, you will encounter a Customs inspection area. A Customs officer will ask to see your passport and will most likely inquire as to why you are entering the country. Your luggage or car may be inspected. Know what items you are prohibited from bringing into the country before you leave home. If asked if you have anything to declare, you say "no," and a search produces undeclared commercial goods (or if you are attempting to transport items you are not allowed to bring into the country), the penalty could range from having to pay duty, to having your goods confiscated, to having your car confiscated, to having to go to jail without passing "GO." It is imperative that you declare all commercial goods before you are stopped and your belongings inspected. (See "Personal versus Commercial Goods" below.)

Crossing with Children

As a parent traveling without your child or children's other parent, you are not allowed to bring your minor children into a foreign country without written (notarized) consent from the other parent.

Crossing with Pets

Some countries allow you to bring your dog or cat with you as long as you have a veterinary certificate showing proof that your pet has had all of his or her required shots. Some countries will require a quarantine process.

Personal versus Commercial Goods

Personal goods would include your clothing, toiletries and anything you might carry with you as a tourist entering another country (such as one still camera, one small CD player, etc.). Commercial goods include equipment or quantities of materials, supplies, wardrobe, etc. One wet suit would be personal; five wet suits would be commercial. NEVER mix personal items with commercial goods or vice-versa, either on the way to or coming back from another country. Commercial goods are handled through a broker or freight forwarder, are documented and crossed through a separate gate. Personal goods are packed in luggage and remain with the individual. Shipments can be held up or confiscated, fines levied and individuals detained for mixing personal and commercial goods.

Crossing with Personal Tools and Equipment

Most countries will not permit you to carry your personal tools, equipment or desktop computers ("tools of trade") with you unless they are preregistered or under a carnet (depending on the country) and you can provide the proper documentation.

Drugs

This is worth mentioning again—even small amounts of marijuana found in luggage or tucked away with the equipment can jeopardize or instigate the shutdown of the entire production.

Crossing with Documents

You are allowed to cross documents (such as mail, files or daily production office pouches), but put them in boxes that are easy to inspect. Label the boxes "Documents Only/No Commercial Value." Videocassettes or small supplies placed in envelopes do not constitute documents and should not be included with boxes of mail or files. If commercial items are discovered within the mail, the box(es) could be held up or confiscated.

Customs and Shipping

Whether you are having equipment, props, set dressing, wardrobe and materials driven over the border in trucks, or you are having everything packed up and shipped in cargo containers via aircraft or ship, the customs and shipping part of your operation is the most time-consuming, complex and crucial part of shooting in another country. It is not unusual for shipments to be held up at ports of entry for weeks at a time (or longer), or for shipments or vehicles to be fined or even seized because someone didn't do their homework, someone didn't receive or follow instructions, one document was not in order or you didn't have the right person handling your shipment. These circumstances, as you can well imagine, can create incredibly costly delays for your production.

Dealing with the regulations and the preparation involved in transporting equipment and materials into another country will involve some amount of input and cooperation from each department on your show, but it is also a full-time job in itself for at least one individual. Some productions will establish an entire shipping department (headed by a shipping coordinator) to interface with brokers, freight forwarders and border personnel; request special permits; disseminate pertinent information to crew members; inform department heads of what is required from their department; coordinate shipments with vendors; schedule deliveries based on border parameters; maintain accurate shipping files and logs; handle or supervise the packing, labeling and paperwork involved; and deal with last-minute emergency needs. Assign at least one person on your staff to deal exclusively with these matters, but don't be surprised if your show requires its own shipping department. The handling of shipping and customs is almost always more time-consuming than one expects and significantly more than what an already busy production coordinator can squeeze into his or her realm of responsibilities.

As important as it is to have a shipping coordinator, it is equally important for someone on the other end to be responsible for receiving your incoming shipments. On smaller shows, one person may be able to handle both shipping and receiving. Mid-size and larger shows will generally require a separate person to oversee receiving. This individual would need to be equally familiar with the shipping and customs process and would:

- monitor the arrival of shipments, alerting the shipping coordinator of any potential hold-ups or problems;
- cross-reference incoming shipments with daily shipping logs to make sure everything that was expected has arrived, and if not, find out why;
- make sure all shipments are delivered to the appropriate departments;
- collect and file all incoming shipping documents; and
- help to coordinate returns.

General Customs and Shipping Guidelines

I can't stress enough the importance of keeping copies of all customs and shipping documents, and accurate, organized records of all incoming and outgoing shipments. You may not only have to refer to this information on a moment's notice, but it will also be essential to the return process. Remember—everything going in on a temporary basis must be accounted for on the way out.

Crew members should not be allowed to make their own shipping arrangements and should be instructed not to carry undeclared equipment or supplies in their cars or luggage. The transportation of goods should be exclusively handled through the shipping department, so all corresponding documentation can be logged and kept on file. Problems arise when undocumented equipment is being returned and there are no records of it ever having entered the country to begin with. Just as one person or department should be designated to supervise and track all shipments crossing the border, each department should designate one individual to interface with the shipping office with regard to all the necessary paperwork, information, delivery schedules, etc., for that particular department. It is also extremely important that each department keep a complete file of their own shipping documents, which they will also need for the return process.

Give yourself as much lead time as possible for all your customs and shipping requirements. As soon as anything is ordered (or even anticipated), contact vendors, shippers and your broker to ascertain the most efficient way to enter the materials, making sure the proper documentation is prepared and special permits are applied for. The more advanced notice you give those coordinating the shipment, the better prepared everyone will be and the more room you will have to accommodate last-minute changes and additions.

When in a hurry, there is a tendency to want to "smuggle" in items without declaring them or obtaining necessary permits. When fighting to meet crucial deadlines, it's natural to want to take shortcuts around customs regulations. Avoid the impulse, because the risks are too great. Your broker or freight forwarder can usually help you work out time-sensitive problems and are often able to secure permission from Customs officials to make special crossings.

Dangerous Goods

Dangerous (or hazardous) goods encompass anything potentially explosive, flammable, toxic or corrosive. It's not just pyrotechnics that qualify as dangerous, but also many hair and makeup supplies, the canned air the camera department uses, batteries, WD-40®, etc. Check with your broker for a complete list of what is considered dangerous. Then, if you will be shipping anything on the list to location, ask your vendors to supply you with MSDS (Material Safety Data) sheets for each product. Shipments of dangerous goods should be manifested separately, with the MSDS sheets attached. The shipment must then be packed and labeled by someone who is specifically licensed to pack dangerous goods. Many brokers and freight forwarders have their own in-house packing departments. You can also find these services listed in the phone book under *crating and packing*. Not only do hazardous materials have to be packed and handled differently, but beyond that, certain types of dangerous materials can be flown on passenger planes and others can only be transported on cargo planes. Your broker can let you know what types of goods can be flown on what type of aircraft. If you try to ship something that has not been legally packed and labeled, or you try to ship something on a passenger plane that is only allowed on a cargo plane, you will jeopardize your entire shipment, which could be held up indefinitely.

Weapons

Most countries have extremely strict regulations pertaining to the importation of weapons. It doesn't matter if they are prop weapons or made of rubber. In many instances, special permits that can take months to obtain are required from both the country exporting and the country importing the weapons. Some countries also require that weapons of any kind be escorted by members of their military. If you wish to transport weapons into another country, check all regulations carefully and plan ahead.

Temporary versus Definite

All shipments of equipment, wardrobe, props, etc. transported to another country and returned to the U.S. (or elsewhere) at the completion of principal photography are considered Temporary Exports. Each shipment is subject to a customs fee going into and out of the other country, but "duties" are not required on temporary exports. Most countries will give you a set length of time in which to return these items (ranging from three months to a year), with the option to renew for another specified amount of time after that. Temporary exports not returned are subject to substantial fines.

Definite exports are those items not expected to return, such as expendable supplies. Some countries will not allow you to export materials on a definite basis, and under these circumstances, you may have to make arrangements with a third-party (local vendor) who will act as the importer of record. Duties are paid on definite exports (ranging anywhere from 10 to 85 percent of the declared value of your goods, depending on the country). Your customs broker may ask for a deposit against duties they anticipate paying out for you.

If you export items on a definite basis that turn out to be defective, the incorrect size or unacceptable in any way, you may return them to the U.S. for purposes of exchange or repair. You will be required to write a letter explaining why you are making the return, and your broker or freight forwarder will help you with this.

Brokers and Freight Forwarders

When transporting equipment, props, set dressing, wardrobe and materials out of the country, retaining the services of a freight forwarder is optional; using a broker is not.

Freight forwarders will consolidate, prepare and arrange for your shipments to be exported to another country. Some have in-house brokers, packing and crating departments and their own bonded warehouses. Others have access to brokers and other services when needed. Certain countries (such as Mexico) will allow a freight forwarder to handle export documents out of the U.S., but they must always work with a broker on the other end to handle the importation of goods into the other country. Exporting to most countries, however, does require a bonded broker to file the proper documents with U.S. Customs. Just as freight forwarders will utilize the services of a broker when necessary, brokers will often utilize the services of a freight forwarder to assist with shipments that have been entrusted to them. Many freight forwarders operate out of offices and warehouses located near specific ports of export (points of departure) or ports of entry and are exceptionally familiar with the import and export regulations relating to specific countries. A broker, on the other hand, generally handles multiple countries.

Get several recommendations on brokers and freight forwarders who specialize in the country (or countries) where you will be filming, and meet with them all. It is vital that you retain the services of people who:

- you feel comfortable with,
- you believe to be honest,
- will be watching out for your best interest and not just their pocket books,

- have good relationships with border authorities,
- are easily accessible,
- you are willing to sign over power of attorney to, and
- you trust to represent you.

When shipping goods to another country, the *Exporter of Record* is the production company or the vendor. Some vendors are great about filling out customs documents, and others, not so great. But while the production is ultimately responsible, many brokers and freight forwarders will (for an additional fee) complete the necessary paperwork for you. If you are doing it yourself, ask your broker or freight forwarder how they want you to prepare the paperwork. If you've done it before, show them the format you use, and make sure it's okay with them. You will find a few forms at the end of this chapter that should be helpful.

Also, make sure to issue additional insured certificates of insurance to your customs broker and/or freight forwarder.

Methods of Importing Goods on a Temporary Basis

There is one set of documentation presented to U.S. Customs when transporting goods out of the U.S., another set upon entering a foreign country, another set when the goods leave that country and yet another when re-entering the U.S. All countries have procedures allowing for the temporary importation of goods to cross their borders; and not only are the procedures different in each country, but they are also frequently subject to change. Incoming goods are all categorized by an assigned "harmonized" code. Some codes cover a broad range of items, while others are quite specific. Many countries have harmonized codes (and related procedures) that are unique to the entertainment industry, but harmonized codes are also subject to change.

Temporary importations are generally valid for three to twelve months. (Your broker will have the latest guidelines for the country you wish to travel to.) Although many countries require carnets with bonds, others require any combination of pro-forma shipping invoices (also known as shipping manifests or commercial invoices), certificates of registration, temporary import bonds (TIBs) and/or cash deposits. The following describes some of these requirements in more detail

Carnets

Accepted in over fifty countries and territories, carnets may be used for unlimited exits from and entries into the U.S. and foreign countries and are valid for one year. They eliminate value-added taxes, duties and the posting of security normally required at the time of importation. They simplify customs procedures by allowing a temporary exporter to use a single document for all customs transactions and to make arrangements in advance at a predetermined cost. They facilitate reentry into the U.S. by eliminating the need to register goods with U.S. Customs at the time of departure. There are three basic components to the Carnet application process: preparation of the General List (inventory of goods being transported—listed by description, serial numbers and value); completion of the carnet application and provision of a security deposit (bond). All Carnet applicants must furnish the USCIB (U.S. Council for International Business) with a security bond, the amount of which varies according to the country (or countries) visited. The bond acts as collateral and will be drawn upon to reimburse the USCIB in the event it incurs a liability or loss in connection with the Carnet of its use. The amount of the bond is based on the total value of the goods listed on the Carnet. The minimum is 40 percent of the value, although 100 percent is required for goods being transported to Israel and the Republic of Korea (the production is expected to pay 1 percent of the security deposit, or a financial statement from the company applying may be sufficient to underwrite the bond). Security deposits are paid in the form of check or money orders, refundable claim deposit or surety bond. The normal processing time for a Carnet is five working days. Basic processing fees range from $120 to $250 and are determined by the value of the shipment. Expedited services range from an additional $35 to $150. You can download application materials from USCIB's website (www.atacarnet@uscib.org).

In addition to listing all goods being transported, a Carnet includes the approximate date of departure from the U.S.; all countries to be visited and the number of expected visits to each; number of times leaving and re-entering the U.S. and additional countries transiting (when merchandise is transported by land and must pass through or stop in a country that lies between the country of departure and the next country of entry).

Carnets do not cover expendable supplies or consumable goods such as food and agriculture.

Additional information on carnets, carnet applications and bond forms can be obtained from one of the following U.S. Council for International Business offices throughout the country.

ATA CARNET HEADQUARTERS AND SERVICE BUREAU

1212 Avenue of the Americas

New York, NY 10036

Tel: (212) 354-4480   Fax: (212) 944-0012

NEW ENGLAND

185 Devonshire Street, Suite 800

Boston, MA 02110

Tel: (800) 233-3620 or (617) 728-9199

Fax: (617) 728-9830

MID-ATLANTIC

61 Broadway, Suite 2700

New York, NY 10006

Tel: (888) 571-1675 or (212) 747-1800

Fax: (212) 747-1948

Executive Plaza I, Suite 105

11350 McCormick Road

Hunt Valley, MD 21031

Tel: (800) 422-9944 or (410) 771-6100

Fax: (410) 771-6104

SOUTHEAST

7205 N.W. 19th Street, Suite 104

Miami, FL 33126

Tel: (800) 468-5467 or (305) 592-6929

Fax: (305) 592-9537

MIDWEST

1501 East Woodfield Road, Suite 302N

Schaumburg, IL 60173

Tel: (800) 227-6387 or (847) 696-8211

Fax: (847) 969-8200

118 Barrington Commons Plaza, Suite 236

Barrington, IL 60010

Tel: (800) ATA-2900 or (847) 381-1558

SOUTHWEST

5112 Morningside Drive

Houston, TX 77005

Tel: (800) 227-6387 or (281) 847-5693

Fax: (281) 847-0700

NORTHERN CALIFORNIA

425 California Street, Suite 700

San Francisco, CA 94104

Tel: (800) 255-4994 or (415) 765-6636

Fax: (415) 391-2716

SOUTHERN CALIFORNIA

100 West Broadway, Suite 100

Long Beach, CA 90802

Tel: (800) 421-9324 or (562) 628-9306

Fax: (562) 590-8523

For more information, contact:

USCIB ATA Carnet Customer Service Department

(212) 354-4480 or atacarnet@uscib.org

Certificate of Registration

Some countries that do not accept carnets will allow you to register equipment, props, set dressing and wardrobe before transporting these goods out of the U.S. Registration is primarily used for goods that were not manufactured in the United States. If you have a manifest containing goods from various countries of origin, then everything can be registered. Stamped on the way out of the country, the original registration documentation is required for reentry into the United States.

You can download a blank Certificate of Registration form directly from the Internet by going to: www.customs.ustreas.gov/travel/forms.htm, and then click on *Downloadable Customs Forms*.

Pro-Forma Shipping Invoices

Also referred to as shipping manifests and commercial invoices, pro-formas are also accepted by countries that do not accept carnets, although some countries require the combination of certificates of registration and shipping manifests. This completed form would indicate a description of goods being sent, a declaration of temporary or definite export, country of origin (country the item was manufactured in), declared value for customs purposes, total weight of each item or box and weight of total shipment.

Descriptions of goods being shipped should:

- Include year, make, model and serial numbers (whenever applicable).
- Include the dimensions of an item (if applicable).
- Include the primary material content of the goods, which is especially important in the exportation of fabric and clothing.

- Note the presence of dangerous goods—anything that could become explosive, flammable, toxic or hazardous. These materials must be manifested and packed separately and accompanied by MSDS—Material Safety Data Sheets (see "Dangerous Goods" section above).
- Be easy to understand. Do not use part numbers or overly-technical descriptions without a brief explanation as to what the materials are and what they are used for. People who are not film technicians must translate and assign code numbers to each item, so make it "border friendly."
- Clearly indicate where each item is, so if you have various crates, boxes, shelves, etc., each location on the truck or cargo container would be numbered. You would, for example, indicate: Box #1, then list the contents of the box underneath that heading. If you have several boxes or crates each containing several items, list the contents of each on one page of the pro-forma. This will make the manifest easier to process, and the shipment easier to inspect at Customs. As you will note on the sample pro-forma shipping invoice form at the end of the chapter, there are spaces to indicate: Page___ of ___ and Box___ of ___.
- It would also speed up the process if you could manifest all U.S.-made goods on one pro-forma, and all foreign-made goods on another. Don't worry about it too much if your equipment packages contain items from various countries of origin, but if you can separate them, it would help.
- If you are manifesting a drawer full of tools, you can list "10 screwdrivers" without having to list the size and type of each one. You can indicate "10 assorted pieces of tubing" without having to record the length of each piece. You can combine descriptions on many small items contained in one drawer or box when describing *like items*. Certain *kits* or *packages* can also be manifested as such without having to describe each piece contained within the kit or package. Check with your broker for more specific guidelines on manifest descriptions.
- If your shipment fills more than one truck or cargo container, you must manifest the shipment by the truckload or container; and each pro-forma should indicate the truck or container number, so it is clear as to which items would be found in which container.
- Indicate the type of packaging. If something should get lost or separated from the rest of the shipment, it's important to know what kind of a case, box or crate it was packed in and what color the case, box or crate is. The more information you provide, the easier it is to keep all the pieces of your shipment together.
- For tracking purposes, each pro-forma should include the name of your production and the production entity. It must also have a *Shipping Manifest Number*. The shipping manifest number, along with a customs entry number, will be what identifies each shipment coming in and going out of a country; and these I.D. numbers will be kept in your files, in your brokers' files and in Customs' files and computers.
- You can devise your own system to use as a shipping manifest number, or use the one described below, which has proved to be quite successful. It's an eight-digit number, followed by a two- or three-letter department code. An example would be:

Shipping Manifest No: 01-09-27-01-PD

01	=	the year
09	=	the month
27	=	the day
01	=	first shipment for that day
PD	=	Production Department (department code)

Suggested department codes are as follows:

Accounting	AC
Aerial	AE
Animals	AN
Art Department	AR
Camera	CAM
Cast-Related	CR
Catering	CA
Communications	CM
Construction	CS
Craft Service	CRS
Editorial	ED
Electric	EL
Extras	EX
Grip	GR
Locations	LOC
Makeup/Hair	MH
Marine	MR
Medical	ME
Miscellaneous	MS
Paint	PT
Production	PD
Props	PR
Publicity	PB

Scaffolding	SF
Security	SC
Set Dressing	SD
Sound	SN
Special Effects	SE
Still Photography	SP
Stunts	ST
Teaching Supplies	TS
Transportation	TR
Video Playback	VP
Visual Effects	VFX
Wardrobe	WD

When completing a pro-forma shipping invoice, you are required to declare the value of each item in the shipment. There is an unwritten understanding that values are reduced for customs purposes. A good guideline would be to declare 40 percent of the actual value on all temporary exports and 30 percent on definite exports; although depending on the item, you may go lower in some instances. On definite exports, the lower your value, the less you will pay in duties. Use your best judgment, keep in mind that it is acceptable to reduce values more on "used" items, but be advised not to go too low on everyday items that Customs officers would be familiar with. Save your creativity for film-related items that people outside of our industry know little about. Remember, however, that if the value you place on something is too ridiculous, it could raise suspicions and delay your shipment.

If possible, each department should be responsible for and prepare their own pro-formas, the process of which is incredibly time-consuming. Consider hiring additional production assistants trained to do shipping invoices to assist your departments and vendors with this operation.

TIB, or Temporary Importation Bond

TIBs are also accepted by certain countries that do not accept carnets. This bond would be based on a percentage of the declared value of an incoming shipment. The bond insures that all appropriate fees will be paid upon returning goods back out of the country.

In-Bond

When merchandise is being sent from a country other than the United States, but must travel through the U.S. to reach its destination, it is sent "in bond," so no duties are paid until the merchandise reaches its final destination. These loads are sealed and transported by a bonded carrier and are generally consigned to a bonded warehouse. Bonded loads must be returned in the same manner.

Shipper Export Declaration

This documentation is necessary for shipments on their way out of the U.S. that are valued at more than $2,500 and/or are temporary exports. You can be hit with a substantial fine for not having a Shipper Export Declaration when necessary. Your broker or freight forwarder will have this form.

Again, each country has different regulations. Canada, for example, has what they call an Equivalency Requirement: If equivalent equipment is available in Canada, you may have difficulty bringing similar U.S. goods across the border. So allow yourself enough lead time to ascertain requirements and restrictions, apply for permits, fill out applications, gather serial numbers and the value of your equipment and post bonds or deposits. Customs and Immigration are government entities, and no matter how urgent our needs may be, they will work within their own time frame and will not make exceptions for anyone, even filmmakers.

Transporting Goods across The Border

This is how it generally works:

- Production submits their portion of the necessary paperwork to the freight forwarder or broker.
- The broker makes sure all required documents are in order and generated.
- A Shipper Export Declaration is issued and registration forms are completed if necessary.
- Arrangements are made for picking up and delivering your shipment(s) to the port of export, or in some cases, right to the border.
- The shipment arrives at the port of export or port of entry (border), and the freight forwarder or broker checks the shipment against the documentation, making sure everything is in order. It is the responsibility of your freight forwarder or broker to make sure your shipment will clear Customs, so if the paperwork doesn't match the load in any way, the shipping documents must be amended or the load possibly separated. Temporary and Definite exports must also be separated, as they are not allowed to cross in the same shipment.
- Duties for definite exports are paid.

- After the merchandise has been checked, duties paid and the load approved for clearance, the shipment is cleared through a U.S. Customs export facility.
- U.S. Customs will not generally inspect outgoing loads other than "in-bond" shipments and heavy machinery. U.S. Shipper Export Declarations and registration forms are presented and stamped at this time.
- Once cleared through U.S. Customs, the shipment is ready to be transported to and cleared through Customs of the other country (with the proper Customs Entry document accompanying the shipment).
- At importation, the shipment is checked against the documentation and the serial numbers are randomly inspected. (Some countries have secondary inspection areas as well.) Once Customs officials have cleared your shipment, the documents are stamped and the load released.

Fees

Those preparing to film out of the country for the first time are often unprepared for the true costs of shipping and customs. Make sure your broker lets you know up front what the anticipated costs will be (door-to-door), and confirm that the price includes any of the following fees that are applicable to your shipments:

- Customs fee (based on value of goods and country of origin)
- MPF—Merchandise Processing Fee at point of entry
- Freight forwarder and/or broker's entry fee
- Fee for freight forwarder or broker special services
- Rush fees
- Duties on definite exports
- Registration fees
- Airline fees
- Delivery or handling fee
- Airport terminal fee
- Inspection Fee

How to Pack and Label

Boxes: All boxes and crates should be labeled with the name of the show and the department it is going to. A contact name would also be extremely helpful. If there is more than one box or crate, three for example, label them, *Box 1 of 3*, *Box 2 of 3* and *Box 3 of 3*. Boxes occasionally get separated from trucks and larger shipments, or arrive at the border without enough information as to what they contain or who they are for, so the more completely they are labeled, the faster they will find their way to you. Advise your vendors (who may be shipping supplies directly to you on location) to label their boxes properly.

If you are packing items that have different countries of origin, it would be helpful to pack U.S.-made goods separately from goods manufactured in other countries.

Trucks: Make sure all drawers, shelves and boxes are labeled (i.e., Box #5, Drawer #1, Shelf #3, Rack #4, etc.), and that each area is both accessible to inspection and easy to locate. The contents of each box, drawer and shelf should be reflected on the shipping manifest.

Cargo Containers: They should be packed with boxes, cases or crates labeled as indicated above. Individual pieces of equipment or set dressing should be tagged and labeled the same way: *Set Dressing—Piece 1 of 3*, etc.

All items in the trucks or cargo containers need to be easily assessable to spot-checking by Customs officials. No crate should be secured so tightly that it cannot be opened and inspected. Trunks and cabinets with keys should be kept unlocked.

Any time you can take a picture of the inside of a packed truck or cargo container or draw a diagram indicating where every numbered box, item, shelf or bin is located—the faster your shipment will move through customs. Know your inventory and be familiar with how it is laid out.

When purchasing new equipment or supplies, make sure to remove all price tags. Having one value on a price tag and a different declared (possibly reduced) value on the accompanying documentation will create a customs headache and may hold up your shipment.

Do not mix temporary and definite exports, do not include personal items with commercial goods and pack dangerous (hazardous) goods separately.

Proving Information to Vendors

Once an order is placed for equipment or materials you will need on location, it is important for your vendors to have a contact to deal with in order to coordinate shipping and customs requirements and to make sure they are aware of all applicable regulations. They need this information, because:

- They will have to supply you with the information you need to prepare your shipping documentation (some vendors, such as Panavision®, will prepare shipping invoices for you).
- They need to know how to pack, label and load correctly, and that not doing so will delay delivery of their shipments.
- They need to know how long it will realistically take to get their equipment and supplies to location.
- If they are shipping or making deliveries to the border, they need to know who your border rep is, where he or she is located and the hours in which deliveries can be made— including the optimal time to arrive in order to cross goods that day.
- A vendor who is unaware of proper procedures may attempt to ship equipment or supplies directly to you on location without knowing the most direct or effective method, and shipments could be delayed.

To save on time and avoid having to explain the same set of instructions over and over again, send or fax your vendors a form letter explaining shipping and customs procedures and include a map (with address, phone number, fax number and contact names) to your border rep's warehouse.

Returns

Your customs broker will give you instructions as to how best to handle your returns. Shipping goods back from a foreign location can be equally as time-consuming as shipping them there to begin with; and this is where having kept complete, well-organized shipping and customs files will be a tremendous asset to the process.

It is significantly easier to return everything all at one time, packed in the same configuration it was sent in. Unfortunately, returns are often made on a piecemeal basis.

Each piece of equipment as it is listed on a carnet must be returned at the same time under that same documentation. Even if you have finished using one or two pieces of equipment sooner than the rest of the package, you cannot return them early. You can stagger returns, but each shipment must include the entire list of goods as documented on each carnet.

Certain types of registrations also require that entire shipments are returned in the exact configuration in which they entered a country. There are other countries that will allow you to return merchandise gradually. As you are ready to return individual pieces of equipment that came as part of larger shipments, you will be canceling just that portion of the Customs entry document on which it came into the country. If you are returning several pieces of equipment, set dressing, props, etc. that all came in at different times as part of different shipments, each item must be matched up to its original pro-forma shipping invoice and customs entry form. Since your brokers must go through the same procedures to cancel an individual item as they do to cancel an entire shipment, returning an item or two at a time could become more costly than waiting to return an entire shipment at once. Weigh the costs of canceling individual items with the value of the item(s) you are returning or the rental you are paying on those items.

Your broker will generate a new customs document for each returning shipment. Once this is issued, the shipment cannot be altered in any way. You cannot decide to add something at the last minute, take something out or switch one piece of equipment for another. If the paperwork does not match the shipment exactly (down to the correct serial numbers), the shipment could be held up at the border indefinitely. Never include personal items with returning commercial goods; that's another sure way to have your shipment held up.

Film and Dailies on a Foreign Location

Raw stock cannot be put on a carnet. It is generally considered a temporary export, gradually accounted for as it leaves the country in its exposed state. Some countries require a bond upon entering. Others assess a tax or duty on the film as it leaves the country based on a percentage of its declared value. Once dailies are sent back to location in the form of a viewing print or videocassette, they are again considered temporary exports and will be canceled out upon return.

Something that was mentioned in Chapter 17, "Distant Location," holds true for international locations as well, and that is this: when transporting exposed film back to the States for processing, make sure it is booked on a direct-through (nonstop) flight. Any time a flight makes multiple stops, there is always a chance that your film will be unloaded before it reaches its final destination. Discuss this with your freight forwarder or broker, because under certain circumstances (even though it's more expensive), it may be prudent to have your film hand-carried onto a flight to insure its arrival.

U.S. Sales Tax Exemptions

Goods purchased in the U.S. to be shipped out of the country may be exempt from sales tax under certain circumstances. You would not be entitled to a tax exemption if you take possession of the materials, pack them and ship them yourself. But if your broker or freight forwarder were to pick up the materials and bring the vendor a copy of the export documents *(bill of lading* or *master airway bill)*, the sales tax would be waived. Certain common carriers can also take possession of tax exempt U.S. goods when presenting a bill of lading that indicates the country to which the goods are being exported.

Check with your broker for more information regarding this regulation, and strongly consider having your broker or freight forwarder pick-up your raw stock orders directly from Kodak or Fuji. Not having to pay sales tax on your film will save you a bundle.

Final Notes

To wrap this section up, I would like to stress the following:

- Do not operate under the assumption that you can impress, intimidate or bribe your way into or out of another country. You are dealing with government agencies and must observe proper protocol while being respectful of agency officials. Gifts are not accepted, arrogant attitudes not appreciated and the entertainment industry is not afforded preferential treatment.
- When dealing with customs and immigrations issues, use common sense; and when in doubt—ASK.
- Every show is different, every country is different and the rules change all the time. DO YOUR HOMEWORK! Do not assume because you did a show in a certain country once before, that the procedures will be the same the next time.

THE UNITED STATES AS A FOREIGN LOCATION

While U.S. citizens are traveling abroad to make films, so are filmmakers from other countries coming to work here. The following summarizes the requirements for bringing cast and crew members from other countries into the United States.

The Immigration Act of 1990 introduced the newly created O and P visa classifications for the entry of artists, entertainers, athletes, performers and related support personnel. Prior to the 1990 act, these individuals would have entered under the H-1B classification of distinguished merit and ability. With the introduction of the O and P visas, the H-1B classification is now limited to individuals in specialty occupations. The H-2B classification, although more complicated to qualify for, remains an option for those who do not qualify in the O Non-Immigrant visa and P Non-Immigrant visa categories.

O VISAS

O-1 Visa: This visa is granted to those who possess extraordinary ability in the arts, sciences, education, business or athletics, or have a demonstrated record of extraordinary achievement in the motion picture and television industry.

O-2 Visa: Granted to those entering the United States temporarily and solely for the purpose of accompanying and assisting an O-1 alien of extraordinary ability. These individuals must be highly skilled, possess all appropriate qualifications and significant prior experience and perform support services that cannot be readily performed by U.S. workers. Documentation is not only required to establish the qualifications of the O-2 petitioner, but also the past working relationship with the O-1 alien.

O-3 Visa: Granted to accompanying family members of O-1 or O-2 aliens.

Before a petition may be approved for the O category, a consultation requirement must be met. In the field of motion pictures and television, consultation with both a labor union or guild and a management organization in the area of the alien's ability is required. The mandatory consultation requirement allows unions to have input on all O-1 and O-2 petitions requiring services in the motion picture and television industry, which affects the adjudication of these petitions. However, it is important to note that consultation with a management organization is also required, which may not be consistent with the union. Further, these consultations are advisory in nature only and are not binding on the ultimate decision of the Immigration Service.

The O-1 and O-2 visa petition may only be approved for the time required to complete a specific event or performance, and may not exceed three years. Extensions are granted one year at a time to continue or complete the same event or activity.

P VISAS

The standard of eligibility is less restrictive than that of the O visas, because the P visas encompass a smaller scope of services.

P-1 Visa: This classification pertains to athletes who perform at an internationally recognized level of performance and seek to enter the United States temporarily for the purpose of competing at a specific competition or tournament, or for a limited athletic season. It also pertains to those who are members of internationally recognized entertainment groups. (The Attorney General may waive the international recognition requirement under special circumstances for a group that is nationally recognized.)

A P-1 entertainment group must have been established for at least one year, and 75 percent of the performers and entertainers in the group must have been performing in the group for at least one year. This classification additionally covers aliens who function as support personnel to individual athletes, an athletic team or an entertainment group. Again, the P-1 visa is granted only for the period of time necessary to complete the performance or event.

P-2 Visa: This category is reserved for an alien who performs as an artist or entertainer, either individually or as part of a group, and is to perform under a Reciprocal Exchange Program that is between an organization(s) in the United States and an organization in one or more foreign states. The P-2 entertainer petition must be accompanied by evidence that the group has been established and performing regularly for a period of at least one year, and must contain a statement from the petitioner listing each member of the group and the exact dates during which that member has been employed on a regular basis by the group. Evidence must also be submitted to substantiate the international recognition of the group. These petitions must also include: (1) a copy of the formal reciprocal exchange agreement; (2) a statement from the sponsoring organization describing the reciprocal exchange as it relates to the specific petition for which P-2 classification is sought; (3) evidence that the appropriate labor organization in

the United States was involved in negotiation, or has concurred with the reciprocal exchange and (4) evidence that the aliens and U.S. artists or entertainers subject to the reciprocal exchange possess comparable skills and experience. Unlike the P-3 visa, it is important to note that the P-2 visa does not require a finding of cultural or ethnic uniqueness.

P-3 Visa: An alien who performs as an artist or entertainer, individually or as part of a group and seeks to enter the United States to perform, teach or coach as such an artist or entertainer, or with such a group, under a commercial or non-commercial program that is culturally unique, may qualify for this classification. A P-3 petition must be accompanied by substantiation from recognized experts attesting to the authenticity and excellence of the alien's or group's skills in performing or presenting the unique or traditional art form. Evidence must also be submitted indicating that most of the performances or presentations will be culturally unique events sponsored by educational, cultural or governmental agencies.

P-4 Visa: The family of a P-1, P-2 or P-3 alien who is accompanying or following to join such alien may enter on this visa.

As with the O non-immigrant category, a consultation requirement is also required with the P non-immigrant category. Written evidence of consultation with an appropriate labor organization regarding the nature of the work to be done and the alien's qualifications is mandatory. The permitted length of stay for all P classifications is generally the time necessary to complete the event or events for which non-immigrant status is sought, with a maximum period of one year. Extensions of stay may be granted for periods of one year to complete the event.

Performers' agents, who routinely negotiate employment for their clients, are allowed to file O and P classification petitions on their behalf. Such petitions must provide a complete itinerary of the event(s) as well as the contract(s) between the third-party employer(s) and the alien. The contract between the agent and the alien specifying the wage offered and the conditions of employment must also be submitted.

Once the Immigration Service approves a petition on Form I-797, the applicant must apply for a visa at a U.S. Consulate abroad by presenting the original Approval Notice and completing a visa application form. When the visa is issued, the applicant may enter the United States and work on the project authorized by the approved petition.

H-2B VISAS

Entertainment personnel who do not qualify as aliens of extraordinary or exceptional ability to be classified in the O and P categories, or as support personnel of an O-1 or P alien, will have to consider using the H-2B classification. For a lesser-known entertainer or technician, or support personnel involved with a project begun abroad that needs to be completed in the United States, when the principal entertainer is a U.S. citizen, this category is the best option available.

Requirements for the H-2B classification are as follows: (1) the position to be filled by the alien is one for which the employer has a temporary need and (2) certification is sought from the U.S. Department of Labor that unemployed persons capable of performing the labor are not available in the United States and the employment of the alien will not adversely affect the wages and working conditions of workers similarly employed in the United States.

The Department of Labor (DOL) has published detailed guidelines for the criteria and procedures to be followed for all H-2 requests in the entertainment industry. Applications for temporary Labor Certification should be filed at least forty-five days prior to the proposed commencement of services to ensure completion and processing by the DOL. In addition to submitting Form ETA-750, Part A, the application must include an itinerary of locations where the alien will work, together with the duration of work in each location, as well as documentation of any recruitment efforts taken by the employer. Proof is required to establish that there are not sufficient U.S. workers able, willing, qualified and available for the employment. Two principal sources of recruitment are always required: an advertisement placed in a national (trade) publication six weeks prior to filing the paperwork, advertising for this particular position or role and a request to the appropriate labor union regarding membership availability.

With regard to talent, casting session information and a letter from the casting director stating the particulars of the casting search in the United States and the reasons for the use of an actor from another country should be included. It must be stressed in the letter that this particular actor is the only one who can properly portray the part as it is written.

The Department of Labor grants labor certifications for periods not exceeding twelve months. If the intended duration of employment is more than one year, a new application must be submitted for any additional year or part thereof; but temporary employment must not exceed three years.

All applications, itineraries, labor certifications, letters and documentation are to be submitted to the Employment Development Department—Alien Certification Office. After reviewing these materials, they will then forward everything to the U.S. Department of Labor. The Department of Labor will then certify or turn down all requests for U.S. work permits.

With regard to talent, a copy of all applications and documentation should also be sent to the Screen Actors Guild, where they are reviewed, and a recommendation of acceptance or denial is then issued and forwarded to the Immigration and Naturalization Service (INS). Check with your local SAG office to find out who your contact is pertaining to the employment of aliens. After certification approval has been obtained from the Department of Labor, the temporary labor certification together with completed I-129H forms are sent to the Regional Service Center of the Immigration and Naturalization Service having jurisdiction over the intended place of employment. This form is three pages long and requires information on the petitioner, the beneficiary and the signature of the petitioner.

As the DOL determination is only advisory, INS can still approve H-2B classification even in the absence of the certification. Petitions submitted to the INS should include a statement from the employer explaining the reasons it is not feasible to hire U.S. workers to fill the position offered and the factors that make the position offered temporary in nature.

Once the I-129H form is processed and labor certification is cleared, applicants can go to the American Consulate in their country and apply for their visa. They cannot apply until it has been approved and cleared in this country. The Immigration Service will notify the petitioning employer, as well as the appropriate consulate, that the said individual has been approved for a visa. With respect to talent, when the Immigration Service has finalized everything, the actors must be cleared with SAG, either checked through Station 12 or Taft-Hartleyed before they can work.

For further information, first contact your attorney and then the Employment Development Department—Alien Certification Office, the United States Department of Labor and the Immigration and Naturalization Service office closest to your base of operations.

NOTE: The first part of this chapter—"U.S. Companies Shooting in Foreign Countries," was completed with the assistance of Milton Reyes of IBC Pacific, a Los Angeles-based global transportation specialist.

The information on visas was provided by Peter Loewy, Esq., Managing Partner of the law firm, Fragomen, Del Rey, Bernsen and Loewy, a national law firm practicing solely in the area of immigration and nationality law. Mr. Loewy is based in the firm's Santa Clara, California office.

FORMS IN THIS CHAPTER

- Pro-Forma Shipping Invoice
- Daily Shopping Log
- Request For Return

PRO-FORMA SHIPPING INVOICE

COMPANY: XYZ PRODUCTIONS

PRODUCTION: HERBY'S SUMMER VACATION

DEPARTMENT: COMMUNICATIONS

MANIFEST DOCUMENT #: OX-10-08-01-CM

DATE: 10-8-XX

[X] TEMPORARY EXPORT [ ] DEFINITE EXPORT (Expendables)

TOTAL NO. OF PIECES: 10   **P.O. #** 2009   **PG.** OF

PORT OF EXPORT: OTAY MESA, CALIF.   **BOX** OF

PORT OF ENTRY: TIJUANA, B.C., MEXICO

SHIPPING AGENT: ABC BROKERS

SHIPPER'S PHONE NO: (619) 555-364   **FAX #:** 555-3665

CONTACT: YOLANDA   **CELL/PGR #:** 555-1114

SHIPPER

Company: XYZ PRODUCTIONS

Address: 1234 FLICK DR.

HOLLYWOOD, CA 90038

Phone No: (323) 555-3331

Fax No: (323) 555-3332

Contact: WAYNE

CONSIGNEE

Company: STUDIOS de la PLAYA, S.A. de C.V.

Address: KM. 32.8 CARRETERA LIBRE

POPOTLA, B.C., MEXICO

Phone No: 011-5266-XX-XX-XX

Fax No: 011-5266-XX-XX-XX

Contact: LUISA

QTY	TYPE OF PACKAGING	DESCRIPTION	SERIAL NO.	COUNTRY OF ORIGIN	WEIGHT	UNIT PRICE	TOTAL VALUE
5	(SILVER CASE)	MOTOROLA HT1000 WALKIE-TALKIES	H-167	MAYLASIA	1½ LB.	$200-	$1,000-
			H-316		1½		
			H-335		1½		
			H-357		1½		
			H-428		1½		
5	(SILVER CASE)	RAPID SINGLE WALKIE-TALKIE CHARGERS	CH-7	USA	1 LB.	$20-	$100-
			CH-9		1		
			CH-12		1		
			CH-25		1		
			CH-40		1		

TOTAL WEIGHT: 12 ½ LBS.   **TOTAL VALUE:** $1,100-

All items listed above are to be used in connection with the motion picture industry

VENDOR: GARY'S WALKIE-TALKIES   **Phone:** (818) 555-4003

Contact: GARY   **Fax:** (818) 555-4004

Tax ID#: 95-1234567   **P.O. or Inv. #:** P.O. # 2005

PRO-FORMA COMPLETED BY _____

The values indicated above are for customs purposes only.

© ELH

Foreign Locations   **301**

DAILY SHIPPING LOG

SHOW: HERBY's SUMMER VACATION

DATE / DEPARTMENT / P.O.# / T=Temporary or D=Definite	DESCRIPTION	VENDOR INFO.	TRANSPORTATION	DECLARED VALUE / NO. OF PIECES / DATE DELIVERED / CUSTOMS ENTRY NO.
DATE: 6·30·XX DEPARTMENT: CONST. P.O.#: 3772 T=Temporary -or- D=Definite: D	CONSTRUCTION EXPENDABLES - DRILL BITS, NAILS, STAPLES, ETC.	RON'S TOOLS & SUPPLIES ATTN: RON 555-7757	TO PORT OF EXPORT (OR BORDER): VENDOR FROM PORT OF EXPORT TO PORT OF ENTRY: BROKER FROM PORT OF ENTRY TO LOCATION: STUDIO DRIVER CARNET OR SHIPPING MANIFEST NO.: 0X-06-20-01-CS	DECLARED VALUE: $735 NO. OF PIECES: 5 BOXES DATE DELIVERED: 6·21 CUSTOMS ENTRY NO.: 32176SX-7
DATE: 6·22·XX DEPARTMENT: GRIP P.O.#: 4331 T=Temporary -or- D=Definite: T	MISC. GRIP PKG.	STUDIO RENTAL EQUIP., INC. ATTN: BARRY 555-4334	TO PORT OF EXPORT (OR BORDER): TRANSPO. FROM PORT OF EXPORT TO PORT OF ENTRY: " FROM PORT OF ENTRY TO LOCATION: " CARNET OR SHIPPING MANIFEST NO.: 0X-06-22-01-GR	DECLARED VALUE: $8,000 NO. OF PIECES: 10 CASES DATE DELIVERED: 6·23 CUSTOMS ENTRY NO.: 32177SX-9
DATE: 6·22 DEPARTMENT: SPEC EFX P.O.#: 4335 T=Temporary -or- D=Definite: T	60' CONDOR	ABC HIGH-LIFT ATTN: ALAN 555-6011	TO PORT OF EXPORT (OR BORDER): USA EXPRESS FROM PORT OF EXPORT TO PORT OF ENTRY: BROKER FROM PORT OF ENTRY TO LOCATION: " CARNET OR SHIPPING MANIFEST NO.: 0X-06-22-02-SE	DECLARED VALUE: $7500 NO. OF PIECES: 1 DATE DELIVERED: 6·23 CUSTOMS ENTRY NO.: 32179X-4
DATE: DEPARTMENT: P.O.#: T=Temporary -or- D=Definite:			TO PORT OF EXPORT (OR BORDER): FROM PORT OF EXPORT TO PORT OF ENTRY: FROM PORT OF ENTRY TO LOCATION: CARNET OR SHIPPING MANIFEST NO.:	DECLARED VALUE: NO. OF PIECES: DATE DELIVERED: CUSTOMS ENTRY NO.:
DATE: DEPARTMENT: P.O.#: T=Temporary -or- D=Definite:			TO PORT OF EXPORT (OR BORDER): FROM PORT OF EXPORT TO PORT OF ENTRY: FROM PORT OF ENTRY TO LOCATION: CARNET OR SHIPPING MANIFEST NO.:	DECLARED VALUE: NO. OF PIECES: DATE DELIVERED: CUSTOMS ENTRY NO.:

© ELH

REQUEST FOR RETURN

RETURN REFERENCE NO: 11050X-R

COMPANY: XYZ PRODUCTIONS

PRODUCTION: Herby's Summer Vacation

ITEM(S) TO BE RETURNED	SERIAL/UNIT NOS.	CARNET OR SHIPPING MANIFEST NUMBER	CUSTOMS ENTRY NUMBER	DECLARED CUSTOMS VALUE	NO. OF PIECES	WEIGHT
(3) MOTOROLA HT100 WALKIE-TALKIES	H-167 H-335 H-357	OX-10-08-01-CM	1234SXX	$600-	3	4½ LBS.
(3) WALKIE-TALKIE CHARGERS	CH-7 CH-12 CH-25	SAME AS ABOVE	SAME AS ABOVE	$60-	3	3 LBS.
TOTALS:				VALUE $660-	PIECES 6	WEIGHT 7½ LBS.

PICK-UP ITEM(S)/LOAD FROM: PRODUCTION OFFICE

DATE OF REQUEST: 11-03-XX

RETURN CUSTOMS DOCUMENTATION NO:

[ ] COMPLETE RETURN
[X] PARTIAL RETURN
[ ] FINAL - PARTIAL RETURN
[ ] RETURN FOR REPAIR

PROJECTED DATE TO LEAVE: 11-05-XX

[X] CAN LEAVE WHEN READY
[ ] HOLD FOR APPROVAL
[ ] MUST LEAVE ON: _____

ESTIMATED DATE OF ARRIVAL: 11-05-XX

WAYBILL NO.

SPECIAL INSTRUCTIONS:

TRANSPORTATION:

LOCATION TO PORT OF EXPORT: TRANSPORTATION

PORT OF EXPORT TO PORT OF ENTRY: ABC BROKERS

PORT OF ENTRY TO DESTINATION: SHIPPERS EXPRESS

FINAL DESTINATION:

SHIPPING AGENT: SHIPPERS EXPRESS

PHONE NO: (310) 555-1100

FAX NO: (310) 555-1101

CELL/PGR#: (310) 555-2014

CONTACT: MILTON

VENDOR: GARY'S

ADDRESS: 123-4TH ST. STUDIO VILLAGE CA

PHONE NO: (818) 555-7322

CONTACT: GARY

HRS. OPEN: 8A-6P

SE 377233TMX

TRANSPO, TRUCK LEAVING STUDIO

TRUCK LICENSE NO: CDE 1346

DRIVER: HUGO

SPOT-CHECKED BY: _(signature)_

APPROVED BY: _(signature)_

© ELH

CHAPTER NINETEEN

Effects

Although the previous edition of this book focused solely on visual effects, this revision incorporates physical and mechanical effects as well. The technologies and processes utilized to create each are often interdependent, and those involved must routinely collaborate and rely on each other's expertise to achieve desired effects.

Visual effects are created when outside elements, such as animation, matte shots and computer-generated images (CGI) are integrated with original photography. The term *visual effect* also refers to the more familiar reverses, dupes, flops, freeze frames, etc. *Physical effects* refers to the fabrication and development of models (miniatures); prosthetics; mechanically-operated vehicles, puppets, robots and creatures and the creation of specialty props. *Special makeup effects*, used in the preparation of prosthetics, is included in this category as well. *Mechanical effects*, better known as *special effects*, encompasses the recreation of rain, wind and snow; explosions; crashes; bullet hits; etc.

For years, when one would refer to "effects," it could be assumed the reference related to special (or mechanical) effects. Few shows do not utilize the services of a special effects crew, even if it's just to create fog or rain; but the term now covers a myriad of connotations. As current production trends and competition for box office revenues create the desire for bigger, better and more innovative effects, this entire aspect of filmmaking is expanding and becoming increasingly complex.

VISUAL EFFECTS

Studios and production companies are now routinely employing visual effects units, headed by a visual effects supervisor, to oversee the entire process. The number of people needed to facilitate the effects on any one show will depend on the number of effects to be created, how complicated the work will be, how many effects houses will be utilized and, most importantly—what all film work boils down to—budgetary and scheduling considerations.

Advancements in computer technology continue to be a tremendous asset to the field of visual effects, and high-speed Internet connections make it possible for CGI artists to live and work from anywhere they desire. Stills and quick-time movies can be e-mailed to and from anywhere with enough resolution to make professionally-qualified decisions, and a fifteen-second CGI shot can be transmitted over the Internet (at full resolution) in an hour. Between now the time of this writing and the time this book is actually published, further technological advancements will have shortened that hour significantly.

Although the possibilities appear to be endless, don't make the mistake of thinking that digital is the way to go just because everyone else is doing it. Depending on your project and budget, it is not always practical, cost-effective or necessary. If traditional techniques can be employed to achieve your shot, go for it. An example of this might include utilizing a simple split screen instead of something that would require complex rotoscoping. Ask your special effects supervisor which effects can be done practically, and consider more traditional photographic elements whenever possible. Do not just assume that anything can be accomplished by means of CGI, because that's not always the case. Be realistic about which effects will truly enhance or advance your story, and understand what can be done and how much it will cost.

If your company does not have its own visual effects department, it's a good idea to bring an independent visual effects supervisor onto your film; or as some smaller-budgeted projects often do—make a deal with an effects house that will assign one of its own supervisors to your show. If your budget is tight and you think you can coordinate the visual effects work yourself, think again. Don't make the mistake of trying to save money by not having a qualified supervisor on-board; and if you have a complicated effects show, it would be extremely prudent to have your own supervisor work with the house supervisor(s). Depending on the effects, you will need at least one person, and possibly more, with a good working knowledge of visual effects (and related methodology) to coordinate and evaluate the work being created from multiple sources, schedule production work that must be done in conjunction with certain effects, monitor costs, make sure delivery dates are met and watch out, at all times, for the interest of the production. An effective supervisor will know where to locate the best quality for the least amount of money by making good deals with the houses that specialize in creating the exact type of effects you're looking for.

Smaller production companies shopping for one effects house to do their entire show will begin the process by asking those under consideration for samples of their work. Those who pass the first hurdle will be sent a script along with storyboards illustrating potential visual effects shots, from which a bid will be submitted. Once the bids are all in and assessed, those still in the running will be asked to come in for a meeting, where, along with discussions of methodology, the director will share his or her creative vision. The chosen house will designate a supervisor who will usually come in for a second meeting where all shots, costs and schedules are discussed and confirmed. This is also the time to identify difficult effects, so the supervisor can focus more attention on achieving the most challenging and intricate shots. By working with only one house, you can often make a flat deal for the entire show. While this will afford some amount of protection against overages for things such as added shots or effects that turn out to be more complicated than originally anticipated, the downside is that you also take the risks associated with remaining with one house and accept the results you get.

Whether it's an independent supervisor or a house supervisor, expect that he or she is knowledgeable in choosing the right techniques and will endeavor to produce photographic realism.

Not choosing the right people in this field may not only leave you with less-than-desired effects but can also adversely affect both your budget and schedule.

One of the most common misconception regarding visual effects is that it is strictly a facet of post production. It isn't! The visual effects process must begin at the very earliest stages of pre-production, and it generally continues right up through the end of post production. Avoid committing to any effects work before confirming that you have a sufficient budget in which to do them correctly and have sufficient time to complete them on schedule. Waiting too long to start the process will, at the very least, create added expenses and scheduling delays.

The steps one takes when contemplating visual effects are as follows:

- Breakdown your script and identify all shots you believe cannot be achieved by conventional production photography or mechanical effects.
- Have someone who specializes in conceptual design storyboard all effects shots with clearly defined drawings.
- List all visual effects shots. Discuss and assess the methods to be used to accomplish each.
- Send the breakdowns and storyboards out to four or five visual effects houses for bids. Select houses that specialize in the type of effects work you are trying to create. The bids should include estimated time frames needed to accomplish the work, as well as estimates on the cost of doing the work.

Once bids have come in, you may want to:
- Make script changes to eliminate or modify effects that are too costly or too time-consuming to create as currently written.
- Go back to studio executives or funding source to request a budget increase if your current effects budget is not sufficient.
- Extend your delivery date to accommodate the time necessary to create certain desired effects.

Once bids have been accepted, your visual effects supervisor will work with the various effects houses in creating an overall schedule. Upon budget and schedule approval, the work must start immediately. Some effects may take six months to a year to develop and perfect; and creating computer-generated effects is also a very lengthy process. Certain effects will take longer to create than anticipated, and concept or design changes are often made along the way. Starting the process as early as possible will enable you to better accommodate these delays and changes.

Your effects supervisor will work with the UPM and first assistant director to schedule portions of effects shots, such as background plates, that must be done during production. A special crew or unit may be required for the shoot. The effects supervisor will also let the UPM know in advance if any special equipment will be needed, such as a blue screen, green screen, a *motion control* camera system, etc. A motion control or MC system is a computer-controlled camera rig used to create complex and repeatable camera movements in visual effects shots. It is an essential tool in VFX (visual effects) photography when different elements of the same shot require identical camera motion, for example when live action is being combined with either miniatures (by scaling down the repeated move to the scale of the miniature), or with CGI elements (when motion data can be exported or imported into or from a 3-D computer graphics system).

All effects-related production needs—shooting, crew and equipment—must be worked into the budget and schedule during pre-production. If the proper time and budgetary requirements are not considered up front, it could become a much more costly and time-consuming process to squeeze them into the schedule at a later date or after the completion of principal photography. Also, not having the necessary production footage in a timely manner may likely hold up the work being done at the effects house.

Certain effects elements, such matte shots, can be added during post production; but remember, visual effects is not just a function of post production—it requires planning and work that must begin during the very earliest stages of pre-production. Not being able to anticipate and integrate the elements essential to achieving the effects you desire may prove to be disastrous to your budget, to your schedule and, perhaps, to your picture.

PHYSICAL EFFECTS

One does not generally hire a physical effects coordinator or department, but will retain the services of individuals or outside companies who specialize in the fabrication of prosthetics, models, puppets, mechanically-operated creatures, etc. Most of these elements are used in conjunction with visual and/or mechanical effects, and examples of this might include the construction of a 3-D model enhanced with digital imagery or a mechanically-operated vehicle rigged to blow up in the heat of an action sequence. Some special effects supervisors have the ability to construct models, props and anything mechanically driven, while others collaborate with those who specialize in these fields.

The use of models (such as model ships, aircraft, bridges, entire towns, etc.) can eliminate the need to build expensive sets and allows you the opportunity to shoot in far-away locations without leaving your own backyard. Well-constructed and well-lit three-dimensional models, photographed in-camera will produce shadows and depth that make the image come alive and appear real. Without getting into costly CGI expenses, a similar digital image with a single light source may appear flat and devoid of lifelike shadows.

Prosthetics are three-dimensional "appliances" affixed to a body to alter the body's image. This would include such things as: aging skin, scars, burns, mutilations, a sixth finger, a mermaid tail or a full creature or animal suit. It's a process that often combines prop-making, special makeup effects and puppeteering. More complicated prosthetics might require a mold of an actor's body (a "life cast"), which is sculpted to create a desired effect. The materials used to create prosthetic pieces will depend on their location on the body and how flexible they need to be. Foam latex is often used for facial appliances, because it's natural looking—although fragile and not reusable. Denser silicones and certain urethanes are also used. They're reusable, but not as naturally flexible. Facial appliances can involve anywhere from a single to dozens of individual prosthetic pieces, depending on the complexity of the desired look. Prosthetics are also sometimes rigged to include cable or radio-controlled facial movements and expressions. These processes can be both time-consuming and expensive.

As with visual effects, locate individuals who specialize in the physical effects you're seeking, see samples of their work and get bids. Those selected should be brought into your project during the early stages of pre-production, as sufficient time must be allowed for development, construction, testing and possible changes. Keep in mind that prosthetics work cannot begin until respective actors have been cast. Arrange meetings between all those involved if models, prosthetics, props, etc. are to be integrated with other effects or departments; and closely monitor the construction of these effects to insure that they are meeting your expectations and are remaining on budget and on schedule.

MECHANICAL EFFECTS

Mechanical effects are most commonly known as special effects, and those who work in this field are responsible for activities such as the:

- recreation of atmospheric conditions such as wind, rain, snow and fog (ranging from mild to extreme);
- handling of fire and steam;
- rigging for accidents, crashes, near-misses, etc.;
- rigging for all types of explosions;
- handling or supervising of hydraulic work;
- rigging of bullet hits ("squibs");
- rigging and handling of all flying work (whether it's a person, creature or vehicle doing the flying);
- rigging of tanks and pools for water work;
- handling and supervision of retractables (such as knives) and breakaways (objects made of rubber, balsa wood, glass, etc. that are manufactured to easily and safely break);
- handling, supervision and possibly the manufacture of synthetic (rubber) props—or "mold making"; and
- miscellaneous maintenance, repairs and rigging for other departments.

Special Effects supervisors and coordinators generally have their own workshops and mobile facilities (usually housed in at least one forty-foot trailer) and are the bearers of several federal, state and local licenses. The primary federal license issued here in the United States is from the BATF (Bureau of Alcohol, Tobacco and Firearms), and it governs the use of explosives and the handling of hazardous materials. Local pyrotechnic licenses are usually obtained through the City Fire Marshall. Certain licenses are required for each state in which you are working, so before shooting on a distant location, make sure your effects crew is certified to work there. Since the regulations associated with licenses issued in different states and municipalities all vary to some degree, and more than one may be required in any one location, the rule is that the strictest regulations take precedent. Other licenses and certifications held by effects personnel include those in welding, scuba, AC/DC electronics and mechanics.

There are special effects supervisors and coordinators who do it all—their own model-making, hydraulic work, molds, etc.—but not all are that versatile. Those who do not do it all, need to know who to bring onto their crew or which company to contract that specializes in exactly what they need. Bringing in the best people available will help to assure the quality, accuracy and safety of any given gag.

Safety is one of the most important factors to consider when incorporating effects into your show—both the safety record of your effects crew and the safe construction and implementation of gags. Pertinent safety bulletins should be attached to call sheets the day before major effects are scheduled, and safety meetings should be held on-set prior to their execution. When it comes to safety—corners should never be cut, schedules compromised, nor money spared to prevent accidents and injuries.

The effects coordinator works closely with both the stunt coordinator in the design and rigging of stunts and with the construction coordinator in the building of structures that are to be rigged for explosions, crashes and other effects. Also, as previously mentioned, he works in conjunction with the visual and physical effects people on the overall creation and implementation of effects. While the physical effects people might provide a model of a house, for example, it's the mechanical team that makes that model come alive with smoke coming out of the chimney or a stream running alongside the house. And while the visual effects crew supervises a shot against a green screen, it's the mechanical crew that rigs the mermaid—allowing her to leap out of the water and through the air in front of the green screen, which is ultimately to be replaced with a shot of the harbor.

Utilizing different methodologies, there are certain effects that can be accomplished either visually or mechanically. It is therefore prudent to have both visual and special effects supervisors provide bids and time tables for accomplishing each gag. It is also helpful to see examples of similar work they have done, so in addition to cost and time factors, you can compare quality and believability as well.

Bring your special effects coordinator on as early as possible during pre-production, and have at least one "effects" meeting (more if time permits), so all effects work—visual, physical and mechanical—can be discussed, coordinated and scheduled.

CHAPTER TWENTY

Wrap

Depending on what department you are in, wrapping up a show and neatly tying up all the loose ends will range anywhere from a day or two to three or four weeks and will depend on factors such as: your budget; the type of show you're doing; applicable union and guild regulations; sets to be struck; practical locations to be repaired and restored; paperwork to be turned in; rentals to be returned; assets to be inventoried and stored (or sold); props, set dressing and wardrobe to be pulled for reshoots or inserts; insurance claims to be prepared and submitted and offices to be closed up.

Production managers, coordinators and accountants will generally take longer to wrap than other crew members, with the accountant the last to leave before turning the files over to a post production accountant. Wrap time for production personnel is often shorter for those working for a studio or established production company than for those on smaller independent projects, as studios and larger companies generally have an in-house production staff that can assume final wrap details. The line producer and/or production manager, taking all variables into consideration, will prepare a staff and crew wrap schedule prior to the end of principal photography.

The disposition of remaining production-owned assets needs to be determined well in advance of the last day of shooting. And if there is a possibility that reshoots, added scenes or inserts will be done at a later date, production must compile a list of pertinent scenes from which items can be pulled, inventoried, boxed and stored separately. If any of these are rental items, arrangements should be made to take them off rental and to purchase them. Also to be established is whether remaining assets are to be stored or sold; and if they are to be stored, where they are to be taken. Should the wardrobe be stored or taken to a resale shop? Should entire sets be dismantled and stored, or just door jams, windows and paint, wallpaper and carpet samples? These are all things that need to be confirmed before wrap procedures can be passed on to your crew.

Approximately two weeks before the completion of principal photography, issue a memo asking each department to check their list of assets against the list that the accounting department keeps. Inform them of how you want their asset inventory prepared; who to submit inventory lists to; which scenes are slated for possible reshoots (thus, which items need to be pulled, purchased, etc.); where everything is to be stored and which items may be sold and for how much (50 percent of purchase price is fairly standard). Ask crew members to start assessing their L&D (loss and damages), and let them know if company assets no longer needed may be traded to vendors to offset L&D charges (reminding them to inform you, in advance, of any such arrangement). This is also a good time to inform crew members that you will be reviewing total wrap mandays with each department in the coming week.

In theory, those departments given a sufficient amount of wrap time should have less L&D due to the fact that they have the time to clean and/or repair certain items themselves, and can search for and retrieve items that have been misplaced. While this is often the case, much also depends on how any given department has been organized and has taken care of its rentals throughout the shoot. Those who are conscientious from the beginning can generally wrap quickly with little or no L&D.

Being able to confirm wrap dates is crucial in determining final shooting costs. Some production managers meet with department heads to discuss the wrap date of each member of their department. On one show I worked on, our Associate Producer, Mark McNair, introduced me to a form, which, with a few minor modifications, has become my new *Departmental Wrap Schedule*. It's a great way to document and authorize a precise wrap schedule, and to make everyone understand that absolutely no one is going to be paid for wrap days that are not preapproved. You'll find a copy of this form at the end of this chapter.

The studio or production company you're working for will ask for a wrap schedule, and instead of or in addition to the individual departmental schedule, you may also wish to prepare an overall schedule, grouping crew members by department and, as above, listing their position, number of weeks/days to wrap and wrap date.

As soon as a show has completed filming, everyone—Production, Accounting, and each department head—needs to double-check all their active purchase orders, making sure all rentals are returned in a timely manner—with the emphasis on "returned." I was on a show last year where a piece of equipment, parked way in the back of a property we had used as a location, had gone totally unnoticed and was left sitting there for several weeks after wrap. The vendor had not been notified that filming was completed, and it had slipped the eye of both the location manager and the property owner. Transportation thought Effects had returned it, and vice-versa. The error would have been discovered much sooner had the responsible department checked to make sure that all their P.O.s were closed out. I strongly suggest using the Equipment Rental Log form (found in Chapter 5, "Pre-Production") to help track returns. Along the same lines, make sure you are given a receipt for all rental items returned by the production or picked up by the vendor, and that all return slips and receipts are kept on file in the accounting office. (For some reason, they tend to get lost quite easily.) On another show I was involved with recently, a vendor charged the production for the replacement of an item three different people swore was returned; but because no one could produce a copy of the return slip, the production was ultimately held liable.

Shows that are not wrapped properly produce major difficulties for studio and production company staff and for post production accountants. Clearing up unresolved matters pertaining to the shoot can be quite challenging and time-consuming (especially for those who were not involved with the project from the beginning), and this can cost valuable time, money and energy needed to complete the picture. You can blame a poorly-wrapped show on a budget that's too tight to sustain a longer wrap period, or on staff and crew members who are in too much of a hurry to leave; but in reality, there should be no excuse. And as well as any one person may perform during the production, our final impression of that person is often based upon how professionally and thoroughly he or she has wrapped his or her last show.

PRE-WRAP

There are many things you can do to start the wrap process prior to the completion of principal photography. The more you can accomplish ahead of time, the smoother and faster the wrap. This will get you started:

- Make a sweep of the office and collect things such as film commission information packets, headshots submitted by Casting, and any type of demo tape—anything that can be returned—and start returning.
- Start cutting down on office supply orders, bottled water, Polariod™ film, etc. Don't order anything more than what is absolutely necessary to get you through till the end of the show.
- Start assembling final crew, cast and contact lists. The crew lists, in particular, should be available to distribute prior to the last day of filming.
- Check with department heads to see if there are any rentals that can be returned early. This would include any office equipment no longer being used.
- After making sure all originals are on file, collect all extra copies of outdated crew lists, cast lists, contact lists, schedules and day-out-of-days, and dump them in the recycle bin.
- Ask department heads to start assessing their L&D (loss and damages).
- Inform vendors of when the last day of filming will be and when returns will be made. Also, start scheduling necessary pick-ups.
- If not already done, decide on and order show gifts. If your budget can afford it, order enough for your favorite vendors, film commission reps and production executives.

Whether the gifts are distributed on the set prior to the last day of filming, on the last day or at the wrap party, tag gifts with the names of cast, crew and staff members and divide them by department. Using cast and crew lists, check off each person's name as they are given their gift. This way, no one is inadvertently left out.

- Call companies that buy raw stock short ends, and find the one that's currently offering the best prices. (Tally your Raw Stock Inventory and check it against camera department totals. Anticipate the amount of short ends you will have for sale before checking prices.)
- Schedule a day to have a cast and crew photo taken. (Try for a day when the majority of the cast will be there. If that isn't possible, call and invite those who aren't scheduled to work that day.) If the photos are not going to be ready before the last day of filming, prepare address labels, so an 8 x 10 print can be sent to each member of the cast, crew and staff.
- Start planning a wrap party. Design an invitation or notice and distribute accordingly.
- Scout around for new productions about to start and talk to their production coordinators. One or two might be interested in buying your leftover office supplies, Polariod™ film and any office items such as lamps, fans, heaters, toaster oven, coffee pots, etc. Prepare an inventory (with prices) and fax it to those interested.

THE REAL THING

Okay—shooting has now been completed, the party was a smashing success, everyone is in a hurry to go on to their next show or catch-up on their sleep—and you're now officially in wrap. Submit written notice to the property or facilities manager as to when you will be vacating the offices and change your office hours. Although shooting days are generally twelve hours or more, wrap days should be no longer than ten hours.

As soon as you can, start collecting:

- walkies
- pagers
- cell phones/Nextels™
- rented computer equipment
- keys
- parking cards and/or passes

Many companies will include a list of wrap requirements in their production manual. Here is one you can use.

Wrap Checklist

Legal
- ❏ All contracts, agreements and releases have been countersigned and returned, and copies distributed and filed

Locations
- ❏ All signed location agreements have been returned, copies distributed and filed
- ❏ All practical locations have been thoroughly wrapped, cleaned and restored to original (or better than original) condition, and owners have signed a Location Release form

Return
- ❏ Equipment
- ❏ Vehicles
- ❏ Walkie-talkies
- ❏ Pagers/cellular phones
- ❏ Props
- ❏ Set dressing
- ❏ Wardrobe
- ❏ Greens
- ❏ Flats/cycs/backdrops

Paperwork
- ❏ Final cast list
- ❏ Final crew and staff list
- ❏ Final script with all change pages
- ❏ Final shooting schedule
- ❏ Final day-out-of-days
- ❏ Final location list
- ❏ Final contact list
- ❏ Prepare wrap books (see section below "Wrap Books")
- ❏ Organize and pack up production files

Collect files from the art department, location department, producer's assistant, UPM, production supervisor and coordinator and discard duplicates (keeping originals whenever possible). Pack files in portable file boxes; label boxes with the name of the show and number the boxes (Box 1 of ___, Box 2 of ___, etc.). Type up an inventory of the files contained in each box (indicating the box number at the top of the page); and in addition to a master inventory list, tape a copy of each box's inventory on the top of that box.

Assets

❑ Collect all asset inventory logs

❑ Balance raw stock inventory, match totals to assistant cameraperson's records; account for differences, if any

❑ Pull items needed for reshoots, added scenes and/or inserts

Sell or Store

❑ Short ends

❑ Polariod™ film

❑ Props

❑ Set dressing

❑ Unused expendables

❑ Computer software

❑ Fans/heaters

❑ Coffee pots/toaster oven

❑ Tools/lumber/building supplies

❑ Wardrobe

❑ Office supplies, lamps, answering machine, etc.

❑ Arrange storage of assets not sold, if company does not already have storage facilities

Prepare a list of items for sale (with prices). This list goes to the producer(s), director and production executives first, as they usually have first dibs on the items being sold. Often, arrangements are also made in advance for cast members to buy articles of their wardrobe or set pieces they have expressed interest in. Remaining items (with price tags) are often displayed in an open area (stage or large office) where staff and crew members can shop. Make sure to let everyone know in advance when these items will be available to look at and buy. Select one person (production coordinator or someone in Accounting) to be responsible for keeping tabs on what is being sold and for collecting the money.

Insurance

❑ Submit all insurance claims not previously submitted

❑ Prepare breakdown of pending and unsettled claims

Guild-Related

❑ All SAG contracts have been countersigned, returned, distributed and filed

❑ Submit all SAG Production Time Reports

❑ Submit final Casting Data Reports

❑ Submit final SAG Cast List

❑ Submit all DGA Weekly Work Sheets

❑ File DGA Employment Data Report

❑ Final DGA and WGA screen credit approval

NOTE: SAG requires submission of final screen credits and music cue sheets at the completion of post production.

Turnover to Post Production

❑ Script supervisor's final notes

❑ Script supervisor's final script

❑ Continuity Polaroids

❑ Final cast list

❑ Final camera reports and sound reports

❑ First draft of screen credits—main titles and end credits (including all credits based on contractual obligations and union and guild regulations)

Accounting-Related

❑ Make sure all final time cards are submitted

❑ Collect all refundable deposits

❑ Close accounts and ask vendors to submit final invoices

❑ Collect all L&D charges

❑ Have all outstanding invoices approved and paid

❑ Send out forwarding address notices

❑ Collect outstanding petty cash

❑ Prepare a 1099 list

❑ Prepare a final vendor list (in alphabetical order)

❑ Prepare a final budget

❑ Prepare a final cost report

❑ Prepare notes regarding all pending issues for the post production accountant

❑ Turn all files over to the post production accountant

Closing the Production Office

❑ Submit change-of-address to post office (if necessary)

❑ Submit forwarding phone number to phone company (if necessary)

❑ Return office furniture

❑ Return office equipment

❑ Disconnect phones and utilities

- ❏ Cancel bottled water and coffee service
- ❏ Return refrigerator
- ❏ Pack up remaining forms and supplies
- ❏ Remove all signs you've posted around the outside of the office and parking lot
- ❏ Have office cleaned well and any necessary repairs made to qualify for reimbursement of your security deposit

Before You Walk Out The Door
- ❏ Send out special thank-you notes to those whose contributions meant the most to you during production
- ❏ Prepare a detailed memo for the production executive summarizing all ongoing or pending issues (anything that might come up) and the status of each
- ❏ Send files to the studio/production company
- ❏ Have a final walk-through the office with the property manager before turning over the keys

WRAP BOOKS

Your Basic Wrap Book

Wrap books are generally prepared for the producer(s), director, UPM, production supervisor, coordinator and accountant. The contents of this book are contained within a large three-ring binder (with dividers) or taken to a printer for binding. It contains the final versions of the following (plus any other pertinent information you might want to include):

- Budget (the coordinator's book may not contain the budget)
- Cast list
- Crew list
- Contact list
- Location list with maps
- Shooting schedule
- One-line schedule
- Day-out-of-days

- Call sheets
- Production reports
- Final script with all change pages
- Inventory of stored items

The Final Production Book

A Final Production Book would be prepared by the studio or parent company after the completion of post production. The contents would take up two three-ring binders. This book condenses enough basic information to often alleviate the need to dig through file boxes searching for information when issues arise long after the show has been completed. These books would include:

- Corporate (signatory papers) information
- Bank information (bank, contact, account number, copy of signature cards, etc.)
- Bank reconciliation
- Trial balance
- Final budget
- Final cost report
- Cast list and final SAG cast list
- Chart-of-account and vendor list
- Contact list (local and location)
- Final staff and crew list
- Crew deal memos
- Location list (including dates and deals)
- Call sheets
- Production reports
- Final shooting schedule
- Final day-out-of-days
- Key correspondence
- Copies of major deals
- Copies of signed union and guild contract agreements
- Information on insurance claims
- Final script
- Dates of delivery and delivery requirements
- Inventory logs and location of inventory

FORMS IN THIS CHAPTER

- Departmental Wrap Schedule

DEPARTMENTAL WRAP SCHEDULE

Show: __HERBY'S SUMMER VACATION__

Scheduled Completion Date of Principal Photography: __9·10·XX__

Date: __9·03·XX__   Department: __CAMERA__

Department Head: __F. STOPP__

Total Wrap/Man Days Budgeted: __5 DAYS__   Work Hours Per Day: __10__

Date of Wrap Completion: __9·12·XX__

NAME	POSITION	# WRAP WKS/DAYS	WRAP DATE
LARRY LENSCAPP	1ST ASSISTANT CAMERA	2 DAYS	9·12
MATT BOXX	2ND ASSISTANT CAMERA	2 DAYS	9·12
PHILM·CANN, JR.	CAMERA LOADER	1 DAY	9·11

Department Head Signature: _F. Stopp_

UPM Approval: _Z. Filmer_

© ELH

CHAPTER TWENTY-ONE

Interactive

Interactive refers to a program that allows participants to control the action, characters and eventual outcome of a scenario being played out by use of a computer keyboard, mouse, remote control, joystick or set of buttons on a pistol grip device attached to a theater armrest. Interactive programs controlled by voice-activated means exists as well. Evidence of this rapidly growing industry can be found on the Internet and in video, computer and arcade games, some of which come complete with virtual-reality glasses and gloves that generate 3-D environments with which viewers can interact. Entertainment-based, informational and service-related interactive displays can also be found at kiosks (booths) found at museums, amusement parks, shopping centers and airports. And while a handful of interactive shows have been produced for television, cable and feature films, they're not quite mainstream yet—although Microsoft's WebTV© does allow television viewers to play along with game shows, participate in polls and chat with other viewers during interactive programming.

All interactive media are computer-based. Now that the interactive software has advanced to the point that live action and video can be incorporated into both computer programs and CD-ROMs, producers of interactive programs have the ability to replace computer-generated characters with live performers. By combining computer-generated graphics and effects with live action, you now have a multimedia program requiring a specific mixture of elements that must be facilitated by a multimedia trained staff. All conventional rules have changed with this non-traditional form of production.

Once an interactive program is designed and its elements are determined, producers and their crews must have the expertise to budget, schedule, coordinate and supervise animators, artists, technicians, live film or video production, editors and a generally intensive post production process. It is the responsibility of the creative director to make sure all graphic and live action elements are interfaced properly and work well together. Software programmers also play a significant role in the development of these projects, as codes (or labels) must be written for every single element (or "asset") integrated into the program—every sound, action, effect, piece of animation, piece of text, every button, etc. These assets create thousands of files and the need for asset management. In addition to software programming, knowledge in the fields of post production technology, computer platforms (Windows, Mac, SEGA, Nintendo, etc.), electronics and basic film and video is extremely beneficial. As the field expands, so does the number of people qualified to oversee the medium.

Interactive production companies do exist, as do interactive divisions of traditional production companies, studios, post production houses and effects houses. Working in conjunction with programmers, these facilities must have the technology to blend and manipulate all the completed elements into a finished product.

Many actors do voiceovers for the animation in interactive programs, but more are becoming involved in live action as well, which is quite different from conventional productions. Schedules generally move much faster and instead of sets, they are often filmed in front of blue or green screens. Each scene must be performed in various versions, ultimately allowing viewers to choose the scenario they wish. (Keeping continuity of multiple takes and versions of each scene is a formidable task for the asset manager or script supervisor.)

As live production for interactive and multimedia programs has increased, so has the involvement of the industry's unions and guilds. The Directors Guild of America and the Writers Guild of America both offer interactive agreements. The DGA has crew stipulations, and both guilds require payment of all appropriate pension, health and welfare benefits. Beyond that, their interactive contracts are negotiated on a project-by-project basis. The most detailed guild contract is the one offered by the Screen Actors Guild.

In June of 1993, SAG created the first Interactive Agreement in the entertainment industry. It covers all forms of media productions, including but not limited to film, videotape and other forms of electronic publishing. SAG's Interactive/Multimedia Agreement is the official contract under which all guild members must be hired and to which producers wishing to use SAG talent must become signatory.

To learn more about this field, a large selection of books and magazines are available on the subject. A wealth of information can be found at a selection of yearly conventions that feature electronic multimedia systems. Examples would be:

- ShowBiz Expo (East and West)—website: showbizexpo.com
- NAB (National Association of Broadcasters)—website: www.nab.org
- E3 (Electronic Entertainment) Expo—website: www.e3expo.com

Classes and seminars are available, and those who have started working in the field may be eligible for membership in the Academy of Interactive Arts and Sciences in Santa Monica, California. Their phone number is (310) 441-2280, and their website can be found at www.interactive.org.

CHAPTER TWENTY-TWO

Commercial Production

Similar to television and feature production in many ways, commercial production is very much a world onto itself. While there are individuals who have the ability to jump back and forth between the two realms, many choose to build their entire careers within this fast-moving industry. Commercial production schedules are much shorter, crews are smaller and salaries are generally higher. Much of the paperwork is different, and studios and networks are replaced by advertising agencies and clients. Because of these differences and the fact that this industry is such big business throughout the world, I thought it appropriate to include a new chapter outlining the basics of commercial production.

A commercial starts with a client who hires an advertising agency to promote a product or service, and the agency decides to include at least one commercial spot as part of its advertising campaign.

DEVELOPING, BIDDING & AWARDING

The following is a brief rundown of the development process from inception to the beginning of pre-production:

- The agency's traffic department purchases air time for the commercial spot(s).
- The agency's creative director assigns creative teams, each comprised of an art director and copywriter, to come up with concepts for the spot(s).
- An account executive is assigned to the project. This person becomes the primary liaison between the client and the agency.
- The creative teams meet with the client to pitch their concepts. Some ideas are rejected and others are developed further before one is finally chosen.
- An agency producer is assigned to the job, and he or she will confer with the art director and copywriter in narrowing down a selection of commercial production companies and directors who might be right for this type of spot. Most production companies consistently employ anywhere from three to eight different directors, while some of the more successful commercial directors have their own production entities.
- Once commercials are approved by the client, the creative team(s) and agency producer confer regarding what type of director they are looking for and they come up with a potential list of those they are interested in. The agency producer then contacts either the executive producer of the production company the director is attached to, or the sales representative (covering their region) for the production company. Requests are then placed for the directors' demo reels.
- The creative team(s) and agency producer review all the reels, narrowing it down to what they call the "short stack."
- After a director's availability is confirmed, scripts and storyboards are sent to the production companies and directors whose reels are liked in the hope that the director will be interested in the project.
- If all parties are interested, the agency will then decide on three directors whom they will invite to bid the job. AICP (the Association of Independent Commercial Producers) guidelines dictate that every production must allow three directors to bid a job.
- The three chosen directors are sent bid packages to complete and send back, and confer-

ence calls are set up between the director and the agency creatives, which allows the creatives to determine which director is best suited for the job. Although the bids include a summary of costs, it is also an overall outline of how the production company plans to execute the job. The basis of the standard bid form is that all live items are marked up by a single number. This number encompasses overhead costs as well as the production company fee. Because this figure is an average that provides for differentials of profit and overhead throughout the job, the bid form is designed for use with a constant number in marking up all line items of the bid.

- More conference calls ensue, and bids are sent back and forth for budget clarifications.
- Bid specs will indicate if this is a "cost plus" job or not. Cost plus is when the agency only pays for actual costs. It works like this: production companies provide an estimate of costs based on the agreed-upon specifications, and this estimate is submitted on a cost-summary form. A fixed fee (a specific dollar amount) is then added to the total cost. When agreed upon, the combination of costs and fee becomes the contract price. At the conclusion of the job, the production company does a cost-accounting, and the agency is billed for all actual direct costs plus the predetermined fixed fee. This way, additional costs for approved overages are added to the final payment; and if the job comes in under budget, the final payment is reduced by the amount saved. Even if the entire job isn't deemed cost plus, certain budget items (generally those where the cost of unknown factors cannot be anticipated in advance) can be negotiated as cost plus during the bidding process.
- Once details of an approach have been agreed upon, a proposal accepted and the commercial awarded to one company, the approved budget becomes the contract price for the job, barring a major change in specifications.
- The production company chooses a producer, who receives the budget, script, storyboards and any other information pertinent to this job. The producer then assembles his or her staff and crew. A typical office staff would include the producer, UPM, production coordinator and a couple of production assistants; and crew sizes range from thirty-five to fifty. A casting director is hired, a location scout starts lining up potential location sites and the pre-production process has begun.

THE PRE-PRODUCTION BOOK

One of the production coordinator's responsibilities is to assemble a pre-production book in time to pass out at the pre-production meeting. The book contains the following:

- a personnel list, including client, agency, production company, editorial, dailies and lab contacts
- a calendar that indicates prep activities (meetings, casting, fittings, scouts, etc.) and all pre-light, construction, shoot and strike days—also a general post production schedule provided by the agency producer
- the script
- all storyboards
- (sometimes) the director's shot list
- location information with maps
- a crew list
- a vendor list (or production directory, as it is sometimes referred to)
- a cast (or talent) list
- and anything else that is pertinent to the spot or location where the production is shooting

THE RELATIONSHIP BETWEEN THE CLIENT, AGENCY AND PRODUCTION COMPANY

The following diagram illustrates how the client, agency and production company (ideally) relate to each other. The arrows indicate the individual each person primarily looks to for information and support.

Video village is an area on the set where the client(s) and agency people view all on-camera activities from video monitors.

DIFFERENCES

There are certain aspects of commercial production that are the same as and others that vary from those of long-form productions. Here are a few key areas to be aware of:

- Depending on the variables involved, prep schedules can range from five days to two weeks. The number of shoot days can range from one day to one month, and wrap is generally two to three days in duration.
- In addition to signing with the Association of Independent Commercial Producers (AICP), commercial companies sign specific commercial agreements with the DGA, IA and Teamsters. While most companies produce union commercials, there are some that operate under non-union arms as well.
- While the production is responsible for casting, booking, fittings, issuing calls and making sure contracts are signed, it is the agency that signs with the Screen Actors Guild, not the production company.
- It is generally the production company that carries the insurance coverage and not the agency.
- Any part of a visual effect that is handled in-camera becomes the responsibility of the pro-

duction. Any CGI work or effects that are done in post production are handled by the agency.

- The production company pays for film processing and the development of dailies, but the negative is turned over to the agency; and the agency is responsible for the editing process.
- Call sheets are much simpler than those used on theatrical or television productions (sample included at the end of this chapter); and with the addition of out times and pertinent notes relating to the day's shooting activities, the same general form is used in lieu of a production report.
- Unlike a feature, television or cable show, the production manager is responsible for tracking all costs. At the completion of wrap, he or she submits a complete financial accounting to the production company by way of a *wrap book*. The payroll is handled by a payroll company, and the accountant's prime responsibility is to issue checks and audit the wrap book.

THE WRAP BOOK

A wrap book would include the following:

- A P.O. log and copy of every purchase order issued. The P.O. would look something like this:

Purchase Order Log						
Job#:						
Job Title:						
Company Name:						
P.O.#	Date	Issued To		Line#	Amount	Check#

- A location check log, which would look something like this:

Location Check Log
Job#:
Job Title:
Company Name:

Date	Ck#	Vendor	Description	Line#	P.O.#	Amount

- A payroll breakdown, which would look like this:

Payroll Breakdown
Job#:
Job Title:
Company Name:

Name	Position	Line#	Amount

- petty cash reconciliations
- original paid invoices and receipts

The commercial industry in the United States is governed by the Association of Independent Commercial Producers (AICP), which focuses on the needs and interests of commercial production companies. Founded in 1972 by a small group of television commercial production companies, today's organization represents 80 to 85 percent of all domestic commercials, whether produced for traditional broadcast channels, nontraditional use, public or private viewing. They serve as a strong collective voice for the $4.5 billion commercial industry. If you would like further information on AICP guidelines, seminars, agreements, payment schedules or forms, you can visit their website at www.aicp.com.

FORMS IN THIS CHAPTER

- Commercial Call Sheet

COMMERCIAL CALL SHEET

				CREW CALL: 7A
DATE: 8.21.XX	JOB TITLE(S): A DAY AT THE LAKE	JOB:		
DAY: 2 of 2		JOB#:	SUNRISE: 6:30A	SUNSET: 7:30P

CLIENT: CHIC SHADES SUNGLASSES	AGENCY: LIGHT & ASSOCIATES 555 SCHOOL ST, SANTA MONICA, CA 90401 (310) 555-3117	PRODUCTION CO: XYZ PRODUCTIONS 1234 FLICK DR. HOLLYWOOD, CA 90038
LOCATIONS: PARADISE BEACH (3 MI. NORTH OF MALIBU)		NEAREST HOSPITAL: LINCOLN MEMORIAL 9876-1ST ST. - L.A.
CREW PARKING: PUBLIC LOT @ SO. END OF BEACH	Executive Producer: ELLIOT LIGHT Producer: SARAH RHODES Business Affairs Manager: BEVERLY FAIRFAX Art Director: LAUREL COLFAX Copywriter: DIANA LIGHT	PRODUCTION PAGERS: 555-1002 555-1007

				PRODUCTION CELL PHONES: 555-3337 + 3339		AGENCY CELL: 555-6000

CREW	NAME	PHONE	PAGER	IN	OUT	EQUIPMENT	VENDOR	PHONE
Director	SID CELLULOID	555-XXXX	XXX-XXXX	O/C				
Producer	SWIFTY DEALS	XXX-XXXX	XXX-XXXX	O/C		ANIMALS	ANIMALS RUS	XXX-XXXX
1st AD	A. DEES	XXX-XXXX	XXX-XXXX	6:30		CAMERA		
Prod. Manager	FRED FILMER	XXX-XXXX		O/C		CAMERA CAR		
Prod. Coordinator	C. COORDINATES	XXX-XXXX	XXX-XXXX	O/C		CATERING	FREDERIC'S	XXX-XXXX
D.P.	F. STOPP	XXX-XXXX	XXX-XXXX	7A		CASTING	DEE CASTOR+CO.	XXX-XXXX
1st Asst. Camera	L. LENSCAPP	XXX-XXXX		7A		CONDORS		
2nd Asst. Camera	PHIL M.CANN JR	XXX-XXXX		7A		CRAFT SERVICE		
Loader	MIKE MAGZINE	XXX-XXXX		7A		CRANE	ABC CRANE CO.	XXX-XXXX
Gaffer	SPARKY PLUG	XXX-XXXX	XXX-XXXX	7A		CELL PHONES		
Best Boy Elec.	CARY CURRENT	XXX-XXXX	XXX-XXXX	6:30A		DAILIES		
Electric	JERRY JUICER	XXX-XXXX		6:30A		DOLLY		
Electric	AARON ARCS	XXX-XXXX		6:30A		DOLLY TRACK		
Electric/Driver	MARK MUSCO	XXX-XXXX		6:30A		EDITORIAL		
Key Grip	C. STANDD	XXX-XXXX	XXX-XXXX	6:30A		ELECTRIC	RWH EQUIP. RENT	XXX-XXXX
Best Boy Grip						EXPENDABLES		
Grip						EXTRAS CASTING		
Grip Driver						GENERATOR	AL'S GENERATORS	XXX-XXXX
Grip						GRIP		
Script Supervisor						INSURANCE	NEAR NORTH	XXX-XXXX
VTR						LAB	CFI	XXX-XXXX
Make-Up						MESSENGER	USA EXPRESS	XXX-XXXX
Make-Up Assistant						MOTORCYCLE CAM. CAR		
Wardrobe						MOTORHOMES		
Wardrobe Assistant						PICTURE CARS		
Production Designer						PAYROLL SER.	PREMIERE	XXX-XXXX
Prop Master						PERMITS		
Set Decorator						PROD. SUPPLIES		
Prop Assistant						RAW STOCK	WESTMAN FILM	XXX-XXXX
Set Dresser						SETS		
Craft Service						VEHICLES		
P.A.						VTR		
P.A.						WALKIES	GARY'S	XXX-XXXX
P.A.						WATER TRUCK		
P.A.						WEATHER	WEATHER CHECK	XXX-XXXX
P.A.						WORKERS COMP.		
2nd AD								
Water Truck Driver								
Teacher						COFFEE/DONUTS:	READY @: 6:30A	
Locations Manager						# OF LUNCHES: 70	READY @: 1P	

TALENT ROLE	TALENT NAME	PHONE	PAGER	IN	OUT	AGENT	PHONE	CONTACT
BOY ON BEACH	HOLLYWOOD MANN	XXX-XXXX	XXX-XXXX	6:30		JOE COOL	XXX-XXXX	JOE
SEXY GIRL	SCARLET STARLET			6:30		" "		
BOY W/ DOG	JON ADAMS			7A		" "		

PRODUCTION SUMMARY	SOUND ROLL	FILM STOCK	STOCK#1:	STOCK#2:	STOCK#3:
CALL TIME		RECEIVED TODAY:			
1 ST SHOT		RECEIVED PREVIOUS:			
LUNCH		TOTAL EXPOSED TODAY:			
1ST SHOT PM	SCENE NOS.	TOTAL EXPOSED TO DATE:			
2ND MEAL		TOTAL UNEXPOSED:			
CAMERA WRAP		S.E. TO DATE UNEXPOSED:			
PROD. WRAP		UNEXPOSED IN CANS:			

PRODUCTION NOTES:

CHAPTER TWENTY-THREE

A Little Post Production

Many production people find that their knowledge of post production and its everchanging technology is somewhat limited. Hired at the beginning of pre-production, they work through the end of production and take a few weeks to wrap before moving on to the next picture. It is assumed that the post production supervisor will handle all necessary tasks associated with completing the film. But even with a good post production supervisor on board, production personnel often find themselves involved with certain facets of post production prior to the end of principal photography.

Post production is a vast and complicated subject, worthy of an entire book in itself. Just as budgets, schedules and the selection of equipment were once based on whether a film was for television or theatrical release, the field grows increasingly more complex as current and developing technologies offer more choices. Moviolas and Kems are almost extinct, editors are now proficient at editing on a computer and post production personnel must keep up with technology that is evolving in leaps and bounds.

Right now, one of the fastest developing fields in our industry includes both digital production and post production. New companies are springing up every day; and books, magazines, seminars and entire conventions are being devoted to evolving digital technology. And although some films are now being shot digitally, the accessibility of equipment that transfers digital video directly to 35mm negative is still somewhat limited (with Sony Hi-Def the current leader in this field). However, the need to make 35mm release prints will eventually diminish as more films are being released directly to video or onto the Inter-

net, and as fifteen test markets around the world are currently experimenting with the projection of films into theatres via satellite and fiber optic lines.

But unless you are working in the field, having a good overview of the various stages and technological processes should suffice as far as effectively performing your job in a production capacity. It is also important to be aware of just how significant post production is to your finished picture.

A fundamental understanding of post production (and post production-related costs) is needed to prepare more accurate budgets. Other basics that are beneficial to know are the differences between film and electronic editing (and the integration of both on your film); how to plan a post production schedule (including the time needed to complete and incorporate complicated visual effects); guidelines for preparing screen credits and some essential terminology.

It is also beneficial to be aware of standard delivery requirements: those elements (i.e., film, sound track, script, contracts, cast list, stills) that must be turned over to the distributor of your film when post production has been completed. Much of the necessary paperwork can be accumulated ahead of time (during principal photography) to save time during post production.

Post production is the time used to assemble and complete your picture. It begins during pre-production with the preparation of a post production budget and schedule, the lining up of crew and facilities and the planning of arrangements that must be made for any necessary special processes (such as visual effects). It is imperative to know what is involved, up front, and to anticipate how long the post production process will take before committing to a delivery date. Changes and delays along the way are not uncommon, but the more thorough the planning, the better chances are that the picture will remain on budget and on schedule. Once your film has been edited, the remaining components needed to complete the picture are as follows: inserts and pick-up shots, sound effects and foley, music, ADR (automatic dialogue replacement), titles (main titles and end credits), opticals, and visual effects. Simplified, these are the elements that are mixed together to create a finished product ready for release. Although there were at one time standard methods utilized to produce this finished product, there are now many more options and considerations. One of the most critical decisions to be made for each show is whether the post production will be done entirely on film, done entirely by electronic methods, or accomplished with a combination of both.

FILM VERSUS ELECTRONIC EDITING

Although rarely done this way anymore, the traditional method of editing had been to cut on film. This is when the work print (selected takes printed from the developed negative) is literally cut, either on a moviola or a flatbed (Kem). The cuts are manually spliced together, and sequences are stored on reels or cores. Changes requiring deletions, additions or alterations require the time-consuming process of going back through trims (pieces of work print not used from cut sequences) and outs (scenes that were printed but not cut or used). When the picture is locked in, the negative is cut to match the edited work print. Release prints are then struck from the conformed negative. This is a much slower process than editing electronically, but the cost of renting moviolas and flatbeds is a fraction of the cost of electronic equipment. An entire second editing crew can, and often is, hired for what it would cost to cut a picture on one of the digital systems. There are still editors who are not yet comfortable using computers and who enjoy physically handling the film during the editing process.

Videotape editing was popular for quite some time and is still used by some. Of the videotape editing systems available, some are linear and some are nonlinear. Digital editing, which is a nonlinear system, is currently very much the system of choice. A nonlinear system allows the editor to insert, remove or alter scenes without affecting any of the scenes preceding or following the change. Linear systems do not easily allow for this option. Cutting digitally equates to cutting on a computer, and the two most popular such systems are AVID and Lightworks.

Digital editing is fast and allows you the time and ease of cutting different versions of each scene, jumping back and forth until one variation is deemed better than the others. There is some amount of instant gratification in being able to restructure scenes and play with different options, as well as being able to create temporary visual and special effects right in the editing room. Using these systems can shave weeks off your schedule, especially in television, where schedules are tight. The faster pace of editing will often eliminate the need for additional editors. You will also realize savings on your sound package, as you will no longer have to order reprints of production takes for sound effects and dialogue editing. Sound tracks can be duplicated digitally directly from your system. In addition, because digital editing systems produce high-quality sound and the ability to incorporate music and effects into the cut, temp dubs may no longer be necessary.

The down side to digital editing is the expense of the equipment, which is considerably higher than that of traditional editing equipment. If the time you save and the additional staff you may not have to hire compensates for the higher costs, then you are well advised to go with one of the digital systems. Even if you are not on a tight schedule, if you can afford the extra cost of the electronic equipment and want the versatility it can offer, then it is also a wise choice. Be aware, however, that using this method does not necessarily equate to saving time and therefore money. As the equipment is so expensive, editing rooms often run twenty-four hours a day, with assistant editors working in shifts—one at night to load footage from the previous day's shoot, and another to work days with the editor.

Having the ability to experiment with and create special and visual effects digitally during the editing process can be a tremendous help; but, while instantly gratifying, the process can easily get out of hand and become expensive. It is easy to forget that all effects must eventually be recreated at an optical or effects house and transferred to negative.

DGA directors exercising their right to a lengthy number of specified director's cut days, retakes and/or visual effects that need to be incorporated into the picture later than anticipated, and producers who schedule several previews and continually experiment with new ways to cut the picture, are all elements that may contribute to a schedule that turns out to be just as lengthy as it would have been cutting the picture by more conventional means.

Dailies and screenings created from electronically edited footage are viewed on the system's computer monitor or downloaded onto videotape for viewing elsewhere. Another factor to consider with the use of digital equipment is that if your dailies or screenings are to be viewed on a big screen or you plan to preview the picture, you will have to have the work print cut to conform to your electronic edit. Once you start adding film elements and the cost of another editor or assistant to conform the work print, any anticipation of savings you might have had become negligible.

New and ever-evolving technology has produced new and varied choices to make concerning every phase of post production. Your post production supervisor and/or producer must be aware of what each alternative offers, including both the benefits and possible problems associated with each. There is much to be considered before budgets and schedules are finalized, systems are selected, a lab is chosen, equipment is ordered, sound and visual effects houses are retained and post production personnel are hired.

POST PRODUCTION SOUND

Sound editing, ADR, foley and dubbing are the components of post production sound. Most of this work is done by sound effects houses, and more than 50 percent of the work done at sound effects houses is done digitally. Sound editing equipment and software have been developed to be compatible with (and to read the files of) digital editing systems such as AVID and Lightworks. Presently, it takes separate software programs to read the files of each system, but new software is being developed that will be able to read the files of any editing system.

Files from a digitally edited show are loaded onto the sound editing system's computer with the help of an edit decision list (EDL). Without an EDL, each take (either on DAT or 1/4-inch mag-netic tape) must be manually loaded into the system, taking three times as long.

The cost of using digital equipment for sound editing is more expensive than the conventional analog-based equipment, but the quality it produces is better. Digital equipment also allows sound editors and sound designers (individuals who specialize in creating sound effects for big action sequences or sequences that require unique and distinctive sounds) the ability to listen to several tracks simultaneously while in the process of building their sound effects units.

Sound effects houses are now frequently getting involved with pictures during pre-production by working in conjunction with sound mixers in relation to production sound and how it will be recorded. Most houses also now offer what is called the ADE System. The ADE produces a database and time code during the normal transfer of dailies, creating an EDL that allows for the automatic loading and assembly of the production sound for sound editorial.

Various release-print sound-track systems such as SRD, SDDS and Dolby have been developed by different studios and companies and are available in both digital and analog formats. (Optical tracks are still used as well.) The producing entity of your picture, where it is being dubbed, the cost of a licensing fee (if applicable) for the use of a specific system, overall budgetary and scheduling considerations and personal preferences, will help you and your post production supervisor determine which system should be used for your film.

DAILIES

Until recently, the traditional meaning of the word dailies (or *rushes*) had only one connotation—the positive (or *work*) print made from the director's selected takes that is screened for the producer, director, D.P. and studio the day after filming. Even if videocassettes were made, they were made in addition to the work print, and dailies were viewed in a screening room on a large screen. When shooting companies screen print dailies on distant location, they travel with a portable projection system and projectionist, sometimes with a custom-made projection trailer or arrangements are made to screen dailies at a local theatre.

Today, unless a work print is struck for the purpose of viewing the film on a large screen, the term dailies generally refers to the director's selected takes that have been transferred onto half-inch VHS cassettes and/or Beta SP cassettes. Some feature productions will order both work print and viewing cassettes, and some may wish to view dailies on a large screen for just the first few days of filming for the purpose of checking camera work and film quality.

I discuss the coordination of shipping dailies to and from distant locations in Chapter 16, "Locations." Again, this was the traditional method. The negative is developed, a work print struck, dailies are synced-up—then boxed and shipped (usually via counter-to-counter air service) to wherever the shooting company happens to be. Today, there is also a process called *streaming*. This is where the negative is developed, transferred and digitized. Dailies are then sent over a T-1 (or high-end fiber optic) line. The lab can only transmit dailies this way to locations that have T-1 lines in place, but they are becoming increasingly available throughout the United States.

THE POST PRODUCTION PROCESS

From camera through delivery, there was a time when all film followed the same route. Not so anymore. Every type of show is handled differently, and changing technologies continuously offer new options. As of now, the following is a basic rule-of-thumb for how shows are currently being processed and delivered, and each example comes with the assumption that the picture is being edited electronically.

Features

- Develop negative
- Print dailies
- Telecine to Beta SP or digi Beta
- Digitize to editing system
- Edit
- Conform work print and negative to match edit
- Strike an IP (interpositive)
- Strike an internegative from the IP
- Strike an average of 1,700 to 2,000 release prints from the internegative

Two-Hour Movie for Television or

One-Hour Television Drama

- Develop negative
- Telecine to digi Beta
- Digitize to editing system
- Edit
- On-line assembly
- Deliver to network on digi Beta master or high definition

Movie for Cable

- Develop negative
- Telecine to digi Beta
- Digitize to editing system
- Edit
- Have a film print made at the end of the edit
- Conform the print and negative
- Strike an IP and internegative for release prints
- Deliver on digi Beta master or high definition and film

SAMPLE POST PRODUCTION SCHEDULES

Post production schedules can vary. Half-hour television shows are being completed in two weeks; one-hour shows in four to six weeks and two-hour movies for television in twelve weeks. Theatrical features have been completed in twelve weeks from the completion of principal photography, and some take eight to ten months. Schedules vary greatly depending on the form in which your picture is to be released (i.e., television, theatrical, video), how it is structured to meet delivery date and budgetary obligations and whether the post production is to be done on film, electronically or using a combination of both.

The following are three different versions of a reasonable post production schedule based on a modestly budgeted film—not overly extravagant, yet allowing enough time to make sure everything is done properly. All are subject to interruption and change, and are to be used as guidelines only.

None of these sample schedules include previewing, which is when a picture that is not locked in (or final) is screened for a full movie audience. The audience's comments and reactions are assessed and changes are made accordingly. Pre-dubbing is necessary prior to each preview, and a certain amount of restructuring is required following each preview to facilitate appropriate changes. Most lower (and some moderately) budgeted films cannot afford the additional time and expense to preview, whereas larger budgeted films often have several previews before a final cut is locked in. Each preview adds at least one week to your post production schedule time.

The first schedule utilizes the traditional method of doing everything on film. The second, which is quite commonly used, illustrates a combined use of film and electronic methods. The third reflects an all-electronic scenario, with delivery on videotape.

The process of editing begins during principal photography. The film shot on the set each day is taken to the lab each evening to be developed. It is printed (creating a work print) and/or transferred in Telecine. It is then transferred to Beta SP, digi Beta or directly onto the editing system's hard drive. Digital audiotapes are synced up and transferred in Telecine (along with the negative). For those still using 1/4-inch sound tapes, the sound is then synced up and transferred to 35mm mag stock or videotape. Even if you are cutting digitally, syncing the sound track to a work print will allow you to screen dailies on a large screen the following day.

The editor can begin cutting as soon as filming has been completed on an entire sequence. The following reflects the weeks following the completion of principal photography.

POST PRODUCTION PROCESS DONE ENTIRELY ON FILM

Week 1

The editor receives the last batch of dailies and the script supervisor's final notes and continues the assembly.

Week 2

The producer starts assembling a list of tentative screen credits. By the end of this week, the editor should have a completed assembly of the picture (sometimes referred to as the editor's cut).

Weeks 3–6

Once the editor's cut is completed, the director then takes the next several weeks to add changes. It is reasonable to assume a first cut will be completed by the end of Week 4 and a final director's cut by the end of Week 6.

DGA regulations specify that the director of a feature film budgeted over $1,500,000 is to receive up to ten weeks or one day of editing time for each two days of originally scheduled photography, whichever is greater (following the editor's assembly of the picture) to complete the director's cut. The director has up to twenty days to complete a cut on a television motion picture running 90 to 120 minutes; and on a television motion picture running more than two hours—twenty days, plus five days for each additional hour in excess of two hours.

Although the director is entitled to the above-specified number of days, those who work well with their editor(s) and are also cognizant of delivery date requirements and the financial concerns of the company will not generally take the full allotted time and will complete their cut within a reasonable time frame.

Week 7

- Producer screens the director's cut and starts adding his or her own changes to the picture.
- Spot the picture with the composer, sound effects and dialogue editors. Although not final, a cassette of the picture (without time code) should be given to each so they can begin their work.

Week 8

- Inserts, retakes and visual effects (other than dissolves and fades) should all be completed and cut in no later than this week.
- Producer should complete his or her changes by the end of this week, constituting the final cut and locking in the picture.
- Transfer the final cut to video (with time code) for sound effects, dialogue and music editors and the composer.

Week 9

- Main titles and screen credits should be finalized.
- Assistant editor starts ordering opticals (dissolves, fades, wipes, etc.).
- If the picture is for theatrical release, the editor starts cutting the television version.
- Negative cutter begins cutting the negative.

Week 11

- Begin looping (ADR) actors.
- Begin color correcting.
- Begin answer printing.

Weeks 10–13

During these weeks (while the sound effects and foley editors, dialogue editor and the composer are preparing their work), the opticals are finalized, the opticals and credits are cut into the picture and the negative cutter continues cutting the negative.

Weeks 14–16

Assuming the sound track of this picture will be recorded in stereo, it will take approximately five weeks to dub the show. It would be cost-effective to spend the first three weeks pre-dubbing. If pre-dubbing is done during these three weeks, this is also the time when the picture is scored (prior to the final dub).

Weeks 17 and 18

- Final dub (or mix)
- View first trial print minus any missing elements, such as end credits not yet approved or opticals not completed.

Week 19

- Add any sound fixes to (or "sweeten") the picture. If there are any major sound fixes, they should be made to the master tracks. Minor fixes can be done at the same time as print mastering.
- Make a print master.
- Make a mono master.
- Make M&E (music and effects) tracks for foreign distribution.
- If required, make a television and stereo version of the picture.
- Time the picture for color.
- Strike a first answer print.

Week 20

- Strike a final answer print.
- Prepare delivery requirements.

Post Production Schedule Based on Editing Digitally and Completing the Process on Film

You can reduce your editing time and subsequent post production schedule by two or three weeks by cutting on digital equipment rather than using a moviola or flatbed and cutting on film. If, however, this reduction infringes upon the DGA's allocated time frame given for the director's cut,

you must receive permission from your director to waive his or full time allotment.

Assuming this schedule is approved by both the producer and director, Weeks 1 and 2 remain the same. Weeks 3 to 6 now become Weeks 3 and 4, and everything else is moved up by two weeks, creating an eighteen-week schedule. If you can cut three weeks off your editing time instead of two, everything is moved up an additional week, producing a seventeen-week schedule.

Again, if dailies are to be viewed on a large screen (even if it is for the first few days), the work print must be cut to conform to the electronic edit from the beginning. If the work print is to be cut for the purpose of a preview, it might be done following a second cut toward the end of Week 4. If you do not preview but still wish to screen a final cut for the producer and director, then the work print should be conformed during Week 5.

Unless you are delivering your picture on a one-inch videotape master only, the negative will need to be cut to conform to the electronic edit (whether you have previously cut the work picture or not). This would be done during the same time frame as would an all film post production schedule. Both the work print and negative are conformed using an edit decision list (EDL) prepared by the assistant editor.

In addition to picture editing, the popularity of editing sound effects and music digitally is also on the rise. Most pictures are being done with a combination of both. The type of equipment being used for each phase of the post production process will help determine both schedule and budget, because speed and versatility are constantly being weighed against costs. A well-informed post production supervisor and editor, along with the producer, should be able to make the best choices for each picture. When using qualified post production facilities and personnel, whether the equipment is film-based or electronic, the end result will remain the same.

ENTIRE POST PRODUCTION SCHEDULE DONE ELECTRONICALLY

Week 1

- The editor receives the last batch of dailies and the script supervisor's final notes. The assembly continues.

- The producer starts assembling a list of tentative screen credits.

Week 2

- By the end of this week, the editor should have a completed assembly of the picture (editor's cut).

Weeks 3 and 4

- The director uses this time for his or her cut. Again, if this reduced schedule infringes upon the allotted DGA time, the remainder of the director's time must be waived.
- Inserts, retakes, etc. should be completed and incorporated into the picture.
- Spot the picture with the composer, sound effects and dialogue editors.

Week 5

- This week should be used for the producer's changes and to lock in the picture.
- It is also the time to finalize the main titles and screen credits.

Week 6

- Order opticals.
- Cut television version.
- If you are required to deliver release prints, the negative cutter should receive a cut list, so he or she can start cutting the negative to conform to the final edit. If the picture is for video or television release, and you are only required to deliver a one-inch master, this step is not necessary.
- By the end of this week, start ADR.

Weeks 7–10

- Begin on-line process in which picture is transferred to a digi Beta master and all color corrections are made.
- If the negative has been cut and the negative cutting has been completed, a first trial print can be struck.
- These are the weeks in which the sound effects, foley and dialogue editors, in addition to the composer, are finalizing their work.

Weeks 11–13

- Pre-dub

Weeks 14 and 15

- Final dub (or mix)

Week 16

- Fixes
- Make M&E tracks for foreign distribution.
- Prepare delivery requirements.

BASIC POST PRODUCTION TERMINOLOGY

Film-Related Terms

These terms are listed in order of progression through the post production process.

Work Print (or Dailies)

A (positive) print made from the director's selected takes. This is what the editor works with in assembling the picture.

Negative Cutter

Negative cutters are responsible for accepting the exposed negative from the lab. They break the negative down into individual scenes and maintain a log of each scene by key numbers (numbers on the edge of the film used to match the work print to the negative). The negative cutter pulls sections of negative for reprints and opticals, and, most importantly, cuts the negative to match the final cut work print. This person is hired prior to the start of principal photography.

Syncing Dailies

The matching or synchronization of the sound track to the picture. This is accomplished by matching the sound of the clapping slate from the sound track with the exact spot in the picture where the slate comes together.

Coding Dailies

Printing matching numbers on the edge of the work print and the sound track for the purpose of maintaining synchronization while cutting the picture.

Inserts

Inserts are brief shots that are used to accentuate a story point. They are usually close-ups or extreme close-ups and can include anything from the time on a wristwatch to a hand writing a note. If time restrictions did not allow for inserts to be shot during production, or if it is decided after the completion of principal photography that an insert is needed, they can easily be shot on a small insert stage anywhere and any time. Depending on the shot, the actual actors are generally not needed. It is important, however, that the props and the wardrobe match exactly.

Opticals

Visual effects such as dissolves, fades, enlargements, etc. This may also include titles when they appear over action.

Spotting

Running the picture with the composer to determine where music will begin and end for each scene. Separately running the picture for the sound effects editors to determine where and what sound effects are to be added or enhanced, and for the dialogue editor to determine where dialogue needs to be replaced or added.

Sound Effects

The adding, replacing or enhancing of sounds of any kind that are not recorded during production or were recorded but deemed unusable. Sound effects can include anything from the sound of a kiss to that of a major explosion.

Foley

A method of recording sound effects that involve physical movement, such as footsteps, that can be duplicated on a sound stage. These effects are recorded by a foley artist, who reproduces the exact movement on the stage while watching the action being projected on a screen.

Looping (or ADR—Automatic Dialogue Replacement)

Re-recording production dialogue that has been deemed unusable for any number of reasons (airplane flying overhead during the take, unintelligible dialogue, etc.). The actors repeat the dialogue while watching themselves projected on a screen and listening to the sound track on earphones as it was originally recorded on the set. The new dialogue that is being recorded must match the lip movement of the actor on the screen.

Looping also encompasses the adding of off-stage dialogue that had not been previously recorded, or miscellaneous crowd or background voices ("walla"). These are also done while the actors view the projected scene.

Scoring

The recording of the music that is to be used in the film.

Pre-dubbing

When there are so many sound tracks being used that it makes it difficult to maintain control, it is advantageous to mix several sound tracks together prior to the final mix. This is usually done with dialogue when mixing in stereo. However, if you have a large number of sound effects tracks, you may also want to premix some of them. Once the dialogue tracks are mixed, the effects and the music are balanced accordingly.

Dubbing

As a film term, this can also be referred to as mixing. It is the blending of dialogue, music and sound effects.

Fixes or Sweetening

This involves going back after the dubbing has been completed to make adjustments to the sound track.

Print Master

Combining all mastered stereo tracks into a single piece of magnetic sound track.

Optical Sound Track

The transferring of the print master from magnetic tape stock to optical stock, which is then combined with the negative to make a release print.

Timing

This is a process in which the color and density of the picture are balanced from one scene to another throughout the picture. It is done at the lab with the lab's color timer, the editor and, occasionally, the director of photography.

First Trial Print

This is a first complete print of the film with sound track, opticals and titles struck from the cut original negative. This print will indicate where additional minor color and density adjustments have to be made. Several trial prints may be necessary before an answer print is struck.

Answer Print (Release Print)

The first acceptable release print struck from the original negative.

ELECTRONIC TERMS

The following list represents the tip of the iceberg. There are many, many more terms associated with electronic post production, which can be found in books, magazines and operational manuals; on the Internet or learned in classes and seminars dedicated to the field. For the purposes of this book, however, a limited and select number of basic terms are sufficient. These terms are listed in alphabetical order.

A/D

Analog to digital converter.

Analog

The common form of any magnetic recording (i.e., audiotape or videotape) in which the recorded waveform signal maintains the shape of the original waveform signal. (Digital recording converts an analog audio or video signal to a digital signal.)

ASCII

American Standard Code for Information Interchange—a standard code used in data transmissions.

Aspect Ratio

The ratio of screen width to screen height.

Bit

Binary digit, the smallest part of information in a binary notation system. A bit contains the information one or zero. A group of eight bits composes a byte.

Byte

A group of eight data bits which are processed together.

Cut List

A list of edits (containing picture key numbers) given to a negative cutter to conform the negative to match an electronically cut picture.

D1 (Component)

A digital method of recording a signal in which the elements of luminance (brightness and darkness) and the three primary colors of red, green, and blue are recorded separately rather than combined, allowing each to be enhanced individually. It provides the highest quality video signal available.

D2 (Composite)

A digital method of recording in which the elements have been combined. D2 (composite video) is easier to transmit, although the quality is not as high as D1 (component video). D1s and D2s are generally used to record completed one-inch master videotapes during the final stages of the post production process, most commonly to fulfill delivery requirements.

DAT

Digital audiotape.

Digital

Converting an analog (waveform) signal to a numerical signal.

Digital Cut

Outputting digitized material (footage, sound and music) onto videotape.

Digitizing

The loading of material—footage (on videotape), sound and music—into a digital editing system.

Dubbing

The process of duplicating a videotape.

Edit Decision List (EDL)

List of edits used to conform the one-inch master to the (off-line) edited version during the on-line process.

Layback

Transferring the finished audio track back to the master videotape.

MJPEG (or Motion JPEG)

Based on the JPEG image compression standard developed by the Joint Photographic Experts Group, which is the standard used for the transfer of a single image or frames over the Internet and World Wide Web. The Motion JPEG standard is actually the JPEG standard applied to all the frames of video in a sequence. MJPEG was primarily developed for broadcast television editing for use with nonlinear video editing systems. It stores all frame information in a compressed format and allows the editor to easily view individual frames in a sequence.

MPEG

A group of standards developed by The Motion Picture Experts Group in order to improve compression capabilities for video and audio used in the entertainment industry.

NTSC (National Television Standards Committee)

This defines the 525-line, 30-frame-per-second television standard currently being used in the United States, Canada, Mexico, Japan and a few other countries.

Off-Line

The process of electronic editing.

On-Line

This process is to an electronic edit what a negative cutter is to a picture completed on film. On-line operators conform videotapes containing daily production footage to the completed (off-line) edited version. It is also possible to mix audio tracks and to add titles and opticals during the on-line process. The end result is a digi Beta master.

PAL (Phase Alternate Line)

The 625-line, 25-frame-per-second television standard used in Western Europe, India, China, Australia, New Zealand, Argentina and parts of Africa.

Pixel

Derived from Picture Elements, this is the smallest unique point of a digital video image. In a digital video, a picture is divided up into thousands of pixels, each identified by its luminance, chrominance and position information.

SECAM (Systeme Electronique pour Couleur Avec Memoire)

The 625-line, 25-frame-per-second television system developed in France and used in France, Eastern Europe, Russia and parts of Africa.

NOTE: When ordering videotapes for distribution requirements, always be aware of which system—NTSC, PAL or SECAM—the videotapes must be transferred to.

(SMPTE) Time Code

An electronic indexing method used for editing and timing video programs. The time code denotes hours, minutes, seconds and frames elapsed on a videotape. SMPTE refers to the Society of Motion Picture and Television Engineers, the organization that set up this time-code system.

Standard Definition Television (SDTV)

Offers the ability to transmit four or more standard-quality programs (equivalent to NTSC) using the same channel. SDTV incorporates stereo sound plus a wide range of data services. It displays picture and sound without noise or interference.

Streaming

The process of playing a file that has been specifically encoded so that it can be played while it downloads, instead of having to wait for the entire file to download. As part of the streaming format, there is usually some form of compression included.

Sweetening

The process of mixing sound effects, music and announcer audio tracks with the audio tracks of the edited master tape.

TC

Short for time code.

Telecine

The process of, or place where, film is transferred to videotape.

Video Compression

A process in which an amount of data being transmitted can be reduced by encoding the data first.

SCREEN CREDITS

One of the things a production manager or coordinator is often asked to do before wrapping a show is to supply the company or producer with a list of tentative screen credits. Screen credits vary greatly from picture to picture, but there are basic guidelines that apply to all productions.

Union and guild requirements govern the placement of certain screen credits. Some credits are given based on an unwritten industry-accepted pecking order, some are negotiated before the beginning of principal photography and others are given at the sole discretion of the producer after the completion of principal photography. The following are basic union and guild regulations pertaining to screen credits and examples of what a reasonable set of credits might look like, both for a motion picture and a movie for television. Note that you are not bound by any of the union and guild requirements if you are not a signatory to that particular union or guild. However, many of the union rules pertaining to screen credit placements are also routinely utilized on non-union shows. Again, be aware that much of the positioning is negotiated and is determined by the producer.

Directors Guild of America (DGA)

Director—Theatrical Motion Pictures

The director of the film shall be accorded credit on a separate card on all positive prints and all videodiscs and videocassettes of the film in size of type not less than 50 percent of the size in which the title of the motion picture is displayed or of the largest size in which credit is accorded to any other person, whichever is greater. Such credit shall be on the last title card appearing prior to principal photography or the first card following the last scene of the picture.

Director—Television

The director shall be given credit in the form *Directed by* on a separate card, which shall be the last title card before the first scene of the picture or the first title card following the last scene of the picture. However, in the case of split credits, where credit is given to any person before the first scene of the picture, the director shall be given the last solo credit card before the first scene of the picture. The director's name on the screen shall be no less than 40 percent of the episode or series title, whichever is larger.

NOTE: The DGA has a provision stating that no one other than the Director can use the word "director" or "direction" in their screen credit title (or in paid advertising credits). Although the titles of Art Director and Director of Photography were established prior to this provision, it would apply to the title of Casting Director (or any other title with "director" in it). A casting director's screen credit would merely read, *Casting by* _____.

Unit Production Manager/First Assistant Director/Second Assistant Director—Theatrical Motion Pictures and Television

Employer shall accord credit in a prominent place (no less than a separate card, or its equivalent in a crawl, shared by no more than three names) on all positive prints of each feature or television motion picture. The only technical credits that may receive a more prominent place shall be those of the director of photography, the art director and the film editor. The order of names on the card shall be the unit production manager, first assistant director and key second assistant director, and each of such names on the card or crawl shall be of the same size and style of type. If you wish to give your unit production manager the screen credit of production manager, it must be with the prior approval of the DGA.

NOTE: The DGA requires that you submit your tentative screen credits to them for approval of "compliance with credit provisions." The above is a brief synopsis of their credit provisions. Check the DGA basic agreement for a complete list of their credit guidelines.

Screen Actors Guild (SAG)

Performers—Theatrical Motion Pictures

Producer agrees that a cast of characters on at least one card will be placed at the end of each theatrical feature motion picture, naming the performer and the role portrayed. All credits on this card shall be in the same size and style of type, with the arrangement, number and selection of performers listed to be at the sole discretion of the producer. In all feature motion pictures with a cast of fifty or less, all performers shall receive credit. In all other feature motion pictures, not less than fifty shall be listed in the cast of characters required at the end of each feature motion picture in connection with theatrical exhibition, excluding performers identified elsewhere in the picture. Stunt performers need not be identified by role.

Performers—Television Motion Pictures

As for theatrical motion pictures, there should be at least one card at the end of each television motion picture naming the performer and role portrayed. Any performer identified by name and role elsewhere in the picture, or any performer playing a major continuing role and identified by name elsewhere in the picture, need not be listed in the cast of characters at the end of the picture.

NOTE: When two lead actors of equal renown star in the same film, their main title screen credits are often placed side by side. In an effort to remain impartial, the position of the credits in the main title of the film are often switched for the paid ads.

Writers Guild of America (WGA)

Writers—Theatrical Motion Pictures

Credit for the screenplay authorship of a feature-length photoplay shall be on a single card and read, *Screenplay by*. When the screenplay is based on a story and no other source material, the screen credit shall read, *Story by*. When the

screenplay is based on source material, the credit shall read, *From a Story by* or *Based on a Story by*. Screen credit on photoplays in which one or more writers has written both the story and the screenplay shall be worded, *Written by*; and screen credit for a screenplay will not be shared by more than two writers. Writing credits as finally determined shall appear on a card immediately preceding the card for the director. No other credit, except source material credit, may appear on the writer's card. Credit for screenplay writer shall be in the same style and size of type as that used for the individual producer or director, whichever is larger.

Writers—Television

Credit shall be given on the screen for the authorship of stories and teleplays, and shall be worded, *Teleplay by*, or *Story by* (based on a story with no source material), or *Written by* (for story and teleplay). Screen credit for teleplay will not be shared by more than two writers. Writing credit, including source material credit, may appear on a separate card or cards immediately following the title card of a particular episode, or immediately prior to or following immediately after the director's credit.

NOTE: Check your Writers Guild Basic Agreement for requirements relating to the submission of Tentative Screen Credits.

Miscellaneous Local Craft Unions

Director of Photography

Credit shall be given on a separate card adjacent to the group of cards for the writer, producer and director, in whichever order such cards appear in such grouping.

Film Editor

Credit shall read, *Edited by*, or *Editor*, and such credit shall be on a separate card in a prominent place (it is generally placed adjacent to the art director credit). This credit is given only to the editor who edits the material for content, continuity, and narration concept.

Art Director

Credit shall be on a separate card adjacent to the director of photography credit and read *Art Director* or *Art Directors*. If the latter is used and joint credit is given, the names shall be joined by the word "and." If you wish to give production designer or production designed by credit, prior permission must be obtained from the local union.

Costume Designer

While this credit is not mandatory, it may only be given to a member of the Costume Designers Guild. If given, it should read, *Costumes Designed by*, *Costumes by* or *Costume Designer*.

Set Decorator

There is no regulation calling for the specific placement of this credit other than in a prominent place. It usually appears directly after or shortly after the DGA (UPM, first assistant director, and second assistant director) card in the end credits.

Makeup Artist/Hair Stylist

The requirement of this local is just that both the makeup artist and the hair stylist receive screen credit. Placement is at the discretion of the producer.

Main Titles and End Credits

Main titles refer to the screen credits that appear before the picture begins, and end credits appear following the picture. If your film is for television, check the network's delivery requirements as to their format, which will indicate the amount of time you have to run screen credits. The number of screen credits a producer is able to give (other than those that are contractual or required by the unions and guilds) is greatly influenced by the limited amount of time allowed to run them. Producers of theatrical features, on the other hand, do not share the same time restrictions and have the freedom to give credit to whomever they wish. Before your screen credits are finalized, have them checked over and approved by your legal and/or business affairs office and your production executive.

SAMPLE MAIN TITLES
Movie For Television

Card #1	(Show Title)	
Card #2	Starring	
	_____	(lead cast)
Card #3	_____	(cast)
Card #4	_____	(cast)
Card #5	_____	(cast)
Card #6	And	
	_____	(last cast member as listed and the "And/as"
	as _____	makes this a "special" credit)
Card #7	Editor (or "Edited by")	_____
Card #8	Production Designer	_____
Card #9	Director of Photography	_____
Card #10	Executive Producer	_____
Card #11	Produced by	_____
Card #12	Written by	_____
Card #13	Directed by	_____

SAMPLE MAIN TITLES
Theatrical Motion Picture

Card #1	_____	Presents	(name of producing entity)
Card #2	A _____	Production	(name of producer or producer's company)
Card #3	A _____	Film (name of director)	
Card #4	_____	(lead cast)	
Card #5	_____	(2nd lead)	
Card #6	(Picture Title)		
Card #7	Starring		
	_____	(cast)	
Card #8	_____	(cast)	
Card #9	_____	(all cast members	
	_____	may not receive	
	_____	single card credit)	
Card #10	And		(the last cast credit is almost as special as the first and is accentuated by the "And...")
	_____		
Card #11	Casting by	_____	
Card #12	Music by	_____	
Card #13	Costume Designer	_____	(this credit is sometimes listed in the end credits)
Card #14	Associate Producer	_____	
Card #15	Edited by	_____	
Card #16	Production Designer	_____	
Card #17	Director of Photography	_____	
Card #18	Executive Producer	_____	
Card #19	Produced by	_____	
Card #20	Screenplay by	_____	
Card #21	Directed by	_____	

SAMPLE END CREDITS
Theatrical Motion Picture

Note: Depending upon your contractual obligations, the amount of time you have to run the end credits, and the producer's "discretion" as to the exact placement of names, your credits will look different. The following sample end credits are merely simplified abbreviated examples of what yours might look like.

Card #1   Associate Producer   _____

Card #2   Co-Starring

                 _____ as   _____

                 _____ as   _____

                 _____ as   _____

                 _____ as   _____

Card #3   Featuring

                 _____ as   _____

                 _____ as   _____

                 _____ as   _____

                 _____ as   _____

                 _____ as

                 _____ as

Card #4   _____   Unit Production Manager

            _____   First Assistant Director

            _____   Key Second Assistant Director

            _____   Second Second Assistant Director

Card #5   _____   Art Director

            _____   Set Decorator

            _____   Chief Lighting Technician

            _____   Property Master

            _____   Script Supervisor

            _____   Sound Mixer

Card #6   _____   Camera Operator

            _____   Costume Supervisor

            _____   Key Grip

            _____   Location Manager

            _____   Production Coordinator

Card #7   _____   Post Production Supervisor

            _____   Assistant Film Editor

            _____   Music Editor

            _____   Sound Editor

            _____   Negative Cutter

            _____   Rerecording Mixer

Card #8   _____   Department Head Make-up Artist

            _____   Head Hair Stylist

            _____   Special Make-up Effects

            _____   Production Accountant

            _____   Transportation Coordinator

            _____   Extra Casting

Card #9   Catering by   _____

            Color by   _____

            Titles & Opticals by   _____

            Lenses & Camera Equipment by   _____

            Rerecorded at   _____

Card #10   Copyright © 19XX by   _____

            All Rights Reserved

            Music Copyright © 19XX by

            All Rights Reserved   _____

                                         I.A.T.S.E. bug (if applicable)

Card #11   (Production Company Logo)

SAMPLE END CREDITS
Movie for Television

Note: These credits would probably run on a "crawl"; and again, remember, this is just an example.

CAST OF CHARACTERS

_____	as	_____
_____	as	_____
_____	as	_____
_____	as	_____

_____	Unit Production Manager
_____	First Assistant Director
_____	Key Second Assistant Director
_____	Second Second Assistant Director
_____	Second Unit Director
_____	Choreographer
_____	Art Director
_____	Set Decorator
_____	Costume Supervisor
_____	Men's Costumer
_____	Women's Costumer
_____	Camera Operator
_____	Steadicam Operator
_____	First Assistant Cameraman
_____	Second Assistant Cameraman
_____	Script Supervisor
_____	Sound Mixer
_____	Boom Operator
_____	Utility Sound Technician
_____	Additional Film Editor
_____	Assistant Film Editor
_____	Apprentice Editor
_____	Supervising Sound Editor
_____	ADR Editor
_____	Sound Editor
_____	Music Editor
_____	Chief Lighting Technician
_____	Assistant Chief Lighting Technician
_____	Lighting Technicians
_____	Key Grip
_____	Second Company Grip (Best Boy-Grip)
_____	Dolly Grip
_____	Grips
_____	Set Designer
_____	Property Master
_____	Assistant Property Master
_____	Lead Person
_____	Set Dressers
_____	Art Department Coordinator

SAMPLE END CREDITS—cont'd
Movie for Television

_____	Department Head Make-up Artist
_____	Make-up Artist
_____	Head Hair Stylist
_____	Hair Stylist
_____	Construction Coordinator
_____	Construction Foreman
_____	Stand-by Painter
_____	Special Effects Coordinator
_____	Stunt Coordinator
_____	Location Manager
_____	Production Coordinator
_____	Assistant Production Coordinator
_____	Production Accountant
_____	Assistant Production Accountant
_____	Unit Publicist
_____	Still Photographer
_____	Set Medic
_____	Extras Casting
_____	Craft Services
_____	Transportation Coordinator
_____	Transportation Captain
_____	Drivers
_____	Assistant to (Producer)
_____	Assistant to (Director)
_____	Production Assistants
_____	Musical Supervision
_____	Music Coordinator
_____	Rerecording Mixers
_____	Music Engineer
_____	Music Scoring Mixer
_____	Orchestrations
_____	Orchestra Conductor
_____	Negative Cutter
_____	Color Timer
_____	Titles & Opticals

(SECOND UNIT CREW)

_____	First Assistant Director
_____	Key Second Assistant Director
_____	Camera Operator
_____	Script Supervisor

(STUNTS BY)

_____	_____
_____	_____
_____	_____
_____	_____
_____	_____

(MUSIC CREDITS)

"Song Title" _____
Written by _____
Performed by _____
Courtesy of _____ Records

SAMPLE END CREDITS—cont'd
Movie for Television

THIS FILM WAS SHOT ON LOCATION IN _____

_____

THE PRODUCERS WISH TO THANK

_____
_____
_____
_____
_____

Color by _____
Lenses & Cameras by _____
Rerecorded at _____

Dolby Stereo (R) (logo)

MPAA (logo)   I.A.T.S.E. (bug)

Copyright © 19XX by _____
All Rights Reserved

The events, characters, and firms depicted in this photoplay are fictitious, any similarity to actual events or firms, is purely coincidental.

Ownership of this motion picture is protected by copyright and other applicable laws, and any unauthorized duplication, distribution or exhibition of this motion picture could result in criminal prosecution as well as civil liability.

A (Name of Producing Entity) Production

Distributed by_____
(Company Logo)

STANDARD DELIVERY REQUIREMENTS

Delivery requirements are those elements that must be turned over to the distributor of your picture at the completion of post production. The sooner you get a list of delivery requirements from your distributor, the sooner you can start assembling the necessary elements.

The following is a list of some standard delivery requirements. You may not be asked for everything on this list, or you may be asked for something that is not here, but the specifications will be similar, as these are fairly standard requirements. Your distributor will let you know the quantity needed of each element requested.

- Composite Answer Print or 35mm Release Print: A complete first-class composite 35mm positive print of the picture, fully color-corrected, with complete main and end titles and composite sound track.
- Negative: The complete 35mm picture negative and the optical sound negative in perfect synchronization with the picture negative cut and assembled to conform in all respects to the work print.
- Interpositive (IP): A fine grain positive print of the picture made from the cut negative and used to make a duplicate (dupe) negative.
- Duplicate Negative (Internegative): A second-generation negative made from the interpositive for the purpose of striking additional release prints.
- Low-Contrast (Low-Con) Print: A positive print of the picture made from the dupe negative on special low-contrast film stock for the purpose of transferring the picture to videotape.
- Digital Videotape: A high-definition D-5 full-frame or letterbox video master of the picture and NTSC and PAL digital Betacam and NTSC VHS copies. A D1 NTSC one-inch videotape format of the picture transferred from the low-contrast print. The one-inch videotape is used to make additional videotapes (dubs) of the picture.
- Original Sound Recording: Complete, original 1/4-inch master magnetic recording of the sound track of the picture (original production sound).
- Magnetic Master Composite Mix: A magnetic 1/4-inch or 35mm master composite recording or original digital audio master of the complete sound track of the picture conforming in all respects to the answer print.
- Magnetic Music Master: A magnetic 1/4-inch track of the original music score for the picture.
- Textless Background: A clear background interpositive and dupe negative of all scenes, including main and end titles, which would normally have lettering superimposed over them (used to make foreign-language prints).
- Work Print: The edited work picture and all corresponding dialogue, music and sound effects work tracks.
- Three-Stripe Magnetic Master: A complete dubbed and re-recorded 35mm magnetic master of the sound track of the picture composed of separate dialogue, music and sound effects tracks (three-stripe), or a six-track or eight-track stereo magnetic master or CD-ROM master.
- English Language Sound Track: A 35mm magnetic print master of the complete English-language sound track in synchronization with the original cut picture negative, suitable for the manufacture of optical sound track negatives and digital stereo master, if applicable.
- Music and Effects (M&E) Track: A 35mm sound track of the dubbed music and sound effects (each on separate channels) for purposes of looping dialogue into foreign language versions of the picture.
- Sound System License: A copy of the Producer's Licensing Agreement (if applicable) for a specific sound system used in the dubbing (final mix) of the picture (i.e., Dolby, Sony, etc.).
- Television and/or Airline Version: The negative and positive print(s) or a D2 video master, and sound tracks for all alternate scenes and/or takes, cover shots, looped dialogue lines and other material that can be used in place of all scenes containing nudity, violence and objectionable language in the picture for the purpose of conforming to *rating*, television or airline requirements.
- Foreign Language Version: The negative, positive print(s) and sound tracks for any alternate scenes and/or takes, cover shots, etc. that may contain nudity, violence or language that were shot for the purpose of foreign distribution.
- Information Pertaining to Foreign Dubbing: Copies of dubbing and subtitling restrictions

relating to the replacement of actors' voices, including the dubbing of dialogue in a language other than that in which the picture was originally recorded.

- Outs and Trims: The negative and positive prints of all outtakes, trims, second takes, tests, sound effects tracks, dialogue tracks and music tracks made in connection with the picture, which may be used to manufacture trailers and for purposes of exhibiting and exploiting the picture.
- Access Letters: Letters sent by the producer to the lab(s) and/or any storage facility where elements of the picture (not already delivered to the distributor) are being stored that give the distributor access to these elements. The distributor will require copies of all access letters in addition to the name(s) and location(s) of the facilities where all undelivered elements are being stored and a detailed inventory of the elements being kept at each location.
- Stills: Original black-and-white and color negatives, black-and-white contact proof sheets, still photographs and color transparencies taken in connection with the picture.
- Publicity Material: All publicity and advertising material that may have been prepared in connection with the picture, including press books; posters; biographies of individual producer(s), director(s), writer(s) and featured players; production notes and interviews.
- Continuity Script: A script containing the exact dialogue and action continuity of the completed picture.
- Screenplay: The final screenplay or shooting script, the script supervisor's lined script and notes and the film editor's notes and code books.
- Synopsis: A brief synopsis of the story of the picture.
- Music Cue Sheets: Copies of the music cue sheets of the picture and any other materials that contain music. The music cue sheets are to include: (1) the title of the musical compositions and sound recordings, if applicable; (2) names of the composers and their performing rights society affiliation; (3) names of the recording artists; (4) the nature, extent, and exact timing of the uses made of each musical composition in the picture; (5) the name and address of the owner of the copy-right of each musical composition and sound recording and (6) the name and address of the publisher and company that controls the sound recording.
- Song Lyrics: Copies of all song lyrics (if applicable) for closed captioning.
- Composer's Score: The entire musical score used by the composer and/or conductor, together with all original music, manuscripts, instrumental and vocal parts and other music prepared in connection with the picture.
- Trailers: If a trailer is made by the licensor or any third party, delivery of all same elements may be required.
- Proof of Copyright Ownership: Copies of the producer's registration, claim to copyright in the picture and the screenplay upon which the picture is based; and, when available, copies of the Certificate of Registration.
- Contracts: Copies of all licenses, contracts, releases, clearances, assignments and/or other written permissions from the proper parties for the use of any musical, literary, dramatic and other materials of whatever nature (including logos, trademarks, art work, brand names, etc.) used in the production of the picture (including but not limited to all employment contracts with actors, directors, producers, writers and composers).
- M.P.A.A. Rating: A paid rating certificate from the Code and Rating Administration of America, Inc., and a production code number.
- Unions and Guilds: A letter stating the names of all American and foreign union and guild members who rendered services on the picture. Copies of SAG's "Final Cast Report," a list of DGA and WGA members, along with main and end title credits, signed and approved by DGA and WGA representatives.
- Screen Credits: A complete list of the final main and end titles of the picture, and the names of all persons to whom the producer is contractually obligated to accord credit in any paid advertising, publicity, or exploitation of the picture.
- Final Cast and Crew Lists
- Final Cost Report
- Proof of Errors and Omissions Insurance
- A certificate of insurance evidencing Producer's Errors and Omissions policy covering the picture and adding the distributor as an additional named insured.

- Television residuals: A statement containing the following information for purposes of determining television residual payments: (1) date principal photography commenced; (2) name and address (and loanout information if applicable) of each writer, director, actor, unit production manager, first and key second assistant directors and any other personnel entitled to residuals, together with the following information concerning each: (1) Social Security number; (2) W-4 classification (marital status and number of dependents claimed); (3) length of employment of SAG personnel; (4) a copy of Notice of Tentative Writing Credits and (5) a list of all DGA personnel employed on the picture.
- Ownership
- A certified statement containing the name and address of each participant in net profits to whom the distributor must account and make payment.

CHAPTER TWENTY-FOUR

Industry Survival Tips

Learning how to do your job, being bright and being talented, are only half the battle in establishing an industry career. The other half will hinge upon your ability to make valuable contacts, build a strong network and successfully sell yourself. It is essential to have the right attitude, temperament and personality—to be willing to play the game and do what it takes not only to succeed, but to survive. The competition is enormous, and for every opening, the line of people vying for that job is a mile long. Being able to get those jobs is just as important to your success in the business as are all your other skills and abilities.

Unless you are fortunate enough to land in the exact right place at the right time, find the perfect mentor, count on nepotism, afford to start your own production company, possess needed skills that few others can provide or are just lucky—finding jobs and staying employed takes a great deal of continuous effort.

We need all the help we can get—rookies and veterans alike. Hopefully, this chapter will provide you with some useful tips and insights into both entering and surviving in the film industry.

GETTING WORK

Unlike many other businesses, relatively few people are hired by one studio or production company and remain there until it's time to retire. Studio positions are typically limited in duration as top management teams come and go (their staffs along with them), and salaries are generally too high for many independents to retain full-time production personnel unless they're in production. Staff jobs within the industry do exist, but the majority of film-related work is freelance. And freelance means that every time the job or show you are working on is over, you are back out looking for a new job or show. Unfortunately, no matter what positions we hold when we are working, our secondary occupation is that of perpetually having to look for future work.

Looking for work is uncomfortable, and doing so often takes us outside of our comfort zone. Selling yourself is scary, and trying to set up meetings with busy, important people who don't even know you exist can be terrifying. But everyone does it, and it's an accepted industry reality. When I get anxious about an impending meeting, I remember an interview I once saw Anthony Hopkins give on a television show. When asked by an acting student how he did something that was incredibly difficult (I can't even remember what the something was), he said, "Just do it! Be bold, and mighty forces will come to your aid!" So venture outside of your comfort zone and go for it! It's not going to happen if you don't. It's okay to be nervous, and the more you're out there meeting people and interviewing, the easier and less terrifying it becomes.

Here is how one begins the search process:

- People you meet are going to ask you what you want to do. Your goal can change every week, but know what you want to do now—at this moment.
- Find your market. Do your homework to discover who's out there doing the type of work or projects you would like to be involved with, then target the companies or producers you would like to work for.
- Think about your personal qualities, what makes you special and what it is that will

make you stand out above the others. Individuals are judged on much more than their past industry-related experience, especially when it comes to entry-level positions. During an interview, you will make an impression if you can express a sense of who you are by conveying past experiences and accomplishments. You may have done something exceptional or interesting that has nothing whatsoever to do with the film industry but says a lot about you, the person. Prospective employers are also drawn to individuals they can relate to. They are looking for a connection, a shared work ethic or attitude. So don't worry about your lack of experience—focus on your special abilities and talents and find ways to convey a sense of who you are.

- Develop your "pitch"—a brief summary of the type of person you are, what you're passionate about, what your special strengths and skills are, your previous experience and the type of job you are seeking.
- Contact anyone you know (including friends of friends) whose recommendations could help you get your foot into doors you might not otherwise have access to. Find out if they would be willing to make a call on your behalf, write you a letter of recommendation or let you use their names.
- Work on a concise, professional-looking cover letter and resume. Make sure to run both through spell check; make sure the name of the person you are addressing the letter to is spelled correctly and also verify the person's proper title (call that person's office if you're not sure). Then start sending the resumes out.
- Follow up with a phone call a few days after sending your resume. Ask for the assistant of the person you would like to meet. Using a brief version of your pitch, let the assistant know who you are and why you are calling. Confirm that your resume arrived and solicit their help in setting up a brief meeting with the boss. If a meeting cannot be arranged at that time, ask permission to check in every couple of weeks. Be charming and be appreciative.

Here are some more job-hunting tips:

- NETWORK! NETWORK!! NETWORK!!!
- If you have a varied background, prepare more than one version of your resume, so that each accentuates a different area of your experience. Submit the resume that best matches the qualifications a prospective employer is looking for.
- If you have gone to film school or have taken related classes or seminars, include your professors and teachers in your network. Use them as references, solicit their advice and ask for introductions to their contacts.
- In addition to teachers, ask friends and acquaintances to introduce you to, or help you to get meetings with, their contacts—people you cannot get in to see on your own.
- Consider asking someone you admire who has succeeded in the field you wish to work in, to become your mentor. People who would never think of offering to become mentors often say "yes" when asked directly. Mentors are special people who take an interest in your career and help in any way they can by way of guidance and/or introductions to others whom you would never be able to meet on your own.
- Regularly check the trade papers and industry websites for information regarding shows in development or in prep that you can submit resumes to.
- Join any organization or group you are eligible to join (e.g., Women in Film) that would enable you to network with other people who do what you do and with people who might be in a position to hire you. Also consider getting involved with industry-supported charities.
- Send notes and make calls to contacts and acquaintances, letting them know you are available and asking them to let you know if they hear of anything you might be right for.
- When calling the offices of prospective employers, remain persistently charming and charmingly persistent. The person on the other end of the phone may try to brush you off or may be rude, but do not respond in kind. Remain polite and upbeat.
- Some people drop off resumes in person, hoping to introduce themselves while there. This only works if the person you want to meet is in at the time and is available to see you.
- Follow up all meetings and interviews with a note thanking the person you met for his or her time. Consider writing your note on a unique-looking notecard. If it's special enough, it might not get thrown away. And if left out, it will be a constant and subtle reminder of who you are.
- It is also fitting to send a thank-you note to an assistant or secretary who has been particu-

larly nice or helpful to you on the phone. Think of these people as gatekeepers, because they are often the ones who will get you in to meet the potential employers you have been trying to connect with.

- There are some job referral services for certain categories of jobs. Check your industry reference books for information on these services.
- Also listed in the reference books are employment agencies that specialize in the placement of production assistants, receptionists, secretaries and sundry "assistants to."
- Find out if you are eligible to apply for the Assistant Directors Training Program. If you can pass their exam and are selected for the program, it is an excellent way to get a start in the business.
- Keep up your contacts by staying in touch, even when you are not looking for work. Send notes, make lunch dates and just call to say hello every so often.
- Remain friendly and helpful to others. You never know who may be in a position to help or recommend you at a later time.
- Make sure you have an answering machine and, if at all possible, a pager. If people can't reach you on a spur-of-the-moment basis, you might lose a job.
- An essential key to job hunting is the ability to remain upbeat, persistent and patient. You will undoubtedly be faced with a certain amount of rejection and will run into your share of rude people. Develop a thick skin. Don't take it personally, and don't get discouraged.

You finally have some meetings lined up. Here are some interviewing tips:

- Come to the meeting well groomed. The recommended dress is nice-casual (not too corporate) and stylish. Women—don't overdo the makeup.
- Make sure you are on time (if not a little early).
- Shake hands, sit as close to the person interviewing you as possible and make direct eye contact.
- Have some idea of what you're going to say. (Write it out ahead of time, read it again and rehearse your delivery.)
- Don't immediately launch into your pitch— start with something personal directed toward the person you are meeting. You

might mention how much you admire this person's previous work (showing him or her you did your homework) or how pleased you are to be having this meeting.

- Being charming and having a sense of humor is good. If you're not interesting, you're going to lose the interviewer's attention quickly.
- If you are nervous, it's okay to say you're nervous.
- Linda Buzzell, author of *How to Make It in Hollywood* (HarperPerennial, a division of HarperCollins Publishers), insists that the two deadliest sins you can commit during an interview are being DULL and appearing DESPERATE.
- Another kiss of death would be walking in with an insecure, meek attitude that screams, *you-wouldn't-want-to-hire-me, would-you?*
- Make sure to mention the person who recommended you.
- Be sincere.
- Ask questions. Don't do all the talking.
- Without sounding desperate, let your prospective employer know how much you would like this job, and given the opportunity, what a terrific job you would do.
- About halfway through the interview, you might ask, "Are you learning what you need to know about me?"
- At the conclusion of the interview you might ask, "Am I the kind of person you're looking for?"; or, if this is just a general meeting, "Am I the kind of person you would hire?"
- Ask those you meet with if they would mind referring you to others and ask for their guidance. Whether they hire you or not at that particular time, turn this into an opportunity to secure new contacts (make them part of your *network*).

If you aren't having much luck landing a job, another option you might want to consider is working as an intern (for the experience in lieu of a salary). It may not sound terribly appealing, but if you can afford to do so, it is one of the very best ways to get your foot in a door. Find a person or company you want to work for, or a specific show you want to work on, and volunteer your services. Make yourself useful, work hard, learn as much as you can while you're there and show everyone how terrific you are. You may be able to exchange your time for free lunches, mileage money and a screen credit on the film. Chances are good that you will be officially hired as soon as there is an opening, or will be hired on the company's next show. If nothing else, you have made some new contacts, gained some needed experience and have a show to add to your resume.

PAYING YOUR DUES

Several years ago, while working at my second job in the industry, I found myself exasperated and complaining to a co-worker. I was spending a great deal of time every day running errands for my boss—getting her coffee, getting her lunch, going to the bank for her, etc. I was bright, had some previous experience and felt that these tasks were a tremendous waste of my time and abilities. My friend just looked at me and asked, "Are you ready to make the big decisions and negotiate the deals?" I had to admit I wasn't, to which he replied, "There are only two of you working in that office. If one of you has to make the deals and one of you has to get the coffee, and you're not ready to make the deals yet—where does that leave you?" What a revelation! Until I was ready, I would have to be the one to get the coffee.

It is perfectly natural to complete film school and/or get your feet wet on a film or two and feel you are ready to start moving up. It doesn't always happen that way, so be prepared to pay your dues. Give yourself time to learn, to learn how to learn more, to network and to gain experience. With your first job comes the good news that you have a job in your chosen field. The bad news is that you are starting at the bottom of the proverbial ladder and will typically be given the most menial tasks for the lowest salary.

The trick is to be the very best production assistant, runner, apprentice or secretary that ever existed. Short of being totally abused and terribly exploited, don't whine or groan when asked to do something you don't want to do. Accept tasks willingly. No one is asking you to do anything just to make your life miserable. If it has to be done and falls within your sphere of responsibility, you don't have much choice. Do not complain. Everyone is busy, and no one wants to hear it. Be a pleasure to have around; be a team player and if you have any extra time, volunteer to help others with their work. Everyone will agree that you are wonderful, and they will all want you to work on their next picture and the next one after that.

Use your time at the bottom to start absorbing information, read whatever you can get your hands on, ask questions when it's appropriate to do so and make an effort to learn a little about everyone else's job. Get a good sense of how a set is run, who does what, what goes on in the production office and how the entire picture-making process works. The exposure will not only allow you to find the one area of filmmaking that really excites you, but it will give you a good foundation for becoming a production coordinator, production manager or producer later on.

Once you get your first job or two, remember that your best source of future employment will come from working hard and developing a good reputation on your current job. When the time is right, start asking to take on tasks above and beyond your normal responsibilities. Let the people you work with know what you would ultimately like to do, and ask for their advice and help. Build lasting relationships with co-workers, learn as much as you can, every step of the way and keep your ears open for opportunities.

DEVELOPING THE RIGHT ATTITUDE & NECESSARY PEOPLE SKILLS

Here are some basic principles that should serve you well:

- Understand that you may not be able to take step after sequential step up the ladder of success. For most of us, it's often one step up and then one or two steps down before you can continue your ascent. Be patient!
- You don't have to know everything—you just have to know where to find everything you need to know. You'll be okay if you do your research, anticipate needs and prepare for various possibilities.
- Avoid phrases like "I don't know" and "I can't." When you've reached a dead-end and can't go any further with a task you've been given, ask for help or advice, find different resources and know there is an answer out there somewhere. If you are absolutely, positively convinced something you've been asked to do can't be done, offer alternatives or a compromise. Try to make it work.
- No one is perfect. Give yourself permission to make mistakes, own up to your mistakes, learn from them and get on with it.
- A sense of humor will take you a long way.
- Don't lie. It will come back to bite you in the butt.

- If you are positive and enthusiastic about your job, you will attract people who will want to work with you again and will want to have you around.
- Production is a team effort—share information and don't feel threatened. The better the team or department, the better you look, and the more you learn.
- Stay calm when all around you are bouncing off walls.
- Don't scream or be rude! Be diplomatic and professional.
- Be accessible.
- If you think you might lose your temper, excuse yourself, take a short break and pull yourself together. Don't fall apart in front of others.
- When dealing with nasty people and short tempers, don't take it personally. Try to understand the pressure they're under, and let them know you're there to support them. If you find yourself in an intolerable situation, you will have to decide if it's worth the experience, credit or paycheck. Sometimes it is, and sometimes it's better to leave. Differences with difficult people or clashes in personality will not generally affect future employment opportunities; and nothing is worth an inordinate amount of stress or making yourself ill over insufferable working conditions.
- When you do work with someone you genuinely like and admire, let them know how much you appreciate them and how much you would like to work with them again. Stay in touch.
- Don't declare an emergency unless it truly is one.
- Don't get so caught up with small details that you lose site of the big picture. Spending too much time weighing the pros and cons of every issue may prevent you from being able to make necessary spur-of-the-moment decisions when unexpected circumstances arise. If you get too caught up in minutiae, you'll lose both valuable time and money.
- Stay healthy and don't forget to take care of yourself.
- Make time (even if it's limited) for the other things in your life that are important to you. It's easy to lose sight of priorities.
- Understand you are not your job. Whether your title sounds important or not, you as an individual are important and have a lot to offer. If you are not being treated with respect,

don't let it prevent you from having a good sense of yourself and your contribution.
- Realize that there are going to be days when you go home at night feeling totally beaten up and stomped on. Be reassured that it does get better.
- Don't ever forget the phrase—IT'S ONLY A MOVIE!

ONCE YOU'VE GOT YOUR FOOT IN THE DOOR, HOW DO YOU LEARN WHAT YOU DON'T ALREADY KNOW?

We all start a new job hoping to learn from the people we'll be working for. Unfortunately, however, even those with the best of intentions may be too busy to teach you much. If you want to learn more, be better at your job and move up faster—take an active role in your own continuing education.

- Again, do not hesitate to ask questions and seek advice.
- Keep up with changing technologies and be aware of new production-related computer software.
- Take notes on things happening around you that you want to remember for future reference.
- On your current show, if you can spare the time, ask to sit in on an occasional meeting.
- Find a bookstore that specializes in industry-related books or one that has a good film section. Start collecting books that will assist you in your work. Purchase industry reference books (e.g., *LA 411* and *New York Production Guide*).
- Get used to reading the trades (*Daily Variety* and *Hollywood Reporter*). If you cannot afford yearly subscriptions, pick up a couple issues each week from a local newsstand.
- Subscribe to other industry-related publications (e.g., *On Production*).
- Regularly check out industry-related websites.
- Obtain union and guild contracts or books that summarize the contracts, and familiarize yourself with basic union and guild rates and regulations. Get to know union and guild representatives.
- Collect production manuals from previous employers, or make copies of manuals your

friends may have from other studios and production companies. Each one has useful information that the other ones do not.

- Talk to representatives from the equipment houses your company has accounts with. Ask questions and, if possible, make arrangements to stop by when it's convenient. Someone should be available to show you the different types of equipment and to explain how the equipment is used. Keep copies of updated equipment catalogs for reference.
- Ask for a tour of the lab your company uses.
- Sign up for production-related classes and seminars.
- Go to annually held production-related conventions, such as ShowBiz Expo and Location Expo. Pick up and keep information on equipment, production services, location services, etc.
- Stay in touch and network with others who work in the same general field as you. It could be through a union, guild, industry-related organization or just a group of friends and acquaintances. Exchange information, share tips on solving common problems, discuss changing industry trends and help each other make new contacts and find new jobs.

In closing, I would like to say that in spite of the many obstacles and the tremendous amount of competition those of us in this business are continuously up against, I am convinced that the recipe for success is this:

1 great attitude

1 large network

plenty of hard work

vast amounts of energy

an abundance of determination

a willingness to start at the bottom

the desire to learn

the patience to get there

1 thick skin

liberal amounts of schmoozing

the time and effort to keep up contacts

1 sense of confidence

1 sense of humor

generous dashes of passion and excitement

GOOD LUCK!

Tear-Out Blank Forms

REQUEST FOR ☐ PICKUP ☐ DELIVERY

SHOW_____ DATE_____

REQUESTED BY_____

ITEM(S) TO BE PICKED-UP/DELIVERED_____

_____

_____

_____

_____

PICK-UP FROM/DELIVER TO (INDIVIDUAL)_____

(COMPANY) _____ PHONE#_____

ADDRESS _____

_____

DIRECTIONS (if needed)_____

_____

_____

_____

_____

PICKUP/DELIVER BY:

☐ _____ (A.M.) (P.M.)   ☐ REFERENCE P.O.#_____
☐ AS SOON AS POSSIBLE   ☐ CHECK REQUIRED FOR PICKUP
☐ TODAY, NO SPECIFIC TIME   ☐ SEE RECEPTIONIST
☐ NO RUSH -- WHENEVER YOU CAN

COMMENTS/SPECIAL INSTRUCTIONS_____

_____

_____

_____

DATE & TIME OF PICKUP/DELIVERY_____

ITEM(S) DELIVERED TO (PRINT NAME)_____

RECEIVED BY (SIGNATURE)_____

© ELH   (ALL PICK-UP & DELIVERY SLIPS ARE TO BE KEPT ON FILE IN THE PRODUCTION OFFICE)

INTERN NOTIFICATION

PRODUCTION COMPANY_____

SHOW_____DATE_____

INTERN'S NAME_____

SOCIAL SECURITY NO._____

ADDRESS_____

_____

HOME PHONE#_____PAGER#_____

HOME FAX#_____MOBILE PHONE#_____

WORK CAPACITY_____

DEPARTMENT_____SUPERVISOR_____

TO WORK AT THE FOLLOWING LOCAITON(S)   IN THE FOLLOWING STATE(S)

_____   _____

_____   _____

_____   _____

DATES OF SERVICE: FROM_____ TO_____

TO WORK _____Days Per Week _____Hrs. Per Day

☐ PAID INTERNSHIP @ $_____ ☐ per hour ☐ per day ☐ per week

☐ UNPAID INTERNSHIP

☐ SCHOOL CREDIT   College/University_____

                    Phone#_____

                    Contact_____

COMPANY TO PROVIDE: ☐ LUNCH - CATERED ON SET OR $____ MAX. OFF SET

                              ☐ MILEAGE REIMBURSEMENT @ _____¢ PER MILE
                                  (DOES NOT INCLUDE DISTANCE TO & FROM REPORT-TO LOCATION)

                              ☐ REIMBURSEMENT OF GAS RECEIPTS

                              ☐ HOTEL ACCOMMODATIONS (IF SO, INTERNS MAY SHARE ROOMS)

                              ☐ OTHER_____

AGREED TO_____
          Intern's Signature

APPROVED BY_____

© ELH

DAILY OFFICE TO DO LIST

CHECK OFF ITEMS AS THEY ARE COMPLETED   DATE _____

IN THE MORNING

FIRST PERSON IN

- [ ] Stop on your way in to buy craft service food (donuts, bagels, fruit, juice, etc.)
- [ ] Check with front gate (or Security) to see if any packages had been dropped off during the night
- [ ] Inform Security you are in (if applicable)
- [ ] Put the coffee and hot water on, set up craft service area, replenish bottled water supply if needed
- [ ] Turn on heat or air conditioning, open windows, unlock doors, turn on lights
- [ ] Check for messages on voice mail, write out and distribute
- [ ] Check for faxes, make copies and distribute
- [ ] Call weather service for today's weather report

LATER IN THE MORNING (DUTIES ASSIGNED BY PROD. COORDINATOR)

- [ ] Finish copying and distributing incoming faxes/messages
- [ ] Copy, file and distribute daily paperwork sent in from set
- [ ] Check office supply area to determine what needs to be replenished/ordered
- [ ] Make sure there is an ample supply of Fed-Ex® envelopes and waybills, mailing supplies and postage
- [ ] Check craft service area to determine what needs to be replenished/ordered
- [ ] Check departmental wall envelopes to determine who did not retrieve yesterday's messages or vital paperwork
  Locate those individuals, relay messages and arrange for pick up or delivery of the paperwork
- [ ] Work out schedule of daily runs with the production coordinator or assistant coordinator

DAILY

- [ ] Make sure there is an ample supply of the latest complete script (with all changes)
- [ ] Make sure there is an ample supply of current schedules, crew lists, maps, script change pages, etc.
- [ ] Monitor the supply of fax cover sheets and other forms used daily. Replenish as needed.
- [ ] Distribute incoming mail
- [ ] File contents of "To File" box
- [ ] Track down and relay important messages to those who may not be in the office
- [ ] Check updated weather report
- [ ] Keep photocopy and kitchen (craft service) areas neat
- [ ] Help with clean-up after lunch
- [ ] Check to see if additional runs need to be made during the day
- [ ] Continually check fax machines for incoming faxes
- [ ] Check area surrounding offices for loose trash and/or cigarette butts. Clean as necessary
- [ ] Take all outgoing mail to post office by 4:30 p.m.
- [ ] Make sure over-night delivery packages are dropped off before scheduled deadline
- [ ] Monitor food and water supplies
- [ ] Monitor paper supplies (white legal and letter and 3-holed white, blue, pink, etc.)
- [ ] If you run out of things to do, **ASK** what you can do to help

AT NIGHT

- [ ] Call sheet distribution
- [ ] Tomorrow's weather report
- [ ] Make sure all copiers, fax machines and printers are fully stocked with paper
- [ ] Clean kitchen area, including: counters, dirty dishes, sink, coffee pots, cutting boards, knives, etc.
- [ ] Close and seal all opened food containers, store in ziplock bags and/or in refrigerator
- [ ] Clean photocopy and fax areas, restack and reorganize paper
- [ ] On nights cleaning service is not due, collect and bag trash and close dumpsters
- [ ] Straighten bullpen areas and replenish forms
- [ ] Prepare sides for the next day

LAST PERSON OUT

- [ ] Close and lock windows, turn off heat or air conditioning
- [ ] Turn off lights
- [ ] Activate voice mail/answering machine
- [ ] Close and lock doors
- [ ] Call Security to let them know you are last man out

FRIDAYS

- [ ] Mail approved Exhibit G's to SAG
- [ ] Mail certificates of insurance (not previously mailed) to insurance company
- [ ] Throw out old food from refrigerator
- [ ] Wash out refrigerator
- [ ] Prepare a list of who will be working over the weekend for Security

REMEMBER... KEEP A NOTEPAD and PEN WITH YOU AT ALL TIMES, TAKE NOTES, AND IF YOU HAVE A QUESTION -- ASK.

INSTRUCTIONS
PLEASE READ ALL INSTRUCTIONS CAREFULLY BEFORE COMPLETING THIS FORM.

Anti-Discrimination Notice. It is illegal to discriminate against any individual (other than an alien not authorized to work in the U.S.) in hiring, discharging, or recruiting or referring for a fee because of that individual's national origin or citizenship status. It is illegal to discriminate against work eligible individuals. Employers **CANNOT** specify which document(s) they will accept from an employee. The refusal to hire an individual because of a future expiration date may also constitute illegal discrimination.

Section 1 - Employee. All employees, citizens and noncitizens, hired after November 6, 1986, must complete Section 1 of this form at the time of hire, which is the actual beginning of employment. **The employer is responsible for ensuring that Section 1 is timely and properly completed.**

Preparer/Translator Certification The Preparer/Translator Certification must be completed if Section 1 is prepared by a person other than the employee. A preparer/translator may be used only when the employee is unable to complete Section 1 on his/her own. However, the employee must still sign Section 1.

Section 2 - Employer. For the purpose of completing this form, the term "employer" includes those recruiters and referrers for a fee who are agricultural associations, agricultural employers or farm labor contractors.

Employers must complete Section 2 by examining evidence of identity and employment eligibility within three (3) business days of the date employment begins. If employees are authorized to work, but are unable to present the required document(s) within three business days, they must present a receipt for the application of the document(s) within three business days and the actual document(s) within ninety (90) days. However, if employers hire individuals for a duration of less than three business days, Section 2 must be completed at the time employment begins. **Employers must record: 1)** document title; **2)** issuing authority; **3)** document number, **4)** expiration date, if any; and **5)** the date employment begins. Employers must sign and date the certification. Employees must present original documents. Employers may, but are not required to, photocopy the document(s) presented. These photocopies may only be used for the verification process and must be retained with the I-9. **However, employers are still responsible for completing the I-9.**

Section 3 - Updating and Reverification. Employers must complete Section 3 when updating and/or reverifying the I-9. Employers must reverify employment eligibility of their employees on or before the expiration date recorded in Section 1. Employers **CANNOT** specify which document(s) they will accept from an employee.

- If an employee's name has changed at the time this form is being updated/ reverified, complete Block A.

- If an employee is rehired within three (3) years of the date this form was originally completed and the employee is still eligible to be employed on the same basis as previously indicated on this form (updating), complete Block B and the signature block.

- If an employee is rehired within three (3) years of the date this form was originally completed and the employee's work authorization has expired **or** if a current employee's work authorization is about to expire (reverification), complete Block B and:
  - examine any document that reflects that the employee is authorized to work in the U.S. (see List A **or** C),
  - record the document title, document number and expiration date (if any) in Block C, and complete the signature block.

Photocopying and Retaining Form I-9A blank I-9 may be reproduced, provided both sides are copied. The Instructions must be available to all employees completing this form. Employers must retain completed I-9s for three (3) years after the date of hire or one (1) year after the date employment ends, whichever is later.

For more detailed information, you may refer to the INS Handbook for Employers, (Form M-274). You may obtain the handbook at your local INS office.

Privacy Act Notice. The authority for collecting this information is the Immigration Reform and Control Act of 1986, Pub. L. 99-603 (8 USC 1324a).

This information is for employers to verify the eligibility of individuals for employment to preclude the unlawful hiring, or recruiting or referring for a fee, of aliens who are not authorized to work in the United States.

This information will be used by employers as a record of their basis for determining eligibility of an employee to work in the United States. The form will be kept by the employer and made available for inspection by officials of the U.S. Immigration and Naturalization Service, the Department of Labor and the Office of Special Counsel for Immigration Related Unfair Employment Practices.

Submission of the information required in this form is voluntary. However, an individual may not begin employment unless this form is completed, since employers are subject to civil or criminal penalties if they do not comply with the Immigration Reform and Control Act of 1986.

Reporting Burden. We try to create forms and instructions that are accurate, can be easily understood and which impose the least possible burden on you to provide us with information. Often this is difficult because some immigration laws are very complex. Accordingly, the reporting burden for this collection of information is computed as follows: **1)** learning about this form, 5 minutes; **2)** completing the form, 5 minutes; and **3)** assembling and filing (recordkeeping) the form, 5 minutes, for an average of 15 minutes per response. If you have comments regarding the accuracy of this burden estimate, or suggestions for making this form simpler, you can write to the Immigration and Naturalization Service, HQPDI, 425 I Street, N.W., Room 4307r, Washington, DC 20536. OMB No. 1115-0136.

EMPLOYERS MUST RETAIN COMPLETED FORM I-9
PLEASE DO NOT MAIL COMPLETED FORM I-9 TO INS

Form I-9 (Rev. 11-21-91)N

Please read instructions carefully before completing this form. The instructions must be available during completion of this form. ANTI-DISCRIMINATION NOTICE: It is illegal to discriminate against work eligible individuals. Employers CANNOT specify which document(s) they will accept from an employee. The refusal to hire an individual because of a future expiration date may also constitute illegal discrimination.

Section 1. Employee Information and Verification.To be completed and signed by employee at the time employment begins.

Print Name: Last	First	Middle Initial	Maiden Name

Address (Street Name and Number)	Apt. #	Date of Birth (month/day/year)

City	State	Zip Code	Social Security #

I am aware that federal law provides for imprisonment and/or fines for false statements or use of false documents in connection with the completion of this form.

I attest, under penalty of perjury, that I am (check one of the following):
- [ ] A citizen or national of the United States
- [ ] A Lawful Permanent Resident (Alien # A_____
- [ ] An alien authorized to work until ___/___/___
  (Alien # or Admission #) _____

Employee's Signature	Date (month/day/year)

Preparer and/or Translator Certification. *(To be completed and signed if Section 1 is prepared by a person other than the employee.) I attest, under penalty of perjury, that I have assisted in the completion of this form and that to the best of my knowledge the information is true and correct.*

Preparer's/Translator's Signature	Print Name

Address (Street Name and Number, City, State, Zip Code)	Date (month/day/year)

Section 2. Employer Review and Verification.To be completed and signed by employer. Examine one document from List A OR examine one document from List B and one from List C, as listed on the reverse of this form, and record the title, number and expiration date, if any, of the document(s)

List A	OR	List B	AND	List C

Document title:_____

Issuing authority: _____

Document #: _____

Expiration Date (if any): ___/___/___

Document #: _____

Expiration Date (if any): ___/___/___

CERTIFICATION - I attest, under penalty of perjury, that I have examined the document(s) presented by the above-named employee, that the above-listed document(s) appear to be genuine and to relate to the employee named, that the employee began employment on(month/day/year) ___/___/___ and that to the best of my knowledge the employee is eligible to work in the United States. (State employment agencies may omit the date the employee began employment.)

Signature of Employer or Authorized Representative	Print Name	Title

Business or Organization Name	Address (Street Name and Number, City, State, Zip Code)	Date (month/day/year)

Section 3. Updating and Reverification To be completed and signed by employer.

A. New Name (if applicable)	B. Date of rehire (month/day/year) (if applicable)

C. If employee's previous grant of work authorization has expired, provide the information below for the document that establishes current employment eligibility.

Document Title:_____ Document #: _____ Expiration Date (if any): ___/___/___

I attest, under penalty of perjury, that to the best of my knowledge, this employee is eligible to work in the United States, and if the employee presented document(s), the document(s) I have examined appear to be genuine and to relate to the individual.

Signature of Employer or Authorized Representative	Date (month/day/year)

LISTS OF ACCEPTABLE DOCUMENTS

LIST A	LIST B	LIST C
Documents that Establish Both Identity and Employment Eligibility	**OR** **Documents that Establish Identity** **AND**	**Documents that Establish Employment Eligibility**

LIST A

Documents that Establish Both Identity and Employment Eligibility

1. U.S. Passport (unexpired or expired)

2. Certificate of U.S. Citizenship (*INS Form N-560 or N-561*)

3. Certificate of Naturalization (*INS Form N-550 or N-570*)

4. Unexpired foreign passport, with *I-551 stamp or* attached *INS Form I-94* indicating unexpired employment authorization

5. Alien Registration Receipt Card with photograph (*INS Form I-151 or I-551*)

6. Unexpired Temporary Card (*INS Form I-688*)

7. Unexpired Employment Authorization Card (*INS Form I-688A*)

8. Unexpired Reentry Permit (*INS Form I-327*)

9. Unexpired Refugee Travel Document (*INS Form I-571*)

10. Unexpired Employment Authorization Document issued by the INS which contains a photograph (*INS Form I-688B*)

OR

LIST B

Documents that Establish Identity

1. Driver's license or ID card issued by a state or outlying possession of the United States provided it contains a photograph or information such as name, date of birth, sex, height, eye color and address

2. ID card issued by federal, state or local government agencies or entities, provided it contains a photograph or information such as name, date of birth, sex, height, eye color and address

3. School ID card with a photograph

4. Voter's registration card

5. U.S. Military card or draft record

6. Military dependent's ID card

7. U.S. Coast Guard Merchant Mariner Card

8. Native American tribal document

9. Driver's license issued by a Canadian government authority

For persons under age 18 who are unable to present a document listed above:

10. School record or report card

11. Clinic, doctor or hospital record

12. Day-care or nursery school record

AND

LIST C

Documents that Establish Employment Eligibility

1. U.S. social security card issued by the Social Security Administration (*other than a card stating it is not valid for employment*)

2. Certification of Birth Abroad issued by the Department of State (*Form FS-545 or Form DS-1350*)

3. Original or certified copy of a birth certificate issued by a state, county, municipal authority or outlying possession of the United States bearing an official seal

4. Native American tribal document

5. U.S. Citizen ID Card (*INS Form I-197*)

6. ID Card for use of Resident Citizen in the United States (*INS Form I-179*)

7. Unexpired employment authorization document issued by the INS (*other then those listed under List A*)

Illustrations of many of these documents appear in Part 8 of the Handbook for Employers (M-274)

Form I-9 (Rev. 11-21-91)N Page 3

LOANOUT AGREEMENT

Film: _____

Prod. Co.: _____

Address: _____

_____ Date: _____

This agreement is between _____ ("Producer") and

_____ ("Company") for the services of _____

_____ ("Employee"), in the position of _____.

Company warrants that it is a bona fide Corporation, incorporated in the State of _____ on _____, 20___. Federal ID# _____, and as a condition precedent to Company's receipt of any payment hereunder, will present a Certificate of Incorporation to Producer evidencing corporate status.

Company and Employee warrant that Employee is under exclusive contract to Company, and that Company has the right to loan Employee's services to Producer as herein provided. Company understands that the lending nature of this agreement prohibits Producer from remitting any compensation for Employee's services, rentals, living allowances, etc. due hereunder to the Employee. By countersigning this agreement, Employee agrees to be bound hereby and agrees to render the services provided herein, to look solely to Company for compensation for all monies due hereunder, and to indemnify Producer against liability for withholding and payroll taxes applicable hereto.

If Company maintains a workers' compensation insurance policy under which Employee is currently covered, Company will present a copy of documentation evidencing such coverage. Otherwise, notwithstanding the lending nature of this agreement, the parties acknowledge that an employment relationship exists between Producer and Employee whereby Producer or Producer's designated Employer of Record is Employee's special employer under this agreement and Company is Employee's general employer (as such terms are understood for purposes of workers' compensation statutes). The parties acknowledge that their rights and the limitations on their liability pursuant to this agreement shall be no different than those rights and limitations which would be applicable under the existing workers' compensation statues had Employee rendered services directly for Producer as Producer's general employee. Producer will pay, or will cause Producer's designated Employer of Record to pay, any pension, health and welfare payments required to be made by applicable guild collective bargaining agreements by reason of Employee's services hereunder.

If there is any inconsistency between this agreement and the terms of any applicable guild collective bargaining agreements, then: the terms of such collective bargaining agreements shall control; this agreement shall be deemed modified to the minimum extent necessary to resolve the conflict; and this agreement as thus modified shall remain in full force and effect. Producer shall be entitled to the maximum benefits permitted to Producer under any such collective bargaining agreements for the minimum payments required, except as may be otherwise specifically provided in this agreement.

Producer's remedies and rights contained in this agreement shall be cumulative and the exercise of any remedy or right shall not be in limitation of any other remedy or right. In the event of any failure or omission by Producer constituting a breach of Producer's obligations under this agreement, Company's and Employee's sole remedy (if any) shall be an action at law for damages, and neither Company nor Employee shall have any right to rescission and/or injunctive and/or other equitable relief.

This agreement may not be altered, modified, changed, rescinded or terminated in any way except by an instrument in writing signed by the parties hereto.

PRODUCER   COMPANY:

By_____   By_____

                                            EMPLOYEE:

                                            By_____

BOX/EQUIPMENT RENTAL INVENTORY

PRODUCTION COMPANY _____

SHOW _____ PROD # _____

EMPLOYEE _____ POSITION _____

ADDRESS _____ SOC.SEC. # _____

_____ PHONE # _____

LOAN OUT COMPANY _____ FED. I.D. # _____

RENTAL RATE $ _____ PER ☐ DAY ☐ WEEK

RENTAL COMMENCES ON _____ ☐ SUBMIT WEEKLY INVOICE
☐ RECORD ON WEEKLY TIME CARD

INVENTORIED ITEMS:

_____

_____

_____

_____

_____

_____

_____

_____

_____

_____

_____

_____

_____

_____

_____

_____

_____

_____

_____

_____

Please note: 1. *Box and equipment rentals are subject to 1099 reporting.*
2. *The Production Company is not responsible for any claims of loss or damage to box/equipment rental items that are not listed on the above inventory.*

EMPLOYEE SIGNATURE _____ DATE _____

APPROVED BY _____ DATE _____

© ELH

VEHICLE RENTAL SHEET

PRODUCTION COMPANY _____ DATE _____

ADDRESS _____

_____

PHONE # _____

The vehicle as described below is to be rented for use on the film tentatively entitled:

_____

TYPE OF VEHICLE _____

YEAR, MAKE, MODEL _____

VIN# _____

LICENSE # _____ VALUE $ _____

SPECIAL EQUIPMENT/ATTACHMENTS _____

_____

RENTAL PRICE $ _____ PER ☐ DAY ☐ WEEK ☐ MONTH

START DATE _____ COMPLETION DATE _____

LEGAL OWNER OF VEHICLE _____

ADDRESS _____

_____

PHONE # _____ FAX # _____

DRIVER OF VEHICLE (if not owner) _____

VEHICLE TO BE USED FOR _____

DEPARTMENT _____

INSURANCE SUPPLIED BY _____

INSURANCE COMPANY _____

POLICY # _____

INSURANCE AGENCY _____

INSURANCE AGENCY REP. _____

PHONE # _____ FAX # _____

CERTIFICATE OF INSURANCE: ☐ TO OWNER   ☐ IN VEHICLE   ☐ ON FILE

COPY OF REGISTRATION IN CAR: ☐ YES   ☐ NO

AGREED TO: _____
      (Vehicle Owner)

APPROVED BY: _____ TITLE: _____

© ELH

PURCHASE ORDER

DATE _____   P.O.# _____

SHOW _____   PROD# _____

COMPANY _____

ADDRESS _____   PHONE# _____

_____   FAX# _____

VENDOR _____   PHONE# _____

ADDRESS _____   FAX# _____

_____   CONTACT _____

VENDOR SOC. SEC. # OR FEDERAL ID#_____   CORPORATION: ☐ YES ☐ NO

☐ PURCHASE ☐ RENTAL ☐ SERVICE (Indicate if amount being charged is per show-day-week- or -month)

DESCRIPTION	CODING	AMOUNT

SET #S: _____   INCL. TAX IF APPLICABLE _____

IF TOTAL COST CANNOT BE DETERMINED   TOTAL COST: $ _____
AT THIS DATE, ESTIMATE OF COSTS
WILL NOT EXCEED $ _____

IF P.O. IS FOR A RENTAL, PLEASE INDICATE RENTAL DATES: FROM _____ TO _____

ORDER PLACED BY_____ DEPT _____

APPROVED BY_____   DATE _____

© ELH

PURCHASE ORDER EXTENSION

DATE _____   ORIGINAL P.O.# _____

SHOW _____   PROD# _____

VENDOR _____   PHONE# _____

CONTACT _____   FAX# _____

☐ RENTAL   ☐ SERVICE

DESCRIPTION	CODING	AMOUNT

INCL. TAX IF APPLICABLE _____

TOTAL COST: $ _____

EXTENDED RENTAL DATES: FROM _____ TO _____

P.O. EXTENDED BY _____   DEPT _____

APPROVED BY _____   DATE _____

© ELH

PURCHASE ORDER LOG

SHOW: _____

P.O. #	DATE	VENDOR	P.O. FOR	PRICE	CHECK ONE			DATE RENTAL RETD.	ASSET ✓	DEPARTMENT P.O. ASSIGNED TO
					PURCHASE	RENTAL	SERVICE			

© ELH

CHECK REQUEST

DATE _____   AMOUNT $ _____

SHOW _____   PROD# _____

COMPANY _____

ADDRESS _____   PHONE# _____

_____   FAX# _____

CHECK PAYEE _____   PHONE# _____

ADDRESS _____   FAX# _____

_____   ATTN _____

PAYEE SOC. SEC. # OR FEDERAL ID# _____   CORPORATION: ☐ YES ☐ NO

☐ PURCHASE   ☐ RENTAL   ☐ DEPOSIT   ☐ ADVANCE   ☐ SERVICE   ☐ 1099   ☐ ASSET

DESCRIPTION	CODING	AMOUNT

INCL. TAX IF APPLICABLE _____

CHECK NEEDED: DAY_____ DATE_____

TIME_____ ☐ A.M. ☐ P.M.

☐ WITHIN NORMAL PROCESSING TIME

TOTAL: $ _____

WHEN CHECK IS READY, PLEASE: ☐ MAIL   ☐ HOLD FOR PICKUP   ☐ GIVE TO: _____

CHECK REQUESTED BY_____   DEPT _____

APPROVED BY_____   DATE _____

(INVOICE SUBSTANTIATION MUST FOLLOW THIS REQUEST)

© ELH

PETTY CASH ACCOUNTING

NAME _____ DATE _____ | ENVELOPE# _____ |

PICTURE _____ AMT. RECEIVED $ _____

POSITION _____ DEPT. _____ [ ] CHECK [ ] CASH   CHECK# _____

DATE	RECEIPT NO.	PAID TO	PAID FOR	ACCOUNT	AMOUNT

| UPM: | APPROVED: | | TOTAL RECEIPTS: _____ |
| AUDITED: | ENTERED: | | AMT. ADVANCED: _____ |

PETTY CASH ADVANCE/REIMBURSEMENT	CASH/CHECK RET'D: _____
RECEIVED IN CASH: $ _____ ON: _____	REIMBURSEMENT DUE: _____
SIGNATURE:	

NOTE: Tape receipts to 8-1/2x11 sheets of paper and number each to correspond with numbers listed above. Receipts are to be originals, and each must be dated and clearly indicate what it is for. Circle date, vendor and total amount on each receipt.

© ELH

AMOUNT $ _____   NO. _____

RECEIVED OF PETTY CASH

DATE _____

NAME _____

DEPARTMENT _____

DESCRIPTION _____

_____

_____

_____

☐ PETTY CASH TO BE ACCOUNTED FOR

APPROVED BY   RECEIVED BY

_____   _____

© ELH

INDIVIDUAL PETTY CASH ACCOUNT

NAME _____   DEPT _____

SHOW _____   PROD # _____

FLOAT $ _____

DATE	CHECK#/CASH RECV'D FROM	AMOUNT RECV'D	ACCOUNTED FOR	BALANCE

© ELH

MILEAGE LOG

NAME _____   WEEK ENDING _____

SHOW _____   PROD # _____

DATE	LOCATION		PURPOSE	MILEAGE
	FROM	TO		

TOTAL MILES _____

_____ MILES @ _____ ¢ PER MILE = $ _____

APPROVED BY _____   DATE _____

PD. BY CHECK # _____   DATE _____

© ELH

INVOICE

TO _____   DATE _____

_____

_____

_____

FROM _____

(Address) _____

_____

(Phone #) _____

PAYEE SS# OR FEDERAL ID# _____   1099 ☐

FOR SERVICES RENDERED ON_____   <u>OR</u> WEEK/ENDING_____

DESCRIPTION OF SERVICE/RENTAL/CAR ALLOWANCE	AMOUNT DUE

TOTAL AMOUNT DUE $ _____

EMPLOYEE SIGNATURE_____

APPROVED BY_____

PAID BY CHECK # _____   DATE _____

© ELH

CASH OR SALES RECEIPT   DATE _____   No. _____

RECIPIENT/
SOLD TO   _____

ADDRESS   _____

_____

PHONE #   _____

FOR PURCHASE OF: _____

_____

WRITTEN
AMOUNT _____ $_____

☐ CASH   ☐ 1099   SS # _____

☐ CHECK   FEDERAL ID # _____

ACCOUNT CODING_____

APPROVED BY _____ RECV'D BY _____

© ELH

DAILY COST OVERVIEW

SHOW _____   PROD # _____

DATE _____   DAY # _____

START DATE _____

SCHEDULED FINISH DATE _____

REVISED FINISH DATE _____

	PER CALL SHEET	SHOT	AHEAD/BEHIND
# OF SCENES			
# OF PAGES			

	AS BUDGETED AND/OR SCHEDULED	ACTUAL	COST (OVER)/UNDER
CAST OVERTIME	_____	_____	_____
COMPANY SHOOTING HOURS	_____	_____	_____
MEAL PENALTY	_____	_____	_____
EXTRAS & STAND-INS	_____	_____	_____
CATERING	_____	_____	_____
RAW STOCK	_____	_____	_____
UNANTICIPATED EXPENSES:			
_____	_____	_____	_____
_____	_____	_____	_____
_____	_____	_____	_____
_____	_____	_____	_____
_____	_____	_____	_____

TOTAL FOR TODAY _____

PREVIOUS TOTAL _____

GRAND TOTAL _____

PREPARED BY _____   APPROVED BY _____

© ELH

CREW DATA SHEET

NAME	POSITION	SOC. SEC. # FEDERAL ID#	ACCNTG. CODE	START DATE	DEAL MEMO	NO. OF WRAP DAYS	WRAP DATE	OVER/UNDER

© ELH

TIME CARDS/INVOICES
WEEKLY CHECK-OFF LIST

NAME	POSITION	SOC. SEC. # FED. I.D. #	TIME CARDS AND/OR INVOICES TURNED IN EACH WEEK							
			W/E	W/E	W/E	W/E	W/E	W/E	W/E	W/E

© ELH

THE CHECK'S IN THE MAIL

CHECK MADE OUT TO	CHECK NUMBER	CHECK DATED	ADDRESS SENT TO	DATE MAILED	PAY-ROLL	INV.

BREAKDOWN SHEET

SHOW: _____

LOCATION: _____

[ ] STAGE [ ] LOCAL LOCATION [ ] DISTANT LOCATION

BREAKDOWN PAGE NO: _____

PRODUCTION NO: _____

DATE: _____

SCENE #S	[ ] INT. [ ] EXT.	DESCRIPTION	STORY DAY: [ ] DAY [ ] NIGHT [ ] DAWN [ ] DUSK	NO. OF PAGES
				TOTAL PGS:

NO.	CAST	ATMOSPHERE	PROPS-SET DRESSING
		CAMERA	WARDROBE
		SPECIAL EFFECTS	VISUAL EFFECTS
	STAND-INS	TRANSPORTATION-PIC. VEHICLES	SOUND-MUSIC
	STUNTS	ELECTRIC-GRIP-CRANES	SPECIAL EQUIPMENT
	MAKEUP-HAIR	ANIMALS-LIVESTOCK-WRANGLERS	OTHER
	SPECIAL MAKE-UP EFFECTS		
			[ ] TEACHER-WELFARE WORKER

DAY-OUT-OF-DAYS

PRODUCTION COMPANY _____

PRODUCTION TITLE _____

EPISODE TITLE _____

PRODUCTION # _____

SCRIPT DATED _____

DATE _____

PRODUCER _____

DIRECTOR _____

UNIT PRODUCTION MGR. _____

FIRST ASST. DIRECTOR _____

NAME	CHARACTER	MONTH →	DAY OF WEEK →	SHOOTING DAYS →										TRAVEL	START	FINISH	WORK	IDLE	TOTAL
1																			
2																			
3																			
4																			
5																			
6																			
7																			
8																			
9																			
10																			
11																			
12																			
13																			
14																			
15																			
16																			
17																			
18																			
19																			
20																			
21																			
22																			
23																			
24																			
25																			
26																			
27																			
28																			
29																			
30																			
31																			

© ELH

ASSET INVENTORY LOG

SHOW: _____

DEPARTMENT: _____

| ITEM(S) | PURCHASED FROM | PURCHASE DATE | PURCHASE PRICE | P.O.# | AT COMPLETION OF PRINCIPAL PHOTOGRAPHY | | | |
					IF PORTION USED, HOW MUCH REMAINS	IF SOLD, FOR HOW MUCH	IF RET'D. TO COMPANY, IN WHAT CONDITION	LOCATION OF ITEM

© ELH

EQUIPMENT RENTAL LOG

ITEM(S)	VENDOR ADDRESS/PHONE/FAX CONTACT	P.O. #	DEPARTMENT ASSIGNED TO	DATE PICKED-UP	LENGTH OF RENTAL	DATE RETURNED	L&D SUBMITTED

© ELH

DATE RECVD. FROM VENDOR	P.O. #	ITEM(S) & MODEL #(S) (INCLUDING ACCESSORIES)	SERIAL #	PHONE #	PRINT NAME	DATE OUT	DATE IN	SIGNATURE	DATE RETD. TO VENDOR

Vendor:

Address:

Phone #:

Contact:

NOTES:

© ELH

WALKIE-TALKIE SIGN-OUT SHEET

DATE RECV'D FROM VENDOR	P.O. #	INDICATE ITEM & MODEL NO. (Walkie-Talkie, Charger, Headset, Bullhorn, Other Accessory, etc.)	SERIAL #	UNIT #	DEPARTMENT ASSIGNED TO	PRINT NAME	DATE OUT	DATE IN	SIGNATURE	DATE RETD. TO VENDOR

NOTES:

Vendor:

Address:

Phone #:

Contact:

© ELH

DISTRIBUTION LOG

NAMES

Document columns:

- SCRIPT & REVISIONS
- BUDGET
- COST REPORTS
- PRE-PROD. SCHEDULE
- SHOOTING SCHED. & ONE-LINER
- DAY-OUT-OF-DAYS
- CONTINUITY BREAKDOWN
- STORYBOARDS
- CREW DEAL MEMOS
- CREW LIST
- CAST & CREW CONTRACTS
- CAST LIST W/O DEALS
- CAST LIST W/DEALS
- CAST PHOTOS
- EXTRAS BREAKDOWN
- VEHICLE BREAKDOWN
- STUNT & EFX. BREAKDOWNS
- CONTACT LIST
- LOCATION AGREEMENTS
- RELEASE FORMS
- PRODUCT PLACEMENT REPORTS
- TRAVEL INFO. & MOVEMENT LISTS
- CALL SHEETS
- PRODUCTION REPORTS
- WRAP REPORTS
- INSUR. & WORKERS COMP CLAIMS
- POST PROD. SCHEDULE
- MUSIC CUE SHEETS
- DELIVERY REQUIREMENTS

TOTAL NO. OF COPIES NEEDED:

© ELH

CREW INFORMATION SHEET

Please fill in the following information completely and return this form to the Production Office. Thank You.

SHOW_____

NAME_____

POSITION_____DEPARTMENT_____

HOME ADDRESS _____

_____

MAILING ADDRESS (If Different)_____

_____

HOME PHONE#_____PAGER#_____

HOME FAX#_____MOBILE PHONE#_____

E-MAIL ADDRESS_____

☐ Check here if you DO NOT want any of the above information on the Crew List

☐ Check here if you just want your pager & mobile numbers on the Crew List

SOCIAL SEC#_____BIRTHDAY (month & day only)_____

LOAN-OUT CO._____FED. ID#_____

START DATE_____UNION_____

EMERGENCY CONTACT_____

RELATIONSHIP_____HOME PHONE#_____

MOBILE PHONE#_____WORK PHONE#_____

TRAVELING PREFERENCES (We will try to accommodate your preferences to be best of our ability)

AIRLINE SEAT (check one)   ☐ Window ☐ Middle ☐ Aisle ☐ Bulkhead ☐ No Preference

AIRLINE MEAL (check one)   ☐ Vegetarian ☐ Non-Dairy ☐ Kosher ☐ No Preference

PLEASE LIST YOUR FREQUENT FLYER ACCOUNT NUMBERS

AIRLINE   ACCNT. NO.

_____   _____

_____   _____

_____   _____

HOTEL ROOM

LOCATION: ☐ Ground Level ☐ In the Back ☐ Near the Front ☐ No Preference

BED STYLE: ☐ King ☐ Queen ☐ 2 Beds   ROOM: ☐ Smoking ☐ Non-Smoking

IF AVAILABLE, I WOULD LIKE THE FOLLOWING IN MY ROOM:

☐ Refrigerator ☐ Microwave ☐ Extra Rollaway ☐ Desk ☐ Modem Line

The above information is solely for Production Office records and will be kept strictly confidential.

© A Stephan A. Marinaccio II form

ACORD™ CERTIFICATE OF LIABILITY INSURANCE

DATE (MM/DD/YY)

PRODUCER

THIS CERTIFICATE IS ISSUED AS A MATTER OF INFORMATION ONLY AND CONFERS NO RIGHTS UPON THE CERTIFICATE HOLDER. THIS CERTIFICATE DOES NOT AMEND, EXTEND OR ALTER THE COVERAGE AFFORDED BY THE POLICIES BELOW.

INSURERS AFFORDING COVERAGE

INSURED

INSURER A:	
INSURER B:	
INSURER C:	
INSURER D:	
INSURER E:	

COVERAGES

THE POLICIES OF INSURANCE LISTED BELOW HAVE BEEN ISSUED TO THE INSURED NAMED ABOVE FOR THE POLICY PERIOD INDICATED. NOTWITHSTANDING ANY REQUIREMENT, TERM OR CONDITION OF ANY CONTRACT OR OTHER DOCUMENT WITH RESPECT TO WHICH THIS CERTIFICATE MAY BE ISSUED OR MAY PERTAIN, THE INSURANCE AFFORDED BY THE POLICIES DESCRIBED HEREIN IS SUBJECT TO ALL THE TERMS, EXCLUSIONS AND CONDITIONS OF SUCH POLICIES. AGGREGATE LIMITS SHOWN MAY HAVE BEEN REDUCED BY PAID CLAIMS.

INSR LTR	TYPE OF INSURANCE	POLICY NUMBER	POLICY EFFECTIVE DATE (MM/DD/YY)	POLICY EXPIRATION DATE (MM/DD/YY)	LIMITS	
	GENERAL LIABILITY				EACH OCCURRENCE	$
	COMMERCIAL GENERAL LIABILITY				FIRE DAMAGE (Any one fire)	$
	CLAIMS MADE ☐ OCCUR				MED EXP (Any one person)	$
					PERSONAL & ADV INJURY	$
					GENERAL AGGREGATE	$
	GEN'L AGGREGATE LIMIT APPLIES PER: ☐ POLICY ☐ PROJECT ☐ LOC				PRODUCTS - COMP/OP AGG	$
	AUTOMOBILE LIABILITY				COMBINED SINGLE LIMIT (Ea accident)	$
	ANY AUTO					
	ALL OWNED AUTOS				BODILY INJURY (Per person)	$
	SCHEDULED AUTOS					
	HIRED AUTOS				BODILY INJURY (Per accident)	$
	NON-OWNED AUTOS					
					PROPERTY DAMAGE (Per accident)	$
	GARAGE LIABILITY				AUTO ONLY - EA ACCIDENT	$
	ANY AUTO				OTHER THAN EA ACC	$
					AUTO ONLY: AGG	$
	EXCESS LIABILITY				EACH OCCURRENCE	$
	☐ OCCUR ☐ CLAIMS MADE				AGGREGATE	$
						$
	DEDUCTIBLE					$
	RETENTION $					$
	WORKERS COMPENSATION AND EMPLOYERS' LIABILITY				WC STATU-TORY LIMITS ☐ OTH-ER ☐	
					E.L. EACH ACCIDENT	$
					E.L. DISEASE - EA EMPLOYEE	$
					E.L. DISEASE - POLICY LIMIT	$
	OTHER					

DESCRIPTION OF OPERATIONS/LOCATIONS/VEHICLES/EXCLUSIONS ADDED BY ENDORSEMENT/SPECIAL PROVISIONS

CERTIFICATE HOLDER	ADDITIONAL INSURED; INSURER LETTER: _____	**CANCELLATION**

SHOULD ANY OF THE ABOVE DESCRIBED POLICIES BE CANCELLED BEFORE THE EXPIRATION DATE THEREOF, THE ISSUING INSURER WILL ENDEAVOR TO MAIL _____ DAYS WRITTEN NOTICE TO THE CERTIFICATE HOLDER NAMED TO THE LEFT, BUT FAILURE TO DO SO SHALL IMPOSE NO OBLIGATION OR LIABILITY OF ANY KIND UPON THE INSURER, ITS AGENTS OR REPRESENTATIVES.

AUTHORIZED REPRESENTATIVE

ACORD 25-S (7/97)   © ACORD CORPORATION 1988

IMPORTANT

If the certificate holder is an ADDITIONAL INSURED, the policy(ies) must be endorsed. A statement on this certificate does not confer rights to the certificate holder in lieu of such endorsement(s).

If SUBROGATION IS WAIVED, subject to the terms and conditions of the policy, certain policies may require an endorsement. A statement on this certificate does not confer rights to the certificate holder in lieu of such endorsement(s).

DISCLAIMER

The Certificate of Insurance on the reverse side of this form does not constitute a contract between the issuing insurer(s), authorized representative or producer, and the certificate holder, nor does it affirmatively or negatively amend, extend or alter the coverage afforded by the policies listed thereon.

ACORD 25-S (7/97)

ACORD™ PROPERTY LOSS NOTICE

DATE (MM/DD/YY)

PRODUCER	PHONE (A/C, No, Ext):		MISCELLANEOUS INFO (Site & location code)	DATE OF LOSS AND TIME	AM	PREVIOUSLY REPORTED
					PM	YES NO

	POLICY TYPE	COMPANY AND POLICY NUMBER	EFFECTIVE DATE	EXPIRATION DATE
	PROP/ HOME	CO:		
		POL:		
CODE: SUB CODE:	FLOOD	CO:		
AGENCY CUSTOMER ID		POL:		
	WIND	CO:		
		POL:		

INSURED

NAME AND ADDRESS

CONTACT

CONTACT INSURED

NAME AND ADDRESS

WHERE TO CONTACT

WHEN TO CONTACT

RESIDENCE PHONE (A/C, No)	BUSINESS PHONE (A/C, No, Ext)	RESIDENCE PHONE (A/C, No)	BUSINESS PHONE (A/C, No, Ext)

LOSS

LOCATION OF LOSS

POLICE OR FIRE DEPT TO WHICH REPORTED

KIND OF LOSS	FIRE	LIGHTNING	FLOOD	OTHER (explain)	PROBABLE AMOUNT ENTIRE LOSS
	THEFT	HAIL	WIND		

DESCRIPTION OF LOSS & DAMAGE (Use reverse side, if necessary)

POLICY INFORMATION

MORTGAGEE

NO MORTGAGEE

HOMEOWNER POLICIES SECTION 1 ONLY (Complete for coverages A, B, C, D & additional coverages. For Homeowners Section II Liability Losses, use ACORD 3.)

A. DWELLING	B. OTHER STRUCTURES	C. PERSONAL PROPERTY	D. LOSS OF USE	DEDUCTIBLES	DESCRIBE ADDITIONAL COVERAGES PROVIDED
					ON

COVERAGE A. EXCLUDES WIND

SUBJECT TO FORMS (Insert form numbers and edition dates, special deductibles)

FIRE, ALLIED LINES & MULTI-PERIL POLICIES (Complete only those items involved in loss)

ITEM	SUBJECT OF INSURANCE	AMOUNT	% COINS	DEDUCTIBLE	COVERAGE AND/OR DESCRIPTION OF PROPERTY INSURED
	BLDG CNTS				
	BLDG CNTS				
	BLDG CNTS				

SUBJECT TO FORMS (Insert form numbers and edition dates, special deductibles)

FLOOD POLICY	BUILDING:	DEDUCTIBLE:	ZONE	PRE FIRM	DIFF IN ELEV	FORM TYPE	GENERAL	CONDO
	CONTENTS:	DEDUCTIBLE:		POST FIRM			DWELLING	

WIND POLICY	BUILDING	DEDUCTIBLE	CONTENTS	ZONE	FORM TYPE	GENERAL	CONDO
						DWELLING	

REMARKS/OTHER INSURANCE (List companies, policy numbers, coverages & policy amounts)

CAT # FICO #	ADJUSTER ASSIGNED		ADJUSTER #	DATE ASSIGNED

REPORTED BY	REPORTED TO	SIGNATURE OF PRODUCER OR INSURED

ACORD 1 (2/95)   NOTE: IMPORTANT STATE INFORMATION ON REVERSE SIDE   © ACORD CORPORATION 1988

Applicable in California

Any person who knowingly presents false or fraudulent claim for the payment of a loss is guilty of a crime and may be subject to fines and confinement in state prison.

Applicable in Florida and Idaho

Any person who Knowingly and with the intent to injure, Defraud, or Deceive any Insurance Company Files a Statement of Claim Containing any False, Incomplete or Misleading information is Guilty of a Felony.*
  * In Florida - Third Degree Felony

Applicable in Indiana

A person who knowingly and with intent to defraud an insurer files a statement of claim containing any false, incomplete, or misleading information commits a felony.

Applicable in Kentucky and New Jersey

Any person who knowingly and with intent to defraud any insurance company or other persons, files a statement of claim containing any materially false information, or conceals for the purpose of misleading, information concerning any fact, material thereto, commits a fraudulent insurance act, which is a crime, subject to criminal prosecution and civil penalties.

Applicable in Michigan

Any person who knowingly and with intent to injure or defraud any insurer submits a claim containing any false, incomplete, or misleading information shall, upon conviction, be subject to imprisonment for up to one year for a misdemeanor conviction or up to ten years for a felony conviction and payment of a fine of up to $5,000.00.

Applicable in Minnesota

A person who files a claim with intent to defraud or helps commit a fraud against an insurer is guilty of a crime.

Applicable in Nevada

Pursuant to NRS 686A.291, any person who knowingly and willfully files a statement of claim that contains any false, incomplete or misleading information concerning a material fact is guilty of a felony.

Applicable in New Hampshire

Any person who, with purpose to injure, defraud or deceive any insurance company, files a statement of claim containing any false, incomplete or misleading information is subject to prosecution and punishment for insurance fraud, as provided in RSA 638:20.

Applicable in New York

Any person who knowingly and with intent to defraud any insurance company or other person files a statement of claim containing any materially false information, or conceals for the purpose of misleading, information concerning any fact material thereto, commits a fraudulent insurance act, which is a crime, and shall also be subject to a civil penalty not to exceed five thousand dollars and the stated value of the claim for each such violation.

Applicable in Ohio

Any person who, with intent to defraud or knowing that he/she is facilitating a fraud against an insurer, submits an application or files a claim containing a false or deceptive statement is guilty of insurance fraud.

Applicable in Oklahoma

WARNING: Any person who knowingly and with intent to injure, defraud or deceive any insurer, makes any claim for the proceeds of an insurance policy containing any false, incomplete or misleading information is guilty of a felony.

Applicable in Pennsylvania

Any person who knowingly and with intent to injure or defraud any insurer files a claim containing any false, incomplete or misleading information shall, upon conviction, be subject to imprisonment for up to seven years and payment of a fine of up to $15,000.

ACORD 1 (2/95)

ACORD™ AUTOMOBILE LOSS NOTICE

DATE (MM/DD/YY)

PRODUCER	PHONE (A/C, No, Ext):	COMPANY		MISCELLANEOUS INFO (Site & location code)	

		POLICY NUMBER		REFERENCE NUMBER	CAT #

CODE:	SUB CODE:	EFFECTIVE DATE	EXPIRATION DATE	DATE OF ACCIDENT AND TIME	AM	PREVIOUSLY REPORTED
AGENCY CUSTOMER ID:					PM	YES	NO

INSURED

	CONTACT	CONTACT INSURED	

NAME AND ADDRESS	NAME AND ADDRESS	WHERE TO CONTACT
		WHEN TO CONTACT

RESIDENCE PHONE (A/C, No)	BUSINESS PHONE (A/C, No, Ext)	RESIDENCE PHONE (A/C, No)	BUSINESS PHONE (A/C, No, Ext)

LOSS

LOCATION OF ACCIDENT (Include city & state)	AUTHORITY CONTACTED:	VIOLATIONS/CITATIONS
	REPORT #:	

DESCRIPTION OF ACCIDENT (Use reverse side, if necessary)

POLICY INFORMATION

BODILY INJURY (Per Person)	BODILY INJURY (Per Accident)	PROPERTY DAMAGE	SINGLE LIMIT	MEDICAL PAYMENT	OTC DEDUCTIBLE	OTHER COVERAGE & DEDUCTIBLES (UM, no-fault, towing, etc)
LOSS PAYEE				COLLISION DED		

UMBRELLA/ EXCESS	UMBRELLA	EXCESS	CARRIER:	LIMITS:	PER CLAIM	PER OCCUR

INSURED VEHICLE

VEH #	YEAR	MAKE:	BODY TYPE:	PLATE NUMBER	STATE
		MODEL:	V.I.N.:		

OWNER'S NAME & ADDRESS	RESIDENCE PHONE (A/C, No):
	BUSINESS PHONE (A/C, No, Ext):
DRIVER'S NAME & ADDRESS (Check if same as owner)	RESIDENCE PHONE (A/C, No):
	BUSINESS PHONE (A/C, No, Ext):

RELATION TO INSURED (Employee, family, etc.)	DATE OF BIRTH	DRIVER'S LICENSE NUMBER	STATE	PURPOSE OF USE	USED WITH PERMISSION?
					YES	NO

DESCRIBE DAMAGE	ESTIMATE AMOUNT	WHERE CAN VEHICLE BE SEEN?	WHEN CAN VEH BE SEEN?	OTHER INSURANCE ON VEHICLE

PROPERTY DAMAGED

DESCRIBE PROPERTY (If auto, year, make, model, plate #)	OTHER VEH/PROP INS?	COMPANY OR AGENCY NAME:
	YES	NO	POLICY #:

OWNER'S NAME & ADDRESS	RESIDENCE PHONE (A/C, No):
	BUSINESS PHONE (A/C, No, Ext):
OTHER DRIVER'S NAME & ADDRESS (Check if same as owner)	RESIDENCE PHONE (A/C, No):
	BUSINESS PHONE (A/C, No, Ext):

DESCRIBE DAMAGE	ESTIMATE AMOUNT	WHERE CAN DAMAGE BE SEEN?

INJURED

NAME & ADDRESS	PHONE (A/C, No)	PED	INS VEH	OTH VEH	AGE	EXTENT OF INJURY

WITNESSES OR PASSENGERS

NAME & ADDRESS	PHONE (A/C, No)	INS VEH	OTH VEH	OTHER (Specify)

REMARKS (Include adjuster assigned)

REPORTED BY	REPORTED TO	SIGNATURE OF PRODUCER OR INSURED

ACORD 2 (2/95) NOTE: IMPORTANT STATE INFORMATION ON REVERSE SIDE © ACORD CORPORATION 1988

Applicable in California

Any person who knowingly presents false or fraudulent claim for the payment of a loss is guilty of a crime and may be subject to fines and confinement in state prison.

Applicable in Florida and Idaho

Any person who Knowingly and with the intent to injure, Defraud, or Deceive any Insurance Company Files a Statement of Claim Containing any False, Incomplete or Misleading information is Guilty of a Felony.*
* In Florida - Third Degree Felony

Applicable in Indiana

A person who knowingly and with intent to defraud an insurer files a statement of claim containing any false, incomplete, or misleading information commits a felony.

Applicable in Kentucky and New Jersey

Any person who knowingly and with intent to defraud any insurance company or other persons, files a statement of claim containing any materially false information, or conceals for the purpose of misleading, information concerning any fact, material thereto, commits a fraudulent insurance act, which is a crime, subject to criminal prosecution and civil penalties.

Applicable in Michigan

Any person who knowingly and with intent to injure or defraud any insurer submits a claim containing any false, incomplete, or misleading information shall, upon conviction, be subject to imprisonment for up to one year for a misdemeanor conviction or up to ten years for a felony conviction and payment of a fine of up to $5,000.00.

Applicable in Minnesota

A person who files a claim with intent to defraud or helps commit a fraud against an insurer is guilty of a crime.

Applicable in Nevada

Pursuant to NRS 686A.291, any person who knowingly and willfully files a statement of claim that contains any false, incomplete or misleading information concerning a material fact is guilty of a felony.

Applicable in New Hampshire

Any person who, with purpose to injure, defraud or deceive any insurance company, files a statement of claim containing any false, incomplete or misleading information is subject to prosecution and punishment for insurance fraud, as provided in RSA 638:20.

Applicable in New York

Any person who knowingly makes or knowingly assists, abets, solicits or conspires with another to make a false report of the theft, destruction, damage or conversion of any motor vehicle to a law enforcement agency, the Department of Motor Vehicles or an insurance company, commits a fraudulent insurance act, which is a crime, and shall also be subject to a civil penalty not to exceed five thousand dollars and the value of the subject motor vehicle or stated claim for each violation.

Applicable in Ohio

Any person who, with intent to defraud or knowing that he/she is facilitating a fraud against an insurer, submits an application or files a claim containing a false or deceptive statement is guilty of insurance fraud.

Applicable in Oklahoma

WARNING: Any person who knowingly and with intent to injure, defraud or deceive any insurer, makes any claim for the proceeds of an insurance policy containing any false, incomplete or misleading information is guilty of a felony.

Applicable in Pennsylvania

Any person who knowingly and with intent to injure or defraud any insurer files a claim containing any false, incomplete or misleading information shall, upon conviction, be subject to imprisonment for up to seven years and payment of a fine of up to $15,000.

ACORD 2 (2/98)

INSURANCE CLAIM WORKSHEET

(THEFT)

STOLEN ☐ EQUIPMENT
☐ WARDROBE
☐ PROPS
☐ SET DRESSING
☐ VEHICLE

PRODUCTION _____

DATE ITEM(S) WERE DISCOVERED MISSING _____

DESCRIPTION OF ITEM(S) STOLEN (Include I.D.#'s If Available) _____
_____
_____
_____
_____
_____
_____

DEPARTMENT USED BY _____
PERSON USED BY _____

WHERE WERE ITEM(S) LAST SEEN _____

WHO DISCOVERED ITEM(S) MISSING _____

ITEM(S) ☐ PURCHASED FOR SHOW—PURCHASE PRICE $ _____
☐ RENTED FOR SHOW
RENTED FROM _____
ADDRESS _____
_____
PHONE# _____
CONTACT _____

VALUE $ _____
RENTAL PRICE $ _____ PER ☐ DAY
☐ WEEK
☐ MONTH

☐ POLICE REPORT ATTACHED
☐ OTHER ATTACHMENTS _____
_____

SUBMITTED TO INSURANCE AGENCY ON _____
ATTENTION _____
CLAIM # _____
INSURANCE COMPANY CLAIMS REP. _____

INSUR. CLAIM WORKSHEET COMPLETED BY _____
DATE _____ TITLE _____

AMOUNT CREDITED TO AGGREGATE DEDUCTIBLE $ _____ DATE _____
REIMBURSEMENT CHECK PAID TO _____
AMOUNT $ _____ DATE _____

© ELH

INSURANCE CLAIM WORKSHEET

DAMAGE TO   ☐ EQUIPMENT
                ☐ WARDROBE
                ☐ PROPS
                ☐ SET DRESSING
                ☐ LOCATION/PROPERTY

PRODUCTION _____

DATE OF OCCURRENCE _____ TIME _____

WHAT WAS DAMAGED _____
_____
_____

LOCATION OF OCCURRENCE _____
_____

HOW DID DAMAGE OCCUR _____
_____
_____
_____
_____

WITNESS _____ POSITION _____
PHONE# _____

DAMAGED ITEM(S)   ☐ PURCHASED FOR SHOW—PURCHASE PRICE $_____
                ☐ RENTED FROM/OWNER _____
                     ADDRESS _____
                                     _____
                       PHONE # _____
                       CONTACT _____

                   RENTAL PRICE $ _____ PER ☐ DAY
                                             ☐ WEEK
                                             ☐ MONTH

VALUE OF DAMAGED ITEM(S) $ _____
ESTIMATE TO REPAIR $ _____
☐ ATTACHMENTS _____
_____

SUBMITTED TO INSURANCE AGENCY ON _____
ATTENTION _____
CLAIM # _____
INSURANCE COMPANY CLAIMS REP. _____

INSURANCE CLAIM WORKSHEET COMPLETED BY _____
DATE _____ TITLE _____

AMOUNT CREDITED TO AGGREGATE DEDUCTIBLE $ _____ DATE _____
REIMBURSEMENT CHECK PAID TO _____
AMOUNT $ _____ DATE _____

© ELH

INSURANCE CLAIM WORKSHEET

☐ CAST
☐ EXTRA EXPENSE
☐ FAULTY STOCK

PRODUCTION _____

DATE OF OCCURRENCE _____ TIME _____

DESCRIPTION OF INCIDENT _____
_____
_____
_____
_____
_____
_____

IF CAST CLAIM, WHICH ARTIST _____

WAS A DOCTOR CALLED IN ☐ YES ☐ NO

NAME OF DOCTOR _____
ADDRESS _____

PHONE # _____

COULD COMPANY SHOOT AROUND INCIDENT ☐ YES ☐ NO
IF YES, FOR HOW LONG _____

HOW MUCH DOWN TIME WAS INCURRED DUE TO THIS INCIDENT _____
_____
_____

AVERAGE DAILY COST $_____

BACKUP TO CLAIM TO INCLUDE _____
_____
_____
_____
_____

SUBMITTED TO INSURANCE AGENCY ON _____
ATTENTION _____
CLAIM # _____
INSURANCE COMPANY CLAIMS REP. _____
INSURANCE AUDITOR _____

INSURANCE CLAIM WORKSHEET COMPLETED BY _____
DATE _____ TITLE _____

AMOUNT CREDITED TO DEDUCTIBLE $_____ DATE _____
REIMBURSEMENT CHECK PAID TO _____
AMOUNT $_____ DATE _____

© ELH

INSURANCE CLAIM WORKSHEET
AUTOMOBILE ACCIDENT

PRODUCTION _____

DATE OF OCCURRENCE _____ TIME _____

LOCATION OF OCCURRENCE _____
_____
_____

HOW DID ACCIDENT OCCUR _____
_____
_____
_____
_____
_____
_____

INSURED VEHICLE (Year, Make, Model) _____
VEHICLE I.D. # _____ LIC. PLATE # _____
OWNER OF VEHICLE _____
ADDRESS _____
PHONE # _____ CONTACT _____

DRIVER _____
POSITION _____
DRIVER'S LIC. # _____ USED W/PERMISSION ☐ YES ☐ NO
ADDRESS _____

PHONE # _____

WHERE CAN CAR BE SEEN _____
WHEN _____

DAMAGE TO CAR _____
_____

ESTIMATE(S) TO REPAIR $_____ $_____

DAMAGE TO OTHER VEHICLE (Year, Make, Model) _____
_____ LIC. PLATE # _____
DRIVER OF OTHER VEHICLE _____
ADDRESS _____

PHONE(S) # _____ # _____

WHERE CAN CAR BE SEEN _____
WHEN _____

DAMAGE TO CAR _____
_____

ESTIMATE(S) TO REPAIR $_____ $_____

© ELH

INJURED _____ _____
ADDRESS _____ _____
PHONE # _____ _____
EXTENT OF INJURY _____ _____
_____ _____
_____ _____

WITNESS(ES) _____ _____
ADDRESS _____ _____

PHONE # _____ _____

☐ POLICE REPORT ATTACHED
☐ OTHER ATTACHMENTS _____
_____
_____

SUBMITTED TO INSURANCE AGENCY ON _____
ATTENTION _____
CLAIM # _____
INSURANCE COMPANY CLAIMS REP. _____

INSURANCE CLAIM WORKSHEET COMPLETED BY _____
DATE _____ TITLE _____

INSURANCE ADJUSTER TO SEE INSURED VEHICLE ON _____
TO SEE OTHER VEHICLE ON _____

AMOUNT CREDITED TO DEDUCTIBLE $_____ DATE _____
REIMBURSEMENT CHECK PAID TO _____
AMOUNT $_____ DATE _____
TO _____
AMOUNT $_____ DATE _____

NOTES:_____
_____
_____
_____
_____
_____
_____
_____
_____

© ELH

CALL SHEET

PRODUCTION COMPANY _____   DATE _____

SHOW _____   DIRECTOR _____

SERIES EPISODE_____   PRODUCER _____

PROD # _____ DAY # _____ OUT OF _____   LOCATION _____

IS TODAY A DESIGNATED DAY OFF? ☐ YES ☐ NO   SUNRISE _____ SUNSET _____

CREW CALL _____   ANTICIPATED WEATHER _____

LEAVING CALL_____   ☐ Weather Permitting   ☐ See Attached Map

SHOOTING CALL _____   ☐ Report to Location   ☐ Bus to Location

SET DESCRIPTION	SCENE #	CAST	D/N	PAGES	LOCATION

CAST	PART OF	LEAVE	MAKEUP	SET CALL	REMARKS

ATMOSPHERE & STAND-INS	

NOTE: No forced calls without previous approval of unit production manager or assistant director. All calls subject to change.

ADVANCE SCHEDULE OR CHANGES

Assistant Director _____   Production Manager_____
© ELH

PRODUCTION REQUIREMENT

SHOW:			PROD #:			DATE:		
Production Mgr.			Gaffer			Cameras		
1st Asst. Dir			Best Boy					
2nd Asst. Dir			Lamp Oper.			Dolly		
2nd 2nd Asst. Dir			Lamp Oper.			Crane		
DGA Trainee			Lamp Oper.			Condor		
Script Supervisor			Local 40 Man					
Dialogue Coach						Sound Channel		
Prod. Coordinator			Prod. Designer					
Prod. Sect'y			Art Director			Video		
Prod. Accountant			Asst. Art Dir.					
Asst. Accountant			Set Designer			Radio Mikes		
Location Mgr.			Sketch Artist			Walkie/talkies		
Asst. Location Mgr.								
Teacher/Welfare Worker			Const. Coord.			Dressing Rooms		
Production Assts.			Const. Foreman			Schoolrooms		
			Paint Foreman			Rm. For Parents		
Dir of Photography			Labor Foreman					
Camera Operator			Const. First Aid			Projector		
Camera Operator						Moviola		
SteadyCam Operator			Set Director					
Asst. Cameraman			Lead Person			Air Conditioners		
Asst. Cameraman			Swing Crew			Heaters		
Asst. Cameraman			Swing Crew			Wind Machines		
Still Photographer			Swing Crew					
Cameraman-Process			Drapery					
Projectionist								
			Technical Advisor			**SUPPORT**		
Mixer			Publicist			**PERSONNEL**		**TIME**
Booman			**MEALS**			Policemen		
Cableman			Caterer			Motorcycles		
Playback			Breakfasts			Fireman		
Video Oper.			Wlkg. Breakfasts rdy @			Guard		
			Gallons Coffee			Night Watchman		
Key Grip			Lunches rdy @ Crew @					
2nd Grip			Box Lunches					
Dolly Grip			Second Meal					
Grip								
Grip								
Grip			**DRIVERS**			**VEHICLES**		
			Trans. Coord.			Prod. Van		
Greensman			Trans. Capt.			Camera		
			Driver			Grip		
S/By Painter			Driver			Electric		
Craftservice			Driver			Effects		
First Aid			Driver			Props		
			Driver			Wardrobe		
Spec. Efx			Driver			Makeup		
Spec. Efx			Driver			Set Dressing		
			Driver			Crew Bus		
Propmaster			Driver			Honeywagon		
Asst. Props			Driver			Motorhomes		
Asst. Props			Driver			Station Wagons		
			Driver			Mini-buses		
Costume Designer			Driver			Standby Cars		
Costume Supervisor			Driver			Crew Cabs		
Costumer			Driver			Insert Cars		
Costumer			Driver			Generators		
			Driver			Water Wagon		
Makeup Artist			Driver			Picture Cars		
Makeup Artist			Driver					
Body Makeup								
Hairstylist			Stunt Coord.					
Hairstylist			Wranglers					
			Animal Handlers			Livestock		
Editor						Animals		
Asst. Editor								
Apprentice Editor								

DEPARTMENT			**SPECIAL INSTRUCTIONS**		

DAILY PRODUCTION REPORT

	1st Unit	2nd Unit	Reh.	Test	Travel	Holidays	Change Over	Retakes & Add. Scs.	Total	Schedule	
No. Days Sched										Ahead	
No. Days Actual										Behind	

Title _____ Prod. # _____ Date _____
Producer _____ Director _____
Date Started _____ Scheduled Finish Date _____ Est. Finish Date _____

Sets _____
Location _____
Crew Call _____ Shooting Call _____ First Shot _____ Lunch _____ Til _____
1st Shot After Lunch _____ 2nd Meal _____ Til _____ Camera Wrap _____ Last Man Out _____
Company dismissed at ☐ Studio ☐ Location ☐ Headquarters   Round Trip Mileage _____ Is Today A Designated Day Off? ☐ YES ☐ NO

SCRIPT SCENES AND PAGES			MINUTES		SETUPS		ADDED SCENES			RETAKES	
	SCENES	PAGES								PAGES	SCENES
			Prev.		Prev.		Prev.		Prev.		
			Today		Today		Today		Today		
Script			Total		Total		Total		Total		
Taken Prev.			Scene No.								
Taken Today											
Taken to Date			Added Scenes								
To Be Taken			Retakes				Sound Tracks				

FILM STOCK	FILM USE	GROSS	PRINT	NO GOOD	WASTE	1/4" ROLLS	FILM INVENTORY	
	Prev.						Starting Inv.	
	Today						Additional Rec'd Today	
	To Date						Total	

FILM STOCK	FILM USE	GROSS	PRINT	NO GOOD	WASTE		FILM INVENTORY	
	Prev.						Starting Inv.	
	Today						Additional Rec'd Today	
	To Date						Total	

FILM STOCK	FILM USE	GROSS	PRINT	NO GOOD	WASTE		FILM INVENTORY	
	Prev.						Starting Inv.	
	Today						Additional Rec'd Today	
	To Date						Total	

CAST - WEEKLY & DAY PLAYERS

Worked – W   Rehearsal - R   Finished - F
Started – S   Hold - H   Test - T
Travel - TR

CAST	CHARACTER	W S R TR	H F T	MAKEUP WDBE.	WORKTIME REPORT ON SET	WORKTIME DISMISS ON SET	MEALS OUT	MEALS IN	LEAVE FOR LOC.	ARRIVE ON LOC.	LEAVE LOCA-TION	ARRIVE AT HDQ.	STUNT ADJ.

XX = N.D. BREAKFAST   * = DISMISS TIME INCLUDES 15 MIN. MAKEUP / WARD. REMOVAL
X = NOT PHOTOGRAPHED   S = SCHOOL ONLY

EXTRA TALENT

No.	Rate	1st Call	Set Dismiss	Final Dismiss	Adj.	MPV	No.	Rate	1st Call	Set Dismiss	Final Dismiss	Adj.	MPV

Assistant Director _____ Production Manager _____
© ELH

NO	STAFF & CREW	TIME	NO	STAFF & CREW	TIME	NO	EQUIPMENT
	Production Manager			Gaffer			Cameras
	1st Assistant Director			Best Boy			
	2nd Assistant Director			Lamp Operator			Dolly
	2nd 2nd Assistant Director			Lamp Operator			Crane
	DGA Trainee			Lamp Operator			Condor
	Script Supervisor			Local 40 Man			
	Dialogue Coach						Sound Channel
	Production Coordinator			Production Designer			
	Production Sect'y			Art Director			Video
	Production Accountant			Assistant Art Director			
	Assistant Accountant			Set Designer			Radio Mikes
	Location Manager			Sketch Artist			Walkie-Talkies
	Assistant Location Manager						
	Teacher/Welfare Worker			Construction Coordinator			Dressing Rooms
	Production Assistants			Construction Foreman			Schoolrooms
				Paint Foreman			Room for Parents
	Director of Photography			Labor Foremen			
	Camera Operator			Construction First Aid			Projector
	Camera Operator						Moviola
	SteadyCam Operator			Set Decorator			
	Assistant Cameraman			Lead Person			Air Conditioners
	Assistant Cameraman			Swing Crew			Heaters
	Assistant Cameraman			Swing Crew			Wind Machines
	Still Photographer			Swing Crew			
	Cameraman-Process			Drapery			
	Projectionist						
				Technical Advisor			
	Mixer			Publicist			
	Boomman			**MEALS**			**SUPPORT PERSONNEL**
	Cableman			Caterer			Policemen
	Playback			Breakfasts			Motorcycles
	Video Operator			Walking Breakfasts ready @			Fireman
				Gals. Coffee			Guard
	Key Grip			Lunches ready @ Crew @			Night Watchman
	2nd Grip			Box Lunches			
	Dolly Grip			Second Meal			
	Grip						
	Grip						
	Grip			**DRIVERS**			**VEHICLES**
				Transportation Coordinator			Production Van
	Greensman			Transportation Captain			Camera
				Driver			Grip
	S/By Painter			Driver			Electric
	Craftservice			Driver			Effects
	First Aid			Driver			Props
				Driver			Wardrobe
	Special Effects			Driver			Makeup
	Special Effects			Driver			Set Dressing
				Driver			Crew Bus
	Propmaster			Driver			Honeywagon
	Assistant Props			Driver			Motorhomes
	Assistant Props			Driver			Station Wagons
				Driver			Mini-buses
	Costume Designer			Driver			Standby Cars
	Costume Supervisor			Driver			Crew Cabs
	Costumer			Driver			Insert Cars
	Costumer			Driver			Generators
				Driver			Water Wagon
	Makeup Artist			Driver			Picture Cars
	Makeup Artist			Driver			
	Body Makeup						
	Hairstylist			Stunt Coordinator			
	Hairstylist			Wranglers			
				Animal Handlers			Livestock
	Editor						Animals
	Assistant Editor						
	Apprentice Editor						

COMMENTS—DELAYS (EXPLANATIONS)—CAST, STAFF, AND CREW ABSENCE

_____
_____
_____
_____
_____
_____

© ELH

DAILY WRAP REPORT

SHOW_____ PROD#_____

DAY_____ DATE_____ SHOOT DAY#_____OUT OF_____

LOCATION_____

CREW CALL_____ SHOOTING CALL_____

FIRST SHOT_____

LUNCH_____TO_____ MEAL PENALTY _____

1ST SHOT AFTER LUNCH_____

SECOND MEAL_____TO_____ MEAL PENALTY _____

1ST SHOT AFTER 2ND MEAL_____

CAMERA WRAP_____ LAST OUT_____

OVERTIME_____

SCHEDULED SCENE NUMBER(S) SHOT_____

UNSCHEDULED SCENE NUMBER(S) SHOT_____

SCENES SCHEDULED BUT NOT SHOT_____

PAGES SCHEDULED_____ PAGES SHOT_____

	SCENES	PAGES	MINUTES	SETUPS
PREVIOUS				
TODAY				
TOTAL				

DAY'S WORK COMPLETED?_____

OF DAYS BEHIND_____

OF DAYS AHEAD_____

FILM FOOTAGE

GROSS TODAY_____ GROSS TO DATE_____

PRINT TODAY_____ PRINT TO DATE_____

NO GOOD_____

WASTE_____

SHORT ENDS_____

NOTES:_____
_____
_____
_____
_____
_____
_____

© ELH

RAW STOCK ORDER LOG

DATE	QTY.	ROLL LENGTH	FOOTAGE PER STOCK				P.O. #	TOTAL FOOTAGE ENTIRE ORDER	TOTAL PRICE
			PRICES: 100' roll: $ 400' roll: $ $1,000' roll: $ 52	PRICES: 100' roll: $ 400' roll: $ $1,000' roll: $ 52	PRICES: 100' roll: $ 400' roll: $ $1,000' roll: $ 52	PRICES: 100' roll: $ 400' roll: $ $1,000' roll: $ 52			

Vendor: Order Desk #:   Account #:

Address: Contact: After-Hours #:

Contact's Dir. #:   Pick-up Hours:

© ELH

RAW STOCK INVENTORY

SHOW_____ PROD#_____

WEEK ENDING_____

	52_____	52_____	52_____	52_____

WEEKLY TOTALS

Good (Print)	_____	_____	_____	_____
No Good	_____	_____	_____	_____
Waste	_____	_____	_____	_____
TOTAL EXPOSED**	_____	_____	_____	_____

PRUCHASED

Previously Purchased	_____	_____	_____	_____
Purchased This Week	+_____	_____	_____	_____
TOTAL PURCHASED	_____	_____	_____	_____

USED

Stock Used To Date	_____	_____	_____	_____
Stock Used This Week**	+_____	_____	_____	_____
TOTAL STOCK USED	_____	_____	_____	_____

Total Purchased	_____	_____	_____	_____
Total Used	-_____	_____	_____	_____
Estimated Remaining Stock	_____	_____	_____	_____
Remaining Stock As per Camera Department	_____	_____	_____	_____

RAW STOCK PURCHASES MADE THIS WEEK

P.O.#_____	_____	_____	_____	_____
P.O.#_____	_____	_____	_____	_____
P.O.#_____	_____	_____	_____	_____
P.O.#_____	_____	_____	_____	_____
P.O.#_____	_____	_____	_____	_____
TOTAL:	_____	_____	_____	_____

© ELH

CAMERA DEPARTMENT
DAILY RAW STOCK LOG

SHOW _____   PROD# _____

DATE _____ SHOOT DAY# _____   FILM TYPE _____

MAG#	ROLL	LENGTH	GOOD	NO GOOD	WASTE	TOTAL EXP.	SHORT ENDS

RECEIVED		GOOD	NO GOOD	WASTE	TOTAL EXP.	SHORT ENDS
	TODAY					
	PREVIOUS					
	TO DATE					
	TOTAL EXPOSED			S.E. EXPOSED TODAY		
	TOTAL UNEXPOSED			S.E. TO DATE UNEXPOSED		
	SHORT ENDS TO DATE UNEXPOSED					
	TOTAL UNEXPOSED ON HAND					

SCRIPT SUPERVISIOR'S
DAILY WRAP REPORT

PRODUCTION CO._____ DATE_____

SHOW_____ SHOOT DAY#_____

LOCATION_____

DIRECTOR_____ 1ST AD_____

UPM_____ SCRIPT SUPV'R_____

CREW CALL_____ SHOOTING CALL_____

1ST SHOT_____

LUNCH_____

1ST SHOT AFTER LUNCH_____ CAMERA ROLLS_____

2ND MEAL_____ _____

1ST SHOT AFTER 2ND MEAL_____ SOUND ROLLS_____

LAST SHOT_____ WILD TRACKS_____

CAMERA WRAP_____ RESHOOTS_____

SET DESCRIPTION   SCENES COMPLETED

_____   _____

_____   _____

_____   _____

_____   _____

	SCENES	PAGES	SETUPS	MINUTES
SCRIPT TOTAL				
SHOT TODAY				
PREVIOUSLY SHOT				
TOTAL TO DATE				
TOTAL REMAINING				

NOTES:_____

_____

_____

_____

_____

_____

SCRIPT SUPERVISOR'S
DAILY LOG

SHOW		SHOOT DAY#
DIRECTOR	DAY	DATE
CAMERA 'A'	SCRIPT SUPERVISOR	
CAMERA 'B'	SET	
CREW CALL SHOOTING CALL	FIRST SHOT WEATHER	

CAMERA ROLL	SCENE	TAKE	SOUND	PRINT	TIME	LENS	PAGE CREDIT	SHOT DESCRIPTION

TIME CREDIT: PAGE CREDIT:

CAMERA ROLL	SCENE	TAKE	SOUND	PRINT	TIME	LENS	PAGE CREDIT	SHOT DESCRIPTION

TME CREDIT: PAGE CREDIT:

CAST DEAL MEMO

PRODUCTION COMPANY_____DATE_____

ADDRESS_____PHONE#_____

_____FAX#_____

SHOW_____EPISODE_____

CASTING DIRECTOR_____PROD#_____

CASTING OFFICE PHONE#_____FAX#_____

ARTIST_____SOC. SEC.#_____

ADDRESS_____PHONE#_____

_____MOBILE#_____

ROLE_____START DATE_____

☐ ACTOR	☐ THEATRICAL	☐ DAY PLAYER
☐ STUNT	☐ TELEVISION	☐ 3-DAY PLAYER
☐ SINGER	☐ CABLE	☐ WEEKLY
☐ PILOT	☐ MULTIMEDIA	☐ D/PU - DAILY TO WEEKLY
☐ DANCER	☐ INTERNET	☐ D/PU - DAILY TO DAILY

COMPENSATION $_____Per ☐DAY ☐WEEK ☐SHOW

	NO. OF DAYS - WEEKS	DATES
TRAVEL		
FITTINGS		
REHEARSAL		
PRINCIPAL PHOTOGRAPHY		
ADDITIONAL SHOOT DAYS		
POST PRODUCTION DAYS		

DRESSING ROOM_____

PER DIEM - EXPENSES_____

_____

TRANSPORTATION - TRAVEL_____

_____

_____

HOTEL ACCOMMODATIONS_____

_____

_____

OTHER_____

_____

_____

_____

BILLING_____

_____

_____

☐ PAID ADVERTISING

© ELH

AGENT_____OFFICE#_____

AGENCY_____FAX# _____

ADDRESS_____MOBILE#_____

_____PAGER#_____

MANAGER_____OFFICE#_____

MANAGEMENT CO._____FAX#_____

ADDRESS _____MOBILE#_____

_____PAGER#_____

PUBLICIST_____OFFICE#_____

P.R. FIRM_____FAX# _____

ADDRESS_____MOBILE#_____

_____PAGER#_____

☐ LOANOUT

CORP. NAME_____FED. ID#_____

ADDRESS (If Different From Above)_____

_____

EMPLOYER OF RECORD_____

ADDRESS_____PHONE#_____

_____FAX#_____

APPROVED BY_____

TITLE_____DATE_____

CREW DEAL MEMO

PRODUCTION CO._____ DATE _____

SHOW _____ PROD # _____

NAME _____ SOC.SEC. # _____

ADDRESS _____ PHONE (Home) _____

_____ (Beeper) _____

START DATE _____ (Fax) _____

JOB TITLE _____ ACCOUNT #_____

UNION/GUILD _____ ☐ Exempt ☐ Non-Exempt *(to be paid on hourly basis only)*

RATE (In Town) _____ Per [Hour][Day][Week] for a [5][6]___-day week

(Distant Loc.) _____ Per [Hour][Day][Week] for a [5][6]___-day week

ADDITIONAL DAY(S) PRO-RATED @_____ (th) Of a week

OVERTIME _____ After _____ hours _____ After _____ hours

BOX RENTAL _____ Per Day/Week

EQUIPMENT/VEHICLE RENTAL _____ Per Day/Week

MILEAGE ALLOWANCE _____ Per Day/Week

> NOTE: Box & Equipment rental & mileage allowance are subject to 1099 reporting.—Any equipment rented by the Production Co. from the employee must be listed or inventoried before rental can be paid.

TRAVEL/ACCOMMODATIONS _____

_____

EXPENSES/PER DIEM _____

_____

OTHER _____

_____

☐ LOAN OUT

CORP. NAME _____ FED. ID# _____

ADDRESS (If Different From Above) _____

AGENT _____ AGENCY _____

ADDRESS _____ PHONE # _____

FAX # _____

EMPLOYER OF RECORD _____

ADDRESS _____ PHONE # _____

FAX # _____

IF AWARDED SCREEN CREDIT, HOW WOULD YOU LIKE YOUR NAME TO READ _____

APPROVED BY _____ TITLE _____

ACCEPTED _____ DATE _____

© ELH

WRITER'S DEAL MEMO

PRODUCTION COMPANY _____ DATE _____

ADDRESS _____ PHONE # _____

_____ FAX # _____

SHOW _____ PROD # _____

EPISODE _____

WRITER _____ PHONE # _____

SOCIAL SECURITY # _____ MESSAGES _____

ADDRESS _____ FAX # _____

_____

DATES OF EMPLOYMENT _____

_____

_____

COMPENSATION _____

_____

ADDITIONAL TERMS OF EMPLOYMENT _____

_____

_____

_____

BILLING _____

_____

_____

☐ PAID ADVERTISING

WRITER'S AGENT _____ DIRECT # _____

AGENCY _____ PHONE # _____

ADDRESS _____ FAX # _____

_____

☐ LOAN OUT

CORPORATION NAME _____

ADDRESS _____

_____

FED. I.D. # _____

CONTRACT PREPARED BY _____

DATE SENT OUT _____

APPROVED BY _____

TITLE _____ DATE _____

© ELH

WRITING TEAM DEAL MEMO

PRODUCTION COMPANY _____ DATE _____

ADDRESS _____ PHONE # _____

_____ FAX # _____

SHOW _____ PROD # _____

EPISODE _____

WRITERS _____ _____

SOCIAL SECURITY # _____

ADDRESS _____ _____

_____ _____

PHONE # _____ _____

FAX # _____ _____

DATES OF EMPLOYMENT _____

_____

COMPENSATION _____

_____

ADDITIONAL TERMS OF EMPLOYMENT _____

_____

_____

BILLING _____

_____

☐ PAID ADVERTISING

WRITER'S AGENTS _____

AGENCY _____ _____

ADDRESS _____ _____

_____ _____

PHONE # _____ _____

☐ LOAN OUT ☐ LOAN OUT

CORP. NAME _____ _____

ADDRESS _____ _____

_____ _____

FEDERAL I.D. # _____

CONTRACT PREPARED BY _____

DATE SENT OUT _____

APPROVED BY _____

TITLE _____ DATE _____

© ELH

Directors Guild of America
7920 Sunset Blvd.
Los Angeles, CA 90046
310-289-2000 / FAX 310-289-2029

Director Deal Memorandum - FILM (Theatrical)

This confirms our agreement to employ you to direct the project described as follows:

DIRECTOR INFORMATION

Name:_____ SS#:_____

Loanout (corp. name)_____ Fed. ID#:_____

Address_____ Tel#:_____

_____

Salary: $_____ ☐ per film ☐ per week ☐ per day

Additional Time: $_____ ☐ per week ☐ per day

Start Date: _____ Guaranteed Period: _____ ☐ days ☐ weeks

If this is your first DGA-covered employment, check here: ☐ Yes

If the Director's compensation will be $200,000 or more, is it possible that the Director's services on the project will span two (2) calendar years (i.e. commence in one calendar year and finish in a subsequent calendar year) between commencement of preparation and delivery of answer print? ☐ Yes ☐ No

PROJECT INFORMATION

Picture Title:_____

Project ID# (if applicable):_____

Budget (if under $6,000,000): $_____

Is this Project covered by a Low Budget Sideletter? ☐ Yes ☐ No

Check (if applicable): ☐ Second Unit ☐ Replacement Director ☐ Trailers, Talent Tests & Promos
☐ Additional Photography ☐ Freelance Shorts & Documentaries

The **INDIVIDUAL** having final cutting authority over the film is:_____

Other conditions (incl. credit above min.)_____

_____

POST PRODUCTION INFORMATION

(Please provide all dates currently scheduled or anticipated; any revisions should be submitted as soon as practicable)

Director's Cut Start Date:_____ Director's Cut Finish Date:_____

Date for Special Photography & Processes (if any):_____ Date for Delivery of Answer Print:_____

Date of Theatrical Release:_____

This employment is subject to the provisions of the Directors Guild of America Basic Agreement of 1999

Accepted and Agreed: Signatory Co (print):_____

Employee:_____ By:_____

Date:_____ Date:_____

Directors Guild of America
7920 Sunset Blvd.
Los Angeles, CA 90046
310-289-2000 / FAX 310-289-2029

| **Director Deal Memorandum - FILM (Television)**
Deal Memos must be submitted <u>no later than</u> commencement of services.

This confirms our agreement to employ you to direct the project described as follows:

DIRECTOR INFORMATION

Name:_____ SS#:_____

Loanout (corp. name)_____ Fed. ID#:_____

Address_____ Tel#:_____

_____

Salary: $_____ ☐ per show ☐ per week ☐ per day

Additional Time: $_____ ☐ per show ☐ per week ☐ per day

Start Date (on or about): _____ Guarnateed Period: _____ ☐ days ☐ weeks pro rata: ☐ Yes ☐ No

If this is the employee's first DGA-covered employment, check here (optional):   ☐ Yes

PROJECT INFORMATION

Project Title:_____

Episode/Segment Title (optional):_____ Project ID#_____

Length of Program: ☐ 30 min.   ☐ 90 min.
                      ☐ 60 min.   ☐ 120 min.   ☐ Other:_____

Produced Primarily for: ☐ Network Prime Time_____   ☐ Basic Cable_____
(Please indicate which Network   ☐ Network, other than Prime Time_____   ☐ Syndication
or Service, as applicable)   ☐ Pay TV_____   ☐ Disc/Cassettes

Is This a Pilot?   ☐ Yes   ☐ No

Budget (for Basic Cable "Dramatic" Projects): $_____

+--+
| **Pay Television:** |
| Is the number of subscribers to the pay television service(s) to which the |
| program is licensed at the time of Director's employment $6,000,000 or less? |
| ☐ Yes ☐ No |
| |
| Is the budget $5,000,000 or more?   ☐ Yes ☐ No |
+--+

Check, if applicable (optional): ☐ Second Unit ☐ Segment ☐ Additional Photography ☐ Replacement Director

The **INDIVIDUAL** having final cutting authority over the Project:_____

Other conditions_____

(inc. credit above min.)_____

POST PRODUCTION INFORMATION (For Projects 90 mins. or longer)_____
(All dates <u>must be provided</u> upon commencement of Principal Photography. Prior to commencement of Principal Photography, please provide all dates known or anticipated. Any revisions should be submitted as soon as practicable.)

Director's Cut Start Date:_____ Director's Cut Finish Date:_____

Date for Special Photography & Processes (if any):_____ Date for Delivery of Answer Print:_____

Date of Network Broadcast (if applicable):_____

This employment is subject to the provisions of the Directors Guild of America Basic Agreement of 1999.

Accepted and Agreed: Signatory Co (print):_____

Employee:_____   By:_____

Date:_____   Date:_____

Directors Guild of America
7920 Sunset Blvd.
Los Angeles, CA 90046
310-289-2000 / FAX 310-289-2029

**Unit Production Manager and Assistant Director
Deal Memorandum - FILM**

This confirms our agreement to employ you on the project described as follows:

AD/UPM INFORMATION

Name:_____ SS#:_____

Loanout (corp. name)_____ Fed. ID#:_____

Address_____ Tel#:_____

_____

Category:
☐ Unit Production Manager   ☐ 2nd Second Assistant Director
☐ First Assistant Director   ☐ Additional Second Assistant Director
☐ Key Second Assistant Director   ☐ Technical Coordinator
                         ☐ Assistant Unit Production Manager

Photography: ☐ Principal   ☐ Second Unit   ☐ Both

Salary (dollar amt): $_____ $_____   ☐ per week
                        (Studio)   (Location)   ☐ per day

Production Fee (dollar amt): $_____ $_____
                                (Studio)   (Location)

Start Date: _____   Guaranteed Period:_____

PROJECT INFORMATION

Film or Series Title:_____

Episode/Segment Title:_____

Length of Program: ☐ 30 min.   ☐ 120 min.
                            ☐ 60 min.   ☐ Other_____
                            ☐ 90 min.

Produced Primarily for: ☐ Theatrical   ☐ Syndication
                               ☐ Network   ☐ Disc/Cassettes
                               ☐ Basic Cable   ☐ Pay-TV (service)_____

Other conditions:
(e.g., credit, suspension,   _____
per diem, etc.)   _____

☐ Studio   ☐ Distant Location   ☐ Both   ☐ Check if New York Amendment Applies

This employment is subject to the provisions of the Directors Guild of America Basic Agreement of 1999

Accepted and Agreed: Signatory Co (print):_____

Employee:_____   By:_____

Date:_____   Date:_____

Directors Guild of America
7920 Sunset Blvd.
Los Angeles, CA 90046
310-289-2000 / FAX 310-289-2029

Special Low Budget Project
Unit Production Manager and Assistant Director
Deal Memorandum - FILM

This confirms our agreement to employ you on the project described as follows:

AD/UPM INFORMATION

Name:_____ SS#:_____

Loanout (corp. name)_____ Fed. ID#:_____

Address_____ Tel#:_____

Category: ☐ Unit Production Manager   ☐ 2nd Second Assistant Director
           ☐ First Assistant Director   ☐ Additional Second Assistant Director
           ☐ Key Second Assistant Director

Photography: ☐ Principal   ☐ Second Unit   ☐ Both

Salary (dollar amt): $_____ $_____   ☐ per week
                          (Studio)   (Location)   ☐ per day

Production Fee (dollar amt): $_____ $_____
                              (Studio)   (Location)

Based on a _____day/week   Based on a _____hr./day
           (5/6/7)

Please indcate the following if applicable: _____% is paid when services are performed
                                            _____% is deferred

Start Date: _____   Guaranteed Period:_____

PROJECT INFORMATION

Film Title:_____

Theatrical Film Budget: ☐ Under $1,200,000
                            ☐ Between $1,200,000 and $2,500,000
                            ☐ Between $2,500,000 and $3,500,000
                            ☐ Between $3,500,000 and $6,000,000

Other conditions: _____
(e.g., credit, per diem,
etc.)   _____

            ☐ Studio   ☐ Distant Location   ☐ Both

This employment is subject to the provisions of the Sideletter to Directors Guild of America Basic Agreement of 1999. Guild members shall understand that all conditions of employment not referenced in the Sideletter Agreement are completely negotiable, and should be specifically set forth in this deal memorandum.

Accepted and Agreed: Signatory Co (print):_____

Employee:_____   By:_____

Date:_____   Date:_____

THE PERFORMER MAY NOT WAIVE ANY PROVISION OF THIS CONTRACT WITHOUT THE WRITTEN CONSENT OF SCREEN ACTORS GUILD, INC.

SCREEN ACTORS GUILD

DAILY CONTRACT
(DAY PERFORMER)
FOR TELEVISION MOTION PICTURES OR VIDEOTAPES

Company _____   Date _____

Production Title _____   Performer Name _____

Production Number _____   Address _____

Date Employment Starts _____   Telephone No.: (___) _____

Role _____   Social Security No. _____

Daily Rate $ _____   Date of Performer's next engagement _____

Weekly Conversion Rate $ _____

Wardrobe supplied by performer   Yes ☐   No ☐

If so, number of outfits _____ @ $ _____

                    (formal) _____ @ $ _____

COMPLETE FOR "DROP-AND-PICK-UP" DEALS ONLY:

Firm recall date on _____

or on or after * _____

("On or after" recall only applies to pick-up as Weekly Performer)

As   ☐ Day Performer   ☐ Weekly Performer

*Means date specified or within 24 hours thereafter.

THIS AGREEMENT covers the employment of the above-named Performer by _____ in the production and at the rate of compensation set forth above and is subject to and shall include, for the benefit of the Performer and the Producer, all of the applicable provisions and conditions contained or provided for in the applicable Screen Actors Guild Television Agreement (herein called the "Television Agreement"). Performer's employment shall include performance in non-commercial openings, bridges, etc., and no added compensation shall be payable to Performer so long as such are used in the role and episode covered hereunder in which Performer appears; for other use, Performer shall be paid the added minimum compensation, if any, required under the provisions of the Screen Actors Guild agreements with Producer.

Producer shall have all the rights in and to the results and proceeds of the Performer's services rendered hereunder, as are provided with respect to "photoplays" in Schedule A of the applicable Screen Actors Guild Codified Basic Agreement and the right to supplemental market use as defined in the Television Agreement.

Producer shall have the unlimited right throughout the world to telecast the film and exhibit the film theatrically and in supplemental markets in accordance with the terms and conditions of the Television Agreement.

If the motion picture is rerun on television in the United States or Canada and contains any of the results and proceeds of the Performer's services, the Performer will be paid for each day of employment hereunder the additional compensation prescribed therefor by the Television Agreement, unless there is an agreement to pay an amount in excess thereof as follows:

_____

_____

If there is foreign telecasting of the motion picture as defined in the Television Agreement, and such motion picture contains any of the results and proceeds of the Performer's services, the Performer will be paid the amount in the blank space below for each day of employment hereunder, or if such blank space is not filled in, then the Performer will be paid the minimum additional compensation prescribed therefor by the Television Agreement. $ _____

If the motion picture is exhibited theatrically anywhere in the world and contains any of the results and proceeds of the Performer's services, the Performer will be paid $_____ , or if this blank is not filled in, then the Performer will be paid the minimum additional compensation prescribed therefor by the Television Agreement.

If the motion picture is exhibited in supplemental markets anywhere in the world and contains any of the results and proceeds of the Performer's services, then Performer will be paid the supplemental market fees prescribed by the applicable provisions of the Television Agreement.

If the Performer places his or her initials in the box below, he or she thereby authorizes Producer to use portions of said television motion picture as a trailer to promote another episode or the series as a whole, upon payment to the Performer of the additional compensation prescribed by the applicable provisions of the Television Agreement.

Initial

By _____
Producer

_____
Performer

Production time reports are available on the set at the end of each day, which reports shall be signed or initialed by the Performer.

NOTICE TO PERFORMER: IT IS IMPORTANT THAT YOU RETAIN A COPY OF THIS CONTRACT FOR YOUR PERMANENT RECORDS.

**MINIMUM THREE-DAY CONTRACT
FOR TELEVISION MOTION PICTURES OR VIDEOTAPES
THREE-DAY MINIMUM EMPLOYMENT**

THIS AGREEMENT is made this _____ day of _____, 20____, between _____ , a corporation, hereinafter called "Producer," and _____ , hereinafter called "Performer."

<u>WITNESSETH</u>:

1. **Photoplay: Role and Guarantee.** Producer hereby engages Performer to render service as such in the role of _____ , in a photoplay produced primarily for exhibition over free television, the working title of which is now _____ . Performer accepts such engagement upon the terms herein specified. Producer guarantees that it will furnish Performer not less than _____ days' employment. (If this blank is not filled in, the guarantee shall be three (3) days.)

2. **Salary.** The Producer will pay to the Performer, and the Performer agrees to accept for three (3) days (and pro rata for each additional day beyond three (3) days) the following salary rate: $_____ .

3. Producer shall have the unlimited right throughout the world to telecast the film and exhibit the film theatrically and in Supplemental Markets in accordance with the terms and conditions of the applicable Screen Actors Guild Television Agreement (herein referred to as the "Television Agreement").

4. If the motion picture is rerun on television in the United States or Canada and contains any of the results and proceeds of the Performer's services, the Performer will be paid the additional compensation prescribed therefor by the Television Agreement, unless there is an agreement to pay an amount in excess thereof as follows:

_____

_____

5. If there is foreign telecasting of the motion picture as defined in the Television Agreement, and such motion picture contains any of the results and proceeds of the Performer's services, the Performer will be paid the amount in the blank space below plus an amount equal to one-third (1/3) thereof for each day of employment in excess of three (3) days, or, if such blank space is not filled in, then the Performer will be paid the minimum additional compensation prescribed therefor by the Television Agreement. $_____ .

6. If the motion picture is exhibited theatrically anywhere in the world and contains any of the results and proceeds of the Performer's services, the Performer will be paid $_____ , plus an amount equal to one-third (1/3) thereof for each day of employment in excess of three (3) days. If this blank is not filled in, the Performer will be paid the applicable minimum additional compensation prescribed therefor by the Television Agreement.

7. If the motion picture is exhibited in Supplemental Markets anywhere in the world and contains any of the results and proceeds of the Performer's services, the Performer will be paid the supplemental market fees prescribed by the applicable provisions of the Television Agreement.

8. **Term.** The term of employment hereunder shall begin on _____ , on or about* _____ and shall continue thereafter until the completion of the photography and recordation of said role.

* The "on or about clause" may only be used when the contract is delivered to the Performer at least three (3) days before the starting date.

9. **Incorporation of Television Agreement.** The applicable provisions of the Television Agreement are incorporated herein by reference. Performer's employment shall include performance in non-commercial openings, closings, bridges, etc., and no added compensation shall be payable to Performer so long as such are used in the role and episode covered hereunder and in which Performer appears; for other use, Performer shall be paid the added minimum compensation, if any, required under the provisions of the Screen Actors Guild agreements with Producer. Performer's employment shall be upon the terms, conditions and exceptions of the provisions applicable to the rate of salary and guarantee specified in Paragraphs 1. and 2. hereof.

10. **Arbitration of Disputes.** Should any dispute or controversy arise between the parties hereto with reference to this contract, or the employment herein provided for, such dispute or controversy shall be settled and determined by conciliation and arbitration in accordance with and to the extent provided in the conciliation and arbitration provisions of the Television Agreement, and such provisions are hereby referred to and by such reference incorporated herein and made a part of this agreement with the same effect as though the same were set forth herein in detail.

11. **Performer's Address.** All notices which the Producer is required or may desire to give to the Performer may be given either by mailing the same addressed to the Performer at _____ , or such notice may be given to the Performer personally, either orally or in writing.

12. **Performer's Telephone.** The Performer must keep the Producer's casting office or the assistant director of said photoplay advised as to where the Performer may be reached by telephone without unreasonable delay. The current telephone number of the Performer is (_____)_____.

13. If Performer places his initials in the box, he thereby authorizes Producer to use portions of said television motion picture as a trailer to promote another episode or the series as a whole, upon payment to the Performer of the additional compensation prescribed by the Television Agreement.

14. **Furnishing of Wardrobe.** The Performer agrees to furnish all modern wardrobe and wearing apparel reasonably necessary for the portrayal of said role; it being agreed, however, that should so-called "character" or "period" costumes be required, the Producer shall supply the same. When Performer supplies any wardrobe, Performer shall receive the cleaning allowance and reimbursement specified in the Television Agreement.

15. **Next Starting Date.** The starting date of Performer's next engagement is _____.

IN WITNESS WHEREOF, the parties have executed this agreement on the day and year first above written.

By _____
Producer

_____
Performer

_____
Social Security Number

Production time reports are available on the set at the end of each day. Such reports shall be signed or initialed by the performer.

Attached hereto for your use is a Declaration Regarding Income Tax Withholding ("Part Year Employment Method of Withholding"). You may utilize such form by delivering same to Producer.

NOTICE TO PERFORMER: IT IS IMPORTANT THAT YOU RETAIN A COPY OF THIS CONTRACT FOR YOUR PERMANENT RECORDS.

**THE PERFORMER MAY NOT WAIVE ANY PROVISION OF THIS CONTRACT
WITHOUT THE WRITTEN CONSENT OF SCREEN ACTORS GUILD, INC.**

SCREEN ACTORS GUILD
MINIMUM FREE LANCE WEEKLY CONTRACT
FOR TELEVISION MOTION PICTURES OR VIDEOTAPES
Continuous Employment – Weekly Basis – Weekly Salary
One Week Minimum Employment

THIS AGREEMENT is made this _____ day of _____ , 20____ , between _____ , a corporation, hereinafter called "Producer," and _____ , hereinafter called "Performer."

WITNESSETH:

1. **Photoplay: Role and Guarantee**. Producer hereby engages Performer to render services as such, in the role of _____ , in a photoplay produced primarily for exhibition over free television, the working title of which is now _____ . Performer accepts such engagement upon the terms herein specified. Producer guarantees that it will furnish Performer not less than _____ weeks employment. (If this blank is not filled in, the guarantee shall be one week.)

2. **Salary**. The Producer will pay to the Performer, and the Performer agrees to accept weekly (and pro rata for each additional day beyond guarantee) the following salary rate: $_____ per "studio week." (Schedule B Performers must receive an additional overtime payment of four (4) hours at straight time rate for each overnight location sixth day).

3. Producer shall have the unlimited right throughout the world to telecast the film and exhibit the film theatrically and in Supplemental Markets, in accordance with the terms and conditions of the applicable Screen Actors Guild Television Agreement (herein referred to as the "Television Agreement").

4. If the motion picture is rerun on television in the United States or Canada and contains any of the results and proceeds of the Performer's services, the Performer will be paid the additional compensation prescribed therefor by the Television Agreement, unless there is an agreement to pay an amount in excess thereof as follows:

_____

_____

5. If there is foreign telecasting of the motion picture, as defined in the Television Agreement, and such motion picture contains any of the results and proceeds of the Performer's services, the Performer will be paid $_____ plus pro rata thereof for each additional day of employment in excess of one week, or, if this blank is not filled in, the Performer will be paid the minimum additional compensation prescribed therefor by the Television Agreement.

6. If the motion picture is exhibited theatrically anywhere in the world and contains any of the results and proceeds of the Performer's services, the Performer will be paid $_____ plus pro rata thereof for each additional day of employment in excess of one week, or, if this blank is not filled in, the Performer will be paid the minimum additional compensation prescribed therefor by the Television Agreement.

7. If the motion picture is exhibited in Supplemental Markets anywhere in the world and contains any of the results and proceeds of the Performer's services, the Performer will be paid the supplemental market fees prescribed by the applicable provisions of the Television Agreement.

8. **Term**. The term of employment hereunder shall begin on _____ , on or about*_____ and shall continue thereafter until the completion of the photography and recordation of said role.

*The "on or about clause" may only be used when the contract is delivered to the Performer at least three (3) days before the starting date.

9. **Incorporation of Television Agreement.** The applicable provisions of the Television Agreement are incorporated herein by reference. Performer's employment shall include performance in non-commercial openings, closings, bridges, etc., and no added compensation shall be payable to Performer so long as such are used in the role and episode covered hereunder and in which Performer appears; for other use, Performer shall be paid the added minimum compensation, if any, required under the provisions of the Screen Actors Guild agreements with Producer. Performer's employment shall be upon the terms, conditions and exceptions of said provisions applicable to the rate of salary and guarantee specified in Paragraphs 1. and 2. hereof.

10. **Arbitration of Disputes.** Should any dispute or controversy arise between the parties hereto with reference to this contract, or the employment herein provided for, such dispute or controversy shall be settled and determined by conciliation and arbitration in accordance with and to the extent provided in the conciliation and arbitration provisions of the Television Agreement, and such provisions are hereby referred to and by such reference incorporated herein and made a part of this agreement with the same effect as though the same were set forth herein in detail.

11. **Performer's Address.** All notices which the Producer is required or may desire to give to the Performer may be given either by mailing the same addressed to the Performer at _____ , or such notice may be given to the Performer personally, either orally or in writing.

12. **Performer's Telephone.** The Performer must keep the Producer's casting office or the assistant director of said photoplay advised as to where the Performer may be reached by telephone without unreasonable delay. The current telephone number of the Performer is (___)_____ .

13. If Performer places his initials in the box, he thereby authorizes Producer to use portions of said television motion picture as a trailer to promote another episode or the series as a whole, upon payment to the Performer of the additional compensation prescribed by the Television Agreement.

14. **Furnishing of Wardrobe.** The Performer agrees to furnish all modern wardrobe and wearing apparel reasonably necessary for the portrayal of said role; it being agreed, however, that should so-called "character" or "period" costumes be required, the Producer shall supply the same. When Performer supplies any wardrobe, Performer shall receive the cleaning allowance and reimbursement specified in the Television Agreement.

15. **Next Starting Date.** The starting date of Performer's next engagement is _____ .

IN WITNESS WHEREOF, the parties have executed this agreement on the day and year first above written.

By _____

Producer

_____

Performer

_____

Social Security Number

Production time reports are available on the set at the end of each day. Such reports shall be signed or initialed by the performer.

NOTICE TO PERFORMER: IT IS IMPORTANT THAT YOU RETAIN A COPY OF THIS CONTRACT FOR YOUR PERMANENT RECORDS.

![SAG logo] SCREEN ACTORS GUILD

STUNT PERFORMER'S
DAILY CONTRACT
FOR TELEVISION MOTION PICTURES

**THE ARTIST MAY NOT WAIVE ANY PROVISION OF THIS CONTRACT
WITHOUT THE WRITTEN CONSENT OF SCREEN ACTORS GUILD, INC.**

STUNT PERFORMER_____ DATE OF AGREEMENT_____

ADDRESS_____

_____

TELEPHONE (____)_____ SOCIAL SECURITY NO._____

COMPANY/PRODUCER_____

PRODUCTION TITLE_____ PRODUCTION NO._____

AGENT/AGENCY_____

ADDRESS_____

_____

DAILY RATE $_____ SERIES_____

WEEKLY CONV. RATE $_____ START DATE_____

1. <u>DESCRIPTION OF SERVICES</u>: Producer hereby engages Stunt Performer to render services as
   _____. Stunt Performer accepts such engagement upon the terms
   herein specified.

2. <u>TERM/GUARANTEE</u>: Producer guarantees to furnish Stunt Performer not less than_____days
   engagement. If this space is not filled in, the guarantee shall be one (1) day.

3. <u>STUNT ADJUSTMENTS</u>: It is understood that the rate of compensation specified may be adjusted depending
   upon the nature of the stunt activities Producer may require. If so, a stunt adjustment will be agreed upon
   between the parties through good faith bargaining and said adjustment shall be noted on Stunt Performer's
   daily time report or time card. The parties shall agree upon the compensation to be paid before the stunt is
   performed if they may readily do so; however, it is expressly agreed that production shall not be delayed for
   the purpose of first determining the compensation for a stunt. Such adjustment shall increase Stunt
   Performer's compensation for the day in the manner prescribed in Schedule H of the Screen Actors Guild
   Codified Basic Agreement.

4. <u>INCORPORATION OF PRODUCER-SCREEN ACTORS GUILD COLLECTIVE BARGAINING AGREEMENT</u>:
   All provisions of the Screen Actors Guild Codified Basic Agreement and Television Agreement as the same
   may be supplemented and/or amended to date shall be deemed incorporated herein. Stunt Performer's
   engagement shall include performance in non-commercial openings, closings, bridges, etc., and no added
   compensation shall be payable to Stunt Performer so long as such are used in the Motion Picture covered
   hereunder and in which Stunt Performer appears or with respect to which Stunt Performer is paid
   compensation hereunder. Stunt Performer's engagement shall be upon the terms, conditions and
   exceptions of said provisions applicable to the rate of compensation and guarantee specified.

5. <u>RIGHTS</u>: Producer shall have the unlimited right throughout the universe and in perpetuity to exhibit the
   Motion Picture in all media, now or hereafter known, and Producer, as employer-for-hire of Stunt Performer,
   shall own all rights in the results and proceeds of Stunt Performer's services hereunder.

6. <u>ADDITIONAL COMPENSATION</u>: If the Motion Picture covered hereby is exhibited, containing any of the
   results and proceeds of Stunt Performer's services hereunder, in any of the following media:
   (i) "Free" television reruns in the United States or Canada, or both;
   (ii) Television exhibition anywhere in the universe outside the United States and Canada;
   (iii) Theatrical exhibition anywhere in the universe;

(iv) Supplemental Market exhibition anywhere in the universe;

(v) Basic Cable exhibition anywhere in the universe,

as to each such medium in which the motion picture is so exhibited, Producer will pay, and Stunt Performer will accept as payment in full, the minimum additional compensation provided therefor in the Screen Actors Guild Codified Basic Agreement or Television Agreement, as the case may be, except as compensation in excess of such minimum, if any, has been provided in this Agreement.

7. CONTINUOUS EMPLOYMENT AND RIGHT TO ROLE (when applicable): If Stunt Performer portrays a role or has dialogue, Stunt Performer shall be entitled to "continuous employment" and "Right to Role," if any, only to the extent prescribed by the Screen Actors Guild Codified Basic Agreement. Stunt Performer shall receive a separate contract for such services.

8. MOTION PICTURE AND TELEVISION FUND: Stunt Performer (does) (does not) hereby authorize Producer to deduct from the compensation hereinabove specified an amount equal to _____ percent of each installment of compensation due Stunt Performer hereunder, and to pay the amount so deducted to the Motion Picture and Television Fund of America, Inc.

9. WAIVER: Stunt Performer may not waive any provision of the Screen Actors Guild Codified Basic Agreement of Television Agreement, whichever is applicable, without the written consent of the Screen Actors Guild, Inc.

10. SIGNATORY: Producer makes the material representation that either it is presently a signatory to the Screen Actors Guild collective bargaining agreement covering the engagement contracted for herein, or that the Motion Picture is covered by such collective bargaining agreement under the "Independent Production" provisions (Section 24) of the General Provisions of the Screen Actors Guild Codified Basic Agreement.

Signing of this Agreement in the spaces below signified acceptance by Producer and Stunt Performer of all of the above terms and conditions hereof and attached hereto, if any, as of the date specified above.

PRODUCER_____STUNT PERFORMER_____

BY_____

Production time reports and/or time cards are available on the set at the beginning and end of each day, which reports and/or time cards shall be signed or initialed by Stunt Performer and must indicate any agreed stunt adjustments.

NOTICE TO STUNT PERFORMER: IT IS IMPORTANT THAT YOU RETAIN A COPY OF THIS AGREEMENT FOR YOUR PERMANENT RECORDS.

SCREEN ACTORS GUILD

STUNT PERFORMER'S
MINIMUM FREELANCE THREE-DAY CONTRACT
FOR TELEVISION MOTION PICTURES

STUNT PERFORMER _____ DATE OF AGREEMENT _____

ADDRESS _____

_____

TELEPHONE ( ) ___ – _____ SOCIAL SECURITY NO. _____ – ___ – _____

COMPANY/PRODUCER_____

PRODUCTION TITLE _____ PRODUCTION NO. _____

AGENT/AGENCY _____

ADDRESS _____

_____

1. **DESCRIPTION OF SERVICES:** Producer hereby engages Stunt Performer to render services as _____ _____ . Stunt Performer accepts such engagement upon the terms herein specified.

2. **COMPENSATION/TERM/GUARANTEE:** Producer will pay Stunt Performer and Stunt Performer agrees to accept the following three-day compensation (excluding location premiums) of $_____(and pro rata services). The total guaranteed compensation shall be $ _____ for the total guaranteed period of _____ . If this space is not filled in, the guarantee shall be three (3) days. Stunt Performer shall receive sixth day location premium where applicable.

3. **START DATE:** The term of engagement shall begin on _____. or "on or about" * _____ .

4. **NEXT START DATE:** The start date of Stunt Performer's next engagement is _____.

5. **STUNT ADJUSTMENTS:** It is understood that the rate of compensation specified may be adjusted depending upon the nature of the stunt activities Producer may require. If so, a stunt adjustment will be agreed upon between the parties through good faith bargaining and said adjustment shall be noted on Stunt Performer's daily time report or time card.

   The parties shall agree upon the compensation to be paid before the stunt is performed if they may readily do so; however, it is expressly agreed that production shall not be delayed for the purpose of first determining the compensation for a stunt. Such adjustment shall increase Stunt Performer's compensation for the three-days in the manner prescribed in Schedule H-II or H-III of the Screen Actors Guild Codified Basic Agreement.

6. **INCORPORATION OF PRODUCER-SCREEN ACTORS GUILD COLLECTIVE BARGAINING AGREEMENT:** All provisions of the Screen Actors Guild Codified Basic Agreement as the same may be supplemented and/or amended to date shall be deemed incorporated herein. Stunt Performer's engagement shall include performance in non-commercial openings, closings, bridges, etc., and no added compensation shall be payable to Stunt Performer so long as such are used in the Motion Picture covered hereunder and in which Stunt Performer appears or with respect to which Stunt Performer is paid compensation hereunder. Stunt Performer's engagement shall be upon the terms, conditions and exceptions of said provisions applicable to the rate of compensation specified.

*The "on or about" clause may only be used when this Agreement is delivered to Stunt Performer at least three (3) days before the Start Date.

7. **RIGHTS:** Producer shall have the unlimited right throughout the universe and in perpetuity to exhibit the Motion Picture in all media, now or hereafter known, and Producer, as employer-for-hire of Stunt Performer, shall own all rights in the results and proceeds of Stunt Performer's services hereunder.

8. **ADDITIONAL COMPENSATION:** If the Motion Picture covered hereby is exhibited, containing any of the results and proceeds of Stunt Performer's services hereunder, in any of the following media:

   (i)   "Free" television reruns in the United States or Canada, or both;
   (ii) Television exhibition anywhere in the universe outside the United States and Canada;
   (iii) Theatrical exhibition anywhere in the universe;
   (iv) Supplemental Market exhibition anywhere in the universe;
   (v)   Basic Cable exhibition anywhere in the universe,

   as to each such medium in which the motion picture is so exhibited, Producer will pay, and Stunt Performer will accept as payment in full, the minimum additional compensation provided therefor in the Screen Actors Guild Codified Basic Agreement or Television Agreement, as the case may be, except as compensation in excess of such minimum, if any, has been provided in this Agreement.

9. **CONTINUOUS EMPLOYMENT AND RIGHT TO ROLE (when applicable):** If Stunt Performer portrays a role or has dialogue, Stunt Performer shall be entitled to "continuous employment" and "Right to Role," if any, only to the extent prescribed by the Screen Actors Guild Codified Basic Agreement. Stunt Performer shall receive a separate contract for such services.

10. **MOTION PICTURE AND TELEVISION FUND:** Stunt Performer [does] [does not] hereby authorize Producer to deduct from the compensation hereinabove specified an amount equal to _____ percent of each installment of compensation due Stunt Performer hereunder, and to pay the amount so deducted to the Motion Picture and Television Fund of America, Inc.

11. **WAIVER:** Stunt Performer may not waive any provision of the Screen Actors Guild Codified Basic Agreement or Television Agreement, whichever is applicable, without the written consent of the Screen Actors Guild, Inc.

12. **SIGNATORY:** Producer makes the material representation that either it is presently a signatory to the Screen Actors Guild collective bargaining agreement covering the engagement contracted for herein, or that the Motion Picture is covered by such collective bargaining agreement under the "Independent Production" provisions (Section 24) of the General Provisions of the Screen Actors Guild Codified Basic Agreement.

Signing of this Agreement in the spaces below signifies acceptance by Producer and Stunt Performer of all of the above terms and conditions and those on the reverse hereof and attached hereto, if any, as of the date specified above.

PRODUCER _____   STUNT PERFORMER _____

BY _____

Production time reports and/or time cards are available on the set at the beginning and end of each day, which reports and/or time cards shall be signed or initialed by Stunt Performer and must indicate any agreed stunt adjustments.

NOTICE TO STUNT PERFORMER: IT IS IMPORTANT THAT YOU RETAIN A COPY OF THIS AGREEMENT FOR YOUR PERMANENT RECORDS.

S-5 (7-92)

![logo] SCREEN ACTORS GUILD

STUNT PERFORMER'S
MINIMUM FREELANCE WEEKLY CONTRACT
FOR TELEVISION MOTION PICTURES

THE ARTIST MAY NOT WAIVE ANY PROVISION OF THIS CONTRACT
WITHOUT THE WRITTEN CONSENT OF SCREEN ACTORS GUILD. INC.

```
STUNT PERFORMER_____DATE OF AGREEMENT_____
ADDRESS_____
_____
TELEPHONE (    )_____SOCIAL SECURITY NO._____
COMPANY/PRODUCER_____
PRODUCTION TITLE_____PRODUCTION NO._____
AGENT/AGENCY_____
ADDRESS_____
_____
```

1. **DESCRIPTION OF SERVICES**: Producer hereby engages Stunt Performer to render services as _____. Stunt Performer accepts such engagement upon the terms herein specified.

2. **COMPENSATION/TERM/GUARANTEE**: Producer will pay Stunt Performer and Stunt Performer agrees to accept the following weekly compensation (excluding location premiums) of $_____ (and pro rata for each additional day beyond the guarantee until completion of services). The total guaranteed compensation shall be $_____ for the total guaranteed period of _____. If this space is not filled in, the guarantee shall be one (1) week. Stunt Performer shall receive sixth day location premium where applicable.

3. **START DATE**: The term of engagement shall begin on_____. or "on or about" *_____.

4. **NEXT START DATE**: The start date of Stunt Performer's next engagement is_____.

5. **STUNT ADJUSTMENTS**: It is understood that the rate of compensation specified may be adjusted depending upon the nature of the stunt activities Producer may require. If so, a stunt adjustment will be agreed upon between the parties through good faith bargaining and said adjustment shall be noted on Stunt Performer's daily time report or time card.

   The parties shall agree upon the compensation to be paid before the stunt is performed if they may readily do so; however, it is expressly agreed that production shall not be delayed for the purpose of first determining the compensation for a stunt. Such adjustment shall increase Stunt Performer's compensation for the week in the manner prescribed in Schedule H-II or H-III of the Screen Actors Guild Codified Basic Agreement.

6. **INCORPORATION OF PRODUCER-SCREEN ACTORS GUILD COLLECTIVE BARGAINING AGREEMENT**: All provisions of the Screen Actors Guild Codified Basic Agreement and Television Agreement as the same may be supplemented and/or amended to date shall be deemed incorporated herein. Stunt Performer's engagement shall include performance in non-commercial openings, closings, bridges, etc., and no added compensation shall be payable to Stunt Performer so long as such are used in the Motion Picture covered hereunder and in which Stunt Performer appears or with respect to which Stunt Performer is paid compensation hereunder. Stunt Performer's engagement shall be upon the terms, conditions and exceptions of said provisions applicable to the rate of compensation and guarantee specified.

The "on or about" clause may only be used when this Agreement is delivered to Stunt Performer at least three (3) days before the Start Date.

7. RIGHTS: Producer shall have the unlimited right throughout the universe and in perpetuity to exhibit the Motion Picture in all media, now or hereafter known, and Producer, as employer-for-hire of Stunt Performer, shall own all rights in the results and proceeds of Stunt Performer's services hereunder.

8. ADDITIONAL COMPENSATION: If the Motion Picture covered hereby is exhibited, containing any of the results and proceeds of Stunt Performer's services hereunder, in any of the following media:
   (i) "Free" television reruns in the United States or Canada, or both;
   (ii) Television exhibition anywhere in the universe outside the United States and Canada;
   (iii) Theatrical exhibition anywhere in the universe;
   (iv) Supplemental Market exhibition anywhere in the universe;
   (v) Basic Cable exhibition anywhere in the universe,

   as to each such medium in which the motion picture is so exhibited, Producer will pay, and Stunt Performer will accept as payment in full, the minimum additional compensation provided therefor in the Screen Actors Guild Codified Basic Agreement or Television Agreement, as the case may be, except as compensation in excess of such minimum, if any, has been provided in this Agreement.

9. CONTINUOUS EMPLOYMENT AND RIGHT TO ROLE (when applicable): If Stunt Performer portrays a role or has dialogue, Stunt Performer shall be entitled to "continuous employment" and "Right to Role," if any, only to the extent prescribed by the Screen Actors Guild Codified Basic Agreement. Stunt Performer shall receive a separate contract for such services.

10. MOTION PICTURE AND TELEVISION FUND: Stunt Performer (does) (does not) hereby authorize Producer to deduct from the compensation hereinabove specified an amount equal to _____ percent of each installment of compensation due Stunt Performer hereunder, and to pay the amount so deducted to the Motion Picture and Television Fund of America, Inc.

11. WAIVER: Stunt Performer may not waive any provision of the Screen Actors Guild Codified Basic Agreement of Television Agreement, whichever is applicable, without the written consent of the Screen Actors Guild, Inc.

12. SIGNATORY: Producer makes the material representation that either it is presently a signatory to the Screen Actors Guild collective bargaining agreement covering the engagement contracted for herein, or that the Motion Picture is covered by such collective bargaining agreement under the "Independent Production" provisions (Section 24) of the General Provisions of the Screen Actors Guild Codified Basic Agreement.

Signing of this Agreement in the spaces below signified acceptance by Producer and Stunt Performer of all of the above terms and conditions hereof and attached hereto, if any, as of the date specified above.

PRODUCER_____STUNT PERFORMER_____

BY_____

Production time reports and/or time cards are available on the set at the beginning and end of each day, which reports and/or time cards shall be signed or initialed by Stunt Performer and must indicate any agreed stunt adjustments.

NOTICE TO STUNT PERFORMER: IT IS IMPORTANT THAT YOU RETAIN A COPY OF THIS AGREEMENT FOR YOUR PERMANENT RECORDS.

SCREEN ACTORS GUILD

DAILY CONTRACT
(DAY PERFORMER)
FOR THEATRICAL MOTION PICTURES

Company _____   Date _____

Date Employment Starts _____   Performer Name _____

Production Title _____   Address _____

Production Number _____   Telephone No.: (____) _____

Role _____   Social Security No. _____

Daily Rate $ _____   Legal Resident of (State) _____

Weekly Conversion Rate $ _____   Citizen of U.S. ☐ Yes ☐ No

COMPLETE FOR "DROP-AND-PICK-UP" DEALS ONLY:

Firm recall date on _____

or on or after * _____

("On or after" recall only applies to pick-up as Weekly Performer)

As   ☐ Day Performer   ☐ Weekly Performer

*Means date specified or within 24 hours thereafter.

Wardrobe supplied by Performer   Yes ☐   No ☐

If so, number of outfits _____ @ $_____

(formal) _____ @ $_____

Date of Stunt Performer's next engagement: _____

The employment is subject to all of the provisions and conditions applicable to the employment of DAY PERFORMER contained or provided for in the Producer-Screen Actors Guild Codified Basic Agreement as the same may be supplemented and/or amended.

The performer [does][does not] hereby authorize the Producer to deduct from the compensation hereinabove specified an amount equal to _____ per cent of each installment of compensation due the Performer hereunder, and to pay the amount so deducted to the Motion Picture and Television Relief Fund of America, Inc.

Special Provisions: _____

PRODUCER _____   PERFORMER _____

BY _____

Production time reports are available on the set at the end of each day. Such reports shall be signed or initialed by the Performer.

Attached hereto for your use is Declaration Regarding Income Tax Withholding.

NOTICE TO PERFORMER: IT IS IMPORTANT THAT YOU RETAIN A COPY OF THIS CONTRACT FOR YOUR PERMANENT RECORDS.

**SCREEN ACTORS GUILD
MINIMUM FREE LANCE CONTRACT
FOR THEATRICAL MOTION PICTURES**

Continuous Employment—Weekly Basis—Weekly Salary
One Week Minimum Employment

THIS AGREEMENT, made this _____ day of _____ , 20_____ , between _____

_____ , hereafter called "Producer," and

_____ , hereafter called "Performer."

1. PHOTOPLAY, ROLE, SALARY AND GUARANTEE. Producer hereby engages Performer to render services as such in the role of _____ , in a photoplay, the working title of which is now _____ , at the salary of $_____ per "studio week" (Schedule B Performers must receive an additional overtime payment of four (4) hours at straight time rate for each overnight location Saturday). Performer accepts such engagement upon the terms herein specified. Producer guarantees that it will furnish Performer not less than _____ week's employment (if this blank is not filled in, the guarantee shall be one week). Performer shall be paid pro rata for each additional day beyond guarantee until dismissal.

2. TERM: The term of employment hereunder shall begin on

   on _____

   on or about* _____

and shall continue thereafter until the completion of the photography and recordation of said role.

3. BASIC CONTRACT. All provisions of the collective bargaining agreement between Screen Actors Guild, Inc. and Producer, relating to theatrical motion pictures, which are applicable to the employment of the Performer hereunder, shall be deemed incorporated herein.

4. PERFORMER'S ADDRESS. All notices which the Producer is required or may desire to give to the Performer may be given either by mailing the same addressed to the Performer at_____ or such notice may be given to the Performer personally, either orally or in writing.

5. PERFORMER'S TELEPHONE. The Performer must keep the Producer's casting office or the assistant director of said photoplay advised as to where the Performer may be reached by telephone without unreasonable delay. The current telephone number of the Performer is_____.

6. MOTION PICTURE AND TELEVISION RELIEF FUND. The Performer [does] [does not] hereby authorize the Producer to deduct from the compensation hereinabove specified an amount equal to _____ per cent of each installment of compensation due the Performer hereunder, and to pay the amount so deducted to the Motion Picture and Television Relief Fund of America, Inc.

7. FURNISHING OF WARDROBE. The (Producer) (Performer) agrees to furnish all modern wardrobe and wearing apparel reasonably necessary for the portrayal of said role; it being agreed, however, that should so-called "character" or "period" costumes be required, the Producer shall supply the same. When Performer furnishes any wardrobe, Performer shall receive the cleaning allowance and reimbursement, if any, specified in the basic contract.

Number of outfits furnished by Performer _____ @ $_____

(formal) _____ @ $_____

*The "on or about" clause may only be used when the contract is delivered to the Performer at least seven days before the starting date. See Codified Basic Agreement, Schedule B, Schedule C, otherwise a specific starting date must be stated.

8. ARBITRATION OF DISPUTES. Should any dispute or controversy arise between the parties hereto with reference to this contract, or the employment herein provided for, such dispute or controversy shall be settled and determined by conciliation and arbitration in accordance with the conciliation and arbitration provisions of the collective bargaining agreement between the Producer and Screen Actors Guild relating to theatrical motion pictures, and such provisions are hereby referred to and by such reference incorporated herein and made a part of this Agreement with the same effect as though the same were set forth herein in detail.

9. NEXT STARTING DATE. The starting date of Performer's next engagement is _____

10. The Performer may not waive any provision of this contract without the written consent of Screen Actors Guild, Inc.

11. Producer makes the material representation that either it is presently a signatory to the Screen Actors Guild collective bargaining agreement covering the employment contracted for herein, or that the above-referred-to photoplay is covered by such collective bargaining agreement under the Independent Production provisions of the General Provisions of the Screen Actors Guild Codified Basic Agreement as the same may be supplemented and/or amended.

IN WITNESS WHEREOF, the parties have executed this agreement on the day and year first above written.

PRODUCER _____ PERFORMER _____

BY_____ Social Security No. _____

Production time reports are available on the set at the end of each day, which reports shall be signed or initialed by the Performer.

Attached hereto for your use are the following: (1) Declaration Regarding Income Tax Withholding ("Part Year Employment Method of Withholding") and (2) Declaration Regarding Income Tax Withholding. You may utilize the applicable form by delivering same to Producer. Only one of such forms may be used.

NOTICE TO PERFORMER: IT IS IMPORTANT THAT YOU RETAIN A COPY OF THIS CONTRACT FOR YOUR PERMANENT RECORDS.

 **SCREEN ACTORS GUILD**

STUNT PERFORMER'S
DAILY CONTRACT
FOR THEATRICAL MOTION PICTURES

STUNT PERFORMER_____DATE OF AGREEMENT_____

ADDRESS_____

_____

TELEPHONE (_____)_____SOCIAL SECURITY NO._____

COMPANY/PRODUCER_____

PRODUCTION TITLE_____PRODUCTION NO._____

AGENT/AGENCY_____

ADDRESS_____

_____

DAILY RATE $_____SERIES_____

WEEKLY CONV. RATE $_____START DATE_____

1. <u>DESCRIPTION OF SERVICES</u>: Producer hereby engages Stunt Performer to render services as
_____. Stunt Performer accepts such engagement upon the terms
herein specified.

2. <u>TERM/GUARANTEE</u>:   Producer guarantees to furnish Stunt Performer not less than_____days
engagement. If this space is not filled in, the guarantee shall be one (1) day.

3. <u>STUNT ADJUSTMENTS</u>: It is understood that the rate of compensation specified may be adjusted depending
upon the nature of the stunt activities Producer may require. If so, a stunt adjustment will be agreed upon
between the parties through good faith bargaining and said adjustment shall be noted on Stunt Performer's
daily time report or time card. The parties shall agree upon the compensation to be paid before the stunt is
performed if they may readily do so; however, it is expressly agreed that production shall not be delayed for
the purpose of first determining the compensation for a stunt. Such adjustment shall increase Stunt
Performer's compensation for the day in the manner prescribed in Schedule H of the Screen Actors Guild
Codified Basic Agreement.

4. <u>INCORPORATION OF PRODUCER-SCREEN ACTORS GUILD COLLECTIVE BARGAINING AGREEMENT</u>:
All provisions of the Screen Actors Guild Codified Basic Agreement and Television Agreement as the same
may be supplemented and/or amended to date shall be deemed incorporated herein. Stunt Performer's
engagement shall be upon the terms, conditions and exceptions of said provisions applicable to the rate of
compensation and guarantee specified.

5. <u>RIGHTS</u>: Producer shall have the unlimited right throughout the universe and in perpetuity to exhibit the
Motion Picture in all media, now or hereafter known, and Producer, as employer-for-hire of Stunt Performer,
shall own all rights in the results and proceeds of Stunt Performer's services hereunder.

6. <u>ADDITIONAL COMPENSATION</u>: If the Motion Picture covered hereby is exhibited, containing any of the
results and proceeds of Stunt Performer's services hereunder, in any of the following media:
(I) "Free" television reruns in the United States or Canada, or both;
(ii) Television exhibition anywhere in the universe outside the United States and Canada;
(iii) Theatrical exhibition anywhere in the universe;

as to each such medium in which the motion picture is so exhibited, Producer will pay, and Stunt Performer will
accept as payment in full, the minimum additional compensation provided therefor in the Screen Actors Guild

Codified Basic Agreement, except as compensation in excess of such minimum, if any, has been provided in this Agreement.

7. <u>CONTINUOUS EMPLOYMENT AND RIGHT TO ROLE (when applicable)</u>: If Stunt Performer portrays a role or has dialogue, Stunt Performer shall be entitled to "continuous employment" and "Right to Role," if any, only to the extent prescribed by the Screen Actors Guild Codified Basic Agreement. Stunt Performer shall receive a separate contract for such services.

8. <u>MOTION PICTURE AND TELEVISION FUND</u>: Stunt Performer (does) (does not) hereby authorize Producer to deduct from the compensation hereinabove specified an amount equal to _____ percent of each installment of compensation due Stunt Performer hereunder, and to pay the amount so deducted to the Motion Picture and Television Fund of America, Inc.

9. <u>WAIVER</u>: Stunt Performer may not waive any provision of the Screen Actors Guild Codified Basic Agreement of Television Agreement, whichever is applicable, without the written consent of the Screen Actors Guild, Inc.

10. <u>SIGNATORY</u>: Producer makes the material representation that either it is presently a signatory to the Screen Actors Guild collective bargaining agreement covering the engagement contracted for herein, or that the Motion Picture is covered by such collective bargaining agreement under the "Independent Production" provisions (Section 24) of the General Provisions of the Screen Actors Guild Codified Basic Agreement.

Signing of this Agreement in the spaces below signified acceptance by Producer and Stunt Performer of all of the above terms and conditions hereof and attached hereto, if any, as of the date specified above.

PRODUCER_____STUNT PERFORMER_____

BY_____

Production time reports and/or time cards are available on the set at the beginning and end of each day, which reports and/or time cards shall be signed or initialed by Stunt Performer and must indicate any agreed stunt adjustments.

NOTICE TO STUNT PERFORMER: IT IS IMPORTANT THAT YOU RETAIN A COPY OF THIS AGREEMENT FOR
                            YOUR PERMANENT RECORDS.

 SCREEN ACTORS GUILD

STUNT PERFORMER'S
MINIMUM FREELANCE WEEKLY CONTRACT
<u>FOR THEATRICAL MOTION PICTURES</u>

STUNT PERFORMER _____ DATE OF AGREEMENT _____

ADDRESS _____

_____

TELEPHONE (___) - _____ SOCIAL SECURITY NO. ____ - __ - _____

COMPANY/PRODUCER _____

PRODUCTION TITLE _____ PRODUCTION NO. _____

AGENT/AGENCY _____

ADDRESS _____

_____

---

1. **DESCRIPTION OF SERVICES:** Producer hereby engages Stunt Performer to render services as _____ _____. Stunt Performer accepts such engagement upon the terms herein specified.

2. **COMPENSATION/TERM/GUARANTEE:** Producer will pay Stunt Performer and Stunt Performer agrees to accept the following weekly compensation (excluding location premiums) of $_____ (and pro rata for each additional day beyond the guarantee until completion of services). The total guaranteed compensation shall be $_____ for the total guaranteed period of _____ . If this space is not filled in, the guarantee shall be one (1) week. Stunt Performer shall receive sixth day location premium where applicable.

3. **START DATE:** The term of engagement shall begin on _____ . or "on or about" * _____ .

4. **NEXT START DATE:** The start date of Stunt Performer's next engagement is _____ .

5. **STUNT ADJUSTMENTS:** It is understood that the rate of compensation specified may be adjusted depending upon the nature of the stunt activities Producer may require. If so, a stunt adjustment will be agreed upon between the parties through good faith bargaining and said adjustment shall be noted on Stunt Performer's daily time report or time card.

   The parties shall agree upon the compensation to be paid before the stunt is performed if they may readily do so; however, it is expressly agreed that production shall not be delayed for the purpose of first determining the compensation for a stunt. Such adjustment shall increase Stunt Performer's compensation for the week in the manner prescribed in Schedule H-II or H-III of the Screen Actors Guild Codified Basic Agreement.

6. **INCORPORATION OF PRODUCER-SCREEN ACTORS GUILD COLLECTIVE BARGAINING AGREEMENT:** All provisions of the Screen Actors Guild Codified Basic Agreement as the same may be supplemented and/or amended to date shall be deemed incorporated herein. Stunt Performer's engagement shall be upon the terms, conditions and exceptions of said provisions applicable to the rate of compensation and guarantee specified.

7. **RIGHTS:** Producer shall have the unlimited right throughout the universe and in perpetuity to exhibit the Motion Picture in all media, now or hereafter known, and Producer, as employer-for-hire of Stunt Performer, shall own all rights in the results and proceeds of Stunt Performer's services hereunder.

The "on or about" clause may only be used when this Agreement is delivered to Stunt Performer at least three (3) days before the Start Date.

8. **ADDITIONAL COMPENSATION:** If the Motion Picture covered hereby is exhibited, containing any of the results and proceeds of Stunt Performer's services hereunder, in any of the following media:

(i)   "Free" television reruns in the United States or Canada, or both;
(ii) Television exhibition anywhere in the universe outside the United States and Canada;
(iii) Theatrical exhibition anywhere in the universe;
(iv) Supplemental Market exhibition anywhere in the universe;
(v)   Basic Cable exhibition anywhere in the universe,

as to each such medium in which the motion picture is so exhibited, Producer will pay, and Stunt Performer will accept as payment in full, the minimum additional compensation provided therefor in the Screen Actors Guild Codified Basic Agreement or Television Agreement, as the case may be, except as compensation in excess of such minimum, if any, has been provided in this Agreement.

9. **CONTINUOUS EMPLOYMENT AND RIGHT TO ROLE (when applicable):** If Stunt Performer portrays a role or has dialogue, Stunt Performer shall be entitled to "continuous employment" and "Right to Role," if any, only to the extent prescribed by the Screen Actors Guild Codified Basic Agreement. Stunt Performer shall receive a separate contract for such services.

10. **MOTION PICTURE AND TELEVISION FUND:** Stunt Performer [does] [does not] hereby authorize Producer to deduct from the compensation hereinabove specified an amount equal to _____ percent of each installment of compensation due Stunt Performer hereunder, and to pay the amount so deducted to the Motion Picture and Television Fund of America, Inc.

11. **WAIVER:** Stunt Performer may not waive any provision of the Screen Actors Guild Codified Basic Agreement or Television Agreement, whichever is applicable, without the written consent of the Screen Actors Guild, Inc.

12. **SIGNATORY:** Producer makes the material representation that either it is presently a signatory to the Screen Actors Guild collective bargaining agreement covering the engagement contracted for herein, or that the Motion Picture is covered by such collective bargaining agreement under the "Independent Production" provisions (Section 24) of the General Provisions of the Screen Actors Guild Codified Basic Agreement.

Signing of this Agreement in the spaces below signifies acceptance by Producer and Stunt Performer of all of the above terms and conditions and those on the reverse hereof and attached hereto, if any, as of the date specified above.

PRODUCER _____ STUNT PERFORMER_____

BY_____

Production time reports and/or time cards are available on the set at the beginning and end of each day, which reports and/or time cards shall be signed or initialed by Stunt Performer and must indicate any agreed stunt adjustments.

NOTICE TO STUNT PERFORMER: IT IS IMPORTANT THAT YOU RETAIN A COPY OF THIS AGREEMENT FOR YOUR PERMANENT RECORDS.

S-2 (7-92)

SCREEN ACTORS GUILD

PERFORMER CONTRACT FOR INTERACTIVE PROGRAMMING

Company _____   Date _____

Production Title _____   Performer Name _____

Production Number _____   Address _____

Date Employment Starts _____   Telephone No.: (____) _____

Role _____   Social Security No.: _____

Daily Rate $_____   Date of Performer's next engagement _____

3 Day Rate $_____

Weekly Rate $_____

Special Provisions $_____

_____

Wardrobe supplied by Performer ☐ Yes ☐ No

If so, number of outfits _____ @ $_____

(formal) _____ @ $_____

Complete for "Drop-And-Pick-Up" Deals ONLY:

Firm recall date on _____

or on or after* _____

("On or after" recall only applies to pick-up as Weekly Performer)

As ☐ Day Performer ☐ Weekly Performer

*Means date specified or within 24 hours thereafter.

THIS AGREEMENT covers the employment of the above-named Performer by _____ in the production and at the rate of compensation set forth above and is subject to and shall include, for the benefit of the Performer and the Producer, all of the applicable provisions and conditions contained or provided for in the applicable Screen Actors Guild Interactive Agreement, and/or the Screen Actors Guild Television Agreement. Performer's employment shall include performance in non-commercial openings, bridges, etc., and no added compensation shall be payable to Performer so long as such are used in the role and project(s) covered hereunder in which Performer appears; for other use, Performer shall be paid the added minimum compensation, if any, required under the provisions of the Screen Actors Guild agreements with Producer.

Producer shall have all the rights in and to the results and proceeds of the Performer's services rendered hereunder, as are provided with respect to "photoplays" in Schedule A of the applicable Screen Actors Guild Codified Basic Agreement and the right to supplemental market use as defined in the Television Agreement.

Producer shall have the unlimited right throughout the world to telecast the film and exhibit the film theatrically and in supplemental markets in accordance with the terms and conditions of the Television Agreement.

By _____   _____
                          Producer   Performer

                                          _____
                                               Performer's Social Security No.

Production time reports are available on the set at the end of each day, which reports shall be signed or initialed by the Performer.

NOTICE TO PERFORMER: IT IS IMPORTANT THAT YOU RETAIN A COPY OF THIS CONTRACT FOR YOUR
#37A   PERMANENT RECORDS.

SCREEN ACTORS GUILD

TAFT/HARTLEY REPORT

ATTENTION: _____ ATTACHED?: ☐ RESUME ☐ PHOTO

EMPLOYEE INFORMATION

NAME _____ SS#_____

ADDRESS _____ AGE (IF MINOR) _____

CITY/STATE _____ ZIP _____ PHONE (____)_____

EMPLOYER INFORMATION

NAME _____ Check one: ☐ CASTING OFFICE

ADDRESS _____   ☐ STUDIO
                                                 ☐ PRODUCTION COMPANY

CITY/STATE _____ ZIP _____ PHONE (____)_____

EMPLOYMENT INFORMATION

CHECK ONE: General Extra ☐   Special Ability Extra ☐   Dancer ☐

WORK DATE(S) _____ SALARY_____

PRODUCTION TITLE _____

SHOOTING LOCATION (City & State) _____

REASON FOR HIRE (be specific) _____

_____

_____

_____

_____

_____

Employer is aware of General Provision, Section 14.G of the Screen Actors Guild Codified Basic Agreement of 1989 for Independent Producers as amended that applies to Theatrical and Television production, wherein Preference of Employment shall be given to qualified professional extras (except as otherwise stated). Employer will pay to the Guild as liquidated damages, a sum which shall be determined by binding arbitration for each breach by the Employer of any provision of those sections.

SIGNATURE_____ DATE _____
          Producer or Casting Director (indicate which)

PRINT NAME _____ PHONE (____)_____

TAFT/HARTLEY REPORT

ATTENTION: _____ ATTACHED?: ☐ RESUME ☐ PHOTO

EMPLOYEE INFORMATION

NAME _____ SS#_____

ADDRESS _____ AGE (IF MINOR) _____

CITY/STATE _____ ZIP _____ PHONE (____)_____

EMPLOYER INFORMATION

NAME _____ Check one: ☐ CASTING OFFICE
                                                  ☐ STUDIO
ADDRESS _____   ☐ PRODUCTION COMPANY

CITY/STATE _____ ZIP _____ PHONE (____)_____

EMPLOYMENT INFORMATION

CHECK ONE: General Extra ☐   Special Ability Extra ☐   Dancer ☐

WORK DATE(S) _____ SALARY_____

PRODUCTION TITLE _____

SHOOTING LOCATION (City & State) _____

REASON FOR HIRE (be specific) _____

_____

_____

_____

_____

_____

Employer is aware of General Provision, Section 14.G of the Screen Actors Guild Codified Basic Agreement of 1989 for Independent Producers as amended that applies to Theatrical and Television production, wherein Preference of Employment shall be given to qualified professional extras (except as otherwise stated). Employer will pay to the Guild as liquidated damages, a sum which shall be determined by binding arbitration for each breach by the Employer of any provision of those sections.

SIGNATURE_____ DATE _____
            Producer or Casting Director (indicate which)

PRINT NAME _____ PHONE (____)_____

SCREEN ACTORS GUILD THEATRICAL & TELEVISION SIGN-IN SHEET

PRODUCER: _____
PROD'N CO: _____
PROD'N OFFICE
PHONE # _____

AUDITION DATE: _____

CASTING REP: _____
CASTING REP. PHONE: _____
PRODUCTION TITLE: _____
EPISODE: _____

CASTING REP:
Please fill in <u>time seen</u> for each actor

_____
Casting Director's Signature

(1) NAME	(2) SOCIAL SECURITY	(3) ROLE	(4) AGENT	(5) PROVIDED? PARK	SCRIPT	(6) ARRIVAL TIME	(7) APPT TIME	(8) TIME SEEN (Cast. rep.)	(9) TIME OUT	(10) TAPED?	(11) ACT. INI.

SCREEN ACTORS GUILD PERFORMERS PRODUCTION TIME REPORT

Exhibit G

Picture Title _____ Prod.# _____ Date _____ Contact _____ Phone No. (___) _____

Shooting Location _____ Is Today a Designated Day Off? *Yes ___ No ___

Please Complete in Ink

WORK - W REHEARSAL - R FITTING - FT TRAVEL - TR
START = S HOLD - H TEST - T FINISH - F

CAST	MINORS	CHARACTER	W - S - R / H - F - T / TR - FT	REPORT MAKEUP WDBE.	REPORT TIME			MEALS						TRAVEL TIME				Stunt Adj.	Minors Turoring Time	Wardrobe No. of Outfits Provided	Forced Call / MPV's	PERFORMER'S SIGNATURE
					Report on set	Dismiss on set	Dismiss Makeup Wardrobe	In / Out / ND MEAL	1st Meal Start	Finish	2nd Meal Start	Finish	Leave for Location	Arrive on Location	Leave Location	Arrive at Studio					

SCREEN ACTORS GUILD

CASTING DATA REPORT

See Reverse
For Instructions

THIS FORM MUST BE COMPLETED FOR EACH MOTION PICTURE AND EACH EPISODE OF EACH
SERIES PRODUCED FOR THE QUARTER IN WHICH PRINCIPAL PHOTOGRAPHY WAS COMPLETED.

1) PRODUCTION COMPANY _____

2) QUARTER and YEAR _____

3) PROJECT (Title, Prod. No., etc.) _____

4) DESCRIPTION (Feature, M.O.W., TV Series, etc.) _____

5) TOTAL NO. OF DAYS OF PRODUCTION (Principal Photography Only) _____

6) DATA SUBMITTED BY _____
   NAME

   TELEPHONE NUMBER _____

7) CHECK IF APPROPRIATE ☐ NO STUNTS

PART I

8)

CATEGORY		FORM OF HIRING			9) CAST TOTALS	10) NO. OF DAYS WORKED	11) AGE:		
		DAILY	WEEKLY	SERIES			UNDER 40	40 and OVER	UNKNOWN
MALE	LEAD								
	SUPPORT								
FEMALE	LEAD								
	SUPPORT								

PART II

12)

CATEGORY		FORM OF HIRING						13) NO. OF DAYS WORKED		14) AGE					
		DAILY		WEEKLY		SERIES				UNDER 40		40 and OVER		UNKNOWN	
		M	F	M	F	M	F	M	F	M	F	M	F	M	F
ASIAN/PACIFIC	LEAD														
	SUPPORT														
BLACK	LEAD														
	SUPPORT														
CAUCASIAN	LEAD														
	SUPPORT														
LATINO / HISPANIC	LEAD														
	SUPPORT														
N. AMERICAN INDIAN	LEAD														
	SUPPORT														
UNKNOWN / OTHER	LEAD														
	SUPPORT														

INSTRUCTIONS

(After reading the following, if you have any further questions, please call 213/549-6644.) (For your convenience, our fax number is 213/549-6647.)

1. Indicate the name of the signatory Production Company (e.g., "THE ABC COMPANY").

2. Indicate the quarter/year when **principal photography** was completed (e.g., "1st quarter 1981"). Make one report only for full project even though it might span more than one quarter.

    The quarters consist of:

January	-	March	(1st)
April	-	June	(2nd)
July	-	September	(3rd)
October	-	December	(4th)

3. Indicate the <u>name</u> of the film for which you are reporting.

4. Indicate the <u>type</u> of project (feature, television movie, television pilot, television series, animation.

5. Use a number to respond to this question.

6. Indicate the name of person completing this form and the telephone number for same.

7. Two separate reports are required, one for <u>Performers</u> only and one for <u>Stunt Performers</u> only. If there were no Stunt Performers employed on the film, check the "No Stunt" box. If Stunt Performers were employed, complete the casting data report form for Stunt Performers.

8. <u>Part I.</u> Indicate the total number of lead and supporting Performers in each of the applicable categories. Series performers column is provided for episodic TV shows only. Daily column is for daily contract & 3-day contract performers only. Weekly column is for weekly contract and run-of-the-picture performers. A day contract performer upgraded to a weekly contract performer in a drop/pick-up situation should be listed in the weekly column (**do <u>not</u> count** the performer twice).

9. Use numbers only to indicate the total number of Performers in the category.

10. Use numbers only to indicate the total number of days worked by <u>ALL</u> Performers in the category. (Include all days paid for including hold, rehearsal days, etc.)

11. Use numbers only to indicate how many Performers were in each age group.

12. <u>Part II.</u> Indicate the total number of males and females in each category.

13. Use number only to indicate the total number of days worked by <u>ALL</u> the Performers in male and female category.

14. Use numbers only to indicate how many Performers were in each age group.

<u>NOTE:</u> PLEASE MAKE EVERY EFFORT TO INSURE THAT YOUR NUMBERS CORRESPOND ACROSS AND AMONG PART I AND PART II.

SCREEN ACTORS GUILD

#48B

See Reverse For Instructions

CASTING DATA REPORT FOR STUNT PERFORMERS ONLY

THIS FORM MUST BE COMPLETED FOR EACH MOTION PICTURE AND EACH EPISODE OF EACH SERIES PRODUCED FOR THE QUARTER IN WHICH PRINCIPAL PHOTOGRAPHY WAS COMPLETED.

(1) PRODUCTION COMPANY _____

(2) QUARTER and YEAR _____

(3) PROJECT (Title, Prod. No., etc.) _____

(4) DESCRIPTION (Feature, M.O.W., TV Series, etc.) _____

(5) TOTAL NO. OF DAYS OF PRODUCTION (Principal Photography Only) _____

(6) DATA SUBMITTED BY _____
NAME

TELEPHONE NUMBER ( ) _____

(7) NAME OF STUNT COORDINATOR _____

PART I

(8) CATEGORY	DAILY	WEEKLY	SERIES	(9) PERFORMER TOTALS	(10) NUMBER DAYS WORKED	(11) AGE UNDER 40	AGE 40 AND OVER	AGE UNKNOWN	(12) STUNT SUMMARY DESCRIPT	STUNT SUMMARY NON-DESCRIPT
MALE										
FEMALE										

PART II

(13) CATEGORY	FORM OF HIRING										(14) NUMBER DAYS WORKED		(15) AGE						(16) STUNT SUMMARY			
	DAILY		WEEKLY		SERIES								UNDER 40		40 AND OVER		UNKNOWN		DESCRIPT		NON-DESCR PT	
	M	F	M	F	M	F					M	F	M	F	M	F	M	F	M	F	M	F
ASIAN/PACIFIC																						
BLACK																						
CAUCASIAN																						
LATINO / HISPANIC																						
N. AMERICAN INDIAN																						
OTHER / UNKNOWN																						

STUNT INSTRUCTIONS

**There are two separate report forms required.
Complete one report for Performers and one report for Stunt Performers.

(After reading the following, if you have any further questions, please call 213/549-6644.) (For your convenience, our fax number is 213/549-6647.)

1.   Indicate the Production Company (e.g., "THE ABC COMPANY").

2.   Indicate the quarter/year (e.g., "1st quarter 1981").

     The quarters consist of:

January	-	March	(1st)
April	-	June	(2nd)
July	-	September	(3rd)
October	-	December	(4th)

3.   Indicate the <u>name</u> of the film for which you are reporting.

4.   Indicate the <u>type</u> of project (feature, television movie, television pilot, television series, animation.

5.   Use a number to respond to this question.

6.   Indicate the name of person completing this form and the telephone number for same.

7.   Provide the name of the stunt coordinator for the film.

Part I

8.   Indicate the total number of males and females in each category.

9.   Use numbers only to indicate the total number of stunt performers in the category.

10. Use numbers only to indicate the total amount of days worked by all stunt performers in the category.

11. Use numbers only to indicate how many stunt performers are in a certain age group.

12. Use numbers only to indicate the stunts as **descript*** or **non-descript***.

     *Descript   =   A stunt performer who doubles for an actor.

     *Non-descript =   A stunt performer doing a utility or faceless stunt.

Part II

13. Indicate the total number of males and females in each category.

14. Use numbers only to indicate the total number of days worked by <u>all</u> the Performers in each category.

15. Use numbers only to indicate how many performers were in each age group.

16. Indicate the stunts as descript or non-descript.

NOTE: **Please make every effort to ensure that your numbers correspond across categories and among <u>Part I and Part II</u>.**

SCREEN ACTORS GUILD

LOW-BUDGET AFFIRMATIVE ACTION CASTING DATA REPORT

THIS FORM MUST BE COMPLETED FOR EACH MOTION PICTURE AND EACH EPISODE OF EACH SERIES PRODUCED FOR THE QUARTER IN WHICH PRINCIPAL PHOTOGRAPHY WAS COMPLETED.

See Reverse
For Instructions

(1) PRODUCTION COMPANY _____

(2) QUARTER and YEAR _____

(3) PROJECT (Title, Prod. Number, etc.) _____

(4) DESCRIPTION (Feature, M.O.W., TV Series, etc.) _____

(5) TOTAL NUMBER OF DAYS OF PRODUCTION (Principal Photography Only) _____

(6) DATA SUBMITTED BY _____ NAME

TELEPHONE NUMBER ( ) _____

(7) CHECK IF APPROPRIATE ☐ NO STUNTS

PART I (8)

CATEGORY		FORM OF HIRING (9)			CAST TOTALS	NO. OF DAYS WORKED (10)	AGE: (11)		
		DAILY	WEEKLY	SERIES			UNDER 40	40 TO 60	60 & OVER
MALE	LEAD								
	SUPPORT								
FEMALE	LEAD								
	SUPPORT								

PART II (12)

CATEGORY		FORM OF HIRING (13)						NO. OF DAYS WORKED		AGE (14)						
		DAILY		WEEKLY		SERIES				UNDER 40		40 TO 60		60 & OVER	
		M	F	M	F	M	F	M	F	M	F	M	F	M	F
ASIAN/PACIFIC	LEAD														
	SUPPORT														
BLACK	LEAD														
	SUPPORT														
CAUCASIAN	LEAD														
	SUPPORT														
LATINO / HISPANIC	LEAD														
	SUPPORT														
N. AMERICAN INDIAN	LEAD														
	SUPPORT														
UNKNOWN / OTHER	LEAD														
	SUPPORT														

INSTRUCTIONS

1. Indicate the Production Company (e.g., "THE ABC COMPANY").

2. Indicate the quarter/year (e.g., "1st quarter 1981").

    The quarters consist of

January	–	March	(1st)
April	–	June	(2nd)
July	–	September	(3rd)
October	–	December	(4th)

3. Indicate the <u>name</u> of the film for which you are reporting.

4. Indicate the <u>type</u> of project (feature, television movie, television pilot, television series, animation).

5. Use a number to respond to this question.

6. Indicate the name of the person completing this form and the telephone number for same.

7. Two separate reports are required, one for <u>Performers</u> only and one for <u>Stunt Performers</u> only. If there were no Stunt Performers employed on the film, check the "No Stunt" box. If Stunt Performers were employed, complete the casting data report form for Stunt Performers.

8. <u>Part I</u>. Indicate the total number of lead and supporting Performers in each of the applicable categories.

9. Use numbers only to indicate the total number of Performers in the category.

10. Use numbers only to indicate the total number of days worked by <u>ALL</u> Performers in the category.

11. Use numbers only to indicate how many Performers were in each age group.

12. <u>Part II</u>. Indicate the total number of males and females in each category.

13. Use number only to indicate the total number of days worked by <u>ALL</u> the Performers in male and female category.

14. Use numbers only to indicate how many performers were in each age group.

NOTE: PLEASE MAKE EVERY EFFORT TO ENSURE THAT YOUR NUMBERS CORRESPOND ACROSS AND AMONG <u>PART I AND PART II.</u>

FINAL CAST LIST INFORMATION SHEET

SCREEN ACTORS GUILD

DATE FILED: _____

PICTURE TITLE _____

SHOOTING LOCATION _____

PRODUCTION COMPANY _____

START DATE _____ COMPLETION DATE _____

ADDRESS _____

FEDERAL I.D. # _____ STATE I.D. # _____

PHONE ( ) _____ CONTACT _____

PICTURE #

Check One: MP ☐ MOW ☐ OTHER TV ☐ INDUSTRIAL ☐ OTHER ☐

DISTRIBUTOR _____

To establish Residual payments, see Section 5.2 of the 1980 Basic Agreement.

PLAYER NAME & SOCIAL SECURITY NUMBER	PLAYER ADDRESS INCLUDING ZIP	(1) PERIOD WORKED WKS * DYS *	(1) START DATE	(1) FINISH DATE	(2) CONTRACT TYPE	(3) PLAYER TYPE	(4) TOTAL GROSS SALARY	(5) BASE SALARY	TIME UNITS	SALARY UNITS	TOTAL UNITS	FOR SAG USE ONLY

(1) Include days not worked, but considered worked under continuous employment provisions. Report contractually guaranteed work period or actual time worked, whichever is longer.

(2) Insert D for Daily or W for Weekly type of contract.

(3) Insert: A = Actor; ST = Stunt; P = Pilot; SG = Singer; ADR = Automated Dialogue Replacement.

(4) Include all salary, Overtime, Premium, and Stunt Adjustments. Do not include any Penalties paid (e.g., Meal Penalties, Forced Calls, etc.).

(5) List base contractual salary (e.g., $1,500.00/week or $500.00/day).

To establish Residual payments, see Section 5.2 of the 1980 Basic Agreement.

PLAYER NAME & SOCIAL SECURITY NUMBER	PLAYER ADDRESS INCLUDING ZIP	(1) PERIOD WORKED WKS	DYS	(1) START DATE	(1) FINISH DATE	(2) CONTRACT TYPE	(3) PLAYER TYPE	(4) TOTAL GROSS SALARY	(5) BASE SALARY	TIME UNITS	SALARY UNITS	TOTAL UNITS	FOR SAG USE ONLY

(1) Include days not worked, but considered worked under continuous employment provisions. Report contractually guaranteed work period or actual time worked, whichever is longer.
(2) Insert D for Daily or W for Weekly type of contract.
(3) Insert: A = Actor; ST = Stunt; P = Pilot; SG = Singer; ADR = Automated Dialogue Replacement.
(4) Include all salary, Overtime, Premium, and Stunt Adjustments. Do not include any Penalties paid (e.g., Meal Penalties, Forced Calls, etc.).
(5) List base contractual salary (e.g., $1,500.00/week or $500.00/day).

SCREEN ACTORS GUILD
MEMBER REPORT
ADR THEATRICAL/TELEVISION

It is the responsibility of the reporting member to file a copy of this report with the Screen Actors Guild within forty-eight (48) hours of each session and to deliver a copy to the employer or the employer's representative at the conclusion of each session. If there is a contractor, he shall assume these responsibilities with respect to each session.

Work Date _____   Title _____

Episode Title _____   Production Number _____

Production Co./   Studio   Sound Supervisor
Employer _____   Facility _____   Editor _____

Address _____   Address _____   Sound Engineer/
                                                                    Mixer _____

         _____   _____   ADR Supervisor _____

         _____   _____   Employer Rep. _____

Phone Number (___) _____   Phone Number (___) _____

Type of Film: Theatrical ☐   TV Series ☐   TV MOW ☐   TV Pilot ☐   Other _____

Performer's Name	Performer's Social Security Number	Character of 6+ Lines (sync)	Additional sets of up to 3 characters under 5 sync lines each	Hours Employed		Meal Period From/To	Performer's Initials
				Studio Time Report/Dismiss			
_____	_____	_____	_____	_____		_____	_____
_____	_____	_____	_____	_____		_____	_____
_____	_____	_____	_____	_____		_____	_____
_____	_____	_____	_____	_____		_____	_____
_____	_____	_____	_____	_____		_____	_____
_____	_____	_____	_____	_____		_____	_____
_____	_____	_____	_____	_____		_____	_____
_____	_____	_____	_____	_____		_____	_____

Reel Numbers Recorded: _____

NOTES: _____

_____

This engagement shall be governed by and be subject to the applicable terms of the Screen Actors Guild Codified Basic or Television Agreement.

Production Co./EMPLOYER _____

Signature of Employer or
Employer Representative _____

SAG Reporter _____   (Print name) _____

SAG Reporter's Phone # (___) _____   Date _____

SCHEDULE A—EXHIBIT I

DIRECTORS GUILD OF AMERICA
WEEKLY WORK LIST

From: _____

(signatory company)

_____

(address)

_____

Return to:
Directors Guild of America, Inc.

Week Ending: _____

Name	Soc. Sec. #	Cat.	Project

Prepared by _____

Phone # _____

RC314/031489

DGA EMPLOYMENT DATA REPORT

DATE: _____ PREPARED BY: _____ PHONE #: _____

SIGNATORY COMPANY: _____

QUARTER COVERED: _____

PROJECT: _____

DIRECTOR

	C	B	H	A	AI	UNKNOWN
MALE						
FEMALE						

UNIT PRODUCTION MANAGER

	C	B	H	A	AI	UNKNOWN
MALE						
FEMALE						

FIRST ASSISTANT DIRECTOR

	C	B	H	A	AI	UNKNOWN
MALE						
FEMALE						

SECOND ASSISTANT DIRECTOR

	C	B	H	A	AI	UNKNOWN
MALE						
FEMALE						

FIRST TIME DIRECTOR

	C	B	H	A	AI	UNKNOWN
MALE						
FEMALE						

INSTRUCTIONS

The minority codes utilized in this report represent the following:

C	-	CAUCASIAN
B	-	BLACK
H	-	HISPANIC
A	-	ASIAN
AI	-	AMERICAN INDIAN

When completing this report the employment statistics must be reported in order that two (2) types of statistics can be obtained; the first statistic will indicate the number of persons employed in the respective category (referenced above) during that quarter. The second statistic will indicate the number of days worked or guaranteed in the respective categories for that quarter. Therefore in each category, there will be two (2) separate sets of statistics, one on top of the other, separated by a horizontal slash (example below). The top statistic will represent the number of employees working, the bottom statistic will be the number of days worked or guaranteed during the same quarter.

Example:

DIRECTOR

	C	B	H	A	AI	UNKNOWN
MALE	1/56					
FEMALE		1/25				

In the above example there was one (1) male Caucasian Director working during the quarter for a total of fifty-six (56) days worked or guaranteed. There was one (1) female Black Director working for a total of twenty-five days worked or guaranteed.

This report is to be submitted on a per-production basis not on a per episode basis. In instances where the same DGA employee is employed for multiple episodes in a continuing series, such employee will only be counted once in the number of employee statistics but such employee's cumulative days worked shall be included in that statistic.

NOTICE OF TENTATIVE WRITING CREDITS—THEATRICAL

TO: Writers Guild of America, west, Inc. 7000 West Third Street, Los Angeles, CA 90048, or to:
   Writers Guild of America, East, Inc. 555 West 57th Street, New York, NY 10019

   AND

   Participating Writer(s) (or current agent, if participant so elects)

NAMES OF PARTICIPATING WRITER(S)   ADDRESS(ES)

_____ _____

_____ _____

_____ _____

_____ _____

TITLE OF MOTION PICTURE:_____

EXECUTIVE PRODUCER:_____

PRODUCER:_____

DIRECTOR:_____

OTHER PRODUCTION EXECUTIVE(S), AND THEIR TITLE(S),

IF PARTICIPATING WRITER(S):_____

_____

Writing Credits on this production are tentatively determined as follows:

ON SCREEN:_____

_____

ON SCREEN SOURCE MATERIAL CREDIT, IF ANY:_____

_____

ON SCREEN AND/OR IN ADVERTISING, presentation and production credit, IF ANY:_____

_____

SOURCE MATERIAL upon which the motion picture is based, IF ANY:_____

_____

The final shooting script is being sent to all participating writers with the notice of tentative writing credits.

The above tentative writing credits will become final unless a protest is communicated to the undersigned not later than 6:00 p.m. on _____.

Company:_____ By:_____

               Name:_____

               Address:_____

               _____

Date:_____ Phone No:_____

NOTICE OF TENTATIVE WRITING CREDITS—TELEVISION

Date _____

TO: Writers Guild of America, west, Inc. 7000 West Third Street, Los Angeles, CA 90048, or to:
      Writers Guild of America, East, Inc. 555 West 57th Street, New York, NY 10019

      AND

      Participating Writers

NAMES OF PARTICIPATING WRITERS   ADDRESS

_____   _____
_____   _____
_____   _____
_____   _____

Title of Episode_____ Production#_____
(If Pilot or MOW or other special or unit program, indicate Network and length)

Series Title_____

Producing Company_____

Executive Producer_____

Producer_____ Assoc. Producer_____

Director_____ Story Editor_____
                                       (or Consultant)

Other Production Executives, If Participating Writers_____

_____

Writing Credits on this episode are tentatively determined as follows:

ON SCREEN:

Source material credit ON THIS EPISODE (on separate card, unless otherwise indicated) if any:

Continuing source material or Created By credit APPEARING ON ALL EPISODES OF SERIES (on separate card):

Revised final script was sent to participating writers on_____

The above tentative credits will become final unless a protest is communicated to the undersigned not later than 6:00 p.m. on_____.

_____
(Company)

By:_____

CAST INFORMATION SHEET

SHOW: _____

ACTOR	#	ROLE	START DATE	D=DAILY, W=WEEKLY, D/P=DROP/PICKUP	# OF DAYS WORKING	DEAL MEMO	SENT SCRIPT	NOTIFIED WARDROBE	NOTIFIED MAKEUP & HAIR	STATION 12	TRAVEL/HOTEL ACCOMMODATIONS	RENTAL CAR -OR- CAR & DRIVER	MEDICAL EXAM	RECEIVED HEAD-SHOTS	CONTRACT PREPARED	CONTRACT TO AGENT/ACTOR	SIGNED CONTRACT RETURNED	CONTRACT CO-SIGNED & DISTRIBUTED	WORK PERMIT, IF MINOR	SCRIPT REVISIONS (BLUE)	SCRIPT REVISIONS (PINK)	SCRIPT REVISIONS (GREEN)	DIALOGUE COACH OR LESSONS, IF NECESSARY

© ELH

EXTRA TALENT VOUCHER

VOUCHER NO:

DATE:	PRODUCTION:		[ ] UNION [ ] NON-UNION
PRODUCTION COMPANY:		PROD. CO. PHONE NO:	UNION NO:
EXTRA CASTING AGENCY:		EMPLOYER OF RECORD (Payroll Co.):	
CONTACT:	PHONE NO:	ADDRESS:	
NAME (Please Print)		AGE:	
ADDRESS:		PHONE NO:	

		[ ] NEW EMPLOYEE [ ] NEW ADDRESS	INTERVIEW: $
PHONE NO:	CELL/PGR. NO:	[ ] MARRIED [ ] SINGLE	FITTING: $
SOCIAL SECURITY NO. (must be completed):		# OF ALLOWANCES:	SPECIAL ABILITY: $

REPORT TIME/IN:	RATE: $	WARDROBE:	QTY:	$	SMOKE WORK: $
FIRST MEAL OUT:	RATE ADJUSTMENT: $	MEAL PENALTY:	QTY:	$	BODY MAKEUP: $
FIRST MEAL IN:	___ HRS. OF S.T. @ $	AUTO:		$	HAIR: $
SECOND MEAL OUT:	___ HRS. OF 1-1/2X @ $	MILES:			WET WORK: $
SECOND MEAL IN:	___ HRS. OF 2X @ $	AMT. PER MILE: $.			BEARD: $
DISMISSED/TIME OUT:					DRESS OR UNIFORM: $
TOTAL MEAL TIME:	TOTAL ADJUSTMENTS: $				OTHER: $
NET HOURS:	**GROSS TOTAL: $**	TOTAL:		$	TOTAL $

I acknowledge receipt of the compensation stated herein as payment in full for all services rendered by me on the days indicated. I hereby grant to my employer permission to photograph me and to record my voice, performances, poses, acts, plays and appearances, and use my picture, photograph, silhouette and other reproductions of my physical likeness and sound in the above-named production and in the unlimited distribution, advertising, promotion, exhibition and exploitation of the production by any method or device now known or hereafter devised in which the same may be used. I agree that I will not assert or maintain against you, your successors, assigns and licensees, any claim, action, suit or demand of any kind or nature whatsoever in connection with your authorized use of my physical likeness and sound in the production as herein provided.

As a condition of my employment by the Production Company on The Production, I agree that I will abide by all rules of employment as dictated by the Production Company or its agents, or by any Safety Coordinators assigned to The Production, especially those rules pertaining to safety including but not limited to: (a) remaining in areas designated as safe areas during any period that I am not asked to perform my duties as an extra, and (b) acting in a safe manner at all times so as not to injure myself or others, and (c) to refrain from taking any illegal substances that might impair my ability to do the job for which I was hired.

As a further condition of employment herein, I agree that I have the ability to perform each and every task, job assignment or special ability I have been asked to perform, and that if I knowingly make false representations that I am qualified to perform these assignments when, in fact, I know that I am not qualified, that such misrepresentation may be grounds for dismissal of any workers compensation claim should I be injured as a result of performing an assignment for which I knowingly was not qualified to perform.

I have read the entire conditions of employment and by signing this voucher, I acknowledge that I understand and agree with the entire conditions of employment.

SIGNATURE: _____

(If minor, parent or guardian must sign)

APPROVED BY: _____ TITLE: _____

SAG EXTRA VOUCHER

PRODUCER:

DATE

SAG NO.

☐ SINGLE ☐ MARRIED ☐ MARRIED but withheld at higher single rate

SOCIAL SECURITY NO. MUST BE PROVIDED TO MAKE PAYMENT

Total number of allowances you are claiming: _____

Additional amount, if any, you want deducted $ _____

If claiming exemption from withholding, write exempt and year in box _____ 19 _____

EMPLOYEE: PLEASE PRINT INFORMATION LISTED ABOVE AND SIGN WHERE INDICATED

"I, the undersigned, certify that the number of income tax withholding exemptions claimed on this certificate does not exceed the number of which I am entitled.

"I agree to accept the sum properly computed based upon the times and the basic wage rate shown as payment in full for all services heretofore rendered by me for said employer.

"I further agree that the said sum, less all deduction required by law, may be paid to me by negotiable check issued by said company, said check to be addressed to me at my last reported address and deposited in the United States mail within the time periods provided by law.

"I hereby give and grant to the company named all rights of every kind and character whatsoever in and to all work heretofore done, and all poses, acts, plays and appearances heretofore made by me for you and in and to all of the results and proceeds of my services heretofore rendered for you, as well as in and to the right to use my name, likeness and photographs, either still or moving for commercial and advertising purposes. I further give and grant to the said company the right to reproduce in any manner whatsoever any recordations heretofore made by said company of my voice and all instrumental, musical, or other sound effects produced by me. I further agree that in the event of a retake of all or any of the scenes in which I participate, or if additional scenes are required (whether originally contemplated or not) I will return to work, and render my services in such scenes at the same basic rate of compensations as that paid me for the original taking.

"By signing this form, I hereby agree that said employer may take deductions from my earnings to adjust previous overpayments if and when said overpayments may occur."

Signature _____ **Date** _____

Address _____ **Apt #** _____

City _____ **State** _____ **Zip** _____

Phone Number _____

BACK OF WHITE COPY MUST BE COMPLETED

YOUR EMPLOYER OF RECORD IS
IF OTHER THAN A PAYROLL COMPANY, EMPLOYER'S FEDERAL I.D. NUMBER IS _____

PRODUCTION NO. OR TITLE

	DISMISSAL TIME
	STARTING TIME

TYPE OF CALL

		PENALTIES	HOURS WORKED	MEAL PERIODS
				OUT IN
BASIC WAGE RATE	TRAVEL TIME ARRIVE LOCATION: LEAVE LOCATION:			OUT IN

ASST. DIR.-APPROVED FOR PAYMENT

	FITTING	MEALS B☐ L☐ D☐	INTERVIEW ☐
	☐		

WARDROBE	PROPS	VEHICLE	MILEAGE

DO NOT WRITE IN THIS SPACE

TYPE OF WORK	PAY CODE	HOURS			BASIC RATE	
		WORK	PAY	AMOUNT		
DAY		·	·			
NIGHT		·	·			ADJUSTMENTS
O/T		·	·			
WET		·	·			OVERTIME
SMOKE		·	·			
OTHER		·	·			ALLOWANCES
OTHER		·	·			
OTHER		·	·			GROSS
OTHER		·	·		·	

white—PAYROLL COPY
yellow—PRODUCTION COPY
pink—SAG COPY
golden rod—EXTRAS COPY

Screen Actors Guild
Kenmar Printing 357
Form No. 451

The Complete Film Production Handbook **457**

PERSONAL RELEASE

Film: _____

Prod. Co.: _____

Address: _____

_____   Date: _____

Ladies and Gentlemen:

I, the undersigned, hereby grant permission to _____ ("Producer") to photograph me and to record my voice, performances, poses, acts, plays and appearances, and use my picture, photograph, silhouette and other reproductions of my physical likeness and sound as part of the _____ tentatively entitled _____ (the "Picture") and the unlimited distribution, advertising, promotion, exhibition and exploitation of the Picture by any method or device now known or hereafter devised in which the same may be used, and/or incorporated and/or exhibited and/or exploited.

I agree that I will not assert or maintain against you, your successors, assigns and licensees, any claim, action, suit or demand of any kind or nature whatsoever, including but not limited to, those grounded upon invasion of privacy, rights of publicity or other civil rights, or for any other reason in connection with your authorized use of my physical likeness and sound in the Picture as herein provided. I hereby release you, your successors, assigns and licensees, and each of them, from and against any and all claims, liabilities, demands, actions, causes of action(s), costs and expenses whatsoever, at law or in equity, known or unknown, anticipated or unanticipated, which I ever had, now have, or may, shall or hereafter have by reason, matter, cause or thing arising out of your use as herein provided.

I affirm that neither I, nor anyone acting for me, gave or agreed to give anything of value to any of your employees or any representative of any television network, motion picture studio or production entity for arranging my appearance on the Picture.

I have read the foregoing and fully understand the meaning and effect thereof and, intending to be legally bound, I have signed this release.

Dated: _____

_____
Signature

_____
If a Minor, Guardian's Signature

_____
Please Print Name

AGREED AND ACCEPTED TO:

_____

By: _____
_____
Address

_____
Phone No.

PERSONAL RELEASE—PAYMENT

Film: _____

Prod. Co.: _____

Address: _____

_____   Date:_____

Ladies and Gentlemen:

In consideration of payment to me of the sum of $_____, receipt of which is hereby acknowledged, I, undersigned, hereby grant permission to _____ ("Producer") to photograph me and to record my voice, performances, poses, acts, plays and appearances, and use my picture, photograph, silhouette and other reproductions of my physical likeness and sound as part of the _____ tentatively entitled _____ (the "Picture") and the unlimited distribution, advertising, promotion, exhibition and exploitation of the Picture by any method or device now known or hereafter devised in which the same may be used, and/or incorporated and/or exhibited and/or exploited.

I agree that I will not assert or maintain against you, your successors, assigns and licensees, any claim, action, suit or demand of any kind or nature whatsoever, including but not limited to, those grounded upon invasion of privacy, rights of publicity or other civil rights, or for any other reason in connection with your authorized use of my physical likeness and sound in the Picture as herein provided. I hereby release you, your successors, assigns and licensees, and each of them, from and against any and all claims, liabilities, demands, actions, causes of action(s), costs and expenses whatsoever, at law or in equity, known or unknown, anticipated or unanticipated, which I ever had, now have, or may, shall or hereafter have by reason, matter, cause or thing arising out of your use as herein provided.

I affirm that neither I, nor anyone acting for me, gave or agreed to give anything of value to any of your employees or any representative of any television network, motion picture studio or production entity for arranging my appearance on the Picture.

I have read the foregoing and fully understand the meaning and effect thereof and, intending to be legally bound, I have signed this release.

Dated:_____

_____
Signature

_____
If a Minor, Guardian's Signature

_____
Please Print Name

_____

AGREED AND ACCEPTED TO:

_____
Address

_____
Phone No.

By:_____

_____
Social Security or Federal ID No.

GROUP RELEASE

Film: _____

Prod. Co.: _____

Address: _____

_____   Date: _____

Ladies and Gentlemen:

I, the undersigned, hereby grant permission to _____ ("Producer")
to photograph me and to record my voice, performances, poses, acts, plays and appearances, and use
my picture, photograph, silhouette and other reproductions of my physical likeness and sound as part of
the _____ tentatively entitled _____
_____ (the "Picture") and the unlimited distribution,
advertising, promotion, exhibition and exploitation of the Picture by any method or device now known or
hereafter devised in which the same may be used, and/or incorporated and/or exhibited and/or exploited.

I agree that I will not assert or maintain against you, your successors, assigns and licensees, any claim,
action, suit or demand of any kind or nature whatsoever, including but not limited to, those grounded upon
invasion of privacy, rights of publicity or other civil rights, or for any other reason in connection with your
authorized use of my physical likeness and sound in the Picture as herein provided. I hereby release
you, your successors, assigns and licensees, and each of them, from and against any and all claims,
liabilities, demands, actions, causes of action(s), costs and expenses whatsoever, at law or in equity,
known or unknown, anticipated or unanticipated, which I ever had, now have, or may, shall or hereafter
have by reason, matter, cause or thing arising out of your use as herein provided.

I affirm that neither I, nor anyone acting for me, gave or agreed to give anything of value to any of your
employees or any representative of any television network, motion picture studio or production entity for
arranging my appearance on the Picture.

I have read the foregoing and fully understand the meaning and effect thereof and, intending to be legally
bound, I have signed this release.

NAME	ADDRESS	SOC. SEC.#

USE OF NAME

Film: _____

Prod. Co.: _____

Address: _____

_____   Date:_____

Ladies and Gentlemen:

For good and valuable consideration, receipt of which is hereby acknowledged, I grant permission to_____("Producer") and its successors, assigns, distributees and licensees forever, throughout the universe, the sole, exclusive and unconditional right and license to use, simulate and portray my name to such extent and in such manner as you in your sole discretion may elect, in or in connection with your_____ tentatively entitled _____(the "Picture") including reissues, remakes of and sequels to any such production, prepared by you or any successor to your interest therein, together with the right to publish synopses thereof, and to advertise, exploit, present, release, distribute, exhibit and/or otherwise utilize said productions and publications throughout the world.

I hereby release Producer, its successors, assigns, distributees and licensees from any and all claims and demands arising out of or in connection with such use including, without limitation, any and all claims for invasion of privacy, infringement of your right of publicity, defamation (including libel and slander) and any other personal and/or property rights.

In granting of the foregoing rights and licenses, I acknowledge that I have not been induced so to do by any representative or assurance by you or on your behalf relative to the manner in which any of the rights or licenses granted hereunder may be exercised; and I agree that you are under no obligation to exercise any of the rights or licenses granted hereunder.

Dated:_____

                                                        _____
                                                        Signature

                                                        _____
                                                        Please Print Name

                                                        _____
AGREED AND ACCEPTED TO:
                                                        Address

                                                        _____
By:_____
                                                        Phone No.

USE OF TRADEMARK OR LOGO

Film: _____

Prod. Co.: _____

Address: _____

_____ Date:_____

Ladies and Gentlemen:

For good and valuable consideration, receipt of which is hereby acknowledged, the undersigned hereby grants to you, your agents, successors, licensees and assigns, the non-exclusive right, but not the obligation to photograph, record, reproduce or otherwise use all or part of our trademark(s), logo(s), and/or animated or identifiable characters (the "Mark(s)") listed below in the _____ tentatively entitled _____ (the "Picture"), and to utilize and reproduce the Mark(s) in connection with the Picture, without limitation as to time or number of runs, for reproduction, exhibition and exploitation, throughout the world, in any and all manner, methods and media, whether now known or hereafter devised, and in the advertising, publicizing, promotion, trailers and exploitation thereof.

The undersign represents that the consent of no other person or entity is required to enable you to use the Mark(s) and that such use will not violate or infringe upon the rights of any third parties. I hereby release to you and your agents, successors, licensees and assigns, from any claim of any kind or nature whatsoever arising from the use of the Mark(s).

In granting of the foregoing rights and licenses, I acknowledge that I have not been induced to do so by any representative or assurance by you or on your behalf relative to the manner in which any of the rights or licenses granted hereunder may be exercised; and I agree that you are under no obligation to exercise any of the rights or licenses granted hereunder.

Mark(s):_____

Very truly yours,

_____
Signature

_____
Please Print Name

_____
Title

_____
Company

AGREED AND ACCEPTED TO:

_____

_____
Address

By:_____

_____
Phone No.

USE OF LITERARY MATERIAL

Film: _____

Prod. Co.: _____

Address: _____

_____ Date: _____

Ladies and Gentlemen:

I am informed that you are producing a _____ tentatively entitled
_____ (the "Picture"), and that you have requested that I
grant you the right to use the title and/or portions of the following literary material owned and
published by the undersigned for inclusion in the Picture:

For good and valuable consideration, receipt of which is hereby acknowledged, I, the
undersigned, do hereby confirm the consent hereby given you with respect to your use of the
above title and/or literary material (the "Materials") in connection with the Picture, and I do hereby
grant to you, your agents, successors, licensees and assigns, the perpetual right to use the
Materials in connection with the Picture. I agree that you may record the Materials on film, tape or
otherwise and use the Materials and recordings in and in connection with the exhibition,
advertising, promotion, exploitation, and any other use of the Picture as you may desire.

I represent that the consent of no other person or entity is required to enable you to use the
Materials, and that such use will not violate or infringe upon the rights of any third parties. I
hereby release you, your agents, successors, licensees and assigns from and against any and
all claims, liabilities, demands, actions, causes of action, costs and expenses, whatsoever, at law
or in equity, known or unknown, arising out of your use of the Materials as provided herein in
connection with the Picture.

In granting of the foregoing rights and licenses, I acknowledge that I have not been induced to do
so by any representative or assurance by you or on your behalf relative to the manner in which
any of the rights or licenses granted hereunder may be exercised; and I agree that you are under
no obligation to exercise any of the rights or licenses granted hereunder.

Very truly yours,

_____
Signature

_____
Please Print Name

AGREED AND ACCEPTED TO:

_____

_____
Address

By: _____

_____
Phone No.

USE OF ARTWORK
(RELEASE FROM COPYRIGHTED OWNER)

Film: _____

Prod. Co.: _____

Address: _____

_____ Date: _____

Ladies and Gentlemen:

For good and valuable consideration, receipt of which is hereby acknowledged, I, the undersigned, grant to you, your agents, successors, licensees and assigns, the non-exclusive right but not the obligation to use my artwork (as described below) in the _____ _____ tentatively entitled _____ (the "Picture"), and to utilize and reproduce the artwork in connection with the Picture, without limitation as to time or number of runs, for reproduction, exhibition and exploitation, throughout the world, in any and all manner, methods and media, whether now known or hereafter known or devised, and in the advertising, publicizing, promotion, and exploitation thereof.

I hereby release you, your agents, successors, licensees and assigns from any claim of any kind or nature whatsoever arising from the use of such artwork, including, but not limited to, those based upon defamation (including libel and slander), invasion of privacy, right of publicity, copyright, or any other personal and/or property rights and agree that I will not now or in the future assert or maintain any claims against you, your agents, successors, licensees and assigns.

I represent that I am the owner and/or authorized representative of the artwork, and that I have the authority to grant you the permission and rights herein granted, and that no one else's permission is required with respect to the rights herein granted.

In granting of the foregoing rights and licenses, I acknowledge that I have not been induced to do so by any representative or assurance by you or on your behalf relative to the manner in which any of the rights or licenses granted hereunder may be exercised; and I agree that you are under no obligation to exercise any of the rights or licenses granted hereunder.

Title of Artwork: "_____"

Very truly yours,

_____
Signature of Owner and/or Authorized Agent

_____
Please Print Name

_____
Title/Company

AGREED AND ACCEPTED TO:
_____
Address

By:_____
_____
Phone No.

USE OF STILL PHOTOGRAPH(S)
(RELEASE FROM COPYRIGHTED OWNER)

Film: _____

Prod. Co.: _____

Address: _____

_____   Date:_____

Ladies and Gentlemen:

For good and valuable consideration, receipt of which is hereby acknowledged, I, the undersigned, grant to you, your agents, successors, licensees and assigns, the non-exclusive right but not the obligation to use and include the still photograph(s) (the "Still(s)") as described below, in the_____tentatively entitled _____
_____(the "Picture"), and to utilize and reproduce the Still(s) in connection with the Picture, without limitation as to time or number of runs, for reproduction, exhibition and exploitation, throughout the world, in any and all manner, methods and media, whether now known or hereafter known or devised, and in the advertising, publicizing, promotion, and exploitation thereof.

I hereby release you, your agents, successors, licensees and assigns from any claims of any kind or nature whatsoever arising from the use of the Still(s), including, but not limited to, those based upon defamation, invasion of privacy, right of publicity, copyright, or any other personal and/or property rights and agree that I will not now or in the future assert or maintain any claims against you, your agents, successors, licensees and assigns.

I represent that I am the owner and/or authorized representative of the poster, and that I have the authority to grant you the permission and rights herein granted, and that no one else's permission is required with respect to the rights herein granted.

In granting of the foregoing rights and licenses, I acknowledge that I have not been induced to do so by any representative or assurance by you or on your behalf relative to the manner in which any of the rights or licenses granted hereunder may be exercised; and I agree that you are under no obligation to exercise any of the rights or licenses granted hereunder.

Description of the Still(s):_____

_____

_____

Very truly yours,

_____
Signature of Owner and/or Authorized Agent

_____
Please Print Name

_____
Title/Company

AGREED AND ACCEPTED TO:

_____

By:_____

_____
Address

_____
Phone No.

USE OF STILL PHOTOGRAPH(S)
(RELEASE FROM PERSON DEPICTED IN PHOTO)

Film: _____

Prod. Co.: _____

Address: _____

_____   Date: _____

Ladies and Gentlemen:

For good and valuable consideration, receipt of which is hereby acknowledged, I, the undersigned, grant to you, your agents, successors, licensees and assigns, the non-exclusive right but not the obligation to use and include my physical likeness in the form of a still photograph(s) (the "Still(s)") as described below, in the_____ tentatively entitled _____ (the "Picture"), and to utilize and reproduce the Still(s) in connection with the Picture, without limitation as to time or number of runs, for reproduction, exhibition and exploitation, throughout the world, in any and all manner, methods and media, whether now known or hereafter known or devised, and in the advertising, publicizing, promotion, and exploitation thereof.

I agree that I will not assert or maintain against you, your agents, successors, licensees and assigns, a claim, action, suit or demand of any kind or nature whatsoever, including but not limited to, those grounded upon invasion of privacy, rights of publicity or other civil rights, or for any other reason in connection with your authorized use of the Still(s) in the Picture as herein provided. I hereby release you, your agents, successors, licensees and assigns from any and all such claims, actions, causes of action, suits and demands whatsoever that I may now or hereafter have against you or them.

In granting of the foregoing rights and licenses, I acknowledge that I have not been induced to do so by any representative or assurance by you or on your behalf relative to the manner in which any of the rights or licenses granted hereunder may be exercised; and I agree that you are under no obligation to exercise any of the rights or licenses granted hereunder.

Description of the Still(s):_____

_____

_____

Sincerely yours,

_____

Signature

_____

Please Print Name

AGREED AND ACCEPTED TO:

_____

Address

By:_____

_____

Phone No.

USE OF POSTER
(RELEASE FROM COPYRIGHTED OWNER)

Film: _____

Prod. Co.: _____

Address: _____

_____   Date: _____

Ladies and Gentlemen:

For good and valuable consideration, receipt of which is hereby acknowledged, I, the undersigned, grant to you, your agents, successors, licensees and assigns, the non-exclusive right but not the obligation to use and include the poster (entitled or otherwise described as _____ _____) (the "Poster") in the _____ tentatively entitled _____ (the "Picture"), and to utilize and reproduce the Poster in connection with the Picture, without limitation as to time or number of runs, for reproduction, exhibition and exploitation, throughout the world, in any and all manner, methods and media, whether now known or hereafter known or devised, and in the advertising, publicizing, promotion, and exploitation thereof.

I hereby release you, your agents, successors, licensees and assigns from any claims of any kind or nature whatsoever arising from the use of the Poster, including, but not limited to, those based upon defamation (including libel and slander), invasion of privacy, right of publicity, copyright, or any other personal and/or property rights and agree that I will not now or in the future assert or maintain any claims against you, your agents, successors, licensees and assigns.

I represent that I am the owner and/or authorized representative of the poster, and that I have the authority to grant you the permission and rights herein granted, and that no one else's permission is required with respect to the rights herein granted.

In granting of the foregoing rights and licenses, I acknowledge that I have not been induced to do so by any representative or assurance by you or on your behalf relative to the manner in which any of the rights or licenses granted hereunder may be exercised; and I agree that you are under no obligation to exercise any of the rights or licenses granted hereunder.

Very truly yours,

_____
Signature of Owner and/or Authorized Agent

_____
Please Print Name

_____
Title/Company

AGREED AND ACCEPTED TO:
_____

By: _____
_____
Address

_____
Phone No.

USE OF VEHICLE

Film: _____

Prod. Co.: _____

Address: _____

_____   Date:_____

Ladies and Gentlemen:

For good and valuable consideration, receipt of which is hereby acknowledged, I, the undersigned, grant to you, your agents, successors, licensees and assigns, the right but not the obligation to use the below-mentioned vehicle, and to include all or part of the trademarks, logos, and/or identifiable characters associated therewith ("Vehicle") in the_____ tentatively entitled _____(the "Picture"), without limitation as to time or number of runs, for reproduction, exhibition and exploitation, throughout the world, in any and all manner, methods and media, whether now known or hereafter known or devised, and in the advertising, publicizing, promotion, and exploitation thereof.

The undersigned represents that the consent of no other person or entity is required to enable Producer to use the Vehicle as described herein and that such use will not violate or infringe upon the trademarks, service marks, trade names, copyright, artistic and/or other rights of any third parties including the rights of publicity and/or privacy. The undersigned hereby releases Producer, Producer's agents, successors, licensees and assigns, from any claim of any kind or nature whatsoever arising from the use of the Vehicle, including but not limited to, those based upon defamation, invasion of privacy, right of publicity, copyright, or any other personal and/or property rights, and the undersigned agrees that the undersigned shall not now or in the future assert or maintain any such claim against Producer, Producer's agents, successors, licensees and assigns.

In granting of the foregoing rights and licenses, I acknowledge that I have not been induced to do so by any representative or assurance by you or on your behalf relative to the manner in which any of the rights or licenses granted hereunder may be exercised; and I agree that you are under no obligation to exercise any of the rights or licenses granted hereunder.

Very truly yours,

_____
Signature of Owner and/or Authorized Agent

_____
Please Print Name

_____
Title/Company

AGREED AND ACCEPTED TO:

_____
Address

By:_____

_____
Phone No.

CROWD NOTICE—RELEASE

TO BE PLACED IN SEVERAL CLEARLY VISIBLE LOCATIONS
IN A STUDIO WHEN FILMING OR TAPING BEFORE A LIVE AUDIENCE

CROWD NOTICE—RELEASE

PLEASE BE ADVISED THAT YOUR PRESENCE AS A MEMBER OF
THIS STUDIO AUDIENCE DURING THE FILMING/TAPING OF THE
PROGRAM _____
CONSTITUTES YOUR CONSENT TO YOUR VOICE AND LIKENESS
BEING USED, WITHOUT COMPENSATION, IN THE UNLIMITED
DISTRIBUTION, ADVERTISING, PROMOTION, EXHIBITION AND
EXPLOITATION OF THE PROGRAM IN ANY AND ALL MEDIA BY ANY
METHOD OR DEVICE NOW KNOWN OR HEREAFTER DEVISED, AND
YOU RELEASE _____
FROM ANY LIABILITY IN CONNECTION WITH SUCH USAGE.

IF FOR ANY REASON YOU OBJECT TO YOUR VOICE AND LIKENESS
BEING SO USED, YOU SHOULD LEAVE THE STUDIO AT THIS TIME.
IF YOU REMAIN, YOUR PRESENCE AT THIS FILMING/TAPING WILL
CONSTITUTE YOUR APPROVAL OF THE FOREGOING.

CROWD NOTICE—RELEASE

TO BE PLACED IN SEVERAL CLEARLY VISIBLE LOCATIONS
IN THE "AREA" IN WHICH FILMING OR TAPING IS TAKING PLACE

CROWD NOTICE—RELEASE

PLEASE BE ADVISED THAT FILMING/TAPING IS TAKING PLACE IN
CONNECTION WITH THE PRODUCTION OF A _____
TENTATIVELY ENTITLED _____
PEOPLE ENTERING THIS AREA MAY APPEAR IN THE PICTURE. BY
ENTERING THIS AREA, YOU GRANT TO _____
_____ THE RIGHT TO FILM AND PHOTOGRAPH YOU AND
RECORD YOUR VOICE AND TO USE YOUR VOICE AND LIKENESS,
WITHOUT COMPENSATION, IN CONNECTION WITH THE PICTURE AND
THE DISTRIBUTION AND EXPLOITATION THEREOF, AND YOU RELEASE
_____ AND ITS
LICENSEES FROM ALL LIABILITY IN CONNECTION THEREIN. YOU AGREE
AND UNDERSTAND THAT _____ WILL
PROCEED IN RELIANCE UPON SUCH GRANT AND RELEASE.

_____ DOES NOT ASSUME
RESPONSIBILITY FOR ANY INJURY TO YOUR PERSON OR DAMAGE OR
LOSS TO YOUR PROPERTY.

**THE USE OF CAMERA AND RECORDING EQUIPMENT IS PROHIBITED DUE
TO UNION AND COPYRIGHT REGULATIONS.**

SMOKING IS PROHIBITED IN THIS AREA. THANK YOU!

SUPPLYING A FILM/TAPE CLIP OF YOUR SHOW
FOR PROMOTIONAL PURPOSES

Date:_____

_____

_____

_____

_____

Ladies and Gentlemen:

The undersigned hereby authorizes you to use a Film/Tape Clip (the "Clip") from the _____
entitled _____
for promotional purposes only in the program entitled _____
currently scheduled for broadcast on _____.

The undersigned hereby affirms that neither he nor anyone acting on his behalf or any company
which he may represent, gave or agreed to give anything of value (except for the Clip) which
was furnished for promotional purposes solely on or in connection with _____
_____to any member of the production staff, anyone associated in any manner
with the program or any representative of _____ for mentioning
or displaying the name of any company which he may represent or any of its products,
trademarks, trade-names or the like.

The undersigned understands that any broadcast identification of the Clip (or the name of any
company, product, etc. which he may represent) which _____
may furnish, shall, in no event, be beyond that which is reasonably related to the program
content.

The undersigned is aware, as is the company which he may represent, that it is a Federal offense
unless disclosed to _____ prior to broadcast if the undersigned
gives or agrees to give anything of value to promote any product, service or venture on the air.

The undersigned represents that he is fully empowered to execute this letter on behalf of any
company which he may represent.

The undersigned warrants that he or the company which he may represent has the right to grant
the license herein granted, and agrees to indemnify you for all loss, damage and liability, excluding
the payment of any guild-related talent fees or performing rights fees in the music included in said
Clip, if any (which you agree to pay or cause to be paid), arising out of the use of the above
material.

Very truly yours,

AGREED AND ACCEPTED TO:

_____
Signature

_____
Please Print Name

By:_____

_____
Title

_____
Phone No.

PRODUCT PLACEMENT RELEASE

Film: _____

Prod. Co.: _____

Address: _____

_____ Date: _____

Ladies and Gentlemen:

The undersigned ("Company") agrees to provide the following product(s) and/or service(s) to _____ for use in the _____ tentatively entitled _____ (the "Picture"):

The Company grants to you, your successors, licensees and assigns, the non-exclusive right, but not the obligation to use and include all or part of the trademark(s), logo(s) and/or identifiable characters (the "Mark(s)") associated with the above listed product(s) and/or service(s) in the Picture, without limitation as to time or number of runs, for reproduction, exhibition and exploitation, throughout the world, in any and all manner, methods and media, whether now known or hereafter known or devised, and in the advertising, publicizing, promotion, trailers and exploitation thereof.

The Company warrants and represents that it is the owner of the product(s) or direct provider of the service(s) as listed above or a representative of such and has the right to enter this agreement and grant the rights granted to _____ hereunder.

In full consideration of the Company providing the product(s) and/or service(s) to _____ _____, _____ agrees to accord the Company screen credit in the end titles of the positive prints of the Picture in the following form:

The Company understands that any broadcast identification of its products, trademarks, trade names or the like which may furnish, shall in no event, be beyond that which is reasonably related to the program content.

As it applies to any and all television broadcasts of the Picture, the Company is aware that it is a Federal offense to give or agree to give anything of value to promote any product, service or venture on the air. The Company affirms that it did not give or agree to give anything of value, except for the product(s) and/or service(s) to any member of the production staff, anyone associated in any manner with the Picture or any representative of _____ for mentioning or displaying the name of the Company or any of its products, trademarks, trade names, or the like.

I represent that I am an officer of the Company and am empowered to execute this form on behalf of the Company.

I further represent that neither I nor the Company which I represent will directly or indirectly publicize or otherwise exploit the use, exhibition or demonstration of the above product(s) and/or service(s) in the Picture for advertising, merchandising or promotional purposes without the express written consent of _____.

Sincerely yours,

_____
Authorized Signatory

_____
Please Print Name

_____
Title

AGREED AND ACCEPTED TO: _____
Name of Company

_____

By:_____   _____
Address

_____
Phone No.

FILM/TAPE FOOTAGE RELEASE

Date:_____

LICENSOR:_____

LICENSEE:_____

DESCRIPTION OF THE FOOTAGE:_____

_____

_____

PRODUCTION:_____ (the "Picture")

LENGTH OF FOOTAGE:_____

LICENSE FEE, if any:_____

Licensor hereby grants to Licensee, Licensor's permission to edit and include all or portion of the above-mentioned Footage in the Picture as follows:

1. Licensor grants to Licensee a non-exclusive license to edit and incorporate the Footage in the Picture. Licensee may broadcast and otherwise exploit the Footage in the Picture, and in customary advertising and publicity thereof, throughout the world in perpetuity in any media now known or hereafter devised.

2. Licensee shall not make any reproductions whatsoever of or from the Footage except as described hereunder.

3. Licensee agrees to obtain, at Licensee's expense, all required consents of any person whose appearances are contained in the Footage pursuant to this agreement, and to make any payments to such persons, guilds or unions having jurisdiction thereof and music publishers, when necessary. Licensor agrees to supply the identity of such persons, if known.

4. Licensor represents and warrants that: (1) Licensor has the right and power to grant the rights herein granted, and (2) neither Licensee's use of the Footage pursuant to this license nor anything contained therein infringes upon the rights of any third parties.

5. Licensor and Licensee each agree to indemnify and hold the other harmless from and against any and all claims, losses liabilities, damages and expenses, including reasonable attorneys' fees, which may result from any breach of their respective representations and warranties hereunder.

6. As between Licensor and Licensee, the Picture shall be Licensee's sole and exclusive property. Licensee shall not be obligated to use the Footage or the rights herein granted or to produce or broadcast the Picture.

7. Licensor acknowledges that, under the Federal Communications Act, it is a Federal offense to give or agree to give anything of value to promote any product, service or venture in the Picture, and Licensor warrants and represents that Licensor has not and will not do so.

8. This agreement constitutes the entire understanding between the parties, supersedes any prior understanding relating thereto and shall not be modified except by a writing signed by the parties. This agreement shall be irrevocable and shall be binding upon and inure to the benefit of Licensor's and Licensee's respective successors, assigns and licensees.

Kindly sign below to indicate our acceptance of the foregoing.

Licensor:

_____
Signature

_____
Please Print Name

_____
Title

CONFIRMED:

_____
Company

_____

By:_____

_____
Address

_____
Phone No.

_____
Soc. Sec. or Federal ID No:

TALENT
USE OF NAME & LIKENESS
IN A FILM OR TV CLIP

Date:_____

_____
_____
_____
_____

Dear _____.

I am writing to you with regard to a _____ being produced by
_____ and tentatively entitled _____
_____ (the "Picture"). The Picture is scheduled
for release on _____.

A brief description of the Picture is as follows:

In conjunction with this Picture, we are requesting permission to use the appearance of _____
_____ in a clip from_____.

In consideration for _____'s permission and in conjunction with the
current SAG Agreement, _____ hereby offers to pay _____
_____ a fee of _____. This sum represents the total
payment for _____'s use of _____'s name and
likeness in the above-described clip in and in connection with the Picture and in promotion for the
picture. Compensation to _____ for any further use of the Picture in
any media shall be governed by the then applicable collective bargaining agreements pertaining
to such use.

I would appreciate it if you would have_____ complete the information
requested below and acknowledge_____ assent to the Agreement by signing below. Once
executed, please return a copy of this letter to us for our records.

Please do not hesitate to call should you have any questions.

Sincerely yours,

ACCEPTED & AGREED TO:

By:_____   Date:_____

_____   SS#:_____

_____   Fed. Tax ID#:_____

_____
Loan-out Corporation Name & Address

REQUEST FOR VIDEOCASSETTE

Date:_____

_____
_____
_____
_____

Dear _____ :

You accept delivery of the_____ ("Recording") of _____
(the "Picture"), and in connection of our delivery of it, agree as follows:

1.   You warrant, represent and agree that the Recording shall be used solely for your private, personal library purpose or for screenings in connection with an in-house demo reel; and the Recording will never be publicly exhibited in any manner or medium whatsoever. You will not charge or authorize the charge of a fee for exhibiting the Recording. You will not duplicate or permit the duplication of the Recording. You will retain possession of the Recording at all times.

2.   All other rights in and to the Picture, under copyright or otherwise, including but not limited to title to, are retained by _____

3.   The permission which we have granted to you for the use of the Recording itself will be non-assignable and non-transferable.

4.   You agree to indemnify us against and hold us harmless from claims, liabilities and actions arising out of your breach of this agreement.

5.   You agree to reimburse us for the cost of making the Recording available to you.

This will become a contract between you and us upon your acceptance of delivery of the Recording.

Sincerely yours,

_____
Signature

_____
Please Print Name

AGREED AND ACCEPTED TO: _____
                                      Address

By:_____   _____ _____
                                      Phone No.

ACKNOWLEDGMENT OF SAFETY GUIDELINES

This will acknowledge that in accordance with the Injury and Illness Prevention Program in place at _____ ,
I have received, read and understand the *Production Safety Guidelines* pertaining to the production of _____ .

I am aware that failure to adhere to these procedures could endanger me and my co-workers, and I will strive to further the company's policy of maintaining a safe work environment.

_____
Employee's Signature

_____
Date

_____
Employee's Name (print or type)

_____
Job Title or Position

(Please return this form to the Production Office when signed.)

DAILY DEPARTMENTAL SAFETY MEETING REPORT

SHOW:_____

DATE:_____SHOOTING DAY#:_____

TODAY'S LOCATION:_____

DEPARTMENT:_____

WAS A DEPARTMENTAL SAFETY MEETING HELD BEFORE SHOOTING? ☐YES ☐NO

WAS THE DAY'S WORK AND REQUIREMENTS TO COMPLETE IT BY
YOUR SPECIFIC DEPARTMENT DISCUSSED? ☐YES ☐NO

WERE ANY SAFETY HAZARDS OR CONCERNS ABOUT SAFETY
RELATED TO THE DAY'S SHOOT DISCUSSED? ☐YES ☐NO

SPECIFICALLY, WHAT SAFETY CONCERNS WERE DISCUSSED?

_____
_____
_____
_____
_____
_____
_____
_____
_____
_____
_____
_____

WERE SAFETY GUIDELINES AND PROCEDURES RELATED TO THESE
CONCERNS DISCUSSED? ☐YES ☐NO

WERE SAFETY BULLETINS ATTACHED TO THE CALL SHEET TODAY? ☐YES ☐NO

HAS YOUR ENTIRE CREW REVIEWED THE SAFETY SHEETS? ☐YES ☐ NO

WERE ANY ADDITIONAL CONCERNS REGARDING THE DAY'S WORK
ADDRESSED BY THE CREW? ☐YES ☐NO

IF SO, PLEASE EXPLAIN THE CONCERNS AND HOW THEY WERE
ADDRESSED:

_____
_____
_____
_____
_____
_____
_____

_____   _____
SIGNED   POSITION

EMERGENCY INFORMATION
(To be posted on the set at all times)

SHOW:_____DATE:_____

PRODUCTION CO:_____

PROD. OFFICE PHONE NO:_____FAX#:_____

TODAY'S LOCATION:_____

ADDRESS:_____

_____

LOCATION PHONE NO:_____

PROPERTY OWNER(S)/MANAGER:_____

OWNER/MANAGER'S PHONE NO:_____

ESSENTIAL PHONE NUMBERS   EMERGENCY CALLS ONLY: **911**_____

POLICE:_____FIRE:_____

NEAREST EMERGENCY MEDICAL FACILITY:_____

_____

_____

EMERGENCY ROOM PHONE NO:_____

Emergency Telephone Procedures:
Indicate if you have a medical or fire emergency that requires an immediate response, then give the following information:
- Type of emergency (fire, medical, police or other) and related details (persons involved, nature of injuries, etc.)
- Location of emergency (including building, floor and room numbers)
- Your name and the telephone number you are calling from

Note: Do not hang up first as the operator may require additional information from you.

UPM:_____

PHONE:_____ PAGER:_____

SET MEDIC:_____

PHONE:_____ PAGER:_____

LOCATION MANAGER:_____

PHONE:_____ PAGER:_____

ON-SET SAFETY COORDINATOR:_____

PHONE:_____ PAGER:_____

CONSTRUCTION SAFETY COORDINATOR:_____

PHONE:_____ PAGER:_____

PRODUCTION SAFETY CONSULTANT:_____

PHONE:_____ PAGER:_____

LOCATION AGREEMENT

Film _____	Scripted Location _____
Prod. Co. _____	Scene No(s) _____
Address _____	_____
_____	
Phone # _____	Date _____

Dear Ladies and Gentlemen:

1. I, the undersigned owner or agent, whichever is applicable, hereby irrevocably grants to _____ ("Producer"), and its agents, employees, contractors and suppliers, the right to enter and remain upon and use the property, both real and personal, located at: _____

_____

(the "Property"), including without limitation, all interior and exterior areas, buildings and other structures of the Property, and owner's name, logo, trademark, service mark and/or slogan, and any other identifying features associated therewith or which appear in, on or about the Property, for the purpose of photographing (including without limitation by means of motion picture, still or videotape photography) said premises, sets and structures and/or recording sound in connection with the production, exhibition, advertising and exploitation of the_____ tentatively entitled _____ (the "Picture").

2. Producer may take possession of said premises commencing on or about _____ subject to change because of weather conditions or changes in production schedule, and continuing until the completion of all scenes and work required.

3. Charges: As complete and full payment for all of the rights granted to Producer hereunder, Producer shall pay to Owner the total amount of $ _____ , broken-down as follows:

	No. of Days				
Prep	_____	X $ _____	= $ _____
Shoot	_____	X $ _____	= $ _____
Strike	_____	X $ _____	= $ _____
Hold	_____	X $ _____	= $ _____
Other	_____		$ _____
	_____		$ _____

All charges are payable on completion of all work completed, unless specifically agreed to the contrary. Producer is not obligated to actually use the property or produce a_____ or include material photographed or recorded hereunder in the Picture. Producer may at any time elect not to use the Property by giving Owner or agent 24 hours written notice of such election, in which case neither party shall have any obligation hereunder.

4. Producer may place all necessary facilities and equipment, including temporary sets, on the Property, and agrees to remove same after completion of work and leave the Property in as good condition as when received, reasonable wear and tear from uses permitted herein excepted. Signs on the Property may, but need not, be removed or changed, but, if removed or changed, must be replaced. In connection with the Picture, Producer may refer to the Property or any part thereof by any fictitious name and may attribute any fictitious events as occurring on the Property. Owner irrevocably grants to Producer and Producer's successors and assigns the right, in perpetuity, throughout the universe, to duplicate and recreate all or a portion of the Property and to use such duplicates and recreations in any media and/or manner now known or hereafter devised in connection with the Picture, including without limitation sequels and remakes,

merchandising, theme parks and studio tours, and in connection with publicity, promotion and/or advertising for any or all of the foregoing.

5. Producer agrees to use reasonable care to prevent damage to the Property, and will indemnify and hold Owner harmless from and against any claims or demands arising out of or based upon personal injuries, death or property damage (ordinary wear and tear excepted), suffered by such person(s) resulting directly from any act of negligence on Producer's part in connection with the work hereunder.

6. All rights of every nature whatsoever in and to all still pictures, motion pictures, videotapes, photographs and sound recordings made hereunder, shall be owned by Producer and its successors, assigns and licensees, and neither Owner nor any tenant, or other party now or hereafter having an interest in said property, shall have any right of action against Producer or any other party arising out of any use of said still pictures, motion pictures, videotapes, photographs and or sound recordings, whether or not such use is or may claimed to be, defamatory, untrue or censurable in nature. In addition, neither Owner nor any tenant, nor any other party now or hereafter having an interest in the Property, shall have any right of action, including, but not limited to, those based upon invasion of privacy, publicity, defamation, or other civil rights, in connection with the exercise of the permission and/or rights granted by Owner to Producer. If there is a breach by Producer hereunder, Owner shall be limited to an action at law for monetary damages. In no event shall Owner have the right to enjoin the development, production, distribution or exploitation of the Picture.

7. Force Majeure: If because of illness of actors, director or other essential artists and crew, weather conditions, defective film or equipment or any other occurrence beyond Producer's control, Producer is unable to start work on the date designated above and/or work in progress is interrupted during use of the Property by Producer, then Producer shall have the right to use the Property at a later date to be mutually agreed upon and/or to extend the period set forth in Paragraph 2, and any such use shall be included in the compensation paid pursuant to Paragraph 3 above.

8. At any time within six (6) months from the date Producer completes its use of the Property hereunder, Producer may, upon not less than five (5) days prior written notice to Owner, reenter and use the Property for such period as may be reasonable necessary to photograph retakes, added scenes, etc. desired by Producer upon the same terms and conditions as contained in this agreement.

9. Owner warrants neither he or anyone acting for him, gave or agreed to give anything of value, except for use of the Property, to Producer or anyone associated with the production for using said Property as a shooting location.

10. Owner represents and warrants that he/she is the owner and/or authorized representative of the Property, and that Owner has the authority to grant Producer the permission and rights granted in this agreement, and that no one else's permission is required. If any question arises regarding Owner's authority to grant the permission and rights granted in this agreement, Owner agrees to indemnify Producer and assume responsibility for any loss and liability incurred as a result of its breach of the representation of authority contained in this paragraph, including reasonable attorneys' fees.

AGREED AND ACCEPTED TO:

_____
Production Company ("Producer")

By: _____
Its Authorized Signatory

_____   By: _____
("Owner")   Its: _____

_____   _____
                                    Social Security or Federal ID No.
Address

_____   _____
Phone No.   Fax No.

NON-FILMED LOCATION AGREEMENT

Property Owner_____   Location _____

Property Address_____   Set#_____

_____

Production Co._____ ("Producer")

Address _____

_____

Re: _____ (the "Picture")

To the Producer:

I, the undersigned owner or agent, whichever is applicable, hereby irrevocably grants to Producer, its employees, agents, contractors and suppliers, and such other parties as it may authorize or designate, to enter and use, for the purpose of:_____
_____
(indicate whether parking, holding, meals, staging, etc.) the Property located at the address set forth above hereinafter referred to as the "Property" which Property consists of: _____
_____
(description), which permission includes access to and from the Property and the rights to bring and utilize thereon personnel, personal property, material and equipment. Producer shall leave the Property in substantially as good condition as when received by Producer, excepting reasonable wear and tear and use of the Property for the purposes herein permitted.

Access to the Property is granted for _____ , commencing approximately _____ ("the Term").

In full consideration of the above, Producer will pay the undersigned the sum of $ _____ .

In the event that any loss and liability is incurred as a direct result of any property damage to the Property occurring on the Property caused by Producer in connection with the aforementioned use of the Property, Producer agrees to pay for all reasonable costs of actual and verifiable damage. In this connection, the undersigned agrees to participate in a walk-through of the Property with Producer's representative (Location Manager) to inspect the property so damaged.

Producer further agrees to hold the undersigned harmless from any and all third-party suits, claims, or loss or liabilities caused by Producer in connection with the aforementioned use of the Property.

It is further agreed that the undersigned's rights and remedies in the event of a failure or an omission constituting a breach of the provisions of this Agreement shall be limited to the undersigned's right, if any, to recover damages in an action at law, but in no event shall the undersigned be entitled by reason of any such breach to terminate this Agreement, or to enjoin or restrain the distribution, exhibition or other exploitation of the Picture or the advertising or publicizing thereof.

This Agreement may not be altered except by a written instrument signed by both parties. This Agreement shall be binding upon and inure to the benefit of the undersigned and Producer and their respective successors and assigns.

The undersigned warrants that the undersigned has the full right to enter into this Agreement and that the consent of no other party is necessary to effectuate the full and complete permission granted herein.

AGREED & ACCEPTED:

By: _____
(Property owner or designated signatory)   AGREED & ACCEPTED for Producer:

Phone#: _____ Fax#:_____   By: _____

Social Security# or Federal ID#:
_____

LOCATION RELEASE

Property Owner _____   Location _____

Property Address _____   Set# _____

_____

Production Co. _____ ("Producer")

Address _____

_____

Re: _____ (the "Picture")

To the Producer:

Owner hereby acknowledges that the Property as referred to in the LOCATION AGREEMENT between Producer and Owner dated _____ , (the "Agreement") has been returned to Owner in substantially the same condition as it was in prior to Producer's use thereof:

Owner hereby acknowledges that:

(a)   all payments required under the Agreement have been paid;

(b)   no additional restoration work is required in connection with the Property;

(c)   Owner and any individual who entered the Property at the invitation or on behalf of Owner, suffered no personal loss or damage in connection with the use of the Property by Producer; and

(d)   Producer has no other responsibilities in connection with the Property other than to continue to hold Owner harmless from any and all third-party suits, claims, or loss or liabilities directly resulting from Producer's use of the Property.

Owner hereby releases and forever discharges Producer, its parent, subsidiary, affiliated and associated companies and its and their officers, employees and agents, and their successors and assigns of and from any and all claims, debts, demands, liabilities, obligations, costs, expenses, damages, actions and causes of action of whatsoever kind or nature, whether known or unknown, which Owner has ever had, now has or which Owner or any of its successors or assigns hereafter can, shall or may have against Producer based on or arising out of, relating to or in connection with the Agreement.

Producer may assign, transfer, license, delegate and/or grant all or any part of its rights, privileges and property hereunder to any person or entity. This Agreement shall be binding upon and shall inure to the benefit of the parties hereto and their respective heirs, executors, administrators, successors and assigns. This Agreement and Owner's rights and obligations hereunder may not be assigned by Owner.

ACCEPTED AND AGREED TO:

_____   _____
Owner   Date

LOCATION INFORMATION SHEET

SHOW _____   PRODUCTION # _____
LOCATION MANAGER _____   (SCRIPTED) LOCATION _____
PERMIT SERVICE _____   _____
     CONTACT _____   DATE(S) _____
     PHONE # _____   ☐ INT.   ☐ EXT.   ☐ DAY   ☐ NIGHT

ACTUAL LOCATION
(Address & Phone #)

CONTACTS

Owner(s)   Name(s) _____
           Address _____

DATE & DAYS

	# of days	dates
Prep:		
Shoot:		
Strike:		

Phone/FAX # _____
Beeper # _____

Representative(s)

Company: _____
Contact: _____
Address: _____
_____

Phone/FAX # _____
Beeper # _____

LOCATION OF NEAREST EMERGENCY MEDICAL FACILITY

LOCATION SITE RENTAL FEE

Full Amount $ _____   O.T. after ____ hrs. per day @ $ _____ per hr.

Amount for PREP days $ _____   _____ Additional days @ $ _____ per day

Amount for SHOOT days $ _____   Additional charges: Phone $ _____

Amount for STRIKE days $ _____   Utilities $ _____

Deposit $ _____ Due on _____   Parking $ _____

☐ Refundable   ☐ Apply to total fee   (Other) _____ $ _____

Balance $ _____ Due on _____

CHECKLIST

☐ Location Agreement	☐ Heaters/Fans/Air Conditioners	**Allocated Parking For**
☐ Certificate of Insurance	☐ Lay-out Board/Drop Cloths	☐ Equipment
☐ Permit	☐ Utilities/Power Supply	☐ Honeywagons
☐ Fire Safety Officer(s)	**Allocated Areas For**	☐ Motor Homes
☐ Police	☐ Extras	☐ Catering Truck
☐ Location Fee	☐ Dressing Rms.	☐ Cast Vehicles
☐ Security	☐ Eating	☐ Crew Vehicles
☐ Intermittent Traffic Control	☐ Hair/Makeup	☐ Buses
☐ Post for Parking	☐ School	☐ Picture Vehicles
☐ Signed Release from Neighbors	☐ Equipment	☐ Extra Tables & Chairs/Tent
☐ Prepared Map to Location	☐ Special Equipment	☐ Locate Parking Lot if
	☐ Animals	Shuttle is Necessary

© FI H

LOCATION LIST

SHOW _____ PRODUCTION # _____

SET LOCATION	ACTUAL LOCATION (ADDRESS & PHONE)	DATE & DAYS (PREP/SHOOT/STRIKE)	CONTACTS (OWNER & REPRESENTATIVE)

© ELH

REQUEST TO FILM DURING EXTENDED HOURS

Dear Resident:

This is to inform you that _____ will be shooting a film entitled
_____ in your neighborhood at the following address:
_____.
Filming activities in residential areas is normally allowed only between the hours of _____ and _____.
In order to extend the hours before and/or after these times, the City requires that we obtain a signature of approval from
the neighbors. The following information pertains to the dates and times of our scheduled shoot and any specific
information you may need to know regarding our filming activities.

We have obtained or applied for all necessary City permits and maintain all legally required liability insurance. A copy of
our film permit will be on file at the City Film Office and will also be available at our shooting location.

FILMING DAYS/HOURS REQUESTED: on _____ (date(s))
    from _____ to _____
    and on _____ (date(s))
    from _____ to _____

THE FOLLOWING ACTIVITIES ARE PLANNED FOR THE EXTENDED HOURS:
_____
_____
_____
_____

We appreciate your hospitality and cooperation. We wish to make filming on your street a pleasant experience for both you
and us. If you have any questions or concerns before or during the filming, please feel free to call our Production Office
and ask for me or the Production Manager.

Sincerely yours,

_____   _____
Location Manager   Production Company

                                                _____
                                                Phone No.

We would very much appreciate it if you would complete and sign where indicated below. A representative from our
company will be by within the next day or two to pick up this form.

☐ I DO NOT OBJECT TO THE EXTENDED FILMING HOURS
☐ I DO OBJECT TO THE EXTENDED FILMING HOURS

COMMENTS:

NAME: _____

ADDRESS: _____

_____

PHONE #: (Optional) _____

TRAVEL MOVEMENT

SHOW _____ PROD # _____

TRAVEL FROM _____ TO _____

DAY/DATE _____

TYPE OF AIRCRAFT _____ AIRLINE _____ MEAL(S) _____ MOVIE _____

FLIGHT # _____ DEPARTURE TIME _____ ARRIVAL _____ FLIGHT STOPS IN _____

CHANGE TO FLIGHT # _____ DEPARTURE _____ ARRIVAL _____

NAME	POSITION	GROUND TRANSPORTATION TO AIRPORT	TO BE PICKED UP @	GROUND TRANSPORTATION FROM AIRPORT

DIRECT # TO PRODUCTION OFFICE _____ FAX # _____

ADDITIONAL INFO. _____

HOTEL _____
Address _____
Phone # _____

QUICK REFERENCE **TRAVEL MOVEMENT**

DATE: _____

SHOW

NOTE—*the following information is subject to change*

NAME	POSITION	DATE LEAVING	GROUND TRANSPORTATION TO AIRPORT	FLIGHT INFORMATION	GROUND TRANSPORTATION FROM AIRPORT	HOTEL ACCOMMODATIONS

© ELH

INDIVIDUAL TRAVEL ITINERARY

SHOW_____ DATE_____

COMPANY_____

ADDRESS_____ PHONE#_____

_____ FAX#_____

NAME_____ POSITION_____

DATE SCHEDULED TO TRAVEL_____

LOCATION(S)_____

Current weather conditions are:_____

We will be shooting_____nights, and the weather at night during this time of year is anticipated to be:
_____. Please pack accordingly.

GROUND TRANSPORTATION TO: [ ] THE AIRPORT   [ ] LOCATION

☐ Company will send a car for you @_____ [ ] a.m. [ ] p.m.

☐ Report to_____to take shuttle bus at_____ [ ] a.m. [ ] p.m.

☐ Please provide your own ground transportation to the airport, and the production will reimburse you
   for the airport shuttle van or cab fare

   Be at the airport no later than_____ [ ] a.m. [ ] p.m. for check-in

---

FLIGHT INFORMATION

Airport_____

Airline_____Flight #_____Departs at_____ [ ] a.m. [ ] p.m.

Change of plane in_____

Airline_____Flight#_____Departs at_____ [ ] a.m. [ ] p.m.

Arrives at_____ [ ] a.m. [ ] p.m.

YOUR AIRLINE TICKET

☐ Pick-up @ the production office

☐ It will be delivered to your home

☐ You have an electronic ticket waiting for you at the airport

Record Locator No:_____

(Note: be sure to bring a picture ID with you to the airport)

YOUR PER DIEM

Your per diem will be $_____per day

☐ Pick-up @ the prod. office before you leave

☐ You will receive it when you get to location

GROUND TRANSPORTATION FROM THE AIRPORT

☐ You will be picked-up by a company driver: ☐ at the arrival gate ☐ in the baggage area ☐ outside of baggage

☐ The driver will have a sign with: ☐ your name on it ☐ the name of the show on it

☐ A rental car will be waiting for you at the airport - Rental Car Company_____

   Type of car_____ Confirmation No._____

☐ Take a cab from the airport to the hotel ☐ Take the hotel shuttle van from the airport to the hotel

---

HOTEL/MOTEL ACCOMMODATIONS

Hotel/Motel_____

Address_____

_____

Phone No._____

Fax No._____

LOCATION PRODUCTION OFFICE

Address_____

_____

_____

Phone No._____

Fax No._____

IF YOU ARE HAVING YOUR MAIL FORWARDED TO YOU WHILE YOU ARE ON LOCATION, HAVE IT SENT:

☐ to the home office (it will be forwarded to location) ☐ to the production office on location ☐ to the hotel

RETURN: You are tentatively scheduled to return on_____

© ELH

HOTEL ROOM LOG

SHOW: _____

HOTEL: _____

ADDRESS: _____

PHONE#: _____   FAX#: _____

DATE(S):   From _____ To _____

WEEK/ENDING: _____

CONTACT: _____

NAME	POSITION	CONF. #	PO/TA#	ROOM TYPE	ROOM #	ROOM RATE	DATE IN	DATE OUT	LATE CHECK-IN NOTES	TOTAL DAYS

© ELH

HOTEL ROOM LIST

SHOW _____   PROD # _____

HOTEL _____   LOCATION _____

ADDRESS _____

_____   LOCATION DATES _____

                                                          Through
PHONE # _____   FAX # _____   _____

NAME	POSITION	ROOM #	DIRECT #
Production Office	----------		
Accounting Office	----------		
Transportation Office	----------		
Editing Room	----------		

© ELH

MEAL ALLOWANCE

SHOW _____

LOCATION _____

PROD # _____

WEEK OF _____

BREAKFAST $ _____
LUNCH $ _____
DINNER $ _____

NAME	MON			TUE			WED			THUR			FRI			SAT			SUN			TOTAL	SIGNATURE
DAY																							
DATE																							
	B	L	D	B	L	D	B	L	D	B	L	D	B	L	D	B	L	D	B	L	D		

APPROVED _____

TOTAL: _____

© ELH

DAILIES SHIPMENT LOG

SHOW: _____   DATE: _____

| DATE | CHECK ONE | | ITEM(S) BEING SHIPPED | AIRLINE | FLIGHT NO. | LEAVES | ARRIVES | # OF PIECES | WAYBILL # | DRIVER-SERVICE DELIVERING TO AIRPORT | DRIVER-SERVICE PICKING UP FROM AIRPORT | ✓ |
	TO OFFICE	TO LOC.										

PRO-FORMA SHIPPING INVOICE

COMPANY:

PRODUCTION:

DEPARTMENT:

MANIFEST DOCUMENT #:

DATE:

[ ] TEMPORARY EXPORT   [ ] DEFINITE EXPORT (Expendables)

SHIPPER		CONSIGNEE	
Company:		Company:	
Address:		Address:	
Phone No:		TOTAL NO. OF PIECES:	P.O.#	PG. ___ OF ___
Fax No:				BOX ___ OF ___
Contact:		PORT OF EXPORT:	
		PORT OF ENTRY:	
		SHIPPING AGENT:	
		Phone No:	FAX #:
		Fax No:	
		SHIPPER'S PHONE NO:	
		Contact:	CELL/PGR#:

QTY	TYPE OF PACKAGING	DESCRIPTION	SERIAL NO.	COUNTRY OF ORIGIN	WEIGHT	UNIT PRICE	TOTAL VALUE

TOTAL WEIGHT: _____

TOTAL VALUE: _____

The values indicated above are for customs purposes only.

All items listed above are to be used in connection with the motion picture industry.

VENDOR:	Phone:
Contact:	Fax:
Tax ID#:	P.O. or Inv. #:

PRO-FORMA COMPLETED BY:

© ELH

DAILY SHIPPING LOG

SHOW: _____

DATE: / DEPARTMENT: / P.O.#: / T=Temporary -or- D=Definite:	DESCRIPTION	VENDOR INFO.	TRANSPORTATION	
			TO PORT OF EXPORT (OR BORDER):	DECLARED VALUE:
			FROM PORT OF EXPORT TO PORT OF ENTRY:	NO. OF PIECES:
			FROM PORT OF ENTRY TO LOCATION:	DATE DELIVERED:
			CARNET OR SHIPPING MANIFEST NO:	CUSTOMS ENTRY NO:
DATE: / DEPARTMENT: / P.O.#: / T=Temporary -or- D=Definite:			TO PORT OF EXPORT (OR BORDER):	DECLARED VALUE:
			FROM PORT OF EXPORT TO PORT OF ENTRY:	NO. OF PIECES:
			FROM PORT OF ENTRY TO LOCATION:	DATE DELIVERED:
			CARNET OR SHIPPING MANIFEST NO:	CUSTOMS ENTRY NO:
DATE: / DEPARTMENT: / P.O.#: / T=Temporary -or- D=Definite:			TO PORT OF EXPORT (OR BORDER):	DECLARED VALUE:
			FROM PORT OF EXPORT TO PORT OF ENTRY:	NO. OF PIECES:
			FROM PORT OF ENTRY TO LOCATION:	DATE DELIVERED:
			CARNET OR SHIPPING MANIFEST NO:	CUSTOMS ENTRY NO:
DATE: / DEPARTMENT: / P.O.#: / T=Temporary -or- D=Definite:			TO PORT OF EXPORT (OR BORDER):	DECLARED VALUE:
			FROM PORT OF EXPORT TO PORT OF ENTRY:	NO. OF PIECES:
			FROM PORT OF ENTRY TO LOCATION:	DATE DELIVERED:
			CARNET OR SHIPPING MANIFEST NO:	CUSTOMS ENTRY NO:
DATE: / DEPARTMENT: / P.O.#: / T=Temporary -or- D=Definite:			TO PORT OF EXPORT (OR BORDER):	DECLARED VALUE:
			FROM PORT OF EXPORT TO PORT OF ENTRY:	NO. OF PIECES:
			FROM PORT OF ENTRY TO LOCATION:	DATE DELIVERED:
			CARNET OR SHIPPING MANIFEST NO:	CUSTOMS ENTRY NO:

© ELH

REQUEST FOR RETURN

RETURN REFERERNCE NO: _____

ITEM(S) TO BE RETURNED	SERIAL/UNIT NOS.	CARNET OR SHIPPING MANIFEST NUMBER	CUSTOMS ENTRY NUMBER	DECLARED CUSTOMS VALUE	NO. OF PIECES	WEIGHT
			TOTALS:	VALUE	PIECES	WEIGHT

PICK-UP ITEM(S)/LOAD FROM: _____

DATE OF REQUEST: _____

RETURN CUSTOMS DOCUMENTATION NO: _____

[ ] COMPLETE RETURN
[ ] PARTIAL RETURN
[ ] FINAL - PARTIAL RETURN
[ ] RETURN FOR REPAIR

PROJECTED DATE TO LEAVE:

[ ] CAN LEAVE WHEN READY
[ ] HOLD FOR APPROVAL
[ ] MUST LEAVE ON: _____

ESTIMATED DATE OF ARRIVAL: _____

WAYBILL NO. _____

SPECIAL INSTRUCTIONS: _____

TRANSPORTATION:

LOCATION TO PORT OF EXPORT: _____
PORT OF EXPORT TO PORT OF ENTRY: _____
PORT OF ENTRY TO DESTINATION: _____

VENDOR: _____

ADDRESS: _____

TRUCK LICENSE NO: _____ DRIVER: _____

FINAL DESTINATION:

SHIPPING AGENT: _____
PHONE NO: _____
FAX NO: _____ PHONE NO: _____
CELL/PGR#: _____ CONTACT: _____
CONTACT: _____ HRS. OPEN: _____

SPOT-CHECKED BY: _____

APPROVED BY: _____

© ELH

DEPARTMENTAL WRAP SCHEDULE

Show:_____

Scheduled Completion Date of Principal Photography:_____

Date:_____ Department:_____

Department Head:_____

Total Wrap/Man Days Budgeted:_____ Work Hours Per Day:_____

Date of Wrap Completion:_____

NAME	POSITION	# WRAP WKS/DAYS	WRAP DATE

Department Head Signature:_____

UPM Approval:_____

© ELH

COMMERCIAL CALL SHEET

			CREW CALL:
DATE:	JOB TITLE(S):	JOB:	
DAY: of		JOB#:	SUNRISE: SUNSET:

CLIENT:	AGENCY:	PRODUCTION CO:
LOCATIONS:		NEAREST HOSPITAL:
	Executive Producer:	PRODUCTION PAGERS:
CREW PARKING:	Producer: Business Affairs Manager: Art Director: Copywriter:	PRODUCTION CELL PHONES: AGENCY CELL:

CREW	NAME	PHONE	PAGER	IN	OUT
Director					
Producer					
1st AD					
Prod. Manager					
Prod. Coordinator					
D.P.					
1st Asst. Camera					
2nd Asst. Camera					
Loader					
Gaffer					
Best Boy Elec.					
Electric					
Electric					
Electric/Driver					
Key Grip					
Best Boy Grip					
Grip					
Grip Driver					
Grip					
Script Supervisor					
VTR					
Make-Up					
Make-Up Assistant					
Wardrobe					
Wardrobe Assistant					
Production Designer					
Prop Master					
Set Decorator					
Prop Assistant					
Set Dresser					
Craft Service					
P.A.					
P.A.					
P.A.					
P.A.					
P.A.					
2nd AD					
Water Truck Driver					
Teacher					
Locations Manager					

EQUIPMENT	VENDOR	PHONE
ANIMALS		
CAMERA		
CAMERA CAR		
CATERING		
CASTING		
CONDORS		
CRAFT SERVICE		
CRANE		
CELL PHONES		
DAILIES		
DOLLY		
DOLLY TRACK		
EDITORIAL		
ELECTRIC		
EXPENDABLES		
EXTRAS CASTING		
GENERATOR		
GRIP		
INSURANCE		
LAB		
MESSENGER		
MOTORCYCLE CAM. CAR		
MOTORHOMES		
PICTURE CARS		
PAYROLL SER.		
PERMITS		
PROD. SUPPLIES		
RAW STOCK		
SETS		
VEHICLES		
VTR		
WALKIES		
WATER TRUCK		
WEATHER		
WORKERS COMP.		
COFFEE/DONUTS:	READY @:	
# OF LUNCHES:	READY @:	

TALENT ROLE	TALENT NAME	PHONE	PAGER	IN	OUT	AGENT	PHONE	CONTACT

PRODUCTION SUMMARY	SOUND ROLL	FILM STOCK	STOCK#1:	STOCK#2:	STOCK#3:
CALL TIME		RECEIVED TODAY:			
1 ST SHOT		RECEIVED PREVIOUS:			
LUNCH		TOTAL EXPOSED TODAY:			
1 ST SHOT PM	SCENE NOS.	TOTAL EXPOSED TO DATE:			
2ND MEAL		TOTAL UNEXPOSED:			
CAMERA WRAP		S.E. TO DATE UNEXPOSED:			
PROD. WRAP		UNEXPOSED IN CANS:			

PRODUCTION NOTES:

Index

mechanical, 304, 307
models, 306, 307
physical, 304, 306
prosthetics, 306
safety, 307
sound, 323
special makeup effects, 304
starting, 305, 307
visual, 304-306
Employer's liability and workers' compensation,
92-93
Employment
consecutive, 193
of minors, 194-195
Equipment rental log, 71, 85
Executive staff list, 72
Extras, 200-206
casting agencies, 200-201
casting on location, 202
as entry level to business, 203-204
large crowds, gathering, 201-202
nonunion to union status move, 203
preparation time for, 201
process, 201-202
SAG categories of, 202-203
specific types, finding, 200-201

F

Fair use defined, 240
Files, 18-21
blank forms needed, 19
day, 21
episode, 21
for features, movies for television, cable, or
Internet, 19-21
series, 21
Film
clips clearance, 210, 228
commissions, 273-274
on foreign locations, 296-297
six phases of, 1
talent clearance from feature films, 212
Filmmaker's Code of Conduct, 259-260
First trial print definition, 329
Fixes definition, 328
Foley definition, 328
Foreign locations. *See* Locations, foreign
Forms given crew members on first day, 27

G

Guilds and unions. *See* Unions and guilds

H

H-2B visas, 299
Harassment, sexual, 251

I

IA. *See* International Alliance of Theatrical Stage
Employees
IATSE. *See* International Alliance of Theatrical
Stage Employees
IIPP. *See On Production* Injury and Illness Prevention Program
Industry-Wide Labor-Management Safety Board,
245, 246
Inserts, 327-328
Insurance requirements, 90-109
aircraft, 96
animals or livestock usage, 96
automobile, 91-92, 103-104, 108-109
bereavement coverage, 94
cast insurance, 93-94
certificates of insurance, 91, 92, 100, 340
checklist for, 80-81
claim worksheets, 105-109
claims reporting procedures, 98
completion bonds, 97-98
comprehensive general liability, 91
direct physical loss, 94
on employee vehicles, 16
entertainment specialty, 90
errors and omissions (E&O) liability insurance,
90-91, 236, 340
essential elements, 94
faulty stock, camera, and processing, 94-95
foreign coverage added to U.S. policy, 286
foreign package policy, 96
guild/union accident coverage, 93
items insurance companies examine, 90
physical loss, direct, 95
political risk insurance, 96-97
production package, 93-95
property loss notice, 101-102
railroads, 96
risk management survey, 90
signal interruption, 96
stunts in film and, 90
supplemental coverage, 95-97
third party property damage, 95
Travel Accident Policy, 93, 270
umbrella (excess liability) policy, 95
valuables usage, 96
water and working on or near, 93
watercraft, 96

Index of Forms

CD Contents

This CD contains PDF files for the U.S. Dept. of Justice Form I-9 and for two sets of file folder labels. These documents are *not* interactive. Viewing and printing them requires that Acrobat Reader (included on this CD) be installed on your computer. Form I-9 must be filled out by hand or with a typewriter.

There are also five Word document files—three for specific checklists and two containing the same file folder labels as two of the PDF files—supplied in case you have trouble printing the PDF files from your specific printer. These files are *not* interactive. They can be viewed and printed from a PC using Word 97 or later, and from a Mac using Word 2001 for Mac.

The other forms on this CD are interactive Word templates. They can be opened using Word and then saved to a disk drive with any name you choose. These interactive forms are designed to be filled out in Word, but they can also be printed and filled out by hand if necessary.

Instructions

1. Select the desired form file from the CD Index.

2. Use File ➤ Save As to save the template file to your hard drive or to a floppy disk, preferably with a new name. If desired, you may save the file in the .doc format.

3. Enter information in the form fields as needed. Use the Tab key or click with your mouse to move between fields. In some cases, clicking a field reveals a scroll box showing various choices. Click the scroll box and select the option you want. Your selection displays.

4. In forms designed to do math functions, the total or result box is automatically updated when you leave an entry field.

5. Save the file or print it out.

Caution: Unprotecting (unlocking) and subsequently reprotecting (relocking) one of these files deletes all the information you have entered in the form fields.

System Requirements

To use this CD on a PC, you need a Pentium I or higher, Windows 95 or later, and Word 97 or later. To use it on a Mac, you need any Mac OS-compatible system (must be PowerPC processor-based) running at 120 MHz or faster, 48MB Ram (with 1MB of Virtual Memory) for OS 9.0 and later (32MB Ram [with 1MB of Virtual Memory] for earlier than OS 9.0). Of course, a CD drive is also required.